GOVERNANCE OF
GLOBAL FINANCIAL MARKETS

The recent financial crisis proved that pre-existing arrangements for the governance of global markets were flawed. With reform underway in the US, the EU and elsewhere, Emilios Avgouleas explores some of the questions associated with building an effective governance system and analyses the evolution of existing structures. By critiquing the soft law structures dominating international financial regulation and examining the roles of financial innovation and of neo-liberal policies in the expansion of global financial markets, he offers a new epistemological reading of the causes of the Global Financial Crisis.

Requisite reforms leave serious gaps in cross-border supervision, in the resolution of global financial institutions and in the monitoring of risk originating in the shadow banking sector. To close these gaps and safeguard the stability of the international financial system, an evolutionary governance system is proposed that will also enhance the welfare role of global financial markets.

EMILIOS AVGOULEAS holds the chair of International Banking Law and Finance at the Law School of the University of Edinburgh. He was previously the Professor of International Financial Markets and Financial Law at the University of Manchester. He also holds a number of visiting professorships and has written extensively in the wider field of financial law and economics, behavioural finance and financial regulation, and EU financial services law.

INTERNATIONAL CORPORATE LAW AND
FINANCIAL MARKET REGULATION

Corporate law and financial market regulation matter. The Global Financial Crisis has challenged many of the fundamental concepts underlying corporate law and financial regulation; but crisis and reform has long been a feature of these fields. A burgeoning and sophisticated scholarship now challenges and contextualizes the contested relationship between law, markets and companies, domestically and internationally. This Series informs and leads the scholarly and policy debate by publishing cutting-edge, timely and critical examinations of the most pressing and important questions in the field.

Series Editors
Professor Eilis Ferran, University of Cambridge
Professor Niamh Moloney, London School of Economics and Political Science
Professor Howell Jackson, Harvard Law School

Editorial Board
Professor Marco Becht, Professor of Finance and Economics at Université Libre de Bruxelles and Executive Director of the European Corporate Governance Institute (ECGI).
Professor Brian Cheffins, S. J. Berwin Professor of Corporate Law at the Faculty of Law, University of Cambridge.
Professor Paul Davies, Allen & Overy Professor of Corporate Law and Professorial Fellow of Jesus College, University of Oxford.
Professor Luca Enriques, Professor of Business Law in the Faculty of Law at the University of Bologna.
Professor Guido Ferrarini, Professor of Business Law at the University of Genoa and Fellow of the European Corporate Governance Institute (ECGI).
Professor Jennifer Hill, Professor of Corporate Law at Sydney Law School.
Professor Klaus J. Hopt, Director of the Max Planck Institute of Comparative and International Private Law, Hamburg, Germany.
Professor Hideki Kanda, Professor of Law at the University of Tokyo.
Professor Colin Mayer, Peter Moores Professor of Management Studies at the Saïd Business School and Director of the Oxford Financial Research Centre.
James Palmer, Partner of Herbert Smith, London.
Professor Michel Tison, Professor at the Financial Law Institute of the University of Ghent, Belgium.
Andrew Whittaker, General Counsel to the Board at the UK Financial Services Authority.
Professor Eddy Wymeersch, former Chairman of the Committee of European Securities Regulators (CESR), former Chairman of the IOSCO European Regional Committee and Professor of Commercial Law, University of Ghent, Belgium.

GOVERNANCE OF GLOBAL FINANCIAL MARKETS

The Law, The Economics, The Politics

EMILIOS AVGOULEAS

CAMBRIDGE UNIVERSITY PRESS
Cambridge, New York, Melbourne, Madrid, Cape Town,
Singapore, São Paulo, Delhi, Mexico City

Cambridge University Press
The Edinburgh Building, Cambridge CB2 8RU, UK

Published in the United States of America by Cambridge University Press, New York

www.cambridge.org
Information on this title: www.cambridge.org/9780521762663

First published 2012

A catalogue record for this publication is available from the British Library

ISBN 978-0-521-76266-3 Hardback

In loving memory of my father Evangelos

CONTENTS

Walter Bagehot's classic, *Lombard Street*, was his response to the financial crisis sparked by the collapse of the Overend Gurney bank and to what he saw as the enormity of the potential liabilities of the City of London, which accompanied its great wealth. He wrote: '[W]e must examine the system on which these, great masses of money are manipulated, and assure ourselves that it is safe and right'. Professor Avgouleas has penned an equally authoritative study of the background to the financial crisis which began in 2007 and the ameliorative steps subsequently taken. He too inquires whether the system is now 'safe and right'. The answer is not totally reassuring as regards the international operation of the world's financial giants and the financial revolution they have spawned. In his view what is necessary is a new system of global financial governance, underpinned by an umbrella international treaty.

But this is to anticipate. The detailed and careful analysis which precedes Professor Avgouleas's conclusion begins with a lucid account of the structures and operation of financial markets, identifying their contribution to economic growth but also highlighting their risks and instabilities. Market phenomena such as bubbles and herding feature regularly but in the modern age there have also been developments such as derivatives transactions and shadow banking. That leads to a cogent dissection of the crisis itself and what proved to be the frail machinery available to handle it, not least in its cross-border dimensions. The context of the crisis, as Professor Avgouleas explains, was what he characterizes as the financial revolution of the preceding decades – liberalized markets, technological advances and financial innovation, all accentuated by a public policy shot through with neo-liberalism. On reading Professor Avgouleas's account of this financial revolution, one draws the obvious parallel with the Industrial Revolution and correlative financial change of Bagehot's day. The financial revolution, misunderstood and badly managed, was fertile ground for a crisis when coupled with factors such as the excessive rent-seeking by those associated with finance, their lobbying against effective capital requirements and other prophylactic regulation, and their promotion of a climate where 'light touch' regulation was the order of the day.

Professor Avgouleas then turns to international financial governance, with a thoughtful history of the Bretton Woods settlement in practice, and of the measures following the Asian Crisis of the late 1990s and the Global Financial Crisis a decade later. As would be expected, the IMF and the constellation of Basel institutions, such as the Financial Stability Board (née Forum) feature prominently. The role of state-to-state groups like the G-20 is also traced. The weaknesses in standard setting and its enforcement post-Asian Crisis are explored, in particular the Basel II standards for bank capital, which in their formulation were captured by the industry. Basel II is also illustrative of the drawback to the soft law approach to international financial regulation. The meat of Part III of the book is Professor Avgouleas's outline and critique of post-Global Financial Crisis measures at national, regional (European Union) and international levels. The reasons for the differences in approach are touched on, as is the constitutional background to the new European Supervisory Authorities and supervisory colleges. Fraught issues are explained such as the countercyclical buffer in Basel III. The reform of the 'too-big-to-fail' financial institution and the new resolution regimes are deservedly given extensive treatment.

This is a book of great scholarship. The wealth of learning is astonishing. It is drawn from a range of disciplines as varied as finance theory, economics, international relations and law. Not everyone will agree with the solutions proffered. In one sense they appear radical but a contextual reading reveals that, like most sensible reforms, they build on what has gone before. Anyone pondering the way forward for global financial governance will need to engage with the considerations Professor Avgouleas advances, based as they are on the mature reflections of a leading authority. The book deals with matters which concern ordinary people; as Professor Avgouleas notes, it is they who have reaped the consequences of the international havoc wrought by the Global Financial Crisis in terms of job losses and economic hardship. Deliberation by public policy makers on the contents of the book will inevitably lead them to conclude that vested interests cannot be allowed to continue with 'business as usual'.

Sir Ross Cranston FBA

PREFACE

The collapse of Lehman Brothers was just the high point of a crisis that started in mid-2007 and continues until this day. This came to be known as the Global Financial Crisis (GFC). Policy-makers, regulators, the industry, academics and other stakeholders throughout the world have been grappling with its root causes and consequences on a daily basis for the past four years. The Eurozone debt crisis is only its latest manifestation/transformation in a dramatic chain of events that has also led to the near collapse of the world's biggest financial institutions and their costly public rescues, a major economic recession and heavy over-indebtedness for most Western countries.

Many of the questions raised following the eruption of the GFC have been answered only in part. Therefore, one of the biggest challenges this work has faced was the possibility of fashioning a new epistemological reading of the causes of the GFC. This new reading had to build on those causes of the GFC that have already been well explained, such as, for instance, trade imbalances, misaligned incentives and unsustainable debt accumulation. But it also had to try to identify the missing link that allowed those causes to be correlated in open global markets with catastrophic consequences.

The eruption of the GFC showed that the preceding regulatory frameworks in the US and the EU were more or less built on sand, when it came to crisis management, especially cross-border crisis management. In addition, the global financial architecture of the pre-crisis era, largely based on a thick network of soft law bodies, lacked the institutional capacity required to deal with a cross-border financial crisis. The rules and standards of those bodies were built on flawed assumptions, which, especially in the case of capital standards, allowed financial institutions to over-leverage their balance sheets operating on a perilously thin equity base. They also did not take into account system-wide developments. Thus, capital adequacy standards intensified rather than contained asset bubbles that in most cases precede financial collapses. Other failures and loopholes clearly observed in the system in the pre-GFC era were narrow representation, lack of accountability and a significant failure to address the problems created by the integration of global financial markets, including issues of regulatory coverage. National, regional and international regulatory systems, largely informed by neo-liberal ideology, left outside of any meaningful public oversight the global OTC derivatives markets and the shadow banking sector, namely, the two most important laboratories/sources of financial innovation and generators of interconnectedness.

A gigantic reform effort is underway in the US, the EU and globally trying to address the aforementioned loopholes in order to minimize systemic risk and contain the impact of the 'too-big-to-fail' institution. Requisite reforms have also led to the establishment of a number of new systemic regulators and financial supervisors at all levels. The mandate of these bodies is often complex and their effectiveness remains unverified. Nonetheless, it is beyond doubt that most of these reforms are in the right direction and will close major loopholes in the regulation and supervision of global finance. However, this effort is bound to be undermined by the absence of formal global governance structures dealing with: (1) the supervision of large cross-border financial institutions, so-called Globally Systemically Important Financial Institutions (G-SIFIS); (2) the resolution of large cross-border financial groups; (3) the extension of global supervisory oversight to the shadow banking sector; and (4) the building of knowledge-based standard-setters for international finance that would closely co-operate and supervise the most effective of the existing soft law bodies, such as the Basel Committee on Banking Supervision, on a legally binding basis.

The Eurozone debt crisis entered its critical phases after the completion of the manuscript. As a result, it is not given full consideration in the book. A weak and severely under-capitalized banking sector is again at the heart of the problem, making several of the obvious solutions, such as large-scale sovereign debt restructuring, unsustainable. Arguably, developments in the Eurozone give additional force to one of the central arguments of this book as regards the need for impartial and effective supra-national governance structures to regulate and supervise global markets and especially large cross-border financial institutions, strengthening the force and effectiveness of ongoing regulatory reforms.

The writing of this book started at the beginning of my study leave in September 2008. A week later Lehman Brothers collapsed and any meaningful writing effort paused for at least two years. In the meanwhile, the world of global finance changed forever. The scholarly and policy-making analysis of global markets and of the global financial crisis that has emerged since 2008 has been fragmented but yet in many cases it has been of peerless quality. In addition, the bulk of relevant analysis has been immense and probably beyond the ability of a sole researcher to read, save understand, what was said there. At the same time, reform was taking shape in a number of areas, especially the regulation of systemic risk and 'too-big-to-fail' institutions, at rapid pace and at all levels: national, regional, international. As a result, keeping up with developments became an impossible task and the idea of dropping the project altogether came to my mind several times. Nonetheless, the immense challenges the modern world presents are inextricably tied up with the good workings of global finance, which since 2007–8 seems to have fallen into a state of irremediable disrepair. Thus, the desire of joining other (much more influential) voices in offering an analysis and possibly a workable first solution to the problem was one of the reasons that kept me going. My mother's great example of fortitude in the face of personal loss and her unfailing support was the second major reason. The third was the encouragement, support and immensely helpful advice I received from very distinguished scholars. Charles Goodhart has frequently shared his invaluable insights with me and shed light on many areas of global markets and their regulation that looked incomprehensive. This work would have been much poorer without being able to 'drill' into his vast well of knowledge in the field of global markets and global finance reform. Joe Norton, one of the founders of international financial regulation as a distinct academic discipline, proved to be the mentor and friend only the most fortunate ever have in their academic lives. In email after email Joe gave me constructive advice, sense of direction, access to his work and incredible emotional support following the death of my father in March 2010. Steven Schwarcz, one of the giants of modern financial law, not only was the kindest of hosts during my stay at Duke Law School, but also has been a good friend and colleague, who has provided inspiration with his original scholarship and work ethic. Eilis Ferran, one of the founders of this series, and a scholar of the highest order in the field of corporate and financial law, was both very supportive in the planning stages of this book and a source of rational and constructive advice during the research and writing stages. Cambridge University Press editor, Kim Hughes with her strict adherence to deadlines constantly reminded me that this book, like any other, should have a completion date and for everything that comes next there is always the possibility of a second edition. I am immensely grateful to all of them.

Special thanks must go to Sir Ross Cranston for finding the time to read the manuscript and provide the foreword for this book. I am also grateful for his advice about the timing and contents of this book and his invaluable insights on global financial reform. Once again it has been an immense privilege to be able to benefit from discussions with Sir William Blair on various aspects of this book.

I had immensely informative and constructive discussions on various parts of this book with a number of distinguished scholars and good friends, especially Douglas Arner, Lawrence Baxter, Ross Buckley and Heracles Polemarchakis. Doug, Larry, Ross and Heracles repeatedly gave me access to their unpublished work and dedicated hours of email and face to face discussions to our mutual effort to understand the whirlwind developments unfolding in front of our eyes and make (scholarly) sense of them. I am deeply indebted to all of them. Similarly I am indebted to my Manchester colleagues, Dora Kostakopoulou and William Lucy, for similar discussions and much appreciated editorial advice. I have also held very stimulating discussions with colleagues from other UK universities and especially Iain MacNeil, Joanna Gray and Dalvinder Singh. I am grateful to them for sharing with me their insights and scholarly work. The same applies to Eva Hupkes of the FSB for kindly giving me access to her unpublished work.

I would also like to thank all the academics and students that have attended my lectures and seminars on several themes of this book in the past three years at the Universities of Oxford, Cambridge, Duke, Copenhagen and Hong Kong. The participants of the conference 'Greening Humanity', held in Athens at the Eugenides Foundation in October 2010, and especially my colleagues in Manchester and co-organizers of this conference John Harris and Jon Sulston (Nobel Prize, Med. Sci., 2002), have taught me a great deal about the moral dilemmas facing our modern world and its multi-faceted challenges. Discussions with them and with OLMMOG are responsible for planting into my mind one of the central ideas of this book.

In writing this book I have also incurred a number of institutional debts. First, I would like to acknowledge the generous financial support I have received from the UK's Arts and Humanities Research Council (AHRC) by means of a study leave research grant. I would also like to thank Manchester Law School and its then Head of School Andrew Sanders for granting me a year-long study leave upon re-joining the law school. I would also like to thank Duke Law School and its Dean David Levi for hosting me as a Global Capital Markets Fellow during the

AY 2008-2009. Last but not least I would like to thank the production team at Cambridge University Press and especially Sarah Roberts for their great work in turning my manuscript into the book you hold in your hands.

The book considers global financial developments up to 20 July 2011 and discusses regulatory proposals issued until that date with only minor updates for follow ups. Furthermore, every effort has been made to state the law as it stood on 30 June 2011.

ABBREVIATIONS

ABCP	Asset Backed Commercial Paper
ABS	Asset Backed Securities
AIFMD	Alternative Investment Fund Managers Directive
AMH	Adaptive Markets Hypothesis
BCBS	Basel Committee on Banking Supervision
BHC	bank holding company
BIS	Bank for International Settlements
BoE	Bank of England
CBO	Collateralized Bond Obligations
CBRG	Cross-Border Resolution Group
CCP	central counterparty
CDO	Collateralized Debt Obligation
CDS	Credit Default Swap
CEBS	Committee of European Banking Supervisors
CESR	Committee of European Securities Regulators
CFTC	Commodity Futures Trading Commission (US)
CLN	Credit Linked Note
CLO	Collateralized Loan Obligation
CoCo	Contingent Capital Instrument
CRA	credit rating agency
CVA	credit valuation adjustment
EAD	exposure at default
EBA	European Banking Authority
EBRD	European Bank of Reconstruction and Development
ECB	European Central Bank
EIB	European Investment Bank
EIOPA	European Insurance and Occupational Pension Authority
EL	Expected Loss
EMH	Efficient Market Hypothesis
ESA	European Supervisory Authority
ESFS	European System of Financial Supervisors
ESMA	European Securities Markets Authority

ESRB	European Systemic Risk Board
EU	European Union
EWS	Early Warning System
FANNIE MAE	Federal National Mortgage Association
FATF	Financial Action Task Force on Money Laundering
FDIC	Federal Deposit Insurance Corporation
FRB	Federal Reserve Board (US)
FREDDIE MAC	Federal Home Loan Mortgage Corporation
FSA	Financial Services Authority (UK)
FSAP	Financial Sector Assessment Program
FSB	Financial Stability Board
FSD	Financial Sector Development
FSF	Financial Stability Forum
FSOC	Financial Stability Oversight Council
FSSA	Financial Sector Stability Assessment
GATS	General Agreement on Trade in Services
GATT	General Agreement on Tariffs and Trade
G-20	Group of 20
GDP	Gross Domestic Product
GFC	Global Financial Crisis
GSE	Government Sponsored Enterprise
G-SIFI	Globally Systemically Important Financial Institution
IAASB	International Auditing and Assurance Board
IAIS	International Association of Insurance Supervisors
IASB	International Accounting Standards Board
IASCF	International Accounting Standards Committee Foundation
IBRD	International Bank for Reconstruction and Development
IFAC	International Federation of Accountants
IFI	International Financial Institutions
IFS	International Financial Standard
IIF	Institute of International Finance
IMF	International Monetary Fund
IOSCO	International Organization of Securities Commissions
IRB	Internal Ratings Based Approach
ISDA	International Swaps and Derivatives Association
ISMA	International Securities Market Association
ISSB	International Standard Setting Body
LCFI	Large Complex Financial Institution
LCR	Liquidity Coverage Ratio
LGD	Loss Given Default
MBS	Mortgage Backed Securities
MDGs	Millennium Development Goals

MOU	Memorandum of Understanding
NAV	net asset value
NIFA	New International Financial Architecture
NSFR	Net Stable Funding Ratio
OBSE	off-balance sheet entity
OECD	Organisation for Economic Co-operation and Development
OLA	Orderly Liquidation Authority
OTC	Over the Counter
PCA	Prompt Corrective Action
PD	probability of default
PSE	Public Sector Entity
RMBS	Residential Mortgage-Backed Securities
ROSC	Reports on the Observance of Standards and Codes
RWAs	risk-weighted assets
SDRs	Special Drawing Rights
SEC	Securities and Exchange Commission (US)
SIFI	Systemically Important Financial Institution
SIV	Special Investment Vehicle
SPE	Special Purpose Entity
SPV	Special Purpose Vehicle
TARP	Troubled Assets Relief Program
TRN	Transnational Regulatory Network
TRS	Total Return Swap
UN	United Nations
UNCTAD	United Nations Conference on Trade and Development
UNDP	United Nations Development Programme
WTO	World Trade Organization

Introduction

1. The autumn of 2008

In mid-July 2007 the global credit markets came to a standstill. On the face of it, the continuous decline in the US housing market and the over-expansion of US and European banks in the US market for sub-prime mortgages led them to accumulate serious and mostly hidden losses. Mounting losses gave rise to a crisis of confidence where no bank would lend money to any other regardless of its credit standing. At the same time, the flows of capital to the global market for structured credit products all but disappeared. Gradually, the liquidity problems encountered by US and European banks were transformed into solvency problems due to their high leverage and low capitalization escalating the confidence crisis. In the process, bank problems became so deep as to develop into a full-blown financial crisis, the worst the world had seen since 1929.

Although an event of unprecedented severity, the Global Financial Crisis(GFC) had rather 'humble' beginnings. The first ominous episode was the collapse of a medium-size mortgage provider in the UK, Northern Rock.[1] It was followed by the collapse of the fifth biggest US investment bank, Bear Stearns, in March 2008, which became the subject of a quasi-compulsory takeover by JP Morgan. However, while the clouds of the unprecedented storm were gathering, most bankers and policy-makers still believed that the crisis would be contained. Then in the space of few weeks from early September (when the collapse of Fannie Mae and Freddie Mac was followed by Lehman Brother's failure) to early October 2008, the global financial system teetered on the brink of collapse on a daily basis.[2] It was rescued at a huge cost to US and European taxpayers and

---

[1] The Run on the Rock, (House of Commons, Treasury Committee, Fifth Report of Session 2007–08, 24 January 2008).

[2] I provide a concise overview of the events of autumn 2008 in Chapter 2, Section 6.2. For an authoritative timeline of the events leading to the GFC and its aftermath from the eruption of the sub-prime mortgage crisis in March 2007, see Council of Foreign Relations,

bail-outs gave rise to a heated debate in most parts of the world, although, in the conditions prevailing at the time, they seemed the only sensible option available. The bail-outs of the autumn of 2008 were followed by a global economic recession that was felt mostly in the developed world.

2.   Why the GFC was not prevented?

The GFC was not the first truly global financial crisis, that 'dubious' honour belongs to the 1929 crisis, and it is not going to be the last, but it was the biggest to date. The questions raised by the GFC permeated all levels and spheres of the global policy debate, touching on the politics, economics and legal/regulatory infrastructure underpinning global finance. Arguably, some of these questions have already been settled. One example is the set of new regulations and market infrastructures that are currently being introduced to deal with Over the Counter (OTC) derivatives trading and the risks associated with it. Other important questions, such as the issue of how to tackle best the 'too-big-to-fail' institution and moral hazard attached to its operation, are still being debated. The body of so-called soft law rules or standards comprising international financial regulation and the structures of the international financial architecture, mostly comprising Transnational Regulatory Networks (TRNs), clearly failed to predict or prevent the crisis. The reasons for this failure vary but two things are clear about pre-GFC international regulatory arrangements: their over-reliance on private sector input and lack of even a rudimentary institutional infrastructure to handle cross-border crises were contributing factors both in building up the conditions that led to the GFC and in exacerbating its consequences. But these observations do not tell the full story.

In the two decades preceding the GFC, a host of deregulation and other market-oriented policies, including monetary policies, inspired by the then unstoppable neo-liberal consensus, were pursued in an environment of relentless market innovation and technological advancement. The combination of these factors led to a gigantic expansion of global markets, a number of which – most critically the OTC derivatives market and

---

'Timeline: Global Economy in Crisis', available at www.cfr.org/economics/timeline-global-economy-crisis/p18709. See also Mauro F. Guillén, 'The Global Economic & Financial Crisis:A Timeline', The Lauder Institute, Wharton School, University of Pennsylvania, available at lauder.wharton.upenn.edu/pages/pdf/Chronology_Economic_Financial_Crisis.pdf. See also Hank Paulson, *On the Brink* (New York: Hachette Books, 2010).

the shadow banking sector – were not subject to any kind of regulatory oversight. It is not surprising that, when malevolent forces in the formal banking sector, namely, excessive credit expansion to unsuitable borrowers, combined with unregulated market activities that concealed excessive leverage in the shadow banking sector and with interconnectedness, arising from largely opaque transactions in the OTC derivatives markets, the wave of destruction became unstoppable. This combination was also largely responsible for the severity of the crisis.

Although regulatory inertia was to a large extent influenced by the neoliberal consensus and, to a certain extent, by 'capture', this is in many ways a very crude explanation of market and regulatory myopia. Therefore, not in order to discard those interpretations but rather to overhaul and shed light on them, it is worth re-examining the main forces that, alongside trade liberalization, shaped the development of global financial markets more than any other: *the financial revolution*. This is defined here as the sum of three contemporary developments: open markets due to liberalization; technological advancements in communications and computing power; and financial innovation. The concurrent emergence of these three seemingly independent developments radically transformed the global marketplace and sealed its fate. The utilization of the three elements of the financial revolution not only generated mega-profits but also colossal amounts of well concealed tiny risks that, if combined with other risks of equally low probability, could bring financial devastation. I provide an analytical examination of the causes of the GFC in Chapter 3.

Even a first reading of the empirical and theoretical studies discussed in Chapter 3 show that the unpredictable combination of all those low probability risks was made possible because of financial innovation and the existence of fast moving and open global markets. I argue in this book that, while a small number of insiders had a fairly good understanding of financial innovation and its possible interaction with the other forces of financial revolution and time-old (and little explained) characteristics of financial markets, such as herding, in most cases policymakers, regulators and even senior bankers preferred to live in a state of 'blissful ignorance'. They did so either because the new developments exceeded their cognitive capacities or because they preferred to take the easy route of merely watching rising market prices and widespread euphoria and not delving deeper, trying to understand what was truly pushing the unprecedented price rises in most global asset markets.

Misunderstanding a major knowledge revolution, as recent financial innovations should be held to be, is nothing new. Not only do communities

of experts tend to be confused as to the actual epistemological properties of new knowledge/technology, but economists have also traditionally
under-estimated its value.[3] Therefore, the possibility of financial innovation (perceived here as a knowledge revolution) being used as a benevo-
lent force to achieve global welfare objectives should not be discarded. On
the contrary, proper research/knowledge structures with a global reach
should be built to help policy-makers and possibly the markets to gain a
better understanding of the properties (and risks) of financial innovation[4]
and of the financial revolution in general in order to manage them in a
way that would not endanger financial stability and would even facilitate
the achievement of other global welfare objectives.

3. Why is finance so important?

3.1   Overview

The financial system provides a large number of critical functions (analytically discussed in Chapter 2) which are inextricably linked with the
welfare of modern economies and day-to-day life. To mention but a few,
financial markets allow private and public actors to fund their consumption and investment needs by means of bank loans or finance provided
by the capital markets, a mechanism that would not have been so readily available in the absence of well functioning markets. The reason is
that the financial system provides investors, through market prices, with
a reliable criterion of value. The interplay of supply and demand allows
price formation (discovery) through the filtering out of trader's heterogeneous expectations as well as the dissemination of privately held market information. In principle, financial markets, through the provision of
a price discovery mechanism, facilitate the efficient allocation of scarce
resources, using savers', and investors' funds most efficiently.

The financial system protects, through the use of futures markets, producers and consumers of physical commodities and traders and users of
financial assets from adverse price movements. In addition, there is a very
strong (mutual causation) link between financial system development

---

[3] See for an overview of relevant studies and explanations, Yong J. Yoon, 'Science, Scientific
Institutions, and Economic Progress', George Mason University Working Paper in
Economics No. 10–36, 3 November 2010, available at papers.ssrn.com/sol3/papers.
cfm?abstract_id=1702675.

[4] Cf. John Gerard Ruggie, 'International Responses to Technology: Concepts and Trends'
(1975) 29 *International Organization* 557.

and economic growth (and possibly poverty eradication), an aspect of financial markets that is extensively discussed in Chapter 2.

The principal financial institutions that tend to have a cross-border presence are: (1) commercial banks; (2) investment banks; (3) savings banks and credit unions, also called thrift institutions; (4) insurance companies; (5) private pension funds; (6) specialized finance companies which deal either with consumer or commercial loans; and (7) investment funds, including mutual funds, money market funds, hedge funds and sovereign wealth funds, which mainly invest their government's disposable wealth accumulated through trade surpluses. All financial institutions perform some of the functions listed above, but only commercial banks perform all of them.

The traditional banking system has three actors: savers, borrowers and banks and provides credit intermediation through the 'recycling' of savers' deposits into loans. Credit intermediation involves credit, maturity and liquidity transformation, since it generally uses highly liquid short-term deposits to provide, in principle, illiquid long term loans. More specifically, in a modern economy, banks provide three critical services that foster economic development:

(1) they ameliorate the information problems between fund providers, such as depositors and investors, and borrowers or securities issuers by monitoring the latter and ensuring a proper use of the providers' funds;
(2) they provide inter-temporal smoothing of risk that cannot be diversified at a given point in time as well as insurance to savers against unexpected consumption shocks; and
(3) they provide payments infrastructure.[5]

For these reasons the sound and safe operation of banks is of strategic importance not only in fostering economic development but also in ensuring social and economic stability. If savers are confident about the safety and sound operation of the formal banking sector, they will avoid channelling their savings to the informal banking sector, which is highly inefficient and is sometimes operated by criminal syndicates. Accordingly, the sound and safe operation of a competitive banking system ensures interested firms can access bank finance at reasonable market-based interest rates, allowing them to implement investment plans that are dependent on such financing and avoid over-borrowing.

[5] Franklin Allen and Elena Carletti, 'The Role of Banks in Financial Systems', March 2008, available at fic.wharton.upenn.edu/fic/papers/08/0819.pdf.

Similar principles relate to the workings of capital markets, where investor confidence in the operation of the price formation mechanism is paramount to the proper allocation of resources performed by those markets. Investor confidence boosts liquidity, one of the main ingredients of capital markets, but it is normally withdrawn when markets malfunction or are ridden with abuse, whether in the form of fraud, insider dealing or market manipulation.

3.2   Should finance be regulated?

Arguably, the most important and sensitive function of financial markets is efficient allocation of resources. Yet this is a fragile mechanism and may easily be disturbed by exogenous and endogenous shocks/distortions or may not perform properly due to market failures. In addition, because of maturity mismatches between their assets and liabilities, and the risk of contagion due to information asymmetries, banks are vulnerable to runs and represent a serious source of systemic risk. Hence the need for extensive regulations which broadly intend to:[6]

(1) preserve the confidence of the providers of finance (whether this means depositors and other creditors or investors) and of consumers of financial services in the function, processes and efficient outcomes of financial markets;
(2) remedy market failures (e.g., disclosure and market integrity regulations); and
(3) protect the financial system from unforeseen but likely shocks such as bank runs (e.g., deposit insurance and capital adequacy regulations).

It follows that one of the main justifications of financial regulation is that the multitude of externalities and failures finance providers and users encounter have such a large impact on the real economy that financial sector institutions should be tightly regulated to make them more resilient and their liquidity has to be subsidized through central bank support.

Securing the sound, safe and efficient operation of the banking system is no easy business. In fact it may be impossible to totally eliminate financial crises and bank failures, although financial systems have over the years

---

[6] See Charles Goodhart, Philipp Hartmann, David T. Llewellyn, Liliana Rojas-Suarez and Steven Weisbrod, *Financial Regulation, Why, How, and Where Now?* (London: Routledge, 1998); Ross Cranston, *Principles of Banking Law* (Oxford University Press, 2nd edn, 2002), Chapter 3; Emilios Avgouleas, *The Mechanics and Regulation of Market Abuse – A Legal and Economic Analysis* (Oxford University Press, 2005), Chapter 5.

been increasingly subject to strict government regulations attempting to prevent bank collapses, which may trigger contagion through generalized lack of confidence. Any given body of rules that is trying to create and preserve a sound and safe banking system must address four concerns:

(1) ensure the efficient and effective operation of banks, since due to the *principal/agent* problem savers do not know the true quality of the management that operates the bank with which they have trusted their savings;
(2) ensure that banks have adequate financial resources either to avoid a *failure* or to compensate their depositors and other creditors properly;
(3) devise a public system of regulations and supervisory techniques which ensure that, in the event of a bank failure, any depositor's run is effectively averted/contained and does not lead to a systemic crisis and the collapse of the banking system due to *contagion*; and
(4) ensure that the financial system is not used to facilitate *criminal activities* and, especially, to legalize the proceeds of crime (money laundering).

While national public authorities might find it easy to build regulatory systems that try to achieve these goals and end up pursuing them with moderate success, they are bound to find it impossible to deal with cross-border contagion and loss of confidence stemming from it in an era of global markets. As a result, a number of formal and informal international bodies, such as the International Monetary Fund (IMF), the European Union (EU), the Group of 20 most developed countrie(G-20), and the Basel Committee on Banking Supervision (BCBS), and a number of other Transnational Regulatory Networks (TRNs) have produced multiple sets of financial standards and regulations that intend to secure the sound and safe operation of international banks and other parts of global financial markets.[7] Where the sources of these rules are TRNs, they normally become binding either through national implementation or EU legislation.

During the 1990s, as finance became increasingly global, so did financial crises. Following the Mexican and Asian financial crises, a set of new arrangements was put in place to meet the needs of global finance, the 'New International Financial Architecture' (NIFA). In essence, these reforms amounted to little more than establishing another TRN, the

---

[7] See, for more extensive analysis, Chapter 4 of this book and Rosa Lastra, *Legal Foundations of International Monetary Stability* (Oxford University Press, 2006), Part III.

Financial Stability Forum (FSF), to co-ordinate the disparate soft law networks. At the same time, a system of voluntary monitoring through the Financial Sector Assessment Program (FSAP)[8] meant that, for the first time, international standard setting would be supported by a rudimentary review process. Yet NIFA structures proved entirely unsuitable to regulate properly the financial revolution and address the challenges this created. In fact, Basel capital standards, which were one of the central parts of NIFA, proved to be terribly flawed. They were very pro-cyclical and fostered regulatory arbitrage that allowed regulated banks to resort to highly leveraged shadow banking activities, which proved a very significant and well concealed source of systemic risk. Indeed, the total absence of any kind of institutional capacity in the field of crisis management and bank cross-border resolution meant that NIFA soft law structures were rendered irrelevant during the GFC.[9]

In the middle of the current crisis, two significant changes have taken place in the edifice of the international financial architecture. The first has been the emergence of the G-20 heads of state level as the predominant body for the co-ordination of international policy responses to the GFC and the second the reconstitution of the FSF that was renamed as the Financial Stability Board (FSB).[10] The FSB is increasingly taking a leadership role in international micro-prudential supervision matters.

4.   The post-2008 reforms

It is not surprising that the GFC triggered a frenetic period of reform in an attempt to mend the broken arms of domestic and global finance and restore its functions. In the UK, the FSA will be abolished to be replaced by two new regulators, one responsible for prudential supervision (Prudential Regulation Authority) and one for investor protection and market conduct (Financial Conduct Authority). There will also be a new Financial Policy Committee in the Bank of England, which will be the macro-prudential supervisor having primary responsibility for maintaining financial stability.[11]

---

[8] See IMF, 'Factsheet- The Financial Sector Assessment Program (FSAP)', 23 March 2011, available at www.imf.org/external/np/exr/facts/fsap.htm.
[9] See Chapters 3 and 5 below.
[10] See also Joseph J. Norton, '"NIFA-II" or "Bretton Woods- II"?: The G-20 (Leaders) Summit Process on Managing Global Financial Markets and The World Economy – Quo Vadis?', (2010) 11 *Journal of Banking Regulation* 261–301.
[11] The UK Treasury intends thus to adopt a 'twin peaks plus' approach to financial supervision. See HM Treasury, A New Approach to Financial Regulation: The Blue Print for Reform (Cm 8083, July 2011).

Switzerland, which is not an EU member but came close to a systemic crisis due to the problems experienced by its two biggest banks (UBS and Credit Suisse), also restructured its system of financial supervision moving in a direction opposite to that in which the UK Treasury intends to move. Since January 2009 a single authority, the Financial Markets Authority (FINMA), has held responsibility for both prudential and investor/consumer protection regulation, succeeding the Swiss Federal Banking Commission and other sectoral regulators. The Swiss National Bank has retained responsibility for the stability of the financial system.[12]

In the US and the EU, legislators have brought about sweeping changes as regards the regulation, supervision and resolution of large banks and other Systemically Important Financial Institutions (SIFIs), OTC derivatives trading and ratings production by the credit rating agencies (CRAs). In addition, the BCBS has produced a radically upgraded capital framework for banks.

After a period of gestation and amid mutual recriminations between Democrats and Republicans as to who is to blame for the collapse of Wall Street, the US Senate approved the massive Dodd–Frank Act in July 2010. The Act brings about significant reforms (analytically discussed in Chapters 6 and 7) as regards the structure of systemic risk supervision in the US, with the establishment of the Financial System Oversight Council (FSOC) and expansion of the Federal Reserve Board's (FRBs) supervisory remit to insurance companies and other non-bank financial institutions that, in the opinion of the new macroprudential supervisor, are systemically important. It also regulates the activities of commercial banks and introduces a strict regime for the standardization of OTC derivatives and centralization of trading and settlement of trades. Another very important reform Dodd–Frank has introduced is the establishment of a new special resolution regime (the Orderly Liquidation Authority or OLA) for SIFIs, whether banks or non-bank financial institutions. These will have to go through compulsory liquidation if they enter the scheme.

The pace of reform has been relentless in the EU as well and at least as wide ranging as in the US. The EU's reliance on a supervisory model that was centred on national supervisors proved to be very ineffective. Three major problems were identified. First, there was a marked lack of any framework for the monitoring of systemic risk on a pan-European basis. Second, 'home country control' proved problematic and exposed

---

[12] See Swiss Financial Market Supervisory Authority Act (FINMASA) (effective 1 January 2009).

the gaps in cross-border supervision of banking groups. Third, the unco-ordinated bank rescues highlighted the lack of pan-European structures for cross-border crisis management. Since these gaps in financial supervision called for a radical rethinking of regulatory structures in the EU, the Commission mandated a High-Level Group chaired by Jacques de Larosière to make recommendations on how to strengthen European supervisory arrangements and improve investor/consumer/depositor/taxpayer protection. The High-Level Group, in its final report of 25 February 2009 (the 'de Larosière Report'),[13] suggested reforms to the structure of financial supervision in the EU and consistent implementation of harmonized rules. Thus, the structure and processes of financial regulation in the EU have undergone very significant transformation, as a result of which:

(1) the newly established European Systemic Risk Board (ESRB) has become the European macro-prudential supervisor, although it has no formal standing in EU law;
(2) the principles of minimum harmonization and mutual recognition have largely disappeared, since the standard setting competence of the new European Supervisory Authorities (ESAs) makes them the central pillars and channels of maximum harmonization; and
(3) certain aspects of the supervision of cross-border groups have (implicitly) shifted from home country control to transnational supervisory structures comprising, essentially, supervisory colleges[14] and the new ESAs.

In addition, the EU has proposed or enacted legislation to bring credit rating agencies under the direct supervision of the new European Securities and Markets Authority (ESMA), to regulate hedge fund managers and to encourage OTC derivatives standardization and centralization of clearing and settlement.

---

[13] The de Larosière Report is available at ec.europa.eu/internal_market/finances/docs/de_larosiere_report_en.pdf.
[14] Directive 2009/111/EC of 16 September 2009 amending Directives 2006/48/EC, 2006/49/EC and 2007/64/EC as regards banks affiliated to central institutions, certain own funds items, large exposures, supervisory arrangements, and crisis management OJ L 302/97 17 November 2009. This Directive maintains that the supervisory powers of national competent authorities are not diluted, Recital 6. However, given the powers of Colleges and of the ESAs, and the authority Colleges may establish over systemically important branches, this claim looks maximalist. See new Art. 42a of Directive 2006/48/EC inserted by means of Art. 1 of Directive 2009/111/EC.

International regulators have also been very active. The BCBS has radically redesigned its capital adequacy standards and has introduced a new supervisory framework to regulate bank capital. It has also designed liquidity and leverage ratios, as well as macro-prudential measures to complement the capital ratio, together called the Basel III framework.[15] In addition, BCBS has issued standards to improve risk management and governance in the banking sector. The main objective of the new capital measures introduced by Basel III is to resolve the chronic problem of bank undercapitalization, a widespread phenomenon during the current crisis, which led to a massive number of bail-outs. Basel III aims to ensure that banks are able to withstand the type of stress experienced during the GFC, including banks' exposure to the economic cycle, bubbles and other macro-economic developments. The preceding Basel framework was exclusively reliant on micro-prudential regulation measures.

Basel III introduces higher levels of capital for banks. As a result, the minimum requirement for common equity, which is regarded as the best form of loss absorbing capital, will be raised from the 2 per cent level of the previous Basel Accords, before the application of regulatory adjustments, to 4.5 per cent of risk-weighted assets (RWAs). To this shall be added a capital conservation buffer of up to 2.5 per cent of RWAs, which will bring the total minimum of common equity in bank capital to 7 per cent of RWAs by 2019 when all reforms will have been implemented. Furthermore, Basel III gives supervisors the discretion to require additional capital buffers during periods of excess credit growth in order to contain asset bubbles, the so-called counter-cyclical buffer, and introduces comprehensive leverage and liquidity ratios that would lead to more resilient banks.

Finally, in an attempt to tackle more effectively moral hazard emanating from public bail-outs of 'too-big-to-fail' institutions, a number of proposals have been set out, chiefly by the IMF and the BCBS, regarding the proper approach to cross-border resolution of financial institutions. The EU has released for consultation its own plans on the same matter (analytically discussed in Chapter 7), which include a pan-European crisis management and cross-border resolution regime.

---

[15] BCBS, 'Basel III: A Global Regulatory Framework for more Resilient Banks and Banking Systems', December 2010.

5.   Whither governance of global financial markets?

5.1   *The book's subject matter*

This book examines the global structures governing international finance in the period from 1944 to 2008 and the substantive and structural reforms that have been proposed or implemented after 2008. The view adopted is that the specific elements underpinning global markets governance comprise, *inter alia*:

(1) national/regional regulations with a cross-border or extra-territorial policy impact or compliance/enforcement dimension, like US and EU financial markets legislation (with the EU being a supra-national structure/organization per se);
(2) International agreements and institutions established under international and European law, such as the IMF or the new (ESAs);
(3) soft law arrangements in the form of international regulatory standards and TRNs, such as BCBS, responsible for global regulatory co-operation and production of standards; and
(4) private sector organizations, such as the Group of Thirty or the International Swaps and Derivatives Association (ISDA) that either provide policy input on matters pertinent to the regulation of global markets or the legal infrastructure on which global market participants conclude their transactions.

Accordingly the arrangements governing international finance involve a constellation of public and private actors and national, European, international and soft law rules and institutions all play an important role. It follows that the only way to provide a credible discussion of these arrangements is by adopting a multidisciplinary approach and to integrate into this study, depending on context, the methodologies, findings, ideas and perspectives of at least three distinct disciplines: legal analysis, economic analysis and international relations theory. Insights of regulatory theory and institutional economics, finance theory and behavioural economics are also utilized in the course of this study but these should be seen as sub-divisions of the three major disciplines mentioned above.

5.2   *Towards a new governance model*

There has never been a better time to discuss the possibility of a supra-national governance system for global financial markets without fearing scornful rejection of such an impractical 'adacemic' exercise. The reason for this assertion is that the problems that the current system presents are very conspicuous and threatening to ignore. Chapters 6 and 7 engage in an in-depth analysis of the reforms that are currently under way. These reforms are, in most cases, a significant step in the right direction. Yet the lack of any governance structures to support them will probably mean that their effective implementation will be undermined.

Furthermore, existing reforms, whether already implemented or just at the planning stage, do little to address a host of issues that have also been at the heart of the current crisis and greatly contributed to its severity. First, current reforms do not secure effective cross-border supervision of SIFIs or even more importantly of the new super class of financial institutions, operating in a multitude of jurisdictions and markets, called Globally Systemically Important Financial Institutions (G-SIFIs).[16] Second, current proposals for effective cross-border crisis management and orderly resolution/insolvency of international financial institutions, and especially financial groups, remain very unconvincing in the absence of fiscal sharing arrangements and arguably of a supra-national authority charged with this task. Third, the newly established systemic risk supervisors in the US and the EU will still be faced with 'blind spots' when it comes to shadow banking activity. This is a major shortcoming, since the volume of transactions taking place in the global shadow banking sector is worth several trillions of dollars more than those taking place in the formal banking sector. Fourth, it is very likely that the design of flawed regulatory standards and regulators' wrongful approach to bank supervision might have been caused by inadequate knowledge of the ramifications of the financial revolution and especially financial innovation.

It is paradoxical that the current soft law structures retain their over-reliance on private sector input for their information/education. As explained in Chapter 3, private sector input can often be unreliable for reasons that go beyond the apparent conflict of interests and have to do with inability of private actors to observe the whole picture and lack of incentives to acquire more knowledge than is necessary for them to carry

---

[16] The FSB defines G-SIFIs as 'institutions of such size, market importance, and global interconnectedness that their distress or failure would cause significant dislocation in the global financial system and adverse economic consequences across a range of countries. Standards for large global financial firms should be commensurate with the system-wide expected losses that their failure would produce.' See FSB, 'Reducing the Moral Hazard Posed by Systemically Important Financial Institutions – FSB Recommendations and Time Lines', 20 October 2010.

out their business. In addition, private actors' understanding of emerging market risks and above all of their correlations with other market phenomena, such as herding, 'irrational exuberance' and widespread loss-aversion or panic (all discussed extensively in Chapter 2 below) might be as low as that of public actors. Finally, the new structures continue to ignore the very big importance to the global development objective of the close causal link between availability of finance and economic growth, well enshrined in the United Nations' Millennium Development Goals.[17] Therefore, there is an urgent need for a new governance paradigm for global financial markets.[18]

This new paradigm should incorporate rather than demolish the effective parts of the current soft law arrangements and especially the rule-making functions of the TRNs and credible private sector input/ co-operation.[19] On the other hand, the new governance regime for global markets and institutions should be based on a formal, hierarchical and multilayered[20] architecture and have at its centre formal international law bodies. I provide in Chapter 8 a proposal for a new governance system for global financial markets that has strong evolutionary characteristics and is based on four regulatory pillars:

(1) a global systemic risk/ macro-prudential supervisor, a role that should be discharged by the IMF;
(2) a micro-prudential supervisor for G-SIFIs with a strong cross-border asset or liabilities base, a role that should be discharged by a reconstituted FSB;
(3) a regulatory policy and risk knowledge management body overseeing the TRNs, a role that may be discharged by the OECD and the research department of the Bank for International Settlements; and
(4) a global resolution authority, which would be exclusively concerned with the resolution of big cross-border institutions or groups.

---

[17] The MDGs seek to, *inter alia*: (1) reduce extreme poverty and hunger by 2015; (2) achieve universal primary education by 2015; (3) reduce by two thirds, between 1990 and 2015, the under-five mortality rate; (4) ensure a sustainable environment, etc. In addition the MDGs call for the creation of a global partnership for development. See UN Human Development Report 2003, 'Millennium Development Goals: A Compact among Nations to End Human Poverty', UN Development Programme, 2003.

[18] On this imperative see David Held, *Cosmopolitanism: Ideas and Realities* (Cambridge: Polity Press, 2010), Chapter 6.

[19] Douglas W. Arner and Ross P. Buckley, 'Redesigning the Architecture of the International Economic System' (2010) 11 *Melbourne Journal of International Law* 185–239.

[20] See Thomas Cottier, 'Multilayered Governance, Pluralism, and Moral Conflict', (2009) 16 *Indiana Journal of Global Legal Studies* 647–79.

Moreover, it is suggested that a new system of governance for global financial markets should identify a core of shared values in the form of general principles and sub-principles underpinning the operation of the system.[21] The most important (and unassailable) of the principles underpinning the proposed governance system ought to be financial stability.[22] Yet there should be room for global regulators to facilitate the development agenda, without compromising systemic stability. It is anticipated that, if the insights of new institutional economics hold true,[23] a governance model like the one proposed here will provide global finance operators with welfare enhancing norms of behaviour, even in the absence of any threat of enforcement.

6. Book structure

This book is a multidisciplinary work. Thus, it has been structured so it facilitates reader understanding of different concepts and developments and also gradually builds its argument on solid foundations. In this respect the book is divided in three parts.

---

[21] Rolf H. Weber, 'Multilayered Governance in International Financial Regulation and Supervision' (2010) 13 *Journal of International Economic Law* 683–704, 689–90.

[22] The terms financial stability and systemic stability are used interchangeably in this book. They are both rather imprecise terms and in most cases defined by reference to what happens in their absence. A formal but not all encompassing definition has been offered by the EU Regulation establishing the European Systemic Risk Board, which defines 'systemic risk' as: '[the] risk of disruption in the financial system with the potential to have serious negative consequences for the internal market and the real economy. All types of financial intermediaries, markets and infrastructure may be potentially systemically important to some degree', EU Regulation 1092/2010 on European Union macro-prudential oversight of the financial system and establishing a European Systemic Risk Board, OJ L 331/11, 15 December 2010, Art. 2(c). An earlier working definition was offered by Garry Schinasi, who defined financial stability as the ability of the financial system to facilitate and enhance economic processes, manage risks and absorb shocks. See Garry J. Schinasi, 'Defining Financial Stability', IMF Working Paper No. 04/187, October 2004, available at papers.ssrn.com/sol3/papers.cfm?abstract_id=879012. For an analytical account see Garry J. Schinasi, *Safeguarding Financial Stability Theory and Practice* (Washington, DC: IMF, 2005), pp. 77–134. For attempts to quantify (model) the different properties of financial stability see C. Goodhart and D. Tsomocos, 'Analysis of Financial Stability', Special Paper 173, Financial Markets Group, London School of Economics, 2007; O. Aspachs, C. Goodhart, M. Segoviano, D. Tsomocos and L. Zicchino, 'Searching for a Metric for Financial Stability', Special Paper 167, Financial Markets Group, London School of Economics, 2006.

[23] See, in general, Douglass North, *Institutions, Institutional Change and Economic Performance* (Cambridge University Press, 1990).

Part I deals with financial markets and financial crises and comprises Chapters 2 and 3. Chapter 2 examines the modern development of global financial markets with particular focus on those that were the product of financial innovation, namely OTC derivatives markets and the shadow banking sector. The chapter is in seven sections. It first explains the economic functions of financial markets and their role in economic development. Then it provides an analysis of the most innovative segments of contemporary financial markets. It proceeds with a critical review of efficient market hypothesis and behavioural finance as the main tools of analysis of market behaviour and asset bubbles. As the analysis of global markets would be incomplete without discussion of policies that stimulated their growth, the chapter also introduces the neo-liberal consensus policies that fostered the continuous expansion of global financial markets and unfettered use of financial innovation. Finally, it offers an analytical discussion of the most common causes of financial crises and examines Hyman Minsky's hypothesis that financial markets are inherently unstable. In this context, it provides concise accounts of the Asian Crisis and of the GFC.

Chapter 3 discusses the causes of the Global Financial Crisis and is in six sections. It first considers the macro-causes of the GFC in accordance with the 'conventional' explanations that have already been offered by academics and policy-makers. It provides an extensive analysis of neo-liberal policies such as deregulation and the Jackson Hole Consensus and considers the impact of the latter on asset bubble formation. It also examines the public housing policies that seem to have contributed to the build up of the GFC. Then, it surveys the micro-causes and sheds light on the issue of misaligned incentives in a variety of contexts ranging from corporate governance and executive compensation to the operation of the 'originate-to-distribute' model. It also considers the flawed regulations that contributed to the GFC. Consequently, it proceeds with a novel look at both the development of global financial markets and the recent crisis. In this context, it suggests that the GFC was above all the result of a little understood financial revolution that was badly mis-managed, due to insider rent-seeking and widespread moral hazard.

Part II is dedicated to a discussion of pre-existing governance structures for global finance (1946–2008) and an evaluation of the soft law aspects of those structures (Chapters 4 and 5). Chapter 4 discusses the evolution of global financial governance and international financial regulation. It first provides an account of early age global governance structures and maps the path that led to the emergence of the BCBS and of the other major TRNs in the sphere of international finance. It also explains the path of trade liberalization and the rise of multilateral development institutions during the same period. It then proceeds to give an analysis of the NIFA and a critical overview of the emerging international finance architecture in the post-GFC period and the role of the G-20 in global regulatory reform and international finance governance.

Chapter 5 provides a critical evaluation of the soft law structures in international financial regulation and highlights the existing supervisory and crisis management deficit in global financial markets. The chapter discusses TRN theory and its importance in international relations. It charts the methods used by TRNs to achieve co-operation in the absence of a binding international treaty. It then proceeds to explain the limits of TRN theory in the sphere of international finance and the failure of the Basel capital framework. It finally provides an exposition of the short-comings of existing soft law structures, especially when it comes to cross-border crisis management and resolution.

Part III examines the most important structural and substantive regu-latory reforms of the post-GFC period, regardless of whether they have already been endorsed and implemented, or they are still at the planning and consultation stage. It also outlines a proposal for a new governance system for global financial markets as an answer to the problems identi-fied in this study. It comprises Chapters 6, 7, and 8. Chapter 6 is in four sections. It provides a critical and in-depth analysis of the most important of the current EU and US reforms, especially as regards the regulation of systemic risk, OTC derivatives and CRAs. It also gives an analytical account of structural reforms in these jurisdictions and of the powers and tasks of the ESRB and of the European Supervisory Authorities. It then proceeds to offer an in-depth view of the Basel III framework.

Chapter 7 provides an analysis of current reform proposals pertain-ing to the supervision of and capital requirements planned to be imposed on 'too-big-to-fail' institutions and the emerging resolution regimes in the US and the EU. It first provides an analysis of the emerging con-sensus for the regulation and supervision of SIFIs expressed through the recommendations of the FSB. It then discusses the size limitations the US Dodd–Frank Act has placed on SIFIs through the Volcker Rule and other provisions and the structural restrictions that the UK authorities are considering imposing on large banks. It proceeds with an in-depth analysis of FSB/BCBS approach to regulating the risk of G-SIFIs through capital surcharges. It also considers the costs and benefits of contingent capital instruments. Consequently, it offers a critical evaluation of BCBS,

FSB and IMF recommendations on cross-border resolution of financial institutions and financial groups, followed by a concise analysis of the Dodd–Frank special resolution regime for SIFIs. The chapter considers the ramifications of the OLA both for the regulation of 'too-big-to-fail' institutions in the US and co-ordination of cross-border resolutions. Finally, the chapter provides a critical analysis and evaluation of the EU Commission proposals for a pan-European crisis management and resolution regime for banks and certain investment firms.

Chapter 8 provides a proposal for a new model of governance for global financial markets in order to address most of the shortcomings of current governance structures and to support effectively and advance recent reforms. It aims to protect the ideal of open global markets and enhance their legitimacy. The proposed global governance structure would have four pillars: (1) macro-prudential; (2) micro-prudential; (3) financial policy, regulation and knowledge supervisor; and, (4) a global resolution authority. The suggested governance system pre-supposes the negotiation and signing of an (umbrella) international treaty governing the most important aspects of international finance. It would be based on a set of general principles and sub-principles that, on the one hand, would stress the paramount importance of financial stability and, on the other, promote the global development objective.

PART I

Financial markets and financial crises

2

Financial markets and financial crises

1. Introduction

The global marketplace changed radically in the 2000s as a result of financial innovation and the development of the global shadow banking industry. While the conditions of excessive liquidity that characterized the markets between 1998 and 2007 and the excessive use of regulatory and tax arbitrage did contribute greatly to the shape of the new market landscape, and more critically to the expansion of the shadow banking sector, financial innovation was not merely the product of the last decade. Financial markets have experienced a number of new breakthroughs since their inception. Distinct advancements in the nineteenth century constitute the formation of the joint stock company, the emergence of international markets for sovereign debt and the establishment of formal arrangements for the trading of forward and futures contracts. Similarly in the twentieth century, the development of syndicated loans and the offshore market for bond issues in dollars, so-called Eurobonds, in the 1960s and the advent of loan transfers in the 1970s set the tune for further innovations in the last two decades of that century.[1] These were the development of the global OTC derivatives markets in the 1980s and the market for securitizations in the 1990s. Three correlated developments greatly facilitated the breakneck pace of financial innovation witnessed in the 2000s: (1) nearly universal abolition of national capital controls, boosting cross-border capital flows; (2) massive advancements in computing capacity and in the speed of communications both due to the technology revolution, which greatly enhanced belief in risk modelling; and (3) international trade liberalization, which led, as a side effect, to further exacerbation of national trade imbalances.

---

[1] See Ross Cranston, *Principles of Banking Law* (Oxford University Press, 2nd edn, 2002), Chapters 12 and 13.

The evolution, development and characteristics of the global financial system have been described in numerous works.[2] As a result, in this chapter I shall only offer a cursory picture of the parts of the global financial system that contributed the most to the Global Financial Crisis (GFC), especially global derivatives markets and the shadow banking sector. The relevant analysis would have been incomplete without a discussion of the prevailing theories relating to the price formation mechanism in financial markets and the behaviour of market participants. This discussion also aids reader understanding of some of the causes of financial market fragility, such as asset bubbles, inextricably linked to boom and bust cycles in the real economy. In the same context, liberalization and policies centred on the Washington Consensus are also examined. These were as central to the explosive growth of modern financial markets as technological advancements and financial innovation.

Financial markets have historically shown strong signs of instability, especially when countries', corporations' and households' indebtedness becomes unsustainable. Thus, this chapter will examine the link between financial markets and financial crises, trying to explain the causes of the latter. It will critically consider theories relating to the perceived inherent instability of financial markets and to other market failures associated with their operation. In this context, the chapter advances the view that in the past three decades the world experienced a financial revolution of unprecedented proportions, which was much misunderstood by policymakers and regulators. As a result, instead of harnessing the potent forces of that revolution and its attendant breakthroughs in knowledge to promote global welfare-enhancing goals, the revolution was left in the hands of insiders.

Partly motivated by greed and partly as a result of their own myopia insiders badly misused the financial revolution, in their search for ever increasing rents, accrued through the increased opportunities presented by deregulated global markets and a free riding on the public guarantee the banking sector has always enjoyed. Finally, this work and the rather

[2] Among the most recent works in the field are: Frederic S. Mishkin and Stanley Eakins, *Financial Markets and Institutions* (Upper Saddle River, NJ: Prentice Hall, 7th edn, 2011); Frederic S. Mishkin, *The Economics of Money, Banking, and Financial Markets* (Upper Saddle River, NJ: Pearson Education, 9th edn, 2010); Stephen Valdez and Philip Molyneux, *An Introduction to Global Financial Markets* (London: Palgrave, 6th edn, 2010); Keith Pilbeam, *Finance and Financial Markets* (London: Palgrave, 3rd edn, 2010). For an overview of capital markets workings, see Emilios Avgouleas, *The Mechanics and Regulation of Market Abuse, A Legal and Economic Analysis* (Oxford University Press 2005), Chapter 2.

prolonged and toilsome effort relating to regulatory reform witnessed in the past three years would have been totally meaningless if international financial markets were not so critical for national and global economic development and the welfare of individuals and nations. Therefore, the ensuing analysis starts with a discussion of the role financial markets play in fostering economic growth and poverty eradication.

The remainder of the chapter is structured as follows. Section 2 explains the economic functions of financial markets and their role in economic development. Section 3 provides an analysis of the most innovative segments of contemporary financial markets, focusing on derivatives, securitizations and the shadow banking sector. Section 4 gives a critical overview of efficient market hypothesis and behavioural finance as the main tools of analysis of market behaviour and asset bubbles. Section 5 introduces the neo-liberal consensus policies that stimulated the continuous expansion of global financial markets and unfettered use of financial innovation. Section 6 provides an analytical discussion of the causes of financial crises and examines the hypothesis that financial markets are inherently unstable. In this context, it provides concise accounts of the Asian Crisis and of the GFC. Section 7 concludes.

2. The important functions of the financial system

2.1 How financial systems foster economic growth

It is widely accepted that financial markets are an efficient means to allocate resources to their most productive use.[3] In this sense, they allow for the renewal of a country's economy by pulling funding from underperforming or ageing sectors and pouring it into newer, more innovative and promising ones, much in accord with Schumpeter's theory of 'creative destruction'.[4] Nonetheless, it is often unclear to the reader of relevant works how finance provides these outcomes. The financial system plays a

---

[3] For an overview, see Jeffrey Wurgler, 'Financial Markets and the Allocation of Capital', Yale International Center Finance Working Paper No. 99–08, 5 August 1999, available at papers.ssrn.com/paper.taf?abstract_id=171921.

[4] See Joseph A. Schumpeter, *Theorie der Wirtschaftlichen Entwicklung* [The Theory of Economic Development] (Leipzig: Dunker & Humblot, 1912); translated by Redvers Opie for the English edition (Cambridge, MA: Harvard University Press, 1934). According to Schumpeter, innovative entrepreneurship leads to gales of 'creative destruction' as innovations cause old inventories, ideas, technologies, skills and equipment to become obsolete.

most critical role in the workings of modern economies and their development[5] through the performance of five functions:

(1) production of *ex ante* information about possible investments;
(2) monitoring of investments and implementation of corporate governance;
(3) management of risk, including risk diversification through trading;
(4) mobilization and pooling of savings, which widen access to finance; and
(5) facilitation of economic exchange (transactions).

Although all financial systems provide these critical functions, there are large differences in how well financial systems provide them. As a result, financial system development is an issue of great importance for the attainment of economic growth. In the next few paragraphs I will discuss the most critical functions of the financial system and then I will proceed with an analysis of the link between financial sector development and two of the most important challenges of the modern world: economic growth and poverty eradication.

2.2   Mobilization, pooling of savings and ease of exchange

Pooling of capital from disparate savers for investment is a costly process. It is widely accepted that mobilizing savings entails: (1) lowering transaction costs attached to collecting savings from different individuals, namely eliminating the need for a multitude of bilateral contracts between suppliers (savers/investors) and users of capital (borrowers/issuers of securities); and (2) overcoming the information asymmetries associated with making savers comfortable in placing their savings out of their control. Thus, in the absence of financial intermediaries, mobilization of investment might have been impossible. Financial systems that are more effective at pooling the savings of individuals can profoundly affect economic development by increasing savings, exploiting economies of scale and overcoming investment indivisibilities. In addition, better savings mobilization can improve resource allocation and boost

---

[5] From the numerous relevant studies I have chosen to use as primary reference what is arguably the best summary of the relevant works prepared in an authoritative way by two World Bank Economists for the Commission on Growth and Development. See Asli Demirgüç-Kunt and Ross Levine, 'Finance, Financial Sector Policies, and Long-Run Growth', Commission on Growth and Development, Working Paper 11, February 2008, pp. 3–4.

technological innovation, since it allows production processes to reach economically efficient scales of production.[6]

Financial arrangements that lower transaction costs can promote specialization, technological innovation and growth.[7] Greater specialization is likely to lead to more efficient production processes.[8] Thus, financial arrangements that lower transaction costs will facilitate greater specialization. In this way, financial markets that lower the cost of exchange encourage productivity and attendant economic development gains.

Financial intermediaries mobilizing savings to be put in a pool have to convince savers of the soundness of the proposed investments.[9] As a result, financial intermediaries strive to establish strong reputations,[10] at least at the outset, since later reduced competition or information asymmetries, especially those created by financial innovation, might make them complacent, or even outright rent-seeking institutions, as was the case in the era before the GFC. Regulation is as important in establishing investor/saver confidence as management's efforts. Thus, banking regulation strives to create sound and safe financial institutions and foster the stability of the system as a whole. Paradoxically, the regulatory burden also restricts competition by raising barriers to entry.

Similarly, securities markets may not be able to expand to their full potential in the absence of some mandatory legal regimes protecting minority shareholder rights.[11] Nevertheless, even in the absence of highly

---

[6] E. R. Sirri and P. Tufano, 'The Economics of Pooling', in D. B. Crane (ed.), *The Global Financial System: A Functional Perspective* (Boston, MA: Harvard Business School Press, 1995), pp. 81–128.

[7] The links between facilitating transactions, specialization, innovation and economic growth were core elements of Adam Smith's work. Smith argued that division of labour – specialization – is the principal factor underlying productivity improvements. See Adam Smith, *The Wealth of Nations* (London: W. Strahan and T. Cadell, 1776), p. 3.

[8] J. Greenwood and B. Smith, 'Financial Markets in Development, and the Development of Financial Markets' (1997) 21 *Journal of Economic Dynamics and Control* 145–81. Greenwood and Smith have modelled the connections between exchange, specialization and innovation.

[9] J. H. Boyd and B. D. Smith, 'Intermediation and the Equilibrium Allocation of Investment Capital: Implications for Economic Development' (1992) 30 *Journal of Monetary Economics* 409–32.

[10] Naomi R. Lamoreaux, *Insider Lending: Banks, Personal Connections, and Economic Development in Industrial New England* (New York: Cambridge University Press, 1994).

[11] Rafael la Porta, Florencio Lopez-de-Silanes, Andrei Shleifer and Robert Vishny, 'Legal Determinants of External Finance' (1997) 52 *Journal of Finance* 1131–50 ; John C. Coffee, Jr., 'The Rise of Dispersed Ownership: The Roles of Law and the State in the Separation of Ownership and Control' (2001), 111 *Yale Law Journal* 1–82, 65.

developed laws, equity markets can, and have, still developed.[12] Yet
securities markets may encounter shocks that result in a loss of investor
confidence. Legal institutions help buffer against this development.[13]
Hence the need for strict and properly enforced mandatory disclosure
rules and market abuse prohibitions in securities regulation and strong
minority protection mechanisms/remedies in company law.[14]

2.3   Information production, facilitation of investor (saver) monitoring and capital allocation

Although many models assume that capital flows towards the most profitable firms, this presupposes that investors have good information about
firms, managers and market conditions. Normally the costs associated
with the evaluation of firms, managers and market conditions before
making savings and investment decisions are rather large. Individual savers may not have the ability to collect, process and produce information
on possible investments. Since savers are reluctant to invest in activities
about which there is little reliable information, high information costs
may keep capital from flowing to its highest value uses. This is especially
the case when entrepreneurs and inventors do not have the skills to communicate (signal) the merits of their idea/technological breakthrough
properly. Not surprisingly one of the main functions of financial intermediaries is to reduce the costs of acquiring and processing information
and thereby improve resource allocation.[15] Without intermediaries, each
investor would face the large fixed cost associated with evaluating firms,
managers and general economic conditions. By improving information,
financial intermediaries can accelerate economic growth. Availability of
information would ideally allow investors to identify the best production technologies and most valuable products/assets. As a result, financial intermediaries may also boost the rate of technological innovation
by identifying those entrepreneurs with the best chances of successfully
initiating new goods and production processes.[16]

---

[12] There are a variety of institutional accounts as to why this is the case. E.g., in China
administrative governance proved a not inferior substitute for formal legal governance. See Katharina Pistor and Chenggang Xu, 'Governing Stock Markets in Transition
Economies: Lessons from China' (2005) 7 *American Law and Economics Review* 184–210.

[13] See Coffee, 'Dispersed Ownership', 65.

[14] Rafael La Porta, F. Lopez-de-Silanes, and A. Shleifer, 'What Works in Securities Laws?'
(2006) 61 *Journal of Finance* 1–32.

[15] Demirgüç-Kunt and Levine, 'Finance, Financial Sector Policies', pp. 3–10.

[16] *Ibid.*

Securities markets also stimulate the production of information about firms. As markets become larger and more liquid, market actors may have greater incentives to expend resources in researching firms, because it is easier to profit from this information by trading in big and liquid markets.[17] Arguably, in larger and more liquid markets it is easier for market actors who have acquired information to disguise their private information and make profit by trading on the market. Thus, larger, more liquid markets boost incentives to produce this valuable information with positive implications for capital allocation.[18] However, as discussed in Section 4 below, the assumptions that financial markets are always efficient resource allocators and that public and private actors in capital markets are consistently rational utility maximizers are highly disputed. Even in the absence of market failures, which to some extent may be remedied through regulation, financial markets present behaviour that often leads to the formation of massive asset bubbles. These, in turn, lead to grand scale wastage of resources rather than efficient allocation.

2.4   Risk management and risk reduction

Lower information and transaction costs facilitate the emergence of financial contracts, markets and intermediaries which enable transfer, hedging and pooling of risk with implications for resource allocation and growth. Thus, as explained above, finance helps growth through the raising and pooling of funds to undertake risky investments. Finance may also facilitate risk management and risk mitigation, through straightforward or innovative financial instruments/techniques (e.g., derivatives, securitization). Essentially, financial systems manage risk through three techniques: cross-sectional risk diversification; inter-temporal risk sharing; and provision of liquidity to contain liquidity risk. Financial systems may mitigate the risks associated with individual projects, firms, industries, regions and countries.[19] Banks, mutual funds and securities markets all provide outlets for trading, pooling and diversification of risk. The financial system's ability to provide risk diversification services can affect long-term economic growth by altering resource allocation and savings

[17] Stanford J. Grossman and Joseph Stiglitz, 'On the Impossibility of Informationally Efficient Markets' (1980) 70 *American Economic Review* 393–408; A. S. Kyle, 'Market Structure, Information, Futures Markets, and Price Formation', in G G. Storey, A. Schmitz and A. H. Sarris (eds.), *International Agricultural Trade: Advanced Readings in Price Formation, Market Structure, and Price Instability,* (Boulder, CO: Westview, 1984).
[18] Demirgüç-Kunt and Levine, 'Finance, Financial Sector Policies', pp. 3–10.
[19] *Ibid.*

rates. While savers generally do not like risk, high-return projects tend to be riskier than low-return projects. Thus, financial markets that facilitate risk diversification tend to induce an investment shift towards projects with higher expected returns.

Moreover, cross-sectional risk diversification can stimulate techno-logical innovation. Engaging in innovation is risky, however. The ability to hold a diversified portfolio of innovative projects reduces risk and promotes investment in growth enhancing innovative activities (with sufficiently risk averse agents). It follows that financial systems which enhance risk diversification can accelerate technological change and economic growth.

Liquidity is a market condition that 'reflects the cost and speed with which market actors can convert financial instruments into purchas-ing power at agreed prices'.[20] Accordingly, liquidity risk arises due to the uncertainties associated with converting assets into a medium of exchange. Informational asymmetries and transaction costs may inhibit liquidity and intensify liquidity risk. These frictions create incentives for the emergence of financial markets and institutions that augment liquid-ity.[21] The standard link between liquidity and economic development arises because some high-return projects require a long-run commitment of capital, but savers do not like to relinquish control of their savings for long periods. Thus, if the financial system does not boost the liquidity of long-term investments, through the maturity transformation function, less investment is likely to be directed to the higher return projects.[22]

The existence of liquid financial markets means that savers can hold liquid assets, such as shares, bonds or demand deposits, which can quickly and easily sell if they seek access to their savings. Simultaneously, capital markets transform these liquid financial instruments into long-term cap-ital investments.[23] In liquid stock markets, equity holders can readily sell their shares, while firms have permanent access to the capital invested

---

[20] *Ibid.*, p. 7.   [21] *Ibid.*
[22] B. Holmstrom and J. Tirole, 'Market Liquidity and Performance Monitoring' (1993) 101 *Journal of Political Economy* 678–709. Indeed, John Hicks, *A Theory of Economic History* (Oxford: Clarendon Press, 1969), pp. 143–5 argues that the products manufactured dur-ing the first decades of the Industrial Revolution had been invented much earlier. Rather, the critical innovation that ignited growth in eighteenth-century England was capital market liquidity.
[23] Ross Levine, 'Stock Markets, Growth, and Tax Policy' (1991) 46 *Journal of Finance* 1445–65 shows that the endogenous formation of equity markets to provide liquidity can affect economic growth.

by the initial shareholders. Such reduction of liquidity risk allows more investment to be channelled to the economy.[24]

2.5 Corporate governance

Financial markets may become, under certain conditions, good agents of strong corporate governance. To the extent that shareholders and creditors effectively monitor firms and induce managers to maximize firm value, this will improve the efficiency with which firms allocate resources and make savers more willing to finance production and innovation. In turn, the absence of financial arrangements that enhance corporate governance may impede the mobilization of savings from disparate agents and also keep capital from flowing to profitable investments. A number of market frictions may keep diffuse shareholders from effectively exerting corporate governance controls, allowing managers to pursue projects that benefit themselves rather than the firm. In particular, large information asymmetries typically exist between managers and small shareholders, while managers also have enormous discretion over the flow of information. Furthermore, small shareholders frequently lack the expertise and incentives to monitor managers because of the large costs and complexity associated with overseeing managers and exerting corporate control. This may induce a free-rider problem, because each stockowner's stake is so small. Every investor relies on others to undertake the costly process of monitoring managers, so there is too little monitoring. The resulting asymmetry between the level of information possessed by corporate insiders and the diffuse body of outside shareholders implies that the voting rights mechanism will not work effectively.

Also, the board of directors may not represent the interests of minority shareholders. Management frequently captures the board and manipulates directors into acting in the best interests of the managers, not of the shareholders. In many countries legal regimes do not adequately protect the rights of small shareholders and legal systems frequently do not enforce the legal rules that actually are in the books concerning protection of diffuse shareholder rights. It follows that large information and contracting costs may keep diffuse shareholders from effectively exerting corporate governance, with adverse effects on resource allocation and economic growth. On the

[24] E.g., V. R. Bencivenga and B. D. Smith, 'Financial Intermediation and Endogenous Growth' (1991) 58 *Review of Economics Studies* 195–209 shows that, by eliminating liquidity risk, banks can increase investment in the high-return, illiquid asset and therefore accelerate growth.

other hand, financial markets through creditor monitoring, stock prices, and the operation of the market for corporate control (hostile takeovers) can become a strong disciplining mechanism,[25] provided that market actors are mostly rational.

2.6   Evidence of the strong link between developed financial systems and economic growth

As implied in the previous discussion, financial development occurs when financial instruments, markets and intermediaries reduce the effects of information search, rule enforcement and transaction costs. Therefore, a developed financial system would be described, under the previous obser-vations, as one that provides financial services that satisfy the needs of most people and affords wider access to finance. The conditions that fos-ter financial system development include a strong legal system with devel-oped property rights where shareholder and creditor rights are protected and properly enforced. [26] Legal, political, cultural, ethnic and geographic differences across countries seem to have an impact on the development of domestic financial institutions and markets.[27]

The link between a developed financial sector and economic growth has been the subject of a large number of (mostly empirical) studies.[28] These

---

[25] See Frank H. Easterbrook and Daniel R. Fischel, *The Economic Structure of Corporate Law* (Cambridge, MA: Harvard University Press, 1996).

[26] Thorsten Beck, Asli Demirgüç-Kunt, Ross Levine and Vojislav Maksimovic, 'Financial Structure and Economic Development – Firm, Industry, and Country Evidence', World Bank Policy Research Working Paper Series 2423. Louigi Zingales, 'The Weak Links' (2003) 85 *Federal Reserve Bank of St Louis Review* 47–52.

[27] From the vast bibliography, see indicatively Kenneth W. Dam, 'Credit Markets, Creditors' Rights and Economic Development', February 2006, Chicago Law School, John Olin Law and Economics Working Paper 281; Rafael La Porta, Florencio Lopes-de-Silanes, Andrei Shleifer and Robert Vishny, 'Investor Protection and Corporate Governance' (2000) 58 *Journal of Financial Economics* 1; Daron Acemoglu, Simon Johnson and James Robinson, 'Institutions as the Fundamental Cause of Long-Run Growth', in P. Aghion and S. Durlauf (eds.), *Handbook of Economic Growth* (Amsterdam: Elsevier, 2005), Chapter 12; La Porta, *et al.*, 'Legal Determinants of External Finance'; Rene M. Stultz and Rohan Williamson, 'Culture, Openness, and Finance' (2003) 70 *Journal of Financial Economics* 313–49; Alberto Alesina, William Easterly, Arnaud Devleeschauwer, Sergio Kurlat and Romain T. Wacziarg, 'Fractionalization' (2003) 8 *Journal of Economic Growth* 155–94.

[28] For an overview of relevant studies, see Ross Levine, 'Finance and Growth: Theory and Evidence', in P. Aghion and S. Durlauf (eds.), *Handbook of Economic Growth* (Amsterdam: Elsevier, 2005); UK Department for International Development, 'The Importance of Financial Sector Development for Growth and Poverty Reduction', Policy Division

have suggested that the deeper a country's financial system the higher its growth potential.[29] One of the first studies to find empirical evidence of the close correlation between financial sector development (FSD) and the overall rate of a country's economic growth was undertaken by the late Professor Goldsmith in 1969.[30] Other empirical analyses have provided further evidence of the positive relationship between financial sector development and growth. For example, King and Levine examined eighty countries over the period 1960–89.[31] After controlling for other factors affecting long-run growth, they examined the capital accumulation and productivity growth channels separately and used various measures of the level of financial development. They found evidence of a strong, positive relationship between the various financial development indicators and economic growth.[32]

By themselves, however, these results do not necessarily imply that FSD leads to higher growth. It may be that growth leads to FSD, as it generates greater demand for financial services that induces an expansion in the financial sector. As a result, many researchers have examined this issue explicitly. King and Levine have found that, even after controlling for other factors that may affect growth, the relationship between the initial level of financial development and growth is strong. Subsequent studies[33] have confirmed that FSD exerts a large positive impact on economic growth. Calderon and Liu also adopted an innovative econometric technique

Working Paper, August 2004, pp. 7–15; Patrick Honohan, 'Financial Development, Growth, and Poverty: How Close Are the Links?', in Charles Goodhart (ed.), *Financial Development and Economic Growth: Explaining the Links* (London: Palgrave, 2004).

[29] Raghuram Rajan and Luigi Zingales, 'Financial Development and Growth' (1998) 88 *American Economic Review* 559–86; Cesar Calderon and Lin Liu, 'The Direction of Causality between Financial Development and Economic Growth' (2003) 72 *Journal of Development Economics* 321–34. For an overview of relevant studies, see Patrick Honohan, 'Financial Development, Growth and Poverty: How Close are the Links?' World Bank Policy Research Working Paper 3203, February 2004.

[30] Raymond W. Goldsmith, *Financial Structure and Development* (New Haven, CT: Yale University Press, 1969). Using data from thirty-five countries covering the period between 1860–1963, Goldsmith found evidence of a relationship between economic and financial development over long periods and that periods of rapid economic growth have often been accompanied by an above average rate of financial development.

[31] Robert G. King and Ross Levine, 'Finance and Growth: Schumpeter Might Be Right' (1993) 108 *Quarterly Journal of Economics* 717–37; Robert G. King and Ross Levine, 'Finance, Entrepreneurship, and Growth: Theory and Evidence' (1993) 32 *Journal of Monetary Economics* 513–42.

[32] King and Levine, 'Finance, Entrepreneurship, and Growth'.

[33] Ross Levine, Norman Loayza and Thorsten Beck, 'Financial Intermediation and Growth Casuality and Causes' (2000) 46 *Journal of Monetary Economics* 31–77.

to analyse this issue,[34] using data from 109 countries over the 1960–94 period. Their results showed that there was bi-directional causality: FSD has a causal impact on growth and growth has a causal impact on FSD. However, the impact of FSD on growth is more important than the impact of growth on FSD. In fact, Calderon and Liu's study suggested that financial sector under-development is more likely to hold growth back in developing countries. Berthelemy and Varoudakis[35] suggested that financial sector underdevelopment could be a serious obstacle to growth even when a country has established other conditions necessary for sustained economic development. This result implies that the lack of a sufficiently developed financial system may even compromise the positive contribution of education to growth. It is very interesting that the more important factor is not which source provides finance, namely bank lending or the capital markets, but how efficiently finance is provided.

2.7   FSD, availability of finance and poverty alleviation

Access to finance is a very difficult term to define and, perhaps, in the case of the poor, not even the most appropriate one. Normally, access to finance is taken to mean access to certain institutions, such as banks, insurance companies or microfinance institutions; or access to the functions (services) that they provide, such as payments services, savings or loans and credits, or use of certain financial products such as credit cards, mortgage and insurance products.[36] It is certain that the availability of financial services has a direct impact on poverty at the micro

---

[34] Calderon and Liu, 'The Direction of Causality'.

[35] J. C. Berthelemy and A. Varoudakis, 'Economic Growth, Convergence Clubs, and the Role of Financial Development' (1996) 48 *Oxford Economic Papers* 300–28. The authors found evidence that countries with a high level of educational achievement, but a low level of FSD, were trapped in relatively low standards of living compared to those countries with a similar level of educational attainment, but a more developed financial sector. Moreover, they found that educational attainment had no significant impact on growth in countries where FSD was weak.

[36] Anne-Marie Chidzero, Karen Ellis and Anjali Kumar, 'Indicators of Access to Finance, Through Household Level Surveys, Comparisons of Data from Six Countries', Paper presented in the World Bank conference: 'Access to Finance: Building Inclusive Financial Systems', 30 May 2006, p.1. For an alternative more conceptual approach see Stijn Claessens, 'Access to Financial Services: A Review of the Issues and Public Policy Objectives', World Bank Policy Research Working Paper 3589, May 2005, pp. 6–12; Augusto de la Torre, Juan Carlos Gozzi and Sergio L. Schmukler, 'Innovative Experiences in Access to Finance: Market Friendly Roles for the Visible Hand?', World Bank mimeo, 30 March 2006, pp. 10–18.

level, primarily by affecting the ability of poor people to accumulate usefully large lump sums – whether for life cycle, emergency or opportunity investment purposes.[37] Access to credit, insurance and savings can reduce the vulnerability of the poor to a number of external shocks, including bad harvests or health difficulties. The mobilization of savings also creates an opportunity for re-lending the collected funds into the community strengthening communal ties.

A number of empirical studies have examined the link between FSD, especially access to finance, and levels of poverty. According to these studies, access to finance can prove an effective (but not exclusive) way to fight poverty, provided that certain conditions are satisfied. A developed financial sector may have an impact on poverty both directly, by raising the income of the poor and making income distribution more equal and indirectly, by stimulating overall economic growth. Cross-country studies on the link between finance and poverty have examined the reverse causality between availability of finance and poverty and found that financial development caused smaller income inequality.[38] Clarke, Xu and Zou have found that inequality decreases as finance develops and the more concentrated income tends to be in a national economy the higher the country's level of poverty. The fact that finance helps to distribute income opportunities more evenly becomes a significant factor in poverty reduction.[39] In the same mode, Beck, Demirgüç-Kunt and Levine, using a broad cross-country sample, have shown not only that financial development raises disproportionately the income of the poor, reducing income inequality but also that countries with more developed financial intermediaries experience faster declines in poverty and income inequality.[40]

---

[37] Daniel C. Hardy, Paul Holden and Vassili Prokopenko, 'Microfinance Institutions and Public Policy', IMF Working Paper 02/159, 2002; Patrick Honohan, 'Financial Sector Policy and the Poor: Selected Findings and Issues', World Bank Working Paper 43/2004; K. Hoff and Joseph Stiglitz, 'Modern Economic Theory and Development', in Gerald Meier and Joseph Stiglitz (eds.), *The Future of Development Economics in Perspective* (Oxford University Press, 2001).

[38] Thorsten Beck, Asli Demirgüç-Kunt and Ross Levine, 'Finance, Inequality and Poverty: Cross-Country Evidence', World Bank Policy Research Working Paper 3338, June 2004. See also Stijn Claessens and Enrico Perotti, 'The Links between Finance and Inequality: Channels and Evidence', Background Paper for the 2005 World Development Report, World Bank, University of Amsterdam, May 2005.

[39] George Clarke, Lixin Colin Xu and Heng-fu Zou, 'Finance and Income Inequality, Test of Alternative Theories', World Bank Policy Research Working Paper 2984, 2003.

[40] Thorsten Beck, Asli Demirgüç-Kunt and Ross Levine, 'Finance, Inequality and Poverty: Cross-Country Evidence', updated version of World Bank Policy Research Working

Moreover, availability of finance has special importance for poor households and smaller firms in a number of other ways. For instance, availability of credit can strengthen the productive assets of the poor by enabling them to invest in productivity enhancing new 'technologies' such as new and better seeds, work equipment or fertilizers etc., or to invest in education and health, all of which may be difficult to finance out of regular household income, although they provide for a higher income in future. The availability of credit can also be an important factor in the creation or expansion of small businesses, thus generating self- and wage-employment and increasing incomes. Eswaran and Kotwal have argued that just the knowledge that credit will be available to cushion consumption against income shocks, should a potentially profitable but risky investment turn out badly, can make households more willing to adopt more risky technologies.[41] Such behaviour will lead to increased use of modern technologies boosting productivity, and hence enhance income. For the same reason, access to credit and other financial services is likely to decrease the proportion of low-risk, low-return assets held by poor households for precautionary purposes (such as jewels), and enable them to invest in potentially higher risk and higher return assets, such as education or tools of trade, e.g., a rickshaw, with serious long-term income enhancing results.[42] Similar are the results of the availability of insurance for the poor,[43] as it protects them from financial vulnerability due to income shocks emanating from an illness or a bad harvest.

Finally, access to finance may become a good agent of economic and social change that improves governance structures decreasing some of the causes of poverty. Rajan and Zingales have suggested that access to finance through, *inter alia*, free and open capital markets is the only means to erode the power of the incumbent elite.[44] Normally, the elite have a vested interest in pushing back economic growth, which would entail the empowerment of the disenfranchised parts of society (normally its biggest part), and thus the erosion of their privileges. For all of the above reasons, securing access to finance is perceived as a catalyst for the

Paper 3338 submitted to the World Bank conference, 'Access to Finance: Building Inclusive Financial Systems', 30 May 2006.

[41] Mukesh Eswaran and Ashok Yeshwant Kotwal, 'Implications of Credit Constraints for Risk Behaviour in Less Developed Economies' (1990) 42 *Oxford Economic Papers* 473–82.
[42] Angus Deaton, 'Saving and Liquidity Constraints' (1991) 59 *Econometrica* 1221–48.
[43] See for the importance of micro-insurance for poverty alleviation, Jonathan Morduch, 'Microinsurance: The Next Revolution?' New York University, mimeo, 2003.
[44] Raghuram Rajan and Luigi Zingales, *Saving Capitalism from the Capitalists* (Princeton University Press, 2nd edn, 2004).

attainability of the Millennium Development Goals (MDGs)[45] and has been the focus of several UN inter-governmental conferences,[46] closely associated with the WTO Doha round of negotiations on international trade liberalization.[47]

3.   Evolution of global markets and financial innovation

3.1   Complex instruments and international financial markets

As mentioned in the introduction to this chapter, the present analysis focuses on those segments of global markets that were the most innovative and least regulated, chiefly derivatives instruments and markets, securitization structures/transactions and the shadow banking sector. These were also the parts of the global market which have been most implicated in the build up and amplification of the GFC. According to the latest estimates, the global derivatives market totals a staggering US $700 trillion measured by the notional value of outstanding contracts.[48] Most of those transactions have been conducted on the lightly regulated (or unregulated) cross-border OTC markets, presenting a massive risk for the global financial system. Thus, one of the main objectives of the financial reform legislation in the US and the EU is to standardize and centralize most OTC derivatives trading.[49]

---

[45] In 2000, in a set of historic agreements, all the country members of the United Nations (UN), with the support of the International Monetary Fund (IMF), the World Bank, the OECD, the G-7, and the G-20, signed up to a set of Millennium Development Goals (General Assembly Resolution 55/2); UN Human Development Report, 'Millennium Development Goals: A Compact Among Nations to End Human Poverty' (2003).

[46] See 'Monterrey Consensus of the International Conference on Financing for Development', United Nations 2003, Mexico, 18–22 March 2002, available at www.un.org/esa/ffd/Monterrey%20Consensus.pdf.

[47] UN, 'Doha Declaration on Financing for Development: Outcome Document of the Follow-up International Conference on Financing for Development to Review the Implementation of the Monterrey Consensus', 9 November–2 December 2008, available at www.un.org/esa/ffd/doha/documents/Doha_Declaration_FFD.pdf.

[48] It is reported that after contracting by 4 per cent in the first half of 2010, total notional amounts outstanding of OTC derivatives rose by 3 per cent in the second half of 2010, reaching US $601 trillion by the end of December 2010. Overall gross credit exposures (a measure that takes into account legally enforceable bilateral netting agreements) stood at US $3.3 trillion. See BIS, Monetary and Economic Department, 'OTC Derivatives Market Activity in the Second Half of 2010', May 2011, pp. 1–2, available at www.bis.org/publ/otc_hy1105.pdf.

[49] For details see Chapter 6, Sections 2.2 and 3.1.

Derivatives are financial instruments whose value is derived from another 'underlying' asset. For example, a stock option[50] is a derivative because it derives its value from the value of the underlying stock. An interest rate swap is a derivative because it derives its value from one or more interest rate indices. Thus, the value of a derivative product normally depends on the price of a cash instrument. Examples of cash instruments include shares in a corporation, bonds, physical stocks of commodities and currencies. However, during recent years this link has been weakened and several classes of derivatives contracts have no underlying asset. Derivatives are used for purposes of risk sharing, hedging, speculation and transformation of the nature and cash flows of long-term claims. Most derivatives transactions are conducted in largely unregulated cross-border OTC markets and are documented using the ISDA Master Agreement architecture.

Derivatives trading does not only serve as an alternative to trading on cash markets, but also permits investors to manage exposures to risks not easily achieved in any other way. A trader can, for instance, obtain, for a certain fee, protection (insurance) against market[51] or interest rate risk limiting his or her exposure to the volatility of the market[52] or change the pattern of payments in a security instrument. On the other hand, derivatives trading can be highly leveraged and run into such large amounts as to exacerbate the risk of counter-party default, threaten the solvency of large financial institutions and ultimately destabilize the financial system.

3.2   The different classes of derivatives contracts

3.2.1   Swaps

The essence of *swaps* is exchange of cash flows. Swaps are flexible in their design. As a result, any exchange of cash flows may become the subject matter of a swap contract. Typically swaps are used to reduce borrowing

---

[50] An option is a contract that gives the right but not the obligation to buy (sell) some underlying cash instrument at a pre-determined rate on a pre-determined expiration date in a pre-set notional amount. A *call option* is a financial contract giving the owner the right but not the obligation to buy a pre-set amount of the underlying financial instrument at a pre-set price with a pre-set maturity date. A *put option* is a financial contract giving the owner the right but not the obligation to sell a pre-set amount of the underlying financial instrument at a pre-set price with a pre-set maturity date.

[51] Stock ownership is perceived as a safer investment when 'insured' with put options. For this reason, put options can increase the demand for stock ownership and thus trading volume on cash markets.

[52] E.g., through the use of cap/floor options.

costs, or to facilitate asset and liability management, e.g., by altering a party's existing liability structure or changing the rate basis of an investment through an asset swap. The most common forms are interest rate, currency and asset or equity swaps, where the cash flows associated with one contract or asset are exchanged for those of another. For example, a corporation that borrows at lower rates in US dollars but needs euros for its investment or supply and distribution requirements may borrow in US dollars and exchange cash flows with a European company that enjoys competitive interest rates in euros but needs US dollars to cover obligations to its own suppliers or other needs. Virtually all commonly used interest rate indices and major convertible currencies are regularly used in swaps. The three basic types of interest rate swaps are: (1) fixed to floating; (2) floating to floating; and (3) fixed to fixed. Swap principles may also be extended to products/assets that may be readily priced such as oil, gold and stock-market indices. The market in swaps was initiated by the now famous Swiss Franc/US dollar swaps between IBM and the World Bank in the early 1980s. The two most important risks arising in the context of a swap agreement are: (1) rate risk, namely that the interest or exchange rates will move against one of the counterparties; and (2) credit risk, which refers to the counterparty's ability to perform the contract.[53]

3.2.2   Forwards and futures contracts

Contracts for future transactions are traded either on futures exchanges (futures contracts) or OTC (forward contracts).[54] Such contracts may be created for any asset. However, they are more likely to cover commodities or goods with large output and inventory requirements, which are susceptible to significant and not easily anticipated price changes.[55] Because contracts for future performance allow producers and other economic agents to buy or sell the underlying asset now for future delivery, they shelter them from price fluctuations and allow rational planning in the production, investment and consumption of the relevant goods or commodities. They also facilitate the hedging of a financial investment's risk exposure.

---

[53] It should be noted that the Dodd–Frank Act 2010 (Section 721) uses the term 'swap' much more widely and the definition used for this term captures most known forms of financial derivatives including credit derivatives. See Chapter 6, Section 2.2.

[54] J. Leslie and G. Wyatt, 'Futures and Options', in D. Cobham (ed.), *Markets and Dealers: the Economics of the London Financial Markets* (London: Longman, 1992), pp. 86–7.

[55] J. M. Burns, 'Futures Markets and Market Efficiency', in M. E. Streit (ed.), *Futures Markets: Modelling, Managing and Monitoring Futures Trading* (Oxford: Blackwell, 1983) pp. 46, 52.

A forward contract is distinguished from a spot contract, that is, a contract for immediate delivery of the asset of the commodity. It is, essentially, an agreement between two parties, e.g., a bank and an importer, or a wheat farmer and a breakfast cereal manufacturer, or an oil producing company and a refinery, or a gold mine and major jeweller in which the seller (the bank/the farmer/the oil producer/the gold mine) agrees to deliver to the buyer (the exporter/the cereal manufacturer/the refinery/ the jeweller) a specified quantity and quality of an asset or commodity (foreign currency/the wheat/the oil/the bullion) at a specified future date at an agreed upon price. A forward contract is normally a privately negotiated bilateral contract that is concluded outside of an organized exchange. The contract terms are not standardized, but are determined by what the parties agree on. The price is generally determined when the contract is entered into, although there are some forward contracts where the parties may agree to transact at a price to be determined later in a manner that is specified on the day the contract is entered into. Thus, forward contracts were, until recently, credited with the ability to stabilize global food prices.[56]

Futures contracts are not very dissimilar to forward contracts, although futures contracts are typically traded on organized exchanges and have standardized terms that are determined by the exchange, rather than by market participants. Futures contracts typically have certain features that make them more useful for hedging and less useful for merchandising than forward contracts. These include the ability to extinguish positions through offset trades rather than actual delivery of the commodity and standardization of contract terms. Futures contracts cover a wide variety of physical commodities (including grains, metals and petroleum products) and financial instruments (such as stocks, bonds, and currencies).

As mentioned above, financial and commodity futures markets serve a host of useful purposes that go beyond hedging.[57] They enhance

[56] 'The grain futures trading system ... insulated American farmers and millers from the inherent risks of their profession. The basic idea was the "forward contract," ... Not only did a grain "future" help to keep the price of a loaf of bread at the bakery – or later, the supermarket – stable, but the market allowed farmers to hedge against lean times, and to invest in their farms and businesses. [As a result] Over the course of the 20th century, the real price of wheat decreased ...' Frederick Kaufman, 'How Goldman Sachs Created the Food Crisis', 27 April 2011 Foreign Policy available at www.foreignpolicy.com/articles/2011/04/27/how_goldman_sachs_created_the_food_crisis.
[57] H. Working, 'New Concepts Concerning Futures Markets and Prices' (1962) 52 American Economic Review 431–59.

the information efficiency of the cash market because the price of futures contracts reflects the weighted average of the disparate information and expectations[58] of all those actively trading on the market. This information could refer to the current and future state of supply and demand for the underlying assets.[59] Arguably, exchange-traded futures reflect market information better than individually negotiated spot transactions. In the absence of an organized spot market, prices quoted on futures markets are used as a reference point for cash market transactions. Futures markets also provide a facility for the rapid dissemination of cross-asset private information.[60] In addition, futures exchanges are far more liquid than commodity/asset spot markets, thus presenting fewer pricing anomalies. This element, along with the higher speed with which prices adjust to new information on futures markets,[61] might lead to a decrease in the volatility of spot market prices.[62]

Before the 1970s, most futures trading related to agricultural goods, such as corn and wheat, and physical commodities such as gold, silver and copper, or natural resources, such as oil and gas. Today, there are successful futures markets in a variety of assets and cash market financial instruments. Transactions in futures made on exchange are cleared through a clearing organization (clearing house), which acts as the buyer to all sellers and the seller to all buyers. Accordingly, all purchases and sales of futures contracts are technically purchased from and sold to the clearing organization rather than the party with whom the transaction has been executed on the trading floor or through an electronic trading platform. Futures traders are not required to pay to their broker the entire value of a contract. Rather, they are required to post a margin that is typically between 2 per cent and 10 per cent of the total value of the contract.

---

[58] For commodity futures markets' reaction to new information, see C. K. Ma, W. H. Dare and D. R. Donaldson, 'Testing Rationality in Futures Markets' (1990) 10 *Journal of Futures Markets* 137–52.

[59] See L. G. Telser and H. N. Higginbotham, 'Organised Futures Markets: Costs and Benefits' (1977) 85 *Journal of Political Economy* 969–1000.

[60] See R. D. Weaver and A. Bannerjee, 'Does Futures Trading Destabilise Cash Prices? Evidence for US Live Beef Cattle' (1990) 10 *Journal of Futures Markets* 41–60.

[61] H. Working, 'Price Effects of Futures Trading' (1960) 1 *Food Research Institute Studies* 3–27.

[62] See M. J. Powers, 'Does Futures Trading Reduce Price Fluctuations in Cash Markets?' (1970) 60 *American Economic Review* 460, 462–3.

3.3   Securitization and structured finance

3.3.1   Background

The finance technique called securitization emerged in the 1970s around residential mortgages, but has since been used with respect to commercial mortgages, credit card receivables, student loans, water bills, lottery ticket receipts and tax payments. It transforms/structures the cash flows of illiquid assets and may be used to provide longer-term funds through traditional forms of issued debt. The same technique is also described as structured finance. In principle, securitization is an ingenious mechanism to spread risk and reduce financing costs especially for small- and medium-size borrowers that are afforded greater access to capital. It may also be utilized for risk transfer purposes or in order to obtain regulatory capital relief by moving bank assets off balance sheet.[63]

Securitization activity experienced a real boost following the implementation of the Basel I capital adequacy framework in the period after 1988, discussed in Chapter 4. The Basel I framework encouraged the breaking down of the link between risk and assets for reasons of regulatory arbitrage. Asset securitization led at the same time to lower capital charges pushing risky assets off balance sheet.[64] Regulatory (and tax) arbitrage was achieved through the utilization of the widely used originate-to-distribute model, which also provided the initial impetus for an explosion of activity in the shadow banking sector, discussed in Section 5 below.

---

[63] This section draws on Vinod Kothari, *Securitization: The Financial Instrument of the Future* (Hoboken, NJ: Wiley Finance, 3rd edn, 2006), Chapters 1,2 and 4; Frank Fabozzi, Henry Davis and Moorad Choudhry, *Introduction to Structured Finance* (Hoboken, NJ: Wiley, 2006); Emilios Avgouleas, 'International Credit Markets: Players, Financing Techniques, Instruments, and Regulation' in Hossein Bidgoli (ed.), *The Handbook of Technology Management* (Hoboken, NJ: Wiley, 2009), Chapter 50. Two very comprehensive works on the legal treatment of securitizations are Steven Schwarcz, *Structured Finance, A Guide to Asset Securitization* (New York: Practising Law Institute, 3rd edn, 2002) and Joseph Tanega, *Securitization Law: EU and US Disclosure Regulations* (London: Lexis/Nexis 2009). A very useful resource to further understanding of technical and regulatory aspects of securitizations and derivatives is the collection of technical papers stored by the specialized Internet portal risk.net, available at www.risk.net/ type/technical-paper.

[64] See Charles Calomiris, 'Financial Innovation, Regulation and Reform' (2009) 29 *Cato Journal* 65–91; Andreas Jobst, 'The Basle Securitisation Framework Explained: The Regulatory Treatment of Asset Securitisation', WP Series 2004/21, Center for Financial Studies, Goethe University of Frankfurt, rev. March 2005, available at www.ifk-cfs.de/ index.php?id=485.

3.3.2 Securitization structures

The 'originate-to-distribute' model is a method of breaking down the process of credit extension from origination to ultimate financing. Starting from origination, the granting of the actual bank loan, the asset created (the borrower's obligation) is normally sold by the 'originator', to another financial institution (the 'packager') and is subsequently merged with other similar assets ('repackaged') to create a marketable security. This process normally involves the creation of a separate legal entity, which is a special purpose vehicle (SPV), also called Special Purpose Entity (SPE). The special entity may be a corporation, a trust or some form of partnership. The sole function of the SPV is to hold the underlying mortgages or other assets in a pool. It may hold the pooled assets on its balance sheet or place them in a separate trust. The pooled assets are called 'collateral'. The SPV normally issues claims (bonds) against itself, backed by the assets held in the pool, issued by the corporate or the trust that holds the portfolio. The SPV uses the proceeds from the sale of the issued bonds or notes to pay the originator or the 'repackager' for the securitized assets (loans). The most straightforward structures involve combining homogeneous or heterogeneous mortgages to create Mortgage-Backed Securities (MBS) or Residential Mortgage-Backed Securities (RMBS). The owners of MBS have a claim on the cash flows arising from the underlying mortgages.

Gradually securitization practice moved to the creation of more complex securities such as Collateralized Debt Obligations (CDOs)[65] or Collateralized Loan Obligations (CLOs),[66] which are backed by a mix of different types of bonds, loans, or other assets and may be covered by various guarantees or hedges. Cash flows from the assets, minus the servicing fees, flow through the SPV to bond holders. In some cases, there are different classes of bonds, which participate differently in the asset cash flows. In simpler arrangements there is only one class of bonds and – except for

[65] CDOs are typically set up by investment banks or fund managers and comprise securitized interests in pools of generally non-mortgage assets. Collateral usually comprises loans or debt instruments called Collateralized Loan Obligations (CLOs) or Collateralized Bond Obligations (CBOs) depending on whether the collateral is loans or bonds respectively. See Avgouleas, 'International Credit Markets'.

[66] CLOs are typically securities issued by an SPV and are backed by loans purchased by the banking institutions sponsoring the issue, or are referenced on such loans. The SPV issues notes or certificates to the investors, the CLOs, which have as collateral the sponsoring bank's loans, rated usually as investment-grade though the collateral may also include some non investment-grade corporate loans. See Andreas Jobst, 'Collateralized Loan Obligations (CLOs) – A Primer', Working Paper Series: Finance and Accounting 96/2002, Department of Finance, Goethe University Frankfurt am Main.

the subtracted processing fees – all investors participate proportionately in the actual cash flows from the assets. When assets are transferred from the originator to the re-packager or the SPV, it is critical that this is done as a legal sale. If the originator has retained some claim on those assets, there would be a risk that creditors of the originator might try to seize the assets in bankruptcy proceedings. Where a securitization is properly implemented, investors face no credit risk from the originator. They also face little credit risk from the SPV, which serves merely as a conduit for cash flows. Whatever cash flows the SPV receives from the collateral are passed along to investors and whatever party is providing servicing. If the collateral entails credit risk, a securitization will often be structured with some sort of credit enhancement. This may include over-collateralization, a third party guarantee or other enhancements.[67]

CDOs and the CLOs were, in turn, bought by investment vehicles set up for this reason, called Special Investment Vehicles (SIVs), or other capital market investors, such as hedge funds. SIVs obtain funds for the said purchases from investors to whom they issue asset backed notes, known as Asset-Backed Commercial Paper (ABCP). Unlike CDOs, ABCP could often enjoy a liquid secondary market. Thus, at the end of the 'originate-to-distribute' chain stood investors, such as hedge funds, banks, pension funds or other financial institutions that provided the ultimate funding of the loans. The bank that advanced the original high-risk or sub-prime loans in the end had transferred most of this risk to the buyers of RMBS, CDOs and other asset backed securities (ABS). Structured securities may be broken into pieces, called tranches, of varying seniority and credit quality.[68] Each tranche is rated separately by one or more credit rating agencies (CRAs). Most of them obtained the highest rating, triple A (AAA). The packager normally kept on their balance sheet the tranches that had the lowest ratings, and thus were not easily marketable.[69] However, as explained below, credit ratings proved to be misleading. Figure 1 shows a typical cash CDO structure and Figure 2 highlights the more complex relationships involved between the various counterparties when ABS are involved.

Synthetic Securitisations allow well-funded originators to protect themselves from some risk by enabling risk transfer through the use of credit derivatives or through the capital markets replicating in part the economic substance of standard securitization transactions. The owner of

[67] See Kothari, *Securitization*, Chapter 17; Jobst, 'Collateralized Loan Obligations (CLOs)'.
[68] IMF, Global Financial Stability Report, 'Containing Systemic Risks and Restoring Financial Soundness', April 2008, 56, Box 2.1.
[69] *Ibid.*, pp. 56–9 and Box 2.2.

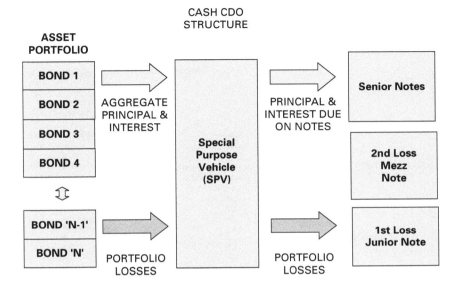

Figure 1   Typical cash CDO structure
Source: Moody's Investors Service Collateralised Debt Obligations: A Moody's
Primer, 7 March 2005.

the assets (the 'Protection Buyer') transfers the credit risk of a portfolio of
assets (a 'Reference Portfolio' or 'Reference Obligations') to another entity
(the 'Protection Seller') or directly to the capital markets. Thus, although
the credit risk of the Reference Portfolio is transferred, actual ownership of the Reference Obligations remains with the Protection Buyer.[70] A
typical synthetic CDO structure is depicted in Figure 3.

3.3.3   All is not good with structured finance

The New York Federal Reserve study on the shadow banking sector
observes that there are at least four different ways in which the securitization process can lower the cost and improve the availability of credit as
well as reduce volatility of the financial system as a whole. First, securitization, which is not conducted merely for reasons of regulatory arbitrage but
involves real credit risk transfer is an important way for an issuer to limit
concentrated exposures to certain borrowers, loan types, and geographic

---

[70] See Vinod Kothari, *Credit Derivatives and Synthetic Securitisation* (New York: Wiley &
Sons, 2003).

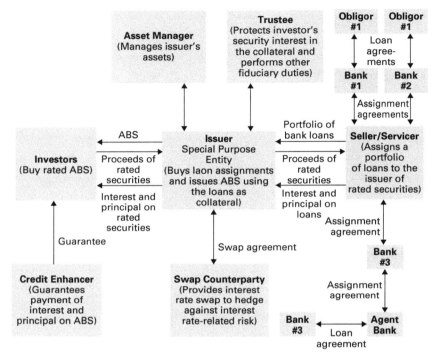

Figure 2   Typical ABS structure
Source: Standard & Poor's, 'Global Cash Flow and Synthetic CDO Criteria', 21 March 2002.

locations on its balance sheet. Second, term asset-backed securitization markets are valuable to lenders who can use them to diversify their
sources of funding and also to raise long-term, maturity-matched funding to better manage their asset–liability mismatch than they could by
solely funding term loans with short-term deposits. Third, securitization
permits lenders to realize economies of scale from over-utilization of their
loan origination facilities (e.g., branches, call centres), which may not be
possible when they retain loans on balance sheet. Fourth, securitization
is a potentially promising way to involve the market in the supervision of
banks, by providing third-party discipline and market pricing of assets
that would be opaque if left on the banks' balance sheets.[71]

[71] Zoltan Pozsar, Tobias Adrian, Adam Ashcraft and Hayley Boesky, 'Shadow Banking',
    Federal Reserve Board of New York, Staff Reports, Staff Report No. 458, July 2010, p. 15.

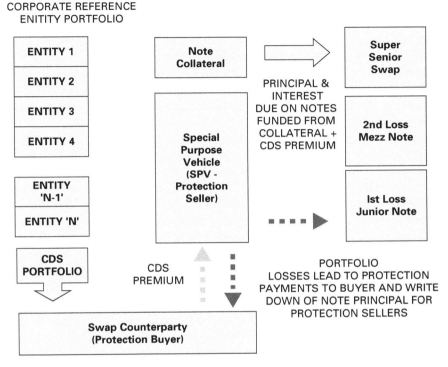

Figure 3   Typical synthetic CDO structure
Source: Moody's Investors Service Collateralised Debt Obligations: A Moody's Primer,
7 March 2005.

However, there are also significant risks in the securitization process. First, valuing the underlying assets is often difficult and most investors are ill-equipped to conduct their own valuations. Thus, there is a risk of investors overpaying for purchases of structured credit securities. Second, the fact that securitization paper has an AAA rating doesn't mean that it is risk free. It only means that the chance of a bond holder incurring a loss attributable to default on the underlying assets is remote. Other risks, which can affect the timing of payments or the deterior-ation of (underlying) borrowers' financial position may be considerable. As a result, during the GFC, the first assets to be downgraded were

AAA-rated securities causing significant losses in investors' portfolios and fire sales.[72] Moreover, flawed credit ratings, due to conflict of interests and incomplete risk models, inadequately capitalized SPVs/SIVs and poorly performing structured credit securities as well as misaligned incentive structures within the 'originate-to-distribute' model have been at the heart of the global financial crisis and the collapse of venerable financial institutions. Also excessive asset securitization for regulatory (and tax) arbitrage reasons led to a weakening of bank balance sheets and excessive leverage since, as explained below, funding available to securitization vehicles tends to be debt driven and short-term, making them vulnerable to wholesale liquidity runs.[73]

Moreover, the 'originate-to-distribute' model provides weak incentives to generate and supply initial and ongoing information on the quality and performance of underlying assets (loans) that were repackaged. Historically, the original lender has also been responsible for carrying the due diligence regarding the borrower's creditworthiness. Traditional lenders had to ensure that the terms of the mortgage appropriately reflect the risks of the transaction and had to be diligent with their client vetting and documentation as they retained exposure to risk of default until repayment of the credit on maturity. However, with the advent of securitization the banks advancing the original loans ('originators') did not retain the risk of the loans they originated but passed it on to other financial institutions, who packaged the loans. Thus, they had no incentive to conduct proper due diligence and borrower monitoring. Namely, credit disintermediation based on the 'originate-to-distribute' model and the consequent severing of the long-term relationship between the originator and the borrower created perverse incentives in the system leading to reckless lending. In addition, the incentive structures often tied originator revenue to loan volume, rather than to the quality of the loans being passed through the chain.[74] Originators were paid by reference to the amount of loans generated regardless of the repayment rate of those loans, which is inextricably linked to the borrower's creditworthiness. It follows that they had every incentive to maximize the volume of loans granted independently of controls on borrower creditworthiness.

---

[72] An analytical account of the illusory investor safety offered by AAA assets is offered in Chapter 5, Section 3.3.
[73] An analytical discussion of the role of financial innovation in the GFC, and of weakening of underwriting standards in mortgage lending is provided in Chapter 3 below.
[74] Mark Carney, Governor of the Bank of Canada, 'Addressing Financial Market Turbulence', Remarks to the Toronto Board of Trade, 13 March 2008.

Gradually credit controls became increasingly compromised at the point of origination. The best-known and most serious case is that of US sub-prime mortgages.[75] To a degree that increased over time, these mortgages were often poorly documented and extended with insufficient attention to the borrower's ability to repay, although this might, in part, have been the result of US government housing policies.[76]

Paradoxically, financial institutions which were thought to have diversified their risk through Off Balance Sheet Entities (OBSEs) and credit derivatives had not realized how much risk they had in fact retained through the provision of guarantees or backstop liquidity lines.[77] Worse, the slice (tranche) they had retained in those entities referred to the riskiest and least worthy part of OBSEs' assets. Subsequently, several banks felt compelled to increase such exposures when the value of those entities collapsed in order to protect their good reputation with investors. So they chose to purchase assets from, or extend credit to, OBSEs that were set up or managed by them,[78] restocking their balance sheets with low quality ('toxic') assets.

3.4   Credit derivatives

3.4.1   Background

Credit derivatives are innovative financial instruments used to mitigate or assume specific forms of credit risk by hedgers and speculators. There are different kinds of credit risk. The most obvious one is the risk of default. Default means that the counterparty to which the other party is exposed will cease to make payments on obligations into which it has entered because it is unable to make such payments for any reason, including bankruptcy or insolvency of the reference asset obligor. However, the credit risk 'insured' in this case (normally called 'credit event') does not mean only the risk of the borrower's default, but also any other risk specified in the contract as credit risk. An intermediate credit risk occurs when the counterparty's creditworthiness is downgraded (beyond a specified

---

[75] An analytical discussion of causes that led to a weakening of underwriting standards is provided in Chapter 3 below.

[76] See Peter J Wallison, 'Dissent from the Majority Report of the Financial Crisis Inquiry Commission', American Enterprise Institute for Public Policy Research, 14 January 2011, available at www.aei.org/docLib/Wallisondissent.pdf.

[77] IMF, Global Financial Stability Report, 'Containing Systemic Risks' pp. 70–2.

[78] President's Working Group on Financial Markets, 'Policy Statement on Financial Market Developments', March 2008.

level) by the credit agencies causing the value of obligations it has issued
to decline in value. Other risks covered by credit derivatives are: financial
restructuring required under bankruptcy protection; technical default; or
the widening of the underlying bond's credit spread over Treasury bills or
bonds or over any other defined asset beyond a specified level. The global
credit derivatives market experienced a massive expansion in the 2000s
and in fact it doubled in value between 2006 and 2007 to US $29 trillion,
just before the eruption of the GFC.[79]

It was assumed that, since credit derivatives synthetically created or
eliminated credit exposures, they allowed institutions to manage credit
risks more effectively. Yet, in the course of the GFC and especially during its latest phase, the subsequent sovereign debt crisis, they also proved
to be instruments of intense speculation and a rather potent and opaque
channel for the transmission of systemic risk, because of the massive
degree of interconnectedness their use gives rise to. Acknowledging the
value of credit derivatives and the risks associated with their use, today
all major G-20 jurisdictions have enacted legislation to bring the bulk of
credit derivatives trading on exchange and clear them through a formal
Central Counterparty.[80]

3.4.2   Species of credit derivatives

The term credit derivatives normally refers to three kinds of financial
instruments: Credit Default Swaps (CDS), Credit Linked Notes (CLNs)
and Total Return Swaps (TRSs).

(a)   Credit Default Swaps   A Credit Default Swap (CDS) is a swap in
which two parties enter into an agreement whereby one party pays the
other a fixed periodic amount for the life of the agreement. The other
party makes no payments unless a specified 'credit event' occurs. The definition of what constitutes a credit event is of fundamental importance to
the operation of these contracts. CDS contracts are normally concluded
under the ISDA architecture and 'credit events' are typically defined to
include a material default, bankruptcy or debt restructuring for a specified

[79] This estimate is based on data released by the BIS. See 'Credit-Default Swaps Spur Fastest
Derivatives Growth', Bloomberg.com, 21 May 2007, available at www.bloomberg.com/
apps/news?pid=newsarchive&sid=aKyV5WdlrDwA.
[80] Title VII (Part II) Dodd–Frank Act and EU Commission, 'Proposal for a Regulation
of the European Parliament and of the Council on OTC Derivatives, Central
Counterparties and Trade Repositories – Explanatory Memorandum', COM(2010) 484
final, 15 September 2010.

Typical Credit Default Swap

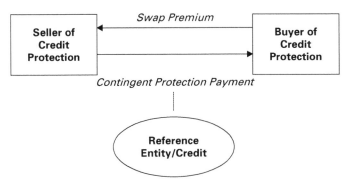

Figure 4   Typical CDS structure

reference asset. If a 'credit event' occurs, the party makes a payment to the first party and the swap then terminates. The size of the payment is usually linked to the decline in the reference asset's market value following the occurrence of such 'credit event'. Figure 4 shows a typical CDS.

For a given swap term the principal factors that determine the theoretical price of a credit swap are: (1) the default probability of each reference credit; (2) the recovery rate; and (3) the counterparty's credit standing. The price is usually fixed as a premium paid in regular intervals calculated as a number of basis points (bps) over the notional amount of the reference credits.

Default probability will be incorporated in the seller's and buyer's models by reference to publicly available data on cumulative historical default rates, usually produced by the major rating agencies. Individual default probability may however, be very tricky to calculate and the rating agencies may be unwilling to provide privately held data on each of the issuer's credits. Recovery rates are often unknown until several months or years have passed since the default has occurred. They may, however, be approximated, if the reference portfolio comprises tradable securities, by the price such securities trade in the post-default period, provided, of course, that trading in them has not been suspended by the relevant exchange or other regulatory authority.[81]

[81] This data is of course very pertinent to the pricing of CDSs. For an overview, see Markit, 'Markit Credit Indices – A Primer', May 2011, Section 1 – Credit Default Swaps, especially pp. 5–6, available at www.markit.com/assets/en/.../Credit_Indices_Primer_May%20 2011.pdf.

Since the purchaser of the credit protection through the CDS has contingent exposure to the seller of the protection in the event of default in the reference credit(s), the credit standing of the swap counterparty (i.e., the party that writes (offers) the swap protection) is an important factor in determining the pricing of the swap. At the same time, this relationship creates opaque links of interconnectedness between financial institutions and investors from different parts of the global economy. For this reason, CDSs (and CDOs) have been widely seen as the manifestations of financial innovation that were most heavily implicated in the amplification of the risks created by the collapse of the US sub-prime mortgage market to other parts of the global financial system.[82]

(b)   Total Return Swaps (TRSs)   TRSs allow two parties to enter into an agreement whereby they swap periodic payments over the specified life of the agreement. One party makes payments based upon the total return – coupons plus capital gains or losses – of a specified reference asset. The other makes fixed or floating payments as with a vanilla interest rate swap. Both parties' payments are based upon the same notional amount. The reference asset can be almost any asset, index or basket of assets, e.g., US corporate bonds trade at a premium (called a credit spread) to the US Treasury curve. The credit spread is volatile in and of itself and it may be correlated with the level of interest rates. Therefore, corporations which have issued debt are eager to find ways to service the cash flows of their bonds more easily and investors are eager to find premiums that they can add to the risk-free rate. The fundamental difference between a CDS and a TRS is the fact that the CDS provides protection against specific credit events. The TRS provides protection against loss of value irrespective of the cause.

(c)   Credit Linked Notes (CLNs)   CLNs are debt instruments backed by the full credit of the selling institution but their performance is based on the performance of a reference loan or group of loans. If the reference credits perform, debt service payments are made on the CLN. If the reference credits default, the CLN is deemed 'defaulted' and payment stops. Thus, the most accurate view of CLNs is to see them as debt instruments bundled with an embedded credit derivative. In exchange for a higher

---

[82] Chapter 3 provides an analytical discussion of the role of financial innovation and CDSs in transmitting and amplifying systemic risk through the opaque ties of interconnectedness they created.

yield on the note, investors accept exposure to a specified credit event. For example, a CLN might provide for principal repayment to be reduced below par in the event that a reference asset defaults prior to the maturity of the note. Most CLNs have additional features that provide for loan recoveries based on a predetermined minimum or the recoveries achieved on the referenced credit(s).

Issuers of CLNs offered in the capital markets usually obtain a rating for their notes before they market them to investors. CLNs, unlike CDSs, are on-balance sheet items and capital exposure is calculated in accordance with the risk-weighting used for assets with similar characteristics, including the nature and country of origin of the issuer. Similarly to CDSs, CLNs are used widely in the context of synthetic securitizations, where the credit risk of a reference asset or portfolio of assets is unbundled and sold separately to those willing to sell credit protection, and no acquisition of the referenced assets is involved.

3.5   Shadow banking

Economists from the New York Federal Reserve have calculated that in early 2008 shadow banking was US $20,000 billion in size, dwarfing the US $11,000 billion traditional banking system. Even today, shadow banking accounts for US $16,000 billion of transactions, which is a much bigger slice of transactions than those going through the traditional banking system, estimated at US $13,000 billion.[83] Like the traditional banking system, the shadow banking system offers credit intermediation. It also offers trading arbitrage possibilities and ample opportunities for regulatory and tax arbitrage. The multi-functional capacity of shadow banks has been evident since their inception.[84] Financial intermediaries that

---

[83] Pozsar, et al., 'Shadow Banking', pp. 3–5.

[84] Stephen Partridge-Hicks and Nicholas J. Sossidis are the two legendary fund managers whose ingenuity pushed the boundaries of the shadow financial sector and are credited by some as its founders. They set up in 1988, as Citibank employees, the first SIV, a limited-purpose finance company with capital from third-party investors that would issue short- and medium-term AAA-rated notes and use the proceeds to buy high-quality, longer-term assets with higher yields. However, even they did not navigate the GFC unscathed. Their flagship fund, Sigma Finance, collapsed in mid-2008. See Paul J Davies, Anousha Sakoui and Gillian Tett, 'Sigma Collapse Ends Shadow Bank Project', *Financial Times*, 2 October 2008, available at www.ft.com/cms/s/0/8c80ff6e-901a-11dd-9890-0000779fd18c.html#axzz1MQOntzkL; and Neil Unmack and Sree Vidya Bhaktavatsalam, 'Pioneers of Structured Investments Fight for Survival of Flagship Fund', *New York Times*, 8 April 2008,available at www.nytimes.com/2008/04/08/business/worldbusiness/08iht-08sigma.11758145.html.

conduct maturity, credit and liquidity transformation without access to central bank liquidity or public sector credit guarantees are normally called shadow banks.[85] Shadow banks tend to be interconnected 'along a vertically integrated, long intermediation chain, which intermediates credit through a wide range of securitization and secured funding techniques such as ABCP, asset-backed securities, collateralized debt obligations, and repo'.[86] The network that binds together institutions acting as shadow banks is what is normally called shadow banking. The Financial Stability Board (FSB) has offered the first authoritative and formal definition of 'shadow banking', describing it as 'a system of credit intermediation that involves entities and activities outside the regular banking system, and raises i) systemic risk concerns, in particular by maturity/liquidity transformation, leverage and flawed credit risk transfer, and/or ii) regulatory arbitrage concerns'.[87] Concerns arise because the credit intermediation services of shadow banks are offered in an environment where 'prudential regulatory standards and supervisory oversight are either not applied or are applied to a materially lesser or different degree than is the case for regular banks engaged in similar activities'.[88]

The shadow banking sector provides credit to households and businesses in much the same fashion as traditional banks, although the clients tend to be bigger and more sophisticated. Accordingly, the shadow banking system, like the traditional banking system, has three actors: savers, borrowers and specialist non-bank financial institutions, performing in many respects functions similar to those of banks. However, in this case, savers place their funds with money market funds, which invest

---

[85] Pozsar, et al., 'Shadow Banking', pp. 2–3. The term was first used by Paul McCulley, a senior economist in a major fund manager, in 2007. McCulley defined shadow banking as: 'unregulated shadow banks [which] fund themselves with uninsured commercial paper [and] which may or may not be backstopped by liquidity lines from real banks' and which stand in contrast to 'regulated real banks, who fund themselves with insured deposits, backstopped by access to the Fed's discount window'. Paul McCulley, 'Teton Reflections' (August/September 2007) PIMCO Global Central Bank Focus, p. 2, available at media. pimco-global.com/pdfs/pdf_sg/GCB%20Focus%20Sept%2007%20SGP-HK.pdf?WT. cg_n=PIMCO-SINGAPORE&WT.ti=GCB Focus Sept 07 SGP-HK.pdf.

[86] Pozsar, et al., 'Shadow Banking', pp. 3–5.

[87] See FSB, 'Shadow Banking: Scoping the Issues – A Background Note of the Financial Stability Board', April 2011, p. 3, available at www.financialstabilityboard.org/publications/r_110412a.pdf.

   To regulate the sector the FSB suggests that the authorities 'should start by casting the net wide, they then should focus on those elements of non-bank credit intermediation where important risks are most likely to emerge'.

[88] Ibid.

these savings in the liabilities of shadow banks. In its essence, 'the shadow banking system decomposes the simple process of deposit-funded, hold-to-maturity lending conducted by banks, into a more complex, whole-sale-funded, securitization-based lending process' that involves a range of shadow banks.[89] Through this intermediation process, the shadow banking system transforms risky, long-term loans (e.g., sub-prime mort-gages) into seemingly credit-risk free, short-term, money-like instruments, which may be 'withdrawable' on demand, much like a demand deposit at a bank.

Yet, unlike the traditional banking system, where credit intermediation is performed under one institutional roof (that of a bank), this function in the shadow banking system is performed through a chain of non-bank financial intermediaries and a series of different activities/functions. According to the New York Federal Reserve study these different functions entail the 'vertical slicing' of traditional banks' credit intermediation process and include: (1) loan origination; (2) loan warehousing; (3) ABS issuance; (4) ABS warehousing; (5) ABS CDO issuance; (6) ABS 'intermediation'; and (7) wholesale funding. The same study notes that the shadow banking system performs these functions in a strict, sequential order with each of the above functions being performed by a specific type of shadow bank and through a specific funding technique.[90] In addition to *cash* investors – which fund shadow banks through short-term repo transactions, and purchases of Commercial Paper (CP) and ABCP instruments – fixed income mutual funds, pension funds and insurance companies also fund shadow banks by investing in their Medium Term Notes and other bonds.[91]

There are, however, significant risks in the operation of the shadow banking system, especially given the short-term nature of some of its funding basis and the absence of any form of deposit insurance, government guarantee and Lender of Last Resort facility. The shadow banking sector is rather susceptible to runs[92] when there is a loss of confidence in financial markets which helps to further amplify the effects of any crisis

---

[89] Pozsar, *et al.*, 'Shadow Banking', pp. 11–12.
[90] *Ibid.* pp. 12–13.   [91] *Ibid.*
[92] 'The shadow banking system is particularly vulnerable to runs – commercial paper investors refusing to re-up when their paper matures, leaving the shadow banks with a liquidity crisis – a need to tap their back-up lines of credit with real banks and/or to liquidate assets at fire sale prices.' *Ibid.* See also Gary Gorton, 'The Panic of 2007'. Yale ICF, Working Paper No. 8–24, 25 August 2008, available at papers.ssrn.com/sol3/papers. cfm;abstract_id=1255362##; Andrew Metrick, 'Regulating the Shadow Banking System', 18 October 2010, available at ssrn.com/abstract=1676947.

in the formal banking sector. These runs do not differ from depositor runs caused by the absence of adequate deposit insurance.[93] It is plausibly suggested that the GFC started as a liquidity (wholesale) run on the shadow banking system. In this respect, Gorton and Metrick have argued that the panic of 2007–8 was triggered by a run on the repo market, which was one of the most important short-term lending markets and provided financing for a large number of structured finance activities.[94]

Furthermore, the leverage built up within the shadow banking system can amplify pro-cyclicality. This has two consequences. First, it increases availability of credit, inflating further asset bubbles. Second, it worsens deleveraging in the event of a confidence crisis and leads to fire sales. In addition, the shadow banking system creates strong links of interconnectedness through the risk sharing techniques utilized in the setting up and operation of shadow banking vehicles (analytically discussed in Chapter 3), which increase the fragility of the formal banking sector.[95] Therefore, it is rather paradoxical that while the Basel III counter-cyclical buffer will be used to curb bank lending during periods of excessive credit growth[96] – a plausible macro-prudential measure – no such measure is applicable to shadow banks. As explained in Chapter 8, the only approach to achieve such intervention would be through a global registration system of shadow banks.

4.   Efficient markets, inefficient markets, adaptive markets

4.1   Introductory remarks

Two competing (and empirically tested) theories have dominated the debate regarding interpretation of the mechanics of the price formation mechanism in financial markets and the rationales/motives of investor behaviour. The first is Modern Finance Theory and the second is Behavioural Finance. More recently, a third wave of theories, of which

[93] The seminal paper on liquidity runs to the banking system is Douglas W. Diamond and Philip H. Dybvig, 'Bank Runs, Deposit Insurance and Liquidity' (1983) 91(3) *Journal of Political Economy* 401–19.
[94] Gary Gorton and Andrew Metrick, 'Securitized Banking and the Run on the Repo', National Bureau of Economic Research Working Paper No. w15223, August 2009, available at papers.ssrn.com/sol3/papers.cfm?abstract_id =1454939.
[95] FSB, 'Shadow Banking: Scoping the Issues,' p. 4.
[96] See BCBS, 'Basel III: A Global Regulatory Framework for more Resilient Banks and Banking Systems', December 2010, pp. 57 *et seq*. Extensive analysis of the mechanics and objectives of the countercyclical buffer is offered in Chapter 6, Section 4.2.

Lo's Adaptive Markets Hypothesis (AMH) stands out, is trying to provide a synthesis of the conflicting views of the other two. Modern Finance Theory is deeply rooted to a rational choice view of the markets. The fundamental assumption of Rational Choice Theory about financial markets is that markets move only on the basis of rational expectations. Namely, asset prices are set by rational investors.[97]

Rational Choice Theory is better defined as an intellectual framework that explains individual preferences,[98] which perceives them as being premised on utility maximization.[99] The theory that, in the face of uncertain outcomes, individuals will choose a course of action that maximizes expected utility, so-called 'Expected Utility Hypothesis', was first clearly expressed by Daniel Bernoulli in 1738.[100] The concept of *expected utility* as the foundation of Rational Choice Theory was further refined by Von Neumann and Morgenstern.[101] Accordingly, the proverbial rational man of neoclassical economics (the famous '*homo economicus*') is supposed to act to maximize expected utility, because his/her preferences are given, consistent and representable in the form of a utility function. Rational agents are assumed to be indifferent between receiving a given financial bundle or a gamble with the same expected value. Moreover, where individuals operate under conditions of uncertainty about the results of their actions, they are assumed to be able to assess the probability distribution in accordance with their level of knowledge. If new information can be collected from the environment, individuals know the information's possible content and assess it, in accordance with Bayes' law, by calculating the probability distribution based on the interplay between the new information's content and their prior knowledge.

Kahneman and Tversky's pioneering research is the foundation of the so-called Psychology of Choice and Judgment which constitutes the

---

[97]   M. Friedman, 'The Methodology of Positive Economics', in M. Friedman (ed.), *Essays in Positive Economics* (University of Chicago Press,1953), pp. 3–43.
[98]   For an analytical account of the difficulty to describe rationality see C. Jolls, C. R Sunstein and R. Thaler, 'A Behavioural Approach to Law and Economics' (1998) 50 *Stanford. L Rev.* 1471–550, 1488.
[99]   See Gary S. Becker, *The Economic Approach to Human Behavior* (University of Chicago Press, 1976), p.14 and Richard Posner, *Economic Analysis of Law* (New York: Aspen Publishers, 6th edn, 2003), Chapters 1–3.
[100]   D. Bernoulli, 'Exposition of a New Theory on the Measurement of Risk', originally published in 1738 and reproduced in (1954) 22 *Econometrica* 23.
[101]   John Von Neumann and Oskar Morgenstern, *Theory of Games and Economic Behavior* (Princeton University Press, 60th anniversary edn, 2007).

first pillar of Behavioural Decision Theory (BDT).[102] The first finding of Kahneman and Tversky's joint work was the so-called 'Prospect Theory', which is a study of how individuals manage risk and uncertainty. The original version of Prospect Theory was designed for gambles with at most two non-zero outcomes. Kahneman and Tversky suggested in their 1979 paper that, when offered a gamble where outcome x has probability p and outcome y has probability q, people assign it with a value of $\pi(p)v(x) + \pi(q)v(y)$ and pick the one with the highest value.[103] This formulation leads to the inference that individuals measure utility over gains and losses rather than over final wealth positions (i.e., they are reference dependent),[104] unlike what is assumed by the Theory of Expected Utility. Therefore, the value assigned to a given state of wealth does vary depending on the individual decision-maker's initial state of wealth.

Moreover, empirical research conducted by psychologists has demonstrated that individuals' judgments originate in impressions as well as in deliberate reasoning. Namely, individuals make decisions using automatic processes (perception), cognitive processes (intuition) and controlled processes (reasoning). The processes of intuition are called 'heuristics' or 'rules of thumb'.[105] The *availability* heuristic controls estimates of the frequency or probability of events, which are judged by the ease with which instances of such events come to mind.[106] In other words, the availability heuristic is an assessment of accessibility. Another heuristic studied systematically by the psychology of judgment and choice is *anchoring*. In forming estimates, people often start with some initial, possibly arbitrary, value and then adjust away from it. In other words, anchoring refers to the process by which an individual decision-maker gravitates to a reference point that he or she subsequently uses as an initial condition for arriving at a final decision. Experimental evidence shows that people anchor too much on the initial value, e.g. on prevailing current interest rates or stock prices, and subsequent adjustment is often insufficient.

---

[102] The other pillar of BDT is experimental economics.

[103] See D. Kahneman and A. Tversky, 'Prospect Theory: An Analysis of Decision under Risk' (1979) 47 *Econometrica* 263–92.

[104] An idea first advanced by Harry M. Markowitz in 'The Utility of Wealth' (1952) 60 *Journal of Political Economy* 151–8.

[105] Daniel Kahneman and Amos Tversky, 'Judgment under Uncertainty: Heuristics and, Biases' (1974) 185 *Science* 1124–31. See also J. T. Harvey, 'Heuristic Judgement Theory (1998) 32 *Journal of Economic Issues* 47–64.

[106] The long list of studies discussing the *availability heuristic* starts with A. Tversky and D. Kahneman, 'Availability: A Heuristic for Judging Frequency and Probability' (1973) 5 *Cognitive Psychology* 207–32.

4.2   *Efficient Markets Hypothesis versus Behavioural Finance*

The Efficient Markets Hypothesis (EMH) constitutes the centrepiece of Modern Finance Theory.[107] It assumes that market prices reflect/equal fundamental value and change on the basis of new information. In an efficient market no investment strategy can yield average returns higher than the risk assumed ('there is no free lunch') and no trader can consistently outperform the market or accurately predict future price levels, as new information is instantly absorbed by market prices.[108] Another EMH assumption is that markets are efficient when transaction costs are relatively low and give 'professionally-informed traders' the opportunity to quickly observe and exploit through arbitrage trading any price deviations from fundamental value, making profit from such discrepancies. The result of arbitrage activity is that prices reach a new equilibrium, which reflects more accurately the traded asset's value and corrects any mis-pricings.[109] Accordingly, inefficient markets are exclusively due to information asymmetries, lack of competition or high transaction costs.

Behavioural Finance challenges most of the assumptions of EMH.[110] The main tenets of Behavioural Finance are that[111]: (1) certain market phenomena, called 'anomalies' or 'puzzles', cannot be explained by EMH, whereas the use of psychology can provide convincing explanations, and

[107] See P. Samuelson, 'Proof that Properly Anticipated Prices Fluctuate Randomly' (1965) 6 *Industrial Management Review* 41–9 and B. Mandelbrot, 'Forecasts of Future Prices, Unbiased Markets, and Martingale Models' (1966) 39 *Journal of Business* 242–55.

[108] See E. F. Fama, 'Efficient Capital Markets: A Review of Theory and Empirical Work' (1970) 25 *Journal of Finance* 383–417; E. F. Fama, 'Efficient Capital Markets II' (1991) 46 *Journal of Finance* 1575–617.

[109] R. J. Gilson and R. H. Kraakman, 'The Mechanisms of Market Efficiency' (1984) 70 *Virginia Law Review* 549, 560 and 565; R. J. Gilson and P. H. Kraakman, 'The Mechanisms of Market Efficiency Twenty Years Later: The Hindsight Bias' (2003) 28 *Iowa Journal of Corporation Law* 715, 723.

[110] See for an overview G. M. Frankfurter and E. G. McGoun, 'Market Efficiency or Behavioral Finance: The Nature of the Debate' (2000) 1 *Journal of Psychology and Financial Markets* 200–10; R. J. Shiller, 'From Efficient Markets Theory to Behavioral Finance' (2003) 17 *Journal of Economic Perspectives* 83, 96–101. See also Emilios Avgouleas, 'Cognitive Biases and Investor Protection Regulation: an Evolutionary Approach' Working Paper, May 2006, available at papers.ssrn.com/sol3/cf_dev/AbsByAuth.cfm?per_id=229512.

[111] See, in general, Nicholas Barberis and Richard Thaler, 'A Survey of Behavioral Finance' National Bureau of Economic Research Working Paper No. 9222, 20 September 2002, pp. 4 and 13, available at papers.ssrn.com/sol3/papers.cfm?abstract_id=327880; D. Hirschliefer, 'Investor Psychology and Asset Pricing' (2001) 56 *Journal of Finance* 1533–97; E. F. Fama, 'Market Efficiency, Long-Term Returns, and Behavioral Finance' (1998) 49 *Journal of Financial Economics* 283–306.

(2) the corrective influence of arbitrage trading is limited due to a number of restrictions. Starting with the second point, convincing evidence has been offered indicating that arbitrage trading may not have the strong corrective role ascribed to it by EMH, as it could prove a risky and expensive activity in a market with less than perfectly rational actors.[112] If we assume two kinds of investors in the market: (1) rational speculators or arbitrageurs who trade on the basis of information; and (2) quasi-rational investors,[113] called 'noise traders',[114] then we accept that some investors act on imperfect information.[115] These cause prices to deviate from their equilibrium values. Nonetheless, the actions of 'noise traders' alone are not sufficient to distort price efficiency. Any price inefficiencies created by 'noise trading' would be exploited by arbitrageurs (so-called 'smart money').

Accordingly, three additional elements are required:

(1) the biases exhibited by noise traders must be consistent[116] (if they are not, most economists would agree that, in a world of heterogeneous biases as much as beliefs, some individuals' biases will cancel out those of others);[117]
(2) the effect of such biases must be so strong as to 'blind' arbitrage traders to the obvious profit opportunities because of widespread 'price inaccuracies' (for instance, hedge funds not only have available to invest very large pools of funds, but also they search on a continuous basis for profit opportunities on a global scale); and
(3) arbitrage is limited by financial or regulatory restrictions.

As regards the first argument, sometimes, 'a single bias extends across most noise traders'. Thus, not only is there no cancelling out of different biases, but also the impact of a single bias, e.g., overconfidence, is exacerbated leading to a price spike or a bubble.[118] Second, the agency relationship

[112] See A. Shleifer and R. Vishny, 'Limits of Arbitrage' (1997) 52 *Journal of Finance* 35–55.
[113] R. H. Thaler, 'The End of Behavioral Finance' (November/December 1999) *Financial Analysts Journal* 12–17.
[114] The issue of 'noise' and its impact on the markets was first analytically discussed by the late Fischer Black. See F. Black, 'Noise' (1986) 41 *Journal of Finance* 529–43.
[115] A. Shleifer and L. H. Summers, 'The Noise Trader Approach to Finance' (1990) 4 *Journal of Economic Perspectives* 19–33.
[116] See Gilson and Kraakman, 'Twenty Years Later', 725, 733.
[117] *Ibid.*
[118] A. Shleifer, *Inefficient Markets: An Introduction to Behavioral Finance* (Oxford University Press, 2000), pp. 173–4; J. B. DeLong, A. Shleifer, L. H. Summers and R. J. Waldmann, 'The Survival of Noise Traders in Financial Markets' (1991) 64 *Journal of Business* 1–19.

that governs the actions of fund managers and of other professional investors (the so-called 'separation of brains from capital')[119] often places limits on arbitrage. Career and compensation concerns closely linked to the need to show short-term profits that are at least comparable with those of competitors force fund managers to herd, i.e., noise traders force professional investors to herd in order to post short-term gains,[120] foregoing arbitrage opportunities. The rationale for such fund manager attitudes/ behaviour is discussed in Sections 4.3 and 4.4 below. Third, arbitrage is often subject to regulatory restrictions on short-sales and considerable transaction costs (e.g., high costs in stock-lending).[121] The so-called Royal Dutch Shell and closed-end funds puzzles constitute strong evidence of the limited impact of arbitrage, due to noise trading.

4.2.1   Royal Dutch Shell

The pricing of the shares of the Royal Dutch Shell Group has been one of the first market phenomena used by Behavioural Finance scholars to show the limitations of the EMH.[122] Royal Dutch Shell is the result of the 1907 merger of Royal Dutch Petroleum and Shell Transport, which were independently incorporated in the Netherlands and Britain respectively. The merger of the two companies' assets was agreed on a 60:40 basis. This ratio roughly remained the basis for the division of cash flows between the two segments of Royal Dutch Shell until 2005. The legacy companies maintained separate listings and Royal Dutch traded primarily in the United States (where it was part of the S&P 500 Index) and the Netherlands. Shell has traded primarily in London, where it has been a major constituent of the Financial Times Stock Exchange Index (FTSE 100). According to the EMH model, the shares of the two components of this company should have traded at a 60:40 ratio, following exchange rate adjustments. Yet, the

---

[119] Shleifer and Vishny, 'Limits of Arbitrage'.

[120] See John Nofsinger and Richard Sias, 'Herding and Feedback Trading by Institutional and Individual Investors' (1999) 54 *Journal of Finance* 2263–95.

[121] See J. Macey, Mark Mitchell and Jeffry Netter, 'Restrictions on Short Sales: An Analysis of the Uptick Rule and its Role in the 1987 Stock Market Crash' (1989) 74 *Cornell Law Review* 799–835; P. M. Dechow, A. P. Hutton, L. Meulbroek and R. G. Sloan, 'Short-sellers, Fundamental Analysis and Stock Returns' (2001) 61 *Journal of Financial Economics* 77–106.

[122] See L. Rosenthal and C. Young, 'The Seemingly Anomalous Price Behavior of Royal Dutch/Shell and Unilever NV/PLC' (1990) 26 *Journal of Financial Economics* 123–41; K. A. Froot and E. M. Dabora, 'How are Stock Prices Affected by the Location of Trade?' (1999) 53 *Journal of Financial Economics* 189–216. This paradox was also examined by Shleifer and Vishny in their article on the limits of arbitrage. See Shleifer and Vishny, 'Limits of Arbitrage'.

history of the price movement of the stocks showed a consistent deviation of over thirty five per cent from the expected ratio. Even when explanations, such as taxes and transaction costs, are taken into account, this
very wide disparity cannot be explained but by reference to noise trading,
clearly illustrating the limits of arbitrage.

4.2.2   Closed-end funds

Arguments concerning the inability of arbitrage to correct pricing inaccuracies, in the presence of noise trader activity, are lent additional force
by the widely observed mis-pricing of the shares/units of closed-end
funds. Unlike open-end funds, closed-end funds issue a fixed number of
shares/units. Thus, the rational way to find a price for their shares is to
divide the net value of the fund's total assets (NAV) by the number of
shares outstanding. Yet the average closed-end fund seems to trade at a
ten per cent discount or premium over NAV.[123] Lee, Shleifer and Thaler,
in a 1991 paper, suggested that some of the individual investors who
are the primary owners of closed-end funds are noise traders, exhibiting irrational swings in their expectations about future fund returns.[124]
Sometimes they are too optimistic, while, at other times, they are too pes-
simistic. Sentiment changes affect fund share prices explaining thus the
difference between share prices and NAV.

This view has been received with serious scepticism by EMH scholars, who have offered a number of rational choice explanations to this
puzzle. They argue that this 'anomaly' is simply the result of transaction
costs (redemption expenses), expectations about future fund manager
performance (agency costs) and tax liabilities. Nonetheless, while these
arguments may explain why funds usually sell at discount, they do not
say why sometimes funds sell at substantial premia, or why discounts
tend to vary on a weekly basis.[125] Furthermore, the noise trader argument
provides a powerful explanation of why it is possible to sell new closed-
end funds at a premium encouraging the establishment of closed-end
funds at times of investor exuberance and why, when a closed-end fund
is liquidated, the share price converges towards NAV. In the latter case,
investors no longer have to worry about shifts in 'noise trader' sentiment

---

[123] Barberis and Thaler, 'A Survey of Behavioral Finance', p. 41.
[124] M. C. C. Lee, A. Shleifer and R. H. Thaler, 'Investor Sentiment and the Closed-end Fund
Puzzle' (1991) 46 *Journal of Finance* 75–109; N. Chopra, M. C. C. Lee, A. Shleifer and R.
Thaler, 'Yes, Discounts on Closed-end Funds Are a Sentiment Index' (1993) 48 *Journal of
Finance* 801–8.
[125] See Barberis and Thaler, 'A Survey of Behavioral Finance', p. 41.

and they cease demanding discounted prices over NAV to compensate for this risk.[126]

4.3   Other puzzles

A number of market 'puzzles' such as; (1) the *equity premium;*[127] (2) *excessive volatility;*[128] (3) *higher* than what would be justified by rational choice assumptions *trading volume;*[129] which is plausibly attributed to *overconfidence;* and (4) the *payment of dividend*, while there are better forms of rewarding a company's shareholders, may all be convincingly explained by reference to the role of *heuristics* and cognitive biases.

In the same context, asset bubbles can be seen as 'anomalies'.[130] Empirical research has shown that individuals frequently exhibit a deep-seated bias towards optimism in predicting future events.[131] In a rising housing or stock market (or any other asset market) individuals embrace unsustainable beliefs that the price rises will continue indefinitely.[132] Resulting overconfidence, otherwise called 'irrational exuberance', can easily grip the markets and it has historically been evident in all major

---

[126] In fact, Lee, Shleifer and Thaler found that there is a strong co-movement in the prices of closed-end funds, which is a powerful indication that noise trader risk is systematic. See above n. 124. Tests carried out by Barberis, Shleifer and Wurgler on the impact of the inclusion of stocks on S&P 500, in the absence of any other information affecting the value of the issuer, have lent further credence to this assumption. See N. Barberis, A. Shleifer and J. Wurgler, 'Why Do Stocks Comove? Evidence from S&P 500 Inclusions' University of Chicago Working Paper, 2001.

[127] R. Mehra and E. Prescott, 'The Equity Premium: A Puzzle' (1985) 15 *Journal of Monetary Economics* 145–61; N. R. Kocherlakota, 'The Equity Premium: It's Still a Puzzle' (1996) 34 *Journal of Economic Literature* 42–71. For a behavioural analysis, see S. Benartzi and R. H. Thaler, 'Myopic Loss Aversion and the Equity Premium Puzzle' (1995) 110 *Quarterly Journal of Economics* 73–92.

[128] R. Shiller, 'Do Stock Prices Move Too Much to Be Justified by Subsequent Changes in Dividends?' (1981) 71 *American Economic Review* 421–36. S. F. LeRoy and R. D. Porter, 'The Present-Value Relation: Tests based on Implied Variance Bounds' (1981) 49 *Econometrica* 555–74.

[129] T. Odean and B. Barber, 'Trading is Hazardous to Your Wealth: The Common Stock Investment Performance of Individual Investors' (2000) 55 *Journal of Finance* 773–806.

[130] See on stock market over-reaction W. F. M. DeBondt and R. Thaler, 'Does the Stock Market Overreact?' (1985) 40 *Journal of Finance* 793–805 and W. F. M. Debondt and R. Thaler, 'Further Evidence on Investor Overreaction and Stock Market Seasonality' (1987) 42 *Journal of Finance* 557–81.

[131] N. D. Weinstein, 'Unrealistic Optimism about Future Life Events' (1980) 39 *Journal of Personality and Social Psychology* 806–20.

[132] See R. J. Shiller, 'Measuring Bubble Expectations and Investor Confidence' (2000) 1 *Journal of Psychology and Financial Markets* 49–60.

bubbles.[133] Institutional investors also seem susceptible to *overconfidence*, since the trading motive is no longer the asset's intrinsic or 'fair' value. Being fully aware that the asset is over-priced, investors pay prices that exceed their own valuation, because they expect to find future buyers to pay a higher price for the asset in question.[134] However, bubbles may also have rational explanations. A very convincing one is that herding, which leads to the creation of bubbles, is investors' reasonable response to *bounded rationality* and information asymmetries.[135]

4.4. Adaptive markets

For many analysts the global financial crisis has spelt the death of the EMH. The same proclamations have also been made in the past, notably after the 1987 crash in US equities. Yet this time it seems that the 'patient' has minimal chances of recovery as a convincing and self-standing explanation of price behaviour in financial markets.[136] Arguably, **Behavioural Finance** has proved a valuable analytical tool in that it shifts attention from analysis of the relationship between prices and information (one of the cornerstones of Modern Finance Theory) to investor behaviour. Thus, the search for new information and the concept of 'fundamental value' become matters of secondary importance. As explained earlier, very large market changes and excessive volatility are attributed to 'irrational' investors who overreact to a given flow of information.[137]

However, in spite of the powerful and ultimately successful challenge that behavioural finance has mounted on the EMH, it is undisputable that learning can reduce the impact of behavioural biases. In addition, sometimes investors do behave rationally and prices take a 'random walk.' Moreover, Behavioural Finance Theory is seriously lacking in predictive

---

[133] Charles P. Kindleberger and Rober Z. Alliber, *Manias, Panics, and Crashes: A History of Financial Crisis* (Hoboken, NJ: New York: Wiley, 5th edn, 2005); Robert J. Shiller, *Irrational Exuberance* (Princeton University Press, 2000).

[134] Jose Scheinkman and Wei Xiong, 'Overconfidence and Speculative Bubbles' (2003) 111 *Journal of Political Economy* 1183–219.

[135] Markus K. Brunnermeier, *Asset Pricing under Asymmetric Information – Bubbles, Crashes, Technical Analysis, and Herding* (Oxford University Press, 2001), Chapter 5.

[136] For a comprehensive historical account of the rise and fall of the EMH, see Justin Fox, *The Myth of the Rational Market, A History of Risk, Reward, and Delusion in Wall Street* (New York: Harper Collins, rep. 2011).

[137] See Shleifer and Summers, 'The Noise Trader Approach to Finance'; L. H. Summers, 'Does the Stock Market Rationally Reflect Fundamental Values?' (1986) 41 *Journal of Finance* 591–601.

value. Thus, it seems that other more inclusive theories, which view markets as evolutionary and adaptive systems that are also susceptible to irrational behaviour due to investors' cognitive limitations and limited self-control, and to strategic trade behaviour (herding), caused by socio-psychological causes or narrow self-interest, provide a better understanding of actual market conditions and investor behaviour.

Andrew Lo of MIT has offered what is currently the best alternative to the battling rivals of Modern Finance Theory and Behavioural Finance. Lo's theory, called Adaptive Markets Hypothesis (AMH),[138] incorporates several assumptions of both theories. Lo submits that markets often can be efficient, but with strong deviations caused by behavioural factors. According to Lo, the forms of market behaviour cited by Behavioural Finance as contradicting the assumptions of EMH, such as loss aversion, overconfidence, overreaction and other cognitive biases, are merely evidence of an evolutionary model of decision-making, where individuals in adapting to a changing environment rely on past experiences (*heuristics* – 'best guesses'). Where AMH differs from Behavioural Finance is that it assumes that if the decision-making challenges that investors face remain stable, the use and outcomes from the use of *heuristics* will gradually adapt, leading in the process to nearly optimal results.[139]

The predominant theme of AMH is that market actors ultimately struggle not for optimal returns (as the EMH holds) – optimization is costly – but for survival, like all living species in an evolutionary framework. AMH holds that market actors behave sometimes rationally and at other times irrationally, depending on which strategy suits best their struggle for survival. Herding may easily become the only survival strategy in a falling market even for professional (rational) investors. Thus, if the more accurate assumption is that markets are complex adaptive systems that encompass both rational and quasi-rational investors,[140] and the latter cause prices to deviate from their equilibrium values, then the majority of investors may in fact be 'momentum' traders who frequently join the herd as their preferred survival strategy.

The assumption that herding constitutes a survival strategy accords well with recent research that herding does not have to be the result of sentiment, such as irrational exuberance. Peer pressure, or attachment to

---

[138] Andrew Lo, 'Reconciling Efficient Markets with Behavioral Finance: The Adaptive Markets Hypothesis', (2005) 7 *Journal of Investment Consulting* 21–44.

[139] *Ibid.*

[140] See also Richard H. Thaler, 'The End of Behavioral Finance', (November/December 1999) 12 *Financial Analysts Journal* 12–13.

short-term gains for career and other reasons relating to the reputation and compensation of the trader or fund manager are also a sufficient and likely factor,[141] because of the agency relationship, or the so-called 'separation of brains from capital'. The agency relationship means that fund managers' and fund investors' interests may be misaligned. Reputations, salaries and career progress are often determined on the basis of short-term profit and comparability with competitors' returns.[142] As a result, fund managers, in fear of the irrational behaviour of 'noise traders' that may force further market falls, leading them to post losses, are likely to decide that foregoing arbitrage opportunities and following the herd is a safer option for themselves,[143] regardless of the long-term damage they may inflict on the fund's investors.

5.   The neo-liberal consensus policies and the growth of global financial markets

5.1   The Jackson Hole Consensus

A number of policies have shaped the development and transformation of global financial markets in the past two decades. The five most important ones were: (1) the so-called great moderation policy, chiefly standing for the targeting of macro-economic stability through monetary policy; (2) the liberalization policies of the Washington Consensus; (3) world trade liberalization, which led to an exacerbation of global trade imbalances and fostered the conditions of excessive liquidity observed in the last decade, (4) financial sector deregulation; and (5) affordable housing policies, which had a certain impact on the explosion of the market for sub-prime mortgages in the US.

---

[141] Paul M. Healy and Krishna G. Palepu, 'Governance and Intermediation Problems in Capital Markets: Evidence from the Fall of Enron' (2003) 17 *Journal of Economic Perspectives* 3–26.

[142] Judith Chevalier and Glenn Ellison, 'Career Concerns of Mutual Fund Managers' (1999) 114 *Quarterly Journal of Economics* 389–432 (examining the labour market for mutual fund managers and managers' responses to the implicit incentives created by their career concerns and showing that the shape of the job separation–performance relationship may provide an incentive for young mutual fund managers to be risk averse in selecting their fund's portfolio).

[143] John R. Nofsinger and Richard W. Sias, 'Herding and Feedback Trading by Institutional and Individual Investors' (1999) 54 *Journal of Finance* 2263–95 (suggesting that herding – a group of investors trading in the same direction over a period of time – and feedback trading – correlation between herding and lag returns – have the potential to explain a number of financial phenomena).

The role of world trade liberalization in the creation of conditions of excessive liquidity in global markets and the impact of US housing policies in the development of shadow banking sector and the creation of the sub-prime market are analytically discussed in Chapter 3. Therefore, in the remainder of this section I shall only examine the impact of great moderation, financial sector deregulation, and Washington Consensus-based liberalization policies on the development of the contemporary financial marketplace.

The decade of the great expansion of global financial markets (roughly from 1997 to 2007) was also the era of great moderation. The policies of the era of great moderation were founded on the so-called Jackson Hole Consensus.[144] The main elements of the Jackson Hole Consensus have been summarized by Professor Charles Bean, a deputy governor of the Bank of England, and his colleagues as comprising seven pillars:[145]

(1) discretionary fiscal policy is an unreliable tool for macroeconomic stabilization;

(2) monetary policy, conducted via setting a path for the expected short-term interest rate, is assigned the primary role for macroeconomic stabilization;

(3) because the transmission mechanism for monetary policy is presumed to operate mainly through longer-term interest rates, expectations of future policy rates are critical and credibility of policy is essential to anchor these expectations;

(4) central bank independence (from the political process) in setting monetary policy is essential to central bank credibility;

(5) flexible inflation targeting under which monetary policy is focused on anchoring expected inflation by keeping realized inflation at or close to its target over an appropriate time horizon;

(6) the efficient markets paradigm is a credible working approximation to the functioning of real world equity and, especially, credit markets. Asset markets are 'efficient at distributing and pricing risk and financial innovations were normally welfare enhancing'. When asset prices become subject to bouts of 'exuberance' on the part of investors, the

---

[144] Jackson Hole is a resort in Wyoming where the international central banking community gathers every year on the invitation of Kansas City Federal Reserve Bank.

[145] Charles Bean, Matthias Paustian, Adrian Penalver and Tim Taylor, 'Monetary Policy after the Fall', Paper given in the Federal Reserve Bank of Kansas City Annual Conference, Jackson Hole, Wyoming, 28 August 2010, pp. 1–3, available at www.kansascityfed.org/publicat/sympos/2010/2010–08–23-bean.pdf.

best monetary policy can do is to limit the fallout when sentiment turns;[146]

(7) price stability and financial stability are complementary and not conflicting objectives. 'Systemic financial crises were seen only in history books and emerging markets; they were unlikely to happen in advanced economies with their developed and well-regulated financial markets.'[147]

A number of economic and political developments reinforced adherence to Jackson Hole Consensus policies. These were:

(1) the handover of monetary policy decisions in June 1997 by the newly elected Labour government in the UK to an independent Monetary Policy Committee (MPC) controlled by the Bank of England. The MPC reversed the trend of high interest rates in the UK;

(2) the introduction of the Euro and the transfer of responsibility for monetary policy by the member states of the European Monetary Union to the European System of Central Banks, headed by the European Central Bank. This change meant that the German approach of tight price controls and relatively low interest rates prevailed across the Eurozone bringing low interest rates and an attendant credit boom to Southern European countries, which in the past had suffered from relatively high inflation and interest rates;

(3) the Federal Reserve's determination to avoid a recession at all costs following the bursting of the bubble in dotcom stocks in the 2000–1 period, which led it to keep interest rates at an unjustifiably low level; and

(4) the Bank of Japan's struggle to counter deflation, following the burst of the huge Japanese asset bubble in the mid-90s, meaning that it had to keep interest rates close to zero throughout the second half of the 1990s and up to the best part of the next decade.

The Jackson Hole Consensus policies are widely seen as being partly (or mainly) responsible for the excessive supply of liquidity that global credit markets experienced up to mid-2007 and, thus, for building the

---

[146] *Ibid.*, p. 2. This bred another fallacy,. i.e., that the growing role of securitization in credit markets, especially in the US, was seen as a stabilizing innovation that reduced systemic risk by distributing and dispersing credit risk away from bank balance sheets and toward a global pool of sophisticated investors.

[147] *Ibid.*, p. 2.

conditions that led to the GFC by allowing asset bubbles to develop in most developed economies, especially in property markets. Its adherents, especially Allan Greenspan, have been widely criticized for their ideological reliance on self-correcting asset markets.[148] While price stability was achieved central banks did not prevent, and may even have contributed to, the GFC. Yet the exercise of monetary policy is a rather complex and nuanced area and some of this criticism may not have been justified. The obvious remedy to prevent the formation of a bubble,[149] namely a monetary policy targeting asset price inflation, such as a rise in interest rates, would certainly have an impact on GDP growth.[150] I provide an analytical account of the dilemma that monetary policy faces in attempting to both maintain price and financial stability in the next chapter.

5.2   Deregulation

Deregulation of the financial services industry in the Western world was founded on the same neo-liberal ideology that informed the Washington Consensus policies discussed below. It led to a significant increase in the size and importance of the financial sector, giving it a disproportionate influence over economic and regulatory policy decisions.[151] However, before the eruption of the GFC deregulation was deemed to be, at least on balance, a policy that had brought strong economic development and

---

[148] See United Nations Conference on Trade and Development (UNCTAD), 'The Global Economic Crisis, Systemic Failures and Multilateral Remedies', New York and Geneva, 2009; United Nations, 'Report of the Commission of Experts of the President of the United Nations General Assembly on Reforms of the International Monetary and Financial System' New York, 21 September 2009.

[149] See Zeno Enders and Hendrik Hakenes, 'On the Existence and Prevention of Asset Price Bubbles' Max Planck Institute for Research Collective Goods Preprint, No. 2010/44, November 2010, available at papers.ssrn.com/sol3/papers.cfm?abstract_id=1705943.

[150] See on the issue Ben S. Bernanke, 'Monetary Policy and the Housing Bubble', Speech at the Annual Meeting of the American Economic Association, Atlanta, Georgia, 3 January 2010, available at www.federalreserve.gov/newsevents/speech/bernanke20100103a.htm.

[151] As Adair Turner, chairman of the FSA and previously director of McKinsey, has observed: '[In recent years] the whole efficient market theory, Washington consensus, free market deregulation system was so dominant that it was somewhat like a "religion". This gave rise to "regulatory capture through the intellectual zeitgeist", enabling the banking lobby to swell in size and power.' Adair Turner, 'How to Tame Global Finance, A Group of Leading Financial Analysts Quiz Britain's Top Regulator on What Went Wrong and How to Sort It Out', (27 August 2009). 162 *Prospect* available at www.prospectmagazine.co.uk/2009/08/how-to-tame-global-finance/.

other welfare gains to the national economies that had liberalized their financial sectors. At the same time, the aggregate benefits to the global economy were the subject of fierce debate and controversy. Deregulation in the financial services sector is surrounded by several conspiracy theories and endless myths. In reality, it was a much more gradual process than is normally assumed, and, in the beginning at least, the principal motive was the search for a new growth engine for post-industrial era economies, such as the UK and the US, which had lost serious ground to goods manufacturers from emerging markets and Japan.

The first formidable step in the direction of deregulation was made in the UK through the so-called 'big bang' of 27 October 1986, which meant the disappearance of traditional stock jobbers.[152] 'Big bang' legislation, probably the centrepiece of the Thatcher era drive towards financial liberalization, abolished the fixed commissions' regime for London Stock Exchange (LSE) and opened access to LSE trading and attendant broking services to all financial houses. This created a chain reaction which gradually led to the acquisition of most of the traditional discount houses and merchant banks, with very few exceptions, either by foreign competitors or large UK commercial banks. The latter meant a huge shift in the business culture of big UK banks, which eventually culminated in the disastrous acquisitions and business policies followed by the Royal Bank of Scotland and the Halifax Bank of Scotland two decades later.[153]

The US, on the other hand, had in place the last relics of Depression era legislation, so called Glass–Steagall Act,[154] until 1999. The core sections of the Banking Act of 1933 (defined as the Glass–Steagall Act) were sections 16, 20, 21 and 32. Section 16, as amended by the Banking Act of 1935, generally prohibited Federal Reserve member banks from purchasing securities for their own account. Sections 16 and 21 also forbade deposit-taking institutions from engaging in the business of 'issuing, underwriting, selling, or distributing, at wholesale or retail, or through syndicate participation, stock, bonds, debentures, notes or other securities', except holdings of US Treasury bills and other public sector debt obligations. According to the US Supreme Court, the Act was intended to

[152] On the disappearance of the LSE's stock jobbers and their business culture, see Bernard Attard, 'Making a Market, The Jobbers of London Stock Exchange, 1800–1986' (2000) 7 *Financial History Review* 5–24.

[153] On the disastrous business policies and fate of the two banks see Section 6.2 below.

[154] Banking Act of 1933, 48 Stat. 162, codified in several sections of the US Code, now repealed.

prevent banks from endangering themselves, the banking system and the public from unsafe and unsound practices and conflicts of interest.[155]

In 1956 the US Congress further mandated, through the Bank Holding Company Act, the separation of banking and insurance underwriting business.[156] However, by the time of its formal repeal in 1999,[157] Glass–Steagall-type restrictions had been seriously eroded, especially as regards the ability of commercial banks to acquire securities affiliates and the trend towards mega-mergers between financial services institutions had already set in. This trend culminated in the 'marriage' of Citicorp (a banking company) with Travellers, a financial conglomerate with several insurance subsidiaries and a securities firm (Salomon Smith Barney), to produce Citigroup. This merger preceded and probably 'coerced' the repeal of the Glass–Steagall Act.[158] It was followed by the subsequent merger of JP Morgan with Chase Manhattan in 2000. These mergers made mega-banks a menacing reality to competitors, consumers and the financial system,[159] greatly increasing the importance of banks and the financial system's interconnectedness. Characteristically, between 1998 and 2008 the number of global banking assets controlled by the five largest international banks grew from 8 per cent to 16 per cent.[160]

The same drive toward deregulation, by means, in this case, of harmonization legislation with the explicit intent of levelling the playing field between continental European universal banking and the informal separation model operated in Britain, meant that EU legislation actively

---

[155] *Investment Co. Inst.* v. *Camp*, 401 US 617, at 630–1 (1971), per Justice Stewart.

[156] Bank Holding Company Act of 1956, Pub. L. No. 511, 70 Stat. 133.

[157] Gramm–Leach–Bliley Financial Services Modernization Act, Pub. L. No. 106–102, 113 Stat. 1338 (1999). For today's reader, who has the benefit of hindsight, it seems inexplicable that so few US senators opposed at the time the repeal of the Glass–Steagall Act. See 'Glass–Steagall Act: The Senators And Economists Who Got It Right', *Huffington Post*, 11 May 2009, available at www.huffingtonpost.com/2009/05/11/glass-steagall-act-the-se_n_201557.html.

[158] See for the influence of the Citigroup merger on the repeal of Glass–Steagall Act and the enactment of the Gramm–Leach–Billey Act, Arthur E. Wilmarth, 'The Dark Side of Universal Banking: Financial Conglomerates and the Origins of the Subprime Financial Crisis' (2009) 41 *Connecticut Law Review* 963–1050, 972–5.

[159] The figures that this consolidation represented in the US are staggering: 'More than 5,400 mergers took place in the U.S. banking industry from 1990 to 2005, involving more than $5.0 trillion in banking assets … [and] the share of U.S. banking assets held by the ten largest banks more than doubled'. 'Wilmarth, The Dark Side', 975–6 (notes omitted).

[160] Andrew G. Haldane, 'Rethinking the Financial Network', Speech, 2009, available at www.bankofengland.co.uk/publications/speeches/2009/speech386.pdf.

promoted the universal bank model.[161] Thus, it fostered the creation of several mega-banks in the UK and the rest of Europe.[162] Finally, liberalization and the dismantling of barriers between commercial and investment banking also meant a large number of cross-border mergers and acquisitions,[163] creating large complex financial conglomerates with very strong international business, asset and deposit bases.

5.3   Washington Consensus policies

Washington Consensus policies, which dominated the development agenda in the 1980s and even more so in the 1990s, focused on rapid market liberalization, the privatization of state dominated industries and macro-stability.[164] They were premised upon a strong faith in free markets and aimed at reducing, or even eliminating, the role of government in economic life.[165] The key policies of the Washington Consensus, as summarized by Williamson in his reformulation of this concept, referred to:

(1) fiscal discipline;
(2) reordering public expenditure priorities;

---

[161] The chief example of EU legislation of this kind is the Second Banking Directive (Second Council Directive 89/646/EEC of 15 December 1989 on the co-ordination of laws, regulations, and administrative provisions relating to the taking up and pursuit of the business of credit institutions and amending Directive 77/780/EEC 30 December 1989, OJ L 386/1, replaced by Directive 2006/48/EC relating to the taking up and pursuit of the business of credit institutions 30 June 2006 OJ L 177/1). The Second Banking Directive allowed deposit-taking European Banks to also engage in the kind of investment market activities that were usually reserved, at least outside of Germany, for securities firms and non-deposit taking investment banks.

[162] 'Nearly 1,800 bank mergers took place in the Eurozone and the United Kingdom (U.K.) from 1990 to 2001. An additional 350 bank mergers were completed in the European Union (EU) from 2002 to 2006. As in the United States, a number of very large bank mergers were completed in the U.K. and Europe ... ' Wilmarth, 'The Dark Side', 977 (notes omitted).

[163] Ibid., 977–8.

[164] This definition was offered by John Williamson, who actually coined the term. See John Williamson, 'What Washington Means by Policy Reform', in John Williamson (ed.), Latin American Adjustment: How Much Has Happened? (Washington, DC: Institute for International Economics, 1990) and John Williamson, 'What Should the Bank Think About the Washington Consensus', Background Paper to the World Bank's World Development Report 2000, July 1999. For a reformulation of the concept see John Williamson, 'A Short History of the Washington Consensus', Conference Paper, 24 September 2004, available at www.iie.com/publications/papers/williamson0904–2.pdf.

[165] Joseph Stiglitz, 'The Post-Washington Consensus Consensus', Working Paper, Initiative for Policy Dialogue, Columbia University, 2004, available at policydialogue.org/files/events/Stiglitz_Post_Washington_Consensus_Paper.pdf.

(3) tax reform;
(4) liberalizing interest rates;
(5) competitive exchange rates;
(6) trade liberalization;
(7) liberalization of inward foreign direct investment;
(8) privatization;
(9) deregulation; and
(10) property rights.

The endorsement of each of these policies meant the eradication of long and deep-seated path-dependent biases in the economic development of countries that had to implement them. A number of those policies, such as fiscal discipline and the establishment of a (legal) system of clearly delineated property rights' and, arguably, trade liberalization did prove to be beneficial for the countries that adopted them. Also, Washington Consensus policies were instrumental in opening up developing country markets, in spite of continuing, and probably justifiable, scepticism about capital controls.[166] This, however, is not to say that several of those policies were not stained by marked weaknesses.

Liberalization of domestic credit markets and policies pertaining to competitive exchange rates – not unfairly compared in their elusiveness to the eternal quest for the Holy Grail – were castigated as the main causes of the East Asian and Russian currency crises in the late 1990s, which brought economic hardship and social strife in the countries concerned. The IMF's insistence on the liberalization of credit markets not through institutional reform, but through market-based interest rates, led to serious financial dislocation. Developing countries often have 'very thin and rudimentary' credit markets and premising interest rates on the whims (or even the genuine conditions) of such markets led often 'to prolonged periods of very high interest rates without improving the availability of credit'.[167]

Another big weakness of the Washington Consensus was that the development policies it dictated were not cognizant of local political, economic and social conditions.[168] In addition, there was lack of substantial experience with the implementation of similar policies, since neither the

[166] Jonathan D. Ostry, *et al.* 'Managing Capital Inflows: What Tools to Use?' IMF Staff Note, SDN/11/06, 5 April 2011.
[167] Stiglitz, 'The Post-Washington Consensus'.
[168] See in general, R. Gilpin, *The Challenge of Global Capitalism: The World Economy in the 21st Century* (Princeton University Press, 2000).

US nor the other developed countries pushing the Washington Consensus agenda had adopted extreme market-oriented policies in the post-World War II era. The speed with which the implementation of these policies was pursued was also a problem. Finally, the Washington Consensus model was not conceptually adaptive to technological change[169] and it wrongfully ignored the development role that can be played by the state.[170]

The debate on the available alternatives to Washington Consensus policies is inconclusive to date. What is really evident though is that a mix of different policies should be used to further the development agenda. In this context, availability of finance and of a strong legal framework that secures the right pre-conditions to facilitate access to external finance (discussed extensively in Section 2 above) plays a rather important role.

6.   Financial markets and financial crises

A number of very important theories have been advanced over the years regarding the propensity of financial markets to fall into a state of instability and even more critically to wreak havoc on the real economy subsequently. Before considering those theories, I proceed below with a cursory discussion of the two most important financial crises of the past two decades: the Asian Crisis and the Global Financial Crisis.

6.1   The Asian Crisis

The Asian Crisis erupted in the summer of 1997, but it was brewing for some time. It caused severe economic turbulence in the South East Asian economies and eventually contagious panic infected other emerging economies. In general, the Asian Crisis is divided into two distinct phases. During the first, from July 1997 to December 1997, the crisis mostly covered the economies of South Korea, Thailand, the Philippines and Indonesia. During the second, from mid-1998 to early 1999, the turbulence spread to other emerging economies, chiefly Russia and Brazil,[171] which experienced difficulties with their sovereign debt repayments

---

[169]   Stiglitz, 'The Post-Washington Consensus Consensus', p. 4.

[170]   R. Wade, *Governing the Market: Economic Theory and the Role of Government in East Asian Industrialization* (Princeton University Press, 2003).

[171]   See, for an overview of the causes of the Asian Crisis, Eshan Karunatilleka, 'The Asian Economic Crisis', Research Paper 99/14, Economic Policy and Statistics Section, House

following over-borrowing, leading in the case of Russia to a temporary default.[172]

The Asian Crisis started as a speculative panic that caused a massive exodus of short-term funds from the aforementioned Asian economies, triggering currency crises. The underlying causes of the crisis were:[173]

(1) flawed foreign exchange policies (informal pegs of local currencies to the dollar), which, in the quest for exchange stability caused serious current account deficits;

(2) massive asset bubbles, which were mainly debt-fuelled and had been caused by short-term speculative flows of funds in the absence of any capital controls; and

(3) a weak banking sector that was largely unregulated[174] and plagued with corruption, and was mainly used to service the purposes of the crony capitalism practices exercised by the quasi-dictatorial regimes in the region.

There is also a strong contingent of economists that sees the Asian Crisis as a mere liquidity crisis since highly liquid short-term debt was used to finance illiquid assets.[175]

of Commons Library, 11 February 1999. See also Paul Krugman, 'What Happened to Asia?' MIT, mimeo, January 1998, available at web.mit.edu/krugman/www/DISINTER.html.

[172] Joseph Stiglitz, *Globalisation and Its Discontents* (London: Penguin, updated edn, 2003), Chapter 5. In fact, the Russian default might have been more the result of domestic policies of credit expansion, widespread corruption, a weak banking sector and crony capitalism than contagion from the Asian Crisis. See Galina B. Hale, 'Lessons from the 1998 Russian Financial Crisis' (2001) 18 *University of California Berkley CSEES Newsletter* 9.

[173] See Morris Goldstein, *The Asian Financial Crisis: Causes, Cures, and Systemic Implications* (Washington, DC: Institute for International Economics, 1998).

[174] See Frederic S. Mishkin, 'Lessons from the Asian Crisis' (1999) 18 *Journal of International Money and Finance* 709–23, 710–12.

[175] Steven Radelet and Jeffrey Sachs, 'The Onset of the East Asian Financial Crisis', Harvard Institute for International Development, 30 March 1998. Radelet and Sachs plausibly argue that the weaknesses of the Asian economies and of their financial sectors were not deep enough to cause a crisis of such magnitude and it was rather loss of confidence and flawed IMF and domestic policies that led to the ensuing investor panic, which due to the illiquidity of assets that had been financed by short-term loans, devastated the economies of the region. See also Steven Radelet, Jeffrey D. Sachs, Richard N. Cooper and Barry P. Bosworth, 'The East Asian Financial Crisis: Diagnosis, Remedies, Prospects' (1998) 29 *Brookings Papers on Economic Activity* 1–90. In fact, flawed exchange policies, illiquidity and the short-term nature of foreign debt (rather than over-indebtedness) seem to have also been at the heart of the Mexican–Argentine debt crisis of 1994–5.

The financial crisis severely undermined public finances in a number of countries and prompted the IMF to organize a rescue package totalling US $112 billion for Thailand, Korea and Indonesia, without, however, controlling the exit stampede.[176] In addition, the IMF prescribed remedies and a sharp increase in interest rates led to further accumulation of debt and a spate of bankruptcies of even healthy, private companies, pushing the South East Asian economies into deep recession.

Moreover, as Mishkin has suggested, the weak regulatory structures of the banking sector in those countries could not cope with the rapid credit growth created by the lending boom. The latter was induced by short-term foreign capital flows, following liberalization of domestic markets and abolition of capital controls, which fuelled excessive risk taking by already unreliable local banks and, in addition, increased pressure on exchange rates since most loans were denominated in a foreign currency. The subsequent deterioration of bank balance sheets is regarded as the most critical reason for driving those countries into the ensuing financial crisis. Finally, the credit rationing that followed the collapse of the South East Asian banking sectors pushed those countries' economies further into recession.[177]

6.2   The Global Financial Crisis

The Global Financial Crisis is an event of unprecedented severity, even though, for a crisis of such magnitude, it had relatively humble beginnings: the collapse of the sub-prime mortgage market in the US due to the geometric rise of delinquent loans. I discuss extensively the causes of the GFC in the next chapter. This means that this paragraph only provides a discussion of the main episodes of the GFC.

In the first half of 2007, the ripple effects from the precipitous fall of house prices in the US and the rise of delinquencies in sub-prime mortgages had crossed the Atlantic Ocean and panic started rearing its head in European and global markets. The first failure of a financial institution beyond the specialized US mortgage providers was only a matter of

---

Ibid., 10–15. Jeffrey Sachs, Aaron Tornell, Andrés Velasco, Francesco Giavazzi and István Székely, 'The Collapse of the Mexican Peso: What Have We Learned?' (1996) 11 *Economic Policy* 13–63.

[176] Radelet and Sachs, 'The Onset of the East Asian Financial Crisis'. For criticism over IMF's policies and conduct during the Asian Crisis, see Stiglitz, *Globalisation and Its Discontents*, Chapter 4.

[177] Mishkin, 'Lessons', 711–12.

time. This came in the form of collapse of UK's Northern Rock, a medium size mortgage provider, due to falling house prices and overreliance on short-term funding from wholesale markets, which in July 2007 simply froze.[178] Due to the small size of the bank, the Northern Rock incident was brushed aside as an unfortunate incident that was mostly due to failure of supervision – an accurate assessment – rather than a forewarning of a generalized collapse of the global financial system – an inaccurate assumption. Then in March 2008 the fifth biggest US investment bank, Bear Stearns, came close to collapse due to losses in its securities portfolio that was strongly linked with the sub-prime mortgage market. Eventually, Bear Stearns became the subject of a quasi-compulsory takeover by JP Morgan, following the purchase by the US central bank, the Federal Reserve, of some of the worst performing assets of Bear Stearns at a cost of US $28 billion.[179] However, although the clouds of the unprecedented storm were gathering, most bankers and policy-makers still believed that the crisis could be contained and when the storm came nobody was ready. What happened next has been described in endless press articles, TV documentaries, academic papers and policy documents. In the space of a few weeks from early September to early October 2008, the global financial system teetered on the brink of collapse on a daily basis.[180]

On 7 September 2008, the US Treasury bailed out the Federal National Mortgage Association, called Fannie Mae, and the Federal Home Loan

---

[178] The Run on the Rock, (House of Commons, Treasury Committee, Fifth Report of Session 2007–8, 24 January 2008). This was the first collapse of a deposit-taking bank in the UK for 150 years. See also Emilios Avgouleas, 'Banking Supervision and the Special Resolution Regime of the Banking Act 2009: the Unfinished Reform' (2009) 4 *Capital Markets Law Journal* 1–35. The last bank panic in England before Northern Rock had occurred in 1866. The collapse of the recklessly managed Overend Guerney and the Bank of England's inability/unwillingness to intervene triggered a generalized banking run. See W. Bagehot, *Lombard Street: A Description of the Money Market* (London: Henry S King & Co.,1873).

[179] M Grynbaum, 'Fed Officials Defend Rescue of Bear Stearns' *NY Times*, 3 April 2008, available at www.nytimes.com/2008/04/03/business/03cnd-fed.html?hp.

[180] For an authoritative timeline of the events leading to the GFC and its aftermath since the eruption of the sub-prime mortgage crisis in March 2007, see Council of Foreign Relations, 'Timeline: Global Economy in Crisis', available at www.cfr.org/economics/timeline-global-economy-crisis/p18709, and Mauro F. Guillén, 'The Global Economic & Financial Crisis:A Timeline', The Lauder Institute, Wharton School, University of Pennsylvania, available at lauder.wharton.upenn.edu/pages/pdf/Chronology_Economic_Financial_Crisis.pdf. See also 'Banking Crisis Timeline, How the Credit Crunch has Led to Dramatic, Unprecedented Events in the City, on Wall Street and Around the World', *Guardian.co.uk*, 30 October 2008, available at www.guardian.co.uk/business/2008/oct/08/creditcrunch.marketturmoil.

Mortgage Corporation (FHLMC), called Freddie Mac, which were regarded as government sponsored enterprises (GSEs),[181] although they had become publicly listed shareholder-owned companies. Fannie Mae and Freddie Mac had accumulated very large losses from their mortgage securities portfolios and the bail-outs were inspired by a need to avoid the massive collateral damage that their collapse would cause to financial markets and the US economy.[182] However, the US Treasury's approach to bail-outs went into reverse when it failed (or declined, depending on whose account should be endorsed) to bail-out Lehman Brothers, a major investment bank and a fixture in the US financial sector for more than 150 years. Following frantic attempts over the previous weekend to find a buyer, Lehman Brothers filed for bankruptcy on 15 September, making it the largest bankruptcy in US history. The announcement of Lehman's collapse triggered a massive crisis of confidence in the markets,[183] as until then investors had assumed that the US Treasury would act to prevent financial institutions the size of Lehman Brothers from failing. It was at this exact moment that share prices in the financial sector took a massive dip and the price of assets relating to the housing market and other forms of bank loans collapsed making the already under-capitalized and highly leveraged European and US banks look bankrupt. As a result, the US sub-prime mortgage crisis and attendant credit crunch turned into a global

---

[181] Fannie Mae was established in 1938 and, its initial mission was to underwrite a portion of mortgage loans granted by US commercial banks and specialized lending institutions. Subsequently, its mission was to maintain a liquid market for securitized mortgages in the secondary market. Freddie Mac was established in 1970 with a mission to expand the secondary market for housing loans. Although both were public companies for a long time (Fannie Mae converted to plc status in 1968), Fannie Mae and Freddie Mac were considered to be government sponsored enterprises because they had been chartered by Congress and were given various privileges (such as exemption from the Securities Act of 1933 and the Securities Exchange Act of 1934) and a line of credit at the Treasury that signalled a special degree of government support. As a result, the capital markets assumed that, in the event of financial difficulties, the government would stand behind them. This implicit government backing gave them access to funding that was lower cost than any AAA borrower and often only a few basis points over the applicable Treasury rate. See Wallison, 'Dissent', pp. 11–12. However, there was nothing in US legislation justifying this view and securing their effective nationalization on 8 September 2008. See on the facts leading to GSEs' bailout and nationalization, Hank Paulson, *On the Brink: Inside the Race to Stop the Collapse of the Global Financial System* (New York: Hachette Book Group, 2010).

[182] Ashley Seager and Phillip Inman, 'US Steps in to Rescue Failing Home Loan Giants', *The Guardian*, 8 September 2008, available at www.guardian.co.uk/business/2008/sep/08/freddiemacandfanniemae.useconomy.

[183] On the massive legal complications of Lehman Brothers's bankruptcy, especially in a cross-border context, see Chapter 5, Section 4.3 below.

financial crisis of unprecedented severity. The remaining Wall Street investment banks either sought buyers, as in the case of Merrill Lynch, which was bought by Bank of America in order to cover its short-term debts and stave off bankruptcy, or turned into bank holding companies in order to obtain access to Federal Reserve liquidity support, as Morgan Stanley and Goldman Sachs did on 22 September 2008. The day after Lehman's collapse (16 September 2008) the insurance giant, American International Group (AIG), which, through a subsidiary, had a massive and solvency-threatening exposure to the CDS market, was subjected to a spate of downgrades. This prompted fears that its failure would trigger the failure of European banks that had bought the CDS cover from AIG and Goldman Sachs,[184] leading to a global financial meltdown. Therefore, the US Treasury provided AIG with an US $85billion USD rescue package on 17 September 2008.

As the situation in stock markets turned desperate and financial sector stocks took a massive 'pounding',[185] US Treasury Secretary Henry Paulson unveiled a rescue plan, named the Troubled Assets Relief Program (TARP) on 17 September 2008. The plan aimed to use US $700 billion of US taxpayer assets to stabilize markets. It also proposed to buy troubled and difficult-to-value assets from the country's largest financial firms, value them and resell them, in the hope of restoring confidence in credit markets.[186] A few days later most developed country regulators, including the SEC and the FSA, released a concurrent prohibition on short sales in financial sector stocks, which came into effect on 21 September 2008.[187]

---

[184] Report of the United States Senate, Permanent Subcommittee on Investigations Committee on Homeland Security and Governmental Affairs, 'Wall Street and the Financial Crisis – Anatomy of a Financial Collapse', 13 April 2011, available at hsgac.senate.gov/public/_files/Financial_Crisis/FinancialCrisisReport.pdf.

[185] Graeme Wearden, 'FTSE 100 Plunges Through 5000-mark as Share Rout Continues, London Index Down Another 178.6 Points HBOS Shares Plummet more than 40%', *The Guardian*, 16 September 2008, available at www.guardian.co.uk/business/2008/sep/16/lehmanbrothers.marketturmoil3?INTCMP=ILCNETTXT3487.

'The London market is having another bruising morning. In opening trade the FTSE 100 was down a massive 10%, touching a low of 3874 points. That was a drop of 439.8 on last night', Chris Tyhorn, 'HBOS Leads FTSE Plunge', *The Guardian* 10 October 2010, available at www.guardian.co.uk/business/marketforceslive/2008/oct/10/hbos-lloydstsbgroup.

[186] TARP was endorsed by US congress on 17 October 2008, following a prolonged, yet minimal by US standards of political bargaining and horse trading, period of consultation due to the urgency of market conditions. Emergency Economic Stabilization Act of 2008 (US) (PL 110–343).

[187] Securities Exchange Act Release No. 34-58592 (18 September 2008) ('Emergency Order Pursuant to Section 12(k)(2) of the Securities Exchange Act of 1934 Taking Temporary

However, the financial drama experienced in global markets continued unfolding at a breathtaking pace. Washington Mutual (Wa-Mu), one of the biggest US savings and loans bank, was seized by the Federal Deposit Insurance Corporation (FDIC) and declared bankrupt on 26 September 2008, underscoring the precarious position of all big high street banks. The next day, the FDIC sold the bank's assets to another bank, JP Morgan Chase for US \$1.6billion, a fraction of the bank's market capitalization just a month ago. On 29 September, Wachovia, another major US commercial bank, entered crisis takeover talks with Citigroup. Wachovia was purchased in early October by Wells Fargo. In the meantime, in the UK, Lloyds TSB had entered into a Treasury induced[188] and vexed takeover of the bankrupt Halifax Bank of Scotland (HBOs).[189] Eventually, since the entire financial sector of most developed countries faced a mortal threat, and most of their major banks, such as Citigroup, Royal Bank of Scotland,[190] Fortis, ING (in the Netherlands) and others faced the prospect of disorderly collapse, a number of countries followed the US example and released massive bank rescue packages in a co-ordinated effort to stabilize the financial sector. [191] These packages included the granting

Action to Respond to Market Developments'); FSA, 'Short Selling (No 2) Instrument 2008' (relating to UK Financial Sector companies), FSA 2008/50 (18 September 2008). For the bans in the EU, see CESR, 'Measures Recently Adopted by CESR Members on short-selling,' CESR/08–742, 22 (September 2008, Updated: 9 January 2009,31 March 2009, 1 February 2010), available at www.cesr.eu/popup2.php?id=5238. Arguably, the bans were misguided, as the market's concerns about financial institutions' solvency were well founded. See for a critical evaluation of the bans, Emilios Avgouleas, 'A New Framework for the Global Regulation of Short Sales, Why Prohibition is Inefficient and Disclosure Insufficient' (2010) 15(2) *Stanford Journal of Law, Business and Finance* 376–425.

[188] The UK Treasury and other European authorities had during the same period to also deal with the failure of Icelandic banks, which intensified the systemic threat to the European (and the global) financial system. The failure of Icelandic banks and the challenges this raised for cross-border bank supervision are discussed in Chapter 5, Section 4.2 below.

[189] Jeff Randall, 'What's Wrong with Lloyds' Takeover of HBOS? Just Follow your Nose', *The Telegraph*, 11 November 2008, available at www.telegraph.co.uk/finance/comment/ jeffrandall/3442788/Whats-wrong-with-Lloyds-takeover-of-HBOS-Just-follow-your-nose.html and Nick Goodway, 'Counting the Cost a Year after Lloyds' Takeover of HBOS', *London Evening Standard*, 17 September 2009.

[190] Graeme Warden, 'British Government Unveils £37bn Banking Bail-out Plan', Guardian. co.uk, 13 October 2008, available at www.guardian.co.uk/business/2008/oct/13/ marketturmoil-creditcrunch.

[191] The UK adopted two rescue packages. The first rescue package (called HM Treasury Credit Guarantee Scheme and Recapitalisation Fund) was passed on 8 October 2008 and totalled £500bn. See 'The Treasury's Statement on a Bailout for British Banks to Rescue the

of extensive state guarantees of bank assets to stabilize the inter-bank market and re-open this channel of liquidity, and in some cases, outright purchase by the state of bad loan assets.[192] Eventually as the immediate threat subsided and the colossal and global nature of the problem became apparent, while the global economy was sliding into a deep recession, the US government invited the heads of state of the G-20 countries to the first summit of this kind convened on 14 November 2008 in Washington. The leaders released a Summit Declaration outlining plans for an ambitious reform agenda for the global financial system.[193]

6.3   Are financial markets inherently unstable?

From the previous discussion of the most recent financial crises and from empirical studies on the causes of such crises, it may be validly argued that debt induced asset bubbles seem to be at the heart of all financial crises.[194] Especially in the past fifty years, financial crises seem to have been caused by a combination of sovereign or private sector over-indebtedness during heady days, which were marked by wide-spread market euphoria, and ended up with colossal misallocation of investment. It is received wisdom that at some point sovereign or private debt becomes unsustainable and at the same time deleveraging strategies followed by over-indebted borrowers not only prick the preceding asset bubbles but also gradually diminish the price of assets acquired through debt, and thus the value of banks' collateral. Subsequently, they push national economies into recession reducing their tax takings at the very same time that revenue is most needed to repay debt. Thus, they lead to a spiral of defaults whereby the private sector's or the state's

Financial Sector from the Turmoil of Recent Days', *The Telegraph*, 8 October 2008, available at www.telegraph.co.uk/finance/financetopics/financialcrisis/3156569/Banking-bailout-The-statement-in-full.html. The second rescue package was adopted in January 2009 and totalled at least £50 billion.

[192] For a detailed account of the global financial crisis during September and October 2008 and a description of the rescue packages see Financial Stability Report (Bank of England, October 2008, Issue 24).

[193] 'Summit Declaration of the Leaders of G20 on Financial markets and the World Economy', 15 November 2008, available at www.g20.org/Documents/g20_summit_declaration.pdf.

[194] A point made in recent literature on financial crises by Nuriel Rubini and Stephen Mihm, *Crisis Economics* (New York: Penguin, 2011); Carmen M. Reinhart and Kenneth Rogoff, *This Time Is Different: Eight Centuries of Financial Folly* (Princeton University Press, 2009).

default pushes the banking sector into default. Alternatively, the bail-
out of the distressed financial sector pushes the country into unsustainable levels of debt, as is currently the case in the US and the UK, or into
default as is the case in Ireland.

6.3.1   Financial instability hypothesis

Arguably, the best account of financial markets' propensity to generate crises has been given by a leading post-Keynesian, the late Professor Hyman
Minsky, whose views were in stark contrast to Chicago School ideas of
efficient markets. Building on earlier work by Fischer and Keynes,[195]
Minsky postulated that economies do not grow or contract independently
of the behaviour of the financial system. On the contrary, the key mechanism that pushes the economy towards contraction is accumulation of
unsustainable debt. He argued that from time to time capitalist economies exhibit a cycle of credit expansion and contraction, which, in the
absence of government controls, such as regulation, central bank supply
of liquidity and monetary policies, may become widespread and impossible to be contained, creating self-perpetuating reactions and amplifying
the effect of debt inflation or deflation in economic activity. The centrepiece of Minsky's theory is the so-called 'financial instability hypothesis',
which is in Minsky's words:[196]

> [A] theory of the impact of debt on system behaviour ... In contrast to the
> orthodox Quantity Theory of money, the financial instability hypothesis
> takes banking seriously as a profit-seeking activity.[197]

[195] Irving Fisher, 'The Debt Deflation Theory of Great Depressions' (1933) 1 *Econometrica* 337–
57 ; John Maynard Keynes, *The General Theory of Employment, Interest, and Money* (New
York: Harcourt Brace, 1936), especially. Chapter 17; John Maynard Keynes, 'The General
Theory of Employment' (1937) 51 *Quarterly Journal of Economics* 209–23; John Maynard
Keynes, 'The Theory of the Rate of Interest', in A. D. Gayer (ed.), *The Lessons of Monetary
Experience: Essays in Honor of Irving Fisher* (New York: Farrar & Rinehart, 1937).

[196] For a restatement and a summary of the 'financial instability hypothesis', see Hyman P.
Minsky, 'The Financial Instability Hypothesis', Jerome Levy Economics Institute of Bard
College, Working Paper 74, May 1992, available at www.levyinstitute.org/pubs/wp74.
pdf. The original conception is described in Hyman P. Minsky, 'Financial Instability
Revisited: The Economics of Disaster', Report Prepared for the Steering Committee for
the Fundamental Reappraisal of the Discount Mechanism, appointed by the Board of
Governors of the Federal Reserve System (1970). See also Hyman Minsky, *Stabilizing
an Unstable Economy* (New Haven, CT: Yale University Press, 1986); Hyman P. Minsky,
'The Financial Instability Hypothesis: Capitalist Production and the Behavior of the
Economy', in C. Kindleberger and J.-P. Laffargue (eds.), *Financial Crises: Theory, History
and Policy* (New York: Cambridge University Press, 1982).

[197] Minsky, 'The Financial Instability Hypothesis', Working Paper, p. 6. The financial
instability hypothesis is a model of a capitalist economy which does not rely upon

According to Minsky's hypothesis, banks seek profits through provision of new loans and try to innovate the ways credit is provided, since 'like all entrepreneurs in a capitalist economy, bankers are aware that innovation assures profits'. Banks and other financial institutions act as 'merchants of debt', who constantly 'strive to innovate' with respect to the assets they acquire and the liabilities they market. Yet, 'changes in [the] supply [of money] have a linear proportional relation to well defined price levels'.[198] Minsky identifies three distinct income–debt relationships for economic actors/units, which he defined as hedge, speculative and Ponzi finance stages. Market actors/units using hedge finance are those 'which can fulfil all of their contractual payment obligations by their cash flows'.[199] It follows that the greater the proportion of equity financing in the liability structure of the economy, the greater the likelihood that the unit is a hedge financing unit. Speculative finance units, on the other hand, are economic units that can meet their payment commitments with respect to their liabilities, even though they would not be able to repay the principal out of income cash flows. Such units have to 'roll over' their liabilities and normally are doing so by issuing new debt to meet commitments on maturing debt. Economic actors/units relying on hedge and speculative finance differ sharply from Ponzi units. In the last case, the cash flows from operations are not sufficient to fulfil either the repayment of principal or the interest due on outstanding debts by their cash flows from operations. In particular, over a protracted period of good times, capitalist economies tend to move from a financial structure dominated by hedge finance units to a structure in which there is large weight to units engaged in speculative and Ponzi finance. Classic examples of such units are over-indebted states with the recent examples of Argentina and Greece standing out.

Ponzi finance units can sell assets or borrow new money. Naturally, borrowing money to pay interest on older loans or selling assets for the same purpose (or in order to pay dividend) creates a debt trap which is tightened through asset sales and pushes asset values downwards. The unit lowers its equity while at the same time it increases liabilities and the

exogenous shocks to generate business cycles of varying severity. On the contrary, business cycles of history are caused by:(1) the internal dynamics of capitalist economies; and (2) the system of interventions and regulations that are designed to keep the economy operating within reasonable bounds, *ibid*. See also contributions by Lawrence H. Summers, Hyman P. Minsky, Paul A. Samuelson, William Poole, and Paul A. Volcker on 'Macroeconomic Consequences of Financial Crises', in Martin Feldstein (ed.), *The Risk of Economic Crisis* (University of Chicago Press, 1991), pp. 135–82.
[198] *Ibid.*   [199] *Ibid.*

prior commitment of future income. Thus, a Ponzi finance unit gradually becomes highly leveraged. Moreover, 'the greater the weight of speculative and Ponzi finance, the greater the likelihood that the economy is a deviation amplifying system'.[200] Therefore, as Minsky notes:[201]

> The first theorem of the financial instability hypothesis is that the economy has financing regimes under which it is stable, and financing regimes in which it is unstable. The second theorem ... is that over periods of prolonged prosperity, the economy transits from financial relations that make for a stable system to financial relations that make for an unstable system.

Accordingly, periods of protracted speculative euphoria (bubbles) lead to accumulation of debts that exceed what borrowers can repay from their income leading to a financial crisis. As lenders reduce the flows of credit to cope with the aftermath of over-lending, they indiscriminately ration credit leading an economy into recession, a condition that in the last crisis was widely described as a 'credit crunch'. Namely, the movement of the financial system from stability to fragility is an integral determinant of business cycles. The gradual movement of the financial system from stability to crisis is commonly referred to as a 'Minsky moment'.

Economists like Paul McCulley have suggested that the sub-prime mortgage crisis was a manifestation of the financial instability hypothesis.[202] McCulley has argued that progression through Minsky's three stages of borrowing was evident as the credit and housing bubbles built through to July–August 2007. Excessive liquidity generated by the shadow banking system funded increased lending turning borrowers to speculative and Ponzi units, generating ever higher levels of leverage, which in turn fuelled the bubble in house prices. According to McCulley, the deleveraging that followed the burst of the bubble meant a return to more hedge finance. McCulley postulates that human behaviour is by nature procyclical, inducing periods of debt inflation and deflation similar to those described by Minsky, which could spin out of control, since individuals tend to be momentum investors rather than value investors, exacerbating the effects of debt and business cycles at the apex of the cycle or its nadir.

---

[200] Ibid.   [201] *Ibid.*

[202] Paul McCulley, 'Global Central Bank Focus, The Shadow Banking System and Hyman Minsky's Journey', *Pimco*, May 2009; George Cooper, *The Origin of Financial Crises: Central Banks, Credit Bubbles, and the Efficient Market Fallacy* (New York: Vintage Books, 2008).

Arguably, McCulley's findings are not dissimilar to behavioural analysis about the way economies and markets work and the creation of boom and bust cycles.[203] The psychological states of overconfidence and risk aversion discussed in Section 4.2 above may especially create periods of massive expansion leading to asset bubbles and periods of sharp contraction. In fact, heightened loss aversion triggered by a confidence crisis which led to excessive liquidity hoarding was evident in the early stages of GFC with deleterious effects for the financial system.[204] However, the notion that sub-prime mortgages were in fact Ponzi finance, as described by Minsky, is disputed, even by followers of Minsky's work.[205] It seems that financial innovation, shadow banking fuelled conditions of excessive liquidity and US housing policies (discussed in Chapter 3), and not only bankers' willingness to lend, were among the many important factors that led to a weakening in loan underwriting standards. In addition, even if the eruption of the sub-prime mortgage crisis was a 'Minsky moment', this would not explain why a US-focused lending crisis threatened the global financial system with extinction.

In general, financial crises seem to be a combination of a number of complicated processes of which debt accumulation is a major but not exclusive part. In addition, the reasons that lead to over-indebtedness might be much wider than merely bankers' willingness to lend and could, at least, in the case of sovereign borrowers, include corruption and crony capitalism, excessive trade imbalances and structural weaknesses. In addition, it is difficult to group together a generalized financial crisis such as that of 1929 or the GFC with several dispersed financial crises of lower severity and less than global reach.[206]

In this context, it is suggested here that the GFC was the combined outcome of a large number of factors and that several of the market conditions that led to the GFC were poorly understood or unpredictable. For instance, the new channels for cross-border transmission of systemic risk

---

[203] George A. Akerlof and Robert J. Shiller, *Animal Spirits: How Human Psychology Drives the Economy, and Why It Matters for Global Capitalism* (Princeton University Press, 2008) especially Chapters 1, 6, and 7.

[204] Emilios Avgouleas, 'The Global Financial Crisis, Behavioural Finance and Financial Regulation: In Search of a New Orthodoxy' (2009) 9 *Journal of Corporate Law* 121–57.

[205] See Paul Davidson, 'Is the Current Distress Caused by the Sub-Prime Mortgage Crisis a Minsky Moment? Or is it the Result of Attempting to Securitize Illiquid Non Commercial Mortgage Loans?' Mimeo, Schwartz Center for Economic Policy Analysis, New School, Mimeo, 2008, available at econ.bus.utk.edu/faculty/davidson/minksy7.pdf.

[206] See about the merits of making this distinction, Barry Eichengreen and Richard Portes, 'The Anatomy of Financial Crises', NBER Working Paper No. 2126, August 1989.

through opaque links of interconnectedness were created by innovative financial instruments, such as CDSs and CDOs, which were largely novel and thus poorly understood. Similarly, the interplay between financial liberalization, trade surpluses, financial innovation and accumulation of systemic risk was largely ignored. Finally, the materialization, at around the same period, of several small and large risks in a correlated manner triggering a generalized loss of confidence, could not possibly have been captured by risk models.

Many of the above conditions were the result of a knowledge revolution,[207] as financial innovation was, which was combined with three further developments to lead to unpredictable risk correlations:

(1) unfettered movement of capital globally, due to abolition of capital controls;
(2) technological breakthroughs that not only led to automated trading processes and rapid communications but also fostered financial innovation and heightened confidence in the robustness of risk models; and
(3) provision of excessive liquidity which was in turn the result of three factors: (a) trade imbalances, which were accumulated as a result of global trade liberalization, (b) Jackson Hole Consensus policies and (c) money market funds channelling savings to the shadow banking sector in search of higher returns.

6.3.2   A financial revolution

Charles P. Kindleberger, arguably the leading economic historian of the last century, argued, in two seminal studies of the causes of financial crises,[208] that exogenous developments such as a major financial or technical innovation precede most crises and play a more catalytic role than debt accumulation. A major innovation such as, for instance, the operation of railways, 'displaces' the expectations of investors, who are unfamiliar with and thus unable to value investments in the new industry, leading first to

---

[207] Borrowing Mankiw's classic definition, the term 'knowledge' is understood to mean the sum total of technological and scientific discoveries, which is transformed into human capital, i.e., 'the stock of knowledge that has been transmitted from those sources into human brains via studying'. Gregory N. Mankiw, 'The Growth of Nations' (1995) *Brookings Papers on Economic Activity*, 275–326.

[208] Charles Kindleberger, *The World in Depression, 1929–1939* (Berkeley, CA: University of California Press, 1973); Kindleberger and Aliber, *Manias, Panics, and Crashes*, pp. 26, 54–8. An exogenous shock eventually turns irrational exuberance into a exit stampede and the bubble is succeeded by panic sales. See for a re-formulation of Kindleberger's argument, Summers et al., 'Macroeconomic Consequences of Financial Crises', pp. 139–146.

overpayment and then to a crash in prices. This is exactly what happened with the overseas trading and exploration industries that were underscoring the wild profit promises attached to the South Sea and Mississippi company shares, both a good example of financial engineering.[209] As Kindleberger suggested, the Crash of 1929 itself followed the introduction of new electrical and transportation technologies.[210] Arguably, the dotcom bubble[211] has been the best illustration of Kindleberger's argument. Kindleberger's view also accords well with behavioural economists arguments about the role of bounded rationality[212] and overconfidence in investor behaviour. Herding behaviour, whether or not induced by irrational exuberance, further fuels asset bubbles exacerbating the displacement effects subsequently caused by the deflation of the bubble.

In this mode, I argue in this book that the best way to understand the GFC is to see it as predominantly the result of unco-ordinated risks which came together[213] because of an economic and knowledge revolution that was badly mismanaged[214] due to ignorance, complexity and opacity, excessive rent-seeking by insiders and an inability to predict the risk correlations that new global trading channels, opened by the financial revolution, would bring about under conditions of widespread panic. Arguably, certain aspects of financial innovation presented a serious breakthrough in knowledge, especially as regards the distribution/diversification of quantifiable credit and project (finance) risk[215] and the revolutionization of the channels available to access finance. The welfare gains of financial

---

[209] See E. Chancellor, *Devil Take the Hindmost, A History of Financial Speculation* (New York: Penguin, 1999), Chapters 1–3. See also, Avgouleas, *The Mechanics and Regulation of Market Abuse*, Chapter 2.

[210] Kindleberger and Aliber, *Manias, Panics, and Crashes*, pp. 26, 160–2.

[211] See Matthew Richardson and Eli Ofek, 'DotCom Mania: The Rise and Fall of Internet Stock Prices' (2003) 58 *Journal of Finance* 1113–38. Cf Dilip Abreu and Markus Brunnermeier, 'Bubbles and Crashes' (2003) 71 *Econometrica* 173–204.

[212] Bounded rationality essentially means that individuals have limited ability to process information because of their limited computational ability and flawed memory. It was introduced as a potential determining factor in the making of economic decisions by Herbert Simon. See Herbert Simon, 'A Behavioral Model of Rational Choice' (1955) 69 *Quarterly Journal of Economics* 99–118; Herbert Simon, 'Rationality as Process and Product of Thought' (1978) 68 *American Economic Review: Papers and Proceedings* 1–16.

[213] See, indicatively, N. Gennaioli, A. Shleifer and R. Vishny, 'Neglected Risks, Financial Innovation, and Financial Stability'NBER Working Paper No. 16068, June 2010.

[214] See indicatively, J. Lerner and P. Tufano, 'The Consequences of Financial Innovation: A Counterfactual Research Agenda', NBER Working Paper No. 16780, February 2011.

[215] See F. Allen and D. Gale, *Financial Innovation and Risk Sharing* (Cambirdge, MA: MIT Press, 1994).

innovation mostly depend on the ends the new 'technology' is used to pursue,[216] quite similarly with all other technological/knowledge revolutions throughout history. For example, if steam had not been used to power factories, there would have been no Industrial Revolution, in spite of the fact that the steam-powered engine amounted to a technological revolution of cardinal importance. The decision to use steam to power factories was made by rational actors who saw the potential for reaping supra-competitive rents by producing goods to a scale unimaginable in the preceding era of windpower, horsepower or even manpower. Similarly, their decision to use the same technology to transport (trains, steamships) cut sharply the time required to transport goods and people around the world. But, unlike the engineers of the financial revolution, they were risking/investing their own money or the money of their financial backers. They were not arbitraging the government guarantees like modern day bankers.

Of course, the same regulators who turned a technological revolution into an economic revolution had no qualms about seeking supra-competitive rents. They did so not only through the use of the new technology but also through absence of (fiercely opposed) public controls regarding worker's salaries or restraints on the pollution generated by their coal burning factories. Since such behaviour was seen as a clear case of market failure, mandatory collective bargaining rules, legislation to protect employees from unfair dismissal and environmental protection laws followed. There was no reason why the financial revolution could not, by analogy, have followed the same path as previous knowledge revolutions, if it had been properly managed.

Arguably, use of structured finance techniques could lead to considerable welfare gains in the field of: (1) poverty eradication, where financial innovation may help transform low-rated micro-finance (or micro-development) credits to higher rated ones increasing their popularity and the quantity of money available from the markets;[217] and (2) financing climate change projects, where the return from the project will be over a considerable period of time and thus investment may not be

---

[216] E.g., it seems that the Industrial Revolution required a financial revolution so that large commitments of capital could be made for long periods, V. R. Bencivenga, B. D. Smith, and R. M. Starr, 'Transactions Costs, Technological Choice, and Endogenous Growth' (1995) 67 *Journal of Economic Theory* 1 53–77.

[217] See, for an example of such a scheme, Emilios Avgouleas, 'International Financial Regulation, Access to Finance, Systemic Stability, and Development' (2008) *LAWASIA Journal* 62–76; Steven Schwarcz, 'Disintermediating Avarice: A Legal Framework for Commercially Sustainable Microfinance' (2011) *University of Illinois Law Review* 1165–201.

forthcoming without a re-engineering/structuring of payments/benefits from, for instance, lower energy bills. And while these are only a few examples of how the financial revolution can facilitate the achievement of global welfare objectives, they are not the only ones.

The massive funding challenges that most Western and some Asian social security systems are bound to face in the next thirty years require innovative solutions, especially in the field of pensions funding. The financial revolution could be fruitfully employed in that field as well, potentially changing the saving and consumption habits of individuals and nations. In this respect, it could prove no different than any other knowledge[218] revolution whether it fits the standard neoclassical growth model or not.[219] In fact, a number of economists have argued that it is innovation rather than accumulation of capital that drives growth and leads to economic revolutions. This is an observation that has especially been made with reference to the impact of the Industrial Revolution on economic growth.[220]

The role of technical change in economic growth is poorly defined in a variety of contexts,[221] and discounting the impact of new knowledge/technological breakthroughs in economics is nothing unusual.[222] Thus, it

[218]   Again as defined by Mankiw. See note 207 above.

[219]   The standard model incorporates Solow, who in his 1956 QJE paper, proposed a model in which outputs are produced by capital K and labour L, but the change in output (i.e., economic growth) is determined by an unexplained residual condition: technical change, i.e., technological innovation. Like all neo-classical economists Solow assumed: constant returns to scale, perfect competition, complete information and no externalities. Solow's theory/model would today be regarded as inadmissible because it gave the consumer no utility function and budget constraints, but it was a significant advancement at its time and provided a very useful analysis of the relative contribution of capital and technological progress to economic growth. See Robert M. Solow, 'A Contribution to the Theory of Economic Growth' (1956) 70 *Quarterly Journal of Economics* 65–94. Solow has assumed technological change as an exogenous event, a view challenged by so-called Endogenous Growth Theory, which is also regarded today as controversial. See Robert E. Lucas, 'On the Mechanics of Economic Development' (1988) 22 *Journal of Monetary Economics* 3–42; Paul Romer, 'Increasing Returns and Long-Run Growth' (1986) 94 *Journal of Political Economy* 1002–37.

[220]   A good analysis is E. A. Wrigley, *Continuity, Chance and Change: The Character of the Industrial Revolution in England* (Cambridge University Press, 1988). See also Deepak Lal, *Unintended Consequences* (Cambridge, MA: MIT Press 1998), although this book focuses more on interaction of factor endowments, culture and politics.

[221]   See Yong J. Yoon, 'Science, Scientific Institutions, and Economic Progress', George Mason University Department of Economics Paper No. 10–36, available at ssrn.com/abstract=1702675.

[222]   Frank Stephen has attributed the domination of Anglo-American firms in the international market for legal services, over the less technology savvy and more traditional German and other big continental European law firms, to the willingness of the former to adapt to and exploit the opportunities created by the new ways to organize and deliver legal services created by the ITC revolution. See F. Stephen, 'The European Single

is not surprising that most economists did not measure the central part of the financial revolution, financial engineering, for what it was but rather focused on its workings in specific high-return areas, ignoring the wider picture. It is also not a novelty at all that an advancement in human knowledge and skills, as in most probability financial engineering is, brings about large-scale economic change and even serious dislocation.

7.   Summary of findings

This chapter has analytically examined the role of financial markets in the modern world and the causes of financial crises. Thus, it first discussed the distributive role of financial markets, especially their role in economic development and poverty eradication. It explained why global finance and its proper governance and regulation merit so much attention. The chapter provided an analytical overview of the most complex segments of modern financial markets, namely, the global derivatives markets and the shadow banking sector, and discussed extensively contemporary forms of financial innovation, which were heavily implicated in building up the risks that led to the GFC and in spreading its catastrophic consequences.

This was followed by analysis of the insights on market behaviour and price formation of the modern finance theory and behavioural finance. It suggested that adaptive theories that see the markets in an evolutionary framework might provide more accurate explanation of market phenomena such as bubbles and herding. Furthermore, the chapter evaluated the neo-liberal consensus policies that facilitated the gigantic expansion of financial markets in the past two decades and stimulated unfettered innovation. It highlighted the distortions these policies brought about in terms of creating oversized global financial institutions, which are inherently 'too-big-to-fail', and interconnectedness.

Finally, the chapter offered an evaluation of the factors that lead to market instability and financial crises. It discussed extensively Minksy's financial instability hypothesis. It postulated that the GFC was rather the product of a poorly understood technological/knowledge revolution, which in combination with liberalization policies led to a financial revolution that was badly mismanaged. It is argued in Chapter 8 that financial innovation may be properly managed and its excesses, inextricably linked to rent-seeking, curbed through, *inter alia*, clever and adaptable global governance structures.

Market and the Regulation of the Legal Profession: An Economic Analysis' (2002) 23 *Managerial and Decision Economics* 115–25.

3

The causes of the Global Financial Crisis

1. Introduction

An examination of the causes of the Global Financial Crisis (GFC) is an inextricable part of any study of global financial governance. Explanations of the GFC have been offered in a fragmented or unified way in a number of works. What this chapter adds is a new look at the connection between financial innovation, deregulation and free capital flows. For such reconceptualization to be possible, first the most widely discussed causes of the GFC must be considered.

Arguably, 'conventional' causes may be divided into two categories. First, causes relating to more general policies and the wider characteristics of the financial system in the past decade, which influenced financial institutions' behaviour, regardless of whether they were developed by the institutions themselves (macro-causes). Second, those that originated from within financial institutions and credit rating agencies, due to misaligned incentives (micro-causes). Particular emphasis will be given to five macro-causes that overlap to some extent:

(1) relaxed monetary policies and trade imbalances which helped to build the conditions that led to the global financial meltdown by fuelling massive asset bubbles and reinforcing irrational exuberance;

(2) well meaning government policies with disastrous end results which either promoted universal housing, as happened in the US,[1] or pursued mono-dimensional approaches to development by placing excessive reliance on one or two industries, as happened in Ireland with real estate developers and the growth of the banking sector and in Spain with the construction industry;

---

[1] Gary Gorton, 'The Panic of 2007', Paper prepared for the Federal Reserve Bank of Kansas City, Jackson Hole Conference, August 2008. See also Peter J. Wallison, 'Dissent from the Majority Report of the Financial Crisis Inquiry Commission', American Enterprise Institute for Public Policy Research, 14 January 2011, available at www.aei.org/docLib/Wallisondissent.pdf.

(3) economic doctrine and regulatory failure, including the absence of institutional capacity to deal with cross-border financial crises, which is discussed extensively in Chapter 5;

(4) flawed use of financial innovation; and

(5) the possible behavioural causes of the crisis.

I will also highlight three micro-causes of the crisis which focus on the problem of the perverse incentives:

(1) traders' and bank executives' compensation structures;

(2) the impact of the originate-to-distribute model on bank credit controls and loan underwriting standards; and

(3) the shortcomings of credit ratings.

Following this analysis, I shall argue that the common theme that bound together most of the above factors to bring about the GFC was the financial revolution. The term financial revolution is used here to describe three phenomena:

(1) *financial innovation*, which was the result of two developments: (a) imaginative uses of finance in the past thirty years, starting with Michael Milken's junk bonds and ending with the production of highly complex financial instruments and techniques, and (b) advancements in mathematical finance (regardless of the accuracy of the models it developed), which were partly made possible by breakthroughs in computing capacity brought about by technology improvements;

(2) *technological breakthroughs*, which created the ability to shift around the globe massive amounts of money within seconds due to the ITC progress from the late 1980s onwards; and

(3) *liberalization*, which led to *free cross-border capital flows* due to the nearly universal abolition of national capital account restrictions in the 1990s and *deregulation* which allowed free access to foreign financial markets and banking systems for the first time since the first globalization period.[2]

The interplay between innovative finance, technology and open markets led to the linking of previously disparate and independent parts of the global financial markets into a homogeneous, interconnected and interdependent system. Moreover, it exacerbated old problems like the

---

[2] Gary Gorton, 'Slapped in the Face by the Invisible Hand: Banking and the Panic of 2007', Federal Reserve Bank of Atlanta, Financial Markets Conference, 11–13 May 2009.

'too-big-to-fail' problem, which became one of the fundamental causes of the GFC,[3] since Large Complex Financial Institutions (LCFIs) took excessive leverage to manufacture a series of systemically important tail risks in an undercapitalized financial system.[4]

There are many explanations dealing with the failure of the market and of policy-makers to manage and regulate the financial revolution properly. The most prevalent are: (1) capture; (2) politicians' and regulators' over-reliance on 'the markets know best' doctrine; and (3) the existence of perverse incentives. Although accurate, these are incomplete explanations. Another powerful explanation of the market and regulatory failures discussed below is that the pre-existing limited understanding of the nature and transmission channels of systemic risk was compounded by nearly total ignorance of the mechanics of the financial revolution. Essentially the financial revolution was in many respects a knowledge revolution

---

[3] According to (the majority of the members of) the Financial Crisis Inquiry Commission of the US Congress, the crisis was man-made and avoidable if warnings had been heeded. The causes of the crisis according to the Commission were: 'Widespread failures in financial regulation, including the Federal Reserve's failure to stem the tide of toxic mortgages; Dramatic breakdowns in corporate governance including too many financial firms acting recklessly and taking on too much risk; An explosive mix of excessive borrowing and risk by households and Wall Street that put the financial system on a collision course with crisis; Key policy makers ill prepared for the crisis, lacking a full understanding of the financial system they oversaw; And systemic breaches in accountability and ethics at all levels'. See Financial Crisis Inquiry Commission, 'The Final Report of the National Commission on the Causes of the Financial and Economic Crisis in the United States', 17 January 2011, Conclusions, p. xv, available at www.fcic.gov/report/conclusions. Wood and Lastra hold that the causes of the financial crisis can be divided in ten groups: '(a) macro-economic imbalances; (b) lax monetary policy; (c) regulatory and supervisory failures; (d) too-big-to-fail (TBTF) doctrine and distorted incentives; (e) excesses of securitization; (f) unregulated firms, lightly regulated firms, and the shadow banking system; (g) corporate governance failures; (h) risk-management failures, excessive leverage, and excessive complexity; (i) the usual suspects: greed, euphoria, and others; and (j) faulty economic theories. The first four groups of explanations put the blame mainly on the authorities (governments, regulators, central bankers). Groups (e)–(i) blame mainly the markets (financial products, managers, risk, greed, poor lending, leverage). The last group (faulty theories) blames economists.' Rosa M. Lastra and Geoffrey Wood, 'The Crisis of 2007–09: Nature, Causes and Reactions' (2010) 13 *Journal of International Economic Law* 531–50.

[4] Viral V. Acharya, Thomas F. Cooley, Matthew P. Richardson and Ingo Walter 'Manufacturing Tail Risk: A Perspective on the Financial Crisis of 2007–09' (2010) 4 *Foundations and Trends in Finance* 247–325. A definition of fat-tail risk in financial markets would define it as the risk of extreme change (swings) in the markets which is rather unusual, as it cannot be predicted solely based on the normal distribution of the return probability, as is the case with other risks which are closer to the mean (value) of the Bell curve. Taleb calls these risks 'black swans'. See Nassim Nicholas Taleb, *The Black Swan: The Impact of the Highly Improbable* (New York: Random House, 2007).

that stretched the cognitive capacity of regulators and policy-makers as well as that of many market actors. As such it revolutionized the way the financial services industry did business, especially when it came to distribution of risk and access to finance. It also opened up new (and largely concealed) transmission channels for systemic risk, whereby the different elements of the financial revolution – financial innovation, advanced (but flawed) risk modelling, rapid communications and news dissemination, and open global markets – could combine and exacerbate the problem by creating invisible institutional interconnectedness and feedback loops.

The remainder of this chapter is divided in six sections. Section 2 discusses the 'macro-causes' of the GFC in accordance with the 'conventional' explanations that have already been offered by academics and policy-makers. It provides an extensive analysis of the neo-liberal consensus policies and public housing policies that seem to have contributed to the build up of the GFC. Section 3 examines the 'micro-causes' and sheds light on the issue of misaligned incentives. Section 4 provides an overview of flawed regulations that contributed to the GFC. Section 5 provides a novel look at both the development of global financial markets and the recent crisis. It offers a critical account of the application of complexity theory on the development of global markets and their regulation. It also advances one of the main arguments of this book, namely, that the GFC was above all the result of a little understood financial revolution that was badly mis-managed due to insider rent-seeking and widespread moral hazard. Section 6 provides the conclusions.

2.   Macro-causes

2.1   Global trade imbalances and lax monetary policies

International trade liberalization and a bubble in global oil and commodity prices led to the accumulation of gigantic trade surpluses in developing countries which could not be invested in underdeveloped domestic financial systems.[5] According to other sources the cause of the surpluses was high savings rates in countries like China.[6] Surplus countries sought

---

[5] Maurice Obstfeld and Kenneth S. Rogoff, 'Global Imbalances and the Financial Crisis: Products of Common Causes', Federal Reserve Bank of San Francisco Asia Economic Policy Conference, 18–20 October 2009.

[6] Ben S. Bernanke, 'The Global Saving Glut and the US Current Account Deficit', Sandridge Lecture, Virginia Association of Economics, Richmond, Virginia, 10 March 2005. However, the UN Commission of Experts notes that one of the reasons for the building

higher yields abroad accumulating assets in foreign economies. The preferred destination of those funds was the US, arguably, because of its more developed financial system which transformed all kinds of claims into financial assets.[7] Although most of those funds were invested in US Treasury bonds and financed the US trade deficit, a substantial part ended up through a number of channels in the shadow banking sector through purchases of ABCP and other related securities. Arguably, the same conditions of loose liquidity combined with low interest rate policies fuelled the appetite of Club Med countries and of their private sectors for overborrowing, which more or less led to the ongoing sovereign debt crisis.

What made this situation (too much money chasing higher returns in the same markets) worse was a truly loose monetary policy, namely a policy, which, through low interest rates and lack of any other controls increased the availability of credit. As explained in the preceding chapter, where the Jackson Hole Consensus was analytically discussed, most of the last decade was marked by a widespread belief that price stability was necessary and (nearly) sufficient for economic growth and financial stability.[8] However, success in stabilizing the price of goods during this period (the so-called era of 'Great Moderation') was often accompanied by inflation in asset prices, leading to unsustainable speculation.[9] This created a policy dilemma to which there was no clear answer. Therefore, most major central banks (e.g., the US Federal Reserve, the European

---

up by developing and especially Asian countries of colossal trade surpluses and foreign currency reserves was to use them as defence against the volatility of financial flows, which made them during the Asian Crisis highly susceptible to external financial shocks and plunged their domestic economies to crises that were partly foreign made. United Nations, 'Report of the Commission of Experts of the President of the United Nations General Assembly on Reforms of the International Monetary and Financial System', New York, 21 September 2009, pp. 24–31, 27, 'Hereinafter the UN Experts' Report'.

[7] Chiefly, Ricardo J. Caballero and Arvind Krishnamurthy, 'Bubbles and Capital Flow Volatility: Causes and Risk Management' (2006) 53 *Journal of Monetary Economics* 35–53. Also, Ricardo J. Caballero, Emmanuel Farhi and Pierre-Olivier Gourinchas, 'An Equilibrium Model of Global Imbalances and Low Interest Rates' (2008) 98 *American Economic Review* 358–93.

[8] See Charles Bean, Matthias Paustian, Adrian Penalver and Tim Taylor, 'Monetary Policy after the Fall', Paper given in the Federal Reserve Bank of Kansas City Annual Conference, Jackson Hole, Wyoming 28 August 2010, available at www.kansascityfed.org/publicat/sympos/2010/2010-08-23-bean.pdf.

[9] For a critical view of the Jackson Hole Consensus, see Paul McCulley and Richard Clarida, 'What Has – and Has Not – Been Learned About Monetary Policy in a Low Inflation Environment? A Review of the 2000s' PIMCO Global Central Bank Focus, October 2010, available at australia.pimco.com/LeftNav/Featured+Market+Commentary/FF/2010/GCB+Focus+October2010+Monetary+Policy+in+a+Low+Inflation+Environment.htm.

Central Bank (ECB), and the Bank of England) chose to focus on price stability and brushed aside the very real systemic threats arising from asset price bubbles, failing to incorporate into their interest rate-setting decisions the asset price growth observed in their economies.

Bringing about price stability was a considerable achievement in itself[10] and it is not unreasonable that central bankers were in a self-congratulatory mood. Moreover, it was Alan Greenspan who first talked about the possibility of 'irrational exuberance' taking a grip on stock markets as far back as 1996. However, in the end central banks choose to adhere to the Jackson Hole Consensus. As a result, many countries were unable to prevent asset bubbles from forming, especially the housing bubble, which kept being fed by the excessive availability of cheap credit.[11] Furthermore, decisions to focus on price behaviour in the real economy led central banks to ignore the broader impact of financial innovations on risk and liquidity and vice versa. For instance, it is plausibly argued that loose monetary policy also led to an explosion in the issuance of CDOs.[12]

The Jackson Hole Consensus had been criticized even before the onslaught of the GFC. But that criticism went unheeded.[13] One argument against the Consensus is that it places excessive reliance on a particular set of models, making unrealistic assumptions concerning market actors' rational behaviour.[14] It also tends to ignore key aspects of the economy,

[10] I have substantially rebalanced my views on this point following stimulating discussions on the monetary policy conundrum with Charles Goodhart.

[11] The view that the US Federal Reserve's very low interest rates fed the housing bubble has also been supported by research offered by one of the world's foremost monetary economists, John Taylor, widely known for the so-called Taylor Rule. See John B. Taylor, 'Housing and Monetary Policy' September (2009) *Housing, Housing Finance and Monetary Policy* 463–76. John B. Taylor, 'The Costs and Benefits of Deviating from the Systematic Component of Monetary Policy', Keynote Address at the Federal Reserve Bank of San Francisco Conference on Monetary Policy and Asset Markets, 22 February 2008.

[12] See Charles Calomiris, Presentation in Yale Law School Center for the Study of Corporate Law, Weil, Gotshal & Manges Roundtable on the Future of Financial Regulation, 13 February 2009. The proceedings of the roundtable were published as John D. Morley and Roberta Romano (eds.), 'The Future of Financial Regulation' John M. Olin Center for Studies in Law, Economics and Public Policy, Research Paper No. 386, 6–7, available at ssrn.com/abstract=1415144.

[13] A number of experts, foremost of whom was Benjamin Friedman had for some years before the crisis offered critiques of the inflation targeting consensus and, since the crisis, they have called for major changes in that consensus. See B. Friedman, 'Why the Federal Reserve Should Not Adopt Inflation Targeting' (2004) 7 *International Finance* 129–36.

[14] United Nations Conference on Trade and Development (UNCTAD), 'The Global Economic Crisis, Systemic Failures and Multilateral Remedies', New York and Geneva, March 2009, pp. 1–3, 'hereinafter UNCTAD Report'. Also UN Experts' Report, p. 35.

including the importance of information asymmetries, diversity of economic agents and the behaviour of banking institutions (endogenous risk).
There is an emerging consensus in economics that most financial crises are
preceded by debt-fuelled bubbles.[15] This one was no exception. While price
stability was achieved, central banks did not prevent, and may even have
contributed to, the GFC.[16] For instance, during the 2001–2 recession US
housing prices did not decrease due to the low levels of interest rates. This
gave rise to the false belief that housing markets were immune to the economic cycle and will continue rising regardless of GDP growth.[17] The risk
models the industry used did not capture long periods and thus the procyclical bias of risk models led to serious mispricing (discounting) of risk.

Eventually, it became impossible for central banks to ignore the impact
of asset inflation on goods inflation,[18] but the appropriate policy response
was not clear. The obvious remedy to prevent the formation of a bubble[19] –
monetary policy targeting asset price inflation, such as a rise in interest rates – would certainly have had an impact on GDP growth.[20] It is,
of course, highly unusual to find central bankers brave enough to raise
interest rates and thus possibly engineer a recession in a previously boom-
ing economy. Central bankers who would dare to take such a decision in
order to prevent or 'prick' asset bubbles should be prepared to withstand
a loud outcry from the markets, the public and politicians. The notable
exception here was a certain Paul Volcker, one of the true central banking
giants of the last century.

---

[15] Karmen M. Reinhart and Kenneth Rogoff, *This Time Is Different: Eight Centuries of
Financial Folly* (Princeton University Press, 2009); Markus Brunnermeier, Andrew
Crockett, Charles Goodhart, Avinash D. Persaud and Hyun Shin, 'The Fundamental
Principles of Financial Regulation', Geneva Reports on the World Economy, 11 January
2009, p. 30, (hereinafter, Geneva Report).

[16] For a good analysis of monetary policy flaws, see Howard Davies and David Green,
Banking on the Future – The Fall and Rise of Central Banking (Princeton University Press,
2010), Chapters 3 and 5.

[17] Emilios Avgouleas, 'The Global Financial Crisis, Behavioural Finance and Financial
Regulation: In Search of a New Orthodoxy' (2009) 9 *Journal of Corporate Law Studies*
121–57.

[18] UN Experts Report, p. 35.

[19] See Zeno Enders and Hendrik Hakenes, 'On the Existence and Prevention of Asset Price
Bubbles', Max Planck Institute for Research Collective Goods Preprint, No. 2010/44,
November 2010, available at papers.ssrn.com/sol3/papers.cfm?abstract_id=1705943.

[20] See on the issue Ben S. Bernanke, 'Monetary Policy and the Housing Bubble', Speech at
the Annual Meeting of the American Economic Association, Atlanta, Georgia, 3 January
2010, available at www.federalreserve.gov/newsevents/speech/bernanke20100103a.htm.
For a more activist view see Davies and Green, *Banking on the Future*, Chapter 12.

2.2   The flawed use of financial innovation

2.2.1.   General observations

As discussed in Chapter 2, the development of innovative financial techniques and instruments in the past twenty-five years (known as financial innovation or financial engineering) was part of a more complex phenomenon that revolutionized the way finance was accessed and intermediated (e.g., securitization, shadow banking, derivatives) and risk was hedged and traded. I have also suggested that financial innovation was, in principle, a neutral development from a social welfare point of view. However, the development of new risk management and investment strategy techniques since the mid 1980s came to be falsely viewed as the answer to most risk management and liquidity generation problems that twentieth-century markets and economies faced. This notion led to a disastrous misuse of financial innovation for five reasons.

First, risk diversification through the use of CDSs or securitization led to homogeneous rather than diverse and well-balanced (hedged) markets. Second, financial innovation led to a serious accumulation of credit risk with capital markets investors, who were the main purchasers of structured credit securities. Most capital market investors could not properly manage the risk of such investments, especially credit risk, because of lack of information and relative lack of quantitative skills. Those market actors lacked accurate information to price the risk wrapped in the structured credit securities. Arguably, mainstream capital market techniques of risk management, hedging the risk of the instrument or selling it, were of little use when the underlying risk was largely unquantifiable – most buyers did not conduct any due diligence regarding the quality of the underlying claims beyond the ratings these had attracted – and the instruments traded on illiquid markets where, eventually, they could not be sold at all or had to be sold at a huge loss. Third, financial innovation increased complexity and lack of transparency in financial markets. This was of crucial importance both in terms of market confidence and mechanisms for prevention of systemic failures. Namely, the length of the financial network and the connections between market participants (interconnectedness) increased exponentially and did so in an invisible manner. This made very difficult any attempt to gauge counterparty's exposures and riskiness. Fourth, the use of the 'originate-to-distribute' model in asset transformation discussed in Chapter 2 tied commission income for asset origination to volume and thus filled the system with perverse incentives. Fifth, highly leveraged derivatives trading, fed on greed and the availability of cheap credit, tended to exacerbate price trends in cash asset markets fuelling irrational exuberance, instead of acting as a counterweight and a hedging mechanism. As a result all markets tended to take one way bets.

The principal example is US sub-prime mortgages. As long as house prices were rising, sub-prime and other borrowers saw the value of their house rise and thus their home equity increase. All other asset markets were rising at the same time and the derivatives market was charging very low risk premia. However, when house prices began to fall and default rates soared, particularly on sub-prime mortgages with adjustable rates, all related markets for structured credit securities and derivatives were affected.[21] Sub-prime mortgages were part of complex structured credit products sold to capital market investors.[22] Thus, the losses associated with mortgage defaults spread throughout the financial system. This led to generalized deleveraging fuelling in the process a downwards price spiral due to forced sales. [23]

The losses from the decline of the US housing market and defaults in sub-prime mortgages also meant massive losses for hedge funds, banks and other capital markets investment vehicles that were buyers of RMBS and CDOs relating to US mortgages. This development necessitated funding calls on behalf of the banks which kept those securities as collateral for the loans they had granted to investment funds, especially to speculative hedge funds that enjoyed very high leveraging in their balance sheets. Banks and hedge funds had then to sell a bigger proportion of their credit

---

[21] President's Working Group on Financial Markets, 'Policy Statement on Financial Market Developments', March 2008, p. 8, (hereinafter PWGFM Policy Statement).

[22] Gorton has shown that between 2001 and 2006 the ratio of sub-prime mortgages securitized by lenders moved from 50.4 per cent to 80.5 per cent, which means that the main financing of such loans was eventually derived from capital market investors through shadow banking operators. Gorton, 'The Panic of 2007', p. 20.

[23] As Lord Turner showed, in the period preceding the GFC: (1) credit spreads on a wide range of securities and loans had fallen to clearly inadequate levels; (2) the price charged for the absorption of volatility risk had fallen because volatility seemed to have declined; (3) falling spreads and volatility prices had driven up the current value of a range of instruments, marked to market value on the books of banks, investment banks and hedge funds. This in turn produced higher apparent profits and higher bonuses, and as a result reinforced management and traders' certainty that they were pursuing sensible strategies. In mid 2007, however, these trends ceased and then went sharply into reverse. The origins of the reverse lay in the US housing market, with growing evidence that excessive credit extension and weak credit standards had resulted in rapidly rising credit losses, with implications for the price of many asset backed securities. FSA, 'The Turner Review, A Regulatory Response to the Global Banking Crisis', March 2009, p. 25, (hereinafter the Turner Review).

securities in a declining market fuelling further the downward price spiral in an illiquid market.[24]

2.2.2   Shadow banking and excessive maturity transformation

As explained in Chapter 2, the shadow banking sector provides credit to households and businesses in much the same fashion as traditional banks, although it is not depositors but money market funds who provide the funding, investing their investors' money, and clients tend to be bigger and more sophisticated. Even today shadow banking accounts for US $16,000 billion of transactions, which is a much bigger slice of transactions than those going through the traditional banking system, estimated to US $13,000 billion.[25]

Apart from a host of policy issues relating to transparency of financial transactions and the role of shadow bank liquidity provision in the creation of asset bubbles, another problem is that, since they lack any government guarantees and deposit insurance, shadow banks are very vulnerable to liquidity runs.[26] These do not differ from those caused by depositor runs.[27] It is plausibly suggested that the GFC started as a liquidity (wholesale) run on the shadow banking system[28] and the ensuing crisis

---

[24] Shleifer and Vishny define a fire sale as 'essentially a forced sale of an asset at a dislocated price. A sale is forced in the sense that the seller cannot wait to raise cash, usually because he owes that cash to someone else. The price is dislocated because the highest potential bidders are typically involved in a similar activity as the seller, and are therefore themselves in a similar financial position. Rather than bidding for the asset, they might be selling similar assets themselves'. Andrei Shleifer and Robert Vishny, 'Fire Sales in Finance and Macroeconomics' (2011) 25 *Journal of Economic Perspectives* 29–48, 30. For the impact of deleveraging on the GFC, see *ibid.* and Gary Gorton and Andrew Metrick, 'Securitized Banking and the Run on the Repo', National Bureau of Economic Research Working Paper No. w15223, August 2009, available at papers.ssrn.com/sol3/papers. cfm?abstract_id =1454939. Moreover, the IMF reported that from October 2007 to April 2008 the prices of Asset Backed Securities (ABS) 'declined between 20 and 40 percent across tranches rated AAA to BBB–, and as much as 50 percent on ABS collateralized debt obligations (ABS–CDOs) across all ratings categories', IMF, 'Financial Stress and Deleveraging, Macrofinancial Implications and Policy', October 2008, p. 11.
[25] Zoltan Pozsar, Tobias Adrian, Adam Ashcraft and Hayley Boesky, 'Shadow Banking', Federal Reserve Board of New York, Staff Reports, Staff Report No. 458, July 2010, p. 5.
[26] See Chapter 2, Section 3.5 and Andrew Metrick, 'Regulating the Shadow Banking System' 18 October 2010, available at ssrn.com/abstract=1676947.
[27] Douglas W. Diamond and Philip H. Dybvig, 'Bank Runs, Deposit Insurance and Liquidity' (1983) 91 *Journal of Political Economy* 401–19.
[28] Gorton and Metrick have argued that the panic of 2007–8 was triggered by a run on the repo market, which was one of the most important short-term lending markets and

of confidence eventually transformed it into a solvency crisis,[29] since bank asset quality started deteriorating and revealed the magnitude of capital shortages.

Financial innovation greatly facilitated the proliferation of shadow banking vehicles. One of the main functions of SIVs and conduits was 'large-scale maturity transformation between short-term promises to note-holders and much longer term instruments held on the asset side'.[30] The main reason was the desire for rapid asset expansion and increased profitability through the use of continuous transformation of long-term assets in banks' balance sheets with short-term claims. Regulatory and tax arbitrage also played a major role in asset transformation, for which credit derivatives were as important as the 'originate-to-distribute' model. Derivatives were designed to replicate the risk distribution effects of securitization (so-called synthetic securitizations) and were also excellent generators of commission income for financial institutions. Thus, the whole process of financial innovation became strewn with perverse incentives, which were reflected all the way down the chain up to executives' massive compensation packages that were based on what proved to be 'bogus' profit. Also, it led banks to believe in perennially liquid (wholesale credit) markets and their own invincibility and immunity to credit risk. Finally, it allowed a massive amount of potentially very risky assets to be essentially hidden away from the eyes of the market and from regulatory oversight.

In addition, as the market started growing, the 'originate-to-distribute' model was replaced by originate-to-arbitrage strategies, where credit securitized and taken off one bank's balance sheet was not simply sold to end investors. Rather securitized debt was 'bought by the proprietary

---

provided financing for a large number of structured finance activities. Repo transactions are mostly collateralized with securitized bonds. They suggest that the juncture between repo financing and securitizations was the main trigger, since concerns about the liquidity of securitized bonds (used as collateral) led to deeper and deeper haircuts – increasing the amount of collateral required for any given transaction. Essentially, with declining asset values and increasing haircuts, the US banking system became insolvent. Gorton and Metrick, 'Securitized Banking and the Run on the Repo'. In fact, there was no chance for highly leveraged operators to find a liquidity respite in other wholesale markets, because the market for commercial paper also dried up, *ibid.*

[29] See, for the increasing importance of this new risk and the fragility of confidence in wholesale/institutional lending markets, Jean-Charles Rochet, 'Systemic Risk: Changing the Regulatory Perspective' (2010) 6 *International Journal of Central Banking* 259–76, 265–9.

[30] Turner Review, p. 21. An analytical discussion of the nature and composition of the shadow banking sector was offered in Chapter 2, Section 3.5.

trading desk of another bank; and /or sold by the first bank but with part of the risk retained via the use of credit derivatives; and/or 'resecuritised into increasingly complex and opaque instruments (e.g. CDOs and CDO squareds); and/or used as collateral to raise short-term liquidity'.[31] Thus, shadow banking activities were highly leveraged, piling up risk on the system and on financial institutions whose balance sheet expansion had come through extensive asset transformation and leverage.[32] Institutions which used asset transformation to manage their capital adequacy obligations also held much lower equity capital than would have been the case if those assets (loans) had been held on balance sheet.[33] Accordingly, banks which at first glance looked particularly sound were, in fact, severely undercapitalized.[34] This was the case because in times of crisis only the levels of equity capital matter.

Leveraged bank balance sheets meant excessive reliance on the continuous existence of short-term funding (liabilities) to finance long-term maturity assets, or the unhindered function of deep and liquid markets for the sale of assets in the event of any funding stresses. However, if there is any shortage of funds available for refinancing, individual institutions are in trouble because they need funds to repay their short-term debt. If they cannot find an alternative source of finance, they must conduct a fire sale of their long-term assets.[35] However, fire sales depress asset prices. The decline in asset prices puts pressure on all institutions that hold such assets to sell more. Under mark-to-market accounting, other institutions will be forced to recognize losses immediately.

Even if financial institutions do not recognize the losses immediately, it suffices that market participants know that these institutions hold such assets and begin to have doubts about them. Such doubts may induce

---

[31] Turner Review, p. 16.

[32] See BCBS The Joint Forum, 'Credit Risk Transfer: Developments from 2005 to 2007', July 2008, available at www.bis.org/publ/joint21.pdf.

[33] '[T]he way securitisation was achieved – especially from 2003 to the second quarter of 2007 – was more for arbitraging regulation than for sharing risks with markets.' Viral Acharya and Matthew Richardson, 'Repairing a Failed System', Vox 7 February 2009, available at www.voxeu.org/index.php?q=node/3015.

[34] A characteristic example is Northern Rock, which was returning capital to its shareholders, with the FSA's approval, just months before it went bust. See Emilios Avgouleas, 'Banking Supervision and the Special Resolution Regime of the Banking Act 2009: the Unfinished Reform' (2009) 4 *Capital Markets Law Journal* 201–35, 204–7 and The Run on the Rock, (House of Commons, Treasury Committee, Fifth Report of Session 2007–8, 24 January 2008).

[35] See note 24 above and Markus Brunnermeier and Lasse H. Pedersen, 'Market Liquidity and Funding Liquidity' (2009) 22 *Review of Financial Studies* 2201–38.

investors to withdraw their funds from these other institutions and there may well be a chain reaction that triggers a domino effect. Such a chain reaction can occur even if there is no doubt about the underlying long-term assets; any shock to the confidence of investors in the refinancing markets can trigger it.[36] And this is exactly what happened at the early stages of the GFC.

Many conduits and SIVs actually had fallback promises of liquidity assistance from the banks that had sponsored them. However, this liquidity assistance did not cover all refinancing needs so that some fire sales had to occur anyway. In view of the illiquid state of the markets for the assets held by conduits and SIVs and of the large amounts that were involved, the assistance that these institutions obtained from their bank sponsors raised doubts about the financial status of the sponsoring banks. Also, as there was saturation of new issues of asset backed securities in 2007, banks kept increasingly higher stakes in the relevant conduits and SIVs. Capital market investors' capacity to absorb the new issues of asset backed/structured credit securities had been exhausted. As a result, the new issues were self-financed and the banks if anything kept 'too much skin' in the game and not too little of it, as was of course their intention. These exposures were well hidden by regulators and possibly badly communicated to the banks' top management.

2.2.3   Risk diversification increases interconnectedness and systemic risk: the role of credit default swaps

The flawed use of financial innovation was nowhere better manifested than the field of risk diversification. Diversification of risk, especially credit risk, was thought to be the beneficial result of structured finance and of financial engineering, especially in the guise of securitizations and trading in credit derivatives. The use of the 'originate-to-distribute' model in securitizations meant the commoditization of risk, especially credit risk, which could then be 'structured', namely, 'sliced, diced, and re-bundled' in order to be readily sold to capital market investors[37] in the form of debt securities, or other instruments. But efficient transfer of risk requires that it is transferred in a diversified way and held in reasonable proportions within diversified portfolios and by institutions able to manage it and absorb losses. None of those principles were upheld in

---

[36] See BCBS, The Joint Forum, 'Credit Risk Transfer: Developments from 2005 to 2007'.
[37] Andrews G. Haldane, 'Rethinking the Financial Network', Speech, 2009, available at www.bankofengland.co.uk/publications/speeches/2009/speech386.pdf. p. 8.

this case. These instruments simply passed between market participants, lengthening the chain of financial transactions and the network of economic relationships to a very significant degree not only by multiplying interconnections but also by increasing the number of market actors that bore a serious amount of systemic risk in their portfolios. As explained above, by the very nature of their business, capital market investors did not have the information to price credit risk nor did they have the skills to manage it.

CDS trading brought together the different parts of the financial system in a very opaque way, strengthening interconnectedness and thus making the system more fragile. In principle, the function of CDS trading is to reduce risk. However, in practice there are important problems with CDS trading. One of the biggest consequences of the proliferation of credit derivatives trading in the 2000s was that they increased complexity while, at the same time, transfer of risk through OTC CDS trading made the markets very opaque, increasing uncertainty.[38] In addition, market participants used CDS trading, in the best of cases, for regulatory arbitrage purposes and, in the worst, as a means of taking speculative bets on asset (property) markets' continuous rise. This was especially the case with naked CDSs, where there was no underlying claim to 'insure' (hedge against).[39] However it should be noted that, while covered CDSs were a strong contributory factor to the intensity and unpredictability of

---

[38] According to the EU Commission: 'the characteristics of OTC derivative markets – the private nature of contracting with limited public information, the complex web of mutual dependence, the difficulties of understanding the nature and level of risks – increases uncertainty in times of market stress and accordingly poses risks to financial stability'. EU Commission Communication, 'Ensuring Efficient, Safe and Sound Derivatives Markets', COM(2009) 332, July 2009, p. 5.

[39] Normally the term 'naked' CDS is used to describe the trading practice 'where the CDS is used by the buyer not to hedge a risk but to take a position (take risk). The buyer of the CDS would gain if the risk materializes or if the price of the CDS subsequently increases due to a perception by the market of an increased risk of default of the issuer.' See EU Commission, Working Document, 'Public Consultation on Short Selling', 2010, p. 9, available at ec.europa.eu/internal_market/consultations/docs/2010/short_selling/consultation_paper_en.pdf. For a discussion of the consequences of prohibition of naked CDS trading see Emilios Avgouleas, 'A New Framework for the Global Regulation of Short Sales, Why Prohibition is Inefficient and Disclosure Insufficient' (2010) 15 *Stanford Journal of Law, Business and Finance* 376–425; Emilios Avgouleas, 'Short Sales Regulation in Seasoned Equity Offerings, What Are the Issues?', in Dan Prentice and Arad Reinsberg (eds.), *Corporate Law and Finance in the UK and EU* (Oxford University Press, 2011), pp. 117–38; Emilios Avgouleas, 'The Vexed Issue of Short Sales Regulation', in K. Alexander and N. Moloney (eds.), *Law Reform and Financial Markets* (London: Edward Elgar Publishing, 2011), Chapter 3.

the crisis, since they led to increased concentration of counterparty risk and interconnectedness. They also reflected the deteriorating quality of the underlying credits,[40] which had not been rated properly by the CRAs or the internal risk management departments when those CDSs were first written.

Three key channels through which the CDS market has contributed to the crisis have been identified:[41]

(a)   **Concentration of counterparty risk**   Some financial institutions such as Lehman Brothers or AIG were able to build up enormous risk positions, hidden from the eyes of regulators and their own shareholders, given also the volume of outstanding CDS, which at the end of 2007 had reached in notional value US$64 billion USD.[42] In addition, it is argued that counterparty risk may increase endogenously because, when liquidity disappears, in an environment of changed expectations, as is the case of a generalized deterioration of credit conditions, e.g., due to developments during the economic cycle, holders of CDSs will choose to hedge their risk by buying more CDSs rather than cancelling out their positions at a loss.[43]

(b)   **The CDS market increased the interconnectedness of global financial markets**   First, the development of an active market for CDS has led to a complicated chain of linked exposures, as an institution may hedge one counterparty risk with another CDS, reducing instead of increasing information about the quality of the underlying credit risk.[44] The resulting complexity made impossible the assessment of counterparty risk and identification of weak links in the financial chain and increased uncertainty.[45] The collapse of a major financial institution dealing in

[40] See on this important distinction Rene M. Stultz, 'Credit Default Swaps and the Credit Crisis' (2010) 24 *Journal of Economic Perspectives* 73–92.
[41] Hendrik Hakenes and Isabel Schnabel, 'The Regulation of Credit Derivatives Markets', in Mathias Dewatripont, Xavier Freixas and Richard Portes (eds.), *Macroeconomic Stability and Financial Regulation: Key Issues for the G20* (CEPR, 2009), pp. 113–27, available as an e-book at www.voxeu.org/reports/G20_ebook.pdf.
[42] Svetlan Boyarchenko and Sergei Levndorski, 'Snowball Effect of a CDS Market'; mimeo, 31 July 2009, available at papers.ssrn.com/sol3/papers.cfm?abstract_id=1440388.
[43] See, for the relevant model, *ibid.*, p. 3.
[44] The situation is different in the case of 'naked' CDS trading where there is no underlying risk to hedge and the motivation is pure speculation on the quality of the underlying credit.
[45] Haldane offers this example: '[C]onsider Bank A seeking insurance from Bank B against the failure of Entity C. Bank A faces counterparty risk on Bank B. If that were the end of

those markets could potentially lead to severe domino effects, and – in an extreme scenario – to a complete unwinding of the CDS market. For instance, Lehman Brothers had numerous CDS counterparty exposures relative to its balance sheet and hundreds of counterparties. AIG was in a similar position. As both institutions came under stress, the markets panicked, worrying less about direct counterparty risk and much more about indirect counterparty risks emanating from elsewhere in the network. However, lack of appropriate legal infrastructure intensified this problem, since, especially during the Lehman bankruptcy, profitable derivatives positions of dozens of billions of dollars were unwound in haste and at a loss, reinforcing phenomena of panic.

(c) **Uncertainty and asymmetric information** Uncertainty was exacerbated by the fact that since financial institutions are normally lenders and borrowers at the same time, they were reluctant to take off-setting action to limit exposure, 'because of concerns about counterparty credit risk'.[46] It is normally difficult to know the identity of all the counterparties of your counterparty and their creditworthiness. Naturally, in times of stress the 'behavioural response to fear of infection' is reflected in declining prices of financial instruments as uncertainty about true counterparty exposure becomes more widespread. Especially in the case of mega-banks, which are normally very complex financial conglomerates with opaque structures, the market's ability to price properly the risk of the bank may face insurmountable obstacles. In addition, the legal status of the netted positions in case of default of one of the counterparties is unclear.[47] The cumulative result of this uncertainty was the disruption in the inter-bank markets discussed above which led to the liquidity crunch

the story, network uncertainty would not much matter. Bank A could monitor Bank B's creditworthiness, if necessary directly, and price the insurance accordingly. But what if Bank B itself has *n* counterparties? And what if each of these *n* counterparties itself has *n* counterparties? Knowing your ultimate counterparty's risk then becomes like solving a high-dimension Sudoku puzzle. Links in the chain, like cells in the puzzle, are unknown – and determining your true risk position is thereby problematic. For Bank A, not knowing the links in the chain means that judging the default prospects of Bank B becomes a *lottery*. Indeed, in some ways *it is worse than a lottery*, whose odds are at least known. In this example, Bank A faces uncertainty in the Knightian sense, as distinct from risk, about the true network structure. Counterparty risk *is not just unknown; it is almost unknowable. And the higher the dimensionality of the network, the greater that uncertainty.*' Haldane, 'Rethinking the Financial Network' (emphasis added).

[46] Markus K. Brunnermeier, 'Deciphering the Liquidity and Credit Crunch 2007–08' (2009) 23 *Journal of Economic Perspectives* 77–100, 78.

[47] Hakenes and Schnabel, 'The Regulation of Credit Derivatives Markets', pp. 115–16.

and ultimately to the panic that necessitated the public bail-out of affected institutions.

Uncertainty greatly increased during the summer of 2007, because of market participants' realization that the prevailing valuation practices – based excessively on ratings – were no longer valid. With liquidity strains characterizing certain market segments, it became impossible for financial firms to value a range of financial assets and off-balance sheet exposures properly using the existing standards on valuation and accounting. As a result of widespread uncertainty about credit valuations, market participants found it difficult to model the expected occurrence of defaults, which led to a widening of credit spreads and a 'freezing' of wholesale credit markets.

2.2.4 Financial innovation and market destabilisation

Financial innovation opened up a new channel for a very old market 'disease' – herding – and intensified its destabilizing consequences. Markets steadily pursued one-way bets (the continuous rise of asset prices) regardless of where those bets were placed, i.e., the spot or the derivatives markets. As an UNCTAD Report has put it: '[there were] too many agents to squeeze double-digit returns out of an economic system that grows only in the lower single-digit range'. Of course, policy makers assumed that the markets would self-correct but this was the wrong assumption because 'financial markets are about the effective use of existing information margins concerning existing assets'.[48] The temporary monopoly over certain information or the ability to guess better an outcome in a market for a certain asset class allows the market actor concerned to gain a monopoly rent based on simple arbitrage. The more agents sense the arbitrage possibility and the quicker they are to react, the quicker the potential gain disappears.[49]

This finding can explain the observed massive scale herding in financial markets throughout the 2000s. Derivatives and spot markets fed each other's price spikes. Although the pattern of rising prices was first observed in the real economy (e.g., the real estate sector and commodities such as grain or oil) and driven by the needs of emerging economies (e.g., India's and China's need for primary commodities to feed their huge manufacturing sectors), derivatives markets jumped on the wagon in order to profit from so-called 'dynamic arbitrage', which in those cases, in simple terms, means taking bets on the continuous rise of prices in

---

[48] UNCTAD Report, p. 3.   [49] *Ibid.*

the relevant sectors. Susequently, derivatives markets were no longer predominantly used to hedge real economy risks but to feed further upward price trends, reinforcing asset bubbles. Gradually the two markets became tightly intertwined when the real economy prices, e.g., housing or commodities, went down because of reduced demand or just because the price momentum simply lost its force and nobody was willing to invest any longer to buy assets or commodities at those prices. This fall was preceded or followed by unwinding of highly leveraged derivatives positions leading to parallel falls in derivatives markets.[50] This meant that traders had to sell assets to cover margin calls on their position in a depreciating market, while at the same time over-leveraged producers and consumers also strove to cut leverage by selling the underlying assets creating a deflationary spiral, which is intensified by reduced borrowing.[51] As a result, financial innovation, an in principle welfare neutral technological breakthrough, became socially wasteful because it was so badly misused.

2.3   Failed government policies

A number of public policies premised on the neo-liberal consensus may be seen as key to developing the conditions that led to the crisis. These can be divided into two categories. First, there were policies motivated by a desire to foster growth in stagnant Western economies and create jobs through the expansion of the financial services industry. The obvious example of governments championing their financial services sector for this purpose are Iceland and Ireland (notwithstanding a certain degree of capture) and to a lesser extent the UK[52] and the US. Second, there were a number of government policies in the US, which fostered credit expansion and proved badly flawed. Rajan argues that in view of falling (real)

---

[50]   The UNCTAD Report describes this trend as follows: 'The bandwagon created by uniform, but wrong, expectations about price trends inevitably hit the wall of reality because funds have not been invested in the productive base of the real economy where they could have generated higher real income. Rather, it has only created the short-term illusion of continuously high returns and a "money-for-nothing mentality"', ibid., pp. 3–4.

[51]   Ibid., p. 4.

[52]   For the privileged position of the financial services industry in the UK, see Charles Moore, 'Mervyn King is Right. If the Banks Face no Risk, We shall all Go Down – They are the Trade Unions of the Modern Era, Sick Dinosaurs that Crush Ordinary Citizens', The Telegraph, 4 March 2011, available at www.telegraph.co.uk/comment/columnists/charlesmoore/8362464/Mervyn-King-is-right.-If-the-banks-face-no-risk-we-shall-all-go-down.html.

wages and stagnant incomes for middle class families in the US and rising inequality the government decided to resort to credit expansion (auto-loans, home-loans etc.) to stimulate the economy and job growth. Of course, the financial sector responded to calls for credit expansion with disastrous consequences.[53] Unrestrained credit expansion led to the formation of asset bubbles and household over-indebtedness.

Furthermore, the great expansion of sub-prime mortgages can be traced in the sound policy of facilitating access to finance for the poor to increase home ownership, which went badly wrong. This policy taken to its extreme caused distortions of the housing market and a relaxation of underwriting standards.[54] More specifically, in 1992, the US Congress enacted Title XIII of the Housing and Community Development Act of 1992 (the GSE Act).[55] This piece of legislation intended to give low- and moderate-income borrowers, who faced serious obstacles to obtaining housing finance, better access to finance through the utilization of the underwriting capacity of a Great Depression institution, the Federal National Mortgage Association (FNMA), so-called Fannie Mae, and of the Federal Home Loan Mortgage Corporation (FHLMC), so-called Freddie Mac,[56] now renamed, which were widely regarded as government sponsored enterprises (GSES), although they had become shareholder-owned companies which offered shares to the public. The GSE Act added a new objective for GSEs, which thus became responsible for the promotion of affordable housing. This new objective required Fannie and Freddie to

[53] Raghuram J. Rajan, *Fault Lines: How Hidden Fractures Still Threaten the World Economy* (Princeton University Press, 2010).
[54] Wallison, 'Dissent', pp. 12–16. Calomiris has also noted: 'numerous government policies specifically promoted subprime risk-taking by financial institutions. Those policies included (a) political pressures from Congress on the government-sponsored enterprises (GSEs), Fannie Mae and Freddie Mac to promote "affordable housing" by investing in high-risk subprime mortgages, (b) lending subsidies policies via the Federal Home Loan Bank System to its member institutions that promoted high mortgage leverage and risk, (c) FHA subsidization of high mortgage leverage and risk, (d) government and GSE mortgage foreclosure mitigation protocols that were developed in the late 1990s and early 2000s to reduce the costs to borrowers of failing to meet debt service requirements on mortgages, and – almost unbelievably – (e) 2006 legislation that encouraged ratings agencies to relax their standards for measuring risk in subprime securitizations. All of these government policies contributed to encouraging the underestimation of subprime risk ...' See Charles Calomiris, 'Financial Innovation, Regulation and Reform' (2009) 29 *Cato Journal* 65–91, 68–9.
[55] Public Law 102–550, 106 Stat. 3672, H.R. 5334, enacted 28 October 1992.
[56] Report of the Committee on Banking, Housing and Urban Affairs, United States Senate, to accompany S. 2733. Report 102–282, 15 May 1992, pp. 34–5.

reduce the mortgage underwriting standards they used when acquiring loans from commercial banks and other loan originators. According to Wallison (and others),[57] the GSE Act, and its subsequent enforcement by the US Department of Housing and Urban Development (HUD), 'set in motion a series of changes in the structure of the mortgage market in the United States and, more particularly, the gradual degrading of traditional mortgage underwriting standards'.[58]

In 1995, the regulations under the Community Reinvestment Act were tightened.[59] And for the first time insured banks and savings and loans institutions had to demonstrate that they were actually making loans in low-income communities and to low-income borrowers. This meant that the competition for the provision of sub-prime mortgages as a ratio of overall mortgage lending intensified and the number of sub-prime mortgages increased exponentially based on an attendant loosening of underwriting standards.[60]

Wallison's dissent from the Report of the FCIC has brought back to forefront of attention the claim that the crisis was primarily the result of US government pressure on the GSEs underwriting US mortgages to expand their asset base and thus house ownership in US by lowering their underwriting standards. According to Wallison, it was the GSEs that led the securitization of sub-prime mortgage markets and not the Wall Street banks.[61] However, this was a claim disputed by the majority of the FCIC which found that banks and not the GSEs were the dominant players in the market for securitized sub-prime mortgages and that bank loans had a much higher delinquency rate than those underwritten by the GSEs.[62] In addition, the Senate Report on Wall Street and the

---

[57] For advancement of arguments similar to those contained in Wallison's 'Dissent', see Giorgio Szegö, 'Can a Flap of a Wing of a Butterfly in Brazil Destroy the Coliseum in Rome ... after 30 Years?' mimeo, January 2011.

[58] Wallison, 'Dissent', pp. 11–14.

[59] Public Law 95–128, Title VIII of the Housing and Community Development Act of 1977, 91 Stat. 1147, 12 USC § 2901 *et seq.*

[60] Wallison, 'Dissent', pp. 13–15.

[61] 'Fannie and Freddie had already acquired at least $701 billion in NTMs [non-traditional mortgages] by 2001. Obviously, the GSEs did not have to follow anyone into NTM or subprime lending; they were already the dominant players in that market before 2002 ... in 2002, when the entire PMBS [private mortgage-backed securities] market was $134 billion, Fannie and Freddie acquired $206 billion in whole subprime mortgages and $368 billion in other NTMs, demonstrating again that the GSEs were no strangers to risky lending well before the PMBS market began to develop', Wallison, 'Dissent', at p. 22.

[62] 'The GSEs participated in the expansion of subprime and other risky mortgages, but they followed rather than led Wall Street and other lenders in the rush for fool's gold.

Financial Crisis has unearthed some very damning evidence about the lending practices followed by high street banks, such as Washington Mutual,[63] the biggest US commercial bank to have been seized by the FDIC and forced into receivership.

Whether the true reason that led the drive to lower underwriting standards for US sub-prime mortgages was unacceptable commercial practices or flawed housing policies and the distortion of the market by the operations of Freddie Mac and Fannie Mae (the strong data in Wallison's 'Dissent' requires further examination), these arguments are merely capable of explaining what triggered the crisis. They also constitute a good explanation of the relatively large number of foreclosures the US faced during this crisis compared with previous housing downturns. However, they can neither account for the global dimensions of the crisis nor for its magnitude.[64] The misuse of financial innovation, discussed below, meant that the right channels opened up for the investment of funds of US and non-US origin in the markets for US mortgage-backed securities regardless of whether the issuers were investment banks or the GSEs. As a result, US sub-prime loans' risk was distributed to and 'infected' a very large number of non-US financial institutions, which because of herding had

They purchased the highest rated non-GSE mortgage-backed securities and their participation in this market added helium to the housing balloon, but their purchases never represented a majority of the market ... They relaxed their underwriting standards to purchase or guarantee riskier loans and related securities in order to meet stock market analysts' and investors' expectations …and to ensure generous compensation for their executives and employees – justifying their activities on the broad and sustained public policy support for homeownership. The Commission also probed the performance of the loans purchased or guaranteed by Fannie and Freddie. While they generated substantial losses, delinquency rates for GSE loans were substantially lower than loans securitized by other financial firms', FCIC Report, pp. xxvi.

63 Report of the United States Senate, Permanent Subcommittee on Investigations Committee on Homeland Security and Governmental Affairs, 'Wall Street and the Financial Crisis – Anatomy of a Financial Collapse' 13 April 2011, pp. 2–5, 48–160 (Part III of the Report), available at hsgac.senate.gov/public/_files/Financial_Crisis/FinancialCrisisReport.pdf. There was no dissent regarding the findings of the Senate Report, which was endorsed by both parties in the US Senate. The Report characteristically states: 'Documents obtained by the Subcommittee reveal that WaMu launched its high risk lending strategy primarily because higher risk loans and mortgage backed securities could be sold for higher prices on Wall Street …. The Subcommittee investigation indicates that unacceptable lending and securitization practices were not restricted to Washington Mutual, but were present at a host of financial institutions that originated, sold, and securitized billions of dollars in high risk, poor quality home loans that inundated U.S. financial markets', ibid., p. 4.

64 Martin Hellwig, 'Capital Regulation after the Crisis: Business as Usual?' Max Planck Institute for Research on Collective Goods, Bonn 2010/31, July 2010, available at ssrn.com/abstract=1645224.

largely taken one-way bets on the continuous rise of the US housing market. The ensuing generalized loss of confidence due to interconnectedness, homogenization and excessive leverage and not the sub-prime mortgage crisis explains why the 2008 turmoil was a true Global Financial Crisis and not merely a serious shock to the US financial system.

2.4   Neo-liberal economic doctrine and deregulation

2.4.1   Regulatory failure

It is widely argued that governments' and regulators' excessive and unjustifiable reliance on the self-correcting mechanism of the markets[65] and on the rationality of market players, the two main ingredients of 'the markets know best' doctrine, were among the most important causes of the global financial meltdown.[66] This belief was influenced by mainstream economic theory of the past three decades, which 'suggested that efficient financial markets would smoothly and automatically solve the most complex and enduring economic problem, namely the transformation of today's savings into tomorrow's investment',[67] thus any public intervention was unnecessary. Of course this view totally ignored three characteristics of financial markets: (1) their inherent susceptibility to frequent crises and dislocation, no less due to widespread information asymmetries; (2) the fact that the markets do not exclusively consist of rational agents; and (3) the fact that the impact of financial innovation on systemic risk was largely unknown.

Yet regulators decided to rely excessively on 'the market knows best' doctrine, which, at the same period, was the main influence behind macroeconomic policies. Not surprisingly, regulatory policy became steeped in the belief that governments 'are inherently less informed and less motivated by sound economic principles' than the market. And, as this argument went, government intervention was likely to distort allocative efficiency, which is normally better achieved by market forces because 'markets are efficient and stable, with a strong ability to absorb shocks'.[68] With respect to financial markets what made matters worse was a quasi-religious belief in the strongly contestable ideas of the Efficient Market

---

[65] See UN Experts Report, p. 17; Richard A. Posner, *A Failure of Capitalism: The Crisis of '08 and the Descent into Depression* (Cambridge, MA: Harvard University Press, 2009), pp. 76–7. Posner is the most surprising of all critics. He provides a half-hearted admission that bounded rationality and irrational exuberance (or failures of rationality as he calls them) were among the underlying causes of the crisis, *ibid.*, p. 77.
[66] UN Experts Report, p. 16.   [67] *Ibid.*   [68] *Ibid.*, p. 24.

Hypothesis (EMH), analytically discussed in Chapter 2. Arguably, this led governments and regulators to a double erroneous belief: (1) that market prices were the best available signal of the state of the markets; and (2) that market prices were the best defence against market failure.[69] Regulators and policy makers chose not to look for signs of market imperfections beyond prices. This was to prove a disastrous decision for a variety of reasons.

To begin with, the quasi-religious belief in efficient (i.e., well priced and liquid) and rational markets was 'false science itself'.[70] First, market efficiency, in the way it is defined by EMH, does not really imply market rationality. It was a large leap of faith to presume that individual rationality leads also to collective rationality.[71] Second, I explained in Chapter 2 how behavioural finance has shown that financial markets, due to irrational exuberance and cognitive biases, are often prone to mispricing, which may cause serious allocative inefficiencies leading to economic dislocation and ultimately to a crisis. Third, the misplaced belief in efficient financial markets was also going counter to past experience that has underscored some of insights of Minsky and Kindleberger (discussed in Chapter 2) that financial markets have embedded instability cycles that spill over into the real economy causing shocks and dislocations that in turn lead to severe crises and loss of confidence.[72]

The same flawed belief in self-correcting rational markets led the powerful drive towards deregulation in the 1990s and most of the present decade. Protective regulations were withdrawn and 'efficient' markets were, to a large extent, left to their own devices to 'regulate' themselves leading to the global financial meltdown. As Lord Turner suggested, [73] this belief in the mythical self-correcting power of the market also gave very considerable clout to big market players, leading to a form of regulatory capture. Capture may explain why regulators did not heed the threats to systemic stability involved in the use of derivatives to lay off credit risk.[74] It may also account for their equally puzzling inertia in the face of the risks posed by the increasing interconnectedness created

---

[69] *Ibid.*, p. 41, 48–9.   [70] Turner Review, p. 40.
[71] *Ibid.*, pp. 40–1.   [72] See Chapter 2, Sections 6.3.1 and 6.3.2.
[73] *Prospect*, Issue 162, 27 August 2009. available at www.prospectmagazine.co.uk/2009/08/how-to-tame-global-finance/.
[74] Yet as explained in subsequent paragraphs, capture is not the only explanation, limited knowledge and almost complete misunderstanding of the interplay of the different elements of the financial revolution were also very big factors behind regulatory adherence to the 'market knows best' doctrine.

by widespread use of financial innovation. Rational markets were supposed to be able to address all these issues by means of self-regulation. Yet capture is also a simplistic and incomplete explanation.

The relaxed regulatory attitude towards derivatives markets and reliance on self-regulation, which characterized the period between 1994–2008, significantly influenced by a Report of the group of experts of an industry group (the G30) on the costs and benefits of derivatives trading, may, of course be attributed to capture.[75] During that period very few regulatory voices were raised arguing that the understanding of derivatives was still very incomplete and the exciting aspects of the new instruments did not obliterate the alarming aspects.[76] Industry lobbying may also explain the regulators' permissive attitude to capital regulations, which allowed banks to use risk modelling to calculate their capital requirements[77] and indulge in excessive asset transformation as a means of regulatory capital arbitrage. This meant that all big banks, at least, were severely undercapitalized before the onset of the GFC[78] having to set aside less and less equity – the only form of capital that can stave off bankruptcy in the event of a crisis. As a result, the erosion of confidence that followed the GFC turned them immediately bankrupt.

---

[75] Group of Thirty Report, 'Derivatives: Practices and Principles', Washington DC, 1 July 1993. For a discussion of the 'cheering welcome' this report received, see Eleni Tsingou, 'The Governance of Over-the-Counter Derivatives Markets', in Peter Mooslechner, Helen Schuberth and Beat Weber (eds.), The Political Economy of Financial Market Regulation: The Dynamics of Inclusion and Exclusion (Aldershot: Edward Elgar, 2006), chapter 7, pp. 168–90, 174–7. See also Derivatives Policy Group, 'A Framework for Voluntary Oversight of the OTC Activities of Securities Firms Affiliates to Promote Confidence and Stability in Financial Markets', Washington DC 1995.

[76] E.g., Brian Quinn, 'Derivatives – Where Next for Supervisors?' (1993) 33 Bank of England Quarterly Bulletin 535–8.

[77] 'The various modifications of "Basel" since the mid-nineties have all been designed to improve the risk calibration of capital requirements. The idea was, in principle, that average capital requirements should be unchanged, but regulatory capital should be ever more closely attuned to actual risks in banking. In fact, these modifications have enabled the large, internationally active banking institutions to reduce regulatory capital, more precisely, to use their capital for ever more levered activities', Hellwig, 'Capital Regulation After the Crisis', p. 5.

[78] Hellwig notes: 'Many institutions had equity amounting to 1 – 3 % of their balance sheets even as they were vaunting themselves as having 10 % "core capital"', ibid., p. 3. This view is confirmed by a BCBS report which found that in the wake of the GFC most big banks had equity amounting to around 2 per cent of total balance sheet assets. BCBS, Consultative Document, 'Strengthening the Resilience of the Banking Sector', Bank for International Settlements, Basel, 2009, p. 7, available at www.bis.org/publ/bcbs164.pdf?noframes=1.

2.4.2   Deregulation fosters the emergence of mega-banks

Influenced by industry's insistence that conglomeration was necessary under new market conditions of global economic integration and financial innovation, regulators disregarded the potential of creating scope for very significant (and insurmountable) conflicts of interest and allowed mega-banks to emerge. The supporters of conglomeration submitted that larger and more diversified financial institutions created better returns for shareholders, due to economies of scale and organizational efficiencies, and strengthened their income base. Therefore, according to this view, consolidation strengthened the stability of financial institutions and thus the stability of the financial system.

The GFC disproved most of those beliefs.[79] Mega-banks resorted to massive use of financial innovation to take speculative gambles in all asset markets and rode in full the wave of excessive liquidity that swept global markets from the late 1990s until 2007, leveraging their balance sheets to unsustainable levels. In the process, they loaded their balance sheets with a large number of impossible to value high-risk assets, especially the OTC-traded CDOs and CDSs, piling up colossal amounts of practically un-diversifiable risk. Thus, they became a ticking time bomb for the stability of the global financial system.

Deregulation led to two adverse outcomes: (1) flawed use of financial innovation (discussed extensively in Section 2.2 above); and (2) the proliferation of 'too-big-to-fail' financial institutions, which, with their herding behaviour, intensified homogenization. Moral hazard associated with the operation and cross-border presence of large financial institutions is regarded as the biggest threat to global financial stability, notwithstanding the competition issues their presence gives rise to in national and international financial markets. A large number of current regulatory reform initiatives are trying to effectively address these issues. These will be considered in Chapters 6 and 7.

Capital adequacy regulations, which essentially replaced restrictions on conglomeration, more or less imposed uniform risk management models[80] for all institutions engaging in credit and capital markets business. Thus,

---

[79]   See Arthur E. Wilmarth, 'The Dark Side of Universal Banking: Financial Conglomerates and the Origins of the Subprime Financial Crisis' (2009) 41 *Connecticut Law Review* 963.

[80]   It is interesting here to consider the circumstances under which a major US bank made freely available its risk management model based on the value at risk principles just before the Basel II framework became the mainstay of bank capital adequacy regulation throughout the world. See Tsingou, 'The Governance of OTC Derivatives Markets', Chapter 7, pp. 168–90.

they exacerbated and cemented the trend towards homogenization.[81] In addition, the 'contamination' of big commercial banks by the operating and management style of investment banks weakened risk management controls and meant that big banks increased their leverage, raising the risk of systemic collapse. Not a direct consequence of conglomeration, but indicative of the casual attitude to risk that it created, was the excessive use by banks of asset securitization and the adoption of the hazardous 'originate-to-distribute' model, which meant that mega-banks were the prime promoters of sub-prime mortgages and the principal drivers behind their growth to disastrous levels.[82] Big banks' proprietary trading desks, which essentially operated as hedge funds, could subsidize their risky ventures into the world of capital markets and markets for exotic OTC derivatives through recourse to the cheap funding base of government guaranteed deposits.[83]

However, neither high leverage nor the questionable value of mega-banks' balance sheets concerned the markets or regulators. Risk modelling and risk calibration, as incorporated in the Basel capital requirements, allowed banks to hold very small amounts of equity, increasing their asset returns over cost of capital and leading to massive profitability in the years preceding the GFC. Analysis of the profitability of financial institutions, which at the time was regarded as a sure sign of their financial health, would in fact have revealed a very strong warning of financial fragility, due to a thinning equity cushion.

Diversification of business lines did not lead to diversification of income sources and investment portfolios that would make banking institutions more resilient. Instead they all adopted a 'follow the leader strategy' and competition made matters worse,[84] increasing, of course, homogenization rather than diversity. The same was true of the second diversification strategy, multiple business activities. Thus, eventually all bank balance

---

[81] See K. Alexander, J. Eatwell, A. Persaud and R. Reoch, 'Financial Supervision and Crisis Management in the EU', prepared for the European Parliament's Committee on Economic and Monetary Affairs, December 2007, IP/A/ECON/IC/2007–069, pp. 3–7.

[82] Wilmarth, 'The Dark Side of Universal Banking' 1017–22.

[83] George Soros, 'Do not Ignore the Need for Financial Reform' *Financial Times*, 25 October 2009, available at www.ft.com/cms/s/0/a12061e0-c196–11de-b86b-00144feab49a.html.

[84] As Haldane puts it: 'Firms migrated activity to where returns looked largest. As each new day dawned – leveraged loans yesterday, CDOs today, proprietary trading tomorrow – the whole sector was drawn to the new source of sunlight. Through competitive forces, finance engaged in a frantic game of follow-the-leader, played for real money'. Haldane, 'Rethinking the Financial Network', p. 7.

sheets looked more or less the same. They engaged in similar trading and investment policies, used similar trading and risk management models and investment methods, and used more or less the same information relying on similar sources and not pursuing alternative research strategies. Furthermore, all those actions were invariably undertaken by highly trained and professional personnel whose mindset, investment behaviour and career goals were similar. Finally, mega-banks' diversification strategies examined from a systemic perspective increased the fragility of the financial system instead of maximizing its resilience because 'the greater the number of eggs, the greater the fragility of the basket – and the greater the probability of bad eggs'.[85]

In the process, mega-banks fostered an organizational culture of short-termism and aggressive speculation in order to boost trader and bank executive compensation as well as returns to their shareholders. Furthermore, increased trading activity (in capital markets) and the excessive use of securitization and financial innovation by mega-banks led to welfare losses instead of the famed gains. With the exemption of advisory and access to finance services, such as underwriting of new securities issues, other forms of investment banking, such as proprietary trading, are nothing more than a classic zero-sum game and incapable of bringing any long-term gains.[86]

Naturally, the gradual elimination of diversity, due to homogenization, in institutions' business and risk management strategies, made 'the whole system less resistant to disturbance'.[87] These developments meant in turn that the financial network, vulnerable as it was by its nature, was, first, deprived of its natural stabilizers that could replenish the markets with capital during the crisis, and, second, became more susceptible to 'feedback effects under stress (hoarding of liabilities and fire-sales of assets)'.[88] This explains why mega-banks, instead of exhibiting the fabled benefits of income and balance sheet diversification were, in fact, very vulnerable to the first change of the wind in the real economy and were at the heart of the 2007–9 crisis.

The total neglect of liquidity by the Basel capital framework, in accordance with its deregulatory spirit and direction, allowed banks both to rely

---

[85] *Ibid.*   [86] See UNCTAD Report, p. 4.

[87] Haldane, 'Rethinking the Financial Network'.

[88] In general, risk traders tend to sell assets in falling markets, whereas risk absorbers tend to buy them at the discount prices. This function was lost when all institutions became risk traders through their shadow banking vehicles and structured credit trades.

excessively on short-term funding to finance their asset expansion and to increase their leverage exponentially. Thus, they became very vulnerable to any liquidity runs due to loss of confidence, which leads to hoarding of liquidity. All institutions that can provide liquidity, with the exception of central banks, feel uncertain about meeting their own funding needs as well as about the solvency of their counterparts. As discussed earlier in this chapter, the drying up of liquidity became the fundamental cause of the collapse of the international financial system once confidence was lost. The fragility of the financial system means that it does not take long before a liquidity crisis is transformed into a solvency crisis. As a result, most US, UK and continental European mega-banks had to be saved from collapse through a substantial infusion of public funds or outright takeovers by the state. An extensive analysis of the Basel standards' shortcomings with respect to liquidity is provided in Chapter 5. It should be noted that the new Basel III framework for liquidity regulation, discussed extensively in Chapter 6, provides a rather satisfactory solution to the problem of financial institution leverage and reliance on short-term funding sources.

Global derivatives markets were another area where the movement towards deregulation and the blind belief in the market's ability to self-regulate prevented the building of adequate defences against systemic risk. Apart from the complexity and interconnectedness that were inextricable by-products of opaque OTC derivatives markets discussed above, regulators also discounted the prevalent short-termism of those markets and the market actors' propensity to herd for various behavioural reasons, including the battle of survival discussed in Chapter 2. Short-termism and herding were greatly encouraged by the absence of any meaningful public controls.

2.4.3   Regulatory failure and market discipline

During the 1990s a large number of restrictions pertaining to permitted banking business and limits on financial conglomeration as well as prudential regulations, such as minimum reserves held with the central bank and minimum deposit coverage ratios over assets, were dismantled.[89] They were replaced by a regulatory template which focused on capital adequacy standards and market discipline. The dismantling of minimum reserves (i.e., minimum liquidity ratios) and flaws in capital

---

[89]   For an excellent overview of the development of bank supervision between the 1970s and the 1990s, see Charles Goodhart, *The Basel Committee on Banking Supervision: A History of the Early Years, 1974–1997* (Cambridge University Press, 2011).

adequacy regulations will be discussed in Chapter 5. The next paragraph merely provides an analysis of the limitations of market discipline as a regulatory tool, since this concept is strongly linked to the doctrine of free market infallibility.

Market discipline and its processes lack a precise definition[90] and seem to have developed more as the product of intuition.[91] Broadly defined, market discipline encompasses the discipline imposed by shareholders and the market for corporate control on bank management and the discipline imposed by subordinated short-term creditors,[92] as well as other creditors,[93] bank customers, and even highly mobile groups of bank employees.[94] All of the above are assumed to have the right incentives to monitor bank behaviour in order to avoid being caught in a bank failure and a messy winding up that would bring them large losses. The most important mechanism to facilitate market discipline is thought to be disclosure of accurate information to the market, and the market's ability to process it properly.[95]

By means of capital adequacy regulations market discipline became an integral part of banking supervision.[96] More specifically, the third pillar of the Basel II Accord required an increased number of regulatory and market disclosures by regulated banks in order to enhance market

---

[90] David T. Llewellyn, 'Inside the "Black Box" of Market Discipline' (2005) 25 *Economic Affairs* 41–7.

[91] Costas Stephanou, 'Rethinking Market Discipline', World Bank Policy Brief, June 2009.

[92] On the role of demandable bank debt in disciplining bankers, see Charles W. Calomiris and Charles M. Kahn, 'The Role of Demandable Debt in Structuring Optimal Banking Arrangements' (1991) 81 *American Economic Review* 497–513. For a refined version seeking to counter the 'too-big-to-fail' problem and deposit insurance, requesting that banks should maintain a minimal proportion of subordinated debt finance while at the same time restricting the means of government recapitalization of insolvent banks, see Charles W. Calomiris, 'Building an Incentive-Compatible Safety Net' (1999) 23 *Journal of Banking and Finance* 1499–519.

[93] Donald P. Morgan and Kevin J. Stiroh, 'Bond Market Discipline of Banks: Is the Market Tough Enough?', Federal Reserve Board of New York Staff Report No. 95, December 1999, available at papers.ssrn.com/sol3/papers.cfm?abstract_id=207148> accessed on 15 June 2009.

[94] David T. Llewellyn and David G. Mayes, 'What is Market Discipline?' in George G. Kaufman (ed.), *Market Discipline in Banking: Theory and Evidence* (Amsterdam: Elsevier, 2003), pp. 186–8.

[95] *Ibid.*, pp. 189–93. This observation is bound to be severely tested by, inter alia, fund managers' propensity towards strategic trade behaviour (herding). See Chapter 2.

[96] For a discussion of the different forms of direct and indirect market discipline, see Daniel Tarullo, *Banking on Basel: The Future of International Financial Regulation* (Washington, DC: Peterson Institute, 2008), Chapter 7.

discipline.[97] This was based on the assumption that, if the regulatory capital positions and risk exposures of banks were regularly disclosed, institutions facing difficulties because, for instance, they pursued risky business, would be restrained / disciplined, at least by their short-term creditors, while, gradually, the rest of the market would become increasingly unwilling to lend them money or do business with them, thereby avoiding the acquisition of an exposure to a failing bank. However, the global financial crisis has proved that there was lots of naivety in this view.

Inadequate protection by deposit insurance may make a bank susceptible to a run, as the Northern Rock incident proved beyond doubt.[98] Thus, it is assumed that deposit insurance fosters systemic stability, although, at the same time, it weakens market discipline,[99] since a big class of short-term creditors (depositors) have very little incentive to perform any kind of market monitoring. Furthermore, because of the very nature of its business, the banking industry creates interconnectedness leading to 'too-big-to-fail' banks, so-called 'interconnectedness spillover'.[100] The failure of one institution may cause a severe disruption in the business of another or a chain of institutional failures ('contagion') due to a crisis of confidence, triggering a cascade of failures. Such an outcome would lead to severe disruption of economic activity and households' livelihood. No modern economy, where most economic activity is dependent on banks, can afford a disruption of those services. This means that, in practice, all big banks enjoy an implicit public guarantee and are 'too-big-to-fail'. It follows that even badly run banks will be rescued with the taxpayer and the deposit insurance scheme covering most creditors' losses. The

[97] Banks were required under the Basel II Accord to regularly disclose, *inter alia*, (1) the composition of their Tier 1 and Tier 2 capital, the total amount of capital, and the accounting policies they use for the valuation of their assets and liabilities; (2) an exposure assessment comprising information about the asset side of balance sheet, the different types of risk to which the bank is exposed and the amounts exposed, the method used for calculating those risks, the external credit agency used for the risk-weighting purposes, in the case of banks using the standardized approach, and general information on the risk assessment methodology used, in the case of banks using the Internal Ratings Based approach and the capital requirements for each different type of risk and the total capital requirements.

[98] The Run on the Rock (House of Commons, Treasury Committee, 24 January 2008). Report of Session 2007–8.

[99] Inter-American Development Bank, 'Unlocking Credit: the Quest for Deep and Stable Bank Lending – Economic and Social Progress in Latin America, 2005 Report', 2004, chapter 7.

[100] Geneva Report 2009, pp. 20–1.

probability of this happening creates strong perverse incentives that significantly weaken market discipline.

The bigger the institution and the more interconnected the more likely that the government will rescue it in the event of failure.[101] This means that bank management have a powerful incentive to expand a banking institution's balance sheet and can afford to behave irresponsibly while its creditors will continue lending it funds without any substantial fear of the losses that any private organization's bankruptcy would entail. Therefore, in the absence of strong disincentives to grow big and of properly calibrated resolution and insolvency regimes, the ever present pressure for public bank rescues of big financial institutions[102] and deposit insurance ameliorate any disciplining power the market could theoretically exert. In this context, it is a very welcome development that the special resolution regime for big financial institutions introduced by the Dodd–Frank Act (analytically discussed in Chapter 7) and the EU Commission proposals for a pan-European resolution regime (also discussed in Chapter 7) target the elimination of moral hazard that comes with bank bail-outs and the minimization of the cost of bank failures to the taxpayer.

Even if it was possible to design appropriate incentives so that, at least, bank creditors became effective monitors of banks, in which case extensive market disclosure would have been very useful, market monitoring would still mean little in terms of preventing institutional failures and/or safeguarding systemic stability for two reasons. First, as Hellwig accurately notes:[103]

> Because of systemic interdependence, the individual bank's risk exposure cannot be ascertained by just looking at the bank's assets and liabilities, on balance sheet and off balance sheet. If the bank's asset position involves a certain risk and the bank has hedged this risk by contracting with a third party, the effectiveness of the hedge depends on the third party's ability to fulfil its obligations when needed. If the risk in question is of macroeconomic dimension, an interest rate risk, exchange rate risk, or a housing-price risk, the counterparty's ability to fulfil its obligation

---

[101] *Ibid.*

[102] *Ibid.*, p. 191. *E.g.*, evidence from the bond markets well before the implementation of Basel II showed that bond markets were taking a softer approach to big banks assuming that they were too big to fail or they were simply too complex in their structure for the bond market to understand and price effectively. See Morgan and Stiroh, 'Bond Market Discipline of Banks'.

[103] Martin Hellwig, 'Systemic Risk in the Financial Sector: An Analysis of the Subprime-Mortgage Financial Crisis', Max Planck Institute for Research on Collective Goods, Bonn 2008/43, November 2008, pp. 59–60.

depends on how many similar contracts it has concluded with other market participants. If risk correlations across contracts are such that the counterparty to the hedge must deliver on many of them at the same time, this in itself may destroy the counterparty's viability.

In today's globalized markets, there is no private institution that possibly has the ability, resources and access to information to be able to conduct a risk analysis of all financial institutions, regulated and unregulated. The advent of financial innovation and attendant opacity of the financial network has made this task nearly impossible, increasing, in the process, uncertainty. Yet, even if such institution existed, the colossal costs of universal monitoring would far exceed the expected benefits. Moreover, for reasons pertaining to banks' susceptibility to runs, business competition, and/or because of confidentiality agreements, crucial data on a bank's business and the performance/profitability of certain business relationships may not be made public on a disaggregated manner. As a result, the effectiveness of individual institution monitoring by the market on the basis of disclosed data becomes of much lesser importance.

There is clear evidence that, in the time leading to the GFC, market discipline, including shareholder control, failed. The two most important market-based indices of a bank's financial health, the CDS premium and the share price showed (with the exception of Northern Rock) no sign of the trouble that lay ahead.[104] Moreover, investors and analysts, instead of exercising any kind of discipline over bank management by asking for the building up of higher capital buffers, were just pushing for higher returns at the height of the boom. Such pressure from the markets provided even bigger incentives to bank management to take ever higher amounts of debt to leverage the bank's balance sheet and expand its profits. Nor did shareholders do anything to prevent disastrous takeover decisions, such as the bid of RBS for ABN AMRO.[105] It is, therefore, doubtful whether shareholders can be trusted first to make wholly rational decisions and not be affected by irrational exuberance and other cognitive limitations

---

[104] Turner Review, pp. 46–7.
[105] See Harry Wilson, Philip Aldrick and Kamal Ahmed, 'Royal Bank of Scotland Investigation: the Full Story of How the "World's Biggest Bank" Went Bust – Using Diary Extracts of the Key Players and Previously Hidden Memos, *The Sunday Telegraph* and *The Daily Telegraph* piece together the full story of RBS's Downfall', *Sunday Telegraph*, 6 March 2011, available at www.telegraph.co.uk/finance/newsbysector/banksandfinance/8363417/Royal-Bank-of-Scotland-investigation-the-full-story-of-how-the-worlds-biggest-bank-went-bust.html.
  The paper's report leaves no doubt that a series of disastrous acquisitions to satisfy investor demands for higher returns and conglomeration were at the heart of RBS's downfall.

and, second, to truly understand the business of very complex organizations like financial institutions and make decisions that go beyond the easily deciphered comparative levels of profitability.

It follows from the aforementioned discussion that the regulator's excessive reliance on market monitoring was flying in the face of a number of severe limitations to the disciplining power of market forces. However, regulatory failure as one of the causes of the GFC is an 'explanation' in need of an explanation. As mentioned above, the obvious way to explain the regulatory failure is, of course, capture. Yet, at best this is an incomplete account of what lay beneath the surface. It fails to give a convincing reason for the total evaporation of the restraining power that loss of reputation entails. It follows that a more multidimensional and thus accurate explanation of regulatory failure is required. I provide such an explanation in Section 5 below where I explain how incomplete and flawed understanding of the financial revolution intensified regulatory complacency and inertia and industry rent-seeking.

2.5   Irrational exuberance and other behavioural causes

I discussed in Chapter 2 how insights from behavioural economics, cognitive psychology and neuroscience reveal that individuals often do not make economic decisions in accord with the image of rational utility maximizers that neoclassical economics has painted for them. Rather they make decisions in a mixed way[106] and the part of the brain that is activated by emotion and instinct also plays a role. At the collective level, such decisions are bound to produce herd effects and irrational momentum swings. Therefore, a number of the causes of the crisis may be well explained by reference to behavioural factors and *bounded rationality*.[107]

---

[106] See Emilios Avgouleas, 'The Global Financial Crisis and the Disclosure Paradigm in European Financial Regulation: The Case for Reform' (2009) 6 *European Company and Financial Law Review* 440–75; Emilios Avgouleas, 'What Future for Disclosure as a Regulatory Technique? Lessons from Behavioural Decision Theory and the Global Financial Crisis', in Iain MacNeil and Justin O'Brien (eds.), *The Future of Financial Regulation* (Oxford: Hart Publishing, 2010), Chapter 12, pp. 205–26.

[107] This concept describes individuals' limited ability to process information, since they possess 'limited computational skills and seriously flawed memories'. See Herbert A. Simon, 'A Behavioral Model of Rational Choice' (1955) 69 *Quarterly Journal of Economics* 99–118; Herbert A. Simon 'Rational Choice in the Structure of the Environment', in Herbert A. Simon (ed.), *Models of Man: Social and Rational* (Hoboken, NJ: Wiley and Sons, 1957), pp. 261, 271.

There is ample empirical evidence which suggests that markets often exhibit signs of large-scale herd effects and overshoot. Behavioural economists have argued for a long time that such empirical evidence proves that financial market prices can diverge substantially and for long periods of time from estimated economic values ('anomalies'), and that the calculated price divergences may be at times so large that policymakers can reasonably conclude that market prices have become irrational. It is, thus, reasonable to ask policymakers to recognize that all asset markets (including those that are not very liquid such as housing) are capable of acting irrationally, and can be susceptible to self-reinforcing herd and momentum effects.[108]

While most markets are capable of irrational pricing and momentum trading, financial markets are more susceptible to them due to high levels of liquidity which mean that momentum trading can develop much faster than in other markets, leading to gross mis-pricings. For this reason, Lo has observed that the ultimate cause of the GFC was human behaviour.[109] This can be broken down into two elements: market euphoria (irrational exuberance), driven also by greed, and the much documented cognitive biases which impact on market actor behaviour.[110] The fact that behavioural causes were in part at play during the last crisis is a view endorsed by several commentators.[111]

Cognitive neuroscientists have provided evidence that financial gain affects the same 'pleasure centers' of the brain that are activated by certain narcotics. This abides well with empirical and impressionistic evidence that market euphoria relaxes human alertness to risks. Arguably, prolonged periods of economic growth and prosperity can induce a collective sense of euphoria and complacency among investors that resembles the

---

[108] Dimitri Vayanos and Paul Woolley, 'An Institutional Theory of Momentum and Reversal', FMG Discussion Paper 621, LSE, November 2008; Robert J. Shiller, *Irrational Exuberance* (Princeton University Press, 2nd edn, 2005).

[109] Andrew Lo, 'Regulatory Reform in the Wake of the Financial Crisis of 2007–2008' (2009) 1 *Journal of Financial Economic Policy* 4–43, 5–6.

[110] For an extensive analysis see Chapter 2 of this book; Emilios Avgouleas, 'Reforming Investor Protection Regulation: The Impact of Cognitive Biases', in M. Faure and F. Stephen (eds.), *Essays in the Law and Economics of Regulation in Honour of Anthony Ogus* (Hague: Intersentia, 2008), pp. 143–76 and Emilios Avgouleas, 'Cognitive Biases and Investor Protection Regulation, An Evolutionary Approach', September 2006, available at papers.ssrn.com/sol3/papers.cfm?abstract_id=1133214.

[111] Lo, 'Regulatory Reform', 19–21; George A. Akerlof and Robert J. Shiller, *Animal Spirits: How Human Psychology Drives the Economy, and Why It Matters for Global Capitalism* (Princeton University Press, 2009), especially chapters 1 and 7; Avgouleas, 'The Global Financial Crisis, Behavioural Finance and Financial Regulation'.

artificial mania that can be induced by mood-enhancing drugs.[112] In fact, in a textbook manifestation of irrational exuberance for a long period of time and up to the summer of 2007, market participants were complacent about the risk of loss in structured credit markets and other neighbouring markets – either through systematic under-estimation of those risks because of recent history, or a decline in their risk aversion due to increasing wealth, or both.

Notwithstanding the excesses of US housing policies discussed in Section 2.3 above, the substantial loosening of underwriting standards that occurred during the peak of the bubble could indicate that irrational exuberance also played a role.[113] Thus, it is likely that, in addition to the aforementioned monetary and housing policies, behavioural factors also contributed to the size of the credit expansion observed until 2007. Mortgage borrowers in the US and other parts of Western world, *anchored* to the prevailing environment of low interest rates and overconfident that rising house prices would last forever, rushed to jump on the property markets' bandwagon. However, in doing so they took no account of whether their borrowings were truly affordable on the basis of their earnings. It is not then surprising that the soaring default rates in those exact loans were the trigger of the present crisis.

Moreover, excessive liquidity is likely to have further stimulated risk discounting. Increasingly overconfident lenders, borrowers and traders believed that liquid markets would last forever providing an outlet for new products to be sold and an ongoing source of funding liquidity for financial institutions, which could thus increase their leverage without any fears of a funding crisis. As a result, market prices did not reflect the underlying long-term nature of the traded assets (housing, commodities) and the falling risk premia (a traditional measure of risk) were taken to mean actual reduction of credit risk.[114]

Market overconfidence was further refuelled by financial innovation. In fact, for some products, such as CDOs, the market was on the face of it right. In their short trading history, CDOs had been profitable and there was no major incident pointing to their hidden risks. Data that covered only a short period of time and peer behaviour provided traders with a false sense of security and gave rise to large-scale herding. After all, as they were are all doing the same thing following the markets' momentum,

---

[112] Turner Review, p. 20   [113] PWGFM Policy Statement, p. 8.
[114] Mark Carney, Governor of the Bank of Canada, 'Addressing Financial Market Turbulence', Remarks to the Toronto Board of Trade, 13 March 2008, p. 3.

they could do no wrong. Career pressures could easily isolate the voices of reason reinforcing herding behaviour and market momentum. Lo provides a textbook illustration of such pressures:[115]

> [Suppose that in] a major investment bank XYZ, a firm actively engaged in issuing and trading CDOs in 2004 …[the Chief Risk Officer (CRO)] was convinced that US residential real estate was a bubble … [and that] there would be devastating consequences for his firm. What possible actions could he have taken to protect his shareholders? He might ask the firm to exit the CDO business, to which his superiors would respond that the CDO business was one of the most profitable over the past decade with considerable growth potential, other competitors are getting into the business, not leaving, and the historical data suggest that real-estate values are unlikely to fall by more than 1 or 2 percent per year … Unable to convince senior management of the likelihood of a real-estate downturn, the CRO suggests a compromise – reduce the firm's CDO exposure by half. Senior management's likely response would be that such a reduction in XYZ's CDO business will decrease the group's profits by half, causing the most talented members of the group to leave the firm … Finally, suppose the CRO takes matters into his own hands and implements a hedging strategy using OTC derivatives to bet against the CDO market. From 2004 to 2006, such a hedging strategy would likely have yielded significant losses, and the reduction in XYZ's earnings due to this hedge, coupled with the strong performance of the CDO business for XYZ and its competitors, would be sufficient grounds for dismissing the CRO.

Excessive investor reliance on credit ratings provides further evidence of herding. Investors could claim that their reliance on credit ratings was a mechanism to economise substantial research costs for buyers of structured securities and thus facilitate transactions. But the flaws of the rating process were well pronounced and serious. CRAs frequently warned the market about the true function of their ratings, although, naturally, their warnings were neither very prominent nor widely publicized.[116] So the mega-paradox is how to explain the fact that, while all the supposedly hyper-rational and certainly highly sophisticated market participants did know very well that the ratings produced by the major CRAs suffered several shortcomings, nevertheless, instead of discounting their role, they placed increased importance on credit ratings. What

[115] Lo, 'Regulatory Reform', p. 21.
[116] IMF, Global Financial Stability Report, 'Containing Systemic Risks and Restoring Financial Soundness', April 2008, p. 55, 'Hereinafter IMF, GFSR 'Containing Systemic Risks'.

was then the reason that led banks and institutional investors to ignore all of the aforementioned faults of the ratings production process and perform little or no in-house credit analysis of their investments? In other words, what forced supposedly hyper-rational market actors to substitute proper analysis and due diligence for 'a subscription to a ratings publication'?[117]

It is the author's view that the incredible amount of trust placed on the ratings of CRAs, which, as a result, 'had grown more powerful than anyone intended',[118] was the result of the operation of *availability* and *representativeness heuristics*. Namely, market participants relying heavily on *heuristics* came to the conclusion that painstaking and accurate calculations of market value were not necessary for structured credit products.[119] The use of *heuristics* was 'justified' by two factors: (1) for certain kinds of structured products, such as CDOs, calculations of value were nearly impossible due to the complexity of such products and the loss of information about risk down the chain from the original credits to the traded instrument; and (2) there was no memory of serious failures of the ratings process, since structured credit securities were predominantly new products without long trading histories. Thus, in the prevailing conditions of market euphoria, credit ratings, in spite of their shortcomings, could be used as a benchmark of value to allow trading and profiteering to continue indefinitely.

Another cognitive factor that might have played a role here is *bounded rationality*. As securitization markets grew and products became more and more complex, expert investors showed limited capacity for understanding structured credit products and developing tools to value them. Instead, as explained above, relying on *availability* and *representativeness heuristics*, they replaced rigorous credit controls and valuation mechanisms with over-reliance on credit ratings. Namely, market actors' cognitive limitations and focus on short-term profit induced sophisticated investors to ignore the warning signals and simply follow the herd.

---

[117] Carney, 'Financial Market Turbulence', pp. 3–4.
[118] IMF, 'GFSR Containing Systemic Risks', p. 56.
[119] The view that credit ratings were used as heuristics was advanced in Avgouleas, 'The Global Financial Crisis, Behavioural Finance and Financial Regulation'. It was strongly supported in Steven Schwartz, 'Regulating Complexity in Financial Markets', Leverhulme Lecture, University of Oxford, 10 November 2010, available at scholarship.law.duke.edu/faculty_scholarship/2352/.

3.   Micro-causes: The issue of misaligned incentives

The micro-causes of the GFC have also been examined by several regulatory bodies and international fora which seem more or less to concur in their findings.[120] Drawing in part on the synopsis offered by the US President's Working Group on Financial Markets, the micro-causes of the GFC may be summarized as follows:[121]

- flaws in the 'originate–to-distribute' model, which led to a significant erosion of market discipline by those involved in the securitization process, including originators, underwriters, CRAs, and global investors;
- flaws in CRAs' assessments of sub-prime residential mortgage backed securities (RMBS) and other complex structured credit products, especially collateralized debt obligations (CDOs) that held RMBS and other asset-backed securities (CDOs or ABS);
- risk management weaknesses at all large financial institutions motivated, in part, by short-term compensation policies and inadequate corporate governance.

It is widely assumed that the majority of the micro-causes of the crisis should be attributed to misaligned incentives. The paragraphs below scrutinize this claim in three contexts: bankers' compensation, the impact of the 'originate-to-distribute' model on credit controls and the information content of credit ratings.

3.1   Executive compensation and corporate governance failures

The issue of bankers' compensation came in to sharp focus with the GFC. It has featured rather prominently in all debates regarding the causes of the GFC and regulatory reforms to prevent its re-occurrence. The main accusation launched against bankers' compensation packages has been that they focused too much on short-term performance, thus creating

---

[120] See IMF, GFSR, 'Containing Systemic Risks'; also Carney, 'Financial Market Turbulence'.
[121] PWGFM Policy Statement, p. 3. See also Ben S. Bernanke, 'Addressing Weaknesses in the Global Financial Markets: The Report of the President's Working Group on Financial Markets', Speech made at the World Affairs Council, 10 April 2008, available at www.federalreserve.gov/newsevents/speech/bernanke20080410a.htm.

perverse incentives.[122] In financial markets in the short term it is possible for the riskier investment to generate the highest (notional) returns with catastrophic long-term consequences. As a result, there has been a very strong trend in favour of regulating bankers' pay instead of leaving it to the market.[123] Most Western countries have adopted or are in the process of adopting stringent compensation rules for bankers, especially in the EU,[124] often following the guidelines of international fora such as the BCBS.[125] Yet the issue of how to regulate bankers' compensation, if at all, remains contentious.[126] Naturally, some form of realignment of bankers'

[122] Among the studies that have evidenced the impact of perverse incentives in bank compensation structures is Lucian Bebchuk, Alma Cohen and Holger Spamann, 'The Wages of Failure: Executive Compensation at Bear Stearns and Lehman 2000–2008', Working Paper, Harvard Law School, 2009. See also Alan Blinder, 'Crazy Compensation and the Crisis – We're all Paying Now Because Skewed Financial Incentives Led to Too Many Big Bets', *Wall Street Journal*, 28 May 2009.

[123] See Lucian Bebchuk and Holger Spamann, 'Regulating Bankers' Pay', Harvard Law School Olin Discussion Paper No. 641, 2009. Lucian Bebchuk, 'Why Financial Pay Shouldn't be Left to the Market', Project Syndicate, August 2009, available at: www.projectsyndicate.org/commentary/bebchuk4. See, in general, Lucian Bebchuk and Jesse Fried, *Pay Without Performance* (Cambridge, MA: Harvard University Press, 2004).

[124] EU Commission, Proposal for a Directive amending Directives 2006/48/EC and 2006/49/EC; Commission Recommendation on Remuneration Policies in the Financial Services Sector, COM (2009) 3159, 30 April 2009; Commission Communication accompanying Commission Recommendation complementing Recommendations 2004/913/EC and 2005/162/EC as Regards the Regime for the Remuneration of Directors of Listed Companies and Commission Recommendation on Remuneration Policies in the Financial Services Sector, COM (2009) 211 final, available at ec.europa.eu/internal_market/company/docs/directors-remun/COM(2009)_211_EN.pdf. Analysts find the new wave of compensation regulations rather restrictive. See Guido Ferrarini, Niamh Moloney and Maria-Christina Ungureanu, 'Executive Remuneration in Crisis: A Critical Assessment of Reforms in Europe' (2010) 10 *Journal of Corporate Law Studies* 73–118.

[125] BCBS, 'Range of Methodologies for Risk and Performance Alignment of Remuneration – final document' 12 May 2011, available at www.bis.org/publ/bcbs194.htm.

[126] 'How people are paid at the top in a free-market system has always been a contentious issue, especially in bad times. [Consider] Babe Ruth's most famous quip ... [w]hen asked in 1930 if it was right that he should be making more money than President Hoover, he replied, "I had a better year than he did"', Steven Brill, 'What's a Bailed-Out Banker Really Worth?' *New York Times Magazine*, 29 December 2009, available at www.nytimes.com/2010/01/03/magazine/03Compensation-t.html?pagewanted=1&_r=1&ref=magazine. This article referred to the difficulty that Kenneth Feinberg, the government's Troubled Asset Relief Program (TARP) 'special master for executive compensation', encountered when he had to set compensation packages for Citigroup and Bank of America executives, although both banks, alongside AIG and the automobile companies, had essentially been bailed out through the use of public money. Babe Ruth was, of course, the most celebrated US baseball player of his time and was the subject of adulation from New York Yankees' fans for hitting his famous 'home runs'.

pay with the long-term interests of shareholders (and of society) as suggested by Bebchuk is both desirable and inevitable.[127]

Yet there are studies that show that banks whose CEOs had large equity stakes, rather than options, in their firms, giving them strong incentives to be guardians of their firms' long-term stability and performance, performed worse or as badly as the rest of the sector during the crisis, despite the fact that such CEOs suffered serious losses in their equity stakes.[128] This finding does not abide well with Bebchuk's main thesis about the alignment of executive pay with performance. But it is rather optimistic to expect institutional investors to act as true market monitors and rely on corporate governance mechanisms to restrain rent-seeking or to remedy the flawed uses of financial innovation. As explained in the next section, there is strong evidence that those within financial institutions who understood the potential of financial revolution, pushed it to its limits in a rent-seeking exercise, inflating institutions' profits and traders' and managers' salaries. Moreover outsiders, mostly institutional investors, did not delve deeper to ascertain the source of financial institutions' strong profitability that generated the hefty dividends and market price appreciation that boosted their returns from financial stocks. They also approved in general meeting after general meeting most executive compensations plans.

Arguably, none of the outside investors had either the inclination or the ability to understand and qualify the long-term risks generated by the ultra-profitability of their 'champions'. Moreover, even if institutional investors had either the incentives – or in an extreme scenario the obligation to do so – they would still have failed in their monitoring duties. First, institutional investors are anything but immune to irrational exuberance and, as a result, as soon as good times return all pretence of effective monitoring will be abandoned in favour of higher returns. Second, they are also constrained by bounded rationality and lack of expertise. Therefore, asking investors to become effective monitors of financial institutions' use and misuses of financial innovation seriously stretches the belief in

---

[127] See for an overview Lucian Bebchuk, 'Fixing Bankers' Pay', *The Economists' Voice*, November 2009, available at www.bepress.com/ev.

[128] Rudiger Fahlenbrach and René M. Stulz, 'Bank CEO Incentives and the Credit Crisis' (2011) 99 *Journal of Financial Economics* 11–26. Other scholars also suggest that compensation structures were not among the principal causes of the crisis. See Guido A. Ferrarini and Maria Crsitina Ungureanu, 'Economics, Politics, and the International Principles for Sound Compensation Practices: An Analysis of Executive Pay at European Banks', ECGI – Law Working Paper No. 169/2010, 1 November 2010.

the disciplining power of shareholder monitoring. Finally, even if institutional investors managed one (improbable) day to become effective monitors of individual financial institutions, this development would provide no protection against systemic risk. As explained in Section 4.1 below, a systemic crisis may even be the outcome of a financial institution's most prudent and reasonable behaviour.

The grand scale rent-seeking by financial institutions and expert insiders that was made possible by the financial revolution and led to the discussed mega-profits was based on their ability to free ride on public subsidies and the existence of the public guarantee. It follows that limiting public subsidies to financial institutions, placing limits on their ability to leverage their balance sheet through the use of debt instead of equity to fund their asset base, and remedying the 'too-big-to-fail' problem are much more effective measures in preventing a new crisis than regulating bankers' pay. Naturally, bankers' pay remains an issue of public fascination and part of the quest for justice, given the devastation the GFC has wreaked on national economies and people's livelihoods. But it is not the only important issue. Thus, it is lamentable that it has stolen the limelight and has taken so much of policy-makers' time during that rare window of opportunity that existed between 2008 and 2010 to redress the chronic defects in the regulation of the global financial services industry.

3.2   The 'originate-to-distribute' model

The way the 'originate-to-distribute' model works was explained in Chapter 2. Essentially, it is a method of breaking down the process of credit extension from 'origination' to ultimate financing. In principle, use of the model spreads risk and reduces financing costs, as it affords to small- and medium-size borrowers greater access to capital.[129] In practice, however, problems arose in recent years throughout the 'originate-to-distribute' chain. Credit disintermediation based on the model led to the severing of the long-term relationship between the originator and the borrower and created perverse incentives in the system leading to reckless lending. Because the bank advancing the original mortgage did not retain the risk of the loan it originated but passed it on to other financial institutions, which packaged the loan into MBS and CDOs, the originator had no incentive to conduct proper due diligence and borrower monitoring. As a result, to a degree that increased over time, mortgages became poorly

---

[129]   Bernanke, 'Addressing Weaknesses in the Global Financial Markets'.

documented and were extended with insufficient attention to the borrower's ability to repay. The best-known and most serious case is that of US
sub-prime mortgages.[130]

Furthermore, the incentive structures often tied originator revenue to
loan volume, rather than to the quality of the loans being passed through
the chain.[131] Namely, originators were paid by reference to the amount
of loans they generated regardless of the repayment rate of those loans,
which is inextricably linked to the borrower's creditworthiness. Thus,
they had every incentive to maximize the volume of loans granted
independently of controls on borrower creditworthiness.

3.3   The flawed information content and use of credit ratings

The problems surrounding credit ratings identified above are both per-
plexing and numerous. The global market for credit ratings is highly
oligopolistic, as three major agencies – Standard & Poors, Fitch, and
Moodys – dominate the market.[132] Perversely competition led to lower
quality ratings and a deterioration of ratings ability to predict default
rather than increased scrutiny.[133] Moreover, the business model of CRAs,
where the rated firm pays the fees for the production of ratings that will
be used by investors for free, has consistently been plagued by conflicts
of interest.[134] The paradox with the use of ratings is why they were relied

---

[130]   The FCIC Report notes: 'Lenders made loans that they knew borrowers could not afford
and that could cause massive losses to investors in mortgage securities ... the report
documents that major financial institutions ineffectively sampled loans they were purchasing to package and sell to investors. They knew a significant percentage of the sampled loans did not meet their own underwriting standards or those of the originators.
Nonetheless, they sold those securities to investors.' FCIC Report, p. xxii. See also ibid.,
p. 20. Cf. Wallison, 'Dissent'.

[131]   Carney, 'Financial Market Turbulence'.

[132]   For an evaluation of their role in the global economy, see Howell E. Jackson, 'The Role
of Credit Rating Agencies in the Establishment of Capital Standards for Financial
Institutions in a Global Economy', in Eilis Ferran and Charles Goodhart (eds.), The
Challenges Facing Financial Regulation (Oxford: Hart Publishing, 2001). For an over-
view of the problems associated with the function of CRAs, see Steven L. Schwarcz,
'Private Ordering of Public Markets: The Rating Agency Paradox' (2002) University of
Illinois Law Review 1–28.

[133]   See Bo Becker and Todd Milbourn, 'How Did Increased Competition Affect Credit
Ratings?', Harvard Business School Working Paper 09–051, 15 September 2010, available at www.hbs.edu/research/pdf/09–051.pdf.

[134]   'Users of ratings, such as investors who consider buying a security, desire accurate ratings. However, firms whose securities are rated prefer favorable ratings as it directly
lowers their cost of capital, and do not necessarily prefer accurate ones. Since rating

on at all? Arguably, all those supposedly hyper-rational and certainly highly sophisticated market participants knew very well that the ratings produced by the major CRAs suffered major shortcomings. I have already argued that the most plausible explanation is that they were used as *heuristics* and their use was evidence of grand scale herding.

Several analysts have addressed the issue of why credit ratings have not been accurate in the market for structured products.[135] They argued that the root of the problem was to be found in ratings inflation, coarse information disclosure and conflicts of interests. CRAs had a legal obligation to regularly disclose information about their models to their issuers. This allowed issuers to fine-tune their packaging strategies, with the possible collusion or at least acquiescence of CRAs, and issue rate-to-measure securities. Namely, issuers could use CRA know how to put together securitized assets that were just on the lower boundary of the range of eligible AAA securities.

On the other hand, ratings inflation was exacerbated by: (1) the use of ratings by regulators, which conferred an intrinsic value to ratings over and above their true ability to measure risk, (2) the presence of an increased number of investors who just followed the herd and mostly used ratings as heuristics, and (3) increased competition. Ironically, the entry of Fitch in the relevant market led CRAs to provide issuers with more favourable ratings.[136]

As information coarseness leads to market opacity and makes monitoring more costly, it fosters adverse selection. The analysis of the typical prospectus for structured credits reveals that the quality (as opposed to quantity) of the information available to investors though the prospectus was poor for two reasons. First, only probability of default (PD) and not Loss Given Default (LGD) was provided.[137] Second, the models used by CRAs were based on assumptions of default correlations that clearly underestimated losses because of price changes due to a downturn, which, however, were as important. Third, their methodologies were both flawed and insufficiently scrutinized. For instance, the 'default and ratings

agencies' revenues come from issuers, a basic tension exists between the desire of raters to please individual paying customers and the raters' need to maintain the overall precision and informativeness of credit ratings.' *Ibid.*, p. 1.

[135] Marco Pagano and Paolo Volpin, 'Credit Ratings Failures: Causes and Policy Options', in Mathias Dewatripont, Xavier Freixas and Richard Portes (eds.), *Macroeconomic Stability and Financial Regulation: Key Issues for the G20* (CEPR, 2009), pp. 129–48, available as an e-book at www.voxeu.org/reports/G20_Ebook.pdf.
[136] See Becker and Milbourn, 'Increased Competition'.
[137] *Ibid.*

transition probabilities of structured products' were not 'consistent with those of corporate and sovereign ratings'.[138] Fourth, CRA methodologies did not really consider the fat tails of the risk distribution curves,[139] i.e., the more extreme default scenarios.

Moreover, while many structured credit securities often bundled together underlying debt obligations emanating from a multitude of obligors, CRAs did not make public the estimated correlation of obligors in the asset pool. This was a major shortcoming, as the cross-correlations could greatly assist investors in assessing whether the rating was based on expectations that were in-line with their own.[140] Arguably, lack of a designated regulator specifically assigned the task of back-testing the rating results further exacerbated the unreliability of ratings. In this context, the new EU legislation governing CRAs that provides both for the back-testing of their ratings[141] and their direct supervision by the newly established European Securities Markets Authority,[142] discussed in Chapter 6, could prove the ultimate reality test regarding the viability of incorporation of ratings within the regulatory framework applicable to financial institutions and investments. CRA failings probably make a very good case for a formal international body that will act as knowledge manager and risk regulator in a global context. Thus, I provide an outline of a relevant proposal in Chapter 8.

Finally, investors often used ratings as a measure to value structured credit products.[143] Ratings were wrongfully perceived as a suitable benchmark to compare different fixed-income instruments. In fact, investors used ratings in order to price fixed income products, when reliable price quotations were unavailable,[144] which in the case of CDOs was not unusual. This was a seriously flawed use of ratings, because asset value is in most cases linked to the marketability/liquidity of the asset and

---

[138] Carney, 'Financial Market Turbulence'.
[139] CESR, 'The Role of Credit Rating Agencies', in Structured Finance Consultation Paper, para. 87.
[140] 'One of the distinctive characteristics of structured products is the fact that changes to these assumptions and the related correlations have an impact on the rating that can be greatly magnified', *ibid.*, para. 86
[141] Regulation (EC) No. 1060/2009 of the European Parliament and of the Council of 16 September 2009 on credit rating agencies OJ L 302/1, 17 November 2009.
[142] Regulation (EU) No. 513/2011 of the European Parliament and of the Council of 11 May 2011 amending Regulation (EC) No. 1060/2009 on credit rating agencies OJ L 145/30, 31 July 2011.
[143] *Ibid.*   [144] IMF, GFSR 'Containing Systemic Risks', p. 55.

prospective levels of liquidity, especially in times of market stress (when liquidity really matters), cannot be measured *ex ante*.

4. Flawed regulations

4.1 *Capital and investor protection regulations*

Bank regulation in the pre-GFC era assumed that policies aimed to guarantee the soundness of individual banks could also safeguard the soundness of the whole banking system. As a result, regulatory policies and risk management focused on individual institutions' behaviour and assumed that protecting the financial health of those would be sufficient to guard against systemic risk. Namely, requisite regulations had a micro-prudential rather than macro-prudential focus. This approach was problematic in many respects.

First, it assumed that the rational behaviour of one market actor could also be used to predict the behaviour of all other market actors and thus of the financial system.[145] As a result, it neglected the fact that there are cases where even rational actions of prudent financial institutions can have negative implications for the system as a whole. Consider the case of a bank that suffers large losses on some of its loans. The prudent choice for this bank is to reduce its lending activities and reduce its assets to a level which is in line with its smaller capital base. If the bank in question is large, or the losses affect several banks at the same time, the individual bank's attempt to rebuild its capital base will drain liquidity from the system. Less lending by some banks will translate into less funding to other banks, which, if other sources of liquidity are not found, might be forced to cut lending levels. Credit restriction will, of course, have an impact on economic growth, lowering output and leading to further decreases in asset values, amplifying the deleveraging process.[146] Yet Basel capital regulations were mostly built on the micro-prudential approach. They also made no attempt to restrain leverage nor did they pay any particular attention to institution and system specific levels of liquidity. Both excessive leverage and a liquidity crunch were, of course, at the heart of the GFC.

Capital regulations presented also a number of other flaws: (1) their pro-cyclical nature; (2) a fostering of disastrous regulatory arbitrage through excessive asset transformation; (3) neglect of liquidity; and

---

[145] UNCTAD Report, pp. 21–2.   [146] See Geneva Report, pp. 5–6.

(4) adherence to a risk-modelling approach which encouraged leverage, through assumption by banks of colossal amounts of short-term debt. All these issues are discussed more extensively in Chapter 5. Basel capital requirements also showed a poor appreciation of the importance and cost of strong equity cushions in the event of a crisis.[147] As a result, most financial institutions were found to be severely under-capitalized and virtually insolvent.

The use of credit ratings was deeply problematic for the reasons mentioned above. Yet, reliance on credit ratings was strongly entrenched in investor protection regulations, which were excessively reliant on rating triggers.[148] Those regulations were deeply flawed. First, they gave ample incentives to hold illiquid assets that appeared to be, according to the prevailing model, low risk and high return. Thus, banks, which can hold and absorb the risk from highly illiquid structured credit products, would instead off-load them to willing buyers who had no skill or ability to manage the risk emanating from those securities. Second, regulations forcing institutional investors to invest only in AAA rated assets led to massive sales following the first downgrades. These 'crowded' sales took place in a declining market and were not dictated by any funding needs but were just forced by institutional investors' legal mandate. As a result, both market prices of such assets and the quality of those investors' balance sheets sharply deteriorated, due to a strong emphasis on mark-to-market accounting, which led to a generalized crisis of confidence and the impression of a universal collapse in asset values, especially those of structured credit securities.[149]

4.2   'Too-big-to-fail' institutions and lack of cross-border special resolution regimes

'Too-big-to-fail' institutions, also called Systemically Important Financial Institutions (SIFIs) have, by all accounts, been at the heart of the crisis.[150] 'Too-big-to-fail' is normally defined as an institution (including

---

[147] 'Critics of these capital regulations have rightly pointed to these capital requirements as having contributed to the subprime crisis by permitting banks to maintain insufficient amounts of equity capital per unit of risk undertaken in their subprime holdings.' Calomiris, 'Financial Innovation', p. 66.

[148] See also Turner Review, p. 22.

[149] Carney, 'Addressing Financial Market Turbulence', p. 4.

[150] UNCTAD Report; Simon Jonhson, 'Too-big-to-fail, Politically', 18 June 2009, available at baselinescenario.com/2009/06/18/too-big-to-fail-politically/. Johnson, an MIT

investment firms, funds and insurance companies) the failure of which would mean serious disruption to the function of the financial system distorting its ability to facilitate orderly payments and settle transactions between institutions and between institutions and consumers within the domestic or the international markets. Such a development may also trigger a crisis of confidence in the financial system leading to a chain of failures (systemic failure).[151]

The orderly operation of the financial system in ensuring economic growth and the proper function of the economy through the channelling of resources and facilitation of payments and settlements of transactions is of vital importance to any modern economy. It follows that any serious disruption in the orderly operation of the financial system would also mean serious disruption in the daily lives of millions and millions of businesses, individuals and families. As a result, 'too-big-to-fail' institutions have operated for a long time under an implicit government undertaking that, although a private business, their continuous existence as a going concern is guaranteed by the taxpayer whatever the circumstances of the institution's failure. The very costly bail-outs that several Western countries undertook in 2008 to rescue their ailing banks have proved this point beyond any doubt. In fact, a (small) number of those banks[152] continue in existence until this day because of taxpayer money. The (inevitable in most cases) bail-out of banks deepened the crisis and led, in part, to the sovereign debt crises being experienced by a number of countries, chiefly Ireland, and to lesser extent many other EU countries and nearly the UK.

The above findings make even more striking the fact that the international banking community lacked, and still lacks, a single resolution and insolvency system for complex SIFIs.[153] The collapse of Lehman

professor and former IMF chief economist, sees regulatory failure leading to the crisis as inextricably interwoven with the fact that regulators allowed banks to become 'too-big-to-fail'.

[151] See also Group 30, 'Financial Reform: A Framework for Financial Stability', 15 January 2009, p. 19, available at www.group30.org/pubs/reformreport.pdf.

[152] So-called 'zombie' banks. See Edward J. Kane, 'Redefining Systemic Risk', Boston College mimeo, May 2010, p. 5, available at www.frbatlanta.org/documents/news/conferences/10fmc_kane.pdf.

[153] Emilios Avgouleas, Charles Goodhart and Dirk Schoenmaker, 'Bank Recovery and Resolution Plans (Living Wills) as the Catalyst of Global Financial Reform' (2012) 8 *Journal of Financial Stability*, in press; Richard Herring, 'Wind-Down Plans as an Alternative to Bailouts: The Cross-Border Challenge', in Kenneth E. Scott, George P. Shultz and John B. Taylor (eds.), *Ending Government Bailouts as We Know Them* (Stanford, CA: Hoover Institution Press, 2010), pp. 125–62.

Brothers clearly showed that, while financial groups are managed on an integrated global basis, their corporate structures are highly fragmented and chaotic, as a result of regulatory and tax arbitrage, national licensing requirements or in order to shield the rest of group from legal claims.[154] Moreover, with the exception of the US, where the FDIC regime only extended to deposit-taking banks and similar institutions, most developed markets lacked even national special resolution regimes for banks.[155] This was a serious regulatory loophole which intensified market uncertainty and ensuing creditor panic leading to depressed market valuations for financial institutions and instant drying up of institutional lending.[156] A number of jurisdictions, chiefly the US through the Dodd–Frank Act (Title II), have introduced special resolution regimes for SIFIs. There are also efforts underway to improve the framework for cross-border resolution of these institutions, but the progress is admittedly fraught with legal obstacles.[157]

5.   Market failure, regulatory failure and the financial revolution

The problem wasn't that Lehman had been allowed to fail; the problem was that Lehman had been allowed to succeed.[158]

5.1   An alternative explanation of market and regulatory failure?

I have already argued that a more nuanced explanation of the discussed market and regulatory failures is required to complement the three

---

[154] Richard Herring and Jacopo Carmassi, 'The Corporate Structure of International Financial Conglomerates, Complexity and Its Implications for Safety and Soundness', in Allen N. Berger, Phillip Molyneux and John Wilson (eds.) *Oxford Handbook of Banking* (Oxford University Press, 2010), pp. 173–204. See also BCBS, 'Report and Recommendations', pp. 14–16.

[155] The Run on the Rock, (House of Commons, Treasury Committee, Fifth Report of Session 2007–8, 24 January 2008). In the UK, this defect was remedied in 2009 with the enactment of the Banking Act 2009. For a discussion of the troubled rescue of Northern Rock and of the 2009 Act's special resolution regime, see Emilios Avgouleas, 'Banking Supervision and the Special Resolution Regime of the Banking Act 2009: The Unfinished Reform' (2009) 4 *Capital Markets Law Journal* 201–35.

[156] For more extensive discussion of this issue see Chapter 5, Section 4.3.

[157] For extensive analysis of reform efforts in the context of cross-border resolution of SIFIs, see Chapter 7, Sections 6 and 7.

[158] Paraphrasing Mike Lewis, *The Big Short: Inside the Doomsday Machine* (New York: W.W. Norton & Co., 2010), p. 234. The same observation applied to Beas Steams, *ibid.*

provided above: possible capture, misaligned incentives; and underestimation of behavioural factors. I have also observed that this explanation must be of such analytical force as to account for the following two puzzles: (1) why reputation restraints and the fear of destroying long-term shareholder value apparently did not play any role in redressing the aforementioned failures? (2) Why regulators (and market actors) did not appreciate the extent to which global markets had become a complex multi-factor game, whose orderly operation was much dependent on the continuous existence of satisfactory levels of liquidity and absence of confidence shocks?

As explained in Chapter 2, in the past twenty years, financial innovation – a term used to describe imaginative uses of finance, starting with Milken's junk bonds, aided by advancements in mathematical finance utilized in risk modelling – technology breakthroughs and the nearly universal abduction of national capital restriction, led to the emergence of a new and poorly understood market landscape. In this landscape capital flows across borders have been free and take place at a very fast speed. They often support transactions in very complex instruments. As a result the disparate roots and branches of the global financial system have become a tightly knit and interdependent whole, rendering financial centres, national economies and individual institutions vulnerable to the volatile winds and moods of global markets. The new market landscape also provided very little room for the untangling of the purpose of individual transactions or for assertion of counterpartys' solvency.

I have already argued that the financial revolution was equal in its importance to other technology driven economic revolutions. An economic revolution is taken here to mean two things: (1) realignment of (or provision of the ability to realign) the means and capacity of production and distribution; and (2) a reconfiguration of wealth accumulation and power relationships within and across societies. Arguably, the financial revolution has the potential to achieve the first by promoting climate change projects and poverty eradication schemes through the revolutionization of access to finance that it has brought about. This not only can substantially shorten the Schumpeterian cycle but more importantly can foster economic and social mobility within and across nations. Moreover, it has strongly exhibited the second characteristic through the massive expansion of the share of the financial services industry in the GDP of many Western countries, including the UK and the US.

Three consequences of the financial revolution stand out: (1) the building of strong links of interconnectedness between financial institutions and economic centres; (2) the ability to shift vast amounts of funds around the globe at the push of a button; and (3) the generation of tradable assets that not only lack any intrinsic value but often are not even linked to anything that has intrinsic value, creating markets for the sake of markets. It was the same products of course that linked the relatively slow world of retail lending markets with the fast reacting universe of capital markets. In that respect, they acted like a conveyor belt, recycling systemic risk across the globe, linking diverse financial centres and tying financial institutions and investors with very dissimilar profiles and goals firmly together. For that reason shocks were transmitted so rapidly from one asset market (US sub-prime credit market) to another (the capital markets), to seemingly unrelated (to investment banks) insurance companies such as AIG, and large financial institutions such as the US, Swiss, UK and European banks. At the same time, nobody had a clear idea about the true impact of trillions of dollars of derivatives trades (in notional value), turned over every day, on the real economy and commodity and other physical asset markets.

Accordingly, another cause of the market and regulatory failures that led to the GFC must be added: flawed/incomplete understanding of the financial revolution. Although neo-liberal politicians and regulators, such as Alan Greenspan, did have a 'mystical' belief in the self-correcting power of free markets and did favour the expansion of the financial sector as a share of GDP, promoting deregulation and financial innovation in order to boost flagging western economies and not fall out with powerful industry interests, they also failed to appreciate the full force and dimensions of the financial revolution.[159] They based their decisions on very limited knowledge of the modern financial world and very limited research, especially as regards the role of the shadow banking sector.[160]

---

[159] This view is also corroborated by former US Federal Reserve Chairman Alan Greenspan's testimony before Congress (the House Committee on Oversight and Government Reform) in October 2008. Responding to the following question by Henry Waxman, Chairman of the Congressional Committee: 'You had the authority to prevent irresponsible lending practices that led to the subprime crisis. You were advised to do so by many others. ... Do you feel that your ideology pushed you to make decisions that you wish you had not made?' Greenspan replied: '*Yes, I've found a flaw ...* Those of us who looked to the self-interest of lending institutions to protect shareholders' equity, myself included, are in a state of shocked disbelief ... The modern risk management paradigm held sway for decades. The whole intellectual edifice, however, collapsed in the summer of last year', available at oversight.house.gov/index.php?option=com_content&view=article&id=3470&catid=42:hearings&Itemid=2.

[160] In this context Gillian Tett has noted: '[A] poster ... created by economists at the New York Federal Reserve ... [e]ntitled *The Shadow Banking System* ... depicts how money

As already explained in Chapter 2 this view constitutes an overhauled and appropriately adapted version of the thesis advanced by Kindleberger regarding the role of exogenous developments (mostly technological breakthroughs) in fostering financial crises, whereby a period of exuberance in valuations is always followed by sharp reductions triggering economic disclocation.[161]

Whether because the proper analytical tools were not in place and the old ones were rusty and patently unsuitable, or because of lack of intellectual curiosity, which also brings a certain amount of comfort, regulators and, for that matter, most academic powerhouses whose job was to challenge doctrine, just swam with the flow. As a result, no light was shed on the potential for disastrous interaction between the aforementioned regulatory actions and omissions and the largely un-codified forces and effects of the financial revolution, as well as the interplay between the different elements of this revolution.[162] It is, therefore, arguable that if they had known better, they would have acted differently to rescue their reputations or in order to save their jobs.

A classic example of such ignorance is the reach of regulation. Systemically important financial institutions (such as insurance companies) had been left out of the framework of prudential regulation. One of the reasons for such omission was that the potential for spillovers between

goes round the modern world, particularly (but not exclusively) in the US ... [it] is a reminder of how *clueless* most investors, regulators and rating agencies were before 2007 about finance ... That was a striking, *terrible omission* ... Little wonder, then, that *so few people immediately appreciated the significance* of the seizing up of shadow banking in 2007'. See Gillian Tett, 'Road Map that Opens up Shadow Banking', Markets Insight Section, *Financial Times*, 18 November 2010, available at www.ft.com/cms/s/0/1a222bf4-f33d-11df-a4fa-00144feab49a.html#axzz15pOcDSC1 (emphasis added).

[161] See Charles Kindleberger, *The World in Depression, 1929–1939* (Berkeley, CA: University of California Press, 1973); Charles P. Kindleberger and Rober Z. Alliber, *Manias, Panics, and Crashes: A History of Financial Crisis* (Hoboken, NJ: Wiley, 5th edn, 2005), especially pp. 26, 54–8.

[162] This is also an admission made by Robert Rubin, an ex Goldman Sachs CEO, ex US Treasury Secretary, ex Citigroup chairman, and arguably the most important man in the global financial services industry in the past two decades after Alan Greenspan. In a question by Financial Crisis Investigatory Commission member Douglas Joltz-Eakin, Rubin replied: '[V]ery few people foresaw the full combination ....You had a large combination of forces that came together .... I think it was this extraordinary combination of many factors that came together ... *What I didn't see, and virtually nobody saw, was that it wasn't only those excesses but it was so many other factors coming together at that time and I think it's that combination that led to this crisis ...*' Robert Rubin, Testimony to the Financial Crisis Investigative Commission, 8 April 2010,Transcript of the testimony available at www.cspan.org/Watch/Media/2010/04/08/HP/R/31560/Govt+officials+testifying+Frmr+Citi+execs+apologize.aspx (emphasis added).

the regulated banking sector and the unregulated hedge funds was underestimated, in spite of the early evidence of such a link provided by the Long-Term Capital Management (LTCM) debacle.[163] Regulators showed a striking inertia to tackle this problem in spite of the increasing interconnectedness created by innovative financial instruments, such as CDOs and CDSs, which were also traded by banks' proprietary trading desks. The behaviour of unregulated entities in the event of a crisis can force these funds to lower their leverage, leading to asset fire sales.[164] Thus, unsupervised entities may eventually become powerful systemic risk dissemination channels. Capture alone cannot, in this case, properly account for regulatory restraint, since it would logically have been cancelled out by a desire to build regulatory empires. Therefore, the misunderstood economic revolution explanation offered above is lent additional force.

One argument that can plausibly be raised here against the limited knowledge/understanding of the financial revolution explanation is that the GFC was not different in its causes and consequences than previous financial crises. An important work by Rogoff and Reinhart[165] has shown with conviction (echoing, to a certain extent, Minsky's argument) that excessive accumulation of debt always leads to a financial

---

[163] For a good description of the LTCM debacle see Roger Lowenstein, *When Genius Failed: The Rise and Fall of Long-Term Capital Management* (New York: Random House, 2001).

[164] It has been convincingly argued that in those cases the largely unregulated hedge funds can become serious sources of contagion. See Zeno Adams, Roland Füss and Reint Gropp, 'Modeling Spillover Effects Among Financial Institutions: A State-Dependent Sensitivity Value-at-Risk (SDSVaR) Approach', European Business School Research Paper No. 10–12, 1 June 2010, available at papers.ssrn.com/sol3/papers.cfm?abstract_id=1705997. The authors show that in times of increased market volatility, like a financial crisis, 'investment banks and, especially, hedge funds play a major role in the transmission of shocks to the other financial institutions'. This view is corroborated by the IMF's report at the height of the crisis on the impact of hedge fund deleveraging due to margin calls and other stresses. See IMF, Global Financial Stability Report, 'Financial Stress and Deleveraging Macrofinancial Implications and Policy', October 2008, Chapter 1, especially Boxes 1.4 and 1.5. One of the earlier studies on how hedge funds can act as systemic risk dissemination channels is Nicholas Chan, Mila Getmansky, Shane M. Haas and Andrew W. Lo, 'Systemic Risk and Hedge Funds', MIT Sloan Research Paper No. 4535–05, 22 February 2005, available at papers.ssrn.com/sol3/papers.cfm?abstract_id=671443.

[165] With an impressive collection of data referring to economic crises since the twelfth century, economics professors Rogoff and Reinhart have highlighted striking similarities between the financial crises they studied, even if the trigger and mechanics of transmission of the economic shocks are different from crisis to crisis. See Reinhart and Rogoff, *This Time Is Different*.

crisis, whether a sovereign or a banking sector crisis. Therefore, Rogoff and Reinhardt argue that 'this time was not different'. Past financial crises had also created international contagion and caused the collapse of financial institutions and reduction of economic output, chiefly during the Great Depression.[166] Nonetheless, 'this time was different' in two crucial aspects: interconnectedness and speed of transmission of shocks. Heightened interconnectedness created by the financial revolution and failure to appreciate the loop feedback effect of shadow banking on risk management were the most critical and unprecedented factors. Also the speed of transmission of systemic shocks from one market to the other and from one financial center to the other, due to heightened levels of homogenization, was unprecedented. These developments essentially necessitated a globally co-ordinated public rescue effort.

The influence of trade liberalization on the financial revolution is indicative. The GFC might have not been so severe in the absence of global trade imbalances. Nonetheless, global trade imbalances also existed in the past but did not have the debilitating impact they had in the 2000s. The reason for this difference was the financial revolution, which led to the development of three trends that had not been evident in the past. First, trade surpluses could easily be invested in the financial systems of other countries, and especially of the US, because of absence of restrictions on capital flows and of the ability of those financial systems to absorb the investment due to their very strong links with shadow banking activities. Second, with the aid of financial innovation, the financial sector could commoditize any kind of physical asset. Thus, investors were spoilt for choice, whether they wanted to speculate in any kind of asset market or (superficially) hedge a risk arising from positions taken in those markets. Third, the mega-profits generated by the financial sector, due to financial innovation and the hidden public subsidies banks enjoyed, meant that investing in the financial sector was, on the face of it, the only 'clever' thing to do.

The explanation offered here of the semi-unknown, misunderstood and misused financial revolution does not suggest that, if politicians and regulators had acted differently, they would necessarily have been successful at preventing or containing the crisis. There is no certainty that they would have managed to devise proper public policy/public intervention tools to regulate/supervise the emerging sources of systemic risk or prevent the interplay of the disparate forces of the financial revolution,

---

[166] *Ibid.*

much like the challenge lawmakers face when they attempt to regulate scientific revolutions.[167] Regulators would also have to have found ways to force financial institutions to abandon excessive rent-seeking. This could have been achieved either through the imposition of a (properly calibrated) tax on such activities or by instilling a strong market discipline mechanism through the elimination of the 'too-big-to-fail' problem. Setting aside the big challenge that the calibration of such a tax and the fashioning of a requisite legal framework would entail, the institutions concerned would have easily resorted to arbitrage between different regulatory regimes. Therefore, both a tax on the financial sector and/or measures to eliminate the 'too-big-to-fail' problem would have failed in the absence of a global agreement.

Moreover, those hypothetically 'wise, well informed, and prudent regulators' would have also faced insurmountable co-ordination and enforcement obstacles, given the fact that global finance is governed by strong domestic regulatory regimes and very weak international supervisory structures. Since most of the problems arising as a result of the financial revolution have a very strong cross-border and global dimension, supervisors/politicians' knowledge and best intentions would still prove insufficient in the absence of strong cross-border governance structures for global finance. It follows that global governance structures are indispensable to any realistic plan to prevent a future crisis that would be based on the ever evolving properties of the financial revolution and their interplay with other factors such as market overconfidence, greed, capture and mainstream market failures such as information asymmetries.

5.2   Complexity, emergence and the GFC

It has been argued that the complex and interwoven properties of the contemporary financial system, which have greatly contributed to the building of the GFC and accounted for its devastating consequences, were the product of evolutionary processes in global finance. According to this view, the financial system should be examined under the same lens that we see eco-systems. As this argument goes, global financial markets

---

[167] See David A. Dana, 'Can the Law Track Scientific Risk and Technological Innovation?: The Problem of Regulatory Definitions and Nanotechnology', Northwestern Public Law Research Paper No. 10–83, 19 November 2010, available at papers.ssrn.com/sol3/papers. cfm?abstract_id=1710928. 'In constructing the definitions of what is regulated, two key challenges are to align the definitions with the risks that motivated the establishment of the regulatory regime and to build in dynamism into the definitions so that they adapt to changes in scientific understanding and technology', ibid., p. 1.

have in the past two decades presented many of the characteristics that are associated with complexity theory[168] and the best way to understand financial crises is to view them as 'unpredictable' natural phenomena, which inevitably occur to all complex and unbalanced systems.[169]

Complexity theory is an interdisciplinary framework used to understand complex systems. The gist of complexity theory (and of its twin chaos theory) is that while some systems are too complex to accurately predict their future, they do, nevertheless, exhibit identifiable underlying patterns that can help individuals cope with those systems' complex workings. Provision of convincing evidence of the assumptions of complexity theory requires extensive computations. Thus, while it was first floated a long time ago, it was only recently with the advent of information technology breakthroughs that the theory was lent credibility. Complexity theory has made its biggest inroads in furthering our understanding of complex adaptive systems[170] using in many areas the assumptions of the older 'systemtheorie'.[171]

[168] See, in general, Herbert A. Simon, 'The Architecture of Complexity' (1962) 106(6) *Proceedings of the American Philosophical Society* 467–82. More recent representative publications include: Stuart Kauffman, *At Home and in the Universe: The Search for the Laws of Self-organization and Complexity* (New York: Oxford University Press, 1996); Michael Waldrop, *Complexity: The Emerging Science at the Edge of Order and Chaos* (New York: Simon & Schuster, 1st edn, 1992); Roger Lewin, *Complexity: Life at the Edge of Chaos* (Chicago University Press, 2000). For a discussion of complexity at the micro-universe of structured finance transactions see, e.g., Steven L. Schwarcz, 'Regulating Complexity in Financial Markets' (2009) 87 *Washington University Law Review* 211–68.

[169] Lo, 'Regulatory Reform'; Michele Zanini, 'Power Curves: What Natural and Economic Disasters Have in Common', *McKinsey & Co. Online Journal* (June 2009), available at www.mckinseyquarterly.com/Power_curves_What_natural_and_economic_disasters_ have_in_common_2376. See also Taleb, *The Black Swan*.

[170] E. Ahmed, A. S. Elgazzar and A. S. Hegazi, 'An Overview of Complex Adaptive Systems' (2005) 32 *Mansoura Journal of Mathematics* 27. The following is among the most comprehensive definitions of Complex Adaptive Systems: '[The term] refers to a field of study and resultant conceptual framework for natural and artificial systems that defy reductionist (top-down) investigation. Such systems are generally defined as being composed of populations of adaptive agents whose interactions result in complex non-linear dynamics, the results of which are emergent system phenomena ... The study of Complex Adaptive Systems (CAS) is the study of high-level abstractions of natural and artificial systems that are generally impervious to traditional analysis techniques. Macroscopic patterns emerge from the dynamic and nonlinear interactions of the systems low-level (microscopic) adaptive agents.' Jason Brownlee, 'Complex Adaptive Systems', Technical Report 070302A, Centre for Information Technology Research, Swinburne University of Technology, March 2007, p. 1, available at www.ict.swin.edu. au/personal/jbrownlee/2007/TR05–2007.pdf.

[171] Two of the most representative publications, which have laid out the foundations of systems theory and at the same time described its applications to social phenomena, are: Ludwig von Bertalanffy, 'An Outline of General Systems Theory' (1950) 1 *British*

Complexity theory has been employed in the study of the global financial crisis either independently[172] or in conjunction with its close relative –
so-called network theory. Unlike most other theories of scientific and
human development, theory of complexity focuses on the evolution of a
system as a whole and less on the study of the behaviour of its individual
constituents. Thus, complexity theory could prove a useful tool to policy
makers dealing with financial markets. A good example for its application
could be capital adequacy regulation, where Basel I and Basel II standards wrongfully focused on the micro-prudential dimension (behaviour
and stability of individual institutions) and failed to take into account
the macro-prudential dimension (behaviour and stability of the financial
system as a whole).

In turn, network theory has been used to explain the three most
important characteristics of global finance in the past decade: complexity, homogeneity and interconnectedness. These phenomena were at the
root of the global financial crisis because their combined effect increased
the fragility of the global financial system (network).[173] First, the nodes of
the global financial system,[174] a term used in natural sciences to explain
a distribution or communication point or endpoint (a hub of activity),
increased exponentially making the system more dense and complex.[175]
This development also increased the interconnectedness of the different
parts of/actors within the system, raising manifold the risk of contagion,
namely, the very risk bank regulation guards against.

Second, financial innovation, in the form of the 'originate-to-distribute'
and 'originate-to-arbitrage' models and derivatives trading increased
further network (mono-)dimensionality leading to massive homogenization of the global financial services industry, thus depriving the system of
its natural stabilizers that could replenish the markets with capital during
the crisis. As mentioned above, homogenization or (mono-)dimensionality
meant that all banks' balance sheets looked more or less the same and

---

Journal for the Philosophy of Science 134–65 and Niklas Luhmann, *Social Systems* (Palo
Alto, CA: Stanford University Press, 1996).

[172] Lo, 'Regulatory Reform', 5.

[173] This, according to Haldane, is also 'a property exhibited by other complex adaptive networks, such as tropical rainforests', Haldane, 'Rethinking the Financial Network', p. 3.

[174] Nodes are scaled by (Total External Assets + Total External Liabilities) for each
node, and links between nodes i and j by (Total External Assetsij + Total External
Liabilitiesij)/(GDPi +GDPj), *ibid.*, p. 12, note 13.

[175] Haldane (at p. 12) characteristically notes: 'Nodes have ballooned, increasing roughly
14-fold. And links have become both fatter and more frequent, increasing roughly
6-fold. The network has become markedly more dense and complex', *ibid.*

their risk management strategies increasingly became similar in order to manage the same risks. Naturally, the gradual elimination of diversity, due to homogenization, made the global financial system less resistant to disturbance. These developments meant in turn that the network was vulnerable to feedback effects under stress (e.g., hoarding of liquidity and fire sales of assets), a characteristic that has also been identified in the spread of certain diseases. Also complexity and (mono-)dimensionality significantly enhanced Knightian uncertainties in the pricing of assets – causing inter-bank lending markets and the market for structured credit securities to come to a complete halt. Third, as the length of the global financial network shrunk, due to (1) the ICT revolution; (2) the ample availability of credit; and (3) the much higher size of cross-border capital flows, national financial systems became ever more connected and thus interdependent. As a result, they also became much more susceptible to cross-border spillovers.

According to a number of commentators, the global financial system also exhibits another property that is central to complex systems and thus complexity theory: emergence. Although this term has been widely used in philosophy since Aristotle – also appearing in the works of John Stuart Mill[176] and Julian Huxley[177] – and has more recently been used in epidemiology, ontology, psychology and the cognitive sciences, it remains notoriously difficult to define.[178] In simple terms, emergence means the novel

---

[176] John Stuart Mill, *A System of Logic* (London: Longmans, 1843) Book III, Chapter 6, §1.

[177] Julian S. Huxley and Thomas Henry Huxley, *Evolution and Ethics: 1893–1943* (London: The Pilot Press, 1947), p. 120.

[178] For many commentators the best definition of emergence has been offered by the philosopher G. H. Lewes (among other things the life partner of writer Mary Anne Evans (aka George Elliot)). Lewes defined emergence as: 'Every resultant is either a sum or a difference of the co-operant forces; their sum, when their directions are the same – their difference, when their directions are contrary. Further, every resultant is clearly traceable in its components, because these are homogeneous and commensurable. It is otherwise with emergents, when, instead of adding measurable motion to measurable motion, or things of one kind to other individuals of their kind, there is a co-operation of things of unlike kinds. The emergent is unlike its components insofar as these are incommensurable, and it cannot be reduced to their sum or their difference', George Henry Lewes, *Problems of Life and Mind* (London: Kegan Paul, Trench, Turbner and Co, 1875), vol. 2, p. 412. Arguably, the most comprehensive attempt to categorize the characteristics of emergence is P. E. Meehl and Wilfrid Sellars, 'The Concept of Emergence', in Herbert Feigl and Michael Scriven, (eds.), *Minnesota Studies in the Philosophy of Science, Volume I: The Foundations of Science and the Concepts of Psychology and Psychoanalysis* (University of Minnesota Press, 1956), pp. 239–52. Cf. Stephen C. Pepper, 'Emergence' (1926) 23 *Journal of Philosophy* 241–5. More recent works in the field are Jaegwon Kim, 'Making Sense of Emergence' (1999) 95 *Philosophical Studies* 3–36; Louise Antony, 'Making Room for

characteristics (qualities and structures) that supervene existing characteristics (qualities and structures) in a distinctive kind of physio-chemical process, being the product of a multitude of relatively simple interactions. Emergence appears always in complex systems during the process of self-organization and is normally empirically observed. In natural systems, emergent qualities display their own characteristic form of activity, while remaining in full accord with the completeness of fundamental physics. Emergent systems are identified by the fact that: (1) they exhibit radical novelty, in the sense that the specific characteristics of the system have not been observed before; (2) they present a certain level of coherence, in the sense that they maintain their specific characteristics over a period of time, they have characteristics of completeness; (3) they are the product of a dynamic (evolutionary) process; and (4) they can be observed and experienced. As this argument goes, the chief emergent property of the global financial system has been structured finance and trading in credit derivatives.[179]

5.3   The role of insider rent-seeking

I have already explained the intellectual and possible practical merits of complexity theory in improving prudential regulation. In addition, there is nothing in network theory that diminishes the argument advanced here that the financial revolution was an economic and knowledge revolution of the first order that stretched humanity to its limits. Nor does it refute the logical extension of this argument, namely that, in the absence of a better understanding of the nature of this revolution and the laying out of structures allowing for co-ordinated global information gathering and crisis prevention and management facilities, the GFC (like the Fukushima incident) was an accident waiting to happen, although the possibility that all different factors of the crisis would combine to a catastrophic effect was very limited, like all tail risks.

Nonetheless, the argument that views the global financial system as an evolutionary process with emergent properties that are not truly capable of being regulated does not provide a totally accurate picture. Not only has the system presented serious discontinuities in its development

the Mental: Comments on Kim's "Making Sense of Emergence"' (1999) 95 *Philosophical Studies* 37–44; Max Kistler (ed.), 'New Perspectives on Reduction and Emergence in Physics, Biology and Psychology' (2006) 151/3 *Synthese*, special issue.
[179]   Haldane, 'Rethinking the Financial Network'.

(unlike other emergent systems), but also the force that influenced the financial revolution most in the past thirty years, in the absence of meaningful regulatory controls, was rent seeking rather than genuine evolution. Individuals within financial institutions that could either understand the mechanics of the financial revolution or, more likely, conceive its potential to generate mega profits (both for the institution and its employees), under certain conditions, pushed the revolution to its limits to serve their own ends, conveniently fostering further obfuscation and complexity.[180]

The existence of a limited number of big players in the market for new financial products meant that a push to extract supra-competitive rents from exclusive access to the new financial technology could be unimaginably successful in the newly integrated global marketplace. There is ample evidence in the recent US Senate Report of how big US banks forced the boundaries of risky (reckless) lending in search of ever higher returns through the use of securitization.[181] Even in the absence of fraud, it is obvious that big banks were taking advantage of their higher sophistication/familiarity with the complex science of structured finance and were selling

---

[180] An SEC complaint against a big Wall Street investment bank, which has now been settled with the bank receiving a large fine without admission of responsibility, provides a characteristic example. According to the SEC's allegations: 'Goldman [Sachs] helped to create an investment fund that was designed to fail – a financial time bomb that eventually lost investors more than $1 billion ... In 2006, hedge fund master John Paulson asked Goldman . . to help him create a fancy type of mortgage-backed security fund, known in Wall Street-speak as a collateralized debt obligation. Paulson believed the nation's housing market was about to collapse, and he wanted a housing-backed investment to bet against. Goldman ... created ABACUS-2007-AC1 – [and] marketed the fund to others as a good buy, the SEC charges. Worse, Goldman never disclosed Paulson's involvement, or that he stood to make big bucks if the fund went south. [Paulson shorted the CDO betting on its failure. Eventually,] ABACUS plummeted in value ... Paulson's "short bet" earned him $1 billion in profits, while duped investors lost a similar sum ... Paulson paid Goldman $15 million for putting ABACUS together. Unlike Paulson, Goldman bet on ABACUS to succeed – and lost $90 million', 'Who's, Why's & How's of Allegations vs. Goldman' NYDailynews.com, 20 April 2010 available at www.nydailynews.com/money/2010/04/20/2010–04–20_whos_whys__hows_of_allegations_vs_goldman.html#ixzz18ZWclYPt. What was striking, in the scheme described in the SEC's complaint, apart from the colossal conflict of interests as per the SEC's allegations, was the extreme complexity of the transactions and the (allegedly) deliberate obfuscation of their true purpose by the investment bank concerned. See also Katherine Burton and Saijel Kishan, 'Paulson & Co. May Face Investor Lawsuits on Goldman Sachs CDO', *Business Week, Bloomberg*, 19 April 2010, available at www.businessweek.com/news/2010–04–19/paulson-co-may-face-investor-lawsuits-on-goldman-sachs-cdo.html.

[181] See Parts II and VI of the US Senate Report, Wall Street and the Financial Crisis.

to investors (even sophisticated investors) products that were known to be loss-making from the outset.[182]

In doing so bankers were motivated by narrow self-interest (greed), although in some cases they were also 'gambling' the bank. One explanation for this high risk behaviour is that, in several banks, senior management had a limited understanding of the financial revolution (though it was much superior to that of regulators, politicians and the public) and could not see/understand the long term risks to the viability of their institution generated by their rent-seeking activity.[183] Another equally convincing explanation is that bankers felt safe to do so. Their feeling of safety was the direct result of three factors: size of the institution, lobbying power and ability to externalize the risk assumed. Once the above had been secured opacity and complexity could be pushed further and further, not as the product of some kind of evolutionary process, but rather as straightforward misuse of the financial revolution in order to hide and protect insiders' rents.

As mentioned earlier, deregulatory policies led to a proliferation of 'too-big-to-fail' institutions. Bankers were also successful at cultivating a political and regulatory environment that minimized regulatory intervention and attendant public controls, a job made easier by the doctrinal adherence of key policy-makers and politicians to 'markets know best' beliefs. In addition, shifting the colossal risks they had assumed to outsiders was not too difficult to achieve because of the (implicit) government guarantee large financial institutions enjoyed. Finally, liberalization of global trade and capital flows'[184] greatly assisted market actors to connect different markets and different financial centres with extreme ease and minimal barriers. Without these developments, the GFC's severity and speed of transmission would have been much lower and the global

---

[182] The US Senate Report takes a very critical view of structured finance activities conducted by Deutsche Bank and Goldman Sachs and of the way they managed conflicts of interest or failed to disclose information to clients, *ibid.*, pp. 330–624.

[183] 'The information setting is complicated ...[t]he sell-side of the market (dealer banks, CDO and SIV managers) understands the complexity of the subprime chain, while the buy side (institutional investors) does not. Neither group knows where the risks are located, nor does either group know the value of every link in the chain. The chain made valuation opaque: information was lost as risk moved through the chain', Gorton, 'The Panic of 2007', p. 4.

[184] For the influence of the imminent Citibank with Travellers merger on the repeal of Glass–Stegall Act and the enactment of the Gramm–Leach–Billey Act, see Arthur E. Wilmarth, 'The Dark Side of Universal Banking: Financial Conglomerates and the Origins of the Subprime Financial Crisis' (2009) 41 *Connecticut Law Review* 963–1050, 972–5.

financial system would not have allowed the transfer of risk from the rent-seekers to the public at such a colossal grade. Therefore, what we have experienced is more or less the product of a totally man-made financial revolution founded on political decisions and technological breakthroughs, which was pushed to its limits due to rent-seeking. This finding does not imply that bankers had themselves an accurate picture of the colossal risks they were accumulating, because of interconnectedness, or had full knowledge of the feedback channels that systemic risk could take. It was sufficient that they had superior knowledge of the financial revolution and safely used it to further rent-seeking since the calculable risks could be borne by somebody else.

Of course, insiders' actions were presented in the outside world as value creation. Today, mostly with the benefit of hindsight, analysts with a serious grasp of the science of those complex products and finance techniques describe the industry's behaviour before the GFC as a classic rent-seeking exercise.[185] Financial institutions used the 'new science' to push risk out of their books to the wider society, lowering the price for assuming it and transferring the gains to insiders. Thus rent-seeking, rather than the change in demographics or the marked increase of Western households in the post-World War II boom years, might also be the better explanation for the exceptional growth of the wholesale financial services sector[186] and in the size of investment banks in the period between the last major recession in the early 1990s and 2008.

---

[185] There is a large number of works that are addressed both to the lay and the expert reader and more or less describe the financial system as a gigantic rent-generation mechanism in the 2000s and view that process (often referred to as bankers' greed) as one of the fundamental causes of the crisis. From the academic output the most forceful analysis of the takeover of the financial system and in that sense of the financial revolution in terms of direction and proceeds by insiders is offered in Simon Johnson and James Kwak, *13 Bankers: The Wall Street Takeover and the Next Financial Meltdown* (New York: Random House, 2010), especially Chapters 5–7. A good account is also provided by Joseph Stiglitz, *Freefall: America, Free Markets, and the Sinking of the World Economy* (New York: W. W. Norton Co., 2010), Chapters 1–2. Not surprisingly, Lewis's book is the most fascinating and informative of the non-expert works. See Mike Lewis, *The Big Short: Inside the Doomsday Machine* (New York: W. W. Norton Co., 2010). Other equally interesting works which canvass on the same theme are Andrew Ross Sorkin, *Too Big to Fail: The Inside Story of How Wall Street and Washington Fought to Save the Financial System – and Themselves* (New York: Viking, 2009) and Gillian Tett, *Fool's Gold: The Inside Story of J. P. Morgan and How Wall St. Greed Corrupted Its Bold Dream and Created a Financial Catastrophe* (New York: Free Press, 2009).

[186] '[T]he importance of financial services as a % of GDP has been swollen by two other factors, one illusory and the other harmful: ... The possible harmful effect is rent

5.4   A knowledge revolution

I have already argued that insufficient knowledge and imperfect understanding of the financial revolution may also account for the observed
regulatory inertia,[187] which was based on the flawed belief that structured
finance techniques and market sectors' superior knowledge had managed
to disperse risk efficiently, especially credit risk.[188] By adopting this seriously flawed belief regulators ignored, as has already been noted, the possibility for fatal correlations between different kinds of markets and their
increasing interconnectedness. They also considered as immaterial the
fact that the main motivation behind trading in innovative instruments
was regulatory arbitrage rather than any serious effort to manage risk.
There is now an emerging consensus that, during the last decade policies
relating to the financial markets were based on assumptions about how

   extraction ... some and perhaps much of the structuring and trading activity involved
   in the complex version of securitised credit, was not required to deliver credit intermediation efficiently. Instead, it achieved an economic rent extraction made possible
   by the opacity of margins, the asymmetry of information and knowledge between end
   users of financial services and producers, and the structure of principal/agent relationships between investors and companies and between companies and individual
   employees. Wholesale financial services ... grew to a size unjustified by the value of its
   service to the real economy.' Turner Review, pp. 47–9. UNCTAD also sees greed as the
   main reason for the implosion of the financial sector in the US, which in 1983 generated
   only 5 per cent of the US GDP and accounted for 7.5 per cent of total corporate profits
   and in 2007 generated 8 per cent of GDP (35 per cent growth) and accounted for 40 per
   cent of total corporate profits (533 per cent growth), UNCTAD Report, pp. 21–2.
[187] A similar explanation of regulatory failure and insider rent-seeking is discussed, in
   among others, Augusto de la Torre and Alain Ize 'Containing Systemic Risk Paradigm-
   Based Perspectives on Regulatory Reform', The World Bank, Policy Research Paper
   5523, January 2011. '[F]inancial bubbles and crises can happen when: (a) nobody really
   understands what is going on, and bad surprises lead to catastrophic mood reversals
   (the collective cognition paradigm); (b) some understand better than others, and they
   take advantage of their superior knowledge (the asymmetric information paradigm);
   (c) everybody understands what is going on, yet no one can do anything about it because
   occasional bubbles and crises occur naturally in a world with enforcement costs, agent
   heterogeneity and asymmetric market access (the costly enforcement paradigm); or
   (d) everybody understands what is going on, yet no one does anything about it because
   private interests do not coincide with those of society (the collective action paradigm)',
   ibid., p. 1.
[188] On regulators' cognitive challenges created by the financial revolution see also Torsten
   Strulik, 'Knowledge Politics in the Field of Global Finance? The Emergence of a
   Cognitive Approach in Banking Supervision', University of Warwick, Centre for the
   Study of Globalisation and Regionalisation Working Paper (195/06), 2006, available at
   wrap.warwick.ac.uk/1910/1/WRAP_Strulik_wp19506.pdf.

the financial system was supposed to work, not upon sufficient knowledge about how the financial system actually worked.[189]

The examples of limited understanding/knowledge that led to destructive risk management strategies are numerous. For instance, the use of structured finance conduits and SIVs gave a false picture both as to its risk divestment effectiveness[190] and its sustainability as a form of short- and medium-term financing.[191] Another characteristic example of this failure to grasp the complex aspects of the financial revolution was failure to realize the importance of hedging the underlying risk in complex structured finance transactions.[192] Finally, a clear indication of partial or otherwise flawed understanding of the financial revolution was the failure of all parties concerned to grasp how the interconnectedness created by the financial revolution pushed beyond all imaginable limits the 'too-big-to-fail' problem.

In general, most of the derivative products and structured securities, which linked the relatively slow world of retail lending markets with the fast reacting universe of capital markets and moved like a conveyor belt systemic risk across the globe ultimately recycling it, were also instruments very poorly understood. This might also be a convincing explanation of why centuries old legal principles, such as the notion of 'insurable interest', were cast aside,[193] in order to allow the market for credit derivatives

---

[189] McCulley and Clarida, 'What Has – and Has Not – Been Learned About Monetary Policy in a Low Inflation Environment?'.

[190] See Joshua D. Coval, Jakub Jurek and Erik Stafford, 'The Economics of Structured Finance' Harvard Business School, Working Paper 09–060, 2008, pp. 4–5, available at ssrn.com/abstract=1287363.

[191] See Hellwig, 'Capital Regulation after the Crisis'.

[192] '[E]quity to risk-weighted assets, is of course useless if the risk weights have not been chosen appropriately. An example is provided by UBS Investment Bank retaining the super-senior tranches of MBS CDOs of their own creation in their own portfolio and avoiding capital charges by engaging in credit defaults swaps against the credit risks of these securities. The correlation of the counterparty risks of these credit default swaps with the underlying credit risks of the MBS CDOs themselves went unnoticed', ibid., p. 3 (notes omitted).

[193] In English law, the concept of 'insurable interest' was fist defined in the Life Assurance Act 1774, which explained that, in the absence of 'insurable interest', taking out an insurance policy is tantamount to a gaming contract, Life Assurance Act 1774, 14 Geo. 3, c. 48 (Eng.). Also the Law Commission has explained that '[a]t its simplest, the doctrine of insurable interest requires that someone taking out insurance gains a benefit from the preservation of the subject matter of the insurance or suffers a disadvantage should it be lost'. See Law Commission & Scottish Law Commission, 'Insurable Interest', Insurance Contract Law Issues Paper 4, 2008, available at www.lawcom.gov.uk/docs/Insurance_Contract_Law_Issues_Paper_4.pdf.

to develop freely.[194] Another example is the passive approach of regulators and politicians. This is how a leading Wall Street professional describes this situation:[195]

> Why do some contracts, tantamount to crimes against humanity, not occasion more expressions of outrage from bankers, analysts, rating agencies, investors and regulators? (They do sometimes incur the wrath of the judiciary). These people often meekly accept a turgid, incestuous, redundant, disorganised and arthritic contract without even a bleat of protest.

It is doubtful that regulatory forbearance with respect to something so serious was merely driven by economic doctrine or even capture. An explanation that does not discard those reasons but also focuses on the fact that financial innovation and its interaction with the other elements of the financial revolution were a 'black hole' for regulators and policy makers ultimately sounds more convincing. It also provides a credible account of the obliteration of forces that would have counter-balanced capture or economic doctrine, such as regulators' self-preservation and empire building incentives/tendencies.

Inevitably, the consequence of these serious misunderstandings was that the spoils from the advent of financial revolution were seized by the few insiders and experts who had nearly monopolistic access to the new technology. As a result, the financial system did not innovate in a way that would enhance growth and manage household risks. Instead financial innovation, driven by tax and regulatory arbitrage, obfuscated bank balance sheets undermining market discipline and regulatory monitoring and increased risk, which was warehoused in opaque parts of the system.

It has been argued that the accrual of rents through innovation in a financial market is of a fundamentally different character than that observed in other areas of economic activity. According to this view, financial markets are about the effective use of existing information margins concerning existing assets and not about technological advances

---

[194] See Lynn Stout, 'How Deregulating Derivatives Led to Disaster, and Why Re-Regulating Them can Prevent Another', UCLA School of Law, Law-Econ Research Paper No. 09–13, November 2009, available at papers.ssrn.com/sol3/papers.cfm?abstract_id=1432654&rec=1&srcabs=1485518.

See also M. Todd Henderson, 'Credit Derivatives Are not "Insurance"', University of Chicago Law & Economics, Olin Working Paper No. 476, 2009, available at ssrn.com/abstract=1440945.

[195] Lee C. Buchheit, 'Did We Make Things Too Complicated?' (2008) 27 *International Financial law Review* 24–26, 26.

into hitherto unknown territory. The temporary monopoly over certain information or the better guess of a certain outcome in the market of a certain asset class allows market actors to gain a monopoly rent based on simple arbitrage. The more agents sense the arbitrage possibility and the quicker they are to make their disposals, the quicker the potential gain disappears. In this case, society also becomes better off, but in a one-off, static sense.[196] The fatal flaw in financial innovation that leads to crises and collapse of the whole system is demonstrated whenever herds of agents on the financial markets 'discover' that stable price trends in different markets (which are originally driven by events and developments in the real sector) allow for dynamic arbitrage, which entails investing in the probability of a continuation of the existing trend. Since many agents disposing of large amounts of (frequently borrowed) money bet on the same 'plausible' outcome (such as steadily rising prices of real estate, oil, stocks or currencies), they acquire the market power to move these prices far beyond sustainable levels.[197]

The above view provides an accurate picture of financial innovation when it is put to the service of speculators in search of rents. But it is very incomplete since it disregards the fact that certain aspects of financial innovation presented very useful breakthroughs in knowledge,[198] especially as regards the distribution/diversification of quantifiable credit and project (finance) risk and the revolutionization of the channels available to access finance.[199] Thus, there was no reason why the financial revolution could not, by analogy, follow the same virtuous path as other economic revolutions.[200]

---

[196] See UNCTAD Report, p. 3. As it is observed in the same report: 'Financial efficiency may have maximized the gains of the existing combination of factors of production and of its resources, but it has not reached into the future through an innovation that shifts the productivity curve upwards and that produces a new stream of income', *ibid.*

[197] *Ibid.*

[198] See Gregory N. Mankiw, 'The Growth of Nations' (1995) *Brookings Papers on Economic Activity* 275–326.

[199] See notes 213–15 in Chapter 2. See also Stelios Michalopoulos, Luc Laeven and Ross Levine, 'Financial Innovation and Endogenous Growth', NBER Working Paper No. 15356, September 2009. Cf. Josh Lerner, 'Innovation, Entrepreneurship and Financial Market Cycles', OECD Science, Technology and Industry Working Papers, OECD, Paris, 18 March 2010, available at dx.doi.org/10.1787/5kmjp6nt8rr8-en.

[200] Cf. R. Litan, 'In Defense of Much, But Not All, Financial Innovation', Brookings Institution, February 2010, available at www.brookings.edu/.../2010/0217_financial_innovation_litan.aspx.

6.   Concluding remarks

This chapter has provided an analytical discussion of the causes of
the global financial crisis highlighting the linkages between the prevailing macroeconomic conditions and the different government and
regulatory policies, market strategies and interests that led to the crisis
as well as the complexity and opacity of systemic risk feedback channels. It has also added a new explanation focusing on the effects of the
semi-unknown and misunderstood financial revolution that facilitated
widespread rent-seeking. This new interpretation of the multitude of
market and regulatory failures that led to the GFC complements the
discussion on the 'conventional' causes of the GFC. It also opens new
lines of critical enquiry. How much do we know about the interplay of
diverse market forces, herding and other behavioural factors and the
four main elements of the financial revolution: financial innovation,
increasing speed and complexity of transactions, open markets and the
resulting interconnectedness?

Although it is argued by a few experts that it is worth suffocating the
financial revolution in order to safeguard global financial stability, such
suffocation is not realistically possible in light of the massive size of the
shadow banking system. Can we then truly build regulatory systems
that protect against the risks generated by the financial revolution by
adopting solutions that only account for domestic or regional interests?
If we cannot, then the next step is to identify the kind of global institu-
tions/arrangements we need, not only to guard against the debilitating
power of the financial revolution but also to harness its creative forces.
Chapter 8 will address this issue by outlining a new model for global
financial governance.

PART II

The evolution of governance structures
for international finance

4

The evolution of global financial governance and development of International Financial Regulation

I. Introduction

In the previous two chapters, I gave an analytical overview of the ways financial markets developed in the past thirty years under the influence of deregulation and financial innovation and discussed the main causes of the Global Financial Crisis (GFC). Flawed regulations, including capital regulations, have been held to be among the principal causes of the GFC. This is a significant paradox, since a host of transnational regulatory networks (TRNs) spent the best part of the last decade building standards that could prevent a financial crisis of the nature and magnitude of the GFC. The only feasible way to provide a comprehensive explanation for this failure is by examining the historical evolution of international financial governance, which has mainly revolved around the production of international financial standards and the operation of TRNs.

We can broadly divide the history of global financial governance into three phases:

(1) the Bretton Woods Phase 1947–97, which also includes the post-Bretton Woods period (from 1972 onwards) when the world moved towards floating exchange rates as the fixed system became unsustainable;
(2) the post-Asian Crisis period 1998–2008, which saw the evolution of loose global financial governance structures into a tighter regulatory framework, called New International Financial Architecture (NIFA); and
(3) the post-2008 period, when national and international policies responding to the causes and consequences of the global financial crisis monopolize the international regulatory reform agenda.[1]

---

[1] During the first globalization phase, roughly the period between 1870 to World War I, there was no international financial regulation and very little domestic regulation so this chapter will not discuss that period in any detail.

This chapter provides an overview of governance developments and a description of how the remit of key institutions, formal and informal regulatory networks, and other relevant bodies evolved and changed during each phase. Attention will also be paid to the evolution of international financial regulation standards and the ways the developing international financial governance framework has interacted with trade agreements and has been influenced by major market events, mostly financial crises, and the shifting sands of ideology.

Global financial governance is based on a diverse 'legal' and organizational universe. This comprises: (1) international treaties, on which the most important International Financial Institutions (IFIs), such as the International Monetary Fund (IMF), the regional development banks, and the World Bank, have been founded; (2) state to state contact and co-ordination groups, such as the Group of 7 most developed countries (G-7) and the Group of Twenty most developed countries (G-20); and (3) 'informal', consensus-based (soft law) standards and structures (TRNs). The latter encompass regulatory agencies and central banks rather than governments. The private sector is either directly represented or has direct information and (often significant) policy input.[2] The existing complex web of TRNs, aided by IFIs and a universe of private sector bodies, is particularly active in three governance spheres:

(1) development of best practice standards, which are generally accepted principles, practices (acting as 'default rules'), and guidelines,[3] ranging from accounting standards to disclosure rules for securities issuers and capital adequacy requirements of banks. International Financial Standards (IFS) are incorporated into TRN member and non-member jurisdictions through national implementation;

(2) production of monitoring reports, which include IMF and World Bank's Financial Sector Assessment Program (FSAP) and Reports on the Observance of Standards and Codes (ROSCs); and

---

[2] For an excellent account of the structure of international financial regulation and the interface between the different TRNs and IFIs and between them and national authorities in each area of international financial regulation, see Rolf H. Weber, 'Mapping and Structuring International Financial Regulation – A Theoretical Approach' (2009) *European Business Law Review* 651–88.

[3] Mario Giovanoli, 'The Reform of the International Financial Architecture after the Global Crisis' (2010) 42 *New York University Journal of International Law & Politics* 81, 84.

(3) enforcement of co-operation through bilateral and multilateral (quasi-binding) Memoranda of Understanding (MoUs).[4]

The ensuing analysis highlights the long distance that the global financial governance wagon has covered and the several stops it has made in the process. As explained in the next chapter, pre-2008 governance structures failed dismally in their main task: the prevention or containment of a large-scale cross-border financial crisis. Therefore, global financial governance needs a radical enrichment of its structures and objectives. Current reform initiatives are very worthwhile. On the other hand, it is also worth arguing that instead of trying to overhaul the current system, new tracks (i.e., directions) and engine (i.e., governance bodies) are required in order to equip future governance structures with much needed capacity to address the challenges of the financial revolution properly and harness its creative forces. Of course, there is no easy way to address such 'lofty' and ambitious goals. Nonetheless, in Chapter 8 of this book I will attempt to sketch a tighter, more hierarchical and more encompassing model of governance for global financial markets.

The remainder of this chapter is divided into four sections. Section 2 provides a discussion of early age global governance structures and maps the emergence of the BCBS and the other major TRNs in the sphere of international finance. It also charts the path of trade liberalization and the rise of the development institutions that gained prominence in the last quarter of the twentieth century. Section 3 gives a critical analysis of the NIFA that came as a result of the Asian Crisis and was centred on IFS production by TRNs and a weak system of monitoring undertaken by the IMF and the World Bank. Section 4 gives a critical overview of the emerging international finance architecture in the post-GFC period and the role of the G-20 in global regulatory reform and international finance governance. Section 5 concludes.

2. The Bretton Woods and post-Bretton Woods phase

2.1. Introductory remarks

The first attempt to provide a comprehensive and universally binding governance framework for the international economic system and economic relations underpinning it was the Bretton Woods Conference and

---

[4] See Chris Brummer, 'Why Soft Law Dominates Finance and not Trade' (2010) 13 *Journal of International Economic Law* 623–43, 628–30.

the resulting Treaty.[5] Unlike what is often suggested, the two architects of the Bretton Woods framework, the US economist Henry Dexter White (first managing director of the IMF and later uncovered as a Soviet spy whilst working at the US Treasury) and John Maynard Keynes (the most celebrated British economist of the twentieth century with a colourful career as a financier) had conflicting ideas as to the institutional structures that should govern post-World War II economic relations. Eventually the structure adopted by the Bretton Woods Treaty was based on three main policy ideas/directions:[6]

(1) formal structures based on international treaties, which allowed for the establishment of international institutions with strong powers and capacity in terms of management of international monetary relations and facilitation of post-World War II reconstruction (and subsequent development) efforts;
(2) restrictions on capital flows, a policy that relied on closed financial markets, which retained a largely domestic focus, at least, until the development of the eurodollar market in the mid-1960s; and
(3) open markets for trade and investment.

These principles have had a paramount influence on the development of the Western world, as the countries of the Eastern bloc gradually withdrew from the arrangements for many decades, re-engaging in the 1980s.

The web of economic interactions/relationships among closed national systems was based on and managed through two interlinked international organizations: the IMF and the World Bank. The third international body that was part of the original framework, the International Trade Organization (ITO), assigned with responsibility to foster liberalization of trade and investment flows, never came to life. In addition, under the original framework, the overall political co-ordination of economic affairs was to take place through the newly established UN and its Economic

---

[5] United Nations Monetary and Financial Conference, Bretton Woods, New Hampshire, 22 July 1944.
[6] The literature on the Bretton Woods agreement, discussions preceding the conference and its impact on the development of global finance in the post-World War II years is vast. Two very useful works are Jacqueline Best, *The Limits of Transparency and the History of International Finance* (Ithaca, NY: Cornell University Press, 2005) and Barry Eichengreen, *Globalizing Capital: A History of the International Monetary System* (Princeton University Press, 2nd edn, 2008). For a concise overview, see Richard N. Gardner, 'The Bretton Woods–GATT System after Sixty-five Years: A Balance Sheet of Success and Failure' (2008) 47 *Columbia Journal of Transnational Law* 26.

and Social Council (EcoSoc), which never acquired in world economic affairs the weight originally envisaged for it. The Bank for International Settlements (BIS) was to be abolished. However, in the early post-World War II years, the BIS had a narrow escape due to the reaction of powerful central bankers who valued the role of the BIS as a neutral institution in what was to become a highly polarized world.[7]

There were no governance arrangements for global finance, a policy choice that is explained by the fact that the system restricted international capital flows, which were regarded as destabilizing, unlike free trade flows. Following the great expansion of unrestricted cross-border capital flows from the middle of the nineteenth century to the beginning of World War I in 1914 (roughly defined as the first globalization phase), international finance fell on harder times. A number of domestic and international economic crises were attributed to bankers and currency speculators.[8] Thus, unfettered international capital flows were viewed with much suspicion, since they could instantly undermine the system of fixed exchange rates envisaged in the Bretton Woods framework. Restrictions on capital flows and hostility towards open markets reinforced the role of the institutions standing at the centre of exchange stability and development finance arrangements. Thus, during the first phase, the IMF and the World Bank operated as the fulcrum of co-ordination of national financial markets and the main channel of capital flows either in the form of foreign exchange loans or development finance.[9]

---

[7] This detail is sure to be found surprising by those who have experienced the rise to global eminence of BIS in its many roles including that of key data collector in the last three decades for international banks (and standard setter).

[8] For two good accounts, see Gottfried Haberler, *The World Economy, Money, and the Great Depression 1919–1939* (Washington, DC: American Enterprise Institute, 1976) and Thomas E. Hall and J. David Ferguson, *The Great Depression: An International Disaster of Perverse Economic Policies* (Ann Arbor, MI: University of Michigan Press, 1998).

[9] For excellent analysis of the turns and twists associated with the mandates of the IMF and of the World Bank at the early stages of their development, due to political calculations and institutional and bureaucracy dynamics, see Anastasia Xenias, 'Wartime Financial Diplomacy and the Transition to the Treasury System 1939–1947', in David M. Andrews (ed.), *Orderly Change – International Monetary Relations Since Bretton Woods* (Ithaca, NY: Cornell University Press, 2008), Chapter 3, pp. 36–52 and Jeffrey M. Chwieroth, 'International Liquidity Provision: The IMF and the World Bank in the Treasury and Marshall Systems, 1942–1957', in David M. Andrews (ed.), *Orderly Change – International Monetary Relations Since Bretton Woods*, Chapter 4, pp. 52–78.

2.2.   *Monetary stability – financial stability and the IMF*

Established in 1945, the IMF's original mandate was to police and facilitate the Bretton Woods monetary arrangements,[10] under which exchange
rates were fixed through a peg of national currencies to the US dollar,
which in turn was fixed to gold.[11] Subject to conditions, a member could
draw on the Fund's resources (drawing rights) to settle part of their
international payments in order to maintain the par value of their currencies. The IMF was not originally designed to deal with non-monetary
matters.

   Following the weakening of the Bretton Woods arrangements and the
proliferation of offshore foreign exchange trade, the IMF introduced the
Special Drawing Rights (SDRs) with the first amendment of its articles
in July 1969. The SDRs were a synthetic currency comprising, initially, a
basket of currencies of the strongest Western economies and Japan. It was
designed to enable the IMF to regain some role in the currency markets.
However, the first fundamental change in the IMF's mission[12] came with

---

[10] Under Art. I of the IMF Agreement– unchanged since 1944 – the purposes of the IMF are:
   (1) to promote international monetary co-operation through a permanent institution
       which provides the machinery for consultation and collaboration on international
       monetary problems;
   (2) to facilitate the expansion and balanced growth of international trade, and to con-
       tribute thereby to the promotion and maintenance of high levels of employment and
       real income and to the development of the productive resources of all members as
       primary objectives of economic policy;
   (3) to promote exchange stability, to maintain orderly exchange arrangements among
       members, and to avoid competitive exchange depreciation;
   (4) to assist in the establishment of a multilateral system of payments in respect of cur-
       rent transactions between members and in the elimination of foreign exchange
       restrictions which hamper the growth of world trade;
   (5) to give confidence to members by making the general resources of the Fund tem-
       porarily available to them under adequate safeguards, thus providing them with
       opportunity to correct maladjustments in their balance of payments without
       resorting to measures destructive of national or international prosperity; and
   (6) in accordance with the above, to shorten the duration and lessen the degree of
       disequilibrium in the international balances of payments of members.
[11] See Rosa Lastra, *Legal Foundations of International Monetary Stability* (Oxford University
   Press, 2006), Part III, and A. F. Lowenfeld, *International Economic Law* (New York:
   Oxford University Press, 2003), pp. 526–7. Unlike the United Nations and WTO, voting in
   the IMF is decided by the member's quotas in the Fund (or shares in the case of the Bank).
[12] The IMF's Articles of Agreement entered into force on 27 December 1945. The Articles
   were first amended, effective 28 July 1969, by the modifications approved by the Board
   of Governors in Resolution No. 23–5, adopted on 31 May 1968. The Second amendment, effective 1 April 1978, was made by the modifications approved by the Board of
   Governors in Resolution No. 31–4, adopted on 30 April 1976. The Third amendment,

the collapse of the Smithsonian Agreement[13] in March 1973. The first oil crisis forced on IMF members' acceptance of floating exchange rates.[14] Following this shift of focus, the IMF amended its Articles (only the Second Amendment to the IMF Articles since Bretton Woods) to reflect its new role in safeguarding global economic stability. So its member countries assigned to the IMF the oversight of the effective operation of the international monetary system[15] and moved its focus to the provision of loans to economies experiencing recurrent exchange crises. In providing those loans the IMF would impose a number of fiscal and structural adjustment conditions, so-called 'conditionality',[16] which rendered it into a major global policy setter. Eventually, the operations of the IMF and of the World Bank started overlapping in a number of areas, including development and poverty eradication.[17] The IMF surveillance role under its original

effective 11 November 1992, was made by the modifications approved by the Board of Governors in Resolution No. 45–3, adopted on 28 June 1990. More details on the IMF Articles amendments are available at www.imf.org/external/pubs/ft/aa/aa.pdf.

[13] The Smithsonian Agreement was concluded in December 1971 in the G-10 Summit and marked the end of the gold peg. Member currencies moved to limited float. Thus, the Smithsonian Agreement amounted to the first re-alignment of the Bretton Woods fixed rate system. It came at the request of the Nixon government because the US currency had become grossly overvalued especially vis-a-vis the Deutsche mark and the Japanese yen. In view of the strong re-emergence of these economies in the post-World War II years and their legendary industrial might, an over-valued dollar grossly undermined the competitiveness of the US economy. See Charles Kindleberger, *A Financial History of Western Europe* (Oxford University Press, 2nd edn, 1993), pp. 452–4.

[14] Eichengreen, *Globalizing Capital*, p. 136.

[15] The second amendment of the IMF articles added Art. IV(1), which supplemented Art. I, and provided the IMF with the additional objective of exchange stability: 'Recognizing that the essential purpose of the international monetary system is to provide a framework that facilitates the exchange of goods, services, and capital among countries, and that sustains sound economic growth, and that a principal objective is the continuing development of the orderly underlying conditions that are necessary for financial and economic stability, each member undertakes to collaborate with the Fund and other members to assure orderly exchange arrangements and to promote a stable system of exchange rates'. The overall effect of the second amendment of the IMF's articles was to give the right to member countries to peg or freely float their currencies as per their policies. See Articles of Agreement, Art. IV 'Obligations Regarding Exchange Arrangements'. For the very interesting history of the demise of the fixed exchange rate system and background to this amendment, see Andreas Lowenfeld, 'The International Monetary System: A Look Back over Seven Decades', (2010) 13 *Journal of International Economic Law* 575–95 581–4. Lowenfeld notes that under the amended Art. IV members assumed no obligation beyond avoiding to manipulate exchange rates, *ibid.*, 583.

[16] IMF, 'IMF Conditionality – A Factsheet', 27 September 2010, available at www.imf.org/external/np/exr/facts/conditio.htm.

[17] In a formal manner the IMF's involvement with poverty reduction started in September 1999 with the establishment of the Poverty Reduction and Growth Facility (PRGF), which

mandate pursuant to Article IV of its Articles was rather narrow and was limited to macroeconomic matters and monetary matters such as balance of payments and exchange rate issues. As IMF surveillance expanded into the financial sector and focused on financial crisis prevention, especially under NIFA, the Fund developed a new set of monitoring procedures under Article IV.[18] Yet there is no evidence that the IMF exercised such surveillance with any success, due also to the unwillingness of member countries to co-operate.[19]

Furthermore, status quo bias, the lack of institutional alternatives due to a marked inability to re-build the international consensus that carried the day in Bretton Woods, a sharply divided world in the Cold War era, neo-liberal economic doctrine and the desire to acquire more influence in international economic affairs put the IMF at the heart of Washington Consensus policy initiatives. As soon as it found itself in the driver's seat, from the late 1980s to the end of the Asian Crisis, the IMF became the principal supporter and institutional facilitator as well as champion of rather controversial capital account liberalization and deregulation in the developed and more crucially in the developing world. Three events strengthened further the IMF's position. First, the collapse of the Soviet Bloc brought into the IMF fold a number of Central and Eastern European countries searching for technical assistance and loans for structural adjustment. Second, the currency crises of the mid-1990s (chiefly the rapid devaluation of Mexican and Argentinean pesos) allowed the IMF to evolve into the main guardian of global financial stability.[20] Third, the

intended 'to make the objectives of poverty reduction and growth more central to [the Fund's] lending operations in its poorest member countries'. Poverty Reduction Strategy Papers were prepared by governments with the active participation of civil society and other development partners and subsequently considered by the 'Executive Boards of the IMF and World Bank as the basis for concessional lending from each institution and debt relief under the joint Heavily Indebted Poor Countries (HIPC) Initiative'. The PRGF has now been replaced by the Fund's Extended Credit Facility, which also makes available loans in times of crisis. Yet there are still a number of PRGFs active around the world. For details see 'Factsheet, The Poverty Reduction and Growth Facility', 31 July 2009, available at www.imf.org/external/np/exr/facts/prgf.htm and 'Factsheet, IMF Extended Credit Facility', 27 September 2010, available at www.imf.org/external/np/exr/facts/ecf.htm.

[18] Art. IV(3)(a) of the amended Articles states that the Fund 'shall oversee the compliance of each member with its obligations under Section 1 of this Article'. Moreover, according to Article IV(3)(b) each member, 'shall provide the Fund with the information necessary for such surveillance, and when requested by the Fund, shall consult with it …' See also IMF 'Surveillance: Factsheet' available at http://www.imf.org/external/np/exr/facts/surv.htm.

[19] Lowenfeld, 'The International Monetary System' 585.

[20] For the transformation of the IMF during this period, see Ross Buckley, 'Improve Living Standards in Poor Countries: Reform the International Monetary Fund' (2010) 24 *Emory International Law Review* 119, 122–5.

advancement of economic globalization and increasing integration of national markets into the international financial system exposed the vulnerabilities of the latter, thereby accentuating further the importance of the IMF during this period.[21] As a result, monetary stability and financial stability gradually merged in the IMF's mandate.[22] Moreover, the role that the IMF had already played as principal facilitator and 'guardian' of global financial stability allowed it to take centre stage during NIFA.

2.3.   The origins of TRNs and of standard setting

2.3.1.   Overview

In general, in the first fifteen years following the end of World War II, the international financial system was no more than a network of commercial banks providing trade and export finance.[23] Thus, the absence of any kind of governance structures did not pose any serious problems. However, the nature and shape of the international financial system started changing rapidly in the 1960s with the development of the (offshore) euromarket for US dollar denominated bonds. The pace of change became faster during the 1970s when most big US and other developed countries' commercial banks established considerable cross-border business lines and active presence abroad.

The increasing internationalization of big commercial bank business meant that several (informal) economic co-operation networks/ groups, with membership comprising a small number of developed countries, emerged in the 1960s and extended their remit to banking issues. The G-7/8, which dominated the informal policy making agenda in the 1990s – just before and well after the collapse of the Soviet Bloc, which, in fact, reinforced the importance of the group – was already prominent in international bank policy affairs. Yet the origins of today's complex web of TRNs sitting at the centre of global financial governance is traced to another informal body, which 'opened for business' in 1974 and gradually dominated the international regulatory agenda. Its core membership came from an 'intriguing' network of central bankers convening their meetings in Basel under the auspices of the BIS and it was called the Committee on

---

[21] See Eichengreen, *Globalizing Capital*.
[22] See, in general, Rosa Lastra, *Legal Foundations of International Monetary Stability* (Oxford University Press, 2006, Chapter 13).
[23] Douglas Arner and Ross Buckley, 'Redesigning the Architecture of the Global Financial System' (2010) 11 *Melbourne Journal of International Law* 185–239.

Banking Regulation and Supervisory Practices. It is of course the initial name of the Basel Committee on Banking Supervision (BCBS).[24]

The continuous internationalization of finance made apparent the need for the establishment of similar informal committees/regulatory fora in other areas of financial activity with formulation of international standards for securities markets and accounting conventions being given clear precedence, due to a substantial increase in the number of companies which wanted to obtain a listing outside their domestic markets. Regulatory initiatives emanating from those committees/fora attempted to address the challenges of an increasingly integrated global marketplace fostering the convergence of national regulatory systems.

Arguably, the most significant of those TRNs were the International Organization of Securities Commission (IOSCO), formed in 1983, and the International Association of Insurance Supervisors (IAIS), formed in 1994. In their respective areas, these organizations promoted discussion and development of common solutions to cross-border financial issues, with domestic implementation of soft law 'international understandings/agreements'. Accordingly, it may be said that the international financial governance structure (architecture) from the middle of the 1980s until 1998 was a loose combination of state-to-state contact groups which comprised the G groupings, formal international organizations such as the IMF and the BIS, and TRNs such as the BCBS and IOSCO.[25]

2.3.2   The G (state-to-state contact) groups

(a)   **The Group of Ten (G-10)**   Interestingly, in the field of international financial governance the origins of TRNs can be traced to the IMF. In the early 1960s the Finance Ministers and central bank governors from the most developed Western countries formed a group to support and to oversee the Fund's General Arrangement on Borrowing (GAB).[26] This

---

[24] See Joseph J. Norton, 'Trends in International Bank Supervision and the Basle Committee on Banking Supervision' (1994) 48 *Consumer Finance Law Quarterly Report* 415 and BCBS, 'History of the Basel Committe and its Membership', August 2009, available at www.bis.org/bcbs/history.pdf.

[25] For a good overview see J. J. Norton, *Devising International Bank Supervisory Standards* (Amsterdam: Kluwer Law International, 1995). For a comprehensive and critical analysis of the work of the BCBS and of IOSCO see Kern Alexander, Rahul Dhumale and John Eatwell, *Global Governance of Financial Systems, The International Regulation of Systemic Risk* (Oxford University Press, 2006), Chapter 2.

[26] The GAB is a special IMF fund financed by the G-10 countries to be used when the IMF's own resources are insufficient.

grouping/network was subsequently called the G-10.[27] In the beginning, the G-10 provided an informal, discrete and flexible forum for central bank governors and Finance Ministers of the ten most industrialized countries, which also had the most developed banking sectors, to discuss matters of common concern, outside the IMF/Word Bank annual conference, where a much larger number of countries participated.[28] Essentially, it pioneered the informal approach to international financial regulation, which was later developed by a constellation of TRNs that would become the main fora for the discussion, production and co-ordinated implementation of financial regulatory standards.

The G-10 has also created several derivative informal networks, the most important of which are: (1) the Committee on the Global Financial System (CGFS)[29] and (2) the Committee on Payment and Settlement Systems (CPSS).[30] These permanent G-10 sub-networks eventually became International Standard Setting bodies (ISSBs) and components of the NIFA. After the onset of the GFC, the G-10 has been submerged by the G-20, which is a much more representative body in geographic terms and as regards concentration of economic power in the twenty-first century, since all four major emerging economies are full members.

[27] The founding members of the G-10 were the US, the UK, Japan, France, West Germany, Canada, the Netherlands, Italy, Belgium and Sweden. Switzerland (which remained a non-IMF member until 1992) joined them in 1984, and, after the collapse of the Soviet bloc, Russia was regularly invited to attend meetings.

[28] E.g., Norton notes that: '[T]he negotiations that led to the establishment of the IMF's "special drawing rights" (SDRs) under the 1969 First Amendment to the Fund's Articles of Agreement, to the short-lived Smithsonian Agreement of 1971 that tried to partially salvage the IMF "par value" system of fixed exchange rates, and to the Fund's Second Amendment to its Articles in 1978 that attempted feebly to provide a transition to the new and current floating exchange rate regime was conducted through the G-10 framework.' Joseph J. Norton, '"NIFA-II" or "Bretton Woods- II"?: The G-20 (Leaders) Summit Process on Managing Global Financial Markets and The World Economy – Quo Vadis?', (2010) 11 *Journal of Banking Regulation* 261–301, 293, note 33.

[29] Formed in 1971 as the Euro-currency Standing Committee for monitoring international banking markets. It was renamed and refocused on financial stability in 1999 as to financial stability concerns. A detailed description of the CGFS mandate and function is available at www.bis.org/cgfs/index.htm.

[30] Established in 1990 as successor to the Group of Experts on Payment Systems, which was, in turn, set up in 1980. The CPSS is 'a standard stetting body for payment and securities settlement systems. It also serves as a forum for central banks to monitor and analyse developments in domestic payment, settlement and clearing systems as well as in cross-border and multicurrency settlement schemes. The CPSS undertakes specific studies in the field of payment and settlement systems at its own discretion or at the request of the Governors of the Global Economy Meeting.' A detailed description of the CPSS is available at www.bis.org/cpss/index.htm.

(b)   The Group of Seven/Eight (G-7/8)   The agenda of G-7 Heads of State and Finance Ministers meetings from 1975 through the mid 1990s mostly focused on global macroeconomic issues including monetary stability, growth, inflation, employment, fiscal responsibility and multilateral trade and investment liberalization, to the exclusion of financial stability, even during the time of the Third World debt crisis in the 1980s. Arguably, the most significant contribution of the G-7 to the international financial architecture during the 1975–90 period came in 1989 at its Paris Summit, when the G-7, in light of increasing concerns over money laundering, called for the creation of the Financial Action Task Force on Money Laundering (FATF).[31]

2.4.   The most important TRNs of the post-Bretton Woods period

2.4.1   The Basel Committee on Banking Supervision

(a)   The early days of the BCBS   As mentioned in Section 2.3 above, the BCBS was founded in 1974 under the auspices of the Bank of International Settlements (BIS). It was accountable to the relevant heads of the member central banks and bank supervisors.[32] The historical events that led to its formation make interesting reading. The establishment of the Committee, an initiative of the G-10 central bank governors, came in the aftermath of the collapse of the American Franklin National Bank, the Israeli-British Bank in London and the Bankhaus Herstatt. The latter was a small German bank that stopped operations in the middle of the trading day, causing a major disruption in currency markets and cross-border payments. Although these were non-systemic bankruptcies of three medium size banks, the G-10 central bank governors became concerned with increased risks to banks due to floating exchange rates and the lack of any co-ordinated cross-border supervision framework. In addition, the Bank of England governor was becoming concerned with the 'capital adequacy' of banking institutions.[33] This marked a shift for bank regulators/supervisors from the traditional focus on institutional liquidity, safeguarded by imposing minimum bank reserve deposits with the central bank, to institutions possessing sufficient capital to address

---

[31] For a detailed description of the workings of FATF, see www.fatf-gafi.org.
[32] For the history of the BCBS, see Duncan Wood, *The Basel Committee and the Governance of the Global Financial System* (Aldershot: Ashgate Publishing, 2004) and Michael Malloy, 'Emerging International Regime of Financial Services Regulation' (2005) 18 *Transnational Lawyer* 329.
[33] Norton, '"NIFA-II"', 266–7.

various bankruptcy risks.[34] As such, the first two tasks that occupied the BCBS's agenda were the cross-border supervision of banks and capital adequacy,[35] mainly focusing on the international banks based in the countries comprising the membership of the BCBS.[36]

The first challenge that national regulators had to address concerned the allocation of supervisory responsibility for international banks, namely, which supervisory authority in the home or host country was responsible for supervising bank branches and subsidiaries across borders. The result of those discussions was the Basel Concordat of 1975, which was a first attempt to allocate international bank supervisory authority among the host and home regulators/supervisors. The Concordat has since undergone numerous refinements and amendments. A number of Western bank failures, chiefly the collapse of Banco Ambrosiano in 1982 and the BCCI debacle in 1991, exposed the framework as inadequate.[37] Thus, the Concordat was further refined in 1983 and was effectively replaced in 1992 with a set of minimum standards on the supervision of international banking groups.[38] These were followed by the publication in 1997 of the Core Principles on Banking Supervision developed by the Committee in co-operation with the IMF and the International Bank for Reconstruction and Development (IBRD).[39]

Also, during the early 1990s it became apparent that bank supervision could not be carried out in a meaningful way if it just focused on big banking institutions, because those banks tended to operate more and more within the structure of bigger banking/financial conglomerates. Thus, a supervisory framework dealing with financial conglomerates was also developed through creation of an ad hoc group called the Tripartite

---

[34] See Charles Goodhart, *The Basel Committee on Banking Supervision: A History of the Early Years, 1974–1997* (Cambridge University Press, 2011).

[35] 'The initial driving forces behind the Committee were the Bank of England, the U.S. Federal Reserve Board of Governors and then the European Community's "Contact Group."' Norton, '"NIFA-II"', 267.

[36] *Ibid.*

[37] See Duncan E. Alford, 'Basle Committee Minimum Standards: International Regulatory Response to the Failure of BCCI' (1992) 26 *George Washington Journal of International Law & Economics* 241; Susan Emmenegger, 'The Basle Committee on Banking Supervision – A Secretive Club of Giants?', in Rainer Grote and Thilo Marauhn (eds.), *The Regulation of International Financial Markets Perspectives for Reform* (Cambridge University Press, 2006), Chapter 10, pp. 224–36.

[38] BCBS, 'Report on Minimum Standards for the Supervision of International Banking Groups and their Cross-Border Establishment', July 1992.

[39] BCBS, 'Core Principles for Effective Banking Supervision', September 1997, revised in October 2006. The revised document is available at www.bis.org/publ/bcbs129.pdf.

Group in 1993 to prepare a report on financial conglomerates. In 1995 this group evolved into a co-operative, informal 'network of networks' called the Joint Forum,[40] comprising the BCBS, IOSCO and the IAIS. The Joint Forum initially focused on the thorny issue of the 'lead regulator' of financial conglomerates.[41] However, the issue of supervision of financial conglomerates remained largely unresolved until the GFC,[42] at least outside the EU. In an attempt to provide a solution to this problem, which led to serious co-ordination challenges in the context of cross-border rescues of financial conglomerates during the GFC, the G-20 has 'sanctioned' the establishment of supervisory colleges,[43] discussed in detail in Section 4.5 below.

The most significant set of standards produced by the BCBS during the 1980s was a risk-based 'Capital Adequacy Accord' published in 1988. The main tenets of this framework are discussed below. Finally, since the late 1980s, the Committee has become concerned with money laundering and, more recently, counter-terrorism, producing attendant regulatory standards.[44] During 1997, the BCBS promulgated a comprehensive and workable set of Core Principles of Bank Supervision. Although over-optimistic in some cases, the Principles also provided the foundations for building sound banking supervision structures both in the developed and more crucially the developing world,[45] and were placed at the heart of the NIFA framework.

From the early 1980s, but more so in the early 1990s, regional, sub-regional and special groups of national bank supervisors/regulators were formed informally to consider how BCBS-based pronouncements could

[40] A description of the workings of the Joint Forum can be found at www.iosco.org/joint_forum/.
[41] See George Alexander Walker, *International Banking Regulation, Law Policy & Practice* (London/NY: Kluwer/Aspen, 2001) discussing the supervision of banking conglomerates and the issue of lead regulator.
[42] See Richard J. Herring, 'Conflicts Between Home and Host Country Prudential Supervisors', in Douglas D. Evanoff, George G. Kaufman and John R. LaBrosse (eds.), *International Financial Instability: Global Banking and National Regulation* (Danvers, MA: World Scientific Publishing Co, 2007), pp. 201–20.
[43] Supervisory colleges formed under the FSB with the 'blessings' of the G-20 are intended as a venue for national supervisors to share information and to co-ordinate monitoring efforts over large and complex (i.e., systemically important) financial institutions.
[44] See BCBS, 'Money Laundering and Terrorist Financing' (document list from 1981–2009), available at www.bis.org/list/bcbs/tid_32/index.htm.
[45] See BCBS, 'Core Principles for Effective Banking Supervision and Related Methodology' (originally adopted 1997, last revised 2006), available at www.financialstabilityboard.org/list/fsb_cos_issuing_body/index.htm.

be translated into the particular region, sub-region or grouping.[46] During the same period the BCBS and IOSCO developed strong links with private bodies (networks) of international accountants, such as the International Federation of Accountants (IFAC) and its standard-setting subcommittee, the International Auditing and Assurance Board (IAASB) and the International Accounting Standards Board (IASB), the standard-setting body of the private, non-profit, International Accounting Standards Committee Foundation (IASCF).[47] This partnership was essential in fostering convergence of accounting standards and raising their quality, both central elements of financial stability and efficient capital markets.

(b)   **The Basel I capital adequacy framework**   In 1988, the BCBS first published a common framework of standards that would foster effective capital adequacy regulation of banks and facilitate convergence of national regulatory standards governing the measurement and enforcement of bank capital adequacy (known as Basel I). This referred to the prescribed capital resources that internationally active banks were required to set aside in order to be deemed as operating on a prudent and sound basis. Capital adequacy requirements largely replaced the regulatory tools that had been developed after the Great Crash, such as cap on interest rates, holding of reserves with the central bank and asset allocation rules as a tool of prudential regulation.[48] Most of these tools had become redundant with capital account liberalization and the advent of ITC. Thus, Basel I capital adequacy standards were a re-regulation effort.[49] The US Federal Reserve and Treasury took a lead role in the consultation proceedings and were particularly active in the drafting and implementation of Basel I standards. Arguably, US regulators were motivated by the fact that the US

---

[46]   See BCBS, 'History and Membership', August 2009, p. 5, available at www.bis.org/bcbs/history.pdf.

[47]   E.g., the IOSCO Technical Committee's Standing Committee 1 on Multinational Disclosure and Accounting works with the IASB on developing and monitoring International Financial Reporting Standards (IFRS). The BCBS also maintains Accounting and Audit and International Liaison subcommittees. A description of the workings of IFAC and IAASB can be found at www.ifac.org. On IASB and IASCF, see www.iasb.org .

[48]   Martin Hellwig, 'Capital Regulation after the Crisis: Business as Usual?' Max Planck Institute for Research on Collective Goods, Bonn 2010/31, July 2010, p.5, available at ssrn.com/abstract=1645224. Other Depression era restrictions (e.g. the Glass–Steagall Act) related primarily to US structural regulations that kept separate commercial from investment banking business.

[49]   *Ibid.*

banks had lost their dominance of international banking markets to the much lighter capitalized Japanese banks.[50]

The main focus of Basel I was on credit (counterparty) risk and much less on other important risks such as currency risk, interest rate risk and market risk. In this respect, the framework required a minimum ratio of certain specified constituents of capital to risk-weighted assets (RWA). The prescribed regulatory capital constituents comprised: (1) Tier 1 (core) capital, which mainly consisted of shareholders equity, disclosed reserves and retained post tax profit; and (2) Tier 2 (supplementary) capital, which mainly consisted of subordinated debt. The Basel I framework endorsed a risk-weighted approach to the assets denominator of the capital assets ratio.[51] It established a relatively simple methodology for bank assets' risk-weighting with only five risk weights – 0, 10, 20, 50 and 100 per cent of asset value – assigned to all types of assets and all types of counterparties, judged by the origin of the counterparty (OECD versus non-OECD countries) and its organizational/legal/economic nature (sovereigns, credit institutions, corporations), without any separate assessment of its creditworthiness. For instance, the risk-weighted ratio for all corporate borrowers was 100 per cent. In addition, following further consultation, the Basel Committee adopted a target standard capital to assets ratio of 8 per cent of which core capital constituted at least 4 per cent.

Due to the institutional weight of participating public organizations, the importance of the countries they represented and the need to level the playing field in the fast growing global market for financial services, the non-binding Basel I Accord was adopted by most countries, first in the developed and then in the developing world, regardless of whether they participated in the workings of the Committee.[52] In fact, most developed countries, including the US and the EU member states, extended the application of the Basel I framework to domestic banks that did not maintain a significant international presence.

However, it soon became apparent that the rather rudimentary risk-weight methods of the Basel I Accord, which, ironically, considering the Basel II and Basel III frameworks, was thought to be a complex approach, suffered from a number of technical weaknesses relating to its narrow

[50] Stavros Gadinis, 'The Politics of Competition in International Financial Regulation' (2008) 49 *Harvard International Law Journal* 447, 501–5.

[51] Malloy, 'Emerging International Regime', 332–3.

[52] See J. J. Norton, 'The Work of the Basle Supervisors Committee on Bank Capital Adequacy and the July 1988 Report on "International Convergence of Capital Standards"' (1989) 23 *International Lawyer* 245.

band of credit risk classifications.[53] It was thought to be especially inept at accommodating the emergent new techniques and instruments used to mitigate risk, such as credit derivatives and securitizations. In addition, the narrow band of borrower classification did not allow lenders to distinguish between major, stable and recognized companies versus risky upstarts.[54] Moreover, little attention was given to correlations and the mitigating effect of uncorrelated credits to well diversified loan portfolios.[55] Finally, Basel I did not properly account for operational risk in banks' loan and securities market portfolios. In Section 3.2 below, I discuss the Basel II framework.

2.4.2 International Organization of Securities Commissions

The International Organization of Securities Commissions (IOSCO) is a transnational association of national securities commissions whose members regulate more than 90 per cent of the world's securities markets. IOSCO is the most influential international standard setter for securities markets. It has its roots in the Inter-American Conference of Securities Commissioners, established in 1974, with the US Securities and Exchange Commission (SEC) being the principal force behind its formation. In 1984, the Conference was transformed into a global co-operative body which eventually became one of the leading financial TRNs. A permanent IOSCO secretariat was established in Montreal in 1987 (now in Madrid) and IOSCO was incorporated under private Quebec parliamentary law.[56] IOSCO, in contrast to the BCBS, was structured as a more universal type of association.[57] It has four regional committees and a

---

[53] E.g., one obvious distortion was the zero weight given to loans to OECD sovereigns irrespective of the riskiness of the country, which allowed countries such as Mexico to be treated the same for capital adequacy requirements as more developed countries with lower ratios of public debt.

[54] Stijn Claessens, Geoffrey R. D. Underhill and Xiaoke Zhang, 'Basle II Capital Requirements and Developing Countries: A Political Economy Perspective', October 2003.

[55] Ibid., pp. 19–23.

[56] For further discussion of IOSCO's evolution see Howard Davies and David Green, Global Financial Regulation: The Essential Guide (Cambridge: Polity Press, 2008), Chapter 2; David Zaring, 'International Law by other Means: The Twilight Experience of International Financial Regulatory Organizations' (1998) 33 Texas International Law Journal 281.

[57] IOSCO has three types of membership which is structured as follows: (1) 114 'ordinary', voting members comprising securities commissions or any public authority responsible for securities markets; (2) 11 non-voting 'associate' members comprising other regulatory bodies having interests in the securities markets; and (3) 74 non-voting, 'affiliate'

two-track interconnected operational committee structure with committees concerned with developed and emerging markets respectively.[58] The objectives of IOSCO are to enable its members to:[59]

(1) co-operate and promote high standards of regulation in order to maintain just, efficient and sound markets;
(2) exchange information on their respective experiences in order to promote the development of domestic markets;
(3) unite their efforts to establish standards and an effective surveillance of international securities transactions;
(4) provide mutual assistance to promote the integrity of the markets by a rigorous application of the standards and by effective enforcement against offences.

Since the late 1980s IOSCO has issued over 300 policy documents covering a broad range of securities market issues, such as capital adequacy, money laundering, securities fraud, information sharing, memoranda of understanding (MoU), financial and non-financial disclosure, auditing and accounting standards, financial conglomerates, market risks, derivatives, asset management, market failures, market intermediaries, non-compliant regimes etc.[60] The most important of IOSCO's policy documents are a set of Objectives and Principles of Securities Regulation (IOSCO Principles), which have been used as the international regulatory benchmarks for all securities markets and, as discussed in Section 3.3.2 below, were employed in the context of FSAP surveys with mixed results. Of considerable importance for the integration of international capital markets were also IOSCO's disclosure standards for cross-border securities offers and listings.[61]

In 2002, IOSCO adopted a multilateral MoU designed to facilitate cross-border enforcement and exchange of information among the international community of securities regulators. The Executive Committee of IOSCO has established two specialized working committees: the

members, comprising self-regulatory bodies – SROs – and international organizations which have an interest or invovlement in securities regulation. A full list of current IOSCO members in all three types of membership is available at www.iosco.org/lists/index.cfm?section=general.
[58] Updated information on IOSCO's organizational structure is available at www.iosco.org/about/index.cfm?section=structure.
[59] The list of IOSCO objectives is available at www.iosco.org/about/.
[60] The full list is available at www.iosco.org/library/index.cfm?section=pubdocs.
[61] See IOSCO, 'International Disclosure Standards for Cross-Border Offerings and Initial Listings by Foreign Issuers', September 1998, available at www.iosco.org/library/pubdocs/pdf/IOSCOPD81.pdf.

Technical Committee and the Emerging Markets Committee. The more influential Technical Committee comprises fifteen agencies that regulate some of the larger, more developed and internationalized markets.

2.4.3   International Association of Insurance Supervisors

The International Association of Insurance Supervisors (IAIS) was formed in 1994 with the implicit objective to provide a BCBS kind of forum for the global insurance industry. Today, the IAIS represents domestic insurance regulators and supervisors of approximately 190 jurisdictions (including fifty-seven US jurisdictions, where the insurance industry is mainly regulated at the state level) and has over 100 'observers' from the public and private sector. The IMF, World Bank and OECD are members of the IAIS. From its inception the IAIS has collaborated closely with the BCBS and IOSCO.

Where standards for international insurance are promulgated, private parties are formally invited to act as observers. In this capacity, most major insurance companies, and some law firms and governmental organizations with interests in insurance supervision, participate in IAIS functions though they have no official vote in the organization. Since the late 1990s, the IAIS has been an integral part of NIFA-I, mostly as the issuer of standards, principles and guidance addressed to the global insurance industry.[62] The IAIS is now listed by the IMF/WB/FSB as one of the major financial sector ISSBs.[63]

2.4.4   Financial Action Task Force

The Financial Action Task Force (FATF) came to life as a result of a G-7 decision in 1989 to establish an informal network dealing with money laundering. It has gradually become central in the anti-money laundering and counter-terrorism financing policies in the financial sector, providing a strong global consensus on standards and measures required to counter these activities.[64] Given heightened global concern with money laundering and financing of terrorist activities, FATF has acquired considerable institutional significance and compliance with its standards has become an integral part of FSAP surveys and financial

---

[62] A full description of the framework is avaialble at www.iaisweb.org/index.cfm? pageID.=440.

[63] See www.financialstabilityboard.org/cos/key_standards.htm .

[64] Cheong-Ann Png, 'International Legal Sources III – FATF Recommendations', in William Blair and Richard Brent (eds.), *Banks and Financial Crime – The International Law of Tainted Money*, (Oxford University Press, 2008) Chapter 5, pp. 87–101.

sector reform efforts carried out by the World Bank and the IMF. Thus, the FATF has become a major component of the NIFA framework as a financial sector ISSB.[65]

In 1990, FATF produced a set of 'Forty Recommendations', which provide a comprehensive plan of action needed to fight against money laundering.[66] In 2001, FATF added 'Eight Special Recommendations' to deal with the issue of terrorist financing, and in 2004 published nine special recommendations, further strengthening the agreed international standards for combating money laundering and terrorist financing – the '40+9 Recommendations'.[67] The task force itself has given rise to two other interlinking networks: one public – the Egmont Group of Financial Intelligence Units[68] – and one private – The Wolfsburg Group: 'an association of eleven global banks, which aims to develop financial services industry standards, and related products, for Know Your Customer, Anti-Money Laundering and Counter Terrorist Financing policies'.[69]

2.4.5   Industry associations

In addition to the international accounting bodies referred to above, there are various other private-based bodies and networks which acquired increasing influence after NIFA but were formed before it. The International Swap Dealers Association (ISDA), which subsequently became the International Swap and Derivatives Dealers Association, is the most important trade body of the global financial services industry. It was established in 1985 to represent the interests of the OTC derivatives industry and provide the legal infrastructure for the cross-border expansion of derivatives trading. Its standards from product definitions

---

[65] Starting originally with sixteen members, in 2007, FATF's membership reached a total of thirty-four member countries and two regional organizations, one of which is the EU. The list of FATF's membership is available at www.fatf-gafi.org/document/5/0,3746,en_32250379_32236869_34310917_1_1_1_1,00.html.

[66] The full *Forty Recommendations* are available at www.fatf-gafi.org/document/28/0,3746,en_32250379_32236920_33658140_1_1_1_1,00.html.

[67] For analysis of the formulation and implementation of FATF standards, see Eleni Tsingou, 'Who Governs and Why? The Making of a Global Anti-money Laundering Regime', in Geoffrey Underhill, Jasper Blom and Daniel Mügge (eds.), *From Reform to Crisis: Financial Integration and the 'New Architecture' of International Financial Governance* (Cambridge University Press, 2010), pp. 172–86.

[68] A detailed description of the group is available at www.Egmontgroup.org.

[69] A description of the standards produced by the group is available at www.wolfsberg-principles.com/index.html.

to risk mitigation mechanisms, such as the ISDA Master Agreement architecture and its close-out netting provisions, are now the globally accepted standards and rules for OTC derivatives trading.[70] As a result, ISDA today exerts an enormous amount of influence and has become an inextricable part of the regulatory edifice of global derivatives markets, leading to calls for it to be placed under some kind of public regulatory oversight.[71]

The International Capital Markets Association (ICMA) is the product of a 2005 merger of the International Primary Market Association (IPMA) and the International Securities Market Association (ISMA, formerly the Association of International Bond Dealers). It is a self-regulatory organization, trade association and standard-setting body for participants in the capital markets, and focuses on European markets, since both ISMA and IPMA were formed as a result of the rise of the European markets in the late 1960s. ICMA promotes the development and efficient functioning of the global capital markets through, *inter alia*, development and maintenance of high standards of market practice, fostering appropriate levels of regulation and education.[72] Essentially, it is the lobbying group of all capital market constituencies with a European focus.

Another example of private groupings with significant influence are creditor clubs. These are informal lenders' groupings that provide expertise, standards and a forum for the restructuring of foreign debt, mostly sovereign debt. The most important creditor groups are the Paris Club (official creditors)[73] and the London Club (commercial bank creditors) which came into existence in the 1980s to deal with international debt restructurings.[74] Specifically, the Paris Club, as an informal group of official creditors, seeks to find co-ordinated and sustainable solutions to the payment difficulties experienced by debtor countries. Subject to debtor countries' adoption of reforms to stabilize and restore their macroeconomic and financial situation, Paris Club creditors provide appropriate debt rescheduling.

---

[70] A detailed description is available at www.isda.org.

[71] See Adam W. Glass, 'Helpful Hints for the New Derivatives Regulators' (2009) 1(11) *Lombard Street*, available at www.finreg21.com/lombard-street/helpful-hints-new-derivatives-regulators.

[72] A detailed description of ICMA's organization and mission is available at www.icmagroup.org.

[73] A detailed description of the Paris Club's organization and mission is available at www.clubdeparis.org.

[74] See www.imf.org/external/np/exr/facts/groups.htm.

2.4.6   Industry think tanks

Arguably, the most influential think-tanks with indirect or direct policy input to the aforementioned TRNs are the Institute of International Finance (IIF), the world's only global association of private financial institutions, formed in 1983,[75] and the Group of Thirty. The latter is a private, non-profit body of experts. It was formed in 1978 in order 'to deepen understanding of international economic and financial issues, to explore the international repercussions of decisions taken in the public and private sectors, and to examine the choices available to market practitioners and policymakers'.[76] The Group of Thirty has, on several occasions, exercised critical influence, for a private organization, on the way international financial regulation is shaped, an attribute mostly owed to the strength of its membership.[77] One such area is the regulation of derivatives. In 1993 it commissioned a study by a group of experts entitled 'Derivatives: Practices and Principles'. This, although a privately financed study,[78] set the tone for light regulation of the derivatives industry and what is now perceived as excessive reliance on self-regulation.[79] The Group of Thirty was also influential in the initiation of the process that led to the more risk sensitive requirements of Basel II.[80] Once a consensus was formed regarding the regulatory flaws that caused, in part, the GFC, the Group of Thirty issued a bold and far reaching report on regulatory reform that has provided a very useful blueprint for G-20 and FSB regulatory initiatives.[81]

---

[75] A detailed description is available at www.iif.com.

[76] A detailed description of the Group's objectives is available at www.group30.org.

[77] E.g., its current chairman of the board of trustees is Paul Volcker and its membership includes central bank governors such as Mervyn King (BoE), Stanley Fisher (Israel), Jean-Claude Trichet (former governor of the ECB), Mario Draghi (ECB, formerly of the Bank of Italy and chairman of the FSB), academics such as Paul Krugman and Kenneth Rogoff, and the heads of some of the biggest international banks.

[78] Eleni Tsingou, 'The Governance of OTC Derivatives Markets', in Peter Mooslechner, Helen Schuberth and Beat Weber (eds.) *The Political Economy of Financial Market Regulation: The Dynamics of Inclusion and Exclusion* (Aldershot: Edward Elgar, 2006), Chapter 7, pp. 168–90, 175.

[79] *Ibid.*, pp. 174–7.

[80] See Eleni Tsingou, 'Transnational Governance Networks in the Regulation of Finance – the Making of Global Regulation and Supervision Standards in the Banking Industry', in Morten Ougaard and Anna Leander (eds.), *Business and Global Governance* (London: Routledge, 2010), pp. 138–53, 143–5.

[81] Group of Thirty, 'Financial Reform: A Framework for Financial Stability', 15 January 2009, available at www.group30.org/pubs/reformreport.pdf.

2.5 Reconstruction, development and the World Bank

2.5.1 World Bank: early years and mandate transformation

Keynes had well realized that the post-World War II world would require very serious investment to be directed to the reconstruction effort, which was essential to achieve lasting peace. This role was assigned to the IBRD, the first of the institutions of the World Bank Group. Its main purpose was to co-ordinate and provide financial support for reconstruction and development. The IBRD's main objectives were:[82]

(1) to assist in the reconstruction and development of member countries by facilitating capital investment for productive purposes, including the restoration of economies destroyed or disrupted by war, the reconversion of productive facilities to peacetime needs and the encouragement of the development of productive facilities and resources in less developed countries;
(2) to promote private foreign investment by means of guarantees or participations in loans and other investments made by private investors and when private capital is not available and provide loans on reasonable terms.

The IBRD's difference from mainstream banks was that its shareholders were governments and its principal objective was not profit maximization. The IBRD issued its first bond in 1947 to finance the reconstruction of Europe. France was one of the first recipients of IBRD loans. The advent of the Marshall plan that also provided reconstruction money to Europe and de-colonization marked a shift of the Bank's focus from Europe to the developing world with project financing becoming the centrepiece of World Bank activities, especially in the 1960s. As the World Bank provided financial support in times of economic crisis in order to enhance social development, it used both funding and transfer of technical assistance to promote policy and institutional reforms within borrower countries. Not only the IMF, but also the World Bank provided loans on the basis of governance and financial reform conditions, with particular emphasis on battling corruption, improvement of the framework for foreign private investment and strengthening of country insolvency and creditor rights laws. Thus, the Bank has gradually become a major standard setter and monitor (mainly through FSAP surveys and Reports on

---

[82] IBRD Articles of Agreement, Art. I – unchanged since 1944.

the Observance of Standards and Codes (ROSCs)),[83] a function that was significantly enhanced during NIFA.

In many cases the World Bank's concentration on (grand scale) project funding has had mixed results. Gradually the World Bank moved into a closer partnership with the private sector, especially private investors and entrepreneurs. As a result, the World Bank (group) now provides seed financing through the International Finance Corporation (IFC) (which was established in 1956 as the venture capital arm of the World Bank group), development aid to very poor countries through its International Development Association (IDA),[84] guarantees through the Multilateral Investment Guarantee Agency (MIGA), established in 1988, private sector loans, and can even lend directly to private sector investors through the IBRD.[85] At the same time, in recognizing the important role of private investment for developing countries, it established the International Centre for Settlement of Investment Disputes (ICSID), which focused on the resolution of cross-border investment disputes.[86]

With the collapse of the Soviet Bloc, the World Bank, like the IMF, added the transition economies to its development assistance portfolio. Naturally, both institutions welcomed the opportunity to turn their attention to setting economic policy instead of merely implementing it, as per the original Bretton Woods design. Nonetheless, the World Bank directly faced many questions about its role and future at the time of the fiftieth anniversary of the Bretton Woods conference in 1994. The reappraisal that followed led it to focus on the overarching objective of

---

[83] For a description of this function of the World Bank see 'ROSC Assessments' available at web.worldbank.org/WBSITE/EXTERNAL/TOPICS/LAWANDJUSTICE/GILD/0,,contentMDK:20086176~menuPK:146209~pagePK:64065425~piPK:162156~theSitePK:215006,00.html. An updated list and description of World Bank principles and guidelines for effective insolvency and creditor rights is available at web.worldbank.org/WBSITE/EXTERNAL/TOPICS/LAWANDJUSTICE/GILD/0,,contentMDK:20196839~menuPK:146205~pagePK:64065425~piPK:162156~theSitePK:215006,00.html.

[84] The IDA was established in 1960 as a tool to advance development grants to the least developed countries. A detailed description of IDA's objectives and projects is available at www.worldbank.org/ida.

[85] See Carl Jayarajah and William H. Branson, 'Structural and Sectoral Adjustment: World Bank Experience, 1982–92', A World Bank Operations Evaluation Study, World Bank, 1995.

[86] International Finance Corporation (IFC), founded in 1956. For a detailed description of its mission and projects, see www.ifc.org. Multilateral Investment Guarantee Agency (MIGA), founded in 1988. For a detailed description of its mission, see www.miga.org. International Centre for Settlement of Investment Disputes (ICSID), founded in 1966. A detailed description of its mission is available at www.worldbank.org/icsid.

poverty reduction and thus the World Bank has become a central player with respect to efforts to achieve the UN's Millennium Development Goals (MDGs). At the same time, with the growth of other multilateral development institutions, bilateral programmes and non-governmental organizations, and especially with the increase in financial flows to developing countries from the private sector, the World Bank now has a much less central role in global capital flows than was originally envisaged in Bretton Woods.

2.5.2   Other international/regional development bodies

The period from the early 1960s to the mid-1990s experienced a proliferation of multilateral development bodies, including:

(1) UN development initiatives such as the United Nations Development Programme (UNDP) and the United Nations Conference on Trade and Development (UNCTAD);

(2) regional development banks, modelled on the IBRD, such as the African Development Bank (AfDB), the Asian Development Bank (ADB), the Inter-American Development Bank (IADB), and (in the 1990s), the European Bank for Reconstruction and Development (EBRD);[87]

(3) a range of other multilateral financial institutions, such as the European Investment Bank (EIB), the International Fund for Agricultural Development (IFAD), the Islamic Development Bank (IsDB), the Nordic Development Fund (NDF), and Nordic Investment Bank (NIB) and the OPEC Fund for International Development; and

(4) national development agencies and aid agencies.[88]

Most of these bodies have played an influential role in shaping the global development agenda, which has culminated in many ways with the endorsement of the UN Millennium Development Goals. Apart from provision of low credit, aid donations, project management expertise and technical assistance, regional banks and development organizations have been very active in the field of law reform with the World Bank in the 2000s and EBRD in the 1990s being the leading examples.

---

[87] A detailed description of the activities of the EBRD can be found at www.ebrd.com/.

[88] Australian Agency for International Development (AusAID), the Canadian International Development Agency (CIDA), the Japan International Cooperation Agency (JICA), the UK Department for International Development (DFID) and the US Agency for International Development (USAID).

The existence of this large constellation of development IFIs and the central place given to the objective of economic growth in the period ranging from the Bretton Woods Conference to the formulation of the MDGs[89] in 2000 reveals a further paradox in the global financial governance edifice. While financial stability is the key to economic development,[90] access to finance and capital flows have been recognized as one of the main tools to achieve that, there is generally no mention of the development objective in most international financial regulation documents and standards. As explained in Chapter 8, this shortcoming of international financial standards ought to be redressed, provided that the overarching objectives of financial stability and investor/consumer protection are not compromised.

2.6   Trade liberalization and financial services: from the ITO to the WTO

2.6.1   Introductory remarks

The ITO, which was intended to serve a formal role in the reduction of trade barriers and facilitation of cross-border investment, never came into existence, because of US Congress opposition. As a result, the General Agreement on Tariffs and Trade (GATT) – established at the 1948 Havana conference – became a self-standing mechanism until the establishment of the World Trade Organization (WTO) in 1995. In spite of its rudimentary institutional infrastructure, GATT was successful in achieving significant liberalization in the field of trade in goods, also taking into account the difficult trade relations that had developed between the rival international camps during the Cold War era. On the other hand, flows of cross-border investment were mostly the subject matter of bilateral agreements and thus in most cases they were dealt with outside the GATT framework.

---

[89]   In a set of historic agreements, all the countries in the United Nations (UN), with the support of the International Monetary Fund (IMF), the World Bank, the OECD, the G-7, and the G-20, signed up to a set of Millennium Development Goals (General Assembly Resolution 55/2). *Inter alia*, the MDGs seek to: (1) reduce extreme poverty and hunger by 2015; (2) achieve universal primary education by 2015; (3) reduce by two thirds, between 1990 and 2015, the under-five mortality rate; (4) ensure a sustainable environment, etc. In addition the MDGs call for the creation of global partnership for development. More information on the MDGs can be found in Human Development Report 2003, 'Millennium Development Goals: A Compact Among Nations to End Human Poverty', UN Development Programme (2003), and on the site: www.developmentgoals.org.

[90]   Douglas Arner, *Financial Stability, Economic Growth, and the Role of Law* (Cambridge University Press, 2007), Chapters 1–2.

The Uruguay round of GATT negotiations culminated with the Marrakesh Agreement, which entered into force on 1 January 1995. Specifically the Marrakesh Agreement comprised the WTO Agreement, which established the World Trade Organization, a new governing body dealing with issues of co-ordination and implementation of international trade agreements and resolution of disputes arising from them. The WTO framework consists of, *inter alia*: the General Agreement on Tariffs and Trade 1994 (GATT), the Agreement on Trade Related Aspects of Intellectual Property Rights (TRIPS), which established an international protection regime for intellectual property rights', and the General Agreement on Trade in Services (GATS),[91] which extended to all service sectors, including financial services.[92] The Fifth Protocol to the GATS, which entered into force on 1 March 1999, provided WTO members' commitments with respect to financial services. This can be revised only as part of a formal revision of the GATS.

It was thought at the time that the WTO agreements would benefit both developed and developing countries. The US essentially opened up its market for goods and services, including manufacturing and agricultural goods in exchange for the creation of a global market for its services sectors, which could not thrive in the global market context without attendant protection of patent rights, trade marks and copyright. Developing countries, on the other hand, thought that they had opened up the Western countries' markets for their agricultural products, but their chief benefit from trade liberalization came in the form of a geo-metric increase in flows of foreign direct investment and manufacturing and service support jobs. Therefore, until the GFC, the chief beneficiaries of trade globalization were China, India, Russia, Brazil, also probably Germany and a small number of other European countries and much less

---

[91] GATS is composed of four parts: (1) the main text of the Agreement (The General Agreement on Trade in Services), (2) eight Annexes, (3) Schedules of specific commitments (4) List of Art. II exemptions.

[92] The main legal components affecting international trade in financial services include: GATS, Annex on Financial Services, Second Annex on Financial Services, Understanding on Commitments in Financial Services, Second Protocol to the GATS, Fifth Protocol to the GATS, Decisions, and Understanding on Rules and Procedures Governing the Settlement of Disputes (DSU). These components contain a number of general obligations respecting trade and financial services contained in the various agreements, including most-favoured nation (MFN) treatment, transparency and the effect of domestic regulation. For further analysis see Panagiotis Delimatsis, 'The Continued Relevance of the GATS in the New Financial Landscape – A Legal Perspective', TILEC Discussion Paper 2010–031, August 2010, pp. 3–5.

the US which has had a large trade deficit for the best part of the last decade. As explained in Chapter 3, this development meant that emerging countries, which built massive trade surpluses in the process, invested those surpluses either directly or indirectly in the financial systems of the developed countries, chiefly in the US, intensifying the housing bubble as well as the bubble in other asset markets.

2.6.2   The 'prudential regulation carve out'

Following the implementation of GATS, foreign entry in national financial services markets is based either on bilateral and regional agreements,[93] or it is centred on GATS. However, unlike areas such as trade in goods, in the area of financial services, because of the 'prudential regulation carve out', which is enshrined in the second paragraph of the Financial Services Annex to GATS, liberalization is at the discretion of individual WTO members and remains quite limited in most cases.[94] The scope of the 'prudential regulation carve out' was and has remained rather imprecise.[95] This is lamentable, since it may be used to exempt the host country from any obligation provided under GATS (and not only in the Financial Services Annex), if the requisite conditions (laid down in paragraph 2 of the Annex) are met.[96] Essentially this means that any restrictive measure that is plausibly founded on prudential grounds can justify decline of access or discriminatory controls. Accordingly, the operation, scope and interpretation of the 'prudential regulation carve out' is rather problematic and needs rethinking,[97] but this cannot be done in isolation from other issues.

[93] Chiefly, the European Union, the Association of Southeast Asian Nations (ASEAN), Mercosur, North American Free Trade Agreement (NAFTA) and Southern African Development Community (SADC).

[94] See Thomas Cottier and Markus Krajewski, 'What Role for Non-Discrimination and Prudential Standards in International Financial Law?' (2010) 13 *Journal of International Economic Law* 817–35.

[95] 'As negotiations during the Uruguay Round were advancing ... negotiators realized that, along with Article XIV on General Exceptions that the framework agreement incorporated, there was a need for a provision *which would exempt from the scope of the GATS regulatory interventions in the financial sector which are based on prudential concerns.* As a result, the GATS drafters adopted a prudential carve-out in paragraph 2 of the Financial Services Annex without however feeling the need to define what this category of measures actually entails.' Delimatsis, 'The Continued Relevance of the GATS', p. 13 (emphasis added).

[96] *Ibid.*, p. 14

[97] For the need to either bring about global harmonization of prudential regulation or conclude agreements of mutual recognition of national prudential regimes through GATS, which would render the 'prudential regulation carve out' inapplicable, see

The WTO framework is an important starting point in supporting foreign competition in financial services. At the same time, it needs to be carefully considered in the context of the relationship between financial liberalization and financial stability. Moreover, it should not be seen in isolation from the wider debate regarding the management of trade imbalances. Thus, financial stability should take centre stage in the wider WTO negotiations. In Chapter 8, I provide a sketch of a governance framework for global financial markets under which, in the context of a new international law agreement, the specific institutions directly covered by the stricter regulatory regime of the suggested global governance scheme will have automatic rights of entry to any national market without being restricted by the 'prudential regulation carve out'.

3. Intermediate phase: a 'New International Financial Architecture' (1998–2008)

3.1 An overview of the NIFA

During the 1990s, as finance became increasingly global, so did the ensuing financial crises. None of the governance structures of the post-Bretton Woods period, which were no more than an incremental evolution of the Bretton Woods framework, were adequate to sustain the pressure emanating from the developing wave of financial innovation, liberalization and market integration that characterized the emergence of financial globalization in the 1990s. In addition, the pre-1998 governance structures were very 'light' and could not provide any kind of forward looking regulatory direction beyond market liberalization. Even in advocating the latter, they were just following market developments as well as Washington Consensus policies fervently embraced by the Bretton Woods' twins and the US Treasury.[98] Those policies, with their focus on liberalization, opening up markets and more importantly abolition of capital restrictions without paying any attention to the level of domestic market development or the competence and expertise of its regulatory institutions meant that the Asian Crisis was an accident waiting to happen. And eventually it

---

Cottier and Krajewski, 'What Role for Non-Discrimination and Prudential Standards in International Financial Law?' 827–33.

[98] For a discussion and critique of Washington Consensus policies and of their impact see Chapter 2, Section 5.3.

happened in the summer/autumn of 1997 and shook global market confidence for some time.[99]

The Asian Crisis made pressing the need for new governance structures for global finance, especially as regards the establishment of early warning systems and regulatory co-operation in the field of crisis prevention and crisis management.[100] Accordingly, in part in order to restore confidence and in part in order to redress some of the weaknesses of the first phase with its lack of any serious market monitoring, discussions centred on the establishment of a New International Financial Architecture. The governance/monitoring/regulatory areas that required strengthening were, according to Camdessus, the then head of the IMF:[101]

(1) surveillance of national economic policies, which should be facilitated by fuller disclosure of all relevant economic and financial data;
(2) regional surveillance in order to encourage countries in the same region to discipline each other in order to prevent contagion;
(3) revamped prudential regulation and supervision leading to (resilient) financial sector reform;
(4) more effective structures for debt workouts, both at the national level and international level;
(5) capital account liberalization to increase the orderliness of and access to international capital markets;
(6) world-wide promotion of good governance and reduction of corruption; and
(7) strengthening IFIs, both in terms of resources, authority and legitimacy, by broadening representation.

In the end, much less happened and resulting governance structures proved markedly weak and ineffective to forecast, prevent or manage the GFC that erupted almost a decade later. Yet most regulatory initiatives (with the exception of Basel II) were in the right direction. It was rather the absence of compulsory monitoring mechanisms and lack of

---

[99] For an overview of the Asian Crisis see Chapter 2, Section 6.1.
[100] See B. Eichengreen, *Toward a New International Financial Architecture: A Practical Post-Asia Agenda* (Washington, DC: Institute for International Economics, 1999). In a sense, the foundation stone of the new architecture had been placed before the Asian Crisis, when the G-7/8 had gradually wrested the role of central policy co-ordinator.
[101] M. Camdessus, 'The Role of the IMF: Past, Present, and Future', IMF Speech 98/4, Remarks at the Annual Meeting of the Bretton Woods Committee, Washington DC, 13 February 1998; M. Camdessus, 'Reflections on the Crisis in Asia', IMF Speech 98/3, Address to the Extraordinary Ministerial Meeting of the Group of 24, Caracas, Venezuela, 7 February 1998.

supervisory capacity and of a binding framework for the management of cross-border crises which largely diminished the importance of good work that had been undertaken in the context of NIFA.

The system adopted was mostly concerned with organizing the disparate soft law networks in a tighter new structure, facilitated by the establishment of a new informal body, the Financial Stability Forum (FSF). Thus, while NIFA arrangements led to the reinforcement of the role of the IMF and of already existing standard-setting bodies, such as the BCBS and IOSCO, the only truly new body to emerge from it was the FSF.

In general, the NIFA system had four levels, incorporating both existing and new international institutions and organizations:

(1) inter-governmental (state-to-state contact) groups, mainly combinations of G-7/G-8-10;[102]
(2) international standard-setting bodies, largely of a technocratic nature;
(3) implementation of standards – in principle a domestic process but in practice developing countries received technical assistance through a variety of international, regional and bilateral sources, which also in some cases lobbied for or 'coerced' implementation (e.g., through the IMF conditionality); and
(4) monitoring implementation of standards, through the IMF/World Bank Financial Sector Assessment Program.

Arguably, the fourth level of NIFA was the biggest advancement over pre-existing arrangements. For the first time, international financial standards were to be supported by a rudimentary level of monitoring at the international level, primarily through the IMF/World Bank/FSAP/ROSC process, moving standards and standard-setting organizations from a purely agreement-based system, to one with a limited level of international review.[103] Namely, the soft law system acquired harder edges.

---

[102] For an overview of the development of the 'G' groups and their impact on the evolution of international financial regulation see Lawrence G. Baxter, 'Internationalization of Law: The "Complex" Case of Bank Regulation', in William Van Caenegem and Mary E. Hiscock (eds.), *The Internationalization of Law: Legislating, Decision-making, Practice, and Education* (Cheltenham: Edward Elgar, 2010).

[103] See, in general, Rolf H. Weber, 'Challenges for the New Financial Architecture' (2001) 31 *Hong Kong Law Journal*. 241; M. Giovanoli, 'A New Architecture for the Global Financial Market: Legal Aspects of International Financial Standard Setting', in M. Giovanoli (ed.), *International Monetary Law: Issues for the New Millennium* (Oxford University Press, 2000); Joseph J. Norton, 'Qualified Self-Regulation in the New Financial Architecture' (2000) 2 *Journal of International Banking Regulation* 9.

On the basis of the foregoing analysis, it can be plausibly argued that standard-setting under NIFA presented six general characteristics:

(1) the emergence of an international consensus on the key elements of a sound financial and regulatory system, at least within the G-10 countries;

(2) the formulation of principles and practices by international groupings of technocratic authorities with relevant expertise and experience, such as the BCBS, IOSCO, IASB and IAIS, where the influence of industry is of critical value;

(3) market discipline, which for the first time becomes an explicit pillar of supervisory practice, probably as a result and natural extension of Washington Consensus policies;

(4) liberalization of access to national markets used as an incentive for the adoption of sound supervisory systems, better corporate governance and other key elements of a robust financial system;

(5) promotion of supervisory independence; and

(6) no formal supra-national supervisory or regulatory body being created with standing in international law meaning that, as a result, ultimate responsibility for policy implementation and supervision rested with national authorities.

Probably the most definitive characteristic of NIFA was the increasing influence that private organizations, especially big banks, through their industry organizations, gradually gained over international standard setting during this period. Norton accurately notes that NIFA-I might be viewed as:[104]

> [A]n evolving policy construct in progress, moving towards a new 'governance structure' and reflecting a 'public–private partnership' among governments, financial sector authorities, international financial institutions and private international financial institutions in the search for grounding a stable, but viable global financial environment.

I explain in the next Chapter that this 'public–private partnership' proved to be a 'double-edged sword'. Private actors, beyond the obvious and very significant conflicts of interest they face, also experience several limitations in the way they perceive and process knowledge about the markets. This means that their input is of course valuable but not always reliable. Thus, uncritical endorsement of their views can prove very detrimental to

---

[104] Norton, '"NIFA II"', 272.

financial stability, as was, for example, their insistence on the accuracy of capital requirements based on risk-modelling.

3.2 The evolution of standard setting bodies and financial standards during NIFA

3.2.1 The role of the G-7 during NIFA

In the 1997 Denver Summit, the G-7 Heads of State and Finance Ministers placed 'financial stability' centre stage, issuing a 'Final Report on Financial Stability'.[105] Greater co-operation among supervisors and among the IFIs was strongly encouraged. The issue of corruption. Anti-terrorism also became main subjects for consideration. The Summit advocated the widespread adoption of the BCBS's 1997 Core Principles (revised in 2006) on bank supervision. At the May 1998 Birmingham Summit, the G-7 Finance Ministers delivered a report to the G-7 Heads of State and Government entitled 'Strengthening the Architecture of the Global Financial System'. This report identified five key areas in need for action:

(1) enhanced transparency;
(2) helping countries prepare for integration into the global economy and for free global capital flows;
(3) strengthening national financial systems;
(4) ensuring that the private sector takes responsibility for its lending decisions; and
(5) enhancing further the role of the International Financial Institutions and co-operation between them.[106]

This report also outlined the implementation steps to be taken in going forward with each of these areas and identified other areas for attention. The G-7 Finance Minister Reports in Cologne (June 1999) and Okinawa (June 2000) specifically followed up, in some detail, and outlined the central components of NIFA targeting financial stability:[107]

---

[105] See Final Report of the G-7 Heads of State and Government on Promoting Financial Stability, 21 June 1997, available at www.g7.utoronto.ca/summit/1997denver/finanrpt.htm .
[106] A detailed description of the Birmingham Report is available at www.g8.utoronto.ca/summit/1998birmingham/g7heads.htm.
[107] See Report of the G7 Finance Ministers to the Köln (Cologne) Summit, 18–20 June 1999, available at www.g8utoronto.ca/finance/fm061999.htm and Report of the G-7 Finance Ministers to the Heads of State and Government (2000 Okinawa Summit), Fukuoka, Japan, 8 July 2000, available at www.g7.utoronto.ca/finance/fm20000708-st.html.

(1) stronger macroeconomic policies for emerging economies;
(2) IFI (in particular the IMF) reform and strengthening of the operating framework;
(3) accurate and timely informational flows and transparency;
(4) strong financial regulation in industrial countries;
(5) strong financial systems in emerging markets;
(6) exchange rate policies;
(7) sound accounting standards;
(8) reform of legal infrastructure;
(9) strengthening of corporate governance;
(10) anticorruption/money laundering;
(11) technological innovation/adaptation; and
(12) risk management.

Although many of the above ingredients of an economic, regulatory and supervisory framework fostering financial stability are rather mainstream, the list above also had surprising inclusions, such as corporate governance.

The main vehicle for the implementation of these initiatives would be a set of 'global principles and standards' touching on the following areas: banking regulation; capital markets regulation; insurance supervision; corporate governance; financial conglomerates; payment, settlement and custody mechanisms; pension funds and collective investment schemes; and accounting and auditing standards. Other areas that were addressed by G-7 Finance Ministers (with mixed results) were such matters as: exchange rate stability; short-term capital flows; regional responses to financial crises; reform of the IFIs; offshore centres; and highly leveraged institutions, such as hedge funds. Other relevant matters that were not tackled with any degree of consistency were the 'prudential regulation carve out', namely the interaction of international prudential standards and the WTO/GATS liberalization process for financial services and, even more critically, as it was shown during the GFC, the consolidated supervision of global banks, banking/financial organizations and financial conglomerates.

At the June 2000 Okinawa Summit, the G-7 Finance Ministers delivered a further report: 'Strengthening the International Financial Architecture'. The report noted, with much support, the recent creation of the FSF and the G-20 to help support the new architecture. More specifically, the report primarily focused on reform of the IMF, including enhancement of its surveillance functions and its lending facilities.[108] However, as the memory of the Asian disaster started fading and the global economy started growing again, other important issues, such as global terrorism, came to the fore. Thus, financial stability became a sideshow and the G-7/8 focus shifted to those other political and security challenges.[109]

3.2.2 The role of the G-20 during NIFA

The G-20 was created as a response both to the financial crises of the late 1990s and a growing recognition that key emerging market countries were not adequately included in the core of global economic policy making and governance.[110] Thus, in September 1999, the G-7 Finance Ministers formally announced the establishment of the Group of 20 Finance Ministers as the successor to the G-22/G-33.[111] The G-20 (Finance Ministers) was conceived as a complement to the G-7 (Finance Ministers), not as a replacement. The Group's mandate was to be (yet another) informal forum that promoted open and constructive discussion between industrial and emerging market countries on key issues related to global economic stability. By contributing to the strengthening of the international financial architecture and providing opportunities for dialogue on national policies, international co-operation and international financial institutions, the G-20 helps to support growth and development across the globe. The primary, but not sole function, of the G-20 (Finance Ministers) was to consider global and emerging market financial matters and assist in overseeing the international financial system in the post-Asian Crisis period and to encourage the implementation of NIFA standards and structures.[112]

The first meeting of the G-20 Finance Ministers and central bank governors was held successfully in Berlin in December 1999. There was no

---

[108] The full report is available at www.g8.utoronto.ca/finance/fm20000708-st.html.

[109] See John Kirton, 'G7/8 Summit Remit Mandates, 1975–2003', G8 Research Group, University of Toronto, 24 June 2003, available at www.g7.utoronto.ca/evaluations/factsheet/factsheet_remits.html and for an overview of the G-7 evolving role during the same period, see Peter I. Hajnal and John J. Kirton, 'The Evolving Role and Agenda of the G7/G8: A North American Perspective', (2000) 7 *National Institute for Research Advancement Review* 5, 6, available at www.g7.utoronto.ca/scholar/hajnal_nira.pdf.

[110] A detailed description of the G-20 mandate is available at www.g20.org/G20.

[111] See G-7 Communiqué, Meeting of the G-7 Finance Ministers and Central Bank Governors, para. 19, 25 September 1999, Washington, DC. The full text of the communiqué is available at www.g7.utoronto.ca/finance/fm992509state.htm.

[112] The inaugural G-20 meeting communiqué, Berlin, 15–16 December 1999, available at www.g20.org/G20/webapp/publicEN/publication/communiques/doc/1999_germany.pdf.

formal secretariat – administrative matters were handled by the country hosting the meeting and then passed on to the next host. No formal communiqué was issued. Subsequently, it was intended that there would be annual meetings of the Ministers and two additional meetings of the deputies (often in the form of workshops or seminars). Members would be considered equal: there would be no formal voting. Group positions would be by consensus. The view of close observers of the group is that the G-20 (Finance Ministers) did provide meaningful leadership and input from 1999 through 2004 in the context of NIFA implementation and monitoring.[113] Financial stability became an issue of lesser importance after 2004, when the underlying issues were thought to have been properly addressed, and broader financial and economic issues came to dominate the Group's agenda, especially the issue of better integration of emerging economies into the globalization process and the world financial system.[114]

From 2005 onwards the G-20 (Finance Ministers) started to focus on 'balanced and orderly world economic development', which included: consideration of the volatility in the price of oil and other commodities; completion of the WTO Doha round of negotiations; a sustainable growth agenda; the internal governance reform of the IMF and World Bank (e.g., quota arrangements, representation/legitimacy, effectiveness and accountability issues); review of IMF's role and facilities respecting emerging economies; energy security; and the nature of development aid programmes.[115] As a result of the GFC the G-20 has become the supreme

[113] According to Norton, during this initial five-year period, the G-20 made significant NIFA-related advancements in the following areas: (1) commitment to and promotion of the IMF/World Bank FSAP and ROSC initiatives, with the concomitant results of supporting the various international codes and standards; (2) co-operation with the FSF; (3) work on sovereign debt restructuring, in particular as to the use of bond collective action clauses (CACs) and voluntary capital markets codes of conduct; (4) work on sustainable exchange rate arrangements and phased abolition of capital controls; (5) efforts to meaningfully involve the private sector in financial crisis prevention; (6) efforts to combat financial abuse (e.g., money laundering and post 9/11 also terrorist financing) in support of market integrity as a precondition to financial stability; (7) fostering of better crisis prevention/resolution mechanisms, such as prudent asset-liability management, adoption of codes and standards, greater transparency, effective and accountable IFIs and enhanced worldwide surveillance and EWSs; and (8) the role of 'institution building' in the financial sector. See Norton, '"NIFA-II"', 278.

[114] Other issues that dominated the agenda of the G-20 (Finance Ministers) were the formulation and implementation of the UN's 2000 MDGs and the issue of 'financing for development' which is part of the MDGs.

[115] See generally G-20 Finance Ministers Communiqué, Xianghe, Hebei, China, 15–16 October 2005. For an insightful analysis on the work of the G-20 from 1999–2007, from

co-ordination and policy making body in the field of global financial reform. The G-20's new role in the emerging global financial architecture is discussed in Section 4.2 below.

3.2.3 The evolution of the IMF

As explained above, since the early 1970s, particularly during the 1980s and the 1990s with the emergence of an array of sovereign debt crises, including the 1994–5 Mexican Crisis and the Asian Crisis, it became apparent that microeconomic, institutional and structural issues had considerable impact on a country's abilities to implement sound macroeconomic and exchange policies. During the same period the IMF was in search of a new mission. In the process, the IMF became the main IFI dealing with global financial stability and crisis prevention also adding standard production to its remit. This shift also meant that the IMF's role as a policy maker and policy giver came under intense criticism. For instance, the Washington Consensus-based liberalization recipe that it gave to most countries in distress during the Asian Crisis was widely regarded to be counterproductive[116] or outright harmful.[117] The IMF became a particularly strong mechanism for the promotion of NIFA standards, since compliance with requisite standards and law reform requests could be tied to its 'conditionality'.[118] In addition, through the NIFA monitoring arrangements, the IMF became a central player in measuring the effectiveness of IFSs in the NIFA period.

The joint IMF/World Bank FSAP and ROSC initiative was intended to promote long-term financial sector reform. The IMF could assess financial sector robustness through: (1) bilateral country consultations and surveillance[119] and a range of 'financial soundness indicators'[120] (included

an emerging economy perspective, see Leonardo Martinez-Diaz, 'The G20 After Eight Years: How Effective a Vehicle for Developing-Country Influence?', Brookings Global Economy and Development Working Paper No. 12, October 2007, available at ssrn.com/sol3/papers.cfm?abstract_Id.=1080280.

[116] See Chapter 2, Section 6.1 and notes therein.
[117] See J. Stiglitz, *Globalization and Its Discontents* (London: Penguin, 2003) and Douglas Arner and Ross Buckley, *From Crisis to Crisis: The Global Financial System and Regulatory Failure* (The Hague: Kluwer Law International, 2011), Chapter 4.
[118] See Stanley Fischer, 'Speech: The IMF and the Financial Sector: Financial Risks, System Stability, and Economic Globalization', June 2000, available at www.imf.org/external/np/speeches/2000/060500.HTM.
[119] See IMF, 'Bilateral Surveillance over Members' Policies – Executive Board Decision', 15 June 2007, available at www.imf.org/external/np/sec/pn/2007/pn0769.htm#decision.
[120] See IMF, 'Financial Soundness Indicators (FSIs) and the IMF', available at www.imf.org/external/np/sta/fsi/eng/fsi.htm.

as part of FSAP programme) and (2) multilateral surveillance involving ongoing analysis of global and regional trends,[121] multilateral consultations on global imbalances, various Early Warning System (EWS)
models,[122] and data quality and dissemination channels. For the reasons
explained below, these tools proved highly ineffective to forecast and
prevent the GFC.

3.2.4   Financial Stability Forum: international oversight and co-ordination

The Financial Stability Forum (FSF) was established under the auspices
of the G-7 in February 1999, with a mandate to: (1) promote international financial stability; (2) improve the functioning of markets; and
(3) reduce systemic risk through enhanced information exchange and
international co-operation in financial market supervision and surveillance.[123] The FSF included five different types of members: national
authorities, international financial institutions, other international
organizations, international financial organizations and committees
of central bank experts. The FSF created a number of ad hoc working
groups to develop recommendations on specific issues, including highly
leveraged institutions, capital flows, offshore financial centres, implementation of standards, incentives to foster implementation of standards, deposit insurance and e-finance. Arguably, the most important
part of the FSF's original mandate was the strengthening of surveillance
and supervision of the international financial system. Specifically, the
FSF was called to:

(1) assess vulnerabilities affecting the international financial system;
(2) identify and oversee the action needed to address these; and

---

[121] Two of the main outputs are the IMF's annual World Economic Outlook and the semi-
annual Global Financial Stability Report. The IMF used to see 'multilateral surveillance'
as being the most important of its functions and described it as: '[T]he surveillance
of economic linkages and policy spillovers between countries as well as international
economic and market developments'. For a detailed description of the IMF, see Office
of Independent Evaluation, 'An Evaluation of the IMF's Multilateral Surveillance',
September 2006, Chapter I, available at www.imf.org/external/np/ieo/2006/ms/eng/
index.htm.

[122] See A. Berg, E. Borenzstein and C. Patillo, 'Assessing Early Warning Systems: How Have
They Worked?' IMF Working Paper (WP/04/52), April 2004, available at Ideas.repec.
org/p/imf/imfwpa/04–52.html.

[123] See George A. Walker, 'A New International Architecture and the Financial Stability
Forum', Essays in International Financial Law and Economics, London Institute, No. 24,
1999.

(3) improve co-ordination and information exchange among the various authorities responsible for financial stability.[124]

Eventually, the FSF constituents agreed upon twelve key areas of standards, grouped into three main categories and known as the Compendium. Each set of key standards was supported by a methodology for assessment and implementation and a variety of related principles, practices and guidelines.[125] The FSB has indicated that it will update the Compendium to add to the list of key standards.[126]

[124] A description is available at www.fsforum.org/about/mandate.htm.

[125] The key standards represent minimum requirements for good practice and often refer to more than one aspect of the financial system. They also vary in terms of level of international endorsement. A broad categorization of the endorsed standards may be grouped as follows:

Macroeconomic Policy and Data Transparency
  (1) Monetary and financial policy transparency: 'Code of Good Practices on Transparency in Monetary and Financial Policies', issued by the IMF.
  (2) Fiscal policy transparency: 'Code of Good Practices on Fiscal Transparency', issued by the IMF.
  (3) Data dissemination: 'Special Data Dissemination Standard/General Data Dissemination System', issued by the IMF.

Institutional and Market Infrastructure
  (4) Insolvency: 'Insolvency and Creditor Rights', issued by the World Bank.
  (5) Corporate governance: 'Principles of Governance', issued by the OECD.
  (6) Accounting: 'International Accounting Standards (IAS)', issued by the IASB.
  (7) Auditing: 'International Standards on Auditing (ISA)', issued by IFAC.
  (8) Payment and settlement: 'Core Principles for Systemically Important Payment Systems' – 'Recommendations for Securities Settlement Systems', issued by CPSS and IOSCO.
  (9) Market integrity: 'The Forty Recommendations of the Financial Action Task Force/9 Special Recommendations Against Terrorist Financing', issued by FATF.

Financial Regulation and Supervision
  (10) Banking supervision: 'Core Principles for Effective Banking Supervision', issued by BCBS.
  (11) Securities regulation: 'Objectives and Principles of Securities Regulation', issued by IOSCO.
  (12) Insurance supervision: 'Insurance Core Principles', issued by IAIS.

See Financial Stability Board, 'Compendium on Standards', available at: www.financialstabilityboard.org/cos/key_standards.htm.

[126] The FSB intends to add the following: 'the Recommendations for Central Counterparties by CPSS and IOSCO, which set out comprehensive standards for risk management of a central counterparty, to facilitate the reform of over-the-counter derivatives markets; (2) the Core Principles for Effective Deposit Insurance Systems by the BCBS and IADI'. The FSB will also add in the future 'one or more standards on resolution regimes for financial institutions'. Furthermore, '[t]he list of key standards will continue to be periodically reviewed and updated by the FSB in light of policy developments at the international level'. See FSB, 'Progress in the Implementation of the G20 Recommendations

Selection of areas and designation of 'key standards' was something of a bottom-up process, with standard setters choosing to address and promote their respective standards to the inter-governmental groupings such as the G-7 and the international financial institutions for adoption and support. Nonetheless, the standard-setting process acquired homogeneous characteristics.

The FSF's legacy is not as successful as it could have been.[127] Apart from problems with the selection of the key standards, its very nature was unclear, perceived by some as a 'think tank with nowhere to go',[128] probably an accurate description given its invisibility and clubbishness.[129] The opaque nature of soft law making was also another factor which undermined the FSF's legitimacy and might have also prejudiced the effectiveness of the selected standards and their implementation. Therefore, it is not surprising that the G-20 (Leaders level) decided at its Washington (November 2008) and London (April 2009) Summits to replace the FSF with the Financial Stability Board in order to strengthen co-ordination of standard production and implementation. Nonetheless, as explained in Section 4.4 below, the FSB suffers many of the shortcomings that plagued the FSF.

3.2.5   BCBS develops a risk-sensitive capital framework

One of the central and least successful parts of NIFA was the Basel II capital adequacy framework. In the late 1990s the weaknesses of Basel I led to an extensive round of negotiations for the drafting of a new accord. Given the many changes in the financial services industry and the growing difficulties experienced by supervisors with the complexity and changing nature of risk in global financial markets, the starting point was to emphasize the role of market discipline in risk management.[130] In

---

for Strengthening Financial Stability – Report of the Financial Stability Board to G20 Finance Ministers and Central Bank Governors', 10 April 2011.

[127] Cally Jordan, 'The Dangerous Illusion of International Financial Standards and the Legacy of the Financial Stability Forum', Melbourne Law School, Legal Studies Research Paper No. 501, 20 August 2010, available at ssrn.com/abstract=1662609. 'After an initial honeymoon period, however, the FSF appeared to lose its way, ultimately proving to be a monumental disappointment … That the FSF was a failure is patently obvious. It has been relegated to the dustbin of history with little ado'. *Ibid.*, pp. 3–4.

[128] John Eatwell, 'The Challenges Facing International Financial Regulation', Western Economic Association, July 2001, p. 14, available at: www.financialpolicy.org/DSCEatwell.pdf.

[129] Jordan, 'Dangerous Illusion', p. 17.

[130] As Daniel Tarullo (a current US Federal Reserve Governor and a Professor of Law) has observed, Basel II consultation resembled trade negotiations and at the outset no national regulator had a clear idea what outcome they desired, Daniel K. Tarullo,

June 1999, the BIS issued a proposal that would significantly change the capital adequacy Accord through extensive revision and refinement of Basel I and by providing an alternative approach to measuring risk that would bring the capital framework closer to global market risk management practices.[131] Following several rounds of consultation, the revised Accord was finally published in June 2004[132] and further additions were released in 2005.[133] The Basel II framework for the assessment of the capital adequacy of international credit institutions and monitoring of their compliance was based on three pillars: Pillar 1 provided *minimum capital requirements*; Pillar 2 described the process for the *supervisory review* of capital adequacy; and Pillar 3 provided the mechanisms to facilitate and enforce *market discipline* through public disclosure.

Pillar 1 involved significant changes in capital adequacy regulation. More specifically, although Pillar 1 reproduced the basic provisions of Basel I, it also introduced important changes in the way aspects of credit risk were to be calculated and expanded the range of risks addressed by capital adequacy standards to include operational risk. Three different options were available to banks to measure the regulatory capital that they had to assign to each asset. The first option was the *standardized approach*, which was intended to be used by less sophisticated institutions. Although it was based on Basel I, it used enhanced risk sensitivity measures, as it differentiated among exposures to different classes of bank clients. 'Risk weightings' for sovereign and corporate exposures could be calculated according to external credit assessments provided by rating agencies or public organizations such as the OECD. The second and third options were based on the new *Internal Ratings Based Approach* (IRB). Under the IRB, international banks were required to establish their own internal methods for assessing the relative risks of their assets in determining the capital requirement for given exposures. In this mode, the *foundation* version of the IRB for risk management made limited use of internal Value at Risk (VaR) models. The *advanced* IRB made much wider use of VaR and was meant for the largest and most sophisticated financial institutions.

Banking on Basel: The Future of International Financial Regulation (Washington, DC: Peterson Institute for International Economics), p. 87.

[131] BIS 'A New Capital Adequacy Framework', Basel, 1999, available at www.bis.org/publ/bcbs50.pdf.

[132] BIS, Press Release, 'G-10 Central Bank Governors and Heads of Supervision Endorse the Publication of the Revised Capital Framework', 26 June 2004, available at www.bis.org/press/p040626.htm.

[133] BCBS, 'International Convergence of Capital Measurement and Capital Standards, A Revised Framework', Updated November 2005, 'Hereinafter Basel II Accord'.

The IRB was based on measures of unexpected losses (UL) and expected losses (EL). The risk components included measures of the probability of default (PD), loss given default (LGD), the exposure at default (EAD) and effective maturity (M). In some cases, banks were required to use a supervisory value as opposed to an internal estimate for one or more of the risk components.[134] In the *foundation* version of IRB, only PD was calculated by the bank and all other risk components were specified by the supervisor. Collateral and loan guarantees were to be taken into account in calculating risk-weighted capital requirements. In the *advanced* version of IRB, all credit risk components were calculated by the bank itself. This meant that the advanced approach relied entirely on 'self- supervision', except that the bank had to qualify the models it used with the supervisor and obtain its approval. Given financial institution's superior expertise with risk-modelling, regulators in most cases would accept their risk-weight assumptions without much modification.

In relation to the application of IRB to risk assessment, a specific framework was created for the treatment of corporate exposures that presented the characteristics of specialized loans (SLs). Corporate credits that relied, for repayment of the loans, upon a stream of income generated by an asset rather than the creditworthiness of the borrower, such as project finance, income-producing real estate, lease financing (or 'object financing'), commodity financing, and high-volatility commercial real estate qualified as SLs. These forms of credit financing were subject to a tailor-made framework of capital standards.[135]

3.2.6   Critique of the Basel II framework

Following the eruption of the GFC the Basel framework was subjected to severe criticism. A full exposition of its flaws is offered in Chapter 5. Thus, only a brief summary will be provided here. First, the GFC proved that Basel II relied excessively on risk-modelling and credit ratings fostering not only regulatory arbitrage (similar to Basel I) but also a relentless push towards ever reduced equity capital cushions, the only form of regulatory capital that matters in the event of a crisis. Second, the sophistication of financial institutions meant that the supervisor had ultimately to rely on the superior risk-modelling expertise of the institution or of the CRAs, making *supervisory review* ineffective. Third, market discipline proved to be much less effective than the previously assumed monitoring mechanism for several reasons. Market participants have

---

[134] Basel II Accord, paras 210–12.   [135] *Ibid.*, paras 220–8 and 275–84.

limited ability to monitor a bank's exposures in light of the very complex instruments financial institutions trade with each other and the ability to hide exposures through shadow banking vehicles. Complexity, opacity and interconnectedness just strengthened the 'too-big-to-fail' problem, weakening, if not obliterating, shareholders' and creditors' incentives to monitor properly the market behaviour and business policies and practices of the banks concerned. Fourth, by focusing on individual banking institutions (the micro-prudential perspective), it largely ignored the impact of trading and investment behaviour of such institutions on the financial system as a whole and its stability (the macro-prudential perspective). Fifth, it provided no framework for the creation of liquidity cushions within highly geared financial institutions. As has already been explained, this was one of the main causes of the GFC. Finally, the framework was procyclical,[136] allowing increased credit flows to the economy during the period of growth, feeding asset bubbles, while banks found themselves inadequately capitalized when the various asset bubbles burst and national economies entered into recession. Both the procyclicality of the Basel framework and the lack of liquidity requirements as causes of the GFC are discussed extensively in the next chapter.

3.3   Implementation – monitoring and the FSAP surveys

3.3.1   The main characteristics of FSAP surveys

An important element of the standard-setting process involves monitoring the implementation of international standards. While primarily a domestic process, implementation is supported by a range of assistance mechanisms. Monitoring mainly takes place at the international level through the international financial institutions, especially the IMF and World Bank. Specifically, the IMF works through its annual Article IV consultations. The World Bank collaborates through ROSCs and FSAPs. The OECD and the FATF are also engaged in monitoring, with the FATF playing quite an influential role in the context of money laundering and

---

[136] The probability that the Basel II capital adequacy requirements would increase procyclicality had been convincingly described even before the finalization of the Basel II framework. See Charles Goodhart, B. Hofman, and M. Segoviano, 'Bank Regulation and Macroeconomic Fluctuations' (2004) 20 *Oxford Review of Economic Policy* 591–615 and Charles Goodhart and A. Taylor, 'Procyclicality and Volatility in the Financial System: The Implementation of Basel II and IAS 39', in Stefan Gerlach and Paul Gruenwald (eds.), *Procyclicality of Financial Systems in Asia* (New York: Palgrave, 2006).

terrorism financing. At the regional level, regional development banks encourage implementation through their respective reviews.

The G-8 mandated, in its Birmingham and Cologne Summits, the development of assessment mechanisms concerning the condition of the financial sector as a whole and recommendations for reform. The idea was that timely identification of financial system strengths and weaknesses and ensuing remedial action based on implementation of NIFA standards would help to promote financial stability and to reduce the potential for crisis. Following the mandate of those Summits, the IMF improved and expanded its surveillance mechanisms and established a joint IMF–World Bank Financial Sector Assessment Program, beginning with a joint pilot program in 1999.[137] FSAP itself consists of three main components: (1) systematic analysis of financial soundness indicators (FSIs) and stress tests; (2) assessments of standards and codes; and (3) assessment of the broader financial stability framework, including systemic liquidity arrangements, governance and transparency and financial safety nets and insolvency regimes.

Upon completion of FSAP surveys, the joint IMF/World Bank team prepares a confidential memorandum presenting their findings. The IMF uses those documents to prepare a Financial Sector Stability Assessment (FSSA) presented to its Executive Board each year. It is also often used in connection with the Fund's surveillance role under its biennial Article IV consultations.[138] Also FSAP surveys are used to facilitate the IMF's role in the production of financial standards and codes of practice as well as the World Bank's development activities enabling it to provide higher quality and more targeted technical assistance. The production of FSAP surveys is a separate activity from the IMF's role in compiling ROSCs, yet the latter is strongly based on FSAP findings. In recent years, the IMF and the World Bank have attempted to integrate the FSAP, FSSA and ROSC processes into their evolving development agenda.

3.3.2   FSAP's shortcomings

FSAP surveys have become the subject of strong criticism due to their failure to give any warning signs before the eruption of the GFC. Their practice in the pre-GFC era had, in general, shown several weaknesses.

---

[137] A detailed description of the IMF's role in carrying out FSAP surveys is available at www.imf.org/external/np/fsap/fsap.asp. A description of World Bank's involvement with FSAP is available at www1.worldbank.org/finance/html/fsap.html.
[138] Norton, "'NIFA-II'", 281.

Arguably, FSAP's inadequacies did not always relate to weak conduct of the surveys but were symptomatic of the bigger global governance weaknesses of the NIFA era and beyond. First, in the absence of an international treaty imposing a compliance commitment or any other contractual (legal) obligation, akin to that which may be imposed on IMF/World Bank borrowers through 'conditionality', co-operation with FSAP was requested voluntarily. The voluntary nature of the FSAP process was of course problematic and was cited as one of the main causes of FSAP's inability to forecast the GFC.[139] As late as 2006 approximately 20 to 25 per cent of countries that were 'systemically important' and/or had vulnerable financial systems – two key criteria endorsed by the IMF and the World Bank Boards for FSAP surveys – had not been assessed, including Turkey, Indonesia, China and, most importantly, the US.[140] In addition, the absence of a global regulatory supervisory authority to follow up FSAP findings and recommend policy under the threat of sanctions meant that timely and accurate observations as part of the FSAP, as was the case with Iceland, went unheeded.[141]

Among the FSAP's many weaknesses was the fact that the voluminous data was of variable quality and not always capable of quantitative processing, since it was also incomplete. In addition, the questions asked in the context of the FSAP process were not always those that should have been asked in the first place. Often this was due to the fact that it tried

---

[139] 'We certainly gave warnings, but these warnings *were not loud or clear enough* ... we failed to pay enough attention to factors like excess leverage, systemic risk, credit booms, and asset prices. At the same time, when we did give warnings, these warnings were often ignored by policymakers ... Moreover, effective surveillance depends on successful outreach as much as sound analysis. Collective action also proved elusive – while we forged ahead with multilateral surveillance, fully recognizing the growing linkages across countries, this exercise had only a modest impact.' Dominique Strauss-Khan, 'Multilateralism and the Role of the International Monetary Fund in the Global Financial Crisis', School of Advanced International Studies, Washington DC, 23 April 2009, available at www.imf.org/external/np/speeches/2009/042309.htm, (emphasis added).

[140] The US finally permitted an FSAP to be conducted in the wake of the global financial crisis. See IMF Independent Evaluation Office, 'Report on the Evaluation of the Financial Sector Assessment Program', 2006, available at www.imf.org/external/np/ieo/2006/fsap/eng/pdf/report.pdf. The IMF has issued a subsequent review explaining what remedial actions the Fund and its members have taken to strengthen FSAP. See IMF, 'The Financial Sectors Assessment Program After Ten Years – Experiences and Reforms for the Next Decade', 28 August 2009, available at: www.imf.org/external/np/pp/eng/2009/082809B.pdf.

[141] On FSAPs' early warning about the precarious state of Iceland's economy, see Jordan, 'Dangerous Illusion', p. 20.

to measure the implementation of 'monolithic' standards on markets of varied structure and depth as are those of developing countries.[142] Also, the carrying out of FSAP inspections suffered from major inconsistencies[143] and the lack of familiarity of IMF and World Bank staff with the national economies under scrutiny made matters even worse. One reason for these inconsistencies is an alleged lack of skills and expertise by the FSAP teams. Another was the fact that FSAP teams were mostly comprised of economists who were called to examine the implementation of financial regulations, a job that is, arguably, much better carried out by suitably qualified lawyers, especially when it involves compliance check box methods. This could have led FSAP staff to draw wrong conclusions on the inspected country's regulatory robustness. In addition, updating FSAPs, especially in view of the constantly evolving methodologies, was problematic. For any country submitting to the highly intrusive and labour intensive FSAP process, which involved facilitating the carrying out of the surveys by large teams of financial experts, FSAP was a significant burden, and even more so for smaller countries with limited resources.

The essentially domestic focus of the FSAP process did not capture cross-border linkages, influences and risk transmission channels or institutional interconnectedness. This eliminated FSAP's usefulness in the case of SIFIs that maintained very large cross-border deposit and asset bases and attendant revenue lines. Namely, the riskiness of the most important institutions in any given economy was largely under-surveyed and, as a result, risks went under-reported. Moreover, the standards themselves were in some cases problematic, backwards looking and, in the case of IOSCO Principles of Securities Regulation dominated, by efficient market ideology and US notions of tight regulation of retail equity markets ignoring the role of other markets, especially where hedge funds were very active.[144] This meant that FSAP surveys missed areas and issues

---

[142] *Ibid.*, pp. 21–3.

[143] 'A more controversial aspect of the FSAP experience, and one which may account for the inconsistencies and variability of the results, focuses on the level of technical skills within the IMF (and The World Bank) to conduct the exercises', *ibid.*, p. 21.

[144] See *ibid.*, pp. 26–8; Press release, 'Global Securities Regulators Adopt New Principles and Increase Focus on Systemic Risk', IOSCO/MR/10/2010, Montreal, 10 June 2010 available at www.iosco.org/news/pdf/IOSCONEWS188.pdf. See Technical Committee of IOSCO, 'Unregulated Financial Markets and Products Final Report', September 2009: 'All systemically important financial markets and instruments should be subject to an appropriate degree of regulation and oversight, consistently applied and proportionate to their local and global significance', p. 3.

of critical interest, especially the role of unregulated markets in propagating systemic risk. Since then IOSCO has taken stock of these inadequacies and revised its standards. The revisions added eight new principles 'based on the lessons learned from the recent financial crisis and subsequent changes in the regulatory environment'.[145]

3.4 A critique of NIFA

Well before the eruption of the GFC, globalized markets had posed very serious challenges to a system that was largely based on national regulatory/ supervisory competence, even within the EU. The three main concerns were:

(1) regulatory arbitrage, which was intensified through the use of shadow banking schemes;
(2) intensification of regulatory competition, caused by the supervisor's tendency or official mandate to attract business to their jurisdiction, which can trigger a race to the bottom; and
(3) the globalized nature of market risks, especially those linked to market abuse, and systemic risks.[146]

In addition, NIFA did not include a comprehensive financial sector/ system reform package that would factor in relevant developmental, trade and investment objectives and there was a striking absence of focus on the actual fragility of developed countries' financial systems. Furthermore, the NIFA structures were especially weak when it came to crisis warnings and cross-border crisis management.[147] As a result NIFA structures proved seriously inadequate to prevent the GFC. An extensive critique of the weaknesses of NIFA's soft law structures and lack of international supervisory capacity is offered in the next chapter.

---

[145] From IOSCO's eight new principles the most pertinent to the causes of the crisis are the following: 'Principle 7: The regulator should have or contribute to a process to review the perimeter of regulation regularly', 'Principle 22: Credit rating agencies should be subject to adequate levels of oversight. The regulatory system should ensure that credit rating agencies whose ratings are used for regulatory purposes are subject to registration and ongoing supervision' and 'Principle 28: Regulation should ensure that hedge funds and/ or hedge funds managers/advisers are subject to appropriate oversight.'

[146] See also Ethiopis Tafara and Robert J. Peterson, 'A Blueprint for Cross-Border Access to U.S. Investors: A New International Framework', (2007) 48 *Harvard International Law Journal* 31, 51.

[147] Arner and Buckley, 'Redesigning the Global Financial Architecture', p. 7.

4. The emerging architecture

4.1 Introductory remarks

While the response to the Asian financial crisis had a very strong international dimension (centred on the IMF), the majority of policies seeking to contain the severity and consequences of the GFC had a strong domestic or regional (in the case of the EU) dimension. At the international level, co-ordination initially took place through the G-7 and, at the multilateral level, through the FSF and the world's major central banks. However, from November 2008 onwards, the G-20 became the main body for co-ordination of policies intended to avert a global economic catastrophe and the melt down of the international financial system. During the initial phases which mainly affected developed countries, the IFIs and the WTO played a marginal role. Only when the tremors spread beyond the G-7 countries and especially when the crisis was transformed into a sovereign debt crisis did the IMF take centre stage. On the other hand, the WTO has remained sidelined, beyond discussions about the completion of the Doha round, possibly a serious strategic mistake as trade liberalization and financial stability should, arguably, be re-aligned at the global level.

The reform initiatives so far have been two-fold: (1) reform of supervisory structures to facilitate regulatory co-operation and crisis management and (2) replacement and enhancement of international standards to radically improve the quality of international financial regulation. The reform of IFSs and especially the new Basel framework are analytically discussed in Chapter 6, together with the new US and EU supervisory structures. In addition, I discuss in Chapter 7 the Basel proposals for the regulation of very big global banks (G-SIFIs) and the new US special resolution regime for big banks and other systemic financial institutions under the Dodd–Frank Act. Thus, the remainder of this section will just focus on the architectural changes in the period after the onset of the GFC in the international context. This new architecture is based on (1) the emergence of the G-20,[148] (2) FSF's successor the Financial Stability Board (FSB), whose main mission is the co-ordination of the standard-setting process and oversight of the standard-setting TRNs,[149] and (3) the

---

[148] See Claudia Schmucker and Katharina Gnath, 'From the G8 to the G20: Reforming the Global Economic Governance System', Garnet Working Paper No. 73/09, 2010, available at www.garneteu. org/fileadmin/documents/working_papers/7310.pdf.

[149] Douglas W. Arner and Michael W. Taylor, 'The Global Credit Crisis and the Financial Stability Board: Hardening the Soft Law of International Financial Regulation?' (2009) 32 *University of New South Wales Law Journal* 488.

reformed IMF.[150] Each of these institutions has a different membership, mission and legal status. Finally, an important role is envisaged for the joint regulatory bodies called 'supervisory colleges', which are assumed to provide co-ordination and leadership in the supervision of large systemically important cross-border financial institutions.

4.2   The emergence of the G-20

In terms of international financial governance, the most important development brought about by the GFC is the emergence of the G-20 as the principal co-ordinating body, following the formation of a government leaders' level within this group.[151] Apart from severe shortcomings of TRNs when it came to cross-border crisis management and co-ordination (analytically discussed in Chapter 5), the limited capacity and ability of IFIs made them an inadequate means for the co-ordination of meaningful international crisis management efforts.[152] Arguably, the wide array of economic policies and regulatory reforms that had to be adopted to counter the effects of the GFC made the assumption of a leading role by the G-20 governments the only reasonable response in the circumstances.

At the April 2009 London Summit, the G-20 leaders reached a broad agreement to enhance the representation of emerging economies to reflect better their economic might. The G-20 now comprises the G-7 countries (Canada, France, Germany, Italy, Japan, the UK and the US) and the biggest emerging economies: Argentina, Australia, Brazil, China, India, Indonesia, Korea, Mexico, Russia, Saudi Arabia, South Africa and Turkey. The EU is represented through the EU Presidency and the European Central Bank (ECB) bringing the membership tally to 20. Moreover, the IMF Managing Director, the Chair of the IMF IMFC, the Chair of the IMF Development Committee and the President of the World Bank are *ex officio* members of the G-20. Other formal international organizations, such as the Organisation for Economic Cooperation and Development

---

[150] For an overview of the emerging architecture see Mario Giovanoli and Diego Devos (eds.), *International Monetary and Financial Law: The Global Crisis* (Oxford University Press, 2010) and Giovanoli, 'The Reform of the International Financial Architecture'.

[151] For an analytical account see Norton, '"NIFA-II"', 281–9. A critical account is provided by Ngaire Woods, 'The G20 Leaders and Global Governance' 27 September 2010, available at www.globaleconomicgovernance.org/wp-content/uploads/Woods-2010-The-G20-and-Global-Governance.doc.pdf.

[152] David Zaring, 'International Institutional Performance in Crisis' (2010) 10 *Chicago Journal of International Law* 475, 493–4.

(OECD), are involved in certain areas. However, the WTO was not formally included – a weakness in the framework.

The nineteen country members of the G-20 plus the EU represent approximately two thirds of the world's population, 80 per cent of world trade, and 90 per cent of the world's GDP. However, the G-20's scant resources and wide and fluid agenda puts in doubt the ability (and willingness) of the G-20 (Leaders' level) to play a leadership role in the field of financial stability on a permanent basis.[153] It follows that since the G-20 represents only a temporary solution to the global challenge of financial stability governance a regulatory vacuum remains to be filled.[154] In Chapter 8, I provide an outline of a formal global governance framework that could fill the most important ideas.

4.3 The IMF

Under the new governance arrangements, mostly agreed by the G-20 (Leaders' level), the IMF is envisaged to play a key role in the global financial architecture emerging as a result of the GFC. First, the IMF has remained the most important global institution for macro-financial supervision. Second, it will conduct a strengthened FSAP, as all G-20 members have agreed to subject themselves to FSAP surveys and to support the transparent assessment of their national regulatory systems. Also it will conduct early warning exercises in co-operation with the FSB. Of course, the IMF is not a selective club of a number of influential countries, but a full-fledged international organization with solid institutional foundations and universal membership, although its quotas based decision-making process still favours the US and European members. It has the potential to be much more representative than any of the 'Gs'. In addition, the G-20 did not rule out the possibility of making FSAPs and ROSCs compulsory through a future revision of the IMF's Articles of Agreement.

Even if the FSAPs and ROSCs were made compulsory for IMF members, the question would remain as to what the IMF should do with that information, since it cannot be acted upon by the Fund itself, which lacks the powers of an international supervisor who could intervene if national authorities showed complacency in the face of stark warnings. Clearly,

---

[153] See Giovanoli, 'Reform of the International Financial Architecture', 105.
[154] Eric J. Pan, 'Challenge of International Cooperation and Institutional Design in Financial Supervision: Beyond Transgovernmental Networks' (2010) 11 *Chicago Journal of International Law* 243–84.

transforming the IMF, which is also the global lender of last resort for sovereign borrowers, into the sole supervisor of global markets would lead to concentration of excessive power into the hands of a global institution, which is already very powerful and has a rather mixed record when it comes to crisis management. Therefore, a different way must be found to build cross-border supervisory and crisis resolution capacity. I suggest in Chapter 8 that this may be done by strengthening of the IMF's supervisory capacity when it comes to monitoring the stability of the global financial system as part of a broader regulatory structure charged with the governance of international finance.

4.4   From the FSF to the FSB

The Washington and, more conclusively, the London Summit of the G-20 (Leaders level) led to the reconstitution of the much maligned FSF, which became a global yet informal Financial Stability Board. The FSB is much more representative than its predecessor, since its membership includes representatives of twenty-four countries. In addition all major IFIs, such as the IMF, the World Bank and the ECB, and all major standard-setting bodies, such as the BCBS, IOSCO and IAIS, are members of the FSB. Also, unlike the BCBS or other TRNs, FSB's membership is subject to regular reviews giving the organization a strong characteristic of openness.

The FSB has inherited the FSF's original mandate of setting standards to assess vulnerabilities affecting the financial system, identifying and overseeing actions required to address such vulnerabilities, and promoting co-ordination and information sharing among authorities responsible for financial stability. It has also been assigned a number of key additional tasks:[155]

(1) monitoring and provision of advice on market developments and their implications for regulatory policy;
(2) monitoring and provision of advice on best practices for meeting regulatory standards;
(3) undertaking joint strategic reviews of the policy development work of the ISSBs to ensure their work is timely, co-ordinated and focused on priorities and addressing gaps;
(4) setting guidelines for and supporting the establishment of supervisory colleges;

---

[155] The full list of FSB tasks is available at www.financialstabilityboard.org/about/mandate. htm.

(5) supporting contingency planning for cross-border crisis manage-
    ment, particularly with respect to systemically important firms; and
(6) collaborating with the IMF to conduct EWS exercises.

The division of responsibility between the IMF and the FSB did not
prove a thorny issue and was resolved through a joint letter by the respective chairmen of the two bodies (Dominique Strauss-Khan and Mario
Draghi).[156] The IMF has remained the principal institution responsible
for surveillance of the global financial system and monitoring of standards implementation through the FSAP and ROSCs. The FSB is taking the
lead in terms of standard setting and co-ordination of standard setting
bodies.

It has been argued by expert commentators that the FSB constitutes
a marked improvement over FSF's fading regulatory profile and weak
mandate.[157] However, the uncertainty surrounding the FSB in terms of
accountability lines and status is considerable, raising the same questions
as the operation of the BCBS. For example, while the FSB was reconstituted by the G-20, there is no clear line of reporting to this body. In addition, like the FSF, the FSB remains an informal organization, which in
itself is neither a (self-standing) standard-setting entity nor a supervisory
authority.[158] As a result, it 'has no institutional powers and can neither
force any country (whether a member of the FSF/FSB or not) to implement the standards approved by it nor impose any sanctions'.[159] In addition, its lack of a standing in international law means that the FSB does not
have any means of formal representation. Also, a number of unresolved
questions surround its standard setting and co-ordination mission. For
instance, it is by no means clear whether the FSB is the ultimate arbiter
with regard to design and adoption of IFSs, nor does its mandate extend
to rendering the other ISSBs accountable to the Board.[160] It is accurately
noted that this lack of clear lines of responsibility in terms of IFS production and implementation could become a rather contentious issue when
a controversial new IFS (or a set of IFSs), which is not based on broad
consensus and generates distributional conflict, is imposed on national
jurisdictions.[161]

---

[156] See Dominique Strauss-Kahn and Mario Draghi, 'Joint Letter to the G-20 Ministers
and Governors', 13 November 2008, available at www.financial stabilityboard.org/
publications/r_081113.pdf.
[157] Giovanoli, 'The Reform of the International Financial Architecture', 108–9.
[158] *Ibid.*, 109–10.   [159] *Ibid.*, 110.
[160] *Ibid.*, 114.   [161] *Ibid.*, 114–15.

It is widely expected that the FSB will provide a smoother framework for standard setting and implementation, although it also adds yet another layer in the already over-complicated decision-making and standard-setting system for global finance. However, its lack of formal legal status, its inability to impose sanctions for non-compliance and its lack of clear accountability lines are bound to prove problematic. Finally, the mandate given to the FSB is not the answer to the biggest questions of international regulatory co-ordination that have arisen in the course of the GFC:

(1) supervision of SIFIs with strong cross-border presence;
(2) burden sharing for resolutions of such institutions, which during the GFC fell disproportionately on home country Treasuries; and
(3) international crisis management co-ordination to contain spillovers created by actions of weak national regulators (as was the case with Icelandic regulators) or regulators that pursue a narrow national interest agenda.

Accordingly, if G-20 governments do not want to keep fighting the last crisis, which is the underlying rationale for the gigantic wave of recent reforms analytically discussed in Chapters 6 and 7, the role of the FSB will have to change. The effortless way in which the FSB has been involved in peer review to test compliance with its standards and its close involvement with supervisory colleges show that the best mission for an FSB re-constituted in the guise of an international law body is to become the formal micro-prudential regulator of G-SIFIs. Another formal body within the regulatory structure proposed in Chapter 8 could perform the FSB's duties in terms of IFS production, bringing under its umbrella of oversight the BCBS, IOSCO and other regulatory TRNs of central importance for the regulation of contemporary financial markets.

4.5   The supervisory colleges

Following the G-20 summit in Washington which stressed the importance of international regulatory co-ordination through the formation of collaborative groups of supervisors, the FSF/FSB initiated the process for the formation of supervisory colleges for (in the first place) thirty large and complex financial institutions judged to have global systemic significance.[162] Supervisory colleges are multilateral working groups

---

[162] The list of the thirty institutions that would be overseen by a college of regulators, while intended to be confidential, was leaked. Patrick Jenkins and Paul J. Davies, 'Thirty

of national authorities involved in the supervision of an international banking group. They are seen as a practical mechanism to closing the gap in the supervision of large cross-border financial groups with multiple stakeholders in a variety of countries. Thus, the colleges are established in order to enhance effective, consolidated supervision of cross-border financial groups on an ongoing basis, including monitoring any threat that the group poses for the stability of the financial system of the countries involved. However, the colleges do not interfere with existing bilateral or multilateral supervisory arrangements, nor do they act as a replacement to national regulators. A substantial part of their work (and key to their success) is overseeing the drafting of recovery and resolution plans by those groups (so-called 'living wills'), which are meant as the principal means to simplify corporate structures, making supervision more effective and to avoid Lehman-type predicaments in the resolution of cross-border groups.

The BCBS concluded its consultation on Good Practice Principles with respect to supervisory colleges in 2010 and published a final set of principles,[163] which provide college objectives, structure and decision-making process, and procedures for communication and information sharing between participating national supervisors. Although a significant improvement over pre-GFC arrangements for cross-border financial group supervision, the colleges are not international supervisors for the groups concerned. All enforcement powers remain vested with national authorities. In addition, there are a number of different colleges supervising the same international banking groups creating room for confusion.[164] Also the colleges do not provide, in the absence of burden-sharing arrangements, any comfort that in the event of a crisis they will not fall apart with each supervisor trying to guard narrowly defined national interest.

5.   Summary and concluding remarks

This chapter has charted the evolution of global governance structures from the Bretton Woods conference in 1944 to date. The relevant analysis

---

Financial Groups on Systemic Risk List', *Financial Times,* 29 November 2009, available at www.ft.com/cms/s/0/df7c3f24-dd19-11de-ad60-00144feabdc0,s01=1.html.

[163] BCBS, 'Good Practice Principles on Supervisory Colleges – Final Document', October 2010, available at www.bis.org/publ/bcbs177.pdf.

[164] For the challenges facing supervisory colleges, see Julia Black, 'Restructuring Global and EU Financial Regulation: Capacities, Coordination and Learning', LSE, Law, Society and Economy Working Papers 18/2010, 23 November 2010, pp. 38–40.

has progressed from the early post-World War II years of protectionism and closed financial markets, when the Bretton Woods twins were shaping their mandates, to the period in the 1970s that the IMF especially had to reinvent its role. The sovereign debt crises of the 1980s and 1990s and the development needs of the post-colonial world meant that, on the eve of the Asian Crisis, the two institutions stood as 'tall' as ever. In the meanwhile, their limited 'regulatory' mandate and the degree of inflexibility ingrained in their statutes and operations meant that much more co-operative forms of international regulation had to be found to address the challenges that the growth of international finance posed in the post-Bretton Woods period. Since the 1970s, when global markets showed the first signs of integration, up to the 1990s and the 2000s, when integration acquired a frenetic pace, the regulation of international finance was mostly based on informal TRNs such as the BCBS and state-to-state contact groups such as the various 'G' groupings.

The Asian Crisis meant a tightening of governance structures but in a way that would co-opt the ever more powerful interests of the global (Western) finance industry. Thus, the NIFA governance paradigm had at its centre the TRNs and their standards in the production of which the private sector had a critical say. This was coupled by a weak system of monitoring undertaken by the IMF and the World Bank. The NIFA structures proved unable to prevent, even predict, the GFC, and some of their most important segments, such as the Basel capital standards, seem to have contributed both to the build up and the severity of the GFC. This accentuated the case for far-reaching reforms. As explained in Chapters 6 and 7, the US, the EU and the TRNs have introduced critical reforms in a number of areas from capital standards to regulation of OTC derivatives trading. They particularly try to address moral hazard emanating from the operation of 'too-big-to-fail' institutions.

However, the governance architecture that has emerged, which has witnessed the rise of the G-20 and the reconsition of the FSF/FSB, does not provide any radical changes from the past. It is plausibly argued that, 'although, the soft law approach clearly failed to prevent or resolve the GFC, the solution adopted so far is an even harder version of the soft law approach'.[165] Standard-setting remains the job of the TRNs such as the BCBS, IOSCO etc, albeit under closer co-ordination through the FSB. As a result, the emerging architecture leaves largely unaddressed the regulatory and supervisory challenges already discussed. In addition, yet again,

---

[165] Arner and Taylor, 'The Global Credit Crisis and the Financial Stability Board', 488.

it neglects the mutually reinforcing relationship between financial stability and economic development. Therefore, the important reforms outlined above might just produce another failure due to the timidity of reforms pertinent to governance structures, ending up as an excellent means for fighting the causes of the last crisis.

The need for forward looking governance structures that will provide formal systemic risk and G-SIFI supervision as well as an international cross-border resolution regime for those financial institutions is as great as ever. In this respect, the dynamic roles assumed by the major parts of emerging architecture, such as the FSB and the IMF, could pave the way for more radical and at the same time evolutionary reforms, which, in the context of an international treaty, could provide effective solutions to the critical challenges international finance continues to raise.

5

The 'softness' of soft law and global financial governance

1. Introduction

In the preceding chapter, I gave an analytical account of the historical evolution of governance structures dealing with global finance. I also discussed the main Transnational Regulatory Networks (TRNs) and the most important regulatory standards they have produced, normally called International Financial Standards (IFS). In this chapter, I shall provide a critique of these structures and standards. Arguably, the challenges facing international financial regulation are not entirely dissimilar from those facing domestic regulation. However, the prevailing view is that, unlike the domestic context where formal structures are the norm, the most effective way to address the regulatory challenges posed by global markets is through the 'soft law' approach that incorporates TRNs as principal regulators with a standard setting mandate that is informal though essentially global in its reach. In accordance with Wellens and Borchardt's widely cited definition, soft law is understood here to mainly refer to:[1]

> [T]he rules of conduct that find themselves on the legally non-binding level (in the sense of enforceable and sanctionable through international responsibility) but which according to the intention of its authors indeed do possess legal scope, which has to be further defined in each case. Such rules do not have in common a uniform standard of intensity as far as their legal scope is concerned, but they do have in common that they are directed at (intention of the authors) and do have as effect (through

---

[1] See K. C. Wellens and G. Borchardt, 'Soft Law in European Community Law' (1989) 14 *European Law Review* 267–321, 274. Snyder's classic definition of soft law states 'rules of conduct which, in principle, have no legally binding force but which nevertheless may have practical effects'. Arguably, this presents a very weak form of soft law that is not representative of the actual function and effect of IFS. See Francis Snyder, 'Soft Law and Institutional Practice in the European Community', in Steve Martin (ed.), *The Construction of Europe – Essays in Honour of Emile Noel* (The Hague: Kluwer Academic Publishers, 1993) pp. 197–225, 198.

213

international law), that the conduct of States, international organisations and individuals is influenced by these rules, however without containing international legal rights and obligations.

As a result, the exact place of each of the discussed IFSs in the sliding scale of bindingness[2] is not of material importance for the purposes of the present study.

TRNs and soft law have been hailed as important mechanisms to resolve the regulatory co-ordination and enforcement challenges posed by globalization in a number of areas ranging from governance of bio-genetic research to financial regulation. TRN theory has its origins in a 'soft power' view of international relations, which was pioneered by leading liberal political theorists Robert Keohane and Joseph Nye.[3] Their analysis was reconceptualized and 'applied' in a number of areas, where international co-operation is of essence, by Anne Marie Slaughter and other international relations scholars, who have proposed a 'soft form' of international co-operation through TRNs as an effective solution to global problems. Slaughter *et al.* have conceived trans-governmental networks, which comprise regulatory networks, legislators, judges, and enforcement officials in the context of 'cooperative arrangements across borders' that 'seek to respond to global issues'.[4] Given the nature of such arrangements in the realm of international finance, this chapter only refers to TRNs that comprise co-operative networks between regulatory agencies, including

[2] Christine Chinkin, 'Normative Development in the International Legal System', in Dinah Shelton (ed.), *Commitment and Compliance – The Role of Non-Binding Norms in the International Legal Systems* (Oxford University Press, 2003), Chapter 1, p. 23.
[3] See Robert O. Keohane and Joseph Nye, *Power and Interdependence: World Politics in Transition* (White Plains, NY: Pearson, 3rd edn, 2001), especially Chapter 10 and Part VI; Robert O. Keohane and Joseph S. Nye, 'Transgovernmental Relations and International Organizations' (1974) 27 *World Politics* 39–62.
[4] Anne Marie Slaughter, *A New World Order* (Princeton University Press 2004), pp 12–14. In Slaughter's view, TRNs facilitate co-ordination and provision of solutions to global problems but they presuppose a much softer approach to states as international actors and weaker sovereignty, where disaggregated state actors delegate responsibility 'to a limited number of supranational government officials' who produce standards of best and commonly agreed solutions to global problems, *ibid.*, p. 263. Another important contribution is Kal Raustiala, 'The Architecture of International Cooperation: Transgovernmental Networks and the Future of International Law', (2002) 43 *Virginia Journal of International Law* 1–92. Raustiala has linked trans-governmental networks to international liberalism. The TRN participants co-operate in so many ways that transcend sovereignty as to lead Raustiala (and Slaughter) to talk about 'disaggregated sovereignty', *ibid.*, 17–26. In the global financial governance context a thorough analysis of the complex way TRNs operated in the pre-GFC period is offered by David Singer, *Regulating Capital: Setting Standards for the International Financial System* (Ithaca, NY: Cornell University Press, 2007).

central banks, but does not extend to other forms of networks discussed by Slaughter such as legislators' or judges' networks.

TRNs and soft law are assumed to represent a shift from formal (Westphalian)[5] international organizations built on pooling of sovereignty to post-sovereign (post-Westphalian)[6] global governance, being the inevitable result of the serious (or desirable) loss of influence experienced by sovereign actors in the modern world. States are at the receiving end of actions of transnational actors, such as multinational enterprises or global financial markets and have limited power of intervention.[7] In such situations and in many other contexts where international co-ordination is required to provide solutions to global problems, TRNs and soft law present, according to their proponents, two distinct advantages. They lower the cost of contracting[8] and entail reduced loss of sovereignty, as they are less restrictive and easier to defect from than a (hard law) international treaty.[9] TRNs are assumed to be a better mechanism to resolve, *inter alia*, cross-border co-ordination and enforcement conundra, especially where issues of sovereignty and national interest protection are of paramount concern. Therefore, due to their organizational and 'legal'

---

[5] 'Westphalian' refers to a set of principles named after the Treaty of Westphalia, which was signed in 1648 and ended the 30 Years' War in Europe. The term tends to refer to the principles of territorial integrity, legal equality among nations, state sovereignty and recognition of nation states' right to self-determination, and non-intervention in the internal affairs of other states. For centuries it was regarded as the fundamental principle of international relations. For a discussion of the principle, see Andreas Osiander, 'Sovereignty, International Relations, and the Westphalian Myth' (2001) 55 *International Organization* 251–87.

[6] See, in general, William Twinning, 'A Post-Westphalian Conception of Law', Review Essay, (2003) 37 *Law and Society Review* 199 and David Held, *Democracy and the Global Order: From the Modern State to Cosmopolitan Governance* (Stanford University Press, 1995). See also Mathias Albert, David Jacobson and Yosef Lapid (eds.), *Identities, Borders, Orders: Rethinking International Relations Theory* (Minneapolis, MN: University of Minnesota Press, 2001).

[7] See Ulrika Morth, 'Introduction', in Ulrika Morth (ed.), *Soft Law in Governance and Regulation: an Interdisciplinary Analysis* (Cheltenham: Elgar Publishing Ltd, 2004), pp. 2–3. Cf. Daniel W. Drezner, *All Politics is Global: Explaining International Regulatory Regimes* (Princeton University Press, 2007).

[8] Kenneth W. Abbott and Duncan Snidal, 'Hard and Soft Law in International Governance' (2000) 54 *International Organization* 421.

[9] See David Epstein and Sharyn O'Halloran, 'Sovereignty and Delegation in International Organizations' (2008) 71 *Law & Contemporary Problems* 77. For the cost advantages of soft law see Charles Lipson, 'Why Are Some International Agreements Informal?' (1991) 45 *International Organization* 495. Also, Christine Chinkin, 'The Challenge of Soft Law: Development and Change in International Law' (2008) 38 *International and Comparative Law Quarterly* 850–66.

flexibility, informal transnational networks are thought to be better placed to produce effective rules and standards for the global marketplace and to be more effective implementation channels than hard law structures.

On the other hand, the most critical areas of national interest interaction in the international relations sphere, such as declaration of lawful war, the protection of human rights and of the environment and international trade, have been placed on a firm international law footing. Also, the pooling of sovereignty in the exercise of core national economic policies within the framework of a formal international law agreement is far from unknown, as testified by IMF members' exchange rate stability commitments, following the Bretton Woods agreements and up to 1972. Furthermore, there is the example of the EU, where, on the basis of a legally binding treaty, member states have pooled sovereignty in a number of areas of national interest, including external trade policy and social policy. In fact, the members of the European Monetary Union have even relinquished their right to set monetary policy. These are all examples of sovereignty concessions made to serve a wider national or international good that advances national interest. Whatever the problems associated with the operation and governance of those international law organizations, nobody has really suggested that co-ordination and enforcement problems observed within them should lead to their replacement by soft law structures and transfer of key decisions to TRNs.

Nonetheless, TRNs and soft law are still very strongly favoured as a form of governance in the context of international finance. Therefore, this chapter examines the strengths and weaknesses of the soft law approach and assesses its contribution to meeting the main challenges facing international financial regulation. For example, are we to assume that finance is so different from trade that it does not need a formal international legal framework which establishes a formal hierarchy of regulatory actors in place of the current 'flat' structure of polycentric regulation? Are the externalities associated with cross-border financial markets so much smaller than those observed in the key areas of national interest mentioned above that it is safe to leave the regulation of global markets to TRNs operating on the basis of soft law? Are the distributional conflicts created by TRNs equitably resolved within the current arrangements, in spite of their legitimacy deficit? Is indeed TRN standard setting, which is based on a 'public–private partnership', enjoying unassailable information advantages over a more formal approach to international financial regulation? And if so, how can the disastrous impact of Basel I and more critically of Basel II standards on the build-up and amplification of the consequences of the GFC be explained?

In this chapter, I shall attempt to answer several of these questions. The discussion will highlight the existing 'supervisory' and crisis management deficit in the context of global financial markets and will argue that it is time for a shift to a more formal and hierarchical approach with respect to the regulation and supervision of international finance.[10] This chapter is in five sections. Section 2 discusses TRN theory and its importance in international relations. It charts the methods used by TRNs to achieve co-operation in the absence of a binding international treaty. Section 3 explains the limits of TRN theory in the sphere of international finance and the failure of the Basel I and II capital frameworks. Section 4 provides an exposition of the shortcomings of existing soft law structures, especially when it comes to cross-border crisis management and resolution. Section 5 provides an outline of a possible solution to the governance challenges already identified.

2.   What is international financial regulation?

2.1   Regulation rationales

Financial markets have a tendency to produce market failures, are vulnerable to contagion and can be susceptible to crises. These can prejudice: (1) the stability of the financial system; and (2) the interests of investors/outsiders in capital markets or financial services consumers. Therefore, it is widely accepted that the main objectives of financial regulation are:[11]

---

[10] Other recent works that have reached a similar conclusion include Eric J. Pan, 'The Challenge of International Cooperation and Institutional Design in Financial Supervision: Beyond Transgovernmental Networks' (2010) 11 *Chicago Journal of International Law* and Luis Garricano and Rosa Lastra, 'Towards a New Architecture for Financial Stability: Seven Principles' (2010) 13 *Journal of International Economic Law* 597–621, 619–20.

[11] For an overview, see George Benston and George Kaufman, 'The Appropriate Role of Bank Regulation' (1996) 106 *The Economic Journal* 688; David Llewellyn, *The Economic Rationale for Financial Regulation*, FSA, Occasional Paper Series No. 1 April 1999; Charles Goodhart, Philipp Hartmann, David T. Llewellyn, Liliana Rojas-Suarez and Steven Weisbrod, *Financial Regulation, Why, How, and Where Now?* (London: Routledge, 1998); Ross Cranston, *Principles of Banking Law* (Oxford University Press, 2nd edn, 2002), Chapter 3; Julia Black, 'Mapping the Contours of Contemporary Financial Services Regulation' (2002) 2 *Journal of Corporate Law Studies* 253–87. For the rationales of capital market regulation, see Emilios Avgouleas, *The Mechanics and Regulation of Market Abuse – A Legal and Economic Analysis* (Oxford University Press, 2005), Chapter 5.

(1) consumer/investor protection;
(2) preservation of market confidence;
(3) protection against systemic risk;
(4) maintenance of economic prosperity.[12]

The risk of systemic collapse is mostly addressed through prudential regulation comprising capital adequacy standards and principles for supervision of bank and non-bank financial entities. Thus, the primary aim of prudential regulation is to maintain the health of the system as a whole and contain systemic risk. Regulation should not seek to create a zero failure environment but an environment where institutional failure can be managed so that it does not endanger the stability of financial system and create market dislocation.[13]

The *raison d'etre* of the constellation of TRNs discussed in the previous chapter is that international financial markets raise different kinds of problems from domestic markets. From the two main pillars of financial regulation, namely, protection of systemic stability and investor/consumer protection, the first has, arguably, been given precedence in the international context, although battling information asymmetries and market abuse are also issues of great importance for cross-border markets. The stability of the international financial system[14] resembles in some respects a *tragedy of the commons* situation,[15] since it is a global public good that may come under threat for three reasons:

(1) international firms' irresponsible behaviour, e.g., selling of highly risky products or engaging in very risky investment strategies (e.g., high leverage);

---

[12] Arguably, recessions that follow banking crises are often more severe and long-lasting than recessions that have their origins elsewhere. Regulation should be especially directed at reducing the scope for these market failures. See United Nations, 'Report of the Commission of Experts of the President of the United Nations General Assembly on Reforms of the International Monetary and Financial System', New York, 21 September 2009, p. 62.

[13] Group of Thirty, 'Financial Reform: A Framework for Financial Stability', 15 January 2009, p. 20, available at www.group30.org/pubs/reformreport.pdf.

[14] See Chapter 1, note 22.

[15] See Iman Anabtawi and Steven Schwarcz, 'Regulating Systemic Risk: Towards an Analytical Framework' (2011) 86 *Notre Dame law Review* 1349. As Schwarcz and Anabtawi accurately note, this type of problem has most of the properties of 'a tragedy of the commons' situation but not all of them, since not all market participants suffer the consequences of their actions equally.

(2) collective action problems,[16] which means that even when individual firms appreciate the desirability of preserving the common good of financial stability, they may be unable to refrain from engaging in legitimate actions that can damage the stability of their fellow institutions and of the financial system as a whole, as is the case with deleveraging and resulting fire sales;[17]

(3) global systemic risk externalities/spillovers due to inability to act or deliberate complacency by national regulators when faced with irresponsible behaviour given the conflicting interests and co-ordination problems facing home and host state regulators.

The first and second externalities may only be battled through regulations that reduce, *inter alia*, moral hazard and solvency and liquidity risk. International financial regulation has striven to achieve that through capital adequacy standards, liquidity requirements, leverage ratios, netting agreements and tight accounting standards (including the recent reforms discussed in Chapters 6 and 7 below).

The third externality clearly raises the question of how to find workable solutions to national supervisors' conflict of interests, communication failures (between home and host supervisors) and attendant cross-border co-ordination challenges or failures. National supervisors may be reluctant to intervene and control a national champion, when the risks of non-intervention (regulatory forebearance) are borne by the investors/depositors of foreign jurisdictions as happened with Icelandic banks (discussed extensively in Section 4 below). Home regulators have strong incentives to engage in complacent behaviour when the costs (e.g., deposit insurance payments)[18] and the fiscal burden of intervention will fall on

---

[16] This point is also made in Yesha Yadav, 'The Spectre of Sisyphus: Re-Making International Financial Regulation After the Global Financial Crisis' (2010) 24 *Emory International Law Review* 83, 88–9.

[17] Kenneth R. French *et al.*, *The Squam Lake Report: Fixing the Financial System*(Princeton University Press, 2010).

[18] A most characteristic example is the case of the Icelandic bank Landsbanki, which also raised EU passporting issues, due to the inability of the UK (as a host regulator) to intervene early to prevent the collapse of the UK branch. Landsbanki's UK branch had raised 'retail internet deposits under the Icesave brand. It had around £4.5 billion of retail deposits outstanding at the time of failure [in October 2008]. These deposits were legally covered by the Icelandic deposit insurance scheme [and] they were covered on a top-up basis by the UK Financial Services Compensation Scheme (FSCS) ... The Icelandic government indicated that it would not be in a position to meet the liabilities of the Icelandic deposit insurance scheme immediately ... In addition, there were £800 million of retail deposits which, because above £50,000,

stakeholders/taxpayers of the home regulator and the beneficiaries are located in foreign jurisdictions. In addition, home supervisors may lack the technical expertise or adequate information to properly understand the business and risk profile of large and complex cross-border financial groups. Again, this failure is common when host supervisors only have a partial picture of the group's operations in their jurisdiction being largely ill-informed about inter-group exposures, as was the case with Lehman Brothers.

As explained in the previous chapter, a number of TRNs and IFIs have undertaken the task of producing suitable regulation for international (and domestic) markets which take legal force through co-ordinated national implementation and peer (or IFI) review of compliance.[19] As this is a non-hierarchical and polycentric structure there is no global authority with a clear mandate to:

(1) supervise systemic risk in an international context, though the European Systemic Risk Board (ESRB) will now fulfil this role in the EU context;
(2) directly supervise cross-border financial institutions (G-SIFIs) and markets on a unitary basis;
(3) monitor national regulators compliance, manage knowledge about emerging risks in the markets and oversee production of regulatory standards by the TRNs, such as the BCBS and IOSCO; and
(4) take resolution action for G-SIFIs and liaise with the G-20 when it comes to international financial crisis management.

Arguably, these shortcomings were among the fundamental reasons for the amplification of the GFC. Therefore, in the remainder of this section I will discuss the advantages and disadvantages of soft law in light of the GFC. In the next section I will consider the implications of the absence of international supervisory and cross-border crisis management capacity.

were covered neither by the Icelandic scheme nor by the FSCS top up. The UK government concluded that these deposits should be protected ... The total initial costs of retail depositor protection arising from the collapse of Landsbanki's UK branch have therefore been met by a combination of the UK government and the FSCS.' See FSA, DP09/2, 'A Regulatory Response to the Global Banking Crisis', DP0912, March 2009, p. 57.

[19] Rolf H. Weber, 'Mapping and Structuring International Financial Regulation – A Theoretical Approach' (2009) *European Business Law Review* 651–88.

2.2 The advantages of soft law and TRNs in the context of global financial governance

The public/private and national/international nature of the economic activities associated with the operation of global financial markets often present intractable challenges and dilemmas and transcend traditional classifications of hard and soft law. In many ways international financial law should not qualify as law at all and in fact it stretches to its limits any notion of what is law, at least in the sphere of international relations, since it is not the product of state actors binding themselves to the promulgated rules and standards.[20] International financial standards are not based on any form of legally binding treaties and are promulgated and implemented mostly by means of informal arrangements.

The traditional view of international law/international relations is that where weak disciplining mechanisms are employed, co-ordination will likely only arise where members have high incentives to co-operate and adjustment costs are small. In areas where significant distributional problems arise, adjustment costs will often be high and non-compliance will not be possible. Instead, only where strong disciplining measures are used – usually through a mix of monitoring mechanisms that impose reputational and market costs – is co-ordination possible. Thus, traditionalists do not see the soft law structures of international financial regulation as being law, but something that is advanced by means of the economic influence of certain nations and the hegemony they exert over world financial affairs.

The traditional view has been criticized as flawed, because it does not provide 'a comprehensive account of the co-ordination challenges underlying cross-border regulation and the function and role of international financial law in the global financial system'.[21] It fails to explain why soft law exists at all in a variety of contexts and chiefly in the realm of international financial regulation. For example, the absence of any formal obligation to comply does not foster opportunism by implying that a cheap exit from commitments may be available.[22] An easy dismissal of soft law overlooks

---

[20] For a good analysis of the issue see Lawrence G. Baxter, 'Internationalization of Law: The "Complex" Case of Bank Regulation', in William Van Caenegem and Mary E. Hiscock (eds.), *The Internationalization of Law: Legislating, Decision-making, Practice, and Education* (Cheltenham: Edward Elgar, 2010).

[21] Chris Brummer, 'How International Financial Law Works (and How It Doesn't)' (2011) 99 *Georgetown Law Journal* 257, 261. See also *ibid.*, 260–4. Cf. Beth Simmons, 'Compliance with International Agreements' (1998) 1 *Annual Review of Political Science* 75–93.

[22] Brummer, 'How International Financial Law Works', 271.

the need for co-operation in global markets and the context in which its rules operate. Markets and firms are in some cases independent actors whose lobbying power and importance can influence the binding force of international financial standards. Therefore, soft law mechanisms often lead to a dynamic incorporation of financial standards, where standards adopted overseas are incorporated domestically without requiring significant involvement by national governments and the legislature,[23] giving them a distinct administrative law dimension.[24]

Slaughter *et al.* as well as a number of legal experts view co-operation through TRNs as key to understanding regulatory rule-making in the realm of international financial regulation.[25] These scholars have extolled the ability of soft-law to resolve conflict and identified international financial regulation as the privileged field of successful application of TRNs and soft law.[26] They have emphasized the distributional consequences inherent in international financial rule-making and identified the various means by which states pursue their own national interests and governance standards. They also highlight how there may often be significant asymmetric benefits in complex co-ordination frameworks.

It has been suggested that the flexibility of mechanisms used by TRNs lowers the costs of regulators, who may engage in standard production without necessarily committing to the adoption of requisite standards. National regulators through their involvement in the drafting process signal (in a non-binding manner) their intention to do so. This informal quality helps the building of understanding between countries that leads to agreement and limits the uncertainty relating to the adoption of a new standard. According to the proponents of TRN theory, the operational flexibility of TRNs helps to promote common and comprehensive regulatory practices/standards by lowering the transaction

---

[23] Michael C. Dorf, 'Dynamic Incorporation of Foreign Law' (2008) 157 *University of Pennsylvania Law Review* 103.

[24] Benedict Kingsbury, Nico Krisch and Richard B. Stewart, 'The Emergence of Global Administrative Law' (2005) 68 *Law & Contemporary Problems* 15; Benedict Kingsbury, 'The Concept of "Law" in Global Administrative Law' (2009) 20 *European Journal of International Law* 23; Nico Krisch and Benedict Kingsbury, 'Introduction: Global Governance and Global Administrative Law in the International Legal Order' (2006) 17 *European Journal of International Law* 1 (discussing the concept of global administrative law).

[25] David Zaring, 'Rulemaking and Adjudication in International Law' (2008) 46 *Columbia Journal of Transnational Law* 563.

[26] David Zaring, 'International Law by Other Means: The Twilight Existence of International Financial Regulatory Organizations' (1998) 33 *Texas Intl Law Journal* 281.

costs associated with any alignment of national regulatory interests.[27] Thus, TRNs appear to be effective in resolving common co-ordination problems in the sphere of international economic relations. The participants' intention to engage is clearly signalled and the danger of wasting resources on standard production without a serious chance of implementation, which would be a strong enough incentive for regulators not to co-operate, is largely avoided.[28] In addition, although international financial (regulatory) agreements are informal, they are taken seriously by signatories, because they are the only medium available to regulators to express commitment to a policy, rule or standard. This is of key importance because even where rules are not legally binding, they may still influence the behaviour of regulators and market participants seeking to make credible commitments of efficiency, value and strong corporate governance or investor protection.

TRNs are said to increase regulatory capacity, since in the context of devising new standards and practices regulators do not start from zero. They share common experiences and learn from each other in a co-operative framework. Thus TRNs render regulation production much cheaper and, arguably, make it much more effective, given also their tendency to conduct long consultations and enrol the views and help of industry organizations such as ISDA and expert groups, many of which were discussed in the previous chapter.

Moreover, while soft law is not regarded by classical international law theory as imposing costs in the event of defection, since it is not binding, it does, nonetheless, give rise to a framework where regulators may be assumed to be bound by reputational constraints. TRNs can publicly signal a member's failure to comply with particular rules or standards, a likely scenario if the infraction is critical. This is not unlike the 'name' and 'shame' policy followed by formal international organizations including the UN. It is also a policy followed by the Financial Action Taskforce (FATF) with respect to jurisdictions, mostly tax havens, which do not adopt FATF dicta targeting money laundering and terrorist finance infrastructure, thereby mandating attendant checks and roadblocks. In addition, agreements frequently reflect consensus on issues with important domestic constituencies. As a result, defection from even informal agreements can have reputational costs that hamper a regulator's ability to supervise the regulated.

[27] Brummer, 'How International Financial Law Works', 283–4.
[28] Ibid., 270–2, 283.

TRNs also have mechanisms to incentivize members and non-members to make strong co-operation commitments. First, prospective TRN membership, or for existing members the opportunity to secure membership of important committees, e.g., IOSCO's Technical Committee, or members' refusal to sign MoUs with non complying countries may prove a sufficient compliance incentive. Second, the commitments of the parties might often be crystallized in multilateral or bilateral memoranda, which are entered into with the clear intention of being observed even if they are not binding in international law. For many regulators, co-ordination is already very much an assurance game that simply requires information sharing for its facilitation and MoUs play this exact role. The MoUs normally provide that signatories will grant each other the assistance required to enforce their respective financial laws and regulations. In doing so, the MoUs solidify participating regulators' commitment to facilitate each other's supervisory and enforcement actions.[29]

MoUs entail low adjustment costs, because they normally cover enforcement and not substantive convergence. The latter translates into higher adjustment costs, due to the radical changes in firm behaviour that convergence normally requires. Yet they can prove particularly useful in strengthening counterparts' supervisory and enforcement capabilities. Where signatories do not have the required domestic authority to assist counterparts seeking to enforce their laws, the MoUs force signatories to seek it from their respective legislators.[30] Therefore, regulators' shared interests expressed through MoUs may grant them considerable institutional leverage.

Although regulators might have to seek additional powers from their home governments/legislatures, as well as the resources to meet their commitments, MoUs allow national regulators to engage in an assurance game, while, at the same time, they impose fewer restraints on a country's self-determination. As a result, both Multilateral and Bilateral Memoranda of Understanding between securities regulators are largely used by IOSCO members as the primary means of enforcement co-operation. Therefore, international financial law can also employ disciplining mechanisms in the face of co-ordination problems involving low adjustment costs.

---

[29] IOSCO, 'Multilateral Memorandum of Understanding Concerning Consultation and Cooperation and the Exchange of Information', May 2002, p. 12, available at www.iosco.org/library/pubdocs/pdf/IOSCOPD126.pdf.

[30] Brummer, 'How International Financial Law Works', 286, 300–3; Pierre-Hugues Verdier, 'Transnational Regulatory Networks and Their Limits' (2009) 34 *Yale Journal of International Law* 113, 144–5.

But these disciplinary mechanisms might, in fact, prove particularly weak in the absence of monitoring mechanisms. For one, no inspection of a country's facilities are required under the bilateral MoUs, and securities authorities do not undertake surveillance of implementation or publish lists of regulators that have failed to implement measures. Instead, as indicated above, countries are largely subjected to *ex post* evaluation and monitoring whenever called on for assistance by their counterparts under the MoU. If inability or unwillingness to render assistance is observed, the reputation of the relevant country may suffer and assistance from the affronted counterparty in the future may not be readily forthcoming. Thus, reputation and the prospect of reciprocal non-compliance can act as strong disciplining mechanisms.

Finally, TRNs have been hailed for their ability to co-opt and utilize the knowledge and expertise of private actors, which is often considered superior to that of public bodies and for good reasons. However, this model also evolved into uncritical endorsement of private sector policy preferences[31] leading to a peculiar and subtle form of capture.[32] Thus it proved to work as a double-edged sword. Beyond the obvious problem of conflict of interests, private actors' knowledge may be distorted for a variety of reasons, discussed extensively in the next section.

2.3   Soft law shortcomings

2.3.1   Regulatory co-ordination

The view that TRNs are the solution to the regulatory challenges facing financial markets is not universally accepted. Strong voices have been raised highlighting the multitude of weaknesses associated with the operation of TRNs as 'global financial regulators'. First, a national regulator's principal concern is not furthering global policy objectives but the protection and advancement of the interests of the national industry.[33] There

---

[31]   See Eleni Tsingou, 'The Governance of OTC Derivatives Markets', in Peter Mooslechner, Helen Schuberth and Beat Weber (eds.), *The Political Economy of Financial Market Regulation: The Dynamics of Inclusion and Exclusion* (Aldershot: Edward Elgar, 2006), Chapter 7, pp. 168–90, 172–3.

[32]   See also Eleni Tsingou, 'Transnational Governance Networks in the Regulation of Finance – the Making of Global Regulation and Supervision Standards in the Banking Industry', in Morten Ougaard and Anna Leander (eds.), *Business and Global Governance*, (London: Routledge, 2010), pp. 138–53.

[33]   Verdier notes: 'national regulators are tied to domestic constituencies by incentives and accountability structures that are much stronger than their links to any "hypothetical global polity." As a result, national regulators acting in TRNs are not free to

is not even evidence of the famed dual duty of regulators within TRNs to both domestic and global interests.[34] But even if there was evidence of such duty, they would still not be entirely impartial actors dedicated to the protection of global public goods such as financial stability. This finding should have been enough to place TRNs under a different light since every rule or standard proposed by TRNs, at least in the realm of international finance, is bound to have distributional consequences that might affect domestic interests and above all domestic financial stability and fiscal outlay.

International regulatory co-operation often involves significant conflicts over the distributive consequences of new standards, since the costs and benefits of alternative proposals fall on different states. As developed countries dominate the TRNs, it is not surprising, although inequitable, that such conflicts are resolved in favour of the industries dominated by TRN members, even where this is at the expense of better regulatory outcomes. The most significant distribution concerns are raised by capital market's disclosure, market integrity rules and cross-border crisis management and bank resolution operations. The latter became rather common during the GFC. Even as regards the regulation of systemic risk, approaches may differ according to national economic interest and the desire to protect key economic sectors[35] or the domestic financial services industry. For instance, some countries may prove net exporters of risk because of the nature of products sold by national institutions and/or the business practices followed by them (e.g., excessive leverage, relaxed credit controls), while maintaining a cross-border presence. In such instances, in the absence of a pre-determined legally binding framework, regulators have very little incentive to co-operate and adopt more stringent regulatory standards or, for instance, take Prompt Corrective Action (PCA). Similarly, some smaller, capital-poor countries may have

---

pursue optimal global public policy for its own sake. Instead, one should expect that their positions will be shaped by the preferences of domestic constituencies.' Verdier, 'Transnational Regulatory Networks', 115.

[34] On the assumption that such a duty exists see Anne-Marie Slaughter, 'Disaggregated Sovereignty: Towards the Public Accountability of Global Government Networks' (2004) 39 *Government and Opposition* 159, 163.

[35] E.g., Verdier notes: 'The impact of domestic pressures on regulatory networks is most dramatically illustrated by instances of direct political intervention. The Basel II negotiations provide a vivid example: it is perfectly clear that Chancellor Schroeder would not have permitted German banking regulators to agree to rules that would harm SMEs, even if they had thought the policy would improve global financial stability', Verdier, 'Trasnational Regulatory Networks', 162.

little other means than weak regulations to attract capital. Without a better alternative for attracting income from financial business, they may feel that maintaining weaker standards gives them a competitive edge and benefits that exceed the risk of fraud or institutional failure. A classic example of such behaviour was, of course, Iceland.

A particular concern is the effect that the endorsement of a particular standard will have on the competitiveness of their relevant markets.[36] Some regulators may find stringent rules and regulations an effective means of attracting firms by allowing them to signal their commitment to a sound regulatory system. Meanwhile, other regulators may find it more appealing to adopt lower regulatory standards in order to attract small financial firms and investment managers seeking to avoid high regulatory costs. In addition, while some regulatory challenges are resolved by TRNs in ways that are beneficial to all states, many do not lend themselves to uncontroversial technical solutions. As a result, most of the adopted standards normally favour the markets/industries of developed countries participating in the TRNs. A characteristic example is Basel II, which, had it been fully implemented, would have adversely affected credit flows to the developing world. First, there were problems with the implementation of Basel II by the less technically advanced financial institutions in emerging market economies. Due to lack of resources and technical sophistication, these were expected to adhere to the *standardized approach* of Pillar 1, which required a higher capital cushion and thus would raise the costs of developing country banks distorting international competition.[37] Second, developing country corporations and other entities naturally have lower ratings, which would attract, under Basel II, higher capital charges, reducing credit flows to those economies.[38]

TRNs are institutionally ill equipped to resolve conflicts that entail distributional consequences.[39] This argument is evidenced beyond any reasonable doubt by the failure to take co-ordinated rescue and resolution action as regards cross-border financial groups, in the absence of a binding framework for international co-operation and fiscal burden

---

[36] See Stavros Gadinis, 'The Politics of Competition in International Financial Regulation' (2008) 49 *Harvard International Law Journal* 447.

[37] Robert Bailey, 'Basel and Development Countries: Understanding the Implications', LSE, Development Studies Institute, Working Paper 05–71, December 2005, pp. 34–5 and 38–9.

[38] Stephany Griffith-Jones and Stephen Spratt, 'The New Basle Capital Accord and Developing Countries, Issues, Implications and Policy Proposals', Discussion Paper No. 2002/36, World Institute for Development Economics Research, March 2002.

[39] Verdier, 'Transnational Regulatory Networks', 115.

sharing. In order to resolve distributive conflicts, international negotiations must involve concessions and trade-offs across areas of national interest and, in some cases, threats and other manifestations of power. These tasks are not normally entrusted to regulatory agencies but are exercised by government bodies, which will essentially determine the said concessions or threat of sanctions. Accordingly, TRNs are neither as apolitical as they are supposed to be, nor can they be effective monitors without exercise of some sort of sovereign power by the governments of participating states.

Although emerging economies may well be affected by international financial rules, wealthier developed countries generally have more at stake in complex financial rule making.[40] For example, some countries may have a relatively small or concentrated domestic investor base, and therefore may have less at stake or even less interest in developing sophisticated disclosure or investor protection regimes. Thus, while TRN theory has assumed relatively seamless co-ordination among securities regulators, this is hardly the case. On the contrary, implementation is often the result of the threat of sanctions.[41]

International standard setters do not always provide clear or effective guidance for emerging challenges/risks. Their pre-GFC standards, especially the Basel capital adequacy framework proved woefully inadequate in many ways, explained in the next section, including a total failure to appreciate the inadequacy of CRAs' models and their glaringly apparent conflicts of interest. Yet lack of accountability structures has meant that the failures of Basel I and especially of Basel II had no impact on the standing of BCBS.

Some of these failures should, in part, be attributed to the quasi-regulatory role assigned to private actors. The input of the latter is

---

[40] 'In such cases, the resulting standards may be globally efficient, but powerful states will enjoy a disproportionate share of the benefits. This was also arguably the case when the United States and the United Kingdom maneuvered to secure adoption of the Basel I. While the higher capital levels mandated by Basel I likely improved global financial stability, the Accord also allowed the two sponsors to maintain their competitive position ...' Verdier, 'Transnational Regulatory Networks', 163.

[41] 'The presence of distributive problems also creates opportunities for powerful states to secure their preferred outcome through incentives and threats, as illustrated by the imposition of money laundering and securities fraud rules on OFCs. [Although OFCs strongly preferred lax regulation their] co-operation was secured through threats of sanctions and loss of access to the markets on which their financial industry depends. In such cases, the resulting standards may be globally efficient, but powerful states will enjoy a disproportionate share of the benefits.' Verdier, 'Transnational Regulatory Networks', 163.

sometimes based on rather imperfect science and is motivated by private interests.[42] Namely, TRNs' excessive reliance on private actor's knowledge and expertise is often misplaced.[43] For example, the strong push by industry to base capital adequacy standards on a risk modelling approach also translated into relentless equity reduction practices in favour of debt, which of course led to over-leveraged and severely under-capitalized banks.[44] Uncritical endorsement of private sector expertise and policy preferences also fostered self-regulation in derivatives markets, which proved woefully inadequate to prevent or contain a large-scale financial crisis.

The trouble with excessive reliance on private sector input is not only that private actors try to promote their own agenda, a pretty legitimate goal on their part. An even bigger problem is that such uncritical endorsement is based on the unfounded assumption that private actors' knowledge is complete, while in fact it is very fragmentary, often steeped in ignorance,[45] and unheeding of true market conditions.[46] These shortcomings are due to two factors. First, private actors, deeply entrenched themselves in the constantly changing winds of the markets, do not

---

[42]   Frank Partnoy, 'How and Why Credit Rating Agencies Are Not Like Other Gatekeepers', in Yasuyuki Fuchita and Robert E. Litan (eds.), *Financial Gatekeepers: Can They Protect Investors?*(Brookings Institution Press and the Nomura Institute of Capital Markets Research, 2006), Chapter 3. Steven L. Schwarcz, 'Private Ordering of Public Markets: The Rating Agency Paradox' (2002) *University of Illinois Law Rev*iew 1.

[43]   'The regulatory community knew that risk calibration was mainly a tool to reduce capital requirements. However, they also knew that, in discussions about risk management, they were no match for the industry', Martin Hellwig, 'Capital Regulation after the Crisis: Business as Usual?' Max Planck Institute for Research on Collective Goods, Bonn 2010/31, July 2010, p 9, available at ssrn.com/abstract=1645224.

[44]   See BCBS, 'The Basel Committee's Response to the Financial Crisis: Report to the G20', October 2010, p. 4; Hellwig, 'Capital Regulation after the Crisis', pp. 2–4.

[45]   'Blankfein ... argued that the real problem was that people had not realised they were taking excessive risk and that in that case a properly constructed leverage ratio may have been an appropriate back-stop against a possible mistake in risk assessment'. See Lloyd C. Blankfein statement in Eurofi Financial Forum 2010, Conference Report: 'Optimizing EU Financial Reforms For Achieving Resilience, Growth, and Competitiveness: What Priorities? What Roadmaps?', September 2010, p. 57, available at www.emcnet.eu/EUROFI_BRU/EUROFI%20FORUM%202010_FINAL%20REPORT.pdf. Blankfein is, of course, the chairman and chief executive officer of the world's best known investment bank.

[46]   Julia Black has noted that: '[T]here is a growing recognition that regulators do not have the resources necessary by way of information, tools and technologies, organisational capacities, leverage, and, at the international level in particular, legitimacy and authority to perform regulation effectively. However, this is also matched by a recognition that firms and markets do not possess these resources either', Julia Black, 'Restructuring Global and EU Financial Regulation: Capacities, Coordination and Learning', LSE, Law, Society and Economy Working Papers 18/2010, 23 November 2010, p. 16.

have enough incentives to gather diverse pieces of data that would provide a more complete picture of the markets, when such data covers areas beyond their immediate business needs. Second, market conditions often differ from what is expected in equilibrium. However, disequilibrium conditions are as much the product of markets actors' own behaviour as of anything else.

Private actors' inadvertent myopia in disequilibrium is witnessed beyond reasonable doubt by their frequent inability to either identify an asset bubble or react to it. Normally it is due to two factors. First, private actors' cognitive biases (extensively discussed in Chapter 2) and socio-psychological pressures distort valuations and trigger strategic trade behaviour (herding), which in turn intensifies disequilibrium conditions. Second, the actions of private actors themselves create the market conditions under scrutiny, a phenomenon known as reflexivity.[47] In those cases, requesting private actors to accurately observe the impact of their own actions and intentions in relaying their analysis of market conditions to their regulatory masters/partners is stretching perceptions of private actors' cognitive ability beyond the limits of credulity.

As noted in Chapter 3, private sector inability (or unwillingness) to close regulator's knowledge gap meant that the financial revolution was very little understood and much misunderstood by policy-makers and supervisors, stretching their cognitive capacity to breaking point.[48] Therefore, TRNs' information advantages due to wider private sector participation may not be overestimated, and the global regulatory community should look at the establishment of more formal structures when

[47] The legendary financier George Soros has offered a good analysis of reflexivity in the context of financial markets: 'Both philosophy and natural science have gone to great lengths to separate events from the observations which relate to them. Events are facts and observations are true or false, depending on whether or not they correspond to the facts … [As a result of applying this view to financial markets] the [prevailing] interpretation of the way financial markets operate is severely distorted … Thinking participants cannot act on the basis of knowledge. Knowledge presupposes facts which occur independently of the statements which refer to them; but being a participant implies that one's decisions influence the outcome. Therefore, the situation participants have to deal with does not consist of facts independently given but facts which will be shaped by the decision of the participants. There is an active relationship between thinking and reality … Reflexivity is, in effect, a two-way feedback mechanism in which reality helps shape the participants' thinking and the participants' thinking helps shape reality …' See George Soros, 'Theory of Reflexivity', MIT Speech, 26 April 1994, available at www.sharpeinvesting.com/2007/08/george-soros-theory-of-reflexivity-mit-speech.html.

[48] See also Black, 'Restructuring Global and EU Financial Regulation'.

it comes to identifying risks and especially the risks arising from time to time from innovative financial techniques and instruments.

2.3.2 Monitoring and enforcement

The success of soft law standards is dependent in large part on the ability of regulators and market participants to identify defections and deviations from what has been agreed. Monitoring is thus a necessary means to facilitate compliance. Only through timely detection of defection can the disciplining mechanism of reputation loss work effectively. Nevertheless, the architecture supporting financial sector monitoring is in many regards quite weak. For one, the surveillance of compliance with international regulatory agreements is available for a relatively finite range of instruments. Regulatory commitments made by political institutions, or through communiqués promulgated by the 'G' groupings in the wake of their Summits, are lightly monitored. Similarly, only basic legislative standards promulgated by TRNs are incorporated into FSAP surveys.

Even where rules are incorporated into financial sector assessments, monitoring of compliance may remain weak. FSAP participation was, for example, entirely voluntary for non-IMF/World Bank borrowers. Also, data provided to international standard-setting bodies is normally self-reported by national authorities and is subject to little verification. As mentioned in Chapter 4, FSAP has provided a weak and defective monitoring mechanism. Although in some rare cases institutions may publicize non-compliance, information gained from the key surveillance mechanisms – the observance reports and the financial sector assessments and informal surveys conducted by national regulators of approaches and techniques of homologues – is published only with the permission of the inspected country.

Accordingly, even when they are adopted in a timely manner, TRN standards still frequently face enforcement problems, as states are tempted to defect from the co-operative framework, especially when they are under pressure from powerful domestic constituencies.[49] Even IOSCO's record is

---

[49] As discussed in Chapter 6, in the author's view, it is very hard to see national regulators who have voted in favour of countercyclical capital regulations ('the counter-cyclical buffer') in Basel to restrict bank lending because the IMF or the BIS tell them that it feeds into an emerging asset bubble, in the absence of formal and legally binding domestic legislation. The uproar from banks and businesses could be so strong as to force to submission even the most powerful and opinionated of regulators. See BCBS, 'Basel III: A Global Regulatory Framework for more Resilient Banks and Banking Systems', December 2010, p. 57. available at www.bis.org/publ/bcbs189.pdf.

less solid than it sounds and most of the convergence has been achieved in areas in which major markets had a strong interest.[50] Similarly in the field of fraud and money laundering the biggest jurisdictions seem to have used FATF to impose their will on smaller jurisdictions hosting tax havens in order to protect their interests. Rules are also unevenly enforced.[51] This can be due to breakdowns in transparency and information, which make the detection of violations difficult, or it can be due to the scope of enforcement. Therefore, the informal and non-binding nature of the rules adopted by TRNs and their restricted capacity to monitor or enforce them limit their effectiveness in circumstances where states have incentives to defect.[52] TRNs in that case are powerless to react without the intervention of governments and the threat of bilateral or multi-lateral sanctions. Incentives to defect do not come bigger than in the context of a major international financial crisis where the resolution of cross-border financial institutions may entail massive fiscal costs for the participating regulators.

2.4   The issue of legitimacy

Another big concern associated with TRNs is their (lack of) legitimacy,[53] and the identification of actions that could be taken to remedy this

[50] As Goodhart observes: 'Thus Basel I, the Accord on Capital Regulation in 1988, was propelled by concern that many of the major international banks, especially in the USA, would have been made insolvent, under a mark-to-market accounting procedure, by the MAB (Mexican, Argentina, Brazil) default crisis of 1982. Congress wanted to impose higher capital regulations on US banks, but was deterred by the Level Playing Field argument that any unilateral move would just shift business to foreign, especially to Japanese, banks. Hence the appeal to the BCBS', Charles Goodhart, 'How Should We Regulate Bank Capital and Financial Products? What Role for "Living Wills"?', in Adair Turner, Andrew Haldane and Paul Woolley, *The Future of Finance: The LSE Report* (London School of Economics, 2010), Chapter 5, pp.165–86. See also Gadinis, 'The Politics of Competition', 449–54.cf. Verdier, 'Transnational Regulatory Networks', 162: '[while] U.S. domestic resistance and a lesser sense of urgency doomed IOSCO's effort to establish capital rules for securities firms.'

[51] E.g., compliance with TRN standards can be enforced much more effectively in the case of countries borrowing from the IMF and the World Bank, which via the conditionality attached to such loans can be forced to commit to or implement international standards promulgated by organizations like the BCBS, IAIS and IOSCO.

[52] E.g., according to Verdier, the 1988 Basel I Accord gradually unravelled as national regulators adopted self-serving exceptions and interpretations, because 'the Committee had little effective leverage to enforce its rules', Verdier, 'Transnational Regulatory Networks', 163.

[53] For an overview of the legitimacy deficit in the specific context of global financial governance, see Geoffrey R. D. Underhill and Xiaoke Zhang, 'Norms, Legitimacy, and Global Financial Governance', ESRC World Economy and Finance Programme, Working Paper Series 0013, September 2006. On the inadequacy of standards of legitimacy

defect.[54] Two leading liberal scholars have defined legitimacy of global governance institutions as follows:[55]

> 'Legitimacy' has both a normative and a sociological meaning. To say that an institution is legitimate in the normative sense is to assert that it has the right to rule – where ruling includes promulgating rules and attempting to secure compliance with them by attaching costs to non-compliance and/or benefits to compliance. An institution is legitimate in the sociological sense when it is widely believed to have the right to rule.

The 'normative view of legitimacy' is essentially posing the question of whether the international organization or body in question was established by state actors and/or organizations recognised under international law which had the competence under national and/or international law to engage in the action in question. Therefore, the 'sociological' view of legitimacy,[56] namely the perception of legitimacy ('believed to have the right to rule') is more important than the normative version for the purposes of the present study.[57]

For a number of commentators the biggest legitimacy concern associated with TRNs is the so-called democratic deficit, normally translated as the absence of serious involvement by national governments in TRN

underpinning global governance institutions, see Daniel Bodansky, 'The Legitimacy of International Governance: A Coming Challenge for International Environmental Law?' (1999) 93 *American Journal of International Law* 596–624. On the issue of legitimacy in international law, see Rudiger Wolfrum, 'Legitimacy in International Law from a Legal Perspective: Some Introductory Considerations', in Rudiger Wolfrum and Volker Robens (eds.), *Legitimacy in International Law* (Berlin: Springer, 2008). A very insightful earlier work is Thomas Franck, *The Power of Legitimacy Among Nations* (New York: Oxford University Press, 1990).

[54] For an overview of the legitimacy challenge see Julia Black, 'Legitimacy, Accountability and Polycentric Regulation: Dilemmas, Trilemmas and Organisational Response', in Anne Peters, Lucy Koechlin, Till Förster and Gretta Fenner Zinkernagel (eds.), *Non-State Actors as Standard Setters* (Cambridge University Press, 2009), pp. 241–69.

[55] Allen Buchanan and Robert O. Keohane 'The Legitimacy of Global Governance Institutions', in Rudiger Wolfrum and Volker Roben (eds.), *Legitimacy in International Law* (Berlin: Springer, 2008), Chapter 2, p. 25.

[56] The 'sociological' view of legitimacy is deeply rooted in the work of Max Weber, the leading sociologist of the twentieth century. See Max Weber, *Economy and Society* (Berkeley, CA: University of California Press, 1978).

[57] Thomas Franck also accentuated the 'sociological' view of legitimacy in the context of international organizations, defining legitimacy as: '[A] property of a rule or rule-making institution which itself exerts a pull towards compliance on those addressed normatively because those addressed believe that the rule or institution has come into being and operates in accordance with generally accepted principles of right process', Franck, *The Power of Legitimacy*, p. 24.

standard setting[58] and lack of political controls.[59] Yet, the thorniest legitimacy question attached to TRNs in the field of global finance is not so much lack of political controls, since heads of state and ministers participate in the G-20 and Treasury departments are represented in BCBS. It is more an issue of lack of accountability mechanisms, since their soft law nature does not allow the establishment of accountability structures similar to those in place for the UN or the WTO. Moreover, building global governance organizations merely on the basis of participating states' consensus, giving them the right to 'rule', is not sufficient. Even if a relevant body was exclusively based on the consent of democratic states, and thus 'democratic accountability structures' were ensured, the main functions of this body would be discharged by a bureaucracy, which would enjoy a wide margin of discretion whether its decisions were made at the national or international level.[60] Thus, such body would not meet the second of the above tests: 'widely believed to have the right to rule'. To meet the second test, global governance institutions should provide benefits that cannot be provided by states.[61] This test could certainly be satisfied by international financial regulators by reference to the evident inability of national regulators to protect the global public good of systemic stability, but not by TRNs. TRNs proved unable to prevent the GFC. In addition, global governance institutions need to be based on a clear set of shared values,[62] and TRN objectives often lack clarity. Finally, being a collection of experts and bureaucrats, TRN legitimacy could be strengthened through the establishment of some form of indirect accountability to the global polity,[63] but formal institutions have proved more successful at achieving that.

[58] Geoffrey Underhill, 'Keeping Governments Out of Politics: Transnational Securities Markets, Regulatory Cooperation, and Political Legitimacy' (1995) 21 *Review of International Studies* 251–78.
[59] Weber notes: 'Nevertheless, the weakness of [TRNs] consists in the lack of political control and the democratic deficit as well as the normative concerns regarding the missing (formal) legal framework', Rolf H. Weber, 'Multilayered Governance in International Financial Regulation and Supervision' (2010) 13 *Journal of International Economic Law* 683–704, 688.
[60] Buchanan and Keohane, 'The Legitimacy of Global Governance Institutions', pp. 39–41.
[61] *Ibid.*, pp. 40–2.   [62] *Ibid.*
[63] See, in general, David Held, 'Law of States, Law of Peoples: Three Models of Sovereignty' (2002) 8 *Legal Theory* 1–44 and Robert O. Keohane, 'Global Governance and Democratic Accountability', Miliband Lectures, London School of Economics, 2002. In the context of International Finance TRNs, see Claire R. Kelly, 'Financial Crises and Civil Society', Brooklyn Law School, mimeo, 4 August 2010, available at works.bepress.com/cgi/viewcontent.cgi?article=1015&context=claire_kelly.

TRNs producing international financial standards fall far short of satisfying the second test of legitimacy for a host of other reasons. As we have already seen, many international standard setters, like the BCBS, are exclusive in their membership or dominated by a narrow band of (usually rich) countries. Even TRNs with very wide and representative membership like IOSCO may have tight knit cores in terms of policy-making, such as IOSCO's Technical Committee.

Regulatory group-think within TRNs and their mono-dimensionality coupled with TRN domination by the larger and more sophisticated members, which represent bigger constituencies and often possess superior expertise, creates serious policy implications. First, they are likely to produce standards that favour members at the expense of non-members. In fact, distributive issues are much more likely to be decided in favour of those with direct policy input. Second, TRNs are very likely to refrain from adopting standards that do not favour their stronger members. For some commentators this inevitable dominance of TRNs by the more advanced economies, until recently the US and a few EU countries, has led to a new form of 'extraterritorial' application of their laws and regulatory traditions.[64]

Some scholars argue that, in recent years, open and extensive consultations held by TRNs before the promulgation of new standards have largely resolved the issue of legitimacy.[65] Moreover, G-20, FSB and BCBS member countries (following membership enlargement) do represent the world's biggest economies and, being hosts to the largest financial services industries, they have more experience and a higher level of expertise in dealing with the most important issues of global finance, such as large and complex financial institutions and markets for sophisticated financial instruments.

On the other hand, Slaughter has noted that TRN democratic accountability and imperfect global representation can be remedied through broader membership and links with global civil society. This is, of course, a useful and interesting proposal that has also been endorsed by other

---

[64] See Weber, 'Multilayered Governance', 695. However, it should be noted that recent activism by China in the context of the G-20 signals the beginning of a more balanced approach to what has more or less been Western regulatory 'imperialism' for three decades.

[65] Michael S. Barr and Geoffrey P. Miller, 'Global Administrative Law: The View from Basel' (2006) 17 *European Journal of International Law* 15, 16. See also Daniel C. Esty, 'Good Governance at the Supranational Scale: Globalizing Administrative Law' (2006) 115 *Yale Law Journal* 1490.

scholars,[66] but may not be sufficient to resolve legitimacy questions when serious distributional questions are raised. This is especially going to be the case with co-ordinated cross-border institutional resolution and rescue operations which involve asset disposal and fiscal expenditure decisions. Any future global governance structures must address, apart from the matters of effective cross-border supervision of global financial institutions, crisis management co-ordination and cross-border resolution and the issue of what principles should guide their operation. I attempt to provide a first answer to these questions in Chapter 8 of this book.

3.   Can soft law financial governance meet the challenges? Lessons from the GFC

3.1   Introductory remarks

Soft law and TRNs are very important and useful components of global governance, especially in areas where a strong pooling of sovereignty would be regarded as intolerable by states. They also have several shortcomings, as explained above. In many ways this form of governance for international finance proved largely ineffective. On the other hand criticism of TRNs should not be generalized and care should be taken not to diminish the valuable role in information sharing and promotion, through soft law, of co-operative forms of governance in a number of other spheres of transnational interaction.

Even notable TRN theorists have pointed out that the soft law structures proved to be ineffective, or at best 'marginally helpful', in managing the GFC.[67] First, Basel capital adequacy standards are widely assumed to have seriously contributed both to the build up and the severity of the crisis.

---

[66]   Kelly, 'Financial Crises and Civil Society'.

[67]   David Zaring, 'International Institutional Performance in Crisis' (2010) 10 *Chicago Journal of International Law* 475, especially pp. 477–85. Also, Giovanoli, a former BIS General Counsel, has noted: 'Looking back, it may seem astonishing that the global financial crisis of 2008 and 2009 ... happened at the *international* level despite the existence of a comprehensive *corpus* of international financial standards (IFSs) ... Did the international financial architecture turn out to be a product of "fair weather architecture"? ... To say the least, the existing IFS, despite their wide scope and sophistication did not prevent the outbreak of the current crisis', Mario Giovanoli, 'The Reform of the International Financial Architecture After the Global Crisis' (2009) 42 *New York University Journal of International Law & Politics* 81, 83–5.

Second, the lack of formal structures for cross-border co-ordination of crisis management and failing bank resolution generated gigantic amounts of confusion and uncertainty resulting in a generalized collapse of confidence in the markets, especially after the messy collapse and winding up of Lehman Brothers. Finally, the standards themselves were in many instances flawed and, as discussed below, they seem to have contributed to instead of preventing the GFC.[68]

3.2   The flaws of the Basel capital framework

I explained in Chapter 3 why the focus of Basel standards on individual institutions' financial standing (micro-prudential regulation) was flawed. Basel capital regulations also proved to be problematic in many other areas, because of factors such as:

(1)   the procyclical nature of capital standards;
(2)   their proclivity to foster regulatory arbitrage;
(3)   the total neglect of liquidity risks under the Basel framework; and
(4)   the provision of incentives to adhere to the risk-modelling approach encouraged leverage, allowing banks to assume large amounts of short-term debt.

All these issues are discussed more extensively in the ensuing paragraphs. Basel capital requirements also showed a poor appreciation of the importance and cost of strong equity cushions in the event of a crisis and the risks of leverage.[69] As a result, when the GFC erupted, most financial institutions were found to be severely undercapitalized and virtually insolvent.

It is sometimes assumed that high leverage (accumulation of debt) and low equity is an inevitable business strategy given the higher costs of equity over debt finance, especially in periods when markets are very liquid and interest rates low. However, there is a strong line of argument that explains that the only reason that debt markets charge banks a lower premium over equity markets and thus banks find debt financing cheaper is because they

---

[68]   *Ibid.*, 85, 87.
[69]   '[T]here is no doubt that if on-balance sheet commercial bank capital regulations had determined the amount of equity budgeted by all subprime mortgage originators, then the leverage ratios of the banking system would not have been as large, and the liquidity risk from repo funding would have been substantially less, both of which would have contributed to reducing the magnitude of the financial crisis', Charles Calomiris, 'Financial Innovation, Regulation and Reform' (2009) 29 *Cato Journal* 65, 66.

enjoy the benefits of public subsidies and tax preferences.[70] Public subsidies make creditors feel relatively secure that, even if the institution concerned failed, they would receive back most of their principal, because of a probable public bail-out. However, the ability to deduct interest payments paid to creditors induces financial institutions' management to choose debt as the preferred form of funding their asset base. Applicable tax laws allow financial institutions to pay lower taxes and increase their profitability and dividend payments, increasing, at the same time, the financial fragility of institutions concerned.

3.3   Regulatory arbitrage through asset transformation, credit ratings and other follies

In principle, Basel risk-weighted capital ratios imposed high capital charges on high-risk assets and low capital charges on low-risk assets. Although such an approach sounds reasonable, it ignores the economic cycle and increases instead of decreasing systemic risk. Namely, it amplifies the leverage cycle leading to debt accumulation in good times and deleveraging, which restricts lending in bad times when credit is scarce. Due to interconnectedness, high leverage increased the fragility of the system as a whole. For instance, Lehman Brothers CDS exposure was eight times bigger than its capital.[71] In addition, during good times certain assets are considered to be less risky than they actually are, and, during bad times, the same assets might be viewed as riskier than they actually are. Mandated capital ratios ended up being too high in good times and too low in bad times, when the capital buffers are needed the most.

The Basel I capital framework encouraged banks to securitize high risk assets through the use of instruments which attracted lower regulatory capital charges. Inevitably, much of bank asset transformation activity was motivated by regulatory (and ratings) arbitrage. As Calomiris has observed:[72]

---

[70]   Anat R. Admati, Peter M. DeMarzo, Martin F. Hellwig and Paul Pfleiderer, 'Fallacies, Irrelevant Facts, and Myths in the Discussion of Capital Regulation: Why Bank Equity is *Not* Expensive', Stanford GSB Research Paper No. 2065, 30 September 2010, available at: ssrn.com/abstract=1669704. Robert A. Jarrow, 'Risk Management Models', Johnson School Research Paper Series No. 38–2010, 19 November 2010, available at SSRN: ssrn.com/abstract=1712086.

[71]   Andrew G. Haldane, 'Rethinking the Financial Network', Speech, 2009, available at www.bankofengland.co.uk/publications/speeches/2009/speech386.pdf.

[72]   Calomiris, 'Financial Innovation', 65.

Originators of the loans were able to maintain lower equity capital against those loans than they otherwise would have needed to maintain if the loans had been placed on their balance sheets. Capital regulation of securitization invited this form of off-balance-sheet regulatory arbitrage, and did so quite consciously. Several of the capital requirement rules for the treatment of securitized assets originated by banks, and for the debts issued by those conduits and held or guaranteed by banks, were specifically and consciously designed to permit banks to allocate less capital against their risks.

To provide an example, the Basel I Accord required that banks hold capital of at least 8 per cent of the risk-weighted assets (RWA) (loans) on their balance sheets; this capital requirement (called a capital charge) was much lower for contractual credit lines. In addition, there was no capital charge at all for reputational credit lines – non-contractual liquidity backstops that sponsoring banks provided to structured investment vehicles to maintain their reputation. Thus, moving a pool of loans into off-balance-sheet vehicles, and then granting a credit line to that pool to ensure a AAA-rating, allowed banks to reduce the amount of capital they needed to hold to conform with Basel I regulations while the risk for the bank remained essentially unchanged.[73]

However, relatively safe assets can have very high systemic risk. It is observed that the assets more likely to be downgraded in a crisis are not the super-safe (e.g., AAA German bunds) or the high-risk ones (e.g., junk bonds) but those assets which are on the margins of AAA.[74] The low risk assets will be in demand in the event of a crisis (due to flight to safety) and the high risk cannot be downgraded by much, unlike those which

---

[73] Markus K. Brunnermeier, 'Deciphering the Liquidity and Credit Crunch 2007–08' (2009) 23 *Journal of Economic Perspectives* 77–100, 79–81, 86.

[74] 'Regulatory capital is meant to be held against unexpected loss ... The rating (should) measure the *expected* probability of default, whereas what matters is the likelihood of migration (downwards) of the rating, and the loss of value should that occur. Assume [two] banks [which] have the same risk-weighted tier one ratios, with say a similar buffer of 2% above the 4% requirement (i.e. 6%), *and* that the risk of downwards migration (of say two notches) is the same for both assets (AAA and BBB) ... The [bank with higher systemic risk] generally is the AAA bank. First, AAA assets ... are truly systemic, in the sense that they only lose value in a system-wide crisis ... Second, the mark-to-market decline in value from the (assumed equal) migration may well be greater. Third, the relationship between rating and CAR is curved ... an equivalent horizontal migration leads to a greater proportionate requirement for extra capital ... So, for a given equal migration and equal capital buffer, the AAA bank will find itself in greater difficulties than the BBB bank', Markus Brunnermeier, Andrew Crockett, Charles Goodhart, Avinash D. Persaud and Hyun Shin, 'The Fundamental Principles of Financial Regulation', Geneva Reports on the World Economy 11, January 2009, p. 8 (hereinafter, Geneva Report).

are borderline safe (e.g., AAA-rated tranches of CDOs).[75] And this is exactly what happened at the beginning of the GFC. These were also the assets that attracted, due to risk weighting, low regulatory capital during the boom. Now retaining them on balance sheet and not selling them at depressed prices in a declining market meant that banks had to find additional capital to set aside. Since they became riskier, because of the downgrade, they attracted a higher regulatory capital buffer. Not surprisingly this coincided with the period when there was a flight of capital from the banking industry and banks found it the hardest to increase their regulatory capital reserves in accordance with capital adequacy requirements. As a result, most banks were considered badly undercapitalized, worsening the crisis of confidence that had afflicted them.

Arbitrage induced asset securitization had two further consequences. First, bank balance sheets were deprived of high quality low risk assets that would provide creditors with comfort during the crisis. This was particularly manifested in the case of Northern Rock that had transferred most of its loan book to a repackaging vehicle called 'the Granite Fund'.[76] Second, bank sponsored SPVs and SIVs were inadequately capitalized and lacked sufficient liquidity support mechanisms. This meant that liability for their funding returned to the banks, which had to commit considerable resources to this task, while the rest of the market and regulators assumed that banks had divested themselves of the risk embedded in securitized assets.

3.4 The systemic implications of neglecting liquidity

During the period up to the summer of 2007 funding liquidity levels were very high, leverage was considered an excellent way to generate additional profits and financial institutions amassed gigantic portions of short-term debt, becoming over-leveraged, through the asset transformation described above. Such behaviour was made possible

---

[75] *Ibid.* United Nations Conference on Trade and Development (UNCTAD), 'The Global Economic Crisis, Systemic Failures and Multilateral Remedies', New York and Geneva, 2009, p. 16.

[76] See Philip Webster, Greg Hurst and Siobhan Kennedy, 'Northern Rock Nationalisation Runs into £49bn Granite Barrier', *The Times*, 21 February 2008, available at www.timesonline.co.uk/tol/news/politics/article3406368.ece; Patrick Wintour, Phillip Inman and Jill Treanor, 'Northern Rock Nationalisation in Turmoil over Offshore Trust', *The Guardian*, 21 February 2008, available at www.guardian.co.uk/business/2008/feb/21/northernrock.banking.

because capital regulations showed a marked neglect for the systemic implications of funding mismatches in the event of a liquidity crunch.

Funding liquidity describes the relative ease with which investors and arbitrageurs can obtain funding from financiers. Funding liquidity risk is due to maturity mismatches and can thus take three forms: (1) margin/ haircut funding risk, or the risk that margins and haircuts will change; (2) rollover risk, or the risk that it will be more costly or impossible to roll over short-term borrowing; and (3) redemption risk, or the risk that depositors of banks or even equity holders withdraw funds. Funding liquidity can become a systemic issue because of two externalities: (1) *Fire sales*, where the price impact from one institution's asset firesales may seriously affect (spillover to) the valuation of other financial institutions' balance sheets in the event of a liquidity crunch; and (2) *Interconnectedness*, which gives institutions incentives to become 'too-big-to-fail', since through the multiplicity of its contractual and other connections to other financial institutions a bank can transmit to them (and the system as a whole) its own funding problems, forcing a public rescue.[77] A diversified asset base does not protect against funding mismatches caused by a system-wide liquidity crunch, even if it strengthens the stability of individual institutions.[78]

Typically, when a leveraged trader, such as a bank or a hedge fund, purchases an asset, it uses that asset as collateral and borrows (short-term) against it. The provider of the loan does not lend the full value of the assets but will impose a margin requirement or a haircut over the value of the pledged instrument as a form of security. That means that a part of the value of the replacement asset will have to be financed by the trader's own equity capital. At the same time, financial institutions that rely substantially on short-term (commercial) paper or repo contracts have to roll over their debt. If the wholesale market dries up and stops giving traders the ability to roll over their short-terms loans, haircuts and margins may increase up to 100 per cent, depriving traders of the opportunity to raise fresh funds by pledging more assets. In those cases, firms must either have in place separate liquidity lines (e.g., from a central bank that is willing

---

[77] '[F]ire-sales by some institutions spillover, and adversely affect the balance sheet of others, causing a negative externality ... In general, a financial institution is also not concerned how many others it will drag down, should it fail ... the failure of big and interconnected institutions would bring down these negative risk-spillover effects on others .. [but the] prospect of a government bailout gives institutions the incentive to become too big to fail and too interconnected to fail', Geneva Report, p. 21, (notes omitted).

[78] Geneva Report, p. 11.

to lend at tolerable rates) or sell assets to shrink their balance sheet. The result is the same when an institution faces a depositors' run (massive withdrawals of demand deposits) or of an investment fund that is subjected to massive capital redemptions. If liquidity levels in the market are also low and the institution has to sell assets at ever declining prices, then liquidity risk is transformed into solvency risk. Basel capital requirements assumed that such an institution could remain solvent through retention of adequate capital buffers.[79] In addition, maintaining individual institutions' solvency was assumed to be sufficient to guard against the risk of systemic disruption.

On the basis of these assumptions, Basel capital requirements merely asked institutions to maintain minimum capital buffers in order to absorb losses on their RWA and remain solvent, thereby protecting their creditors, chiefly retail depositors. Both the original Basel capital Accord of 1988, with its unsophisticated risk category classifications, and the more advanced Basel II framework[80] were entirely focused on individual institution stability, neglecting the macro-prudential dimension. Nonetheless, this thinking was deeply flawed when it came to protection against systemic risk. Assuming that inter-bank markets would always function in the normal way or the lender of last resort would always be able to counter any liquidity shocks ignored two externalities. First, it did not consider the possibility of liquidity hoarding because of lack of confidence and thus the drying up of wholesale markets. Second, it overlooked the possibility that liquidity demands may be so high as to raise the spectrum of fire sales.[81]

Banks entered the crisis with a large portfolio of risky assets. As risks materialized, banks rationally sought to protect themselves from infection from other banks by hoarding liquidity rather than on-lending it, leading to an enduring stress in money markets that evolved into a liquidity crunch. Banks' mutual interdependence in inter-bank networks meant that individually rational actions generated a collectively worse funding position for all. Unable to easily fund their asset portfolio, some

---

[79] Behind Basel's thinking was the belief that the solvency of a financial institution may be secured if regulation protects against the likelihood that the realized value of assets falls below the notional value of creditor claims.

[80] The Basel II framework was more risk sensitive because it relied on risk gradations (risk modelling) of bank assets and linked regulatory capital to the risks of the assets held by each bank. See Chapter 4, Section 3.2.5.

[81] See Markus Brunnermeier and Lasse H. Pedersen, 'Market Liquidity and Funding Liquidity' (2009) 22 *Review of Financial Studies* 2201–38.

financial firms instead opted for the flight from financial assets through sales, depressing prices. However, Basel capital standards did not consider this possibility and thus they failed to capture the deleveraging spiral[82] and the ensuing fire sales avalanche.

3.5   Flawed risk models and procyclicality

Most of the risk models employed by the financial services industry, which were subsequently incorporated into Basel II, were based on so-called Value at Risk (VaR). But VaR had serious shortcomings for a number of reasons and probably constituted a flawed way to capture asset riskiness.[83] First, the model was not based on sound empirical grounds. Its timeline was short and thus in certain asset markets, such as housing, where prices had been rising constantly for twenty years, it systematically underestimated the risk of default.[84] Second, it failed to capture correlations among assets.[85] Third, it did not distinguish between risk and uncertainty.[86] As the model assumed normal distributions of events, it could not capture tail risk, namely, rare extreme loss events – so-called fat tails or black swans – which, in fact, may not be

---

[82] 'The deleveraging spiral was particularly pronounced because the multipliers for deleveraging were enormous. If equity amounts to 2.5 % of the balance sheet, one dollar's worth of losses creates a need to sell forty dollars' worth of assets on average in order to bring the capital ratio back into line. If equity amounts to 2.5 % of the balance sheet, it also doesn't take long for concerns about solvency to arise', 'Hellwig, Capital Regulation after the Crisis', p. 4, (note omitted).

[83] *Ibid.*

[84] It is characteristic of a statement by former US Fed chairman Alan Greenspan: 'It was the failure to properly price such assets that precipitated the crisis.... The modern risk management paradigm held sway for decades. The whole intellectual edifice, however, collapsed in the summer of last year [2007] because the data inputted into the risk management models generally covered only the past two decades, a period of euphoria. Had instead the models been fitted more appropriately to historic periods of stress, capital requirements would have been much higher and the financial world would be in far better shape today ... ', available at oversight. house.gov/index.php?option=com_content&view=article&id=3470&catid=42:hearings&Itemid=2.

[85] See BCBS, 'Consultative Document Strengthening the Resilience of the Banking Sector', December 2009, pp. 37–8, available at www.bis.org/publ/bcbs164.pdf. 'The Committee, based on its empirical work, found evidence that asset value correlations were at least 25% higher for financial firms than for non-financial firms', *Ibid.*, p. 38. Cf. Hellwig, 'Capital Regulation after the Crisis', p. 7

[86] The best illustration is given in Frank Knight, *Risk, Uncertainty, and Profit* (Boston, MA: Houghton Mifflin Co, 1921). Knight is widely regarded as the founder of the so-called Chicago School and this book was based on his award winning doctoral dissertation at Cornell University!

modellable.[87] Moreover, what risk models could not capture is the very risk that regulation should be alert to guard against.[88] Fourth, it was very procyclical and thus patently unsuitable for use in regulatory models that tried to protect financial institutions and the financial system from, *inter alia*, the risk of economic downturns, which is inevitable in all economic cycles. Fifth, it focused on defaults, which are less frequent events, and not on the much more frequent asset price changes, which may prove as dangerous for banks' financial health.[89] Sixth, it failed to capture endogenous risk, namely, the risk emanating from the behaviour of actors within the system, as a response to an exogenous or endogenous development, which could lead to contagion and domino phenomena. A domino or cascade event can force even perfectly hedged and soundly managed financial institutions to fail and is, arguably, the biggest risk for the banking system. VaR assumed independence in the actions of each institution and did not measure the impact of those actions on the behaviour of other institutions and of the market. Namely, it did not capture self-reinforcing cycles.

---

[87] It has been accurately observed that: '[the view that] past distribution patterns carry robust inferences for the probability of future patterns is methodologically insecure. It involves applying to the world of social and economic relationships a technique drawn from the world of physics, in which a random sample of a definitively existing universe of possible events is used to determine the probability characteristics which govern future random samples. But it is unclear whether this analogy is valid when applied to economic and social relationships, or whether instead, we need to recognise that we are dealing not with mathematically modellable risk, but with inherent "Knightian uncertainty"', FSA, 'The Turner Review, A Regulatory Response to the Global Banking Crisis', March 2009, p. 21 (hereinafter the Turner Review).

[88] '[T]he precept that each individual bank's own risk management should be brought up to the level of, and harmonised with … the (best) practices of the most technically advanced individual banks … was wrong for two main associated reasons. First, the risk management concerns of individual banks are, and indeed should be, quite different from those of regulators. A banker wants to know what his/her individual risk is under normal circumstances, 99% of the time. If an extreme shock occurs, it will anyhow be for the authorities to respond. For such normal conditions, the VaR measure is well designed. But it does not handle tail-risk adequately, (see Danielsson 2002). It is the tail risk of such extreme shocks that should worry the regulator.' See Goodhart, 'How Should We Regulate Bank Capital', p. 165. See also Jon Danielsson, 'The Emperor has no Clothes: Limits to Risk Modelling', (2002) 26 *Journal of Banking and Finance* 1252–72.

[89] As Brunnermeier, *et al.* note: [D]efaults need not even be *necessary* to generate contagion. Price changes themselves may be enough. When financial institutions mark their balance sheets to market, changes in prices lead to losses that may be sufficient to transmit the shocks to other institutions even when they do not hold claims against each other. Losses worsen funding liquidity for many financial institutions, forcing them to shed even more assets which further depresses prices and increases losses, and so on', Geneva Report, p. 14 (emphasis added).

A good example is provided by correlations that link the micro to impossible to hedge macro-risks, such as the impact of the economy's long term performance on the value of assets. Such inability may also be due to the fact that the identification of correlations is sometimes beyond the ability of market players. In some cases risks are so tiny[90] or so remote as to be virtually invisible. Yet, given the size of asset intermediation and the broad use of derivatives (especially credit default swaps),[91] risks unrelated to the risk hedged can become correlated allowing relevant shocks to materialize, even if this outcome is rather random and unpredictable. This situation can lead financial institutions to bankruptcy even when they try to hold a well-hedged balance sheet.

Moreover, there is another class of risks which is ever present and likely to occur but cannot really be measured with any degree of accuracy in order to be able to calculate how it would correlate with other risks to ascertain their impact on the probability of those other risks materializing. For instance, is it really possible for any model measuring credit risk to capture the severity of endogenous risk, which depends on the behaviour of market actors (which are also counterparties to a multitude of contracts) and the reaction of the markets?[92]

This weakness is made even worse by the already discussed interdependence/interconnectedness of the different parts of the financial system and the impact of systemic shocks like deleveraging which may lead to fire sales and large deterioration of asset prices.[93] Another adverse

---

[90] Anabtawi and Schwarcz have discussed how such tiny risk correlations can escalate into a systemic problem. See Anabtawi and Schwarcz, 'Regulating Systemic Risk' (2011).

[91] 'Insufficient account was taken of risks arising from correlations between counterparty credit risks and underlying risks in derivatives and other hedge contracts. Such correlations arise naturally when the counterparty is concluding many similar contracts at the same time', Hellwig, 'Capital Regulation After the Crisis', p. 7.

[92] *Ibid.*

[93] On the impact of deleveraging and fire sales on the liquidity freeze during the crisis, see Douglas W. Diamond and Raghuram Rajan, 'Fear of Fire Sales and the Credit Freeze' (2011) 126 *Quarterly Journal of Economics* 557–92; Gary Gorton and Andrew Metrick, 'Securitized Banking and the Run on the Repo', National Bureau of Economic Research Working Paper No. w15223, August 2009, available at papers.ssrn.com/sol3/papers.cfm?abstract_id =1454939. See also Andrei Shleifer and Robert Vishny, 'Fire Sales in Finance and Macroeconomics' (2011) 25 *Journal of Economic Perspectives* 29–48 and Andrei Shleifer and Robert Vishny, 'Asset Fire Sales and Credit Easing' (2010) 100 *American Economic Review* 46–50. A good first approach to regulating fire sales is offered in Anil Kashyap, Richard Berner and Charles Goodhart, 'The Macroprudential Toolkit', Chicago Booth, The Initiative on Global Markets, Working Paper No. 11–2, January 2011, available at ssrn.com/abstract=1735445.

effect of risk modelling that has escaped attention is that a belief in flaw-less risk models may encourage complacency leading to assumption of ever increasing risks undermining the stability of both the individual institution and of the system.[94]

Most of the above flaws reinforce the argument that since regulation should guard against unexpected loss – expected loss can be protected against through the charge of adequate interest premia – the risk mod-elling approach to capital regulation was outright wrong. Yet, Basel cap-ital requirements, especially Basel II, sought to make regulatory capital move closer to banks' choice of economic capital, which was based on risk models. As a result, CARs left credit expansion unchecked during the boom, allowing banks to provide, in an unfettered way, further fuel to overheated economies. For the same reason, banks would not set aside any additional capital during the upswing, finding themselves severely under-capitalized when the crisis hit.

Basel III is trying to redress this defect through new liquidity cover-age and leverage ratios, higher quality Tier 1 capital and the infusion of more equity in bank capital, and the 'capital conservation'[95] and 'countercyclical' buffers,[96] all extensively discussed in Chapter 6. Basel III reforms constitute a substantial improvement over the pre-existing Basel framework and, when implemented – there is a prolonged transi-tional period – they should lead to more resilient and better capitalized banks. Yet the private sector championed risk approach to the calcula-tion of the capital requirement has remained raising concern.[97]

4.   Supervisory failures, cross-border crisis management and 'too-big-to-fail' institutions

4.1   Overview of the issue

The involvement of the two most important international financial institutions, the IMF and the World Bank, in the current governance

---

[94] See also Hellwig, 'Capital Regulation After the Crisis', pp. 7–8.
[95] BCBS, 'Basel III', p. 54.   [96] *Ibid.*
[97] Hellwig argues that risk models should not be used in capital regulations because they cannot provide an accurate picture of the probability (and thus of the size of required capital) for the least visible, and thus most dangerous of the risks assumed by banks. See Hellwig, 'Capital Regulation After the Crisis', pp. 7–8, 10, 14–15.

framework for global finance does not extend beyond standard-setting and monitoring of compliance, because they lack any kind of legal standing to act as global financial regulators. On the other hand, TRNs have no supervisory capacity.

Supervision in financial markets is a competence/function, the discharge of which has predominantly been confined within national borders. Also, there has not been a clear distinction between two different functions of regulation: rule making/standard setting on the one hand and supervision on the other, even in the domestic context.[98] The latter is roughly defined as the day to day monitoring of regulated firms compliance with applicable regulations and imposition of sanctions. This was not regarded as a major failing until the eruption of GFC. The fact that TRNs were not involved in supervision and had no enforcement powers was viewed as an issue of little importance, although certain commentators had either highlighted this absence or advocated the need for the establishment of a global systemic regulator.[99] The lack of any capacity to supervise cross-border institutions and of any clear co-operation in a crisis management (and burden sharing) framework at the international level, which could reconcile home and host country interests, became a serious problem during the GFC.

There are good reasons to believe that Icelandic authorities at least (and possibly Irish regulators as well) were particularly permissive regulators, viewing their banks as their 'national champions'. Icelandic banks maintained a very widespread geographic distribution of assets rather disproportionate to size of the country's GDP.[100] But host

---

[98] See Pan, 'The Challenge of International Cooperation'. Perceptive earlier works which drew such a distinction between the two different concepts are Rosa M. Lastra, 'The Governance Structure for Financial Regulation and Supervision in Europe' (2003) 10 *Columbia Journal of European Law* 49 and Cynthia Crawford Lichtenstein, 'The Fed's New Model of Supervision for "Large Complex Banking Organizations": Coordinated Risk-Based Supervision of Financial Multinationals for International Financial Stability' (2005) 18 *Transnational Lawyer* 283, 287–8.

[99] Kem Alexander, Rahul Dhumale and John Eatwell, *Global Governance and Financial Systems: The International Regulation of Systemic Risk* (Oxford University Press, 2006), Chapter 5.

[100] The Icelandic bank Kaupthing was active through branches and subsidiaries in thirteen jurisdictions. The Internet based Kaupthing Edge attracted many customers with savings accounts and fixed-term deposit accounts offering high interest rates. As of end of 2007, the bank had total assets of €58.3 billion. According to the bank, about 70 per cent of its operating profits originated outside Iceland in 2007 (31 per cent in the United Kingdom, 26 per cent in Scandinavia, 8 per cent in Luxembourg and 2 per cent

country authorities had no effective tools for early intervention under the prevailing framework.[101] Early intervention was however exactly what was required in order not to place host country banking systems under serious threat.

Moreover, where national authorities were being faced with colossal cross-border bank rescue dilemmas and expensive conflicts of interest, MoUs and other soft law structures could play no meaningful role. Characteristic examples are the acrimonious cross-border treatment of the failure of Icelandic banks and the messy rescue of Fortis, a large European bank with a strong presence in three countries.[102] Both cases are surprising examples, as they happened within or just outside the borders of the EU, the region with the highest level of harmonization of national banking laws. The EU's response to the crisis was the creation of the European System of Financial Supervisors (ESFS), which is analytically discussed in Chapter 6. The new EU financial regulators created by the ESFS either do not have formal standing in EU law, like the ESRB, or do not discharge cross-border supervisory powers, like the European Supervisory Authorities (ESAs). Nevertheless their establishment underscores the inadequacies of the previous regime and the need for stronger supra-national supervisory and regulatory structures that go beyond MoUs. These are lessons that can be taken into account in the context of wider global financial reform and thus I examine the cases of Kaupthing, Fortis and Dexia in some detail in the paragraphs that follow.

in other countries). See BCBS, 'Report and Recommendations of the Cross-border Bank Resolution Group', Basel, September 2009, p. 12.

[101] See FSA, Discussion Paper 09/2, 'A Regulatory Response to the Global Banking Crisis', March 2009, pp. 16, 56, 154.

[102] 'Fortis Group was a Belgian/Dutch financial conglomerate with substantial subsidiaries in Belgium, the Netherlands and Luxembourg. The consolidating and co-ordinating supervisor was Belgium's Commission bancaire, financière et des assurances (CBFA), as the banking activities within Fortis Group, headed by the Belgium-based Fortis Bank SA/NV, were the largest part of Fortis's operations. Fortis was deemed to be systemically relevant in the three countries . . [i]n 2007, Fortis acquired portions of the operations of ABN AMRO through a consortium with Royal Bank of Scotland and Santander. In 2008 ... Fortis had difficulties realising its plans to strengthen its financial position and to finance the acquisition and integration of its acquisitions ...[since] June 2008, there was increasing uncertainty in the market whether Fortis would be able to realise the intended steps. Over the summer, its share price deteriorated and liquidity became a serious concern.' BCBS, 'Report and Recommendations', p. 10.

4.2   A closer look at the Kaupthing, Fortis and Dexia cases

4.2.1   Kaupthing

In October 2008, the expensive and messy rescue of two other Icelandic banks by the country's government[103] raised concerns about Kaupthing.[104] As a result, Kaupthing, Singer & Friedlander (KSF), the UK subsidiary of Kaupthing, suffered a continual loss of confidence, leading to massive deposit withdrawals from its Internet banking arm. On 8 October 2008, the FSA decided that KSF did not meet the threshold conditions for operating as a credit institution and should close to new business. On the same day, the FSA obtained an administration order in relation to KSF. As KSF seemed unable to satisfy claims against the UK Financial Services Compensation Scheme (FSCS), the UK government used its special powers to transfer the deposits in KSF's Internet business to ING Direct, with the UK government taking the place of the transferred depositors as creditors of KSF. This action created serious problems for KSF's subsidiary in the Isle of Man, a jurisdiction separate from the UK, which was substantially funded by retail deposits placed by UK residents. Half of the Isle of Man subsidiary's balance sheet referred to a claim on KSF in London. The precarious state of the entire group led UK authorities to freeze the subsidiary's assets located in the UK.[105]

---

[103] In September 2008 the government of Iceland, which had a very cosy relationship with the management of the local banks, decided to buy a 75 per cent stake for €600 million in Glitnir Bank. 'This led to downgrades of Iceland's long-term foreign-currency sovereign credit rating by S&P and Fitch on 29 and 30 September. The combined size of the local banks' balance sheet raised concerns … On 7 October 2008, the Icelandic Financial Supervisory Authority (FME) took control of another bank, Landsbanki, and on 8 October 2008, put Glitnir Bank into receivership …' BCBS, 'Report and Recommendations', pp. 11–12.

[104] Iceland's central bank supported Kaupthing with a €500 million loan and the bank explored the possibility of selling some of its units. 'Despite Icelandic authorities' assurance that Kaupthing would not require the same measures as its domestic competitors, Kaupthing Edge had been affected by a mass withdrawal of funds in the United Kingdom since the first measures had been taken concerning Glitnir Bank in September 2008', BCBS, 'Report and Recommendations', p. 12.

[105] 'On 23 October 2008, the Isle of Man announced it would spend up to GBP 150 million – which compares to the Island's total published reserves and invested funds (less national insurance and pensions) of GBP 922 million and 7.5% of GDP – to partially compensate savers in the Isle of Man branch of KSF. Shortly before the collapse of the bank, the Isle of Man authorities had raised the level of protection of the Depositors' Compensation Scheme from GBP 15,000 to GBP 50,000. An estimated 10,000 depositors had about GBP

Other Kaupthing subsidiaries, and especially the Luxembourg subsidiary, suffered from deposit withdrawals but the management of the bank assured local supervisors that it had sufficient credit lines in place. On the same day as the FSA's action, Kaupthing informed the German Federal Financial Supervisory Authority (BaFin) that the German subsidiary had sufficient liquidity lines put in place and all deposits would be covered. As Iceland took control of Kaupthing the next day, it declared that all domestic deposits were fully guaranteed and the bank could continue its domestic operations. On 9 October 2008, BaFin ordered a stoppage of disposals and payments for the German branch of Kaupthing Bank HK, Iceland, and prohibited the branch from receiving payments not intended for payment of debts because there were risks that the branch was no longer able to meet its obligations towards its creditors. In Luxembourg, a special body ordered, at the request of Kaupthing Bank Luxembourg SA, a stoppage of payments and appointed administrators. Since the Luxembourg subsidiary had branches in Belgium and Switzerland, on the same day, the Swiss Federal Banking Commission appointed (special administration) commissioners at the Geneva branch of Kaupthing Bank Luxembourg SA and prohibited the making of payments. The Swiss Deposit Insurer reimbursed depositors their insured deposits. Action to protect depositors of Kaupthing's local subsidiaries was also taken in Finland and Sweden.[106]

4.2.2   Fortis

Following Lehman's collapse (in the last week of September 2008) Fortis' share price declined rapidly and a run against the bank materialized, mostly by big institutional clients, which threatened the bank with collapse, since it lost at the same time access to the already malfunctioning overnight interbank market. Fortis obtained lending from the ECB through the National Bank of Belgium (NBB), but it was in a rather precarious position making rescue inevitable in order to prevent its collapse. Thus, public authorities from the three countries concerned intervened. However, while they initially did so in a co-ordinated way, soon thereafter each of the three countries (Belgium, the Netherlands and Luxemburg) *just concentrated on the part of the group that was most important for its*

---

840 million in KSF. Only about GBP 100 million of their funds remain in the Isle of Man. More than GBP 590 million of the bank's assets were frozen in the United Kingdom', BCBS, 'Report and Recommendations', p. 13.

[106] *Ibid.*

market.[107] As a result, they failed to preserve franchise value, while the process became very protracted since authorities had to balance 'private shareholder rights with the public interest in systemic stability through swift and decisive bank resolution'.[108]

4.2.3   Dexia

The rescue of Dexia, a Franco-Belgian bank with strong presence in Luxemburg, has shown the value of cross-border co-operation. Like several other US and European banks, Dexia ran into funding difficulties during 2008 both because of inability to fund its asset book and because its US subsidiary Financial Security Assurance (FSA), a mono-line insurer, ran into serious difficulties. On 30 September 2008, Dexia increased its capital by € 6.4 billion, of which Belgian and French public and private sector investors subscribed € 3 billion each and Luxembourg subscribed € 376 million. On 9 October 2008, Belgium, France and Luxembourg concluded an agreement on a joint guarantee mechanism – covered 60.5 per cent by Belgium, 36.5 per cent by France and 3 per cent by Luxembourg – to facilitate Dexia's access to financing. On 14 November 2008, additional public Belgian and French guarantees were announced in the context of the sale of FSA. The three countries concerned agreed to share the burden of guarantees on the basis of percentage of share ownership held by the institutional investors and

---

[107] The Dutch government purchased Fortis Bank Netherlands, Fortis Insurance Netherlands, Fortis Corporate Insurance and the Fortis share in ABN AMRO. The Belgian government raised its holding in Fortis Bank Belgium up to 99%. 'The Belgian government also agreed to sell a 75% interest to BNP Paribas (BNP) in return for new BNP shares, keeping a blocking minority of 25% of the capital of Fortis Bank Belgium. BNP also bought the Belgian insurance activities of Fortis and took a majority stake in Fortis Bank Luxembourg. A portfolio of structured products was transferred to a financial structure owned by the Belgian State, BNP and Fortis Group', BCBS, 'Report and Recommendations', p. 10. On 12 December 2008, the Court of Appeal of Brussels suspended the sale to BNP, which was not yet finalised, and decided that the finalised sales to the Dutch State and to the Belgian State as well as the subsequent sale to BNP had to be submitted for approval by the shareholders of Fortis Holding in order for these three sales to be valid under Belgian Law. After initial rejection by the shareholders, certain transactions were renegotiated and financing of the portfolio of structured products was modified. The renegotiated transaction with the Belgian State and BNP was approved at the second general meeting of shareholders and the latter transaction was finalised on 12 May 2009. *Ibid.*
[108] IMF, 'Resolution of Cross-Border Banks – A Proposed Framework for Enhanced Coordination', 11 June 2010, p. 13, available at www.imf.org/external/np/pp/eng/2010/061110.pdf.

public authorities of the three countries.[109] Dexia's first rescue – there was a second and more expensive rescue in September 2011 – showed that effective cross-border co-operation is possible. However, it is generally impossible, in the absence of a formal structure for cross-border co-operation, especially when the costs involved in the rescue/resolution of an institution/group exceed a certain size.

4.3   Lack of cross-border resolution regimes and 'too-big-to-fail' institutions

The failure of Northern Rock showed, according to the Bank of England and the requisite Parliamentary Committee, how important is the existence of a special resolution regime for banks, which bypasses generally applicable insolvency, property and security laws.[110] Subsequently, the failure of Lehman Brothers showed the importance of having in place contingency arrangements and special legal and regulatory regimes that would allow international banks to fail in an orderly manner, especially in the case of complex SIFIs.[111] I will discuss and evaluate the proposals for reform of cross-border crisis management frameworks and resolution of SIFIs emanating from Basel,[112] the EU,[113] the IMF,[114] and the new US regime for the orderly liquidation of SIFIs under the Dodd–Frank Act in Chapter 7.

One issue on which all these reforms concur is that the combination of organizationally complex cross-border systemically important ('too-big-to-fail') institutions and lack of special resolution and insolvency regimes

---

[109] BCBS, 'Report and Recommendations', p. 11.

[110] House of Commons, Treasury Committee, 'The Run on the Rock', Fifth Report of Session 2007–8, 24 January 2008. In the UK this defect was remedied in 2009 with the enactment of the Banking Act 2009. For a discussion of the troubled rescue of Northern Rock and of the 2009 Act's special resolution regime, see Emilios Avgouleas, 'Banking Supervision and the Special Resolution Regime of the Banking Act 2009: The Unfinished Reform' (2009) 4 *Capital Markets Law Journal* 201–35.

[111] Stijn Claessens, Richard Herring and Dirk Schoenmaker, 'A Safer World Financial System: Improving the Resolution of Systemic Institutions', 12th Geneva Report on the World Economy, International Center for Monetary and Banking Studies, Geneva and CEPR, London, 2010.

[112] BCBS, 'Report and Recommendations'.

[113] EU Commission Communication, 'An EU Framework for Crisis Management in the Financial Sector' (2010), COM 579, 20 October 2010.

[114] IMF, 'Resolution of Cross-Border Banks – A Proposed Framework for Enhanced Coordination', prepared by the Legal and Monetary and Capital Markets Departments, 11 June 2010.

dealing with them on a unitary (group-level) basis proved a lethal mix. Arguably, the most important lesson learnt from the collapse of Lehman is that, while the business of a banking group is run on an integrated global basis, its corporate structure is highly fragmented and labyrinthic. This is normally the result of regulatory and tax arbitrage or of local legal requirements, or is put in place in order to evade legal liability spilling over from one corporate entity to the other within the same group.[115]

After a number of failed merger attempts, Lehman Brothers Holdings International (LBHI) filed for protection under Chapter 11 of the US Bankruptcy Code on 15 September 2008. It was the largest bankruptcy in US history. Although Lehman Brothers was probably the smallest and one of the least complex financial institutions in the list of systemically important institutions maintained by the Bank of England and the IMF, its collapse caused ripple effects that led the global financial system to the brink of collapse. Essentially the Lehman collapse made evident the possibility of significant direct losses to bank creditors and trading counterparties. This realization triggered an intense and widespread loss of confidence, which was further fuelled by heightened fear of contagion, due to financial sector interconnectedness.

Lehman Brother's total reported assets (roughly US$700 billion) did not seem sufficient to satisfy all the claimants. In addition, its complex corporate structure (comprising almost 3,000 separate entities operating in fifty countries)[116] 'greatly impeded the orderly resolution of the firm and created significant spillovers to other institutions and markets'.[117] Through co-ordinated effort most of Lehman's positions in derivatives markets were quickly wound down and settled on the basis of prices achieved following a series of emergency auctions. But that was not the case at all with its bondholders and sellers of CDSs pegged on Lehman, who lost substantial amounts of money.[118] Even more disruptive proved

---

[115] Richard Herring and Jacopo Carmassi, 'The Corporate Structure of International Financial Conglomerates, Complexity and Its Implications for Safety and Soundness', in Allen N. Berger, Phillip Molyneux and John Wilson (eds.), *Oxford Handbook of Banking* (Oxford University Press, 2010), pp. 173–204. See also BCBS, 'Report and Recommendations', pp. 14–16.

[116] BCBS, 'Report and Recommendations', p. 14.

[117] Richard J. Herring, 'Why and How Resolution Policy Must be Improved', in John D. Ciorcari and John B. Taylor (eds.), *Monetary Policy: The Road Ahead* (Stanford University: Hoover Institution Press, 2009), Chapter 11, p. 172.

[118] 'Losses were much greater, however, with regard to credit default swap contracts written on LB. Those selling protection on LB are in a similar position to bondholders and received a similar price: sellers lost $8.625 per $100 of coverage', *ibid.*, p. 173.

to be trades placed by portfolio managers with Lehman Brother's broker dealer entity, Lehman Brothers International (LBI), which were subsequently transferred for settlement to LBI global affiliates. Many of those thousands of trades failed to settle following the declaration of the holding company's bankruptcy leading to litigation which has spread to three continents.

All insolvency practitioners and regulators agree that the greatest problem with Lehman Brother's bankruptcy was that while claims had to be exercised against individual Lehman Brother entities based in different jurisdictions, each having separate legal personality due to the doctrine of incorporation, the group was managed as an integrated entity and borrowed money through the holding company in the same manner.[119] As a result, when bankruptcy was declared, most of subsidiaries' cash became part of the LBHI's estate and got caught up in US bankruptcy proceedings. Moreover, Lehman Brothers, like most other big banks, run their back-up systems and trading platforms on an integrated basis, which meant that information for different products and different subsidiaries was comingled.[120] In addition, there was no clear division of intra-group assets, making the continuous operation of the subsidiaries, following the parent company's bankruptcy, a very arduous task. For example, the administrator of the four London subsidiaries complained that he had not received a confirmation of the assets owned by those subsidiaries as long as nine weeks after LBHI's bankruptcy.[121] The complexity and difficulty of the situation was further exacerbated by the multitude of jurisdictions involved and the different and often conflicting national bankruptcy, property and corporate security laws applicable. Not surprisingly litigation against various Lehman entities is still ongoing and the legal disputes over the assets of the various parts of the group continue unabated.[122]

---

[119] 'LBHI, in effect, served as banker for its affiliates, running a zero balance cash management system. LBHI lent to its operating subsidiaries at the beginning of each day and then swept the cash back to LBHI at the end of each day.' Herring, 'Why and How Resolution Policy Must be Improved', p. 175.

[120] Ibid., p. 175.

[121] See Jennifer Hughes, 'Lehman Highlights Need for Planning', Financial Times, 7 November 2008.

[122] 'Administrators to the London arm of Lehman Brothers, the investment bank that collapsed last September, are preparing a $100bn (£61.5bn) claim against its former parent company in the US', Jonathan Sibun, 'PricewaterhouseCoopers preparing $100bn claim against Lehman Brothers', The Telegraph, 29 August 2009, available at www.telegraph.

The Lehman and Fortis cases have highlighted the incompatibility of cross-border group structures with national resolution regimes and insolvency procedures.[123] This is one of the biggest threats to financial globalization,[124] since it has become obvious that, in the absence of clear cross-border supervisory structures and a single insolvency regime, the operation of SIFIs on a cross-border basis entails serious dangers. An example of the difficulties that may be encountered in the context of a cross-border bank resolution is the conflict of powers over asset transfers, which in some jurisdictions are vested with the insolvency authorities and in others with the courts.[125] The EU and the IMF have moved towards adoption of a more harmonized approach to bank resolution and insolvency,[126] as the only realistic alternative to the co-ordination chaos and risk of systemic collapse observed during the Lehman failure and the Fortis rescue. These plans are discussed analytically in Chapter 7. What is clear from the EU proposals and IMF recommendations is that lack of

co.uk/finance/newsbysector/banksandfinance/6112399/PricewaterhouseCoopers-preparing-100bn-claim-against-Lehman-Brothers.html and Jennifer Hughes, 'Lehman Creditors to Face Years of Waiting', *Financial Times*, 14 November 2008.

[123] Stijn Claessens, Richard Herring and Dirk Schoenmaker, 'A Safer World Financial System: Improving the Resolution of Systemic Institutions', Geneva Report on the World Economy 12, International Center for Monetary and Banking Studies, Geneva and CEPR, London, 2010.

[124] One obvious remedy is of course to ring-fence branches and subsidiaries in the host jurisdiction. But as Avgouleas, Goodhart and Schoenmaker have argued it is unlikely that even ring-fenced subisidiaries will survive the reputation contagion of apparent failure, which will cause a retail or wholesale creditor run on the subsidiary causing in the beginning severe funding problems and eventually forcing it into bankruptcy. See E. Avgouleas, C. Goodhart and D. Schoenmaker, 'Bank Resolution Plans as a Catalyst for Global Financial Reform' (2012) 8 *Journal of Financial Stability*, in press. Also it has been observed that ring-fencing may prove costly and complicated, instead of simplifying, cross-border group resolutions. The segregation of intra-group internal funding and liquidity flows will create operating inefficiencies and may amplify rather than resolve the problem of cross-border bank failures and even impose extra costs on a host country's economy. See E. Cerutti, A. Ilyina, Y. Makarova and C. Schmieder, 'Bankers Without Borders? Implications of Ring-Fencing for European Cross-Border Banks', IMF Working Paper No. WP/10/247, 2010.

[125] Centre for European Policy Studies (CEPS), 'Overcoming Too Big to Fail – A Regulatory Framework to Limit Moral Hazard and Free Riding in the Financial Sector', Report by the CEPS-Assonime Task Force on Bank Crisis Resolution, Brussels, March 2010.

[126] European Commission, 'An EU Framework for Crisis Management in the Financial Sector', COM(2010) 579; European Commission, 'Working Document: Technical Details of A Possible Framework for Bank Recovery and Resolution' IP/11/10 Brussels, 6 January 2011. IMF, 'Resolution of Cross-Border Banks – A Proposed Framework for Enhanced Coordination', 11 June 2010, available at www.imf.org/external/np/pp/eng/2010/061110.pdf.

a supra-national authority and of a binding international framework for cross-border resolution mean that most of the existing obstacles to international crisis management and resolution remain.

Another very thorny issue is how to share the burden in the case of rescuing a cross-border bank or other financial institution. As the TARP Congressional Oversight Panel Report (2010) has shown,[127] in this era of global finance inter-connectedness there is always the possibility that the institutions of a country other than the country providing the rescue money are the main beneficiaries of a rescue operation. Using taxpayers' money in one country to bail out the institutions of another country is an unjust approach and often politically untenable.

5.   What should be done?

The discussion thus far should have brought home that global financial markets are in urgent need of a new governance paradigm to enable stronger cross-border supervision of SIFIs and effective cross-border crisis management, including a framework for the orderly resolution/insolvency of international financial groups. This new paradigm should incorporate rather than demolish the effective parts of its predecessor soft law regime and especially certain of the rule-making functions of the TRNs and reliable private sector input/co-operation. Mere utilization of hard law structures would both lead to regulatory hubris[128] and maximize the cost of regulatory errors. It should also try to tackle the important

---

[127] The Report notes: '[I]t appears likely that America's financial rescue had a much greater impact internationally than other nations' programs had on the United States. This outcome was likely inevitable given the structure of the TARP, but if the U.S. government had gathered more information about which countries institutions would most benefit from some of its actions, it might have been able to ask those countries to share the pain of rescue. For example, banks in France and Germany were among the greatest beneficiaries of AIG's rescue, yet the U.S. government bore the entire $70 billion risk of the AIG capital injection program. The U.S. share of this single rescue exceeded the size of France's entire $35 billion capital injection program and was nearly half the size of Germany's $133 billion program.' TARP Congressional Oversight Panel (COP) Report, 'The AIG Rescue, Its Impact on Markets, and the Government's Exit Strategy', 2010, p. 4. As the TARP is now defunct the document is available at cybercemetery. unt.edu/archive/cop/20110401232818/http://cop.senate.gov/reports/library/report-061010-cop.cfm.

[128] Douglas W. Arner and Ross P. Buckley, 'Redesigning the Architecture of the International Economic System' (2010) 11 *Melbourne Journal of International Law* 185–239.

legitimacy questions that remain, although the expansion of FSB and BCBS membership and the active involvement of the G-20 make them less acute than in the pre-GFC era.

Arguably the new governance regime for global markets and institutions must be based on a formal, hierarchical[129] and multilayered[130] architecture and have at its centre a formal international law structure with four interconnected bodies comprising:

(1) a systemic risk/ macro-prudential regulator that should extend systemic risk oversight to the shadow banking sector – a role that should be discharged by the IMF; [131]
(2) a micro-prudential supervisor for G-SIFIs that should be seen as the natural evolution of FSB's current role, which (as discussed in Chapter 8) is fast moving to a de facto role of peer review co-ordinator and overseer of supervisory colleges;
(3) a regulation and knowledge management body overseeing the TRNs, a role that may only be discharged by the OECD and part of the BIS, due to their reputation for impartiality and technical competence; and
(4) a global resolution authority, which would undertake the task of cross-border group resolution.

The serious obstacles that a shift to more hierarchical and multilayered structure would face would not be limited to strong political opposition but would also extend to practical and institutional architecture challenges of utmost importance. Beyond the massive national economic interests that would have to be reconciled for such structure to ever come to life, there is also the issue of effectiveness. For example, the global systemic regulator would have to have access to the liquidity lines of big central banks, which as a result would sit on its board, limiting its independence. It would also

---

[129] This multiplicity of actors and the mushrooming of international fora create a very complex network structure ... given the rise in systemic risks noted by all the reports on the current system and the interconnectedness of the global financial system the way forward must involve the substitution of this loose network with a hierarchical structure more akin to the one used in the WTO.' Garricano and Lastra, 'Towards a New Architecture', 619 (note omitted).
[130] See also Thomas Cottier, 'Multilayered Governance, Pluralism, and Moral Conflict', (2009) 16(2) *Indiana Journal of Global Legal Studies* 647.
[131] Others see the IMF as the body discharging the role of global regulator in all four areas. Garricano and Lastra, 'Towards a New Architecture', p. 620.

have to identify a core of shared values, which would provide the foundations of such a structure.[132] I attempt to provide an answer to several of these issues in Chapter 8.

---

[132] Weber notes: 'The concept of multilayered governance requires common foundations applicable to all relevant layers, while at the same time it must respect diversity … Consequently, multilayered governance needs to develop normative guidance as to how relations between different layers of governance should be framed in a coherent and not fragmented manner … multilayered governance relies upon a common and shared body of underlying constitutional values and legal principles, which penetrate all layers of governance', Weber, 'Multilayered Governance', 689–90.

PART III

Regulatory reform and a new governance model
for global financial markets

6

Regulatory and supervisory reform: US, EU, BCBS

1. Introduction

1.1 Overview

I gave a brief overview of structural reforms taking place at the level of international financial regulation, where soft law bodies are being tied into a tighter new architecture that has at its centre the Financial Stability Board and at its apex the G 20, in Chapter 5. Structural reforms as a response to the GFC have also taken place in most Western economies. The US Dodd–Frank Act has established a new macro-prudential regulator, the Financial Stability Oversight Council (FSOC). The structure of financial supervision has radically changed in the EU as well with the introduction of the European System of Financial Supervisors.

Even more wide-ranging and far-reaching have been the reforms to the substantive rules governing the financial sector. The Dodd–Frank Act and the EU legislators have brought about sweeping changes as regards the regulation, supervision and resolution of large banks and other Systemically Important Financial Institutions (SIFIs), OTC derivatives trading and ratings production by the Credit Rating Agencies (CRAs). In addition, the Basel Committee on Banking Supervision (BCBS) has produced a radically upgraded capital, liquidity and leverage regulatory framework. I provide in this chapter an analytical discussion of the most important of these reforms. As the new regulations are rather labyrinthic, by way of introduction to them I provide below brief summaries before moving to more detailed analysis. Furthermore, since the regulation of and resolution of SIFIs, inextricably related to the 'too-big-to-fail' problem gives rise to a separate class of problems, IMF, FSB and BCBS proposals to tackle this problem are discussed in the next chapter. In the same chapter, I offer an analysis of the Dodd–Frank special resolution regime for SIFIs and of the EU's proposals for a pan-European crisis management regime that contain measures which range from early intervention to resolution of banks and certain (systemically important) investment firms.

1.2   Summary of reforms

1.2.1   The US reforms

The Dodd–Frank Act was enacted on 9 July 2010 after a prolonged period of public and Congressional debate.[1] The final Act was in many respects the culmination of several political compromises[2] and has since become the subject of serious criticism from both sides of the increasingly polarized political landscape in the US. The main goal of the Act is to address the risks that relate to eventual failure of 'too-big-to-fail institutions' (SIFIs) and the risks relating to financial innovation and the shadow banking sector. It also tries to create a strict framework for consumer protection, including the establishment of the Consumer Financial Protection Bureau (CFPB), in order to avoid a repeat of the sub-prime mortgage scandal.

With respect to SIFI regulation, the Dodd–Frank Act's main innovation is the creation of a number of new regulators and establishment of a new resolution regime that will be dedicated to systemically important institutions regardless of whether they hold a bank licence or not. The Act also curbs, through the so-called Volcker Rule, the ability of regulated banks to engage in the most speculative forms of investment banking and reduce their involvement with/exposure to the shadow banking

---

[1] The Dodd–Frank Act is a 2,300 page long document. A number of US law firms have released extensive summaries of and commentary on the Act. For example, see Skadden, Arps, Slate, Meagher & Flom LLP & Affiliate, 'The Dodd–Frank Act – Commentary and Insights', 2010; Mayer Brown, 'Understanding the Financial Reform Legislation – The Dodd–Frank Wall Street Reform and Consumer Protection Act', 2010; Davis Polk, 'Summary of the Dodd–Frank Wall Street Reform and Consumer Protection Act, Passed by the House of Representatives on June 30, 2010', 9 July 2010. For a good analysis of the issues Dodd–Frank attempts to regulate and the policy/regulatory tools that it employs, see Viral Acharya, Thomas Cooley, Matthew Richardson and Ingo Walter (eds.), *Regulating Wall Street: The Dodd–Frank Act and the New Architecture of Global Finance* (Hoboken, NJ: Wiley Finance, 2011). An excellent analysis of the various aspects of the Dodd–Frank Act is provided in David Skeel, *The New Financial Deal: Understanding the Dodd–Frank Act and Its (Unintended) Consequences* (Hoboken, NJ: Wiley & Sons, 2011).

[2] For the political battles surrounding the enactment of the Dodd–Frank Act and its underlying political goals see David Skeel, 'The New Financial Deal: Understanding the Dodd–Frank Act and its (Unintended) Consequences', Research Paper No. 10–21, Institute for Law and Economics, University of Pennsylvania, October 2010, pp.1–4, available at ssrn.com/abstract=1690979.

sector.[3] With respect to this task, the Act mandates a framework for the standardization of OTC derivatives contracts introducing on exchange trading and clearing requirements for most classes of such contracts. While the Act is by all accounts a major step forward in the regulation of the US financial services industry, it has been validly criticised on three grounds: (1) it does not eradicate 'too-big-to-fail' problem, (2) the cost of compliance is very considerable and thus the implementation of the Act is likely to have an adverse impact on the competitiveness of the US financial services industry,[4] and (3) the Act is largely unhelpful when it comes to international regulatory co-operation and is bound to generate strong regime conflicts and obstacles to supervisory co-ordination, through its extraterritorial reach as well as compliance loopholes.

1.2.2   Reform in the EU

I discussed in Chapter 5 the serious co-ordination issues and supervisory flaws the GFC exposed in the regulatory edifice governing the EU financial sector.[5] The EU's reliance on a supervisory model that was centred on national supervisors proved to be terribly flawed, justifying those who doubted whether a stable financial system, an integrated financial system and national financial autonomy (so-called financial stability 'trilemma') were compatible.[6] The structures for co-operation, co-ordination and consistent application of EU law were very weak. They were particularly ineffective when it came to managing the challenges arising from failing financial institutions operating cross-border both within Europe and globally.[7] These exhibited strong links of interconnectedness

---

[3] An analysis of the Volker Rule is offered in the next chapter where I discuss the emerging regimes for the regulation of SIFIs.

[4] E.g., because of heightened derivatives regulation. See Hal S. Scott, 'Testimony Before the Committee on Financial Services', United States House of Representatives, 16 June 2011, p. 12.

[5] 'The financial crisis in 2007 and 2008 exposed important shortcomings in financial supervision, both in particular cases and in relation to the financial system as a whole', Recital 1, Regulation (EU) No. 1093/2010 of the European Parliament and of the Council, 24 November 2010 establishing a European Supervisory Authority (European Banking Authority), amending Decision No. 716/2009/EC, and repealing Commission Decision 2009/78/EC OJ L331/12, 12 December 2010. For a good overview of those gaps, see Louis W. Pauly, 'The Old and the New Politics of International Financial Stability', (2009) 47 *Journal of Common Market Studies* 955–75.

[6] See D. Schoenmaker, 'The Trilemma of Financial Stability', Duisenberg School of Finance Working Paper, February 2009, available at papers.ssrn.com/sol3/papers. cfm?abstract_id=1340395.

[7] See, for an overview, Fabio Recine and Pedro Gustavo Teixeira, 'The New Financial Stability Architecture in the EU', Institute for Law and Finance, Working Paper Series No. 110, December 2009, especially pp. 7–10.

and were major sources of systemic risk for a host of national markets. The failure of those institutions also exposed a marked lack of trust among national supervisors. Even regulators from (neighbouring) EU member states, who also had established, via the Lamfalussy Committee of European Banking Supervisors (CEBS), a good understanding with their counterparts, chose, nevertheless, to follow a national approach when it came to dealing with distressed cross-border financial institutions, as in the Icelandic banks' and Fortis' cases.

In this context three main problems were identified. First, there was a marked lack of any framework for the monitoring of systemic risk (macro-prudential oversight) in the entire EU. Second, the loopholes of 'home country control' came into sharp focus. The failure of Icelandic banks especially exposed the gaps in cross-border supervision of banking groups in the EU and the European Economic Area (where Iceland belongs) and, in particular, the failure of home country control. Foreign bank branches, which proved to be systemically critical and a menace to host country's systemic stability, were, nevertheless, supervised by their home regulator.[8] Even more damning was the fact that the identified loopholes in supervision were left unattended while the level of harmonization of national prudential regulation regimes was getting increasingly dense. Third, the unco-ordinated bank rescues, and especially the Fortis case, highlighted the lack of cross-border structures for crisis management and bank resolution.

These gaps in EU financial supervision called for a radical rethinking of regulatory structures in the EU. In November 2008, the Commission mandated a High-Level Group chaired by Jacques de Larosière to make recommendations on how to strengthen European supervisory arrangements in order to improve investor/consumer/depositor/taxpayer protection and rebuild trust in the financial system. The Group identified big gaps in the supervision of EU markets, including the absence of a systemic risk oversight body. The High-Level Group recommended reforms to strengthen the supervision of the EU financial sector and ways to facilitate consistent implementation of harmonized rules in its final report, presented on 25 February 2009 (the 'de Larosière Report').[9] The

---

[8]   FSA, Turner Review, 'A Regulatory Response to the Global Banking Crisis', March 2009, pp. 37–9; House of Lords, European Committee, 14th Report, 'The Future of EU Financial Regulation and Supervision', Chapter 7, Session 2008–9, 9 June 2009, available at www.publications.parliament.uk/pa/ld200809/ldselect/ldeucom/106/10610.htm.

[9]   The de Larosière report is available at ec.europa.eu/internal_market/finances/docs/de_larosiere_report_en.pdf. See also Ieke van den Burg and Daniel Dăianu, 'Report

Group recommended the establishment of pan-European supervisory structures comprising three European Supervisory Authorities (ESAs), one for the banking sector, one for the securities sector, and one for the insurance and occupational pensions sector, to replace the corresponding Lamfalussy process committees (CEBS, CESR, CEIOPS).[10] It also recommended the creation of a European Systemic Risk Council.

Following the recommendations of the de Larosière Report and substantial further consultations, financial supervision in the EU has undergone very extensive reform. The general characteristics of the EU reforms may be summarized as follows:

(1) macro-prudential oversight and systemic risk monitoring have predominantly become the job of the newly established European Systemic Risk Board (ESRB);

(2) the EU has abolished the last remnants of the principles of minimum harmonization and mutual recognition in EU financial services regulation. The standard-setting competence of the new ESAs makes them the central pillars and channels of maximum harmonization through their competence to draft the new EU regulatory standards for financial markets and the provision of financial services with a view to establishing common EU rulebooks. The ESAs are also the monitors of consistent application of harmonized rules at the national level;

(3) certain aspects of the supervision of cross-border groups have (implicitly) shifted from home country control to transnational supervisory structures comprising essentially supervisory colleges[11] and the

with Recommendations to the Commission on Lamfalussy Follow-up: Future Structure of Supervision', European Parliament, Committee on Economic and Monetary Affairs (2008/2148(INI)), 18 September 2008, available at www.europarl.europa.eu/sides/getDoc.do?pubRef=-//EP//NONSGML+REPORT+A6–2008–0359+0+DOC+WORD+V0//EN&language=EN.

[10] For an overview of the work carried out by the Lamfalussy Committees until their re-establishment, see Eilis Ferran, 'Understanding the Institutional Architecture of EU Financial Market Supervision', Working Paper, 20 December 2010, pp. 12–24, available at ssrn.com/abstract=1701147.

[11] Directive 2009/111/EC of the European Parliament and of the Council 16 September 2009 amending Directives 2006/48/EC, 2006/49/EC and 2007/64/EC as regards banks affiliated to central institutions, certain own funds items, large exposures, supervisory arrangements, and crisis management OJ L 302/97, 17 November 2009. This Directive maintains the supervisory powers of national competent authorities are not diluted, Recital 6. However, given the powers of colleges and of the ESAs, and the authority colleges may establish over systemically important branches, this claim looks maximalist. See new Article 42a of Directive 2006/48/EC inserted by means of Article 1 of Directive 2009/111/EC.

new ESAs. These changes have made the supervision of cross-border financial groups a more collaborative effort;

(4) until an EU-wide bank resolution and insolvency regime is implemented with fiscal burden sharing arrangements attached to it, the resolution of cross-border institutions remains a national responsibility, notwithstanding the collaborative arrangements for crisis management and bank resolution the EU Commission proposes to implement.[12]

1.2.3   A radically new Basel Accord

(a)   **The shift to macro-prudential regulation**   In the aftermath of the crisis the BCBS has radically redesigned its capital adequacy standards and has introduced a new supervisory framework to regulate liquidity (adequacy) and a global leverage ratio.[13] BCBS has also issued standards to improve risk management and governance in the banking sector. The main objective of the new capital measures introduced by Basel III is to resolve the chronic problem of bank under-capitalization, a widespread phenomenon during the crisis, which led to a massive number of bail-outs. This behaviour was also, as explained in Chapters 4 and 5, a by-product of the application of the previous Basel Capital Accords.[14] Basel III aims to ensure that banks are able to withstand the type of stress experienced during the GFC, including banks' exposure to the economic cycle, bubbles and other macroeconomic developments. The preceding Basel framework was exclusively reliant on micro-prudential regulation measures, although micro-prudential regulation sees risk as exogenous caused as a result of the behaviour of financial institutions and 'neglects the systemic implications of common behaviour' of banks in the economy.[15] The GFC has not only underscored the importance of

---

[12] EU Commission Communication, 'An EU Framework for Crisis Management in the Financial Sector', 20 October 2010, COM(2010) 579. See also DG Internal Market and Services, 'Working Document, Technical Details of a Possible EU Framework for Bank Recovery and Resolution', 6 January 2011, available at ec.europa.eu/internal_market/consultations/docs/2011/crisis_management/consultation_paper_en.pdf.

[13] BCBS, 'Basel III: A Global Regulatory Framework for more Resilient Banks and Banking Systems', December 2010.

[14] See BCBS, 'The Basel Committee's Response to the Financial Crisis: Report to the G20', October 2010, available at www.bis.org/publ/bebs179.pdf.

[15] Avinash Persaud et al., 'The Warwick Commission on International Financial Reform: In Praise of Unlevel Playing Fields', University of Warwick, December 2009, p. 12, available at www2.warwick.ac.uk/research/warwickcommission/finanacialreform/report/uw_warcomm_intfinreform_09.pdf.

resilient financial institutions for the stability of the system, since individual institution failure can always trigger a cascade effect due to loss of confidence, but also has highlighted the importance of guarding against endogenous risks to the system (as discussed in Chapters 3 and 5). For instance, prudent decisions to raise new funds or sell assets made by individual institutions can give rise to negative (liquidity and fire sales) externalities which have the potential to destabilize the financial system. The new Accord has both a micro-prudential focus and a macro-prudential focus. Therefore, it aims to enhance bank resilience at periods of stress and address system-wide risks as well as the pro-cyclical amplification of these risks over time.[16]

However, defining the actual role, tools and boundaries of macro-prudential policy is not as straightforward as it might sound in spite of the significance this policy has acquired in the surveillance and reinforcement of the stability of national financial systems and thus of the international financial system.[17] The joint FSB, IMF and BIS report has offered the following definition of macro-prudential policy:[18]

[16] Philip E. Davis and Karim Dilruba, 'Macroprudential Regulation – The Missing Policy Pillar', (2010) 211 *National Institute Economic Review* 67–80, 73. Macro-prudential surveillance may also help alert central banks to imminent financial instability, *ibid.*, p. 71. Others however argue that over reliance on macro-prudential regulation might lead to a neglect of market discipline that is, allegedly, a desirable by-product of micro-prudential capital adequacy rules. See Anil Kashyap, Raghuram Rajan and Jeremy Stein 'Rethinking Capital Regulation', Paper Prepared for Federal Reserve Bank of Kansas City Symposium, Jackson Hole, Wyoming, 21–23 March 2008, available at www.kc.frb. org/publicat/sympos/2008/KashyapRajanStein.03.12.09.pdf.

[17] In the Seoul G-20 Summit in November 2010, G-20 Leaders asked the FSB, IMF and BIS for a joint report, elaborating on progress achieved in identification of best practices on macro-prudential policy frameworks. In February 2011, the three organizations provided a first report defining the basic elements of macro-prudential policies and summarized the work underway internationally and nationally to develop effective macro-prudential policies and frameworks. See FSB, IMF and BIS, 'Macroprudential Policy Tools and Frameworks, Update to G20 Finance Ministers and Central Bank Governors', February 2011.

[18] *Ibid.*, p. 2. However, Jaime Caruana, General Manager of BIS, has offered this more encompassing definition: '[M]acroprudential policy [is] the use of primarily prudential tools to limit system-wide financial risk, and so prevent disruption to key financial services and the economy … [it] is defined by its aim (limiting system-wide financial risk), the scope of analysis (the financial system as a whole and its interactions with the real economy), a set of powers and instruments and their governance (prudential tools and those specifically assigned to macro-prudential authorities).' See 'Monetary Policy in a World with Macroprudential Policy', Speech at the SAARCFINANCE Governors' Symposium 2011, Kerala, 11 June 2011, available at www.bis.org/speeches/sp110610. htm.

> [A] policy that uses primarily prudential tools to limit systemic or sys-
> tem-wide financial risk, thereby limiting the incidence of disruptions in
> the provision of key financial services that can have serious consequences
> for the real economy, by dampening the build-up of financial imbalances
> and building defences that contain the speed and sharpness of subsequent
> downswings and their effects on the economy; identifying and addressing
> common exposures, risk concentrations, linkages and interdependencies
> that are sources of contagion and spillover risks that may jeopardise the
> functioning of the system as a whole.

Macro-prudential policy is a complement to *micro*-prudential policy and it interacts with other types of public policy that have an impact on financial stability, such as monetary or fiscal policy, but it is no substitute for them.[19] Therefore, the role of macro-prudential policy is not to manage ('dampen') aggregate demand. When it comes to safeguarding macro-economic stability, it is no substitute for monetary and fiscal policies. Macro-prudential policy may not act as a defence against inflation or macro-economic imbalances.[20] It merely intends to buttress the stability of the financial system by controlling the credit growth that normally leads to asset price growth, which, in combination with increasing risk appetite, often driven by irrational exuberance, is a fundamental source of financial instability.

The defining elements of macro-prudential policy are:

(1) its objective – limiting systemic or system-wide financial risk;
(2) the focus of analysis – the financial system as a whole and its interactions with the real economy; and
(3) the set of powers and instruments used for this purpose and their governance, namely, prudential tools and those specifically assigned to macro-prudential authorities.

The FSB, IMF and BIS hold that non-prudential tools are regarded as part of the macro-prudential policy toolkit only if they target on a continuous basis systemic risk and are part of the institutional framework used to 'conduct macro-prudential policy'.[21] A key component of successful macro-prudential policies is effective diagnosis of systemic risk build up.

Macro-prudential policy may pursue either a narrow objective – increasing the resilience of the financial system – or a broader objective – 'to constrain the upswing of the financial cycle itself'. Choosing which

---

[19] FSB, IMF and BIS, 'Macroprudential Policy Tools and Frameworks', p. 2.
[20] Caruana, 'Monetary Policy'.
[21] FSB, IMF and BIS, 'Macroprudential Policy Tools and Frameworks', p. 2.

of the two objectives the macro-prudential policy should be designed to pursue is of the essence. The first objective does not seek to do much more than to build defences (capital buffers) during the boom so that they can be used as risks materialize during the bust. It is not intended to act as a restraint during the boom. The achievement of the broader objective would ask for the buffers to act as an effective mechanism to slow down the pace of credit and asset price booms. The narrow objective would accept that financial cycles and imbalances could materialize despite the best efforts of policymakers.[22] The Basel III framework has clearly chosen to pursue the narrower objective through the building up of the counter-cyclical buffer, also called the macro-prudential overlay, discussed analytically in Section 4.2.2 below, which aims to restrain the build-up of systemic risk.[23]

BCBS also intends to limit interconnectedness. According to BCBS, several of the Basel III capital requirements, which mitigate risks arising from firm-level exposures, also help to address systemic risk and interconnectedness. These include:[24]

(1) capital incentives for banks to use central counterparties for OTC derivatives;
(2) higher capital requirements for trading and derivative activities, as well as complex securitizations and off-balance sheet exposures (e.g. structured investment vehicles);
(3) higher capital requirements for inter-financial sector exposures; and
(4) the introduction of liquidity requirements that penalize excessive reliance on short-term, interbank funding to support longer dated assets.

A further consideration that has been voiced in consultations that go beyond the Basel III framework is whether a tailor-made system of protections should be extended to certain institutions that may have systemic

---

[22] Caruana, 'Monetary Policy'.

[23] FSB, IMF and BIS, 'Macroprudential Policy Tools and Frameworks', p. 3. 'Macroprudential polices aim to address two dimensions of system-wide risk: first, the evolution of system-wide risk *over time* – the "time dimension"; and second, the distribution of risk in the financial system *at a given point in time* – the "cross-sectional dimension"', *ibid.*, p. 2. Moreover, '[T]he key issue in the cross-sectional dimension is to reduce systemic risk concentrations, which can arise from similar exposures across financial institutions (from assets, liabilities, dependence on common services) or because of the direct balance-sheet linkages among them (e.g., counterparty risk)', *ibid.*, p. 3.

[24] BCBS, 'Basel III: A Global Regulatory Framework', p. 7.

importance.[25] BCBS has developed a proposal on a methodology comprising both quantitative and qualitative indicators to assess the systemic importance of financial institutions at a global level,[26] which the FSB will endorse.[27] Regulatory proposals addressing the problem of Globally Systemically Significant Institutions (G-SIFIs)[28] by means of a co-ordinated cross-border resolution regime and additional capital requirements are discussed extensively in the next chapter.

(b)   **Substantive reforms**   Basel III introduces higher levels of capital for banks. First, the minimum requirement for common equity, which is regarded as the best form of loss absorbing capital, will be raised from the 2 per cent level of the previous Basel Accords, before the application of regulatory adjustments, to 4.5 per cent of risk-weighted assets (RWAs) after the application of stricter adjustments. To this shall be added a capital conservation buffer of up to 2.5 per cent of RWAs, which will bring the total minimum of common equity in bank capital to 7 per cent of RWAs by 2019, when all reforms will have been implemented. The Tier 1 capital requirement, which includes common equity and other qualifying financial instruments, selected on the basis of strict criteria, that give them loss absorption capacity equal to equity, will increase from 4 to 6 per cent (before factoring in the conservation buffer). This higher level of capital is coupled with a stricter definition of common equity and an increase in capital requirements for trading activities, counterparty credit risk and capital markets-related activities, for which a higher capital charge shall apply. Furthermore, Basel III gives supervisors the discretion to require

---

[25] Jean-Charles Rochet, 'Systemic Risk: Changing the Regulatory Perspective', (2010) 6 *International Journal of Central Banking* 259–76. In the Seoul G-20 Summit, held on 12 November 2010, the G-20 Leaders endorsed a requirement that SIFIs and initially in particular G-SIFIs should have higher loss absorbency capacity to reflect the greater risks that these firms pose to the global financial system. See, The Seoul Summit Document, Seoul, 12 November 2010, para. 30, available at www.g20.utoronto.ca/2010/g20seoul-doc.html.

[26] BCBS Press Release, 'Measures for Global Systemically Important Banks Agreed by the Group of Governors and Heads of Supervision', 25 June 2011, available at www.bis.org/press/p110625.htm. See also FSB, 'Reducing Moral Hazard Posed by Systemically Important Financial Institutions – Interim Report to G20 Leaders', 18 June 2010, p. 5, available at www.financialstabilityboard.org/publications/r_100627b.pdf.

[27] FSB, 'Progress in the Implementation of the G20 Recommendations for Strengthening Financial Stability – Report of the Financial Stability Board to G20 Finance Ministers and Central Bank Governors', 10 April 2011.

[28] See FSB, 'Reducing the Moral Hazard posed by Systemically Important Financial Institutions – FSB Recommendations and Time Lines', 20 October 2010.

additional capital buffers during periods of excess credit growth in order to contain bubbles (countercyclical buffer). In addition, competent supervisors may require systemically important banks to increase their loss absorbency capacity.

As explained in Chapters 3 and 5, incontrollable procyclical leverage was partly responsible for the extreme fragility of the global financial system and the extent and depth of the GFC. Basel III is trying to remedy this situation through the welcome introduction of restrictions on banks' leverage. Unlike the Basel III regulatory capital framework, which, like its predecessor, remains risk-based, the new Basel III leverage ratio is a simple number which captures both on- and off-balance sheet exposures and net derivatives positions and is not related to any risk adjustment calculations. Namely, the non-risk-based leverage ratio is meant to serve both as a safety valve and a means to contain regulatory arbitrage, which increases leverage through off-balance sheet assets transformation, serving as a backstop to the risk-based capital requirement.[29]

The GFC started as a credit crunch which meant that wholesale lending markets became very illiquid forcing the failure of financial institutions like Northern Rock, which were highly dependent on short-term funding. The continuing liquidity hoarding also forced all banks to become dependent on central bank liquidity schemes for their short-term funding. Lack of any regulatory standards that would require banks to hold a minimum of liquid assets as liquidity reserves came to be regarded as one of the most important loopholes of the Basel capital adequacy regimes. In response, Basel III has introduced minimum liquidity standards to make banks more resilient to potential short-term funding disruptions. The liquidity coverage ratio (LCR) will require banks to have sufficient high-quality liquid assets to withstand a stressed funding scenario that is specified by supervisors over a period of thirty calendar days. Basel III liquidity standards also address the longer-term structural liquidity mismatches normally encountered in bank balance sheets, which, in part, are due to the business of banking that mainly consists of transforming short-term liabilities (deposits) to long-term assets (loans). Thus, the net stable funding ratio (NSFR) will serve as a measure to address longer-term (structural) liquidity mismatches. Banks will have to show that they

---

[29] 'The use of a supplementary leverage ratio will help contain the build-up of excessive leverage in the system. It will also serve as an additional safeguard against attempts to "game" the risk-based requirements and will help address model risk', BCBS, 'The Basel Committee's Response to the Financial Crisis: Report to the G20', p. 5.

can provide a sustainable maturity structure of assets and liabilities over a period of one year. NSFR covers the entire balance sheet and its clear objective is to incentivize banks to use stable sources of funding.

The remainder of this chapter is structured in three sections. Section 2 provides a critical analysis of select parts of the US reforms focusing on the new provisions for systemic risk oversight in the US. Section 3 examines the EU substantive and structural reforms. It provides an analytical account of the powers and tasks of the European Systemic Risk Board (ESRB) and of the European Supervisory Authorities (ESAs). Section 4 examines in some depth the reforms introduced by Basel III.

2.   Critical aspects of the Dodd–Frank Act

2.1   Supervision of SIFIs and systemic risk oversight under the Dodd–Frank Act

2.1.1   Introductory remarks

Title I of the Dodd–Frank Act addresses the issue of financial stability and systemic risk through:

(1) the establishment of the Financial Stability Oversight Council (FSOC), whose task is to oversee the financial services industry, monitor for systemic risk and promote market discipline;[30] and
(2) the creation of a two-tier supervision system, under which the financial institutions most likely to cause system wide problems in the event of failure are subjected to a more intensive supervisory regime than other institutions.

In the first class belong systemically significant bank holding companies (BHCs)[31] and non-bank financial companies. As systemically significant are deemed, in principle, (1) BHCs with at least $50 billion in consolidated assets; and (2) non-bank financial institutions such as investment banks or insurance holding companies that the new FSOC deems to be systemically important, subjecting them to Federal Reserve Board (FRB) oversight.[32] These two kinds of institutions are often also referred to as Systemically

---

[30] Section 111, Dodd–Frank Act.
[31] Under Section 102(a)(1) a bank holding company (BHC) is a group of affiliated companies that has at least one commercial bank in the group, or has chosen to be subject to bank holding company regulation. As said in Chapter 2, Goldman Sachs and Morgan Stanley chose to take this path in September 2008 in order to secure access to Federal Reserve liquidity funding.
[32] Section 113(a)(1), Dodd–Frank Act.

Important Financial Institutions (SIFIs). The FSOC may also subject a 'US nonbank financial company' to FRB supervision and to FRB's 'prudential standards' if the FSOC decides that it is systemically significant, namely, that 'material financial distress' at the non-bank financial company, or the 'nature, scope, size, scale, concentration, interconnectedness' or mix of activities could pose a threat to US financial stability.

Section 113(a)(2) of the Act enumerates factors that the FSOC must consider in making a decision for non-bank entities:[33]

(1) the degree of leverage the company presents;
(2) the extent and nature of the off-balance-sheet exposures of the company;
(3) Interconnectedness: the extent and nature of the transactions and relationships of the company with other significant non-bank financial companies and significant bank holding companies;
(4) the importance of the company as a source of credit for households, businesses, and state and local governments and as a source of liquidity for the US financial system;
(5) the importance of the company as a source of credit for low-income, minority or underserved communities, and the impact that the failure of such company would have on the availability of credit in such communities;
(6) the extent to which assets are managed rather than owned by the company, and the extent to which ownership of assets under management is diffuse;
(7) the nature, scope, size, scale, concentration, interconnectedness and mix of the activities of the company;
(8) the degree to which the company is already regulated by one or more primary financial regulatory agencies;
(9) the amount and nature of the financial assets of the company;
(10) the amount and types of the liabilities of the company, including the degree of reliance on short-term funding; and
(11) any other risk-related factors that the Council deems appropriate.

---

[33] See also FSOC, 'Advance Notice of Proposed Rulemaking, Authority to Require Supervision and Regulation of Certain Nonbank Financial Companies', 75 Fed. Reg. 61,653 (proposed 6 October 2010); FSOC, 'Authority to Require Supervision and Regulation of Certain Nonbank Financial Companies', 76 Fed. Reg. 4,555 (proposed 26 Janurary 2011). The notice on (draft) Fed Reg. 4,555 outlines the criteria that will inform, and the process and procedures established under the Dodd–Frank Act for, designation of US and foreign non-bank financial companies as systemically important bringing them under the supervision of the FRB.

Non-bank financial companies may only be made subject to FRB supervision, if they are: (1) organized under the laws of the US or of any state in the Union, (2) not a BHC or a subsidiary of a BHC; and (3) 'predominantly engaged' in financial activities.[34] As a result of inclusion of insurance activities in the definition of institutions 'predominantly engaged' in financial activities, large insurance companies (even if they have no bank or thrift subsidiary) might fall into the net, seeking to ensure that an AIG kind of debacle is not repeated. On the other hand, commercial firms with only limited financial activities will not be subject to FRB supervision only as a result of their size, interconnectedness or overall importance to the US economy. Such firms, however, may be required to establish an intermediate holding company through which the financial activities of such company and its subsidiaries shall be conducted. The intermediate holding company will then be subjected to FRB supervision.[35]

Non-US banks that either (1) are BHCs by virtue of their ownership of a US bank; or (2) are treated as BHCs under the IBA because, for example, they operate a US branch or agency, will be treated as Systemic BHCs under the Dodd–Frank Act and be subjected to the FRB's 'prudential standards' if they have at least US$50 billion in consolidated assets on a worldwide basis.[36] As mentioned above, foreign non-bank companies will be deemed to have systemic significance for the US financial system, either because they have significant exposure to the US financial system, they are important providers of liquidity or there are strong links of interconnectedness with US firms.[37]

The FSOC and the FRB have broad powers to request information from those companies to determine if they are systemically significant. In this

---

[34] Under Section 102(6) of the Dodd–Frank Act, a non-bank company is predominantly engaged in financial activities if 85 per cent or more of the consolidated annual gross revenues or consolidated assets of the company are attributable to (1) activities that are 'financial in nature' (as defined in Section 4(k) of the Bank Holding Company Act (BHCA)), and (2) if applicable, from ownership of an insured depository institution. Activities that are 'financial in nature' include (1) all kinds of lending and other forms of financing; (2) underwriting, dealing in and brokering securities; (3) derivatives activities; (4) investment management; and (5) insurance activities. To avoid meaningless extension of banking supervision in all areas of a non-bank company's business, Section 167(a) provides that the non-financial activities of a Systemic Nonbank will not be subject to the general prohibition on nonbanking activities of Section 4 of the BHCA. However, the FRB may require that financial activities be placed beneath an intermediate holding company fully subject to the BHCA.

[35] Section 113(c)(3), Dodd–Frank Act.

[36] Section 115(a), (b), Dodd–Frank Act.

[37] Section 113(b), Dodd–Frank Act.

context, the Act mandates the establishment of a formal industry research body and potential think tank called the Office of Financial Research (OFR), which will collect, analyse, and share information pertinent to the size, systemic threat and interconnectedness of the aforementioned institutions.[38] The OFR will also standardize the types and formats of data reported and collected, perform research, and develop tools for risk measurement and monitoring, which shall be made available to financial regulatory agencies.

2.1.2   FSOC powers and duties

The FSOC was established and became active on the day the Act was enacted (under Section 111 of the Act). Section 112 of the Act gives the FSOC broad duties, which include, *inter alia*, monitoring of systemic risk, facilitation of information sharing among regulatory agencies, designation of non-bank financial companies as systemically significant, formulation of regulatory policy proposals directed at the domestic and international market and provision of recommendations to the FRB on prudential standards. The FSOC has broad powers to collect information, including collection of information from non-bank financial companies to determine whether they should be subject to prudential supervision. Also it may act (unlike the ESRB) as a front line supervisor requesting reports from systemic BHCs or systemic non-banks concerning their financial condition and the extent to which their activities could, under adverse circumstances, have the potential to disrupt financial markets or affect US financial stability.[39] All information and reports submitted to the FSOC (including the OFR) must be kept confidential.[40]

FSOC membership includes ten voting members,[41] comprising the key US financial sector regulators (the FRB, the Securities and Exchange Commission (SEC), the Commodity Futures Trading Commission (CCFT)),

[38] The OFR, acting on behalf of the FSOC, can request information on any financial company, including insurance companies, and financial activities from sources including member agencies and financial companies. The OFR will also assist the regulatory agencies to determine the types and formats of data authorized by the Dodd–Frank Act that they should be collecting, Section 112(d), Dodd–Frank Act.

[39] Section 112(d)(3)(A), Dodd–Frank Act.

[40] Section 112(d) (3)(B), of the Dodd–Frank Act.

[41] The chairperson of the FSOC, the secretary of the FSOC, the comptroller, the director of newly established BCFP, the director of the Federal Housing Finance Agency (FHFA), an independent member with insurance expertise who will serve a six-year term, the chair of the FRB, the chair of the FDIC, the chair of the SEC, the chair of the CFTC, and the chair of the National Credit Union Administration Board (NCUA). Section 111(b)(1), Dodd–Frank Act.

and five non-voting members.[42] The FSOC meets at least on a quarterly basis and its ordinary business decisions may be taken by a majority vote. However, actions designating specific firms or activities for enhanced regulation or supervision, such as designating a 'US nonbank financial company' as a SIFI and subjecting it to FRB supervision, generally require a quorum of two-thirds, including the affirmative vote of the Chairperson.

2.1.3   Enhanced 'prudential standards'

With the Dodd–Frank reforms, the FRB essentially became the frontline bank supervisor of the US financial services industry. This development has attracted much attention, since it further reinforces the power and influence of an unelected institution[43] that was already yielding enormous power over the US economy, mainly, through its mandate to set monetary policy. Title I of the Act (especially Section 115) sets out the 'prudential standards' that the FRB must impose on insured depository institutions and their holding companies, as well as systemic non-banks. Section 165(b)(1)(A)(i) requires the FRB to adopt risk-based capital and leverage limits for systemically significant companies higher than those applicable to non-systemic institutions. In addition, Section 165(j) requires the FRB to impose a 15–1 debt to equity (leverage) ratio on a SIFI that poses a grave threat to the US financial system. Another important reform is that, under Section 165(k), SIFI off balance sheet 'activities', which includes most activities relating to securitizations and other forms of asset intermediation and transaction in derivatives (including Credit Default Swaps (CDSs)),[44] will be taken into account in calculating the institution's capital

---

[42] These are the director of the OFR, the director of the FIO, and a state insurance commissioner, state banking supervisor and a state securities commissioner, each of whom will serve a two-year term. Section 111(b)(2) of the Dodd–Frank Act.

[43] For an overview of the debate regarding the Federal Reserve's (un)accountability within and outside Congress, see Roya Wolverson, 'Debating a New Role for the Fed', Report of the Council on Foreign Relations, 4 January 2011, available at www.cfr.org/international-finance/debating-new-role-fed/p21020#p6.

[44] Section 165(k)(3) Dodd–Frank Act defines 'off-balance-sheet activities' as 'an existing liability of a company that is not currently a balance sheet liability, but may become one upon the happening of some future event, including the following transactions, to the extent that they may create a liability: (A) Direct credit substitutes in which a bank substitutes its own credit for a third party, including standby letters of credit. (B) Irrevocable letters of credit that guarantee repayment of commercial paper or tax-exempt securities. (C) Risk participations in bankers' acceptances. (D) Sale and repurchase agreements. (E) Asset sales with recourse against the seller. (F) Interest rate swaps. (G) Credit swaps. (H) Commodities contracts. (I) Forward contracts. (J) Securities contracts. (K) Such other activities or transactions as the Board of Governors may, by rule, define.'

requirements. This is a very significant reform since it closes an important loophole of the capital adequacy regime and limits considerably the room for regulatory arbitrage. Finally, Section 115(c) considers the introduction of contingent capital requirements for Systemic Nonbanks and Systemic BHCs and requires the FSOC to conduct a relevant feasibility study. Other FRB implemented prudential standards will refer to liquidity, short-term debt limits and credit exposure requirements for SIFIs, which will be regularly subjected to stress-testing and will have an obligation to draw up recovery and resolution plans.[45]

Section 171, the so-called 'Collins Amendment', named after Senator Collins who sponsored it, requires several changes to the previous regulatory capital regime applicable to all BHCs and thrift holding companies and also applies to Systemic Nonbanks. In this context Section 171 requires that the appropriate federal banking regulators establish minimum leverage and risk-based capital requirements applied on a consolidated basis to insured depository institutions, depository institution holding companies,[46] and Systemic Nonbanks, based on the risks of the activities conducted by these entities, taking into consideration volume of activity, asset concentration and market share. Namely, the regulatory agencies are required to apply minimum capital requirements that mirror the requirements that currently apply to insured banks, including regulatory capital components to 'insured depository institutions' holding companies. This is a marked departure from prior practice and amounts to a serious tightening of holding company requirements.[47] It is also poised to lead to an elimination or marked reduction in use of hybrid instruments as components of Tier I capital. Finally, the FRB is considering the introduction of a capital surcharge over SIFIs, which may be as high as 7 per cent.[48]

---

[45] Section 165(b)(1)(A) and (C), Dodd–Frank Act.

[46] FRB standards, which will be issued in 2012, will largely reflect the provisions of Basel III which the FRB was very active in drafting. See Daniel K. Tarullo, 'Capital and Liquidity Standards', Testimony before the Committee on Financial Services, US House of Representatives, Washington, DC, 16 June 2011.

[47] According to the Dodd–Frank Report prepared by Mayer Brown this provision was introduced following a FDIC request, which felt 'that assistance provided to insured depository institution subsidiaries was used to strengthen their holding companies, which during the height of the crisis were unable to act as a source of strength', Mayer Brown, 'Understanding the New Financial Reform Legislation', p. 18.

[48] Daniel K. Tarullo, 'Speech at the Peter G. Peterson Institute for International Economics: Regulating Systemically Important Financial Firms', 3 June 2011, available at www.federalreserve.gov/newsevents/speech/tarullo20110603a.htm. Tarullo is a governor of the Federal Reserve System Board of Governors.

Title I brings a revolution to the US model of financial supervision, since it is the first time that financial institutions other than banks will be subjected to the strict prudential standards normally reserved for commercial banks and be subjected to FRB oversight. The clear objective is that large, interconnected firms, whether they are banks, insurance companies, investment banks or other financial intermediaries, will be subject to a stringent regulatory framework that will reduce and mitigate (through a resolution specifically focused on SIFIs) the risk that SIFI activities or failure would threaten the stability of the US financial system.

Although the Dodd–Frank Act is a rather bulky and lengthy document in many respects, it is also framework legislation. Thus, banking regulators must issue rules establishing capital requirements to address certain risk activities, including risks arising from:

(1) significant volumes of activity in derivatives, securitized products and financial guarantees;
(2) securities borrowing and lending, and repos;
(3) concentrations in assets for which reported values are based on models; and
(4) concentration in market share for any activity that would substantially disrupt financial markets if the institution were forced to unexpectedly stop engaging in the activity in question.[49]

By requesting additional capital requirements for these activities, it is clear that the Act signals the increased risks these activities give rise to as well as recognizing that their prohibition would seriously affect the funding efficiency and business models of financial institutions. On the other hand, it is debatable whether increased capital requirements are the best means to guard against risk emanating from these activities and especially the interdependence/interconnectedness they create. Furthermore, in an attempt to tighten the capital adequacy framework the Act orders a study of the feasibility of treatment of hybrid capital instruments as a component of Tier 1 capital for banking institutions and bank holding companies.

2.1.4   Supervision of systemically important activities

In an attempt to seriously increase the level of supervision (and regulatory burden) of operation of market infrastructure services which are essential for the uninterrupted workings of the financial system and of the

---

[49] Section 171(b)(7)(A)–(B), Dodd–Frank Act.

economy, the FSOC is authorized, under Title VIII of the Act, to designate a payment, clearing or settlement activity[50] or financial market utilities (FMUs)[51] as systemically important.[52] The relevant provisions of the Act clearly vest the FSOC with considerable discretion regarding the kind of payment and settlement activities and FMUs that it will consider systemically important. The FSOC will take its decision upon a two-thirds vote of its members[53] taking into account certain specified considerations such as the aggregate monetary value of transactions processed, the aggregate exposure of an FMU or financial institution engaged in covered financial activities, the interdependence of these FMUs or activities, the systemic impact of a failure or disruption of an FMU or covered financial activities and other factors deemed appropriate by the FSOC.[54]

Systemically important financial market utilities and payment, clearing and settlement activities that are regulated by the SEC or CFTC or

---

[50] This is defined under Section 803(7)(A) and (C) of the Dodd–Frank Act as any payment, clearing and settlement of a financial transaction. It includes the process customarily associated with such functions (trade calculations, netting, funds transmittals and movements, final transaction settlement activities) as well as functions such as 'provision and maintenance' of trade information, risk management activities associated with continuing financial activities and any other 'similar functions' that the FSOC may determine.

[51] Under Section 803(6)(A) of the Dodd-Frank Act, an FMU is defined as a person that manages or operates a multilateral system for the purpose of transferring, clearing or settling payments, securities or other 'financial transactions' among financial institutions or between financial institutions and itself. In this context, the definition of 'financial transactions' in Section 803(7)(B) is rather broad and includes funds transfers, securities and commodity contracts, swaps, repurchase agreements and derivatives contracts, as well as 'any similar transaction' that the FSOC determines to be a financial transaction under Title VIII. Under Section 803(6)(B)(i), SEC or CFTC regulated securities and commodities exchanges, designated contract markets, trading or execution facilities or data repositories are *not* included in the definition of an FMU solely by reason of their performance of activities that require their registration as such. Under Section 803(6)(B)(ii), regulated securities and commodities entities and professionals, such as broker dealers, investment companies, transfer agents, and similar persons providing such services or acting on behalf of an FMU in connection with the furnishing of FMU services, similarly are not included in the definition of an FMU, provided that such services do not constitute 'critical risk management or processing functions' of the FMU.

[52] Section 804(a); see also Section 802(a), (b), Dodd–Frank Act. In this context 'systemically important' and 'systemic importance' mean 'a situation where the failure of or a disruption to the functioning of a financial market utility or the conduct of a payment, clearing, or settlement activity could create, or increase, the risk of significant liquidity or credit problems spreading among financial institutions or markets and thereby threaten the stability of the financial system of the United States', Section 803(9).

[53] Section 804(a)(1), Dodd–Frank Act.

[54] Section 804(a)(2)(A)–(E), Dodd–Frank Act.

certain other federal regulators will be subject to prudential regulation, including rule-making, examination and enforcement by such regulator, with back-up authority provided to the Federal Reserve.[55] Where appropriate, the standards must establish a threshold level of engagement in the activity at which the financial institution will become subject to the standards.

2.2   Regulation of derivatives markets under the Dodd–Frank Act

2.2.1   Background and summary

A fair amount of debate in the US has been devoted to the issue of how to regulate OTC derivatives markets. US banks have traditionally been among the principal innovators in the field of finance and in more ways than one the inventors of the shadow banking sector (discussed in Chapter 2). As a result, a regulatory framework that would curb OTC derivatives trading was also assumed to lead to an operating environment that would stifle innovation, market welfare and US financial firms' business. On the other hand, the voices that called for a total ban of certain forms of derivatives trading and strong restrictions on others were much louder and more authoritative in the US than in Europe.[56] The vigorous public discussion of the issue of regulation of OTC derivatives markets also influenced Congressional debates leading to a legislative compromise that is reflected in the Act. Still, the compromise provisions are bound to significantly increase the transparency of OTC derivatives markets and diminish counterparty risk, reducing in the process the sources of systemic risk emanating from OTC derivatives trading.[57] The Act regulates both derivatives dealers, subjecting them to capital and margin requirements, position limits, business conduct rules[58] and post-trade transparency

---

[55] Section 805, Dodd–Frank Act. To avoid duplication regarding the requirements applicable to systemically important non-bank financial companies and companies that engage in systemically important payment, clearing or settlement activities, the Federal Reserve will issue rules to exempt certain types or classes of non-bank financial activities from the prudential and other requirements applicable to systemically important non-bank financial companies in Title I.

[56] Lynn Stout, 'How Deregulating Derivatives Led to Disaster, and Why Re-Regulating Them can Prevent Another', UCLA School of Law, Law-Econ Research Paper No. 09–13, November 2009, available at papers.ssrn.com/sol3/papers.cfm?abstract_id=1432654&rec=1&srcabs=1485518.

[57] Title VII, Dodd–Frank Act, the 'Wall Street Transparency and Accountability Act'.

[58] CFTC/SEC will enact rules to set business conduct standards, including, among others: the duty for swap dealers and major swap participants to verify eligible contract

requirements, and derivatives trading, where it fosters product standard-ization through mandated centralization of trading and clearing.

The term 'swap' is used under the Act to encompass a wider array of derivatives instruments and not merely the different classes of swap contracts. Thus, it not only includes equity swaps, interest rate, energy, commodity and currency swaps but also extends to credit default swaps, which for the first time come under a centralized trading and clearing obligation. The Section 721 definition also covers options and forward contracts.[59] The far reaching Dodd–Frank framework also raises the issue of international harmonization of regulations governing OTC derivatives markets, which should have been seen as the natural consequence of the GFC. In any event, the Act has extraterritorial repercussions as its reach will inevitably extend to entities located outside the US that enter into transactions with US counterparties or otherwise use US jurisdictional means.[60]

The Act does not terminate the traditional division of responsibility in the US for oversight of derivatives trading between the SEC and CFTC. The CFTC retains jurisdiction over swaps, swap dealers and major swap participants. The SEC will have jurisdiction over security-based swaps, security-based swap dealers and major security-based swap participants. Mixed swaps will be regulated by the SEC as security-based swaps. Thus, the Act refers to the CFTC and the SEC as the 'Applicable Agency' with

participant status; disclosure of swap characteristics such as risks and material incentives or conflicts of interest; and fair and balanced communication.

[59] Under Section 721, the definition of 'swap' extends to any agreement, contract or transaction that is an option for the purchase or sale, or is based on the value, of an underlying financial or economic interest or property, or that provides for any purchase, sale, payment or delivery that is dependent on the occurrence, non-occurrence or the extent of the occurrence of an event associated with a potential financial, economic or commercial consequence. Section 761 defines as a security-based swap any agreement, contract or transaction that is a swap and is based on a narrow-based security index, a single security or loan, or the occurrence, non-occurrence or the extent of the occurrence of an event relating to a single issuer of a security or the issuers of securities in a narrow-based security index, provided that such event directly affects the financial statements, financial condition or financial obligations of the issuer. Mixed swaps include security-based swaps that are also based on the value of one or more financial or economic interests or property, or the occurrence, non-occurrence, or the extent of the occurrence of any event or contingency associated with a potential financial, economic or commercial consequence. The principal exclusions from the definition of 'swap' are sales of non-financial commodities for deferred shipment or delivery, so long as the transaction is intended to be physically settled.

[60] Mayer Brown, 'Understanding the New Financial Reform Legislation', pp. 93–4. Skadden Arps, 'The Dodd–Frank Act – Commentary and Insights', p. 59.

respect to each type of product. Section 712 requires the CFTC and the SEC to consult with each other and with the 'prudential regulators' (i.e., the federal banking regulators) in developing regulations and orders applicable to swaps, swap dealers, major swap participants and other swap entities, to ensure regulatory consistency. The FSOC is authorized to resolve disputes between the CFTC and the SEC in a role similar, to a certain extent, to that entrusted to ESAs under new regulations when it comes to disagreement between member state regulators in the EU.

2.2.2   Regulation of swap dealers

This part of the Act clearly regards OTC derivatives trading not only as a source of systemic risk but also as one of the most speculative and highly leveraged financial activities. As a result, it introduces a number of restrictions that will apply to 'swap' dealers in order to curb the involvement of banks in such activities. Section 731 provides that any person may act as a swap dealer or a major swap participant only if the person is registered as such with the Applicable Agency, regardless of any prior registration as a bank or with the SEC as a securities firm. A person may be designated as a swap dealer for a single type or single class or category of swap or activity, and considered not to be a swap dealer for other types, classes or categories of swaps or activities. Under Section 721, a swap dealer is regarded as any person who:

(1) holds itself out as a dealer in swaps;
(2) makes a market in swaps;
(3) regularly enters into swaps with counterparties as an ordinary course of business for its own account; or
(4) engages in any activity causing the person to be commonly known in the trade as a dealer or market maker in swaps.

Critically, entering into a swap agreement in the context of granting a bank loan does not trigger a swap dealer registration obligation for the loan provider. The same applies to a person that enters into swaps for their own account, either individually or in a fiduciary capacity, but not as a part of a regular course of business. There is also a *de minimis* exemption referring to the quantity of swap dealing in connection with transactions with or on behalf of customers.

A major swap participant is any person, other than a swap dealer, who:

(1) maintains a substantial position in swaps, excluding positions held for hedging or mitigating commercial risk or (in the case of certain pension plans) plan risk;

(2) whose outstanding swaps create substantial counterparty exposure that could have serious adverse effect on the financial stability of the US banking system or financial markets; or

(3) is a financial entity that is highly leveraged relative to the amount of capital it holds, is not subject to capital requirements established by an appropriate federal banking agency and maintains a substantial position in outstanding swaps.[61]

The definition of 'substantial position' is left to the Applicable Agencies at the threshold that they determine is prudent for oversight of entities that are systemically important. An entity whose primary business is financing a parent entity's products and which hedges related interest rate and currency risk may be excluded.[62]

Clearly the definition of swap dealers targets big commercial and investment banks. Similarly the definition of swap participant clearly extends to other big swap traders including hedge funds, SIVs and other shadow banking operators. As a result, the registration requirements of the Act will eventually reach hedge funds and other similar operators or impact on their ability to trade the classes of derivatives instruments described above in the US market or via US entities, which will be substantially curbed. Therefore, the benefits for the transparency and stability of the (otherwise) unregulated global derivatives markets is bound to increase substantially. Swap dealers and major swap participants are, subject to certain exceptions, required to clear swaps through a clearinghouse and execute their transactions on a centralized exchange

Another critical reform is the prohibition of 'Federal Assistance' under Section 716(a). The prohibition refers to the use of the Federal Reserve credit facility or discount window with respect to any swap or security-based swap or other activity of the swaps entity.[63] This prohibition is of profound importance, since a major source of public support/subsidy to the derivatives market is cut off, forcing the banks who are active participants

---

[61] New para. 33 of Section 1a, Commodity Exchange Act (7 UBC 1a), amended by Section 721 of the Dodd–Frank Act.

[62] New para. 33(D) of Section 1a, Commodity Exchange Act (7 UBC 1a), amended by Section 721 of the Dodd–Frank Act.

[63] Under Section 716(b), Dodd–Frank Act, 'Federal assistance' means the 'use' of most kinds of advances from any Federal Reserve credit facility or discount window, or FDIC insurance or guarantee. A 'swaps entity' is defined to include any swap dealer, security-based swap dealer, major swap participant or major security-based swap participant. It excludes insured depository institutions that are major swap participants but not swap dealers, as well as depository institutions and covered financial companies that are in a conservatorship, receivership or a bridge bank operated by the FDIC.

in derivatives markets to 'alter fundamentally' the way they 'conduct their business in the OTC derivative markets'.[64] As a result, banking institutions that are required to register as swap dealers or major swap participants by virtue of their swap activities stand to lose their eligibility for federal assistance, in what amounts to yet another major policy tool used by Dodd–Frank to battle interconnectedness and restrict (coupled with the Volcker Rule restrictions on proprietary trading) the exposure of big banks to the highly speculative derivatives markets. In practice, since an insured bank is not permitted to decline federal deposit insurance, this would mean, as a practical matter, that, unless otherwise exempt, banks will be required to 'push out' all derivatives activities to non-bank affiliates, which enjoy no access to federal assistance and thus are not covered by the prohibition, for as long as they are part of a bank holding company or savings and loan holding company and Sections 23A and 23B of the Federal Reserve Act are complied with.[65] Following a last minute compromise, an exemption has been added which allows FDIC-insured depository institutions to retain certain activities relating to transactions in derivatives, mitigating the impact of the push out. Thus, depository institutions will not be forced to push out the following kinds of swap activities:[66]

(1) hedging the depository institution's risk;
(2) engaging in any kind of permitted swap transaction involving rates or reference assets, such as interest rate swaps and currency swaps; and
(3) trading CDSs that are cleared by a clearinghouse.

It follows that depository institutions may not deal in /are required to push out swaps that are based on reference assets that banks may not invest in, such as most commodities and equity securities, as well as uncleared CDSs, unless they enter into these transactions for hedging purposes.[67] The effective date for the 'push out' obligation is 10 July 2012 giving banks sufficient time to divest of their derivatives business.

---

[64] Mayer Brown, 'Understanding the New Financial Reform Legislation', p. 81. Characteristically, the title of Section 716 of the Act is: Prohibition Against Federal Government Bailouts of Swaps Entities.
[65] Section 716(c), Dodd–Frank Act.
[66] Section 716(d), Dodd–Frank Act.
[67] Mayer Brown, 'Understanding the New Financial Reform Legislation', p. 82.

2.2.3   Prudential and reporting obligations of derivatives dealers

Registered swap dealers and major swap participants are required to comply with position limits, business conduct rules[68] and post-trade transparency requirements, including reporting and record-keeping obligations. All registered swap dealers and major swap participants, including banks, must maintain daily trading records of swaps and all related records and recorded communications. Each registered swap dealer and major swap participant will also be required to maintain a complete audit trail for conducting comprehensive and accurate trade reconstructions. Moreover, the Applicable Agency may make swap transaction and pricing data available to enhance price discovery. Swaps and security-based swaps that are subject to mandatory clearing (including those subject to the commercial end user exemption of Section 723(a)), and swaps and security-based swaps that are not subject to the mandatory clearing requirement but are cleared are subject to real time reporting.[69]

Sections 731 and 764 empower federal banking regulators for swap dealers and major swap participants that are banks, and the Applicable Agency for swap dealers and major swap participants that are not banks, to set minimum capital requirements and minimum initial and variation margin requirements. The minimum requirements shall be subject to regular reviews by the banking regulators, the CFTC, and the SEC (at least once per year). Section 724 requires that margin for swaps cleared on a CFTC-regulated clearinghouse may be held only by CFTC-registered Futures Commission Merchants (FCMs). These are under a duty to segregate all money, securities and property of any swaps customer received as margin and cannot commingle with their own funds or use it to margin, secure, or guarantee any trades or contracts with other swaps customers or persons.[70] Any such funds that are held by FCMs may be invested in certain governmental obligations, obligations fully guaranteed by the US, and other approved investments.

---

[68] Sections 731 and 764, Dodd–Frank Act.
[69] Sections 727 and 763, Dodd–Frank Act. Also Sections 726 and 765 require the Applicable Agency to adopt necessary rules to improve the governance of, or to mitigate systemic risk, promote competition or mitigate conflicts of interest in connection with a swap dealer or major swap participant's conduct of business with a derivatives clearing organization, clearing agency, contact market, national securities exchange or swap execution facility that clears, posts or makes swaps available for trading and in which such swap dealer or major swap participant has a material debt or equity interest.
[70] Section 724(a), Dodd–Frank Act.

Section 737 requires that for swaps which perform or affect a significant price discovery function with respect to registered entities, the CFTC should establish limits on the number of positions, other than bona fide hedge positions, that may be held by any person for the spot month, and for each other month, as well as on the aggregate number of positions that may be held by any person, including any group or class of traders. The swap execution facilities are to establish for each of the swaps of the facility position limits, which should be no higher than those established by the CFTC.

2.2.4   Trading and clearing requirements

Either the SEC or the GFTC, depending on the kind of swap concerned, on an ongoing basis, will review each swap, or any group, category, type or class of swap, to make a determination as to whether it should be required to be cleared.[71] Clearing houses must submit each swap, or any group, category, type or class of swaps, that they plan to accept for clearing to the CFTC / SEC. After making a determination, the CFTC / SEC may stay the clearing requirement for a group, category, type or class of swaps for up to 90 days pending a review of its terms.[72] In reviewing a submission, the Applicable Agency will review whether the submission is consistent with the core principles of the relevant derivative clearing organization (for swaps) or clearing agency (for security-based swaps), as applicable. The Applicable Agency must also take into account the following factors in its reviews:[73]

(1) the existence of significant outstanding notional exposures, trading liquidity and adequate pricing data;
(2) the availability of a rule framework, capacity, operational expertise, resources and credit support infrastructure to clear the contract on terms that are consistent with the material terms and trading conventions on which the contract is then traded;
(3) the effect on the mitigation of systemic risk, taking into account the size of the market for such contract and the resources of the clearinghouse available to clear the contract;
(4) the effect on competition, including appropriate fees and charges applied to clearing;
(5) the existence of reasonable legal certainty in the event of the insolvency of the relevant clearinghouse, or one or more of its clearing

[71] Section 723(c), Dodd–Frank Act.
[72] *Ibid.*   [73] *Ibid.*

members, with regard to the treatment of customer and swap counterparty positions, funds and property.

All swaps that the CFTC or SEC has determined should be cleared must be submitted to a clearinghouse for clearing, unless an exception applies.[74] However, a swap transaction is not required to be cleared where the 'commercial end user exemption' applies. The requirements for the application of the exemption are: (1) one of the counterparties is not a financial entity; (2) that entity uses swaps to hedge or mitigate commercial risk; and (3) it notifies the CFTC / SEC of how it generally meets its financial obligations associated with entering into non-cleared swaps.[75] However, the counterparty that satisfies the criteria for the exemption will still retain the option to clear, in its sole discretion, and will have the option to choose the clearinghouse.[76] Moreover, a counterparty to a swap that is not cleared must report the swap to a registered swap repository or, if there is no repository that accepts the swap, to the CFTC / SEC.[77]

2.2.5   Trading centralization

Section 723 provides that all swaps that are subject to the clearing requirement must be traded on a regulated exchange or on a swap execution facility.[78] A swap execution facility is a trading system or platform in which multiple participants have the ability to execute or trade swaps by accepting bids and offers made by other participants. The execution requirement will not apply if no board of trade or swap execution facility makes the swap available to trade. It will also not apply in the case of swaps that are not cleared because one of the counterparties satisfies the commercial end user exemption. Sections 733 and 763 provide that no person may operate a facility for the trading or processing of swaps, unless the facility is registered as a swap execution facility or as a designated contract market. To be registered and maintain registration as a swap execution facility, such facility must comply with the requirements and core principles specified in the Dodd–Frank Act, as well as

---

[74] Sections 723 and 762, Dodd–Frank Act.

[75] Section 723(a), Dodd–Frank Act inserting Section 2(h)(7)(A) in the Commodity Exchange Act (7 USC 2).

[76] Section 723(a), Dodd–Frank Act inserting Section 2(h)(7)(B) & (H)(ii) in the Commodity Exchange Act (7 USC 2).

[77] Section 729, Dodd–Frank Act (amending the Commodity Exchange Act and inserting Section 4(r). (Reporting and Recordkeeping for Uncleared Swaps)).

[78] Section 723(a), Dodd–Frank Act inserting Section 2(h)(8) in the Commodity Exchange Act.

any additional requirements imposed by the Applicable Agency. Section 725 provides that a depository institution or clearing agency registered with the SEC that is required to be registered as a derivatives clearing organization with the CFTC is deemed to be registered with the CFTC to the extent that, before enactment of the Dodd–Frank Act, the depository institution cleared swaps as a multilateral clearing organization or the clearing agency cleared swaps. The CFTC may exempt, conditionally or unconditionally, a derivatives clearing organization from registration if the CFTC determines that the derivatives clearing organization is subject to comparable, comprehensive supervision and regulation by the SEC or the appropriate government authorities in the home country of the organization.

2.2.6   Reporting

Sections 727 and 763 provide that each swap (whether cleared or uncleared) shall be reported to a registered swap data repository. A swap data repository is any person that collects and maintains information or records with respect to transactions or positions in, or the terms and conditions of, swaps entered into by third parties for the purpose of providing a centralized record-keeping facility for swaps. Sections 728 and 763 provide that, to be registered, and maintain registration, as a swap data repository, the swap data repository must comply with the requirements and core principles specified in the Dodd–Frank Act (which include requirements as to governance, conflicts of interest and antitrust), as well as any additional requirements imposed by the Applicable Agency.

2.3   Registration of hedge fund advisers

Another critical reform introduced by the Dodd–Frank Act (Title IV) is the elimination of a prior exemption[79] and introduction of registration requirements for investment advisers. This closes a serious loophole in the US regulatory framework and settles a long-running dispute between different stakeholders in the US regarding the need to register hedge fund advisers.[80] Accordingly, advisers to funds of over US$100 million have to register with the SEC as investment advisers and be subject to reporting and record-keeping requirements,[81] which are specified by the

---

[79] Section 403, Dodd–Frank Act.
[80] See SEC Staff Report, 'Implications of the Growth of Hedge Funds', September 2003, available at ftp.sec.gov/news/studies/hedgefunds0903.pdf.
[81] Sections 402 and 404, Dodd–Frank Act.

SEC.[82] The Act exempts advisers that act solely as investment advisers to venture capital companies.[83] There is also an exemption for investment advisers that (1) act solely as advisers to private funds; and (2) have assets under management in the US of less than US$150 million.[84]

In order to obtain and maintain registration they must disclose all data about their trades and portfolios which is necessary to monitor and assess systemic risk and ultimately protect investors. Thus, the data that has to be disclosed extends to the amount of assets under management; use of leverage, including off-balance-sheet leverage; counterparty exposure; trading and investment positions; valuation policies and practices; types of assets held; side arrangements or side letters; and trading practices and other information deemed necessary by the SEC.[85]

3.   Regulatory and supervisory reform in the EU

3.1   The first attempt to reform EU financial regulation

3.1.1   Capital adequacy regulation and remuneration policy

The immediate reaction by the European Commission to the financial crisis was to propose amendments to the Credit Institutions Directive (Directive 2006/48/EC) and the Capital Adequacy Directive (Directive 2006/49/EC). On 1 October 2008, the European Commission issued a proposal for amending the two Directives.[86] The Commission proposal addressed four main issues: (1) criteria for the treatment of hybrid capital instruments as original own funds; (2) adjusted limits to large exposures; (3) new rules on securitization; and (4) new supervisory arrangements. This proposal resulted in Directive 2009/111/EC of 16 September 2009,[87] which introduced a number of important reforms:

---

[82] Section 406, Dodd–Frank Act.   [83] Section 407, Dodd–Frank Act.
[84] Section 408, Dodd–Frank Act.   [85] Section 404, Dodd–Frank Act.
[86] European Commission, 'Proposal for a Directive of the European Parliament and of the Council amending Directives 2006/48/EC and 2006/49/EC as regards banks affiliated to central institutions, certain own funds items, large exposures, supervisory arrangements, and crisis management', COM (2008) 602 final, 1 October 2008.
[87] Directive 2009/111/EC of the European Parliament and of the Council of 16 September 2009 amending Directives 2006/48/EC, 2006/49/EC and 2007/64/EC as regards banks affiliated to central institutions, certain own funds items, large exposures, supervisory arrangements, and crisis management, OJ L 302/97, 17 November 2009. On 20 July 2011, the Commission adopted a legislative package to strengthen the regulation of the banking sector. The proposal replaces the current Capital Requirements Directives (2006/48 and 2006/49) with a Directive and Regulation. The Directive governs access to deposit-taking activities while the regulation establishes the prudential requirements institutions need

(1) It laid down specific rules with regard to the treatment of so-called 'hybrid capital' as own funds, which the Credit Institutions Directive 2006 had left at the discretion of Member States,[88] and harmonized the criteria for determining whether such hybrid instruments are eligible as 'original own funds';[89]

(2) It amended the provisions on large exposures and extended the definition of 'connected clients'.[90] The Directive introduces one single exposure limit of 25 per cent of the value of the own funds.[91] The same limit (in combination with a maximum of €150 million, whichever is higher) will also apply to exposures by credit institutions to other credit institutions or investment firms.[92]

(3) Responding to the role of financial innovation in the GFC and especially of Collateralized Debt Obligations (CDOs) issuance and trading, Directive 2009/111/EC provides that credit institutions are only allowed to invest in securitized debt issues if a number of conditions are satisfied, ensuring that originators or the sponsors maintain enough 'skin in the game'. Accordingly, the originators of the underlying assets or the sponsors of the issue must 'retain, on an ongoing basis, a material net economic interest and in any event not less than 5 %'.[93] The credit institution must demonstrate to the competent authorities that it understands risks in the securitization and has procedures in place for analysing all aspects of these transactions.[94] The originators or sponsors must also disclose the level of their commitment to maintain a net economic interest and must make available all materially relevant data on the underlying assets.[95] Finally, the competent

to respect, largely reflecting the Basel III reforms. See EU Commission, Press Release, 'Commission wants Stronger and More Responsible Banks in Europe', 1 p 11/9/15 of 20 July 2011. As work on the instruments continues and their transposition will come long after the completion of this book, they are not part of the book's analysis.

[88] See Article 57(a)–(c), Directive 2006/48/EC of the European Parliament and of the Council of 14 June 2006 relating to the taking up and pursuit of the business of credit institutions (recast), OJ L1777/1, 30 June 2006, (hereinafter Credit Institutions Directive).

[89] See Commission Staff Working Document accompanying the Proposal for a Directive of the European Parliament and of the Council amending Directives 2006/49/EC and 2006/48/EC as regards banks affiliated to central institutions, certain own funds items, large exposures, supervisory arrangements, and crisis management, COM (2008) 602 final, at p. 4 (footnote 7).

[90] See amended Article 4, Credit Institutions Directive, point 45, (b).

[91] Amended Article 111(1), Credit Institutions Directive.

[92] Amended Article 111(1), Credit Institutions Directive.

[93] New Article 122a(1), Credit Institutions Directive.

[94] New Article 122a(4)–(5), Credit Institutions Directive.

[95] New Article 122a(7), Credit Institutions Directive.

supervisory authorities must also have methodologies and measures in place to review compliance with the new obligations.

Further amendments to the Credit Institutions Directive and the Capital Adequacy Directive were proposed by the European Commission in a Communication of 13 July 2009.[96] The proposal sought to strengthen the capital requirements for assets that credit institutions hold in the trading-book for short-term resale. Credit institutions will be required to calculate potential losses on these assets in a 'worst-case scenario'.[97] The Commission has proposed to establish higher capital requirements and strengthened disclosure requirements for repackaging securitizations.[98]

Finally, the Commission has required that credit institutions have remuneration policies which are consistent with and promote sound and effective risk management.[99] In this context, the Commission proposed to add to Article 22 of the Capital Requirements Directive the obligation of the competent authorities to require that the credit institution has 'remuneration policies and practices that are consistent with and promote sound and effective risk management'.[100] At first reading, this seems to leave ample room of discretion for national supervisors. However, the competent authorities must make this assessment on the basis of nine principles set out in Section 11 of Annex V to the Credit Institutions Directive. The principles concern remuneration for staff whose professional activities have a material impact on the risk profile of the credit institution.[101]

---

[96] EU Commission, 'Proposal for a Directive amending Directives 2006/48/EC and 2006/49/EC as regards capital requirements for the trading book and for re-securitisations, and the supervisory review of remuneration policies', COM (2009) 362 final, 13 July 2009.

[97] See *ibid.,* Annex II, (3).

[98] Proposed Articles 122b and 136(2), Credit Institutions Directive.

[99] EU Commission, 'Proposal for a Directive amending Directives 2006/48/EC and 2006/49/EC'; Commission Recommendation on remuneration policies in the financial services sector C(2009) 3159, 30 April 2009; Commission Communication accompanying Commission Recommendation complementing Recommendations 2004/913/EC and 2005/162/EC as regards the regime for the remuneration of directors of listed companies and Commission Recommendation on remuneration policies in the financial services sector. The forthcoming amendments of the Capital Requirements Directive will not supersede the Recommendation, but will complement it. See also 'Report on the application by Member States of the EU of the Commission 2009/384/EC Recommendation on remuneration policies in the financial services sector', COM (2010) 286 final.

[100] Article 22 (1), *in fine.* See Article 1(2)(a) of the European Commission Proposal for a Directive of the European Parliament and of the Council amending Directives 2006/48/EC and 2006/49/EC as regards capital requirements for the trading book and for re-securitisations, and the supervisory review of remuneration policies, COM (2009) 362 final, 13 July 2009.

[101] See proposed point (22) of Annex V, Credit Institutions Directive.

Furthermore, the Committee of European Banking Supervisors (CEBS) (which has now been succeeded by the European Banking Authority (EBA)) was given the task of developing guidelines to align the assessments by the national supervisors of the remuneration policies.[102]

3.1.2   The regulation of credit rating agencies in the EU

Like most world regulators, the EU Commission took a very damning view of the role of CRAs in building up the conditions that led to the GFC by greatly underestimating the risk of default and even more importantly the possibility that the rated assets quality would deteriorate. Also as market conditions worsened, CRAs failed to reflect this promptly in their ratings.[103] On 7 December 2009 the EC Regulation on Credit Rating Agencies came into force. It introduced a harmonized approach to the regulation of credit rating activities in the European Union and established a registration system for CRAs.[104]

In June 2010, the European Commission adopted a proposal to amend the CRA Regulation, which came into force in May 2011.[105] The new CRA Regulation has brought CRAs under the direct (and exclusive) supervisory oversight of the new European Securities and Markets Authority (ESMA). ESMA forms part of the new European supervision structure for financial services, discussed below. ESMA will be responsible for approving the registration of CRAs, their ongoing supervision and taking appropriate enforcement action.[106] Thus, under the amended CRA Regulation,

---

[102] Article 22(3), Credit Institutions Directive.

[103] The behaviour of CRAs during the Eurozone debt crisis has come under scrutiny both by the EU Commission and national parliaments. E.g., see 'Credit Rating Agencies and EU Sovereign Debt', Inquiry initiated by the UK's House of Lords' EU Economic and Financial Affairs and International Trade Sub-Committee looking into CRAs and their influence on sovereign borrowing, May 2011, available at www.parliament.uk/business/committees/committees-a-z/lords-select/eu-economic-and-financial-affairs-and-international-trade-sub-committee-a/inquiries/credit-rating-agencies-and-eu-sovereign-debt/.

[104] Regulation (EC) No. 1060/2009 of the European Parliament and of the Council of 16 September 2009 on credit rating agencies OJ L 302/1, 17 November 2009.

[105] Regulation (EU) No. 513/2011 of the European Parliament and of the Council of 11 May 2011 amending Regulation (EC) No. 1060/2009 on credit rating agencies OJ L 145/30, 31 May 2011.

[106] To carry out effective supervision of CRAs, ESMA will be in the position to: (1) require CRAs and all persons involved in rating activities to provide all necessary information; (2) examine any records, data, procedures and any other relevant material, including records of telephone and data traffic; (3) take copies of records, data, procedures and other material; (4) ask for an oral explanation, interview or summon and hear a person; (5) carry out on-site inspections at the premises of CRAs; and (6) seal business premises, books and records. New Article 23(b) and (c), Regulation (EC) No. 1060/2009.

all CRAs that would like their credit ratings to be used in the EU will need to apply for registration with ESMA.[107] In many respects this is the first illustration of a formal pan-European supervision regime in financial markets and, according to the Commission, it is justified by the fact that CRAs do not maintain territorial links with any specific EU member states.

The original CRA Regulation introduced disclosure requirements to increase the amount of information available to all competing agencies and provide investors with greater choice. It also aimed to encourage greater competition in the market by reducing the barriers to entry for potential new participants. The new CRA Regulation upgrades this regime. CRAs are expected to comply with strict standards of ratings integrity, quality and transparency. In specific, registered CRAs have to comply with rigorous rules to ensure that:[108]

(1) their ratings are not influenced by conflicts of interest;
(2) they remain alert about the quality of their methodology and ratings by subjecting them to historical validation (back-testing); and
(3) they act in a transparent manner.

ESMA will monitor compliance with those standards and help investors obtain the information required to assess the integrity and impartiality of credit ratings.[109] More specifically CRAs shall be subject to the following restrictions:[110]

(1) CRAs may not provide advisory services;
(2) they will not be allowed to rate financial instruments if they do not have sufficient quality information to base their ratings on;

---

[107] Amended Articles 4, 5 and 15, 17–18, 20, Regulation (EC) No. 1060/2009.

[108] Article 1 and Recitals 2, 6, 22–3, 26, Regulation (EC) No. 1060/2009.

[109] ESMA is expected to prepare for approval by the Commission draft regulatory technical standards concerning the information to be provided by a CRA in its application for registration, 'the information that a credit rating agency must provide for the application for certification and for an assessment of its systemic importance to the financial stability or integrity of financial markets, the presentation of the information, including structure, format, method and period of reporting, that a credit rating agency must disclose, concerning the assessment of compliance of credit rating methodologies with the requirements set out in Regulation (EC) No. 1060/2009, and the content and format of ratings data periodic reporting to be requested from a credit rating agency for the purpose of ongoing supervision by ESMA'. Recital 11, Regulation (EU) No. 513/2011.

[110] Article 6, 8–10, Annex I and Recitals 22–7 and 37–8 of Regulation (EC) No. 1060/2009. These rules are largely based on the standards set in International Organization of Securities Commissions, 'Code of Conduct – Fundamentals for Credit Rating Agencies', revised October 2008.

(3) they must disclose the models, methodologies and key assumptions on which they base their ratings;
(4) they must differentiate the ratings of more complex products by adding a specific symbol;
(5) they must publish an annual transparency report;
(6) they will have to create an internal function to review the quality of their ratings; and
(7) they should have at least two independent directors on their boards whose remuneration cannot depend on the business performance of the rating agency.

As most of the major CRAs are located outside the EU, the original CRA Regulation has adopted a number of criteria for accepting as equivalent credit ratings by CRAs based in third countries.[111] These include, inter alia, requirements that CRAs must be subject to registration obligations and to an effective ongoing supervision and enforcement regime which also 'prevents interference by the supervisory authorities and other public authorities of that third country with the content of credit ratings and methodologies'.[112]

3.1.3   New rules for derivatives trading and clearing

The close association of credit derivatives with the near collapse and subsequent bail-out of AIG as well as their role in the Lehman Brothers collapse has already been clearly illustrated. Following the promulgation of the Pittsburgh G-20 Summit[113] and the enactment of Dodd–Frank that more or less implements a similar framework, the EU has endorsed a proposal Regulation for OTC derivatives which imposes a number of transparency, reporting, and clearing requirements, as well as position limits. Once adopted, the Regulation would apply from end 2012.

---

[111] Article 5, Regulation (EC) No. 1060/2009.
[112] Article 5(6), Regulation (EC) No. 1060/2009.
[113] In September 2009, G-20 Leaders agreed in Pittsburgh that: 'All standardised OTC derivative contracts should be traded on exchanges or electronic trading platforms, where appropriate, and cleared through central counterparties by end-2012 at the latest. OTC derivative contracts should be reported to trade repositories. Non-centrally cleared contracts should be subject to higher capital requirements', available at www.g20.org/Documents/pittsburgh_summit_leaders_statement_250909.pdf. 'In June 2010, G20 Leaders in Toronto reaffirmed their commitment and also committed to accelerate the implementation of strong measures to "improve transparency and regulatory oversight of over-the-counter derivatives in an internationally consistent and non-discriminatory way".'

The Regulation follows Commission thinking on the role played by derivatives in the financial crisis and the benefits and risks of derivatives markets set out in its Communication of 3 July 2009, which was succeeded by a Communication of 20 October 2009[114] detailing the Commission's intentions to propose a comprehensive regulatory framework for the minimization of risks from OTC derivatives trading.[115] In September 2010 the Commission released its proposal Regulation,[116] which has a broadly similar scope of application with the Dodd–Frank Act, discussed analytically in Section 2.2 above. It contains similar provisions requiring the reporting of OTC derivative contracts and the clearing of eligible contracts. Information on OTC derivative contracts should be reported to trade repositories and be accessible to supervisory authorities. Standardized OTC derivative contracts will be cleared through central counterparties (CCPs) to reduce credit risk. Furthermore, it puts in place strict capital and collateral requirements for OTC derivatives that will be cleared bilaterally. Regulators will require investors to disclose their identity if they take up large short positions in the market, and will be allowed to obtain information from national authorities about any particular position or trading party. Regulators will also have the power to limit or ban naked short-selling if required.

(a) Centralization of OTC derivatives clearing and 'eligible' contracts   The proposed Regulation, reflecting the aforementioned G-20 commitment to clear all standardized OTC derivatives imposes a duty on all 'financial counterparties' to clear through a CCP all OTC derivatives, contracts that are considered eligible and that are concluded with other financial counterparties.[117] The definition of 'financial counterparty' is

---

[114] EU Commission, 'Ensuring Efficient, Safe and Sound Derivatives Markets', COM (2009) 332, available at eur-lex.europa.eu/LexUriServ/LexUriServ.do?uri=COM:2009:0332:FIN:EN:PDF.

[115] EU Commission, 'Ensuring Efficient, Safe and Sound Derivatives Markets: Future Policy Actions', COM (2009) 563, available at eur-lex.europa.eu/LexUriServ/LexUriServ.do?uri=COM:2009:0563:FIN:EN:PDF.

[116] EU Commission, 'Proposal for a Regulation of the European Parliament and of the Council on OTC Derivatives, Central Counterparties and Trade Repositories – Explanatory Memorandum', COM (2010) 484 final, 15 September 2010.

[117] Until the end of 2010, only 10 per cent of derivatives contracts were traded through a clearing house. See Elena Moya, 'Brussels Proposes Tougher Regulation of Derivatives Market, European Commission Unveils Proposed Rules on Short-selling but Steps back from Ban Demanded by France and Germany', The Guardian, 15 September 2010, available at www.guardian.co.uk/business/2010/sep/15/brussels-proposes-tougher-regulation-derivatives.

broad, capturing banks, investment firms, insurance companies, registered Undertakings for Collective Investment in Transferable Securities (UCITS) funds, pension funds and alternative investment fund managers, although many of those institutions are also end users. Central banks, national debt managers and multilateral development banks are exempted. There is no exemption for intra-group transactions entered into by a financial counterparty. Industrial or other non-financial companies that use derivatives contracts to hedge in stock, bond or commodity markets are to be exempted from the new rules.

The colossal amount of systemic risk that shall be concentrated within CCPs means that there should be in place a process to determine which OTC derivative contracts are eligible for mandatory clearing in order not to force CCPs to clear contracts which they are not able to risk-manage. The Regulation introduces two approaches to determine which contracts must be cleared:

(1) a '*bottom-up*' approach, according to which a CCP decides to clear certain contracts and is authorized to do so by its competent authority, who is obliged to inform ESMA, once it approves the CCP to clear those contracts. ESMA will then decide whether a clearing obligation should apply to all of those contracts in the EU. ESMA will need to base that decision on certain objective criteria;
(2) a '*top-down*' approach according to which ESMA, together with the ESRB, will determine which contracts should potentially be subject to the clearing obligation. This process is important to identify and capture those contracts in the market that are not yet being cleared by a CCP.[118]

Counterparties that are subjected to the clearing obligation cannot simply avoid the requirement by deciding not to participate in a CCP. If those counterparties do not meet the participation requirements or are not interested in becoming clearing members, they must enter into the necessary arrangements with clearing members to access the CCP as clients.

(b)   Clearing obligations of non-financial counterparties   A counterparty that is not a financial counterparty is only subject to the clearing obligation if it takes positions in OTC derivatives exceeding a 'clearing threshold' to be specified by the Commission. In calculating this threshold, the proposal Regulation requires the Commission to take into

---

[118]   Paras. 4.3.1 and 4.3.2 EU Commission, 'Explanatory Memorandum'.

account the systemic relevance of the sum of net positions and exposures by counterparty per class of contract.[119] If a non-financial counterparty's positions exceed the clearing threshold then it will be subject to the clearing obligation for all its eligible derivative contracts. In calculating the positions of a non-financial counterparty for this purpose, any derivative contracts entered into by the non-financial counterparty that are 'objectively measurable as directly linked to the commercial activity of the counterparty' will not be included.[120] Yet the scope of the exemption is unclear and requires further clarification if it is not to open serious loopholes. In this regard, the proposed Regulation is less restrictive than the US Dodd–Frank Act.[121]

(c)   **Regulation and supervision of CCPs, non-discrimination, and interoperability**   The proposed Regulation requires any CCP which is established in the EU to be authorized in its home state.[122] To ensure that CCPs established in the European Union are safe, the authorization of a CCP will be subject to a requirement that the CCP has access to adequate liquidity whether as a result of access to central bank or to creditworthy and reliable commercial bank liquidity, or a combination of both. Naturally, such a restriction would raise serious barriers to entry for CCPs based in countries outside the Eurozone.

CCPs may also take other steps to limit credit and liquidity risks. They may choose either to deliver financial instruments and receive delivery or to indemnify participants for losses incurred in the delivery process. Where a CCP opts for assuming the obligation to make or receive deliveries of financial instruments, the proposal Regulation requires the CCP to use the delivery versus payment mechanism to eliminate settlement risk.

[119] The proposal Regulation provides that the Commission, ESMA and the other ESAs shall asses the systemic importance of transactions of non-financial firms in OTC derivatives by 31 December 2013.
[120] See Clifford Chance (Chris Bates), 'Proposed EU Regulation on OTC Derivatives – Client Briefing', 16 September 2010.
[121] The Dodd–Frank Act allows non-financial entities to avoid the clearing obligation only when they are hedging commercial risk and certain other conditions are met (the 'commercial end user' exemption, see note 75 above).
[122] Para. 4.3.3. Title III (Authorisation and supervision of CCPs) of EU Commission 'Explanatory Memorandum'. The home state regulator may only authorize a CCP following an opinion from ESMA and a positive joint opinion from the 'college of competent authorities' established by the CCP's home state regulator and consisting of, amongst others, the regulator itself, ESMA and the competent authorities responsible for the supervision of the CCP's clearing members established in the three member states with the largest contributions to the CCP's default fund.

The proposal Regulation also introduces capital requirements for CCPs. The minimum initial regulatory capital will stand at €5 million. Moreover, the proposal Regulation requires a CCP to have in place robust governance arrangements to respond to any potential conflicts of interest between owners, management, clearing members and indirect participants.[123]

As regards CCPs from third countries, ESMA will also have the direct responsibility of recognizing such CCPs if certain conditions are met. In particular, the recognition will require that (1) the Commission has ascertained the legal and supervisory framework of that third country as equivalent to the EU one; (2) the CCP is authorized and subject to effective supervision in that third country, and (3) ESMA has established co-operation arrangements with the third country competent authorities. A CCP of a third country will not be allowed to perform activities and services in the Union if these conditions are not met.

Furthermore, in order to intensify competition for clearing services and foster further integration of the internal markets for post-trading services the Commission has adopted an open clearing approach to 'eligible' contracts and interoperability. Thus, CCPs shall not be allowed to accept only those transactions concluded on execution venues with which they have a privileged relationship or which are part of the same group. A CCP that has been authorized to clear eligible derivative contracts is required to accept clearing such contracts on a non-discriminatory basis, regardless of the venue of execution.[124] Also, CCPs are required to have non-discriminatory, transparent and objective criteria for admission of clearing members so as to ensure fair and open access to the CCP. However, given the risks involved the proposal Regulation does not grant unfettered access to CCPs, requiring instead that clearing members have sufficient financial resources and operational capacity. Also access may be restricted on the basis of risk control criteria.

Interoperability is an essential tool to achieve effective integration of the post-trading market in Europe. Thus, the proposal Regulation adopts the recommendations of the Giovannini Group report[125] regarding the

---

[123] Para. 4.3.4. Title IV (Requirements for CCPs) of EU Commission 'Explanatory Memorandum'.

[124] For a political economy analysis of competition in clearing markets and a perceptive critique of the proposed EU arrangements, see Gerrard Hertig, 'Post-Financial Crisis Trading and Clearing Reforms in the EU: A Story of Interest Groups with Magnified Voice', Paper presented at Financial Regulation and Supervision in the New Financial Architecture Conference, Taormina, May 2010.

[125] The Giovannini Group, 'Second Report on Clearing and Settlement Arrangements in the European Union', Brussels, April 2003.

breaking down of barriers to cross-border clearing of transactions in transferable securities and money in the EU and allowing CCPs to enter into arrangements to provide clearing services to specified trading venues (inter-operability).[126] The issues of interoperability however has raised objections in the European Parliament from the Rapporteur, Werner Langden, who raised concerns that it would lead to the building up of systemic risk in certain CCPs.[127] For this reason regulatory approval is required before entering into an interoperable arrangement subject to the conditions provided in the Regulation.[128]

(d)   Risk management for non-cleared contracts   For OTC derivative contracts which are not considered to be eligible for clearing by a CCP, financial counterparties and non-financial counterparties that are subject to the clearing obligation should adopt a number of risk mitigation techniques. They must have arrangements in place to measure, monitor and mitigate operational and credit risk. These include requirements for electronic confirmation, portfolio valuation and reconciliation, daily mark-to-market, as well as procedures for an appropriately segregated exchange of collateral or an appropriate and proportionate holding of capital. It is suggested that financial counterparties would choose to hold capital against an uncleared transaction with an end-user, instead of requiring margin.[129] This could also act as a strong disincentive for financial counterparties that are not eligible for clearing to enter into transactions for OTC derivatives. If that is the case the relevant market will subsequently experience very illiquid conditions, and with the exception of contracts entered for purely commercial purposes or hedging, this may prove a good approach to extinguish trades of highly speculative and impossible to value and clear complex derivative contracts of dubious welfare value. To the argument that this approach may suffocate valuable financial innovation, it should of course be countered that if that is the case sooner

---

126   The Giovannini Group has defined 'interoperability' as: '[A] situation in which payment instruments belonging to a given scheme may be used in other countries and in systems installed by other schemes. Interoperability requires technical compatibility between systems, but can only take effect where commercial agreements have been concluded between the schemes concerned', *ibid.*, p. 54.

127   Committee: Economic and Monetary Affairs, 'Lawmakers Begin work on Derivatives Regulation', Economic and Monetary Affairs, 1 March 2011, available at www.europarl. europa.eu/en/pressroom/content/20110228IPR14443/html/Lawmakers-begin-work-on-derivatives-regulation.

128   Para. 4.3.5., Title V (Interoperability) of EU Commission, 'Explanatory Memorandum'.

129   Clifford Chance, 'Proposed EU Regulation on OTC Derivatives', p. 8.

or later a CCP in its drive to increase the volume of its risk 'manageable' business will ask to clear any viable new breed of derivatives contracts.

(e)   **Reporting obligations and trade depositories**   Financial counterparties will have to report to a trade repository the details of any transaction in an OTC derivative contract, including modification and termination, regardless of whether the contract is eligible for clearing. If no trade repository can record the details of the contract, the counterparty must make the report to its home state regulator. A non-financial counterparty is also subject to the reporting obligation where it takes positions that exceed an 'information threshold' and explain to the relevant regulator why it exceeds the 'threshold'. This is clearly a measure intended to curb the exposure of non-financial counterparties to OTC derivatives trading.[130]

In view of their central role in the collection of regulatory information, the Regulation gives ESMA the power to register, withdraw registration from and perform surveillance of trade repositories. As there are no fiscal implications connected to the surveillance of trade repositories the role of local regulators will be very limited in this context.[131] ESMA's role will also ensure unfettered access to all the relevant European authorities and a unique counterparty representing Europe to deal with the competent authorities dealing with third country trade repositories.

A trade repository established in a third country can be recognized by ESMA if it meets a number of requirements designed to establish that such trade repository is subject to equivalent rules and appropriate surveillance in that third country. In order to ensure that there are no legal obstacles in place that would prevent an effective mutual exchange of information and unfettered access to data maintained in a trade repository located in a third country, the Regulation foresees the need to conclude an international agreement to that effect. If such an agreement is not in place, a trade repository established in that third country would not be recognised by ESMA.

---

[130] As is the case with the clearing threshold, the Commission will determine the information threshold on the basis of the systemic relevance of the sum of net positions and exposures by counterparty per class of contract. Unlike the clearing threshold, hedging contracts are not excluded, and are, instead, fully taken into account in determining whether a position exceeds the information threshold.

[131] See para. 4.3.7. Title VII (Requirements for trade repositories) of EU Commission 'Explanatory Memorandum'. Trade repositories will be subject to organizational and operational requirements and ensure appropriate safeguarding and transparency of data. *Ibid.*

It is clear that the draft EU Regulation requires OTC derivative trans-actions to be reported in order to increase the transparency of the market and eliminate the opacity that has so far characterized the OTC deriva-tives market. However, it should not be forgotten that increased trans-parency in financial markets often creates costs.[132] The biggest of these costs is loss of trading volume and liquidity[133] as OTC trading may be driven overseas to jurisdictions that do not have 'concentration' rules. If this happens the need for a regulatory regime for OTC derivatives with formal global coverage will become bigger than ever.[134]

3.1.4   Hedge funds

Another clear sign of the politicization of financial services reform in the EU[135] has been the enactment of Alternative Investments Financial Managers Directive (AIFMD), which establishes a new regime for the reg-ulation of hedge managers and private equity operators established in the EU.[136] The Directive will have to be implemented by member states by July 2013. The Directive has a dual objective. First, it aims to enhance investor protection through the creation of an extensive disclosure and marketing regime. Second, it provides the tools for the identification, mitigation and monitoring of systemic risks arising from the activities of the alternative investment fund management industry, particularly hedge funds and pri-vate equity funds. Thus, it is a welcome development over the previous regime. However, the EU Commission's insistence on widening its ambit and a requirement that third country operators should abide with EU standards significantly 'soured' the legislative process.[137]

---

[132] See Hertig, 'Post-Financial Crisis Trading and Clearing Reform', p. 12.
[133] For this trade off see Emilios Avgouleas and Stavros Deyanakis, 'Trade Transparency and Trading Volume' (2009) 1 *International Journal of Financial Markets and Derivatives* 96–123.
[134] See Section 2.2.1 above.
[135] Ferran calls this process: '[O]pportunistic use of crisis situations to achieve unrelated goals, and crisis induced regulatory over-reaction', see Eilis Ferran, 'The Regulation of Hedge Funds and Private Equity: A Case Study in the Development of the EU's Regulatory Response to the Financial Crisis', European Corporate Governance Institute, Law Working Paper No. 176/2011, February 2011, p. 1.
[136] See Directive 2011/61/EU of the European Parliament and of the Council of 8 June 2011 on Alternative Investment Fund Managers and amending Directives 2003/41/EC and 2009/65/EC and Regulations (EC) No. 1060/2009 and (EU) No. 1095/2010, OJ L 174/1, 1 July 2011, (hereinafter AIFMO).
[137] See Ferran, 'The Regulation of Hedge Funds', pp. 13–18. See also 'The AIFM Directive – Another European Mess – Plans to Regulate Private Equity and Hedge Funds take Two Steps Forward', *The Economist*, 18 May 2010, available at www.economist.com/node/16156357.

The AIFMD introduces authorization and regulation requirements for Alternative Investment Fund Managers (AIFMs)[138] not for Alternative Investment Funds (AIFs) themselves. It imposes on AIFMs an initial own funds obligation and minimum capital requirements related to portfolio size,[139] and governance, conflicts of interest,[140] risk management,[141] and organizational requirements.[142] AIFMD also provides regulatory standards for depositaries,[143] which must be financial institutions: banks, investment firms or any other eligible financial institution, provided that it is not an AIFM. Finally, AIFMD mandates enhanced transparency standards provision to investors, by means of an annual report[144] and disclosure of AIF characteristics, including investment strategies and fees,[145] before they invest in AIFs, and reporting to supervisors, which extends to reporting of levels of leverage.[146]

Following its implementation in 2013, the AIFMD will provide alternative investment managers with a single passport to allow an EU-wide regime for the marketing of hedge funds.[147] The passport scheme that shall be made available to EU AIFMs is to be extended to non-EU AIFMs two years later (subject to advice from ESMA), provided that the third country AIFM is subject to a regulatory regime 'equivalent' to that of the Directive.[148]

The Directive applies a *de minimis* threshold for its application and AIFs with less than €100 million assets under management, namely, the really small funds, are exempt from full authorization. They may register with their home member states and only provide their competent authorities with relevant information regarding the main instruments in which they are trading and on the principal exposures and most important concentrations of the AIFs they manage. If they subsequently wish to benefit from the rights granted under this Directive, then exempt AIFMs can opt and benefit from AIFMD's 'passport' regime.[149]

3.2   *The European system of financial supervision*

3.2.1   Introductory remarks

Following the recommendations of the de Larosiere Report and successive and extensive rounds of consultation, the new EU supervisory

---

[138]   Articles 6–9, AIFMD.   [139]   Article 9, AIFMD.
[140]   Article 14, AIFMD.   [141]   Article 12, 14–16, AIFMD.
[142]   Article 18, AIFMD.   [143]   Article 21, AIFMD.
[144]   Article 22, AIFMD.   [145]   Article 23, AIFMD.
[146]   Article 24, AIFMD.   [147]   Articles 31–2, AIFMD.
[148]   Chapter VII, AIFMD.   [149]   Article 3(a) and Recital 17, AIFMD.

structures were formally established in December 2010.[150] The new arrangements comprise the ESRB and so-called European System of Financial Supervisors (ESFS), which links national supervisors within an EU network. More analytically,

(1) the main mission of the ESRB is the identification of risks to EU financial stability. Where necessary, the ESRB will issue risk warnings and recommendations for action to address such risks;[151]

(2) the former Lamfalussy Committees (regulatory networks) have been transformed into EU bodies with legal personality, so-called European Supervisory Authorities (ESAs), comprising: (a) the European Banking Authority (EBA),[152] (b) the European Insurance and Occupational Pensions Authority (EIOPA),[153] and (c) the European Securities and Markets Authority (ESMA);[154]

(3) the Joint Committee of the European Supervisory Authorities (Joint Committee),[155] which is a forum jointly established by the ESAs to

---

[150] For an overview of the new structures, see Eddy Wymeersch, 'Europe's New Financial Supervisory Bodies', University of Ghent, Financial Law Institute, WP 11/01, January 2011 and Niamh Maloney, 'The European Securities and Markets Authority and Institutional Design for the EU Financial Markets – a Tale of Two Competences: Part (1) Rule-Making' (2011) 12(1) *European Business Organization Law Review*, 41–86. For a critical evaluation, Niamh Maloney, 'EU Financial Market Regulation after the Global Financial Crisis: "More Europe" or more Risks?' (2010) 47 *Common Market Law Review* 1317.

[151] Regulation (EU) No. 1092/2010 of the European Parliament and of the Council of 24 November 2010 on European Union macro-prudential oversight of the financial system and establishing a European Systemic Risk Board, OJ L 331/1, 15 December 2010, (hereinafter the ESRB Regulation). See also Council Regulation (EU) No. 1096/2010 of 17 November 2011 conferring specific tasks upon the European Central Bank concerning the functioning of the European Systemic Risk Board, OJ l 331/162, 15 December 2010.

[152] Established by Regulation (EU) No. 1093/2010 of the European Parliament and of the Council 24 November 2010 establishing a European Supervisory Authority (European Banking Authority), amending Decision No. 716/2009/EC and repealing Commission Decision 2009/78/EC, OJ L 331/12, 15 December 2010.

[153] Established by Regulation (EU) No. 1094/2010 of the European Parliament and of the Council 24 November 2010 establishing a European Supervisory Authority (European Insurance and Occupational Pensions Authority), amending Decision No. 716/2009/EC and repealing Commission Decision 2009/79/EC, OJ L 331/48, 15 December 2010.

[154] Regulation (EU) No. 1095/2010 of the European Parliament and of the Council of 24 November 2010 establishing a European Supervisory Authority (European Securities and Markets Authority), amending Decision No. 716/2009/EC and repealing Commission Decision 2009/77/EC, OJ L 335/84, 15 December 2010.

[155] Provided for by Article 54 of Regulation (EU) No. 1093/2010, of Regulation (EU) No. 1094/2010, and of Regulation (EU) No. 1095/2010 (hereinafter the ESA founding Regulations).

co-ordinate their actions when cross-sectoral rule-making/supervisory issues arise;

(4) the competent or supervisory authorities of the Member States, which, under Article 4(3) of the Treaty on European Union, should co-operate with trust and full mutual respect.[156]

3.2.2   The ESRB

(a)   Objectives and tasks/powers   Until the eruption of the GFC, supervisory arrangements at the EU level had placed 'too little emphasis on macro-prudential oversight and on inter-linkages between developments in the broader macro-economic environment and the financial system'.[157] Another serious shortcoming of pre-existing arrangements was that there was no single body conducting analysis of the macro-prudential environment, a task that was normally performed by member state central banks. As a result, there was no mechanism at the EU level that would 'ensure that macro-prudential risks are adequately identified and that warnings and recommendations are issued clearly, followed up and translated into action'.[158]

The ESRB has been established as an independent body with no legal personality,[159] given strong opposition to the establishment of a formal pan-European systemic risk supervisor. It is responsible for macro-prudential oversight across the EU financial system, in order to contribute to the prevention or mitigation of systemic risks to financial stability in the EU with the explicit purpose of avoiding 'periods of widespread financial distress' in order to 'contribute to the smooth functioning of the internal market' by ensuring the financial sector's sustainable contribution to economic growth.[160] The ESRB Regulation acknowledges that risks to the financial system[161] do not arise only from developments within the financial system but also due to macro-economic developments. For that reason another area where the ESRB is expected to have considerable influence is macro-economic and financial surveillance of the EU member states. This

---

[156] Article 1(4), ESA founding Regulations.
[157] Recital 11, ESRB Regulation.   [158] Recital 11, ESRB Regulation.
[159] The establishment of the ESRB is premised on Article 114 of Treaty on the Functioning of the European Union (TFEU) and has as justification that in the pursuit of its objectives the ESRB will facilitate the implementation of financial services harmonization legislation, Recital 31 of the ESRB Regulation.
[160] Article 3(1), ESRB Regulation.
[161] Article 2(b), ESRB Regulation defines the 'financial system' as encompassing 'all financial institutions, markets, products and market infrastructures'.

surveillance is a responsibility reserved for the EU Commission under the Treaty and the presence of the President of the EU Economic and Financial Committee (EFC) on the ESRB General Board (with no voting rights) strengthens its role in the above matters.[162] The ESRB should provide a link between systemic stability policies and national economic policies pursued by the finance ministries and their collective oversight exercised by the EU Council.[163] Notwithstanding the ERSB's lack of formal standing under EU law, its close ties of co-operation with the ECB, the ESAs, the EU Commission and the Council, national central banks and national supervisors give a distinct hard law edge to its warnings and recommendation.[164]

With respect to systemic risk, ESRB's task is to monitor and assess systemic risk[165] and suggest measures and policies to enhance the resilience of the financial system, in order to secure the maintenance of financial stability, 'mitigating the negative impact of financial shocks on the internal market and the real economy'.[166] The ESRB will also identify SIFIs in the EU, using the criteria contained in guidance issued by IMF, the BIS and the FSB.[167] An assessment based on those three criteria should be supplemented by a reference to the financial vulnerabilities and the capacity of the institutional framework to deal with financial

---

[162] The EFC is a committee of the European Union comprising senior officials from national administrations and central banks, the ECB and the Commission. It was set up by the Treaty of Maastricht and it was initially called the Monetary Committee. A detailed description of the mandate and function of the EFC is available at europa.eu/efc/about/index_en.htm.

[163] Recital 25, ESRB Regulation.

[164] See Eilis Ferran and Kern Alexander, 'Can Soft Law Bodies be Effective? Soft Systemic Risk Oversight Bodies and the Special Case of the European Systemic Risk Board', (2010) *European Law Review* 751–76, available also at papers.ssrn.com/sol3/papers.cfm?abstract_id=1676140.

[165] Article 3(2)(a), ESRB Regulation. The ESRB Regulation defines 'systemic risk' as the 'risk of disruption in the financial system with the potential to have serious negative consequences for the internal market and the real economy', *ibid.*, Article 2(c).

[166] Recital 10, ESRB Regulation.

[167] IMF, BIS and FSB, 'Report of the G-20 Finance Ministers and Central Bank Governors, Guidance to Assess the Systemic Importance of Financial Institutions, Markets and Instruments: Initial Considerations', 28 October 2009. The guidance clarifies that there are no one size fits all criteria. Financial institutions may be systemically important for local, national or international financial systems and economies. The key criteria helping to identify the systemic importance of markets and institutions are size (the volume of financial services provided by the individual component of the financial system), substitutability (the extent to which other components of the system can provide the same services in the event of failure) and interconnectedness (linkages with other components of the system).

failures.[168] There is no *numerus clausus* regarding the institutions that could be systemically important.[169] However, unlike the Dodd–Frank Act, the EU does not create a regulatory regime tailor made to SIFIs.

On the other hand, the FSOC and the ESRB mandates present large similarities when it comes to systemic risk monitoring. Thus, ESRB monitoring is conducted with 'the purpose of mitigating the exposure of the system to the risk of failure of systemic components'. In this respect the ESRB shall:

(1) *Determine and collect the type of information that is important* for discharging this task and for the processing and analysis of such information.[170] The ESRB will have to analyse relevant information in close co-operation with the ECB, the new ESAs, and national central banks.[171] As regulators' knowledge may often lag behind market developments, the private sector and market participants will also be able to have an input, especially as regards the evolving nature and risks of the financial system;[172]

(2) *Identify and prioritize systemic risks;*[173]

(3) *Issue warnings*[174] where systemic risks are deemed to be significant, and where it is appropriate to do so, make those warnings public.[175] The General Board of the ESRB may decide, on a case by case basis, with a majority of two-thirds, and after having informed the Council sufficiently in advance that a warning or a recommendation may be made public;[176]

(4) *Issue recommendations for remedial action (including calls for legislative initiatives) in response to the risks identified* and, where appropriate, make those recommendations public.[177] ESRB recommendations shall be addressed either: (a) to the entire EU, or, (b) to one or more

---

[168] Recital 9, ESRB Regulation.

[169] 'Any type of financial institution and intermediary, market, infrastructure, and instrument has the potential to be systemically significant', Recital 27, ESRB Regulation.

[170] Article 3(2)(a) and Recital 10, ESRB Regulation.

[171] Article 15 and Recitals 6, 24, ESRB Regulation.

[172] Recital 29, ESRB Regulation.

[173] Article 3(2)(b), ESRB Regulation.

[174] Articles 3(2)(C) and 16, ESRB Regulation. When it comes to 'warnings', the ESRB will use a colour code in order to allow interested parties better to assess the nature of the risk, Article 16(4) and Recital 18.

[175] Article 3(2)(c), ESRB Regulation.

[176] Article 18(1), ESRB Regulation. The addressees of warnings and recommendations made public by the ESRB shall also be provided with the right of making public their views, *ibid.* If the general board decides to make a warning or recommendation public, it will inform the addressees in advance, Article 18(2), ESRB Regulation.

[177] Articles 3(2)(d) and 16(1), ESRB Regulation.

member states, or, (c) to one or more ESAs, or, (d) to one or more of the national supervisory authorities. These, although of a non-binding nature, shall attach a specified timeline for the relevant policy response. In order to increase the 'bindingness' and legitimacy of ESRB recommendations, these shall also be confidentially communicated to formal EU bodies like the Commission, the Council and the ESAs;[178]

(5) *Monitor the follow-up to warnings and recommendations*: The ESRB will be able to monitor compliance with its warnings and recommendations, 'in order to ensure that its warnings and recommendations are effectively followed'.[179] ESRB recommendations will have a built-in 'act or explain' mechanism. Thus, addressees of ESRB recommendations should either act upon them or provide adequate justification for not taking action.[180] If the ESRB considers that the reaction is inadequate, it should communicate its views, under strict confidence, to the addressees, the Council and the Authority concerned;[181]

(6) *Inform the EU Council by means of a confidential warning, if it determines that an emergency situation may arise*,[182] especially when it 'detects a risk which could seriously jeopardise the orderly functioning and integrity of financial markets or the stability of the whole or part of the Union's financial system'.[183] The warning must provide the European Council with an assessment of the situation to enable the Council 'to assess the need to adopt a decision addressed to the ESAs determining the existence of an emergency situation'[184] and requiring them to take action;[185]

(7) *Co-operate closely with all the other parties to the ESFS* and, where appropriate, provide the ESAs with the information on systemic risks required for the performance of their tasks; and, in particular, in

---

[178] Article 16(2) and Recitals 19, ESRB Regulation.

[179] Recital 20, ESRB Regulation.

[180] 'If a recommendation referred to in Article 3(2)(d) is addressed to the Commission, to one or more Member States, to one or more ESAs, or to one or more national supervisory authorities, the addressees shall communicate to the ESRB and to the Council the actions undertaken in response to the recommendation and shall provide adequate justification for any inaction', Article 17(1), ESRB Regulation. See also Recital 20.

[181] Article 17(2) and Recital 20, ESRB Regulation. Following the publication of the unheeded recommendation, the European Parliament may invite the Chair of the ESRB to present that decision and the addressees may request to participate in the ensuing exchange of views, Article 17(3), ESRB Regulation.

[182] Article 3(2)(e), ESRB Regulation.

[183] Recital 22, ESRB Regulation.   [184] *Ibid.*   [185] *Ibid.*

collaboration with the ESAs, develop a common set of quantitative and qualitative indicators (risk dashboard) to identify and measure systemic risk;[186]

(8) *Participate, where appropriate, in the Joint Committee* co-ordinating the work of the ESAs on issues of cross-sectoral supervision;[187]

(9) *Co-ordinate its actions with those of international financial organizations*, particularly the IMF and the FSB as well as the relevant bodies in third countries on matters related to macro-prudential oversight[188] and monitor implementation of their recommendations in the EU.[189]

In addition, the European Parliament and the Council have the power to ask the ESRB to examine issues relating to financial stability.[190] In terms of accountability, the ESRB will report to the European Parliament and the Council at least annually, and more frequently in the event of widespread financial distress.[191] The ESRB's annual report to the European Parliament shall only contain the information that the general board decides to make public in accordance with Article 18 of the ESRB Regulation,[192] and the general public shall be able to access the Report.[193] The operation of the ESRB will be reviewed together with that of the other EU supervisory structures within three years following the adoption of relevant Regulations, i.e., by 17 December 2013.[194]

(b)   Structure and decision-making process   During the first five years of its life, the ESRB shall be chaired by the President of the ECB and will also have two vice-chairs. The first vice-chair will come from the ECB, will be elected by and from the members of the General Council of the ECB for a term of five years and may be re-elected once; the second vice-chair will come from the ESAs and will be the Chair of the Joint Committee.[195] In spite of its lack of legal personality, the ESRB has the

---

[186]   Article 3(2)(g), ESRB Regulation.
[187]   Article 3 (2)(h), ESRB Regulation.
[188]   Article 3(2)(i), ESRB Regulation.
[189]   Recital 7, ESRB Regulation. ESRB will also have a role with respect to implementing the recommendations of the IMF, the FSB and the Bank for International Settlements (BIS) to the G-20, *ibid*.
[190]   Recital 23, ESRB Regulation.
[191]   Article 19, ESRB Regulation. For means of informal communication, see Article 19(5), ESRB Regulation.
[192]   'The European Parliament may request the Chair of the ESRB to attend a hearing of the competent Committees of the European Parliament', Article 19(4), ESRB Regulation.
[193]   Article 19(2), ESRB Regulation.
[194]   Article 20, ESRB Regulation.
[195]   Article 5, ESRB Regulation.

structure of a fully fledged high-level regulatory body without any day to day supervisory and enforcement tasks. The ESRB comprises:[196]

(1) the General Board, which is the decision-making body with respect to the tasks assigned to the ERSB by Article 3(2) of Regulation 1092/2010;[197]
(2) a Steering Committee, which assists in the decision-making process of the ESRB by preparing the meetings of the general board, reviewing the documents to be discussed and monitoring the progress of the ESRB's ongoing work;[198]
(3) a Secretariat which is responsible for the day-to-day business of the ESRB. 'It shall provide high-quality analytical, statistical, administrative and logistical support to the ESRB under the direction of the Chair and the Steering Committee';[199]
(4) an Advisory Scientific Committee (ASC) to provide advice to the General Board,[200] comprising a group of external experts, who will have to comply with independence and confidentiality safeguards applicable to members of the General Board;
(5) an Advisory Technical Committee,[201] to provide the technical assistance and advice to the ERSB. It comprises experts from the ECB, national central banks, the ESAs and national supervisors, the EU Commission and the ASC.[202]

The general board has two types of membership:[203]

(1) members with voting power, comprising (a) the President and the Vice-President of the ECB; (b) the governors of the national central banks; (c) a member of the Commission; (d) the Chairperson of the European Banking Authority; (e) the Chairperson of the EIOPA; (f) the Chairperson of ESMA; (g) the Chair and the two Vice-Chairs of the Advisory Scientific Committee; and (h) the Chair of the Advisory Technical Committee, and
(2) members without voting power, comprising: (a) one high-level representative per member state of the competent national supervisory authorities, who will rotate depending on the item discussed; and (b) the President of EFC.

---

[196] Article 4 and Recital 16, ESRB Regulation.
[197] Article 4(2), ESRB Regulation.   [198] Article 4(3), ESRB Regulation.
[199] Article 4(4), ESRB Regulation.   [200] Article 4(5), ESRB Regulation.
[201] *Ibid.*   [202] Article 13, ESRB Regulation.
[203] Article 6(1), (2), ESRB Regulation.

All members of the general board and other 'persons who work or who have worked for or in connection with the ESRB' are subject to a continuous duty of professional secrecy even after completion of their duties.[204] The general board takes decisions on the basis of the one member one vote rule and decisions are taken by simple majority, provided that at least two-thirds of voting members have cast their votes.[205] However, a majority of two-thirds of the votes cast is required to adopt a recommendation or to make a warning or recommendation public. The members of the ESRB must perform their duties 'impartially and solely in the interest of the Union as a whole'.[206] ESRB members should, following the observation of a broad set of EU wide 'macro-economic and micro-financial data and indicators',[207] base their recommendation or warning on possible 'risks of disruption to financial services caused by a significant impairment of all or parts of the Union's financial system that have the potential to have serious negative consequences for the internal market and the real economy'.[208]

The private sector's views should be given due attention and the ESRB should conduct consultations 'with private sector stakeholders, including financial sector representatives, consumer associations' and consumer groups and give them a fair opportunity to make observations.[209] In addition, the fifteen experts of the Advisory Scientific Committee should provide ESRB with independent and substantial technical expertise.[210] However, the balance of votes means that the view of 'insiders' prevails. Thus, safeguards should have been put in place to ensure that independent expert advice would be given due weight and be properly heeded, even if it conflicted with the views of the ESAs or of the ECB.

3.2.3   The European Supervisory Authorities (ESAs)

The Lamfalussy Level 3 committees were regulatory networks with a limited mandate and mainly advisory powers. They could only issue non-binding guidelines and recommendations. However, answering industry demand for speed and efficiency and reflecting their adaptability into

---

[204] Article 8, ESRB Regulation.
[205] Article 10(1), (4), ESRB Regulation. By derogation 'If the [two thirds] quorum is not met, the Chair of the ESRB may convene an extraordinary meeting at which decisions may be taken with a quorum of one-third'. Article 10(4).
[206] Article 7 and Recital 26, ESRB Regulation.
[207] Recital 27, ESRB Regulation.   [208] *Ibid.*
[209] Recital 29, ESA founding Regulations.
[210] Recital 24, ESA founding Regulations.

market conditions, the openness of their consultations and the quality of their reviews, they quickly became an essential part of the EU regulatory edifice with influence much bigger than their formal powers. Nonetheless, the EU still suffered from inconsistent application of harmonized financial regulation and fragmented supervision. Many technical rules were determined at the national level, and there was considerable divergence between member states. Finally, while supervisors of cross-border financial groups have already been subject to an obligation to cooperate within colleges of supervisors, there was no formal mechanism to resolve eventual disagreements among college members. The new ESAs, comprising national regulators and the EU Commission, are designed to address the majority of these issues. According to the former chairman of CESR, Eddy Wymeersch, 'the creation of the authorities, although initially with relatively limited powers, is a crucial step in the organisation of a European system of financial supervision'.[211]

The principles guiding the ESAs' discharge of their tasks and powers are:[212]

(1) the improvement of the function of the internal market by ensuring a high, effective and consistent level of financial regulation and supervision;

(2) the maintenance of the integrity, transparency, efficiency and orderly functioning of financial markets;

(3) the protection of the public values of financial stability, and market and product transparency;

(4) the protection of depositors, investors, policyholders, pension scheme members and beneficiaries;

(5) the prevention of regulatory arbitrage by guaranteeing a level playing field and strengthening international supervisory co-ordination, for the benefit of the economy, including financial institutions and other stakeholders, consumers and employees; and

(6) when carrying out their tasks, the ESAs shall act independently and objectively and in the interest of the EU alone.

(a)   **Tasks and powers of the ESAs**   The tasks assigned to the ESAs by the founding Regulations and the powers granted to them to pursue their task are extensive; in the case of consumer protection they could even

---

[211] Wymeersch, 'Europe's New Supervisory Bodies', p. 9.
[212] Article 1(5) and Recital 10, ESA founding Regulations.

lead to drastic actions. The ESAs' tasks and powers may be summarized as follows:

(1) *Drafting high-quality common regulatory and supervisory standards and practices.* This will be achieved through the development of draft proposals for regulation and implementing technical standards in the areas defined in legislation,[213] on the basis of a delegation of powers by the EU Commission,[214] and by drawing up interpretative guidelines to assist national authorities in taking individual decisions.[215] These ESA powers should help to ensure consistency of national rules within the EU, with the ultimate aim of building a common European rulebook for financial services. The standards drafted by the ESAs will have to be endorsed by the EU Commission in the form of decisions or regulations in order to have binding power;[216]

(2) *Co-ordinating supervision*, in order to avoid regulatory arbitrage and ensure the consistent application of EU legislation and the creation of a common supervisory culture through: (a) facilitation of exchange of information between national supervisors and formulation of common supervisory approaches and, where necessary,[217] (b) settling any disagreements between national supervisors on cross-border matters,[218] including disagreements that occur within colleges of supervisors, through a legally binding mediation process.[219] Where there is persistent disagreement, following a 'conciliation' period,[220] the matter will be settled through an ESA decision that takes into account the views of all supervisors involved;[221]

(3) *Safeguard the consistent application of harmonized legislation* to ensure incorrect or inconsistent application is dealt with quickly and effectively.[222] The ESAs role in this area could stretch as far as issuing

---

[213] Article 10, ESA founding Regulations.
[214] Article 11, ESA founding Regulations.
[215] Article 8(1)(a), 8(2)(a)–(d), 10–17, ESA founding Regulations.
[216] Article 10(1) and (4) of the ESA founding Regulations. 'Regulatory technical standards shall be technical, shall not imply strategic decisions or policy choices and their content shall be delimited by the legislative acts on which they are based', *ibid.*, Article 10(1).
[217] Article 29, ESA founding Regulations.
[218] Article 8(1)(b) and 19, ESA founding Regulations.
[219] Article 21(4), ESA founding Regulations.
[220] Article 19(2), ESA founding Regulations.
[221] Article 19(3), ESA founding Regulations.
[222] '[T]o organise and conduct peer review analyses of competent authorities, including issuing guidelines and recommendations and identifying best practices, in order to strengthen consistency in supervisory outcomes', Article 8(1)(e), ESA founding Regulations.

decisions directly to financial institutions,[223] in cases where there is directly applicable EU legislation,[224] to ensure the correct and consistent application of EU law;[225]

(4) *Contributing to the discharge of the following supervisory tasks:*[226] (a) the consistent and coherent functioning of colleges of supervisors; (b) the monitoring, assessment and measurement of systemic risk; and (c) the development and co-ordination of recovery and resolution plans and development of methods for the resolution of failing financial institutions;

(5) *Supervising CRAs;*[227]

(6) *Co-ordinating national authority actions in emergency situations.*[228] The latter are deemed to arise in the case of adverse developments which may seriously jeopardize the orderly functioning and integrity of financial markets or the stability of the whole or part of the financial system in the EU. In this case, the ESA concerned (in co-operation with the ESRB) may issue a confidential recommendation addressed to the EU Council and provide it with an assessment of the situation.[229] The ESA concerned may even adopt individual decisions requiring competent authorities to take the necessary action;[230]

---

[223] In the specific cases referred to in Article 17(6), in Article 18(4) and in Article 19(4) of the ESA founding Regulations. See Article 6(2)(f), ESA founding Regulations.

[224] ESAs may require the competent national authorities concerned to take specific action or to refrain from action in order to settle the matter and ensure compliance with EU law. A requisite request has a binding effect for the competent national authorities concerned. If a competent authority does not comply with the settlement decision addressed to it, the relevant ESA has the power to adopt decisions directly addressed to financial market participants in areas of EU law directly applicable to them. Article 19(3)(5) and Recital 32, ESA founding Regulations. See also Section 3.1.2 above.

[225] *Ibid.*   [226] Article 8(1)(i), ESA founding Regulations.

[227] Under the proposed Regulation on Credit Rating Agencies and Recital 5, ESA founding Regulations.

[228] Articles 8(1)(b) and 18, ESA founding Regulations.

[229] Article 18(2), ESA founding Regulations.

[230] Article 18(3), ESA founding Regulations. A characteristic example of how this power might be used would be to adopt harmonized bans on short selling on EU securities markets, in place of non-co-ordinated prohibitions and other measures adopted by different member states in September 2008 and May 2010. See EU Commission, 'European System of Financial Supervisors (ESFS): Frequently Asked Questions', MEMO/09/404, 23 September 2009, available at europa.eu/rapid/pressReleasesAction. do?reference=MEMO/09/404. For the problems created by the inconsistent application of (asymmetric in their reach) short sales bans by EU member states, see Emilios Avgouleas, 'The Vexed Issue of Short Sales Regulation and the Global Financial Crisis', in K. Alexander and N. Moloney (eds.), *Law Reform and Financial Markets* (London: Edward Elgar Publishing, 2011), Chapter 3.

(7) *Promoting depositor/investor/policy-holder protection;*[231]
(8) *Monitoring and assessing market developments in their respective areas of competence* and especially of credit flows to households and SMEs and undertaking economic analyses of markets to inform the discharge of ESA functions;[232]
(9) *Discharging of a number of important tasks relating to systemic risk monitoring and building of mechanisms to prevent/contain a systemic crisis,*[233] and co-operating closely with the ESRB, especially as regards provision of information that is necessary for the achievement of the ESRB's tasks;[234]
(10) *Discharging of a number of tasks relating to consumer protection,* including the collection and analysis of consumer trends, co-ordination of financial literacy and education initiatives undertaken by national regulators, development of training standards for the industry, and contribution to the development of common disclosure rules.[235] The ESAs' powers in this area go as far as having the right to temporarily restrict or prohibit a financial activity that threatens the orderly functioning and integrity of financial markets or the stability of the whole or part of the financial system or in situations of emergency;[236]
(11) *Developing common methodologies* for assessing the effect of product characteristics and distribution processes on the financial position of financial market participants and on consumer protection;[237]
(12) *Issuing opinions* to the European Parliament, the Council or the Commission as provided for in Article 34 of the founding Regulations;[238]
(13) *Providing a centrally accessible database of registered financial market participants in the area of its competence.*[239]

---

[231] Article 8(1)(h), ESA founding Regulations.
[232] Article 8(1)(f),(g), ESA founding Regulations. This competence is really odd as it is more related to fostering credit expansion in the EU economies, and especially lending to the SMEs sector, rather than a prudential policy preventing the formation of bubbles, highlighting the sometimes conflicting nature of the supervisory goals assigned to the ESAs.
[233] Articles 22–4, ESA founding Regulations.
[234] Article 8(1)(d), ESA founding Regulations.
[235] Article 9(1), ESA founding Regulations.
[236] Article 9(5), ESA founding Regulations.
[237] Article 8(2)(i), ESA founding Regulations.
[238] Article 8(2)(g), ESA founding Regulations.
[239] Article 8(2)(j), ESA founding Regulations.

(b)   The supervision of EU financial institutions   The first attempt to effect a change in the structure and co-ordination of supervision of cross-border institutions in the EU was Directive 2009/111/EC.[240] The Directive established, following relevant decisions at the Washington and London G-20 Summits, colleges of supervisors for cross-border institutions to improve co-operation between the consolidating supervisor and the supervisors of the member states where the entities of a banking group are present. The colleges had to be set up by the consolidating supervisor and be based on written co-operation agreements between all supervisors involved.[241] The supervisory authorities of third countries may participate in the colleges, where appropriate. However, the colleges do not replace the consolidating supervisor.[242]

Furthermore, the Directive specifies the circumstances under which the consolidating supervisor of an EU parent credit institution (or of a financial holding company) and the supervisors of the subsidiaries should reach a joint decision regarding the adequacy of the consolidated level of own funds held by the group. Another important reform of the Directive is that it gave improved access to information rights to the host country authorities where a 'systemically relevant branch' of a credit institution is located, remedying, to a certain extent, some of the shortcomings of home country control exposed by the failure of Icelandic banks. The Directive provides three criteria to take into account in determining whether a branch is 'systemically relevant': the size of the market share of the branch,[243] the impact of closure of operations on payment and clearing and settlement in the host Member State[244] and the size of the branch in terms of number of clients in the host Member State.[245] However, other reasons for considering the branch as systemically relevant may also be given. The decision on whether a branch should be considered systemically relevant is a joint decision of the authorities concerned.[246]

---

[240] See note 87 above. The Commission Proposal went as far as to propose a (largely impractical) obligation for the competent authorities of each Member State to take into account 'the potential impact of their decisions on the stability of the financial system in all other member states concerned and, in particular, in emergency situations, based on the information available at the relevant time'. Proposed Article 40 (3). See note 86 above.

[241] New Article 131a.   [242] New Article 131a(1).

[243] A branch may be considered systemically relevant if the market share of the branch in terms of deposit exceeds 2 per cent in the host member state, New Article 42a(1), (a).

[244] New Article 42a(1), (b).   [245] New Article 42a(1), (c).

[246] The decision should be taken within two months of the receipt of the request by the authorities of the host country. If no joint decision is reached within this period of time, the authorities of the host Member State will themselves take a decision, New Article 42a(1) (4).

As regards the state of supervision following the establishment of ESAs, in spite of the EU Commission's preliminary intentions, the new Authorities do not have direct supervisory powers over any financial institution in the EU (apart from ESMA's supervision of CRAs), although the founding Regulations leave open the possibility of granting them such powers in the future. As a result, supervision of financial institutions has remained the responsibility of national authorities. ESAs do not replace the supervisory colleges, yet they have a leading role in 'ensuring the consistent and coherent functioning of colleges of supervisors for cross-border financial institutions' across the EU and participate in the workings of colleges with full rights, including the carrying out of on-site inspections.[247] Also, they will share information they gather with colleges. More importantly, ESAs shall monitor the workings of colleges and ensure that they adopt and follow consistent practices for all cross-border groups.

With respect to financial stability, the ESAs will be the high-level micro-prudential supervisors, although they will not engage in day-to-day supervision. They will focus on the identification, at an early stage, of trends, potential risks and vulnerabilities stemming from financial institutions' conduct, across borders and across sectors. In addition, the ESAs, in co-operation with the ESRB, will initiate and co-ordinate EU-wide stress tests to assess the resilience of financial institutions to adverse market developments.[248] It is the ESAs' task to ensure the consistency of methodologies applied to stress tests at the national level. Therefore, the ESAs should also have research functions and employ groups of experts to conduct analyses of the markets and the impact of potential market developments.

Notwithstanding the powers given to supervisory and resolution colleges and the drawing up of group level recovery and resolution plans by credit institutions and systemically important investment firms, member states retain core responsibility for ensuring co-ordinated crisis management and preserving financial stability in crisis situations, in particular with regard to stabilizing and resolving failing financial institutions. Any decisions by ESAs in emergency situations affecting the stability of a financial institution should not impinge on the fiscal responsibilities of Member States. A mechanism shall be established whereby Member States may invoke this safeguard and ultimately bring the matter before the EU

---

[247] Article 21(1) and Recital 36, ESA founding Regulations.
[248] Article 21(2)(b), ESA founding Regulations.

Council for a decision.[249] However, the safeguard mechanism should not be abused, in particular in relation to a decision taken by the ESAs, which does not have a significant or material fiscal impact, such as a reduction of income linked to the temporary prohibition of specific activities or products for consumer protection purposes.[250]

(c)   Systemic risk monitoring and resolution of financial institutions

As mentioned earlier the ESAs will also play a key role in systemic risks monitoring and above all in building mechanisms to prevent/contain a systemic crisis in the financial sector as well as responding to warnings and recommendations made by the ESRB, in accordance with Article 17 of Regulation (EU) No. 1092/2010.[251] More specifically the ESAs will contribute to the enhanced supervision regime, espoused by the EU Commission,[252] through the development of an adequate stress-testing framework, to help identify those institutions that may pose systemic risk and evaluate the potential for systemic risk posed by financial institutions to increase in situations of stress.[253] These institutions are then subject to the strengthened supervision regime, discussed in Chapter 7 below.[254] The ESAs, in collaboration with the ESRB, will develop a common set of quantitative and qualitative indicators (risk dashboard) to identify and measure systemic risk. Upon a request from one or more competent authorities, the European Parliament, the Council or the Commission, or on its own initiative, the ESAs may conduct an inquiry into a particular type of financial institution or type of product or type of conduct in order to assess potential threats to the stability of the financial system and make appropriate recommendations for action to the competent authorities concerned.[255] The ESAs will draw up, as necessary, additional guidelines and recommendations for financial institutions, to take account of the systemic risk posed by them, which will be incorporated in the context of the strengthened supervision framework discussed below.[256]

(d)   ESA organization, decision-making, accountability and appeals   The founding Regulations prescribe the powers of the bodies

---

[249] Article 38, Recitals 5 and 50, ESA founding Regulations.
[250] *Ibid.*   [251] Article 22(2), ESA founding Regulations.
[252] See Article 25, ESA founding Regulations.
[253] Article 23, ESA founding Regulations.
[254] Article 23(1), ESA founding Regulations.
[255] Article 22(2)–(4), ESA founding Regulations.
[256] Article 24, ESA founding Regulations.

and officers of the ESAs, selection criteria and independence safeguards. The ESAs have identical organizational/administrative structures comprising a board of supervisors, a management board, a chairperson and an executive director,[257] the latter being the chief executive officer of the ESAs. The founding Regulations prescribe the powers of the ESA bodies and officers of the ESAs, selection criteria and independence safeguards. The most important of these bodies is the board of supervisors which discharges the majority of tasks and duties discussed above.[258] It also approves the budget of ESAs and exercises disciplinary power against the chairperson and the executive director.

Under Article 40(1) of the founding Regulations, the board of supervisors comprises voting and non-voting members. These are:

(1) the Chairperson, who is non-voting;
(2) the heads of national public authorities competent for the supervision of credit, securities and insurance institutions in each Member State, who have voting rights and must meet in person at least twice a year;
(3) one representative of the Commission, who is non-voting;
(4) one representative of the European Central Bank, who is non-voting;
(5) one representative of the ESRB, who is non-voting;
(6) one representative of each of the other two ESAs, who are non-voting; and
(7) the executive director may participate in meetings of the board of supervisors, without the right to vote.

When carrying out the tasks conferred upon them by the founding Regulations, the chairperson and the voting members of the board of supervisors must act objectively and independently from any national or other interests. Their only guide should be '[the] interest of the Union as a whole'.[259] The decisions of the board are taken with simple majority and on the basis of one member one vote principle. However, as regards the drafting of regulatory technical standards and guidelines and recommendations (under Articles 10 to 16 of the founding Regulations) and measures and decisions that refer to a prohibition or restriction of a financial activity (adopted under the third subparagraph of Article 9(5) of the founding Regulations) or relating to the ESAs' budget, the board of supervisors will take decisions on the basis of a qualified majority of its members.

---

[257] Chapter III, ESA founding Regulations.
[258] Article 43, ESA founding Regulations.
[259] Article 42, ESA founding Regulations.

The founding Regulations also establish a forum comprising the chairpersons of the ESAs, called the Joint Committee, where the ESAs will meet regularly to co-operate and ensure cross-sectoral consistency with the EIOPAand ESMA, in particular regarding: financial conglomerates, accounting and auditing, micro-prudential analyses of cross-sectoral developments, risks and vulnerabilities for financial stability, retail investment products, measures combating money laundering, and information exchange with the ESRB and developing the relationship between the ESRB and the ESAs.[260] The executive directors of each ESA and a representative of the Commission and the ESRB will also attend the meetings of the Joint Committee. The ESAs should utilize the Joint Committee to reach common positions and joint action with regard to all of the aforementioned powers and actions where there is cross-sectoral overlap or in order to settle disagreements between the different ESAs on cross-sectoral actions.[261]

Like the ERSB the ESAs will be accountable to the European Parliament and the Council.[262] The decisions of the ESAs especially as regards actions they have taken in connection with breaches of EU law (Article 17 of the founding Regulations), emergency situations (under Article 18 of the founding Regulations), and settlement of disputes between national supervisors in the context of cross-border supervision may be appealed[263] to the newly established board of appeal, a joint body of the ESAs comprising outside legal experts.[264]

3.2.4   Evaluation of the new arrangements

EU reforms have not led to the establishment of pan-European regulators for large cross-border banks and financial groups, although this was possibly the most pressing of the reforms mooted.[265] On the other hand, the regulatory loopholes exposed by the GFC have been widely used to promote the agenda for centralization of the regulation process in a number of areas, such as investor/consumer protection, although there was no

---

[260] Articles 54 and 55, ESA founding Regulations.
[261] Article 56, ESA founding Regulations.
[262] Articles 3 and 50, ESA founding Regulations.
[263] Article 60, ESA founding Regulations.
[264] Article 58, ESA founding Regulations.
[265] Among the many interesting papers on the subject, the earliest and possibly most perceptive was Carmine Lamanda et al., 'Cross-border Banking in Europe: What Regulation and Supervision?', Unicredit Group Forum on Financial Cross-border Groups, Discussion Paper 1/09, March 2009.

evidence that such reform was required because of a systemic threat. This
observation reveals that, while the EU reform process appears to be more
driven by necessity and less by politics, it has, in fact, been as politicized
a process as reform in the US. The major difference is that in the case of
the EU reforms the critical issue was not just avoidance of bail-outs but
rather the balance of power between the European bodies and the member states.

This complex and sometimes conflicted policy agenda is not the only
challenge the new EU bodies are bound to face. First, the ambiguous
structure of the ESRB is bound to give rise to problems that may seriously
hamper its effectiveness and even affect its reputation. Its informal nature
and its reliance for information gathering on national authorities may
prevent it from discharging its powers properly ending up as yet another
'soft law' institution, while at the same time, due to its close association
with formal EU bodies, may not enjoy the flexibility of the soft law bodies
discussed in Chapters 4 and 5.[266] It is not only that the information provided by national and EU authorities may provide an incomplete picture
but also the danger that the ESRB may lose credibility as a result of flawed
action taken by the implementers of its warnings and recommendations.[267] The ESRB's dependence on other bodies to carry out its 'wishes'
also means that it may easily become involved in national and European
level political struggles and reputation damaging litigation. In addition,
its closeness to the ECB, which is also the effective lender of last resort in
the Euro-zone, means that its independence and credibility may be compromised by the ECB's policy priorities regarding the Eurozone banking
sector. These considerations make the case for eventually overcoming
the current political and legal hurdles and transforming the ESRB into
an independent systemic supervisor for the EU[268] or promoting a global
structure for macro-prudential supervision compelling.

The establishment of the ESAs in place of the Lamfalussy Committees
has plausibly been characterized as an evolutionary as well as

[266] Ferran and Alexander, 'Can Soft Law Bodies be Effective?', pp. 4, 31–2.
[267] *Ibid.*
[268] See also Larry Wall, Maria J. Nieto, and David Mayes, 'Creating an EU Level Supervisor for Cross-Border Banking Groups: Issues Raised by the U.S. Experience with Dual Banking', Federal Reserve Bank of Atlanta, Working Paper Series, WP 2011–06, March 2011, available at www.frbatlanta.org/documents/pubs/wp/wp1106.pdf. Cf. Gerard Hertig, Ruben Lee and Joseph A. McCahery, 'Empowering the ECB to Supervise Banks: A Choice-Based Approach' TILEC Discussion Paper No. DP 2009–001, August 2009, available at ssrn.com/abstract=1327824. This paper contains an interesting contractual (opt in) solution to the supervision of cross-border groups in the EU.

transformative and transitional process.[269] Although regulatory and supervisory centralization has been stretched to the limit of what was politically tenable,[270] regardless of effectiveness, yet complete centralization will remain the final goal. However, even under the agreed framework there is no guarantee of success for ESAs given their small size and limited resources. Moreover, instead of establishing a framework under which cross-border financial groups in Europe are directly regulated by the ESAs, the final outcome is a complex and bureaucratic structure with several over-lapping competences, which might lead to critical delays in taking drastic action. Finally, the issue of cross-border group supervision and resolution at the global level remains unresolved and it is not clear how the ESAs will manage cross-border spillovers or what is going to be their role when third country regulators are involved, beyond the obvious device of supervisory/resolution colleges. This weakness is accentuated by the failure of the proposed EU resolution regime to establish clear fiscal burden sharing arrangements (analytically discussed in the next chapter).[271]

4.   The new Basel capital and liquidity framework

4.1   Minimum capital requirements and composition of capital

4.1.1   Overview

As explained in Chapters 3 and 5, the GFC has clearly demonstrated two things regarding capital regulations. First, the existence of a high equity base is essential for the continuous solvency of any bank. Second, the definition of capital across jurisdictions was rather inconsistent and, coupled with a lack of disclosure, it prevented the market from fully assessing and comparing the quality of capital between institutions. As a result, the BCBS has decided that under Basel III the predominant form of Tier 1 capital will be common shares and retained earnings. The remainder of Tier 1 capital should comprise subordinated perpetual (no maturity/no incentive to redeem) instruments which provide for fully

---

[269] Ferran, 'Understanding the Institutional Architecture', p. 62.

[270] Ferran highlights the critical issue of opposition to further centralization of financial supervision by politicians and industry members based in the UK, the most important financial services market in the EU, *ibid.*, pp. 63–5.

[271] Zdenek Kudrna, 'Regulatory Aftermath of Banking Rescues: More Europe or Business as Usual?', Conference paper presented in EUSA Twelfth Biennial International Conference, 3 March 2011, available at www.euce.org/eusa/2011/papers/12e_kudrna.pdf.

discretionary non-cumulative dividends or coupons. Other forms of innovative hybrid capital instruments will be phased out. Tier 2 capital instruments will be harmonized and so-called Tier 3 capital instruments, which were only available to cover trading book risks, have been eliminated. Finally, to improve market discipline, the transparency of the capital base will be improved, with all elements of capital required to be disclosed along with a detailed reconciliation to the reported accounts.[272]

4.1.2   Capital components

Under Basel III total regulatory capital will consist of the sum of the following:

(1) Tier 1 Capital (going-concern capital), comprising: (a) Common Equity Tier 1 (CET1) and (b) Additional Tier 1.
(2) Tier 2 Capital (gone-concern capital).

Common Equity Tier 1 must be at least 4.5 per cent of RWAs at all times. Tier 1 Capital must be at least 6.0 per cent of RWAs at all times. Total Capital (Tier 1 Capital plus Tier 2 Capital) must be at least 8.0% of RWAs at all times. Common Equity Tier 1 capital consists of the sum of the following:[273]

(1) common shares issued by the bank that meet the criteria for classification as common shares for regulatory purposes;[274]
(2) stock surplus (share premium) resulting from the issue of instruments included in CET 1;

---

[272] BCBS, 'Basel III: A Global Regulatory Framework', p. 2. Basel III retains the three pillars of Basel II discussed in Chapter 4: Pillar I provides the regulatory rules/standards, Pillar II's regulatory review provides scope for supervisory discretion, while Pillar III seeks to enhance market discipline through disclosure.

[273] BCBS, 'Basel III: A Global Regulatory Framework', p. 13.

[274] BCBS provides a number of criteria for the inclusion of common shares in CET 1, which include the following requirements: the shares must represent the most subordinated claim in liquidation of the bank; they should provide entitlement to a claim on the residual assets that is proportional with its share of issued capital, after all senior claims have been repaid in liquidation; the principal involved is perpetual and never repaid outside of liquidation, notwithstanding any discretionary buy backs or other legal means of effective capital reduction; the bank has not created an expectation at issuance that the instrument will be bought back, redeemed or cancelled nor do the statutory or contractual terms provide any feature which might give rise to such an expectation; the shares are directly issued and paid-in and the bank has not directly or indirectly funded the purchase of the instrument. For the full list, see BCBS, 'Basel III: A Global Regulatory Framework', pp. 14–15.

(3) retained earnings;
(4) accumulated other comprehensive income and other disclosed reserves;
(5) common shares issued by consolidated subsidiaries of the bank and held by third parties (i.e., minority interest) that meet the criteria for inclusion in Common Equity Tier 1 capital;
(6) regulatory adjustments applied in the calculation of Common Equity Tier 1;
(7) retained earnings and other comprehensive income including interim profit or loss.

Additional Tier 1 capital consists of the total of the following elements:

(1) instruments issued by the bank that meet the criteria for inclusion in Additional Tier 1 capital (and are not included in Common Equity Tier 1);
(2) stock surplus (share premium) resulting from the issue of instruments included in Additional Tier 1 capital;
(3) instruments issued by consolidated subsidiaries of the bank and held by third parties that meet the criteria for inclusion in Additional Tier 1 capital and are not included in Common Equity Tier 1;
(4) regulatory adjustments applied in the calculation of Additional Tier 1 capital.

4.1.3   Tier 2 capital

According to BCBS, the objective of Tier 2 regulatory capital is to provide loss absorption on a gone-concern basis. Tier 2 capital comprises the total of the following elements:[275]

(1) instruments issued by the bank that meet the criteria for inclusion in Tier 2 capital (and are not included in Tier 1 capital);[276]

---

[275] BCBS, 'Basel III: A Global Regulatory Framework', p. 17.
[276] The issue of which instruments issued by the bank are eligible for inclusion in Tier 2 capital is of great importance as a number of hybrid or debt instruments will not have the desired loss absorbing capacity. Thus, Basel III includes a long list of criteria for inclusion in Tier 2 capital instruments issued by the bank. The most important of the relevant criteria cover the following requirements: the instruments must be issued and paid in; they must be subordinated to depositors and general bank creditors; the investor must have no rights to accelerate the repayment of future scheduled payments (coupon or principal), except in bankruptcy and liquidation. For the full list of criteria for inclusion of instruments into Tier 2 capital, see BCBS, 'Basel III: A Global Regulatory Framework', pp. 18–19.

(2) stock surplus (share premium) resulting from the issue of instruments included in Tier 2 capital;
(3) instruments issued by consolidated subsidiaries of the bank and held by third parties that meet the Basel III criteria for inclusion in Tier 2 capital and are not included in Tier 1 capital;
(4) certain loan loss provisions as specified in the Basel III document; and
(5) regulatory adjustments applied in the calculation of Tier 2 Capital.

4.2   Capital buffers

4.2.1   The capital conservation buffer

Banks will be required to hold a *capital conservation buffer* comprising Common Equity Tier 1 above the regulatory minimum capital requirement. According to BCBS, 'the capital conservation buffer ... is designed to ensure that banks build up capital buffers outside periods of stress which can be drawn down as losses are incurred'.[277] The buffer essentially puts a constraint on discretionary distributions of earnings, including dividend payments, share-backs and staff bonus payments. Alternatively, banks may choose to raise new capital from the private sector as an alternative to conserving internally generated capital.

The capital conservation buffer is indispensable in addressing the collective action problem associated with payment of discretionary bonuses and higher dividends, even in the face of deteriorating capital positions.[278] In the period before (but also during) the crisis it was not unusual to see banks making generous discretionary payments in the middle of the crisis, with the leading example being the case of Northern Rock, which returned capital to its shareholders just weeks before its collapse. Retention of a greater proportion of earnings during a downturn ensures that capital remains available to support the ongoing business operations of banks through subsequent periods of stress, reducing the procyclicality of capital reserves.

If the bank does not wish (or is unable) to raise capital from the private sector, then the lower a given bank's actual capital and the nearer to the minimum requirement the higher the share of earnings that will have to be retained by banks for the purpose of rebuilding their capital buffers.

---

[277] BCBS, 'Basel III, A Global Regulatory Framework', p. 54.
[278] BCBS notes that the buffer 'will reinforce the objective of sound supervision and bank governance and address the collective action problem that has prevented some banks from curtailing distributions', *ibid.*

On the other hand, a bank with Common Equity Tier 1 capital near its highest level (7 per cent or higher) will not have any obligation to comply with any minimum capital conservation ratios.[279] Nonetheless, banks with depleted capital buffers may not use future predictions of recovery as justification for maintaining generous distributions to shareholders, other capital providers and employees. Nor should they use share buy backs or increased dividend payments to signal their financial strength, since such a decision would put shareholders interests above those of depositors and would encourage other banks to follow the same route, wasting capital at a time that they need to conserve it. Thus, Basel III makes a clear policy choice that it should be shareholders, creditors and other usual recipients of distributions rather than depositors who will aid the recovery of bank capital buffers.[280]

4.2.2   The countercyclical buffer

The new capital framework also introduces a *countercyclical buffer* within a range of 0 to 2.5 per cent of RWAs, comprising common equity or other fully loss absorbing capital.[281] This is essentially an extension of the capital conservation buffer, but with stronger macro-prudential characteristics. The buffer will be triggered/implemented according to the state of national economies based on a credit to GDP ratio, which has been chosen over several other variables as the most reliable measure of credit growth in the economy. It provides a clear differentiation from other capital requirements that focus on individual institutions and their risk profile. The objective of the countercyclical buffer is to protect the banking sector (and the broader financial system) from excessive risks built up during periods of excess aggregate credit growth.[282] It is, thus, the most potent

---

[279] For the table illustrating the relationship between the levels of CET 1 and the required capital conservation ratio, see BCBS, 'Basel III: A Global Regulatory Framework', p. 56, para. f.

[280] *Ibid.*

[281] While the maximum countercyclical buffer of 2.5 per cent of RWAs is the international reciprocity standard, it is not a ceiling for national regulators who might wish to impose a higher buffer or use additional macro-prudential tools. BCBS is still reviewing the question of permitting other fully loss absorbing capital beyond CET 1 and what form it would take. Until the Committee has issued further guidance, the countercyclical buffer is to be met with CET 1 only.

[282] BCBS, 'Basel III: A Global Regulatory Framework', p. 57. BCBS notes: 'Losses incurred in the banking sector can be extremely large when a downturn is preceded by a period of excess credit growth. These losses can destabilise the banking sector and spark a vicious circle, whereby problems in the financial system can contribute to a downturn in the real economy that then feeds back on to the banking sector. These interactions highlight the

regulatory weapon so far to counter bubbles and the debilitating effects these have on the financial sector once they diminish through deleveraging to reduce excessive debt built up during the bubble, an increase in the rate of non-performing loans, depreciation of asset values and fire sales.[283] As the buffer is country specific, it will be triggered only when there is excessive credit growth, which leads to a system-wide build up of risk. Conversely, the buffer capital will be released when there is no risk to systemic stability by credit expansion. This would help reduce the risk that available credit is constrained by regulatory capital requirements.

This focus on excess aggregate credit growth means that jurisdictions are likely to deploy the buffer on an infrequent basis. On the other hand, the buffer for internationally active banks will be a weighted average of the buffers deployed across all the jurisdictions to which it has credit exposures. Therefore, they will find themselves subject to the buffer requirement on a more frequent basis than smaller banks, since credit cycles are not always highly correlated across jurisdictions. The countercyclical buffer regime consists of the following elements:[284]

(1) national authorities will monitor credit growth and other indicators that may signal a build up of system-wide risk and make assessments of whether credit growth is excessive and is leading to the build up of system-wide risk. Based on this assessment they will put in place a countercyclical buffer requirement when circumstances warrant. This requirement will be released when system-wide risk crystallizes or dissipates.
(2) internationally active banks will look at the geographic location of their private sector credit exposures and calculate their bank specific countercyclical capital buffer.
(3) the countercyclical buffer requirement to which a bank is subject will extend the size of the capital conservation buffer. Banks will be subject to restrictions on distributions if they do not meet the requirement.

Accordingly, if in the judgment of the relevant national authority its economy goes through a period of excess credit growth, mainly (but not exclusively) based on a properly calibrated credit to GDP ratio, that would

---

particular importance of the banking sector building up additional capital defences in periods where the risks of system-wide stress are growing markedly', *ibid.*
[283] Chapters 2 and 3 have provided an extensive analysis of the relationship between asset bubbles and the advent of financial crises, which seem to have been preceded by such bubbles on most occasions.
[284] BCBS, 'Basel III: A Global Regulatory Framework', p. 57.

lead to the build up of system-wide risk, the authority should, together with any other macro-prudential tools at its disposal, impose a counter-cyclical buffer requirement on the banking sector. This will vary between zero and 2.5 per cent of RWAs, depending on their judgment as to the extent of the build up of system-wide risk. The decision will be implemented gradually, over a period of up to 12 months, to give banks time to adjust. The buffer add-on will apply equally to all banks with credit exposures to the jurisdiction concerned and there is no distinction between banks which are responsible for the credit boom and which are not.

Apart from the imposition of a sector wide countercyclical buffer, national authorities may subject individual banks to a countercyclical buffer that varies between zero and 2.5 per cent to total RWAs. The bank specific buffer will reflect the geographic composition of its portfolio of credit exposures. Banks must meet this buffer with Common Equity Tier 1 or other fully loss absorbing capital or be subject to restrictions on distributions.[285] Naturally, this will generate a number of complex calculation problems for international banks which maintain a strong presence in a number of countries. Basel III holds that international banks should look at the geographic location of their private sector credit exposures (including non-bank financial sector exposures) and 'calculate their countercyclical capital buffer requirement as a weighted average of the buffers that are being applied in jurisdictions to which they have an exposure'.[286] The weighting applied to the buffer in each of the relevant jurisdictions will be the bank's total credit risk charge that relates to private sector credit exposures in that jurisdiction, divided by the bank's total credit risk charge that relates to private sector credit exposures across all jurisdictions. The mechanism to comply with the countercyclical buffer requirement is by extending/triggering the capital conservation buffer described above.[287]

The credit to GDP ratio for the purposes of imposing the buffer add-on should be calculated in three steps:[288]

---

[285] *Ibid.*, p. 58.

[286] *Ibid.* Credit exposures in this case include all private sector credit exposures that attract a credit risk capital charge or the risk-weighted equivalent trading book capital charges for specific risk, IRC and securitization.

[287] The table in para. 147 of the Basel III document provides an illustration of how compliance with the countercyclical buffer requirement will be phased in.

[288] For an analytical exposition of how national authorities should conduct these calculations, see BCBS, 'Guidance for National Authorities Operating the Countercyclical Capital Buffer', December 2010, pp. 12–14 and pp. 15–24 for tables measuring how these ratios would have performed per country during previous banking crises.

Step 1: Calculate the aggregate private sector credit-to-GDP ratio;

Step 2: Calculate the credit-to-GDP gap (the gap between the ratio and its trend);

Step 3: Transform the credit-to-GDP gap into the guide buffer add-on.

The definition of credit used for the purposes of this calculation should capture all sources of debt funds for the private sector. Although available credit data varies across jurisdictions precluding uniformity, the BCBS proposes that the definition of credit should include 'all credit extended to households and other non-financial private entities in an economy independent of its form and the identity of the supplier of funds'.[289] This definition includes credit provided by domestic and international banks as well as non-bank financial institutions either domestically or directly from abroad. It also extends to all debt securities issued domestically or internationally to fund households and other non-financial private entities (including securitizations), regardless of who is the holder of the securities. This approach recognizes that banks can suffer the consequences of a period of excess credit, even if they have not directly driven its growth. Also the broad ambit of this definition restricts any incentives banks could have to divert credit supply to other parts of the financial system.[290]

It should be noted that the credit to GDP ratio is not the only tool that may be used to set the buffer nor should it be over-relied on in the identification of bubbles. The BCBS has also underscored the value of other variables in this context, such as: (1) various asset prices; (2) funding spreads and CDS spreads; (3) credit condition surveys; (4) real GDP growth; and (5) data on the ability of non-financial entities to meet their debt obligations on a timely basis. Moreover, there are occasions when the behaviour of the GDP denominator may not reflect the build-up of system-wide risks, as the ratios' rise may be due to a decline of the GDP due to a recession. To counter these problems BCBS suggests that national macro-prudential authorities 'should form their own judgments about the sustainable level of credit in the economy'.[291] This is also very vague but early indicators suggested by Goodhart, which include growth in property prices and income levels, could prove useful and reliable measurements.[292] Inflated

---

[289] See ibid., pp. 10–11.   [290] Ibid., p. 10   [291] Ibid., p. 11.
[292] '1. A rate of growth of (bank) credit which is significantly faster than average, and above its normal trend relationship to nominal incomes; 2. A rate of growth of housing (and property) prices which is significantly faster than normal and above its normal trend relationship with incomes. 3. A rate of growth of leverage, among the various sectors

asset prices are the essence of asset bubbles and these might be more due to loose monetary policies than bankers' irresponsible lending. In a downturn, asset inflation goes into a reverse and causes severe price corrections, deleveraging and recessions. Thus, price indicators should not be ignored nor should the role of the countercyclical buffer be overestimated as, ultimately, bubbles might only be countered through monetary policy tools.

To avoid distorting competition, jurisdictional reciprocity will be applied when it comes to internationally active banks, although the reciprocity obligation does not extend to buffer requirements that are over 2.5 per cent of RWAs. Host country authorities set the level of the buffer requirement applicable to credit exposures held by local entities located in their jurisdiction. Home authorities are responsible for ensuring that the banks they supervise correctly calculate their buffer requirements based on the geographic location of their exposures. Home authorities always have the right to require the banks they supervise to maintain higher buffers if they judge that the buffer imposed is insufficient. On the other hand, home authorities may not implement a lower buffer add-on in respect of credit exposures of banks they supervise for other (host) jurisdictions, in order to avoid having foreign branches operating at a lower cost base to local banks.[293]

However, as the Basel standards are soft law and reciprocity provisions will essentially be monitored and 'enforced' outside the EU through MOUs, problems of co-ordination are bound to arise undermining the effectiveness of the countercyclical buffer. In addition, national authority

---

of the economy which is significantly faster than usual and above its normal trend relationship with incomes'. Charles Goodhart, unpublished written statement submitted in the context of Oral Evidence given to the House of Commons Treasury Committee 'Accountability of the Bank of England', 23 May 2011, available at www.publications. parliament.uk/pa/cm201012/cmselect/cmtreasy/uc874-ii/uc87401.htm.

[293] BCBS, 'Guidance for National Authorities', p. 4. The countercyclical buffer regime is also subject to a transitional period and will be phased-in in parallel with the capital conservation buffer between 1 January 2016 and year end 2018 becoming fully effective on 1 January 2019. The maximum countercyclical buffer requirement will begin at 0.625 per cent of RWAs on 1 January 2016 and increase each subsequent year by an additional 0.625 percentage points, to reach its final maximum of 2.5% of RWAs on 1 January 2019. Countries that experience excessive credit growth during this transition period may consider accelerating the build-up of the capital conservation buffer and the countercyclical buffer. In addition, where jurisdictions choose to implement larger countercyclical buffer requirements, the reciprocity provisions of the regime will not apply to the additional amounts or earlier time-frames. See BCBS, 'Basel III: A Global Regulatory Framework', p. 60.

discretion in identifying the conditions that may trigger the buffer requirement is bound to give rise to friction between overcautious regulators and regulators with a more liberal approach to credit expansion. Therefore, it should not be overlooked that the countercyclical buffer of Basel III is clearly designed to serve the narrower objective of macroprudential policy and that monetary and fiscal policy remain the principal tools for preventing the formation of asset bubbles. Finally, it would be interesting to see if national regulators who supported the buffer in Basel, are as willing to implement it. Regulators will be bound to face a strong reaction from the growing industries and the banks, which will see their lending being restricted in good times on the basis of regulatory policy – the buffer – while market prices are rising everywhere giving the false impression of similarly rising asset quality.

4.3   Containing leverage

As mentioned in Chapters 3 and 5, one of the major underlying causes of the GFC was the build-up of unsustainable on- and off-balance sheet leverage in the banking system, while banks with excessive leverage could still maintain strong risk based capital ratios.[294] During the most severe part of the crisis, banks were forced to reduce their leverage, amplifying downward pressure on asset prices, and further exacerbating the positive feedback loop between bank losses, declines in bank capital and contraction in credit growth that forced a recession. Since Basel II facilitated instead of curbing leverage, BCBS has introduced a non-risk based leverage ratio (of 3 per cent of Tier 1 for the period from 1 January 2013 to 1 January 2017) that should act as a credible supplementary measure to the risk-based capital requirements. According to the BCBS, the leverage ratio is intended to achieve the following objectives:

(1) constrain the build-up of leverage in the banking sector in order to avoid subsequent excessive deleveraging which can destabilize the broader financial system and the economy; and

(2) reinforce the risk based requirements with a simple, non-risk based 'backstop' measure.

The basis of calculation is the average of the monthly leverage ratio over the quarter based on the definitions of capital (*the capital measure*)

---

[294] See also Martin Hellwig, 'Capital Regulation after the Crisis: Business as Usual?', Max Planck Institute Collective Goods Pre-print, No. 2010/31, July 2010, available at ssrn.com/abstract=1645224>, accessed 12/1/2011.

and total exposure (*the exposure measure*) as specified in the Basel III document (paragraphs 154 to 164). The *capital measure* of the leverage ratio is based on the Basel III new definition of Tier 1 capital, discussed above. The Committee will also collect data during the transition period to track the impact of using total regulatory capital and Common Equity Tier 1.[295] Items that are deducted completely from capital do not contribute to leverage, and should therefore also be deducted from the measure of exposure in order to avoid double counting. The *exposure measure* of the leverage ratio complies with the following rules, which are similar to the accounting measure of exposure:[296]

(1) it should include on-balance sheet, non-derivative exposures, net of specific provisions and valuation adjustments;
(2) physical or financial collateral, guarantees or credit risk mitigation purchased is not allowed to reduce on-balance sheet exposures; and
(3) netting of loans and deposits is not allowed.

Banks should include items using their accounting balance sheet for the purposes of the leverage ratio. In addition, the exposure measure should include:

(1) securities financing transactions, such as repo agreements, which can often be an important source of balance sheet leverage;
(2) derivatives (whether on-or-off balance sheet),[297] including where a bank sells credit protection using a credit derivative, under the special treatment rules contained in the Basel III document;[298] and
(3) all off-balance sheet items, including liquidity facilities and other similar commitments, unconditionally cancellable commitments, direct credit substitutes, acceptances, standby letters of credit, trade letters of credit, failed transactions and unsettled securities. Since OBS items are a source of potentially significant leverage, banks should calculate the above OBS items for the purposes of the leverage ratio by applying a uniform 100 per cent credit conversion factor (CCF), which is

---

[295] BCBS, 'Basel III: A Global Regulatory Framework', p. 4.
[296] *Ibid.*, p. 61.
[297] BCBS clarifies that: 'Derivatives create two types of exposure: an "on-balance sheet" present value reflecting the fair value of the contract (often zero at outset but subsequently positive or negative depending on the performance of the contract), and a notional economic exposure representing the underlying economic interest of the contract', *ibid.*, p. 62, para. 160.
[298] *Ibid.*, p. 62.

measure of bank counterparty exposure. For any commitments that are unconditionally cancellable at any time by the bank without prior notice, banks should apply a CCF of 10 per cent.

Through the inclusion of the above to the 'leverage ratio', Basel III tries to prevent 'system-wide build up' of supposedly low risk or highly rated instruments and also to limit excessive concentration of such instruments.[299] It also limits bank incentives for regulatory arbitrage by driving assets off-balance sheet. Another benefit that might arise from the implementation of the leverage ratio is of a macro-prudential nature. Since during times of credit growth, economic leverage builds in the system causing systemic disruptions during the unwinding phase of the leverage cycle, limiting leverage means that the reduction of credit growth during the deleveraging phase might become much less severe. This could afford the real economy a softer landing, making recessions that normally follow periods of debt accumulation much less pronounced, and the ensuing increase in bank non-performing loans less threatening. Thus, it can be used to contain the consequences of Ponzi finance, as per Minsky's 'financial instability' hypothesis, discussed in Chapter 2, and enhance the financial system's macro-stability.

The BCBS will use the transition period to monitor banks' leverage data on a semi-annual basis in order to assess whether the proposed design and calibration of the minimum Tier 1 leverage ratio of 3 per cent is appropriate over a full credit cycle and for different types of business models. Accounting standards and practices will also be closely monitored to address any differences in national accounting frameworks that are material to the definition and calculation of the leverage ratio.

4.4   Liquidity ratios

As mentioned earlier, Basel III requires, subject to a transitional period, the introduction of minimum liquidity standards to make banks more resilient to potential short-term funding disruptions. These are the

---

[299] See Hervé Hannoun, 'The Basel III Capital Framework: a Decisive Breakthrough', BOJ–BIS High Level Seminars on Financial Regulatory Reform: Implications for Asia and the Pacific, Hong Kong SAR, 22 November 2010, p. 5, available at www.bis.org/speeches/sp101125a.pdf; Stefan Walter, 'Basel III: Stronger Banks and a more Resilient Financial System', 2011, p. 4, available at www.bis.org/speeches/sp110406.pdf. Conference on Basel III, Financial Stability Institute, Basel, 6 April. Such instruments include tranches of AAA structured products such as CDOs and ABS, CDSs and highly rated sovereign debt.

liquidity coverage ratio (LCR) and the net stable funding ratio (NSFR). To facilitate consistent implementation of liquidity standards by national regulators, BCBS has harmonized the parameters used in the standards with predetermined values. Yet in the case of a few parameters, national discretion remains. Also the ratios must be supplemented by detailed supervisory assessments of other aspects of banks' liquidity risk management framework in line with the BCBS 'Sound Principles',[300] without preventing supervisors from adopting more stringent standards or parameters to reflect a bank's liquidity risk profile.[301]

4.4.1   Liquidity coverage ratio

As mentioned above the objective of this standard is to ensure that banks maintain an adequate level of 'unencumbered, high-quality liquid assets that can be converted into cash to meet its liquidity needs for a 30 calendar day time horizon under a significantly severe liquidity stress scenario specified by supervisors'.[302] At a minimum, the stock of liquid assets should enable the bank to survive until day 30 of the stress scenario. This gives management and supervisors sufficient time to take appropriate corrective actions. In the event of a liquidity crunch, Basel III defines this standard as follows:

$$\frac{\text{Stock of high-quality liquid assets}}{\text{Total net cash outflows over the next 30 calendar days}} \geq 100\%$$

Accordingly, the LCR has two components: (1) the value of the stock of high-quality liquid assets in stressed conditions; and (2) total net cash outflows, calculated according to the scenario parameters discussed below. The standard is quite stringent as it requires that the value of the LCR is at all times, over thirty calendar days, no lower than 100 per cent,[303] namely,

---

[300] BCBS, 'Principles for Sound Liquidity Risk Management and Supervision', September 2008. This BCBS guidance – arranged around seventeen principles for managing and supervising liquidity risk – takes account of lessons learned during the crisis and is based on a fundamental review of sound practices for managing liquidity risk in banking organizations. The guidance for supervisors has also been augmented substantially. It emphasizes the importance of supervisors assessing the adequacy of a bank's liquidity risk management framework and its level of liquidity, and suggests steps that supervisors should take if these are deemed inadequate. The principles also stress the importance of effective co-operation between supervisors and other key stakeholders, such as central banks, especially in times of stress.

[301] BCBS, 'Basel III: International Framework for Liquidity Risk Measurement, Standards and Monitoring', December 2010, pp. 2–3.

[302] BCBS, 'International Framework for Liquidity Risk Measurement', p. 3.

[303] BCBS explains that LCR is based on traditional liquidity 'coverage ratio' methodologies used internally by banks to assess exposure to contingent liquidity events. *Ibid.*

that the stock of high-quality liquid assets does not fall below the value of total net cash outflows over the specified period. To meet this requirement on a continuous basis banks must hold a stock of unencumbered, high-quality liquid assets, which would shield them from any severe liquidity stresses. Given the uncertain timing of cash outflows and inflows, bank supervisors should also monitor any potential mismatches within the thirty-day period and ensure that sufficient liquid assets are available to meet any cash-flow gaps throughout the period. [304] The liquidity stress scenarios taken into account by the BCBS proposals refer to combined idiosyncratic and market-wide shocks, which incorporate many of the shocks experienced during the GFC (into one stress scenario). Thus, they are rather severe.[305] They include:

(1) a depositors' run leading to loss of a proportion of retail deposits: (a) Stable deposits (run-off rate = 5 per cent and higher), (b) Less stable deposits (run-off rates = 10 per cent and higher);
(2) a partial drying-up of wholesale lending markets, leading to a partial loss of unsecured wholesale funding;[306]
(3) a panic or a run on the repo market, which would result in a partial loss of secured,[307] short-term financing based on certain collateral and counterparties;
(4) additional contractual outflows that would arise from a downgrade in the bank's public credit rating by up to and including three notches, including collateral posting requirements;
(5) increases in market volatilities that impact on the quality of collateral or potential future exposure of derivative positions and thus require

---

[304] *Ibid.*, p. 3.
[305] In spite of their stringency, BCBS views its stress testing scenarios as a minimum supervisory requirement and banks are expected to conduct their own stress tests to assess the level of liquidity they should hold beyond this minimum, in accordance with the specific nature of their business activities. Internal stress tests should incorporate longer time horizons than the one mandated by LCR. Banks should share the results of their internal liquidity stress tests with their supervisors. *Ibid.*, p. 4.
[306] This includes the following run-off rates for each of the following types of funding: unsecured wholesale funding provided by small business customers: 5 per cent, 10 per cent, and higher; unsecured wholesale funding with operational relationships: 25 per cent; unsecured wholesale funding provided by non-financial corporates and sovereigns, central banks and public sector entities: 75 per cent; unsecured wholesale funding provided by other legal entity customers: 100 percent. BCBS, 'International Framework for Liquidity Risk Measurement', pp. 14–17.
[307] '"Secured funding" means liabilities and general obligations that are collateralised by legal rights to specifically designated assets owned by the borrowing institution in the case of bankruptcy, insolvency, liquidation or resolution', *ibid.*, p. 17.

larger collateral haircuts or additional collateral, or lead to other liquidity needs;

(6) unscheduled drawings on committed but unused credit and liquidity facilities that the bank has provided to its clients; and

(7) the potential need for the bank to buy back debt or honour non-contractual obligations in the interest of mitigating reputational risk.

The numerator of the LCR is the 'stock of high-quality liquid assets', which means the stock of unencumbered high-quality liquid assets to cover the total net cash outflows over a thirty-day period under the afore-mentioned stress scenario. In order to qualify as a 'high-quality liquid asset', assets should be liquid in markets during a time of stress and, if possible, be central bank eligible, which essentially means that they must be assets that can be easily and immediately converted into cash at little or no loss of value. Basel III describes as assets that are more likely to generate funds without incurring large discounts due to fire sales even in times of stress, assets that present the following characteristics:[308]

(1) *Low credit and market risk*: this characteristic is possessed by assets whose issuer has a high credit standing and which possess a low degree of subordination as well as by short-term assets, in easily convertible currencies with low volatility and exchange risk;

(2) *Ease and certainty of valuation*: an asset's liquidity increases if market participants are more likely to agree on its valuation, which, in practice, excludes most of structured credit products;

(3) *Low correlation with risky assets*: this characteristic excludes holding short term debt issued by financial institutions, which is likely to be illiquid in times of liquidity stress in the banking sector;

(4) *Assets listed on a developed and recognized exchange market*: such a listing may increase the transparency of asset pricing and provide stable prices, but a number of short-term liquid instruments are unlikely to be listed;

(5) *Active and sizable market*: the asset should have active outright sale or repurchase agreement (repo) markets at all times (which means having a large number of market participants and a high trading volume). There should be historical evidence of market breadth (price impact per unit of liquidity) and market depth (units of the asset that can be traded for a given price impact).

---

[308] *Ibid.*, p. 5.

Basel III also adds market (micro-)structure elements to the list of characteristics of 'highly liquid assets', such as, (1) the presence of committed market makers, who are bound to provide a liquid market and reasonable prices for the assets concerned; (2) low market concentration which would prevent market price distortions due to monopolistic price behaviour or liquidity hoarding; and (3) flight to quality properties.[309] Accordingly, the test of whether liquid assets are of 'high-quality' is centred on whether, by way of sale or secured borrowing, 'their liquidity-generating capacity is assumed to remain intact even in periods of severe idiosyncratic and market stress'. There are also *operational requirements* in order to regard assets as 'highly liquid'. These mainly refer to asset ability to convert into cash at any time to fill funding gaps between cash inflows and outflows during the stressed period. Thus, the assets must be unencumbered[310] and should be under the control of the specific function or functions charged with managing the liquidity risk of the bank (typically the treasurer).

Furthermore, Basel III describes two categories of assets that can be included in the stock of 'highly liquid assets'. 'Level 1' assets can be included in the pool without limit. They comprise assets held at market value and not susceptible to haircut such as: (1) cash; (2) central bank reserves, if they can be drawn down in times of stress; (c) marketable securities representing claims on or claims guaranteed by sovereigns, central banks, non-central government Public Sector Entities (PSEs), the Bank for International Settlements, the International Monetary Fund, the European Commission, or multilateral development banks.[311] 'Level 2' assets can only comprise up to 40 per cent of the overall stock of 'highly liquid assets' after haircuts have been applied. Level 2 instruments are corporate and covered bonds and marketable securities representing claims on or claims guaranteed by sovereigns, central banks,

---

[309] *Ibid.*, pp. 5–6.

[310] 'Unencumbered' means not pledged (either explicitly or implicitly) to secure, collateralize or credit-enhance any transaction. However, assets received in reverse repo and securities financing transactions that are held at the bank, have not been re-hypothecated, and are legally and contractually available for the bank's use can be considered as part of the stock. In addition, assets which qualify for the stock of high-quality liquid assets that have been pledged to the central bank or a public sector entity (PSE) but are not used may be included in the stock. *Ibid.*, p. 7.

[311] Such marketable securities must satisfy the following conditions: (1) they must have been assigned a 0 per cent risk-weight under the Basel II Standardized Approach; (2) they must be traded in large, deep and active repo or cash markets characterized by a low level of concentration; (3) they must have a proven record as a reliable source of liquidity in the markets (repo or sale) even during stressed market conditions; and (4) they should not be an obligation of a financial institution or any of its affiliated entities, *ibid.*, p 8.

non-central government PSEs or multilateral development banks that satisfy specific conditions.[312]

4.4.2   Net stable funding ratio

(a)   **Objective**   The NSFR is meant to promote more medium- and long-term funding of bank assets and activities. This metric establishes a minimum acceptable amount of stable funding based on the liquidity characteristics of an institution's assets and activities over a period of one year. This standard is designed to act as a minimum enforcement mechanism to complement the LCR and reinforce other supervisory efforts by promoting structural changes in the liquidity risk profiles of institutions away from short-term funding mismatches and toward more stable, longer-term funding of assets and business activities.

In particular, the NSFR standard is structured to ensure that long term assets are funded with at least a minimum amount of stable liabilities in relation to their liquidity risk profiles. Thus, it aims to limit over-reliance on short-term wholesale funding during times of buoyant market liquidity and encourage better assessment of liquidity risk across all on- and off-balance sheet items. Thus, it promotes longer term planning of a bank's funding needs and reinforces supervisory efforts to promote structural changes in the liquidity risk profiles of institutions, forcing them to move away from short-term funding mismatches experienced before and during the GFC. In addition, the NSFR approach offsets incentives for institutions to arbitrage by funding their stock of liquid assets with short-term funds that mature just outside the thirty-day period required by the LCR.

(b)   **Definition of the standard**

$$\frac{\text{Available amount of stable funding}}{\text{Required amount of stable funding}} > 100\%$$

Under this standard the minimum acceptable amount of stable funding based on the liquidity characteristics of an institution's assets and activities over a one year horizon should be 100 per cent. In computing the amount of assets that should be backed by stable funding, the methodology includes required amounts of stable funding for all illiquid assets and securities held, regardless of accounting treatment (e.g. trading versus available-for-sale or held-to-maturity designations). Additional stable funding sources are also required to support at least a small portion of the

---

[312] *Ibid.*, p. 9.

potential calls on liquidity arising from off-balance sheet commitments and contingencies.

Stable funding is defined as the portion of those types and amounts of equity and liability financing expected to be reliable sources of funds over a one-year time horizon under conditions of extended stress.[313] Available stable funding (ASF) is defined as the total amount of a bank's:

(1) capital;
(2) preferred stock with maturity of equal to or greater than one year;
(3) liabilities with effective maturities of one year or greater;
(4) portion of non-maturity deposits and/or term deposits with maturities of less than one year that would be expected to stay with the institution for an extended period in an idiosyncratic stress event; and
(5) portion of wholesale funding with maturities of less than a year that is expected to stay with the institution for an extended period in an idiosyncratic stress event.

Moreover, the objective of the standard is to ensure stable funding on an ongoing, viable entity basis, over one year in an extended firm-specific stress scenario where a bank encounters, and investors and customers become aware of:[314]

(1) a significant decline in the profitability of the institution concerned or its financial state (solvency) arising from heightened credit risk, market risk or operational risk and/or other risk exposures;
(2) downgrading of its debt, counterparty credit or deposit rating by any nationally recognized credit rating organization; and/or
(3) a material event that calls into question the reputation or credit standing/quality of the institution.

The amount of stable funding required by supervisors is calculated as the sum of the value of the assets held and funded by the institution, multiplied by a specific required stable funding (RSF) factor assigned to each particular asset type, added to the amount of off-balance sheet activity (or potential liquidity exposure) multiplied by its associated RSF factor. The RSF factor applied to the reported values of each asset or OBS exposure is the amount of that item that supervisors believe should be supported with stable funding. Naturally, assets that are more liquid and more readily available to act as a source of extended liquidity in the stressed environment identified above receive lower RSF factors (and require less stable

---

[313] *Ibid.*, pp. 25–6.   [314] *Ibid.*, p. 27.

funding) than assets considered less liquid in such circumstances and, therefore, require more stable funding.[315]

4.4.3   Liquidity monitoring tools

In addition to the aforementioned standards,the BCBS has proposed a number of tools to monitor liquidity in the form of metrics that capture specific information related to a bank's cash flows, balance sheet structure, available unencumbered collateral and certain market indicators. The main objective of these metrics is to provide supervisors with important information required to assess the liquidity risk of a bank. In addition, supervisors may use additional tools and metrics to capture elements of liquidity risk specific to their jurisdictions. The main liquidity metrics suggested by the BCBS as monitoring tools, in addition to LCR and NSFR, are:[316]

(a)   **Contractual maturity mismatches**   This metric profiles contractual cash and security inflows and outflows from all on- and off-balance sheet items, mapped to defined time bands based on their respective maturities. It, thus, identifies the gaps between the contractual inflows and outflows of liquidity for defined time bands. These maturity gaps indicate how much liquidity a bank would potentially need to raise in each of these time bands if all outflows occurred at the earliest possible date. The metric provides insight regarding the extent of the bank's reliance on maturity transformation under its current contracts;

(b)   **Concentration of funding**   This metric[317] is designed to identify those sources of wholesale funding that are of such significance that its withdrawal could trigger liquidity problems. Essentially, the metric

---

[315] The metric for the calculation of RSF for various types of on-balance sheet and off-balance sheet items may be found in Tables 2 and 3 respectively of BCBS, 'Basel III: International Framework for Liquidity Risk Measurement, Standards and Monitoring', pp. 29–31.

[316] *Ibid.*, p. 31. There is a transitional period for liquidity ratios as well. Thus, 'the LCR will be introduced on 1 January 2015. The NSFR will move to a minimum standard by 1 January 2018. The Committee will put in place rigorous reporting processes to monitor the ratios during the transition period and will continue to review the implications of these standards for financial markets, credit extension and economic growth, addressing unintended consequences … Both the LCR and the NSFR will be subject to an observation period and will include a review clause to address any unintended consequences.' BCBS, 'Basel III: Global Regulatory Framework', p. 10.

[317] BCBS, 'International Framework for Liquidity Risk Measurement', p. 33.

encourages the diversification of funding sources recommended in the BCBS's 'Sound Principles'.[318] It is illustrated as follows:

A. Funding liabilities sourced from each significant counterparty
The bank's balance sheet total

B. Funding liabilities sourced from each significant product/instrument
The bank's balance sheet total

C. List of asset and liability amounts by significant currency

The numerator for A and B refers to funding concentrations by counterparty or type of instrument/product. Banks and supervisors should monitor both the absolute percentage of the funding exposure, as well as significant increases in concentrations. A significant counterparty is regarded as 'a single counterparty or group of connected or affiliated counterparties accounting in aggregate for more than 1% of the bank's total balance sheet, although in some cases there may be other defining characteristics based on the funding profile of the bank'.[319] A 'significant instrument/product' is defined as a single instrument/product or group of similar instruments/products that in aggregate amount to more than 1 per cent of the bank's total balance sheet.[320] For numerator C banks are required to provide a list of the amount of assets and liabilities in each significant currency. It is intended to capture structural currency mismatches in bank assets and liabilities, which could create a liquidity problem that specifically refers to availability of funding in a specific currency. A currency is considered 'significant' if the aggregate liabilities denominated in that currency amount to 5 per cent or more of the bank's total liabilities. To make them more effective, the above metrics should be reported separately for the time horizons of less than one month, on to three months, three to six months, six to twelve months, and for longer than twelve months.

(c)   **Available unencumbered assets**   This metric measures the amount of available unencumbered assets that are marketable as collateral in secondary markets and/or eligible for central banks' standing facilities. Banks must report the amount, type and location of available unencumbered assets that could (1) serve as collateral for secured borrowing in secondary markets at prearranged or current haircuts at reasonable costs;

---

[318] BCBS, 'Principles for Sound Liquidity Risk Management'.
[319] BCBS, 'International Framework for Liquidity Risk Measurement', p. 35, para. 154.
[320] *Ibid.*, para. 156.

or (2) are eligible for secured financing with relevant central banks at pre-arranged (if available) or current haircuts at reasonable costs for standing facilities only. It follows that emergency assistance arrangements are excluded from this calculation.

(d)   LCR by significant currency   To avoid liquidity problems emanating from currency mismatches between assets and liabilities, banks and supervisors will also monitor the LCR in significant currencies to allow the bank and the supervisor to track potential currency mismatch issues that could arise.[321] The metric is illustrated as follows:'

$$\text{Foreign Currency LCR} = \frac{\text{Stock of high-quality liquid assets in each significant currency}}{\text{Total net cash outflows over a 30-day time period in each significant currency.}}$$

(e)   Market-related monitoring tools   This tool refers to the use of market data as an early warning indicator in monitoring potential liquidity difficulties at banks.[322] The data most pertinent for purposes of liquidity monitoring would include: (1) *market-wide information* referring to the absolute level and direction of major markets; (2) *information on the financial sector* which mirrors broader market movements or indicates whether the sector is experiencing difficulties (e.g., equity and debt market information for the financial sector, broadly the movement of specific financial sector indices); (3) *bank-specific information* which may indicate whether the market is losing confidence in a particular institution or has identified risks at an institution (e.g., information on equity prices, CDS spreads, money-market trading prices, lengths of funding, the price/yield of bank debenture and/or subordinated debt in the secondary market).

4.5   Risk management and supervision

The Basel III framework has stressed the need for stronger capital and liquidity standards to be accompanied by better risk management and supervision, the failure of which was at the heart of the GFC, especially with respect to the use of financial innovation. In July 2009, the BCBS conducted a review of the Pillar 2 supervisory review process to address

---

[321] See *ibid.*, p. 37 for a full illustration of this metric.
[322] *Ibid.*, pp. 37–8.

several notable weaknesses that were revealed in banks' risk management processes during the financial crisis. The areas addressed included:[323]

(1) firm-wide governance and risk management;
(2) capturing the risk of off-balance sheet exposures and securitization activities;
(3) managing risk concentrations;
(4) providing incentives for banks to better manage risk and returns over the long term; and
(5) sound compensation practices.[324]

In response to the findings of this consultation, the Basel II framework increased the risk sensitivity and coverage of the regulatory capital requirement, allowing to capture (previously neglected) key exposures, such as complex trading activities, resecuritizations and exposures to OBS activities. Accordingly in order to address the excess cyclicality of the minimum capital requirement, key risk measures such as probability of default (PD) and loss-given-default (LGD) will be calculated over long-term data horizons.

Furthermore, the BCBS is promoting stronger provisioning practices, which are thought to protect better against increased risk of default during a downturn. The BCBS advocates a change in the way accounting standards measure loss, and strongly supports the IASB initiative to move to an expected loss (EL) approach in lieu of the current incurred loss approach. The EL approach captures actual losses more transparently and is less procyclical than the 'incurred loss' approach. It also provides incentives for stronger provisioning in the Basel III capital framework.[325]

The BCBS also tries to extend the capital framework to capture major on- and off-balance sheet risks, as well as derivative-related exposures, which were largely ignored by the Basel II framework and proved a key destabilizing factor during the GFC. In July 2009 it introduced a number of critical reforms to the Basel II framework in order to raise capital requirements for the trading book and complex securitization exposures, which, as explained in Chapter 3, proved to be a major source of losses

---

[323] BCBS, 'Basel Committee's Response to the Financial Crisis: Report to the G20', October 2010, p. 6, available at www.bis.org/publ/bcbs179.pdf.
[324] For BCBS recommendations on the issue of banker compensation and its alignment with performance and risks employees take on behalf of the bank, see BCBS, 'Range of Methodologies for Risk and Performance Alignment of Remuneration – Final Document' 12 May 2011, available at www.bis.org/publ/bcbs194.htm.
[325] BCBS, 'Basel III: A Global Regulatory Framework', p.6.

for big banks. The enhanced treatment introduces a stressed value-at-risk (VaR) capital requirement based on a continuous twelve-month period of significant financial stress. In addition, the BCBS has introduced higher capital requirements for resecuritizations with respect to both the banking and the trading book.[326]

A number of other reforms raise the standards of the Pillar 2 supervisory review process and strengthen Pillar 3 disclosures. The Pillar 1 and Pillar 3 enhancements have short implementation timetables; the Pillar 2 standards became effective when they were introduced in July 2009. In addition the BCBS is conducting a radical review of the trading book concept and capital requirements with a view to introducing measures to strengthen the capital requirements for counterparty credit exposures arising from banks' derivatives, repo and securities financing activities, and to raising the capital buffers relating to these exposures. The new rules that will derive from the review would also reduce procyclicality and provide additional incentives to move OTC derivative contracts to central counterparties to reduce systemic risk across the financial system.

The new rules also provide incentives to strengthen the risk management of counterparty credit exposures. Thus, under Basel III:

(1) banks must determine their capital requirement for counterparty credit risk using stressed inputs. This will address concerns about capital charges becoming too low during periods of compressed market volatility and help address procyclicality, promoting more integrated management of market and counterparty credit risk;[327]

(2) banks will be subject to a capital charge for potential mark-to-market losses (i.e., credit valuation adjustment (CVA) risk) associated with a deterioration in the credit worthiness of a counterparty. While the Basel II standard covers the risk of a counterparty default, it does not address such CVA risk, which during the financial crisis was a greater source of losses than those arising from outright defaults;[328]

(3) banks with large and illiquid derivative exposures to a counterparty will have to apply longer margining periods as a basis for determining the regulatory capital requirement.[329]

To address the systemic risk arising from the interconnectedness of banks and other financial institutions through the derivatives markets, BCBS is supporting the efforts of the Committee on Payments and

---

[326] *Ibid.*, p. 3.   [327] *Ibid.*, paras. 97–8.
[328] *Ibid.*, paras. 99–102.   [329] *Ibid.*, paras. 103–12.

Settlement Systems (CPSS) and IOSCO to establish strong standards for financial market infrastructures, including central counterparties (CCPs). The capitalization of bank exposures to CCPs will be treated favourably and mark-to-market exposures to approved CCPs will be subject to a low risk weight, proposed at 2 per cent; and default fund exposures to CCPs will be subject to risk-sensitive capital requirements. It is expected that this favourable approach, together with strengthened capital requirements for bilateral OTC derivative exposures, will create strong incentives for banks to move exposures to such CCPs and in this respect the BCBS measures are much in accord with the US and EU reforms of derivatives markets discussed above.[330]

The BCBS has considered a number of measures to mitigate the reliance on external ratings of the Basel II framework. The measures include requirements for banks to perform their own internal assessments of externally rated securitization exposures and the incorporation of key elements of the IOSCO 'Code of Conduct Fundamentals for Credit Rating Agencies' into the Committee's eligibility criteria for the use of external ratings in the capital framework.[331] Finally, following a fundamental review of the securitization framework, including its reliance on external ratings, BCBS will reconsider the use of ratings in the capital framework for securitizations.

4.6   Evaluation of Basel III

As mentioned earlier Basel III capital requirements constitute a significant improvement over Basel II. The definition of capital is clearer, the portion of CET1 has increased considerably raising institutions' loss absorption capacity and the capital conservation buffer can act as an effective break to harmful 'distributions', when the institution faces serious financial difficulties. In addition, the introduction of (non-risk weighted) leverage and especially liquidity ratios is bound to increase the resilience of banking institutions.

On the other hand, Basel III has several shortcomings. The countercyclical buffer is bound to prove controversial both with respect to differentiated national ratios and effectiveness. It might even lead

---

[330]   *Ibid.*, p. 4 and para. 113. See also BCBS, 'Capitalisation of Bank Exposures to Central Counterparties – Consultative Document', 4 February 2011, available at www.bis.org/publ/bcbs190.htm.

[331]   *Ibid.*, paras. 118–21.

to regulatory races to the bottom (in this case the Basel III minimum requirements). Also it might prove unable to restrict credit growth if it is not aided by fiscal or monetary tools. Moreover, apart from a long transitional period, which largely reflects the general weakness of bank balance sheets in this period, three major weaknesses of the Basel III framework might undermine its effective implementation.

First, the value of Tier 2 capital comprising non-convertible debt is strongly disputed. The reason that financial institutions prefer debt is that it is cheaper to them, due to the fact that banks can receive better tax treatment and other incentives for issued debt, since interest payments tend to be tax deductible, as opposed to dividends paid on equity. Thus, it might just be an issue of misaligned regulatory incentives and unjustified public subsidies through tax.[332]

Second, it is always open to doubt whether the continuation of a capital measurement approach that is based on risk weights, which was the Basel II foundation and is embraced also by Basel III, can ever be really credible.[333] Either the banks will feel obliged to manipulate their internal ratings or reporting methodologies or the CRAs will furnish them with procyclical or unreliable ratings that distort risk calculations.[334] In addition, the advancements in risk modelling, even if it has not increased their ability to measure risk or capture uncertainty, problems discussed extensively in Chapters 3 and 5, has increased its complexity.[335] The resulting risk weightings might be no more that an 'article of faith as fact, as much

[332] This claim about the cost advantage of debt issuance has been disputed by Anat R. Admati, Peter M. DeMarzo, Martin F. Hellwig and Paul C. Pfleiderer, 'Fallacies, Irrelevant Facts, and Myths in the Discussion of Capital Regulation: Why Bank Equity is not Expensive', Stanford Graduate School of Business Research Paper No. 2065, 20 March 2011, available at papers.ssrn.com/sol3/papers.cfm?abstract_id=1669704&rec=1&srcabs=1645224.

[333] 'The most serious failure in Basel III is that it doesn't address the principal contribution of Basel II to the last financial crisis, namely, the calculation of risk-weights.' See 'Basel III Third Time's the Charm?' The Economist, Economics/Free Exchange, 13 September 2010, available at www.economist.com/blogs/freeexchange/2010/09/basel_iii. Also Martin Hellwig (the new chairman of the advisory scientific committee of the ESRB) argues that risk models should not be used in capital regulations because they cannot provide an accurate picture of the probability (and thus of the size of required capital) for the least visible, and thus most dangerous, of the risks assumed by banks. See Hellwig, 'Capital Regulation After the Crisis', pp. 7–8, 10, 14–15.

[334] For a note of how Basel III risk-weightings can be twisted and manipulated see Tracy Alloway, 'How to Tinker with Bank Risk-weightings' Financial Times/Alphaville, 8 June 2011, available at ftalphaville.ft.com/blog/2011/06/08/588106/how-to-tinker-with-bank-risk-weightings/.

[335] Andrew Haldane, 'Capital Discipline', Speech given at the American Economic Association, Denver, 9 January 2011, p. 4. available at www.bis/org/review/r110325a.pdf.

art as science' inhibiting both regulatory review and market discipline, in spite of full disclosure.[336] Moreover, there is the issue of robustness that most models fail to achieve, leaving the application of new Basell III ratios that are based on RWAs open to model error, which also weakens regulatory review and market monitoring of bank compliance with the required standards.

Third, like Basel II, Basel III risk modelling does not deal effectively with 'fat tails'. As banks now move to business practices that will not add measurable risk, risk could be pushed to the 'tails', because 'tail risk' (very low risk of default) is normally ignored.[337] Yet, as explained in Chapter 3, correlations of tail risk, which are notoriously unpredictable and unstable, were at the heart of the GFC. In the same mode, Basel III is, arguably, not an effective way to counter endogenous risk, due to herding and other mechanisms that lead the financial services industry to homogeneity. It is, therefore, doubtful whether capital regulation reduces the risk of systemic collapse,[338] especially, in the absence of comprehensive (and binding) mechanisms for the effective resolution of cross-border financial groups.

Fourth, the financial stability benefits the new Accord brings must be weighed against costs of implementation both in terms of bank increased operating costs and loss of output. The benefits of a more stable financial system and more resilient banks that lead to reduction of future banking crises are, of course, obvious but at the same time very difficult to model and quantify.[339] The BCBS insists in its special studies that the increase in bank operating costs resulting from the implementation of the new capital standards and loss of output will be very small (up to 35 basis points for every capital increase of 1 per cent)[340] and will be easily offset by the economic benefits arising from enhanced financial stability.[341] However, these

---

[336] Ibid., p. 4.

[337] See Felix Salmon, 'The Biggest Weakness of Basel III', Reuters, 24 September 2010, available at blogs.reuters.com/felix-salmon/2010/09/15/the-biggest-weakness-of-basel-iii/.

[338] See Hal S. Scot, 'Reducing Systemic Risk Through the Reform of Capital Regulation' (2010) 13 Journal of International Economic Law 763, pp. 777–8.

[339] See BCBS, 'An Assessment of the Long-term Economic Impact of Capital and Liquidity Regulations', August 2010, pp. 5–7, available at www.bis.org/publ/bcbs173.htm.

[340] FSB/BCBS Macroeconomic Assessment Group, 'Assessing the Macroeconomic Impact of the Transition to Stronger Capital and Liquidity Requirements', August 2010; BCBS, 'An Assessment of the Long-term Economic Impact', pp. 3, 9–12.

[341] First, each 1 percentage point increase in the capital ratio raises loan spreads by 13 basis points. Second, the additional cost of meeting the liquidity standard amounts to around 25 basis points in lending spreads when risk-weighted assets (RWA) are left unchanged; however, it drops to 14 basis points or less after taking account of the fall in RWA and

findings are strongly disputed by the Institute of International Finance, which shows a substantial loss of output and job losses.[342] Therefore, the full quantification of actual increases in the cost of banking and loss of output, due to the new capital, liquidity, and leverage provisions of Basel III are still open to question.

the corresponding lower regulatory capital needs associated with the higher holdings of low-risk assets. 'BCBS, An Assessment of the Long-term Economic Impact', p. 4.

[342] IIF projects that implementation of the new capital standards will reduce the real GDP of the US, Euro Area, and Japan by about 3.1 per cent below what it otherwise would be, and that there would be 9.5 million fewer jobs. See Institute of International Finance, 'The Net Cumulative Economic Impact on the Global Economy of Proposed Changes in the Banking Regulatory Framework', June 2010, pp. 9, 49. See also Institute of International Finance, 'The Net Cumulative Economic Impact of Banking Sector Regulation: Some New Perspectives', October 2010, pp. 12–17, available at www.iif.com/download.php?id=/0eTxourA+A=.

7

Global reform of the 'too-big-to-fail' institution and the new resolution regimes in the US and the EU

1. Introduction

The failure of Lehman Brothers and the near collapse of some of the world's mightiest financial institutions together with the public cost involved in their rescue, which in some cases has forced entire countries into bankruptcy (e.g., Iceland) or near bankruptcy (e.g., Ireland), has given rise to endless policy discussions considering the best policies to address the moral hazard and other catastrophic externalities that may arise from the operation of 'too-big-to-fail' institutions (also called Systemically Important Financial Institutions (SIFIs)) and from their cross-border presence. Proposed reforms revolve around five overlapping policy prescriptions whose main objective is to contain the risk from the operation of SIFIs and even more from that of the super class of financial institutions with a strong cross-border presence, called G-SIFIs. These policy proposals may be grouped as follows:[1]

(1) a requirement for additional capital to be held by SIFIs in the form of contingent capital instruments (CoCos) and a capital surcharge imposed on G-SIFIs;

---

[1] The policy framework for SIFIs recommended by the FSB is slightly different, since it does not include structural measures. It combines: (1) a resolution framework and other measures to ensure that all financial institutions can be resolved safely, quickly and without destabilizing the financial system and exposing the taxpayer to the risk of loss; (2) a requirement that SIFIs and initially, in particular, global SIFIs (G-SIFIs) have higher loss absorbency capacity to reflect the greater risks that these institutions pose to the global financial system; (3) more intensive supervisory oversight for financial institutions which may pose systemic risk; (4) robust core financial market infrastructures to reduce contagion risk from the failure of individual institutions; and (5) supplementary prudential and other requirements determined by the national authorities. See FSB, 'Reducing the Moral Hazard Posed by Systemically Important Financial Institutions – FSB Recommendations and Time Lines', 20 October 2010, p. 2.

(2) forms of separation of commercial from investment banking;
(3) limitations on bank size and on engagement in certain risky activities;
(4) imposing on SIFIs a stricter supervision regime that includes regular stress tests and the obligation to prepare *ex ante* recovery and resolution plans (so-called 'living wills');[2] and
(5) introduction of special resolution regimes facilitating the orderly liquidation (or re-organization) of SIFIs, which operate outside of the restraints of ordinary insolvency (and company) law, and minimizing the cost of bank failures to the taxpayer and the disruption to the functions of the financial system.

The Basel Committee on Banking Supervision (BCBS) and the Financial Stability Board (FSB) have been heavily involved with the formulation of most of the above proposals, although this is no guarantee, due to their soft law nature, that their standards will in the end be consistently implemented by national legislators and regulators. The FSB and BCBS are developing an integrated approach to address the risks emanating from the operation of SIFIs through a combination of capital surcharges and bail-in debt.[3] The latter is 'debt that converts to equity in stages as particular financial thresholds are breached'.[4]

The FSB/BCBS approach to SIFI regulation through CoCos has, in part, been endorsed by the US Dodd–Frank Act, which authorizes the Federal Reserve Board (FRB) to mandate the use of contingent capital (Section 165(b)(1)(B) of the Dodd–Frank Act), and the EU Resolution framework proposed by the Commission.[5] In addition, through the Orderly Liquidation Authority (OLA) procedure in the Dodd–Frank Act

---

[2] Living wills not only strengthen the effectiveness of supervision but also make easier the navigation of the multitude of regulators around the legal maze of complex corporate structures and business relationships that cross-border financial groups maintain, facilitating the speed and effectiveness of resolutions of cross-border groups especially.

[3] See BCBS, 'Measures for Global Systemically Important Banks Agreed by the Group of Governors and Heads of Supervision' Press Release, 25 June 2011, available at www.bis.org/press/p110625.htm. BCBS suggestions were first discussed in FSB, 'Progress in the Implementation of the G20 Recommendations for Strengthening Financial Stability – Report of the Financial Stability Board to G20 Finance Ministers and Central Bank Governors', 10 April 2011.

[4] BCBS, 'Proposal to Ensure the Loss Absorbency of Regulatory Capital at the Point of Non-viability', Consultative Document, August 2010.

[5] EU Commission, 'An EU Framework for Crisis Management in the Financial Sector' COM (2010) 579; EU Commission Working Document, 'A Possible EU Framework for Bank Recovery and Resolution', 6 January 2011.

(Title II), the US authorities have at their disposal tailor-made tools and processes to deal with SIFI failure. Also, several EU countries have introduced bank resolution regimes.

The FSB and the BCBS have issued general principles that national resolution regimes should follow not only to provide effective resolution but also to build the foundations for a co-ordinated resolution of cross-border groups. However, reform efforts in the area of cross-border resolutions remain incomplete with Dodd–Frank being very thin on the issue of co-ordination for the resolution of cross-border groups and the proposed EU regime relying mostly on the IMF model of harmonization of general principles and the introduction of a contractual (mutual recognition) group resolution model. Several other loopholes may be identified in the process.[6] Arguably this may not be surprising in the absence of an international treaty providing a global resolution framework for G-SIFIS, an independent global resolution authority administering it and fiscal burden sharing arrangements between key states.

SIFIs mainly become 'too-big-to-fail' due to four factors: size, interconnectedness, the psychological impact of their failure and provision of systemically critical payment and other financial infrastructure services. I have discussed in the previous chapter the US and EU legislation initiatives to centralize OTC derivatives trading and clearing, which will both increase the derivative market's transparency and reduce interconnectedness. Other reforms targeting the size of SIFIs and the kind of activities they should be allowed to pursue also limit interconnectedness. In the US, the relevant Dodd–Frank provisions (e.g., the so-called Volker Rule) limit very significantly the ability of banks to engage in proprietary trading and shadow banking activities, including sponsoring or financing hedge funds and private equity funds. Dodd–Frank also supplements the Volcker Rule with restrictions on future increases in bank size. The UK, on the other hand, seems keen to lean on a form of ring-fencing of commercial bank operations from riskier banking activities.

The remainder of this chapter is divided into seven sections. Section 2 provides an analysis of the emerging consensus for the regulation and supervision of SIFIs, expressed through the recommendations of the FSB. Section 3 discusses the restrictions the US Dodd–Frank Act has

---

[6] IMF, 'Resolution of Cross-Border Banks – A Proposed Framework for Enhanced Coordination', 11 June 2010, available at www.imf.org/external/np/pp/eng/2010/061110.pdf.

placed on SIFIs through the Volcker Rule and other provisions and the structural restrictions that the UK authorities are considering imposing on large banks. Section 4 provides an in depth analysis of the FSB/BCBS approach to regulating the risk and (implicitly) the size of G-SIFIs through capital surcharges. It also considers the costs and benefits of contingent capital instruments and of bail-in mechanisms. Section 5 considers BCBS, FSB and IMF recommendations on the cross-border resolution of financial institutions and financial groups. Section 6 provides a concise analysis of the Dodd–Frank special resolution regime for SIFIs, the OLA, and its ramifications both for the regulation of 'too-big-to-fail' institutions in the US and co-ordination of cross-border resolutions. Section 7 provides a critical analysis and evaluation of the EU Commission proposals for a pan-European crisis management and resolution regime for banks and certain investment firms. Given the complexity and size of the topics covered in this chapter, Section 8 provides a summary of the chapter's findings and a brief conclusion.

2. FSB principles for the supervision of SIFIs

Closer supervision of SIFIs is plausibly regarded as the first line of defence against SIFI failure. According to the FSB, every country must have a supervisory infrastructure that allows it to conduct effective risk assessments and enforce attendant regulations, including the new regulations emerging as a result of Basel III, especially as they relate to SIFIs. The FSB has clarified that supervisors are expected to detect problems proactively, and intervene early to reduce the impact of potential stresses on financial institutions and therefore on the financial system as a whole. More specifically the FSB has recommended the following principles for the supervision of SIFIs:[7]

(1) national supervisors should have the power to apply differentiated supervisory requirements and intensity of supervision to SIFIs based on the risks they pose to the financial system;
(2) all national supervisory authorities should have appropriate mandates, independence and resources to identify risks early and intervene to require changes within an institution, as needed, to prevent unsound practices and take appropriate counter-measures to safeguard against the additional systemic risks;

---

[7] FSB, 'Reducing the Moral Hazard Posed by Systemically Important Financial Institutions – FSB Recommendations and Timelines', pp. 7–8.

(3) national authorities should review supervisory methodologies in the light of the lessons and improved techniques set out in the FSB 'SIFI Supervisory Intensity and Effectiveness Recommendations'[8] and make changes as needed. They should also alert themselves and other authorities to potential weaknesses in their oversight processes in a timely fashion;[9]

(4) FSAP/ROSC surveys should take into account assessments against all essential and additional criteria of the existing Basel Core Principles as they relate to the supervision of SIFIs;

(5) national supervisory frameworks should enable effective consolidated supervision. They should address ambiguity regarding responsibility and remove obstacles relating to information gathering and assessment when multiple supervisors are overseeing the institution and its affiliates;

(6) as regards G-SIFIs, home jurisdictions should: (a) enable a rigorous co-ordinated assessment of the risks facing the G-SIFIs through international supervisory colleges; (b) make international recovery and resolution planning mandatory for G-SIFIs and (c) negotiate institution-specific crisis co-operation agreements within cross-border crisis management groups.[10]

3.   Targeting bank size and speculative banking activities

3.1   The Volcker Rule

Section 619 of the Dodd–Frank Act adds a new Section 13 to the Bank Holding Company Act of 1956. Its main objective is to check the growth of big banks and curb licensed (commercial) banks involvement with the riskiest forms of banking, as proprietary trading in derivatives is often perceived to be, and the shadow banking sector. To insiders it is known as the Merkley–Levin provisions on proprietary trading and conflicts of interest, but it is widely referred to as the 'Volcker Rule', due to the fact that this reform started as a proposal by former Federal Reserve Chairman Paul Volcker. It was endorsed by President Obama. Essentially, Volcker proposed a return to the principles of the Glass–Steagall Act, but not a restoration of the Act itself. The rationale behind Volcker's proposal was that commercial banks' risk-taking activities had

---

[8] *Ibid.*   [9] *Ibid.*, p. 7   [10] *Ibid.*

to be curbed, preventing them from taking advantage of government guarantees by engaging in highly speculative investment activities.

Section 619 is narrower in its scope than the initial Volcker proposal. It bans commercial banks ('banking entities' as defined in Section 619 of the Act)[11] from engaging in proprietary trading – that is, trading and speculating for the bank's own account – and limits their investment in hedge funds or equity funds. Non-bank financial companies, which engage predominantly in financial activities and have been designated as 'systemically important' by the FSOC pursuant to Title I of the Act, are not covered by the ban. However, the Rule requires the FRB to implement rules imposing additional capital requirements and other quantitative limits with respect to their proprietary trading and private fund activities and investments.[12] The Volcker Rule is expected to become effective on 21 July 2012, but banks have at maximum a seven-year grace period to comply with the Rule by 'pushing out' certain derivative business to their subsidiaries. Also related to the Volcker Rule is a limitation of further consolidation of the US financial sector through acquisitions.[13] This constitutes a marked policy reversal from the policies of deregulation of the late 1990s that led to the formation of mega-banks and a massive consolidation of the US financial services industry discussed in Chapters 2 and 3.

More specifically, under Section 622(b) 'a financial company may not merge or consolidate with, acquire all or substantially all of the assets of, or otherwise acquire control of, another company, if the total consolidated liabilities of the acquiring financial company upon consummation of the transaction would exceed 10 per cent of the aggregate consolidated liabilities of all financial companies at the end of the calendar year preceding the transaction'. Section 622(c) exempts from this limitation the acquisition of banks in default or in danger of default, any assistance provided by the Federal Deposit Insurance Corporation (FDIC) under

---

[11] See note 14 below.
[12] See new Section 13(a)(2) of the Banking Holding Company Act of 1956.
[13] President Obama described the rationale behind the rule that limits the size of financial institutions: '[A]s part of our efforts to protect against future crises, I'm also proposing that we prevent the further consolidation of our financial system ... The American people will not be served by a financial system that comprises just a few massive firms. That's not good for consumers; it's not good for the economy. And through this policy, that is an outcome we will avoid.' Remarks by President Barack Obama, 'Additional Reforms to the Financial System, 21 January 2010', available at blogs.wsj.com/deals/2010/01/21/full-text-of-obamas-remarks-on-financial-reform/.

Section 13(c) of the Federal Deposit Insurance Act (12 USC 1823(c)) or an acquisition that would result only in a *de minimis* increase in the liabilities of the financial company.

3.2   Ban on proprietary trading

The Volcker Rule ban on proprietary trading by banking entities[14] defines as 'proprietary trading' the act of 'engaging as a principal for the trading account' of a banking entity in any transaction to buy or sell, or otherwise acquire or dispose of, any 'covered instrument'. The ban extends to trading in any security, derivative or future, or option on any of the foregoing, or any other security or financial instrument designated by the federal banking agencies, the SEC and the CFTC, which are defined as 'covered instruments'.[15] The ban does not apply to commodities such as precious or base metals, or energy or agricultural products, nor does it apply to foreign exchange or loans. The 'trading account' is defined as any account used for acquiring or taking positions in covered instruments 'principally for the purpose of selling in the near term' or otherwise with the intent to resell in order to profit from short-term price movements, and any such other accounts as regulators may determine.[16] 'Covered instruments' held for investment, as opposed to trading, are not covered by the ban.

The concept of proprietary trading is so vague that it will remain dependent on regulatory interpretation which, in turn, will be the subject of ongoing negotiations between the largest banks and the regulators.[17] Moreover, the Act contains a number of exemptions from the ban, which

---

[14] 'Banking entity' is defined to include any insured depository institution, any company that controls an insured depository institution or is treated as a bank holding company for purposes of Section 8 of the International Banking Act 1978, and any affiliate or subsidiary of any such entity. Certain institutions that function solely in a trust or fiduciary capacity and accept deposits on a limited basis are expressly exempted from the definition of 'banking entity'. See new Section 13(h)(1), Bank Holding Company Act 1956. A very good summary of the Volcker Rule is offered in Covington & Burling LLP, 'Dodd–Frank Act – Final Volcker Rule Provisions', 20 July 2010.

[15] New Section 13(h)(4), Bank Holding Company Act 1956.

[16] New Section 13(h)(6), Bank Holding Company Act of 1956.

[17] Skeel accurately observes that this continuous interaction with industry over the interpretation of the ban on 'proprietary trading' will 'reinforce the partnership between the two, with the government softening its definition of proprietary in return for an implicit agreement by the banks not to shift their proprietary trading operations overseas', David Skeel, 'The New Financial Deal: Understanding the Dodd–Frank Act and its (Unintended) Consequences', Research Paper No. 10–21, Institute for Law and Economics, University

may lead to the ban being bypassed, although most of them are quite plausible. The introduction of the 'proprietary trading' ban raised very serious and real concerns regarding the availability of finance to the US government and state entities, the ability of financial firms to manage and hedge their risks, firm's ability to provide underwriting services in order not to distort capital formation, and firm's ability to offer lucrative trading and intermediation services to their customers. These concerns made some of the Act's exemptions inevitable. Accordingly, the Act contains four exemptions from the Volker Rule, called 'permitted activities', which are generally available to all banking entities:[18]

(1) transactions in US government or agency obligations, obligations of the GSEs and obligations of any state or political subdivision;
(2) transactions in securities and other financial instruments in connection with underwriting or market-making activities, to the extent those activities are designed not to exceed the 'reasonably expected near term demands' of clients, customers or counterparties;
(3) risk-mitigation hedging activities in connection with individual or aggregate positions, contracts or other holdings of a banking entity; and
(4) transactions in securities and other financial instruments on behalf of customers.

In addition, the Act exempts transactions in securities and other financial instruments conducted by a regulated insurance company, or its affiliate, for the general account of the insurance company, subject to compliance with applicable state insurance laws. Proprietary trading conducted by a banking entity when the trading occurs 'solely outside of the United States' (offshore trading) and the banking entity is not directly or indirectly owned or controlled by a banking entity organized under US or state law is also exempted. However, as US banking groups and their non-US affiliates will be subject to the ban on a global basis, the offshore trading exemption cannot be used by US banks to 'push out' otherwise prohibited trading to offshore subsidiaries or affiliates, and is rather designed to

of Pennsylvania, October 2010, p. 11, available at ssrn.com/abstract=1690979. Another thorny issue is, of course, monitoring of compliance with the Volcker Rule. See Simon Johnson, 'Proprietary Traders Earn Trust, but Verify', Bloomberg, 7 October 2010, available at www.bloomberg.com/news/2010-10-08/proprietary-traders-earned-trust-but-verify-simon-johnson.html.
[18] New Section 13(d), Banking Holding Company Act 1956.

allow non-US banks to exempt their own proprietary trading activities from an extra-territorial application of the Volcker Rule.

3.3   Limited sponsoring or investing in private equity and hedge funds

Activities covered by the Rule (Section 13(7)(1)) include 'investing' and 'sponsoring' a 'covered fund'. A banking entity 'invests' in a 'covered fund' if it acquires or retains any equity, partnership or other ownership interest in a hedge fund or a private equity fund.[19] A banking entity 'sponsors' a covered fund by: (1) serving as a general partner, managing member or trustee of the fund; (2) selecting or controlling (or having employees, officers or directors, or agents who constitute) a majority of the directors, trustees, or management of the fund; or (3) sharing with the fund for corporate, marketing, promotional or other purposes, the same name or a variation of the same name.[20] In addition, a banking entity that serves, directly or indirectly, as the investment manager, investment adviser or sponsor of a hedge fund or private equity fund, or that organizes and offers a fund as a permitted activity (and any affiliate of such banking entity) is prohibited from entering into a Section 23A of the Federal Reserve Act covered transaction with any such fund,[21] subject to an exemption for prime brokerage transactions.[22] Thus, the ban seems to extend to private funds that would not ordinarily be considered to be the market equivalent of hedge funds or private equity funds, such as venture capital funds.[23] Systemically important non-bank financial companies,

[19] Under new Section 13(h)(2) of the Bank Holding Company Act 1956, a 'hedge fund' or 'private equity fund' is (i) any issuer that would be an investment company but for the exemptions provided by section 3(c)(1) or 3(c)(7) of the Investment Company Act 1940, and (ii) any similar fund as the applicable regulators may determine. Section 3(c)(1) of the Investment Company Act 1940 is available to funds owned by 100 or fewer investors. Section 3(c)(7) is available to funds owned solely by 'qualified purchasers'.

[20] New Section 13(h)(5), Bank Holding Company Act 1956.

[21] New Section 13(f)(1), Banking Holding Company Act 1956. 'Covered Transactions' include: (1) any loan or extension of credit to an affiliate; (2) any purchase of, or investment in, securities issued by an affiliate; (3) any purchases of assets, including assets subject to an agreement to repurchase from an affiliate, unless specifically exempted by the FRB; (4) any transaction in which the covered bank holding company accepts securities issued by an affiliate as collateral for a loan or extension of credit to any entity; and (5) the issuance of a guarantee, acceptance, or letter of credit, including an endorsement or standby letter of credit, on behalf of an affiliate.

[22] New Section 13(f)(3), Banking Holding Company Act 1956.

[23] Mayer Brown, 'Understanding the Financial Reform Legislation – The Dodd–Frank Wall Street Reform and Consumer Protection Act', May 2010, p. 67. However, the Dodd–Frank

which are not subject to the ban per se, will be subject to additional capital charges and restrictions addressing risks and conflicts of interests.

Similarly with the proprietary trading ban, the Dodd–Frank Act also includes several exemptions to the ban on investing in or sponsoring covered funds, which are in addition to the general exemptions of underwriting and market making, hedging and risk mitigation and management of client funds, discussed above. First, there is the *fiduciary* exemption. A banking entity is permitted to organize and offer a private equity or hedge fund, and may serve as sponsor to such a fund, if:

(1) the banking entity provides *bona fide* trust, fiduciary or investment advisory services as part of its business;
(2) the fund is organized and offered only in connection with such services and only to customers of such services;
(3) the banking entity does not guarantee or otherwise assume or insure the obligations or performance of the fund;
(4) the banking entity does not share the same name, or variation of the same name, with the fund;
(5) no director or employee of the banking entity has an ownership interest in the fund unless he or she is directly engaged in providing services to the fund; and
(6) certain other conditions are met.[24]

Second, the Act permits a banking entity to make investments in covered funds organized and offered by the banking entity for purposes of: (1) establishing the fund and providing it with sufficient initial equity (seed capital) for investment to permit the fund to attract unaffiliated investors; or (2) making a *de minimis* investment. A banking entity is allowed to organize and to serve as a general partner or managing member of a covered fund, provided that within one year of establishing a fund:[25]

(1) the banking entity's ownership interest in the fund represents no more than three per cent of the fund's total ownership;
(2) the banking entity actively seeks unaffiliated investors to dilute its investment in the fund to such level;

Act includes what appears to be a blanket exception for a banking entity's sale or securitization of loans permitted by law, *ibid.*
[24] New Section 13(d)(1)(G), Banking Holding Company Act 1956.
[25] New Section 13(d)(4)(B), Banking Holding Company Act 1956. The FRB may extend the one-year period for an additional two years under certain circumstances, new Section 13(d)(4)(C), Banking Holding Company Act.

(3) the banking entity's investment in any private equity or hedge fund must be 'immaterial' to the banking entity, as defined by the applicable regulators; and

(4) in any event the aggregate amount of all such investments may not exceed three percent of its Tier 1 capital.[26]

Third, there is an exemption for investments in private funds, which take place 'solely outside of the United States'. Similarly with the offshore exemption from the proprietary trading ban, this exemption also requires that the bank relying on the exemption is not owned or controlled directly or indirectly by a banking entity organized under US or state law, and is thus designed to prevent the Act's prohibition from reaching the activities of non-US based parent companies of US bank subsidiaries or branches. There is finally an exemption permitting a banking entity to make investments in small business investment companies, which are 'designed primarily to promote the public welfare'. The Securities and Exchange Commission (SEC) and the Commodity Futures Trading Commission (CFTC) may also exempt other activities that they determine 'would promote and protect the safety and soundness of the banking entity and the financial stability of the United States'.[27]

The above exemptions from the Volcker Rule proprietary trading ban and private fund restrictions are not available if the exempt transaction or activity would:[28]

(1) involve or result in a 'material conflict of interest';
(2) result in material exposures by the covered banking entity to 'high-risk assets' or 'high-risk trading strategies';
(3) would pose a threat to the safety and soundness of the banking entity; or
(4) would pose a threat to the financial stability of the US.

3.4   The regime for non-bank financial companies

Any non-bank firm that is engaged predominantly in financial activities, and which is designated as 'systemically significant' under Title I of the Dodd–Frank Act, would be subject to heightened capital adequacy requirements and quantitative limits adopted by the FRB with respect to

---

[26] This is of course a serious derogation from the initial drafting of the Rule which provided a total ban and thus a victory for the US banks lobbying for relaxation of the Volcker Rule.
[27] New Section 13(d)(1)(J), Banking Holding Company Act 1956.
[28] New Section 13(d)(2), Banking Holding Company Act 1956.

its proprietary trading and private fund activities. The Dodd–Frank Act does not specify any capital requirements or quantitative limits, leaving it to the FRB to determine these requirements through the rulemaking process. Thus, the Federal Reserve is required, subject to transition periods and exceptions for 'permitted activities', to impose additional capital requirements and other quantitative limits on their proprietary trading activities.[29]

It is unclear how these limits would be applied in the case of designated non-US non-banking firms such as insurance companies. It is postulated that in these cases the FRB is likely to look to whether there are comparable capital requirements in the home country.[30] If such additional capital requirements have not been adopted in other countries, the FRB may have to decide whether to apply the higher requirements to a non-US company's global capital or just to the US operations of the company. It should be noted that the Volcker Rule is designed to be used by regulators to impose further obligations on banks or systemically important non-bank financial companies. Thus, if regulators determine that additional capital requirements and quantitative limits, including diversification requirements, are appropriate to protect the safety and soundness of banking entities or systemically important non-bank financial companies engaged in proprietary trading and/or permitted sponsoring or investing, they can adopt rules imposing additional requirements and limitations on those activities. Finally, if regulators find that a permitted activity involves material conflicts of interest, or exposure to high-risk trading strategies, or it poses a threat to the stability of the banking entity or of the US financial system, they must issue rules to limit it.

3.5   UK proposals on the structure of the banking industry

During the financial crisis, the UK government bailed out banks with a combined balance sheet of more than two times the UK GDP, which was around US$ 2.7 trillion at the end of 2008.[31] On 16 June 2010, following

---

[29] New Section 13(f)(4), Banking Holding Company Act 1956.

[30] Mayer Brown, 'Understanding the Financial Reform Legislation', p. 71.

[31] In the first half of 2011 the UK government still owned 83 per cent of the Royal Bank of Scotland Group and 100 per cent of Northern Rock. For a concise description of events that led to the effective nationalization of a large part of the UK's banking industry, see Roger McCormick, 'United Kingdom', in The International Bar Association's Task Force on the Financial Crisis, 'A Survey of Current Regulatory Trends', October 2010, pp. 55–88, available at www.ibanet.org/Article/Detail. aspx?ArticleUid=2C72F588-7222-47C9-83E4-7DB0A0A8BF1C.

the formation of a coalition government between the Conservative and the Liberal Democratic parties, the UK's Chancellor set up an Independent Commission on Banking chaired by John Vickers. The Vickers' Committee's mandate was to consider structural and related non-structural reforms to the UK banking sector including a possible separation of retail and investment banking and/or placing limits on proprietary trading and investing, as well as measures to promote competition and reduce market concentration. The tentative suggestions of the Committee's Interim Report, published in April 2011, were endorsed by the Chancellor in a public speech on 15 June 2011.[32] The crux of the Vickers' Committee proposals is that big banks will be required to ring-fence certain riskier operations from their consumer businesses. This will be done by setting up separate commercial bank subsidiaries within the wider groups. The subsidiaries will be separately capitalized and will have liquidity pools or lines separate from those maintained for the business of the entire group in order to safeguard the continuous operation of this part of the bank should the investment banking arm fail.[33]

This is, of course, a lighter version of Glass–Steagall type separation, but much more straightforward than the complicated model pursued under the Volcker Rule. On the other hand, serious issues for regulatory arbitrage are bound to arise unless the UK proposals are adopted by the EU bodies. Otherwise, the branches of EU banks that observe no ring fencing obligations will be able to operate in the UK under the EU 'passport' possibly enjoying a cost advantage in offering both commercial and investment banking services.

4.   Increased capital requirements for SIFIs and G-SIFIs

4.1   Contingent capital instruments

4.1.1   Overview

I have already discussed the proposals to impose capital requirements on SIFIs that go beyond the Basel III minimum in order to increase their loss absorption capacity with a view to increasing the resilience of distressed

---

[32] George Parker, Patrick Jenkins and Brooke Masters, 'Osborne Backs High Street Bank Firewalls', *Financial Times*, 15 June 2011, available at www.ft.com/cms/s/0/f9cf7b86–96b6–11e0-baca 00144feab49a.html#axzz1PtjGGbNH.

[33] See The Vickers Commission (UK Independent Commission on Banking), 'Interim Report, Consultation and Reform Options', 11 April 2011, available at s3-eu-west-1.amazonaws.com/htcdn/Interim-Report-110411.pdf.

institutions and enhancing their chances of remaining a going concern. The FSB has endorsed the BCBS proposals and considers that the greater loss-absorption capacity for SIFIs could be drawn from a menu of alternatives, which should include a combination of capital surcharges, quantitative requirements for contingent capital instruments (so-called Co-Cos) and a share of debt instruments or other liabilities represented by 'bail-in-able' claims, which are capable of bearing loss at the point of non-viability, i.e. within resolution, enabling recapitalization and recovery while maintaining vital business functions of the distressed institution. The proposed EU resolution framework (discussed in Section 7 below) strongly endorses this solution and consults on the preferred approach to authorizing and issuing bail-in-able instruments. In this context, the EU Commission proposes a mechanism that converts debt into equity or the write-off of debt (including unsecured senior debt), based on: (1) contractual agreements between banks and investors; or (2) supervisors' statutory powers in the context of bank resolution.[34] In addition, both the FSB and the BCBS have conducted studies regarding the optimum magnitude of additional loss absorbency that G-SIFIs should have and of the legal and operational market capacity and other issues relating to the viability of contractual and statutory bail-in.[35]

The BCBS proposals describe a framework under which CoCos will serve as a mechanism that would lead financial institutions that experience difficulties to automatic equity capital increases and debt reduction. Specifically, it is proposed that all non-Common Equity Tier 1 instruments and Tier 2 instruments at internationally active banks must have a clause in their terms and conditions that requires them to be written-off on the occurrence of the trigger event,[36] being replaced by common stock which the holders of the instruments to be written-off will be issued as compensation. The issuing banks must maintain on a continuous basis all necessary authorizations to immediately issue the relevant number of shares specified in the instrument's terms and conditions should the

---

[34] An excellent table comparing the different features of most current regulatory and academic proposals relating to CoCos is offered in Charles W. Calomiris and Richard J. Herring, 'Why and How to Design a Contingent Convertible Debt Requirement', Wharton School, Financial Institutions Center, Working Paper 11–41, April 2011, Table 1, pp. 41–5.

[35] It is expected that the FSB, in consultation with the BCBS, will recommend an additional degree of G-SIFI loss absorbency and the instruments by which these can be met by December 2011.

[36] BCBS, 'Proposal to Ensure the Loss Absorbency of Regulatory Capital at the Point of Non-viability', August 2010.

trigger event occur.[37] Any common stock paid as compensation to the holders of the instrument can either be common stock of the issuing bank or the parent company of the consolidated group. The issuance of the new shares as a result of the conversion must take place prior to any public sector injection of capital so that the capital provided by the public sector is not diluted. Namely, the write-off of the capital instruments increases the common equity of the bank and removes the possibility of the capital instrument holders remaining senior to any common equity injected by the public sector.

The proposals regarding the introduction of CoCos are underpinned by prior work undertaken by the Squam Lake group[38] and other academic works.[39] Although there is marked lack of consensus regarding both the characteristics and the triggers of CoCos, their advantages may be summarized as follows.[40] First, CoCos enable raising capital at times when other options are impossible, either owing to unfavourable market conditions or because they are unattractive to shareholders. Second, automatic conversion prevents fire sales and thus it limits contagion triggered by deleveraging in times of systemic stress. Third, CoCos that lead to dilution of existing shareholders' stake are regarded as very good mechanism to incentivize the (voluntary) prompt recapitalization of banks if they have experienced serious loss of equity but before the bank has been shut out of the capital markets. Finally, CoCos dis-incentivize excessive risk-taking and, thus, they might become an effective market discipline mechanism.

---

[37] This requirement is only relevant to instruments whose terms include a conversion mechanism on the occurrence of the trigger event and essentially means that the bank must have sufficient authorized share capital to issue to cover the shares specified in the terms of the convertible instrument that will be subject to the write off, avoiding any legal caps on unissued share capital, *ibid.*, p. 6.

[38] Squam Lake Working Group on Financial Regulation, 'An Expedited Resolution Mechanism for Distressed Financial Firms: Regulatory Hybrid Securities', Council on Foreign Relations, Center for Geoeconomic Studies, Working Paper 2009.

[39] John Coffee, Jr., 'Bail-Ins Versus Bail-Outs: Using Contingent Capital to Mitigate Systemic Risk', Columbia Law and Economics Working Paper No. 380, 22 October 2010, available at papers.ssrn.com/sol3/papers.cfm?abstract_id=1675015. J. Flannery, 'Stabilizing Large Financial Institutions with Contingent Capital Certificates', 2009, available at papers.ssrn.com/sol3/papers.cfm?abstract_id=1485689. Giuseppe De Martino, Masimo Libertucci, Mario Marangoni, and Mario Quagliariello, 'A Proposal for Countercyclical Contingent Capital Instruments', *VOX* 30 October 2010, available at www.voxeu.org/index.php?q=node/5728.

[40] See Ceyla Pazarbasioglu, Jianping Zhou, Uanessa Le Lesté and Michael Moore, 'Contingent Capital: Economic Rationale and Design Features', IMF, Monetary and Capital Markets Department, 25 January 2011.

The three main objectives of CoCos have been summarized by Calomiris and Herring as follows: (1) provision of a contingent cushion of common equity that results from the conversion of debt when the CoCo is triggered safeguarding the bank's existence as going concern, the so called 'bail-in' objective; (2) provision of a credible signal of default risk, which takes the form of the observed yield spread on convertible debt prior to conversion, the so called 'signalling' objective; and (3) incentivization of the voluntary, pre-emptive and timely issuance of equity in order to avoid a highly dilutive CoCo conversion, the so-called 'equity-issuance' objective.[41]

4.1.2   The policy debate

To the advantages of CoCos described above, a caveat must be added. CoCos are largely untested instruments. It is notable that during the recent crisis, most hybrid capital instruments with characteristics similar to CoCos did not absorb losses as they were designed to do.[42] Moreover, it is unclear which of the above objectives should be given the highest weight and the different proposals adopt different approaches. Also the unintended consequences of conversion may be very significant if the trigger event (which relates directly to the objective given the most weight) is not properly designed, especially in times of high market volatility and uncertainty.[43] Properly designing the trigger event is of fundamental importance in ensuring the CoCo's effectiveness and avoiding risks, since conversion could have negative signalling effects, lead to contagion and be subject to price manipulation.[44] In addition, designing as conversion or write-off triggers systemic instead of bank specific events would mean that the disciplining power of CoCos on bank management would dissipate. Critically, designing triggers that are based on systemic events or unfettered regulatory discretion would make the pricing of these instruments really difficult, raising marketability and liquidity issues, especially if traditional investors, such as pension funds, do not find CoCos attractive investment.

---

[41] Calomiris and Herring, 'Why and How to Design a Convertible Debt Requirement' p. 16.
[42] Pazarbasioglou *et al.*, 'Contingent Capital', p. 7. The authors of the IMF study postulate that this failure was (partly) due to 'banks' reluctance to send negative signals to the markets and partly due to regulatory forbearance, overestimated capital ratios and/or capital injections from the governments, which prevented the breach of regulatory ratios'.
[43] *Ibid.*, pp. 8–10.
[44] Charles Goodhart, 'Are CoCos from Cloud Cuckoo-Land?', 10 June 2010, available at www.voxeu.org/index.php?q=node/5159. Suresh Sundaresan and Zhenyou Wang, 'Design of Contingent Capital with Stock Price Trigger for Conversion', New York Federal Reserve, Staff Report 448, May 2010.

An automatic trigger for conversion/write-off, such as when credit spreads or share prices hit certain specified levels, or when regulatory ratios fall below certain levels,[45] has the advantage of transparency and objectivity, removing much mistrusted by the market regulatory discretion. Moreover, Calomiris and Herring argue that the dynamic incentive feature of properly designed CoCos could 'provide a more effective solution to the "too-big-to-fail" problem, reduce forbearance risk (supervisory reluctance to recognize losses), and address uncertainty about the appropriate amount of capital banks need to hold, and the changes in that amount over time',[46] subject to incorporating a market ratio as trigger. In addition, CoCos structured this way should lead SIFIs to build strong risk governance systems and timely asset sales to avoid violation of minimum capital requirements.[47] However, since there is no prior knowledge of the nature of a future crises it will prove very difficult to design conversion triggers that are robust to all possible outcomes and which do not have, as facts actually unfold, unintended and hard-to-manage consequences. Futhermore, the conversion/write-off mechanism is not intended to be used indiscreetly. In principle, even systemic banks should be allowed to fail and enter the traditional insolvency/resolution procedures.

Another alternative to contingent capital instruments could be the elimination of Tier 2 capital for SIFIs. The BCBS notes this would mean that SIFIs would have to be indentified *ex ante*, something that could both prove ineffective and increase moral hazard as it could lead to a lowering of supervisory monitoring for institutions that would be left outside the framework. It would also penalize banks that do not take excessive risks for which Tier 2 subordinated debt is normally cheaper than common equity.[48] In addition, spreads on a bank's subordinated debt are an important market indicator of the bank's financial health, enhancing market discipline and aiding supervisory monitoring that should be alert to price movements in this market. Of course, the second argument is more an issue of calibration of tax incentives, since payments to bondholders

---

[45] The Squam Lake Working Group suggested a double trigger: regulators must declare the existence of a systemic crisis, and the bank must fall below a given capital ratio, Squam Lake, 'An Expedited Resolution Mechanism'. In contrast, Flannery argues that the trigger should not depend on the state of the financial system, but rather on the contemporaneous market value of the firm's outstanding common equity, Flannery, 'Stabilizing Large Financial Institutions'.

[46] Calomiris and Herring, 'Why and How to Design a Convertible Debt Requirement', p. 1.

[47] *Ibid.*, p. 6.

[48] BCBS, 'Proposal to Ensure the Loss Absorbency of Regulatory Capital', p. 5.

are given preferential treatment.[49] Thus, the whole issue of whether Tier 2 capital should be abolished or not hinges on how useful it would be to identify SIFIS *ex ante* and the reliability of spreads in the subordinated debt market, given also that issuance of subordinated debt is only one of a host of mechanisms that may be used to reinforce market discipline.

As mentioned earlier, the various regulatory (and academic) proposals differ as to which of the three objectives ('bail-in', 'signalling', equity issuance') should be given the biggest value. Thus, a few observations are due there. First, the equity issuance motive is based on a combination of market price or CDS triggers which did not work as accurate predictions of the financial condition of banks in the wake of the GFC.[50] Second, CoCos serving this objective will inevitably incorporate as a trigger some measure of value of bank equity capital over value of assets. However, a trigger threshold mixing multiple criteria is bound to create confusion or even make such instruments impossible to price.[51] Third, CoCos targeting this objective may be effective only if a substantial dilution of existing shareholdings through a pre-emptive issue is provided.[52] But it is rather difficult to provide a concrete dilution percentage making this another vague criterion. Fourth, CoCos could provide a credible mechanism to serve the signalling objective only when all public guarantees extended to SIFIs have been eliminated and this time has not come yet.

On the other hand, instruments designed to serve the 'bail-in' objective may be used to credibly withstand substantial default risk and especially tail risk,[53] which was at the heart of the institutional collapse during the GFC. Such instruments also have four additional advantages. First, the existence of substantial debt that is capable of converting into equity to absorb losses would reduce moral hazard and should boost market confidence in the event of failure, averting contagion. Second, it could provide, to some extent, a useful market signal about market estimates

---

[49] Anat R. Admati, Peter M. DeMarzo, Martin F. Hellwig, and Paul C. Pfleiderer, 'Fallacies, Irrelevant Facts, and Myths in the Discussion of Capital Regulation: Why Bank Equity is not Expensive', Stanford Graduate School of Business Research Paper No. 2065, 20 March 2011, avaialble at papers.ssrn.com/sol3/papers.cfm?abstract_id=1669704&rec= 1&srcabs=1645224.

[50] See Chapter 3, p. 120.

[51] Sundaresan and Wang, 'Design of Contingent Capital'.

[52] Steve Strangin, Amanda Hindlau and Sandra Carson, 'Ending "Too Big To Fail"', Goldman Sachs Global Markets Institute, December 2009, available at www2. goldmansachs.com/our-thinking/public-policy/regulatory-reform/effect-reform-part-5.pddf.

[53] Pazarbasioglou *et al.*, 'Contingent Capital', p. 18.

of future risk of default. Third, if the trigger event is designed to relate to the time that other safeguards have been put in place to absorb the funding stress that such institution will immediately experience, due to loss of confidence, as most resolution schemes are designed to do, the impact of the liquidity stress will be negligible and will not trigger market wide panic. Fourth, market discipline remains a strong goal as 'bail-in-able' instruments are dilutive, but it is not over-relied on, given the market tendency to overreact (discussed in Chapter 2), depending on specific market conditions and perceptions.

In this context, the BCBS proposes, in the case of individual institutions, as a trigger event the earlier of: (1) the decision to make a public sector injection of capital, or equivalent support, without which the firm would have become non-viable, as determined by the relevant authority; and (2) a decision that a write-off, without which the firm would become non-viable, is necessary, as determined by the relevant authority. However, where an issuing bank is part of a wider banking group and the issuing bank wishes the instrument to be included in the consolidated group's capital, there must be specified an additional trigger event (group approach),[54] which is the earlier of:

(1) the decision to make a public sector injection of capital, or equivalent support, in the jurisdiction of the consolidated supervisor, without which the firm receiving the support would have become non-viable, as determined by the relevant authority in that jurisdiction; and

(2) a decision that a write-off, without which the firm would become non-viable, is necessary, as determined by the relevant authority in the home jurisdiction.

Therefore, under the suggested BCBS framework contingent instruments will be triggered when an institution is very close to becoming a gone concern and in order to avoid this outcome. This means that the market

---

[54] The conversion/write-down should be triggered by the jurisdiction in which it is given credit as regulatory capital. Therefore, if Tier 2 convertible instruments are issued out of a subsidiary in a foreign jurisdiction and the issuing bank wishes those to be included in group Tier 2 capital, its conversion/write-off will need to be triggered by the earlier trigger event regardless of whether it occurs in the home or the host jurisdiction. However, if the bank only wishes the Tier 2 capital to be included in regulatory capital at the subsidiary level, and not at the consolidated level, it would only need conversion/write-off to be triggered by the host jurisdiction and instruments issued out of the subsidiary will not be recognized as regulatory capital at the consolidated level. See BCBS, 'Proposal to Ensure the Loss Absorbency of Regulatory Capital', p. 7.

will price these instruments accordingly and link the probability of a conversion/write off event to the probability of the issuing institution's future default. Accordingly the safer the institution and the more effective the prudential regulations to make it safe and prevent cyclical risk building into the system, the lower the premium for these instruments.[55] Yet, institutions do fail from time to time and, if history is a guide, the risk of conversion shall not be seen as negligible.

Notwithstanding general concerns about CoCos marketability,[56] it is also arguable that only investors who can bear this form of risk would enter the relevant market, and the returns to such investors for assuming the risk of convertible capital instruments should be significant. Also, it may not prove sensible to offer such instruments to traditional investors, such as pension funds. Such a restriction might have an impact on liquidity but not on market discipline. Specialized investors will almost certainly prove better monitors than mainstream institutional investors in understanding the complex business of modern banking institutions.[57]

A number of additional concerns remain about CoCos[58] suitability as an effective risk absorption instrument. These refer to, first, credit rating agencies' (CRAs') ability and willingness to adequately rate these instruments and second to the tax treatment of CoCos. Second, recognizing CoCos as debt, in spite of their contingent convertibility to equity, would afford them the preferential treatment of tax-deductible interest raising the instruments popularity among banks. Third, regulators would need to have wide statutory powers to write down existing claims of equity and debt holders, override pre-emption rights and change management, interfering, in the process, with shareholders and creditors' property rights. As a result, 'bail-in' schemes will require changes in current legislation 'to legitimize the interference'.[59] Finally, differences in the legal treatment of CoCos across jurisdictions will have to be streamlined

---

[55] *Ibid.*, p. 10.

[56] E.g., Swiss regulators have expressed concerns as to whether there will ever be a market for CoCos even after the two biggest Swiss banks completed with success the issue of CoCos worth several billions of dollars. See Patrick Jenkins and Haig Simonian, 'Swiss Urge Capital Boost for Banks', *Financial Times*, 4 October 2010, available at www.ft.com/cms/s/0/4a24a1c8-cf26-11df-9be2-00144feab49a.html#axzz1QhAq8lsU.

[57] Cf. BCBS, 'Proposal to Ensure the Loss Absorbency of Regulatory Capital', p. 11.

[58] See, for an overview of these issues, Frederick Ryan Castillo, 'The Coconundrum', Harvard Business Law Review Online, 18 January 2011, available at www.hblr.org/2011/01/the-coconundrum/#_ftn24.

[59] See Pazarbasioglu *et al.*, 'Contingent Capital', p. 18.

for this instrument to work properly in the context of cross-border institutions and groups.[60]

4.2   Capital surcharges

The BCBS consultation on capital surcharges for G-SIFIs seems to target increases in Core Equity Tier 1 capital to the exclusion of CoCos.[61] The FSB, BIS and IMF hold that one of the objectives of macro-prudential policy should be 'to reduce systemic risk concentrations, which can arise from similar exposures across financial institutions (from assets, liabilities, dependence on common services) or because of the direct balance-sheet linkages among them (e.g., counterparty risk)'.[62] Thus, protections at individual institutions should be commensurate 'with their contribution to system-wide risk and containing spillovers from their failure'.[63] In other words, the BCBS approach over capital surcharges imposed on G-SIFIs should be based on principles similar to those applicable to restraining pollution on the basis of capacity to pollute, which in this case translates into capacity to generate systemic risk.[64]

Plans for the imposition of such surcharge were at an early stage in June 2011 when this work was completed. From what can be surmised from the early plans, G-SIFIs will be divided into different buckets on the basis of a sliding scale of riskiness. The assessment methodology for G-SIFIs is based on an indicator-based approach and comprises five broad categories: size, interconnectedness, lack of substitutability, global (cross-jurisdictional) activity and complexity.[65] The surcharge for the riskiest institutions will range between a minimum of

---

[60] E.g., '[r]egulators in a home country with the "bail-in" statutory power may not be able to write down the debt that is booked in a foreign country or is governed by a foreign law. In this case, the effectiveness of the "bail-in" could be reduced significantly, unless states are willing to adopt laws recognizing the statutory power of the resolution authorities in other jurisdictions', *ibid.*, p. 18.

[61] See BCBS, 'Measures for Global Systemically Important Banks'. See also FSB, 'Reducing Moral Hazard Posed by Systemically Important Financial Institutions – Interim Report to G20 Leaders', 18 June 2010, p. 5, available at www.financialstabilityboard.org/publications/r_100627b.pdf.

[62] FSB, IMF and BIS, 'Macroprudential Policy Tools and Frameworks – Update to G-20 Finance Ministers and Central Bank Governors', 14 February 2011, p. 3, available at www.bis.org/publ/othp13.pdf.

[63] *Ibid.*

[64] See Andrew G. Haldane, 'The $100 Billion Question', Speech, March 2010, available at www.bankofengland.co.uk/publications/news/2010/036.htm.

[65] *Ibid.*

1 per cent and a maximum of 2.5 per cent of Common Equity Tier 1 capital over total assets on top of the 7 per cent Common Equity Tier 1 buffer banks will be required to hold under the new Basel III capital standards[66] once they are fully phased in at the end of 2018.

The surcharge will clearly act as a restraint of future bank growth through asset expansion, since such expansion will become very expensive. Apart from boosting institutions' stability through an expanded equity base, a rise in the cost of banking as a result of the surcharge and an adverse impact on economic growth may not be ruled out.[67] Moreover, merely relying on the surcharge as a means to contain 'too-big-to-fail' institutions and restrict big bank growth might prove a self-defeating strategy. Arguably, the new super class of global financial institutions is bound to look to investors as much safer than smaller institutions and much more likely to become the subject of a public bail-out pushing down significantly the cost of borrowing for G-SIFIs. Therefore, the capital surcharge might in the end prove to be another channel for the return of moral hazard into the system.[68]

In addition, the Basel surcharge is going to be a minimum and major jurisdictions are considering different surcharge levels above the Basel minimum. In contrast to the BCBS staggered approach, the UK and the Swiss regulators are considering the imposition of a flat surcharge of 3 per cent of risk weighted assets (RWAs) comprising common equity, bringing Tier 1 capital to 10 per cent of RWAs.[69] The total of the Swiss requirement

---

[66] According to the *Financial Times* if the proposal is adopted, Citigroup, JP Morgan, Bank of America, Deutsche Bank, HSBC, BNP Paribas, Royal Bank of Scotland and Barclays would have to maintain core Tier 1 capital ratios of 9.5 per cent. Goldman Sachs, Morgan Stanley, UBS and Credit Suisse would be in the next category down, facing a surcharge of 2 per cent and total minimum ratio of 9 per cent. 'Another 10 to 15 banks are likely to face surcharges ranging from 0.5 to 2 per cent as part of the effort to make "global systemically important financial institutions" more resilient. These banks are considered so big and important to the global economy that they would probably have to be rescued by taxpayers if they got into trouble.' See Brooke Masters and Patrick Jenkins, 'Biggest Banks Face Capital Clampdown', *Financial Times*, 16 June 2011, available at www.ft.com/intl/cms/s/0/521d4450–9859–11e0-ae45–00144feab49a.html#axzz1PjnDNCjF.

[67] Institute of International Finance, 'SIFI Surcharges: Fundamental Issues and Empirical Estimates', 20 April 2011.

[68] E.g., Bloomberg reported that 'Douglas Flint, group chairman of HSBC Holdings Plc, said in March he "absolutely" wanted Europe's biggest lender to be classified as systemically important as it would make the bank more attractive to investors and clients'. See Liam Vaughan and Gavin Finch 'Biggest Banks May Get Boost From Basel', *Bloomberg*, 23 June 2011, available at www.bloomberg.com/news/2011–06–22/biggest-banks-may-get-funding-help-in-basel-regulators-bid-to-shrink-them.html.

[69] Vickers Commission, 'Interim Report', pp. 70–1.

for SIFIs will be 19 per cent of RWAs, and the authorities contemplate that the remaining 9 per cent will comprise CoCos or other debt instruments.[70] The US Federal Reserve, on the other hand, is considering a capital surcharge of up to 7 per cent.[71] Accordingly, the proposed surcharge could also create serious level playing field issues. As Hal Scott has accurately observed, 'SIFIs in countries with low surcharges might have a significant advantage over competitors in countries with fewer SIFIs or over competitors in countries with many SIFIs with high surcharges'.[72]

5.   BCBS-FSB principles on cross-border SIFI resolution

5.1   What is the problem?

Any regulatory approach to addressing the 'too-big-to-fail' problem needs to have effective resolution at its core. Such a regime must be able to prevent the systemic damage caused by a disorderly collapse of financial institutions without exposing the taxpayer to the risk of loss. The national regimes must, as a basic starting point, provide the authorities with the tools to intervene safely and quickly to ensure the continued performance of the firm's essential financial and economic functions, including uninterrupted access of depositors to their funds wherever they are located, and to transfer and sell viable portions of the firm while apportioning losses in a manner that is fair and predictable in order to avoid panics or destabilization of financial markets.[73]

Yet, the complexity and integrated nature of financial group structures and operations, with multiple legal entities spanning national borders and business lines, make rapid and orderly resolutions under current regimes extremely problematic. First, there is the issue of which country's laws will govern the resolution process and whether the decision of national

---

[70] See Nick Sawyer, 'Basel Committee Will not Impose CoCo Requirement for Sifis' *Risk Magazine*, 28 June 2011, available at www.risk.net/risk-magazine/news/2082036/basel-committee-impose-coco-requirement-sifis#ixzz1QhtN1CK3.

[71] Daniel K. Tarullo, 'Regulating Systemically Important Financial Firms', Speech at the Peter G. Peterson Institute for International Economics, 3 June 2011, available at www.federalreserve.gov/newsevents/speech/tarullo20110603a.htm.

[72] See Hal S. Scott, 'Testimony Before the Committee on Financial Services United States House of Representatives', 16 June 2011, p. 22.

[73] See, in general, IMF, 'Resolution of Cross-Border Banks – A Proposed Framework for Enhanced Coordination', 11 June 2010, available at www.imf.org/external/np/pp/eng/2010/061110.pdf.

resolution authorities will be respected by another country's courts. This becomes a major problem because of the second issue arising in this context: grossly incompatible national bank insolvency regimes.

There are two different approaches to resolving cross-border institutions. Under the territorial approach, each country resolves the domestic parts of a cross-border bank within its borders. This essentially leads to ring-fencing of the assets located within the jurisdiction concerned. This is the US approach with respect to branches of foreign banks. Under the universal approach, the institution as a whole, that is including its foreign branches (but not subsidiaries), is resolved across borders.[74] The principal example of the 'universal' approach are the EU Winding up Directives.[75] The two approaches are not clear cut. For instance, the US follows the 'universal' approach for locally domiciled banks but it follows the 'territorial' approach with respect to branches of foreign banks. Similarly, although the Winding Up Directives follow an EU-wide 'universal approach' for EU banks, it is within the discretion of member states to adopt a 'territorial' approach with respect to non-EU bank branches.[76]

The conflicting approaches are serious impediments to effective cross-border resolutions not only because of the danger that foreign resolution/insolvency proceedings may not be recognized, but also because of the aforementioned incompatibility of national resolution regimes. The insolvency regimes of different jurisdictions may have different objectives (some may have a pro-debtor bias, while others may be pro-creditor); they

---

[74] The IMF describes the two approaches as follows: 'Universality – Under an "universal" approach, the insolvency proceedings initiated against the debtor in its home country will purport to have "universal reach." … the home country trustee will seek to gain control over all of the debtor's assets and liabilities – including those located in other countries … To be effective, "universality" of the home country depends on different host countries recognizing this extraterritorial effect of the home country proceedings … Territoriality – [under the] "territorial" approach … a host country will initiate separate insolvency proceedings against a foreign debtor, instead of participating in, or deferring to, the insolvency proceedings opened by the home country. Typically, "territorial" jurisdictions will "ring-fence" the assets and liabilities of foreign entities that are located in its territory in order to satisfy the claims of local creditors.' IMF, 'Resolution of Cross-Border Banks', p. 10, Box 2.

[75] Directive 2001/24/EC of the European Parliament and of the Council of 24 April 2001 on the reorganisation and winding up of credit institutions, OJ L 125/15, 5 May 2001; and Directive 2001/17/EC of the European Parliament and of the Council of 19 March 2001 on the reorganisation and winding up of insurance undertakings, OJ L 110/28, 20 April 2001. Both Directives are currently under review.

[76] IMF, 'Resolution of Cross-Border Banks', p. 10, Box 2.

may apply different ranking of priorities or different treatment of claims. These differences are reflected in the different statutory tools, grounds for intervention and scope of authority for restructuring troubled financial institutions provided to national authorities.

The consequences of these differences in approach are further aggravated by procedural and substantive differences in national insolvency laws. Some countries use general corporate insolvency law for the reorganization and winding up of financial institutions, while others have special proceedings for banks and other financial institutions which provide for tailor-made resolution measures. There are important public policy and legal differences between corporate bankruptcy proceedings and special resolution regimes for financial institutions. The former is not concerned with achieving continuity of key functions of the institution entering bankruptcy proceedings or reducing the potential for a disorderly resolution which would disrupt the workings of the financial system.[77] A number of countries lack resolution powers and tools that facilitate continuity in the key financial functions of the troubled financial institution in order to avoid a disorderly collapse that increases the likelihood of contagion effects across borders. Differences in resolution regimes also affect the *ex ante* behaviour of financial market participants. For instance, if one jurisdiction treats unsecured bond holders more favourably than other jurisdictions in the event of a resolution, bond holders will likely be more willing to offer such financing during periods of financial distress in the most lenient jurisdiction.

The conflicts of procedural and substantive laws and resolution philosophies described above lead to a highly inefficient resolution framework for cross-border institutions and make resolution of cross-border groups on a unitary basis virtually impossible. Apart from the very disruptive legal implications, this marked lack of speed and effectiveness heightens the risk of contagion and thus increases moral hazard, as authorities might be forced to intervene and rescue an institution to avert a systemic crisis.[78] Therefore, an effective solution needs to be found to this problem. In the paragraphs below I critically discuss the IMF, FSB and BCBS proposals to overcome the challenges associated with effective cross-border resolution.

---

[77] See CBRG, 'Report and Recommendations of the Cross-border Bank Resolution Group – Final Papers', March 2010, p. 26, available at www.bis.org/publ/bcbs/69.pdf.
[78] See also IMF, 'Resolution of Cross-Border Banks', p. 12.

5.2 BCBS, FSB and IMF recommendations
on cross-border resolution

5.2.1 BCBS Cross-Border Resolution Group
recommendations

The principal objective of the Cross-Border Resolution Group (CBRG) recommendations is the strengthening of national resolution powers and their cross-border implementation. They provide guidance for firm-specific contingency planning since banks, as well as key home and host authorities, should develop practical and credible plans to promote resiliency in periods of severe financial distress and to facilitate a rapid resolution should that be necessary. The recommendations also aim to reduce contagion by advocating the use of risk mitigation mechanisms such as netting arrangements, collateralization practices and the use of regulated central counterparties. Strengthening the use of these and other measures would help limit the market impact of a bank failure.[79] A summary of the CBRG's ten recommendations is provided below:

(1) *Effective national resolution powers*: National authorities should have appropriate tools, such as the power to create bridge financial institutions, transfer assets, liabilities and business operations to other institutions, and resolve claims to deal with respect to all types of financial institutions in difficulties so that an orderly resolution can be achieved that helps maintain financial stability, minimize systemic risk, protect consumers, limit moral hazard and promote market efficiency;

(2) *Frameworks for a co-ordinated resolution of financial groups*: Each jurisdiction should establish a national framework to co-ordinate the resolution of the legal entities of financial groups and financial conglomerates within its jurisdiction. National authorities should consider a special resolution regime for financial groups and conglomerates to provide an effective mechanism for decisive intervention, when necessary, and for assuring continuity in systemically significant functions performed by the group or conglomerate;[80]

---

[79] CBRG, 'Report and Recommendations of the Cross-border Bank Resolution Group'. For a good analysis of the principles, see Eva Hupkes, 'Rivalry in Resolution: How to Reconcile Local Responsibilities and Global Interests' (2010) 7 *European Company and Financial Law Review* 216.

[80] This includes the power to resolve the legal entities of financial groups and financial conglomerates in a co-ordinated manner to reduce the likelihood of such contagion.

(3) *Convergence of national resolution measures*: National authorities should seek convergence of national resolution tools and measures in order to facilitate the co-ordinated resolution of financial institutions active in multiple jurisdictions and promote a level playing field;

(4) *Cross-border effects of national resolution measures*: To promote better co-ordination among national authorities in cross-border resolutions, national authorities should consider the development of procedures to facilitate the mutual recognition of crisis management and resolution proceedings and/or measures, including more effective recognition of foreign crisis management and resolution proceedings at the bilateral, regional or international level;

(5) *Reduction of complexity and interconnectedness of group structures and operations*: Supervisors should work closely with relevant home and host resolution authorities in order to understand how group structures and their individual components would be resolved in a crisis. If national authorities believe that financial institutions' group structures are too complex to permit orderly and cost-effective resolution, they should consider imposing regulatory incentives on the institutions, through capital or other prudential requirements, designed to encourage simplification of the structures in a manner that facilitates effective resolution;

(6) *Planning in advance for orderly resolution*: The contingency plans of all systemically important cross-border financial institutions and groups should address as a contingency a period of severe financial distress or financial instability and provide a plan, proportionate to the size and complexity of the institution's and/or group's structure and business, to preserve the firm as a going concern, promote the resiliency of key functions and facilitate rapid resolution or wind-down should that prove necessary. Resilience and wind-down contingency planning should be a regular component of supervisory oversight and take into account cross-border dependencies, implications of legal separateness of entities for resolution and the possible exercise of intervention and resolution powers;

(7) *Cross-border co-operation and information sharing*: Key home and host authorities should agree, consistent with national law and policy, on arrangements that ensure the timely production and sharing of the needed information, both for purposes of contingency planning during normal times and for crisis management and resolution during times of stress. There is a need for information to be exchanged before and during a crisis to assist in dealing with a crisis. Authorities should

exchange information on the relevant aspects of their legal and regulatory frameworks and the different national authorities' powers and
responsibilities for regulation, supervision, liquidity provision, crisis
management and resolution. Material adverse developments should
be shared among key authorities as and when they arise;

(8) *Strengthening risk mitigation mechanisms*: Jurisdictions should promote the use of risk mitigation techniques that reduce systemic risk
and enhance the resilience of critical financial or market functions
during a crisis or resolution of financial institutions. These risk mitigation techniques include enforceable netting agreements, collateralization and segregation of client positions;

(9) *Transfer of contractual relationships and temporary 'freezing' of transfers*: National resolution authorities should have the legal authority
to temporarily delay the operation of contractual early termination
clauses in order to complete a transfer of certain financial market contracts to another sound financial institution, a bridge financial institution or other entity. Relevant laws should be amended, where necessary,
to allow a short delay in the operation of such termination clauses in
order to promote the continuity of market functions. Where a transfer
is not available, authorities should ensure that contractual rights to terminate, net and apply pledged collateral are preserved;[81]

(10) *Exit strategies and market discipline*: In order to restore market
discipline and promote the efficient operation of financial markets, national authorities should consider, and incorporate into
their planning, clear options or principles for the exit from public
intervention.[82]

---

[81] The rationale for this principle is that while financial contract early termination and
close-out netting clauses may reduce the risk of contagion during normal times, in the
event of a crisis, when it is likely that all counterparties of a failing bank will exercise
the right to terminate financial contracts immediately, and shall liquidate collateral
upon the initiation of resolution measures, automatic exercise of these rights shall
amplify contagion undermining the stability of the financial system. CBRG recommends in order to fulfil this objective that supervisory authorities and industry groups,
such as ISDA, should find ways to develop standardized contract provisions that support such transfers as a way to reduce the risk of contagion in a crisis. CBRG 'Report and
Recommendations', p. 3.

[82] As CBRG notes: 'where temporary public ownership is necessary, authorities should seek
to return assets to private ownership and management as soon as possible'. On the other
hand, the duration of exit strategies and the risks arising from the termination of public intervention should be well balanced, since an 'abrupt or too hasty exit from public
intervention could impair the financial and operational condition of a troubled financial
institution'. CBRG 'Report and Recommendations', p. 6.

It should be noted that the CBRG recommendations, rather realistically, do not rule out the possibility of public bail-outs, and thus stand in stark contrast with the Dodd–Frank regime (discussed in Section 6 below) and the proposals for an EU resolution regime.

5.2.2   The FSB recommendations

The FSB has endorsed and elaborated further on the CBRG recommendations grouping them into four general principles:[83]

(1) *Comprehensive resolution regimes and tools should be in place*
   (a) All jurisdictions should undertake the necessary legal reforms to ensure that they have in place a resolution regime which would make feasible the resolution of any financial institution without taxpayer exposure to loss from solvency support while protecting vital economic functions through mechanisms which make it possible for shareholders and unsecured and uninsured creditors to absorb losses in their order of seniority;
   (b) Each country should have a designated resolution authority, which should have the powers and tools proposed in the FSB and CBRG recommendations;
   (c) National authorities should consider restructuring mechanisms to allow recapitalization of a financial institution as a going concern by way of contractual and/or statutory (i.e., within-resolution) debt–equity conversion and write-down tools, as appropriate to their legal frameworks and market capacity;
(2) *Effective cross-border coordination mechanisms*
   (a) National resolution authorities should be mandated to seek co-operation with foreign resolution authorities;
   (b) Jurisdictions should provide resolution authorities with the capacity in law to co-operate and to share information across borders. They should eliminate national law obstacles to fair cross-border resolution. Examples of such rules constitute depositor priority rules that give preferential treatment to domestic depositors over those of foreign branches;
   (c) For each G-SIFI, there should be institution-specific (group) co-operation agreements between relevant home and host authorities. These agreements should provide for clarity as regards the

---

[83] FSB, 'Reducing the Moral Hazard Posed by Systemically Important Financial Institutions – FSB Recommendations and Time Lines', pp. 4–5.

roles and responsibilities of home and host authorities in planning for and managing the resolution of the institution at all stages of the crisis;

(d) National law should provide both the mandate and the capacity to co-operate and share all relevant information among home and host supervisors, central banks and resolution authorities. National authorities should enter into formal agreements, namely, not just MOUs, to make them more binding;[84]

(3) *Sustained recovery and resolution planning,* which should be manifested in the following legal framework:

(a) All financial institutions should be able to be resolved in an orderly manner and without recourse to public funds under the applicable resolution regimes. Recovery and resolution plans that assess G-SIFIs resolvability should be mandatory and G-SIFIs should continually update their recovery and resolution planning;

(b) Supervisors and resolution authorities should have the power, exercisable under clear criteria, to require financial institutions to make changes to their legal and operational structure and business practices to facilitate the implementation of recovery and resolution measures;

(c) The ability to orderly resolve an institution under existing resolution regimes in an orderly fashion and co-operation agreements should be an important consideration in host authorities' determination of whether to permit a foreign branch presence, or to permit a subsidiary presence,[85] or to make resolution a local responsibility, but with co-ordination with the home (or group) regulatory and resolution authority;

(d) Big financial groups (i.e., SIFIs with multiple significant legal entities), should: maintain information on a legal-entity basis; minimise any undue intra-group guarantees, in particular undue use of blanket guarantees; ensure that service agreements are

---

[84] The FSB has requested all relevant (FSB member) home and host authorities to have drawn up for all G-SIFIs institution-specific co-operation agreements that specify the respective roles and responsibilities of the authorities at all stages of a crisis by end-2011. FSB, 'Reducing the Moral Hazard Posed by Systemically Important Financial Institutions – FSB Recommendations and Time Lines'.

[85] This restriction does not of course override the EU Treaty freedoms of establishment and free movement as specified in the relevant EU financial services directives, but it does seem to augment and buttress the GATS, 'prudential regulation carve out'. For discussion of the carve out, see Chapter 4, Section 2.6.

appropriately documented and cannot be abrogated by the service provider in resolution; and ensure that significant global payment and settlement services are legally separable and continued operability is safeguarded.

5.2.3   IMF recommendations

The CBRG, which has examined the solutions to the cross-border resolution conundrum for over a year, identified three possible solutions . First, *full 'universality' via a binding legal instrument.* For this solution to be effective an international treaty is required resolving key issues, including the imposition of burden sharing arrangements and the selection of the lead authority. The second solution is a full blown 'territorial' approach, which would essentially lead to the *de-globalization of financial institutions.* Under this approach cross-border financial groups would have to set up, in host jurisdictions, separately incorporated and capitalized subsidiaries ring fencing their assets. The third, or *'middle ground'* approach, entails enhanced co-ordination among resolution authorities mainly through the mutual recognition of crisis management and resolution proceedings and/or measures. From the previous discussion it is obvious that the CBRG and the FSB have opted for variations of the third approach. The IMF plausibly regards this classification as inexact, although it has endorsed the CBRG recommendations. The IMF has clearly gone a step further than all other bodies recommending a voluntary global resolution co-ordination framework based on minimum harmonization of resolution regimes of participating jurisdictions that largely reflect the principles of the United Nations Commission on International Trade Law (UNCITRAL) model law on cross-border insolvencies,[86] which, however, does not extend to cross-border groups. The IMF has suggested that this approach should be underpinned by a non-binding multilateral understanding reached among those countries that are in position to adhere to the various elements of a commonly agreed resolution framework. The IMF suggests that the essential elements of such a resolution framework should be:[87]

---

[86] UNCITRAL, 'Practice Guide on Cross-Border Insolvency Cooperation' 2009. The latest set of recommendations may be found in Working Group V (Insolvency Law), Thirty-seventh session, UNCITRAL Legislative Guide on Insolvency Law, Part three: Treatment of Enterprise Groups in Insolvency, Note by the Secretariat, 31 August 2009, A/CN.9/WG.V/WP.90, available at www.uncitral.org/uncitral/en/commission/working_groups/5Insolvency.html.

[87] IMF, 'Resolution of Cross-Border Banks', pp. 17–18. An academic study has also suggested a similar model for the harmonization of resolution regimes in G-20 countries.

(1) the modification of domestic laws that would require national author-
    ities to co-ordinate with foreign jurisdictions – but only to the extent
    that, in the judgment of the national authority in question, such
    co-ordination would be consistent with the interests of creditors and
    domestic financial stability;
(2) the identification of 'core co-ordination standards' that would be used
    to identify those countries with whom a more co-ordinated cross-
    border resolution would be expected to take place;
(3) recognition that public funding in the resolution process may, on
    occasion, be required, if only on a temporary basis;
(4) the establishment of principles that would set the criteria guiding
    the burden sharing process among the members of the enhanced
    co-ordination framework; and
(5) the specification of co-ordination procedures to be relied upon by those
    countries that adhere to the enhanced co-ordination framework.

The IMF accurately observes that 'host country authorities will only
be willing to co-operate with home country authorities if their national
frameworks have a reasonable level of high quality convergence'.[88] For
this reason it has recommended a set of general principles that should
govern the framework for resolution of cross-border financial institutions
and financial groups. These reflect to a large extent the CBRG recommendations and include:[89]

(1) *non-discrimination against foreign creditors*, which should be
    extended to depositor treatment by local deposit guarantee
    schemes;[90]
(2) *effective intervention tools* comprising special bank resolution
    regimes and official administration procedures that allow competent

---

However, the authors of that paper have expressed a clear preference for a binding framework based on international law rather than the fragile mechanism of MOUs. See Emilios
Avgouleas, Charles Goodhart and D. Schoenmaker, 'Bank Recovery and Resolution
Plans as a Catalyst for Global Financial Reform' (2012) 8 *Journal of Financial Stability*,
in press.

[88] IMF, 'Resolution of Cross-Border Banks', p. 17.
[89] *Ibid.*, pp. 19–25. Cf. Emilios Avgouleas, Charles Goodhart and D. Schoenmaker, 'Living
Wills as a Catalyst for Action,' DFS Policy Paper No. 4, May 2010. See, especially, the
Annex to this paper.
[90] Under this principle there should be no room for '[d]omestic depositor preference in the
home country, based upon the nationality or location of the depositor'. IMF, 'Resolution
of Cross-Border Banks', p. 20.

authorities to intervene rapidly and in a manner that both preserves the critical functions of the institution and avoids contagion; [91]

(3) *appropriate creditor safeguards*, giving, *inter alia*, creditors the right to judicial review and claiming compensation when intervention powers of resolution authorities interfere with private contractual and property rights;[92]

(4) *sufficiently robust and harmonized rules on priority*, which recognize the interests of host country insured depositors and deposit guarantee schemes (DGS). If this principle is not upheld and home country laws do not ensure equal priority for the host country insured depositors and DGS, the resolution authorities of the latter will have a strong incentive to choose the territorial approach;

(5) *provisions for financing of cross-border resolutions,* which do not exclude the possibility of public funding, and facilitate cross-border burden sharing arrangements;[93]

(6) *co-ordination should be based on the home country principle,* allowing home authorities to take the leadership in resolution proceedings

---

[91] These according to the IMF refer to the granting by public authorities of the following powers: (1) the power of early intervention to allow relevant authorities to take action before insolvency; (2) the power to unilaterally restructure the various claims of an institution including a power to order conversion CoCos; (3) the power to conclude mergers and acquisitions without shareholder consent; (4) the unilateral power to transfer assets and liabilities to other institutions, including the establishment of a bridge bank, without requiring the consent of third parties; (5) the power to provide bridge financing to facilitate the transactions relating to resolution; (6) the ability to assume public ownership of the institution on a temporary basis, once the shareholders and unsecured creditors have absorbed the necessary losses; and (7) the power to temporarily suspend various termination provisions contained in financial contracts, in order to limit contagion and preserve critical operations, *ibid.*, p. 20. This template is fully adopted by the proposed EU resolution framework discussed in Section 7 below

[92] These safeguards should, *inter alia*, ensure that: (1) secured property is not transferred out of a failing bank without the benefit of security moving with it; (2) netting and financial collateral arrangements are respected (subject potentially to the temporary suspension of close-out netting rights in respect of financial contracts transferred to a solvent third party); (3) no creditor (domestic or foreign) of a resolved bank is left any worse off as a consequence of the resolution action than they would have been had the bank not been resolved and foreign creditors are not discriminated against on the basis of their nationality or location. IMF, 'Resolution of Cross-Border Banks', p. 22, Box 7.

[93] *Ibid.*, pp. 23–4. The IMF paper suggests that '[i]deally, agreement on burden sharing should be reached by the authorities of the principal jurisdictions on an institution-specific basis *before* a crisis occurs, especially if such agreements were to be supported by institution-specific recovery and resolutions plans (RRPs) or "living wills"', *ibid.* This reflects a similar proposal made in Avgouleas, Goodhart and Schoenmaker, 'Bank Recovery and Resolution Plans'.

covering financial institutions that maintain cross-border branches.[94] This principle reflects a similar choice in UNCITRAL Model law.

The IMF's model for co-ordination of cross-border resolutions constitutes significant progress over pre-existing frameworks but it does not resolve the issue of effective cross-border group resolution. Since it is based on co-ordinated national resolution actions, it is rather ineffective when it comes to group resolution, a shortcoming that it shares with the proposal for an EU resolution regime discussed below, which reflects most of the features of the IMF model.

6.   The Dodd–Frank Act resolution regime for SIFIs

In the US, much more than in Europe the resolution regime had to balance strong political agendas advanced by an increasingly militant Republican party and the liberals who were highly critical of bank bail-outs in light of the US government doing much less to rekindle the recovery of the real economy which had led to serious suffering for US households.[95] The focus of the Dodd–Frank Act resolution regime is on preventing SIFI failures and, if that fails, to lay down the foundations of an orderly resolution process that would not disrupt the function of the rest of the financial system and of the economy.

6.1   Enhanced supervision and failure prevention

The Dodd–Frank Act requires the FRB to issue, in consultation with the FSOC, rules providing for early remediation of financial distress that increase in stringency as the financial condition of the company declines. The FRB must prescribe rules to limit the risks posed to any systemically important non-bank financial company by the failure of any individual company. The rules prohibit a systemically important non-bank financial company from having credit exposure to any unaffiliated company that exceeds 25 per cent of the capital stock.[96] Also, the FRB and FDIC require systemically important non-bank financial companies to submit periodic reports to them and the FSOC regarding the nature and extent to which the company has credit exposure to

---

[94] IMF, 'Resolution of Cross-Border Banks', pp. 25–6.
[95] See David Skeel, *The New Financial Deal: Understanding the Dodd–Frank Act and Its (Unintended) Consequences* (Hoboken, NJ: Wiley & Sons, 2011), pp. 1–8.
[96] Section 165(e)(2), Dodd–Frank Act.

other 'significant' non-bank financial companies and 'significant' bank holding companies.[97]

Section 165 (d) gives the FRB the power to to require each SIFI to file periodic reports with itself, the FSOC and the FDIC describing its plans for rapid and orderly resolution in the event of material financial distress or failure, which shall include:

(1) information regarding the manner and extent to which any insured depository institution affiliated with the company is adequately protected from risks arising from the activities of any non-bank subsidiaries of the company;
(2) full description of the ownership structure, assets, liabilities and contractual obligations of the company;
(3) identification of the cross-guarantees tied to different securities, identification of major counterparties and a process for determining to whom the collateral of the company is pledged; and
(4) any other information that the FRB and FDIC jointly require.

Moreover, the Act introduces a number of steps that lead to enhanced supervision, in addition to the prudential standards discussed in the previous chapter. Section 165(i) provides for the conduct of annual stress tests over SIFIs. In this context, the FRB, in co-ordination with the appropriate primary financial regulatory agencies and the Federal Insurance Office, will conduct annual analyses in which non-bank financial companies supervised by the board of governors and bank holding companies are subject to evaluation of whether such companies have the capital, on a total consolidated basis, necessary to absorb losses as a result of adverse economic conditions. SIFIs will also have to conduct semi-annual internal stress tests. Other financial companies with US$10 billion or more in assets must conduct annual internal stress tests. In addition to the annual stress tests, on-site supervision of banks is also strengthened. The FDIC is authorized to conduct special examinations of any insured depository institution, systemically important non-bank financial company or bank holding company with US$50 billion or more total consolidated assets pursuant to its authority under the liquidation authority of Title II. The FDIC is also granted back-up authority with respect to any depository institution holding company that engages in conduct or threatens conduct, including any

---

[97]   Section 165(d)(20), Dodd–Frank Act.

acts or omissions that pose a foreseeable and material risk to the Deposit Insurance Fund.[98]

Under Section 165(d) all 'covered companies' qualifying as SIFIs have an obligation to prepare annual recovery and resolution plans ('living wills'),[99] which is meant to be used as a powerful tool for the evaluation by the supervisor (FRB) and the resolution authority (FDIC) of the Covered Company's structure, interconnections and possible problem areas. Thus, 'living wills' must contain critical information about the corporate and organizational structure, the business lines, the operations and the financial position of SIFIs. 'Living wills' will be jointly reviewed by the FRB and the FDIC to determine whether the plan meets minimum information requirements and is (1) credible and (2) would facilitate the orderly liquidation of a 'covered company'. If the FRB and the FDIC are not satisfied, they are entitled to ask for amendments.[100]

The FRB's new preventive powers go as far as having the right to dictate certain business actions to be taken by SIFIs that pose a grave threat to the financial stability of the US. Thus, the board of governors, with an affirmative vote of no less than two-thirds of the voting members of the Council then serving, may take the following mitigating action:[101]

(1) limit the ability of the company to merge with, acquire, consolidate with or otherwise become affiliated with another company;
(2) restrict the ability of the company to offer a financial product or products;
(3) require the company to terminate one or more activities;
(4) impose conditions on the manner in which the company conducts one or more activities; or
(5) if the board of governors determines that the above actions are inadequate to mitigate a threat to the financial stability of the US to require the company to sell or otherwise transfer assets or off-balance sheet items to unaffiliated entities.

---

[98] Section 121(a), Dodd–Frank Act.
[99] 'Covered companies' means all financial institutions that are regarded as systemically important either because they are bank holding companies with at least US$50 billion in total global consolidated assets or are foreign banks which are treated as such under Section 8(a) of the International Banking Act, or non-financial companies designated as systemically important by FSOC, under the procedure described in the preceding chapter. See FDIC Proposed Rule, 'Living Wills', 12 CFR Part 360 RIN 3064-AD77, 29 March 2011.
[100] Ibid.   [101] Section 121(a) and Section 163, Dodd–Frank Act.

6.2   Orderly Liquidation Authority

6.2.1   Overview

Title II of the Dodd–Frank Act has introduced a SIFI specific resolution regime and creates a new mechanism for their liquidation called 'Orderly Liquidation Authority' (OLA).[102] The new regime is intended to eliminate taxpayer bail-outs of institutions that are 'too big to fail' by providing the FDIC with the tools necessary to conduct an orderly liquidation of systemically important non-bank financial companies. Under the OLA, the FDIC is given the power to liquidate 'covered financial companies',[103] including banks and FRB supervised non-bank financial institutions which have been deemed to be systemically important. However, the Title II liquidation authority shall only be used in very limited circumstances and the process of the Bankruptcy Code shall remain the primary mechanism for resolving non-bank financial companies. Moreover, given the controversy surrounding the massive US bail-outs of 2008 and TARP, the new regime requires that all financial companies put into receivership under Title II are liquidated and it limits the FRB's Section 13(3) authority to aid individual companies. These changes are designed to prevent preferential government or FRB bail-outs.

At first reading the new regime is a marked improvement over the pre-existing framework whereby it was very difficult to deal with the failure of a financial institution that was not FDIC regulated, as was the case of Lehman Brothers, or where the cost of resolution was much in excess of FDIC funds, necessitating a public bail-out. Yet the differences from the pre-existing regime do not seem to be as great as Dodd–Frank legislators have suggested.[104] The receivership authority is granted as

---

[102] Section 204, Dodd–Frank Act.
[103] Section 201(a)(11) of the Dodd–Frank Act defines a 'financial company' as a company that is incorporated or organized under any provision of federal or state law and is a BHC; non-bank financial company supervised by the FRB; company that is 'predominantly engaged' in activities the FRB has determined to be financial in nature under Section 4(k) of the Bank Holding Company Act; or any subsidiary of the foregoing that is predominantly engaged in activities the FRB has determined to be financial in nature under Section 4(k) of the Bank Holding Company Act. A company is 'predominantly engaged' in activities the FRB has determined to be financial in nature under Section 4(k) of the Bank Holding Company Act if the consolidated revenues of the company from such activities constitute at least 85 per cent of the total consolidated revenues of the company and its subsidiaries (including insured depository institutions), as the FDIC, in consultation with Treasury, will established by regulation.
[104] Skeel argues that the new framework looks not very dissimilar to the previous one and the inexplicable rush to regulate is easily explained if it is viewed as an attempt by the

part of the orderly liquidation process and essentially it constitutes a remodelling of the FDIC's resolution authority for insured depository institutions under the FDIA coupled with several US Bankruptcy Code concepts made to suit the liquidation needs of non-bank financial companies.

6.2.2   The special liquidation process

Title II establishes a comprehensive process for determining whether the FDIC should be appointed as receiver and the financial company liquidated in accordance with the orderly liquidation process. This process generally requires the consent of the Treasury, FDIC and the FRB, and an up-front review of this determination by a federal district court. On their own initiative or at the request of Treasury, the FRB and the FDIC must consider whether to make a written recommendation with respect to whether Treasury should appoint the FDIC as receiver of a financial company. Any such recommendation must be approved by a supermajority of two-thirds of the members of the FRB and two-thirds of the members of the FDIC's Board of Directors.[105] In the case of a broker-dealer, or for financial companies where the broker-dealer is the largest US subsidiary, the recommendation must be approved by two-thirds of the members of the FRB and two-thirds of the members of the SEC; for insurance companies, the recommendation must be approved by two-thirds of the members of the FRB and the Director of the Federal Insurance Office (FIO), in consultation with the FDIC.[106]

Having received the written recommendation of the FRB and FDIC (or other relevant agency), the Treasury may make a determination that the FDIC should be appointed as receiver for a financial company if, in consultation with the President, it finds that:[107]

(1) the financial company is in default or in danger of default;
(2) the failure of the financial company and its resolution under the otherwise applicable law would have serious adverse effects on financial stability in the US;
(3) there is no viable private sector alternative to prevent the financial company's default;

same regulators/politicians that conducted the controversial bail-outs to cover their tracks, David Skeel, 'The New Financial Deal Understanding the Dodd–Frank Act', Research Paper.
[105] Section 203(a), Dodd–Frank Act.   [106] *Ibid.*
[107] Section 203(b), Dodd–Frank Act.

(4) the impact of liquidation by the FDIC on creditors, counterparties and shareholders of the financial company and other market participants would be appropriate given the impact of such liquidation on financial stability in the US;

(5) the orderly liquidation under Section 204 would avoid or mitigate adverse effects on financial stability; and

(6) a federal agency has ordered the financial company to convert all its convertible debt instruments to equity.

In order to secure wider accountability when a decision of so much importance is made, the Treasury Secretary must notify Congress leaders of his/her decision within 24 hours and send a full report justifying his/her decision.[108] A subsequent report must be filed with Congress within sixty days from the appointment of FDIC as receiver.[109] Any appointment of the FDIC as receiver terminates in three years subject to two possible one-year extensions if the FDIC certifies in writing to Congress the need for such an extension. Subject to certain limitations, this period can be extended for the purpose of completing ongoing litigation involving the FDIC as receiver.[110]

6.2.3   OLA triggers/thresholds

OLA triggers/thresholds tend to be objective but they also leave room for regulatory discretion. Accordingly, a financial company would be in default or in danger of default if:[111]

(1) a bankruptcy case with respect to the financial company has been, or is soon likely to be, filed;

(2) the financial company has incurred, or is likely to incur, losses depleting all or substantially all of its capital, and there is no chance of avoiding such capital depletion;

(3) the assets of the financial company are, or are likely to be, less than its liabilities; or

(4) the financial company is not able to pay its obligations in the normal course of business.

To the extent that the FDIC is appointed as receiver for a covered financial company, the provisions of Title II will govern all matters and no

---

[108] Section 203(c)(2), Dodd–Frank Act.
[109] Section 203(c)(3), Dodd–Frank Act.
[110] Section 202(d), Dodd–Frank Act.
[111] Section 203(c)(4), Dodd–Frank Act.

provisions of the US Bankruptcy Code will apply. In the event that upon notification of the Treasury's decision that the FDIC should be appointed receiver for a financial company, the board of directors expresses disagreement with the decision, Treasury shall confidentially petition the US District Court for the District of Columbia to issue an order authorizing the appointment of the FDIC as receiver.[112] The decision of the court is subject to appeal but no stay or injunction is granted pending appeal.[113] The Dodd–Frank Act provides that the board of directors of a financial company are not liable for any acquiescing or consenting decision they take in good faith to the appointment of the FDIC as receiver.[114] Naturally, this provision is meant to provide the board of the company in question with an incentive to consent, eliminating the need for judicial review.[115]

6.2.4   FDIC powers under the OLA

As said above, one of the most important aspects of the OLA is that the FDIC shall exercise its authority under Title II only when such action is necessary to preserve the financial stability of the US rather than for the purpose of preserving the covered financial company. As a result, all financial companies put into receivership under Title II shall be liquidated.[116] The FDIC in the exercise of this authority should:[117] (1) ensure that the shareholders do not receive payment until all other claims are paid; (2) ensure that unsecured creditors bear the losses in accordance with the legal priority of claims; (3) ensure that the management and the board of directors of the covered company have been removed; and (4) not take any equity interest or become a shareholder of the covered financial company. However, reflecting the politicized nature of bank bail-outs in the US, the objectives of the resolution framework are not only to minimize losses to the public and moral hazard by forcing creditors and shareholders, rather than the public, to bear the cost of the institution's failure, as is the case with the proposed European framework, but also 'punitive'.[118] For this reason, those responsible for the failure of the institution should be held accountable. The latter may be required to redress requisite losses.[119] This

---

[112] Section 202(a)(1)(A)(i), Dodd–Frank Act.
[113] Section 202(a)(1)(B), Dodd–Frank Act.
[114] Section 207, Dodd–Frank Act
[115] Mayer Brown, 'Understanding the Financial Reform Legislation', p. 34.
[116] Section 204(a), Dodd–Frank Act.
[117] Section 206, Dodd–Frank Act.
[118] Section 204(a) and Section 206, Dodd–Frank Act.
[119] Section 204(a)(3), Dodd–Frank Act states: 'the Corporation and other appropriate agencies will take all steps necessary and appropriate to assure that all parties, including

objective is different from the one underlying similar proceedings under the US Bankruptcy Code.[120]

The FDIC's special 'liquidation authority' may be extended to the entire group.[121] Thus, the FDIC may appoint itself as receiver of any covered subsidiary that is organized under federal law or the laws of any state, if the FDIC and Treasury jointly determine that: (1) the covered subsidiary is in default or danger of default; (2) such action would avoid or mitigate serious adverse effects on the financial stability or economic condition of the US, and (3) such action would facilitate the orderly liquidation of the covered financial company. A covered financial subsidiary does not include an insured depository institution, an insurance company or a covered broker or dealer. Following its appointment as a receiver of a subsidiary the FDIC treats the subsidiary as a covered financial company with all the powers given to it under Title II.[122]

Universal succession shall ensue and upon appointment as receiver for a covered financial company the FDIC shall succeed the failing entity to: (1) all rights, titles, powers, and privileges of the covered financial company and its assets, and of any stockholder, member, officer or director of such company; and (2) title to the books, records, and assets of any previous receiver or other legal custodian of such covered financial company.[123] This also means that all rights and claims that the shareholders and creditors of the covered financial company may have against the assets of the covered financial company or the FDIC arising out of their status as shareholders or creditors shall be terminated, without affecting rights for compensation uder Title II. The FDIC has a duty to ensure that shareholders and unsecured creditors bear losses, consistent with the priority of claims, as set out in Title II.[124]

Moreover, the powers of the FDIC as a receiver under Title II of the Dodd–Frank Act are modelled on the resolution authority for insured depository institutions under the Federal Deposit Insurance Act.[125] These powers would permit the FDIC to:[126]

management, directors, and third parties, having responsibility for the condition of the financial company bear losses consistent with their responsibility, including actions for damages, restitution, and recoupment of compensation and other gains not compatible with such responsibility'.
[120] Mayer Brown, 'Understanding the Financial Reform Legislation', p. 35.
[121] Sections 210(a)(1)(E) and 202(d), Dodd–Frank Act.
[122] Ibid.   [123] Section 210(a)(1)(A), Dodd–Frank Act.
[124] Section 210(a)(1)(M), Dodd–Frank Act.
[125] Federal Deposit Insurance Act 1950 (PL 81–797, 64 STAT. 873), as revised.
[126] Section 210(a)(1)(B)-(D), (F), (G), Dodd–Frank Act.

(1) take over the assets of and operate the financial company;
(2) set up a bridge financial company;[127]
(3) sell or transfer assets to a bridge financial company;
(4) merge the covered financial company with another company;
(5) value and prioritize claims;
(6) avoid fraudulent transfers and preferences;
(7) seek injunctive relief against any asset anywhere (without the necessity of showing irreparable harm);
(8) prioritize administrative expenses of the receiver;
(9) repudiate contracts, including qualified financial contracts, and limit damages for such repudiation;
(10) transfer qualified financial contracts and give notification of transfer;
(11) impose a one business-day (effectively allowing a weekend to transfer) automatic stay of termination rights for qualified financial contracts (as opposed to the three days in the original Senate-passed bill);
(12) recognize security interests and customer interests;
(13) enforce contracts;
(14) invalidate *ipso facto* clauses;
(15) require consent for the termination, acceleration or declaration of default under any contract to which the covered financial institution is a party; and
(16) pursue directors and officers of a covered financial company for gross negligence or intentional tortious conduct.

6.2.5   Bridge bank

The FDIC, as receiver for one or more covered financial companies or in anticipation of being appointed as receiver, may organize one or more bridge financial companies.[128] Such bridge financial company may, at the FDIC's discretion:

(1) assume such liabilities (including liabilities associated with any trust or custody business, but excluding any liabilities that count as regulatory capital) at FDIC's discretion;

---

[127] Under Section 201(a)(3), of the Dodd–Frank Act a 'bridge financial company' means a new financial company organized by the FDIC in accordance with Section 210(h) of the Dodd–Frank Act for the purpose of resolving a covered financial company.
[128] Section 210(h), Dodd–Frank Act.

(2) purchase such assets (including assets associated with any trust or custody business) of such covered financial company; and

(3) perform any other temporary function which the FDIC may prescribe.

The FDIC may grant a federal charter to and approve articles of association for one or more bridge financial company or companies, with respect to such covered financial company. Upon its establishment, a bridge financial company is under the management of a board of directors appointed by the FDIC.

Any succession to or assumption by a bridge financial company of rights, powers, authorities or privileges of a covered financial company given to it by FDIC shall be effective without any further approval under federal or state law, assignment or consent. The FDIC is not required to pay capital into a bridge financial company or to issue any capital stock on behalf of a bridge financial company. However, if the FDIC determines that such action is advisable, it may cause capital stock or other securities of a bridge financial company to be issued and offered for sale.

6.2.6   Financing resolution and repayment plan

Section 214 of the Dodd–Frank Act mandates that no taxpayer funds should be used to prevent the liquidation of any financial company under this title. All funds spent in the liquidation of a financial company under this title should be recovered from the disposition of assets of such financial company, or shall be the responsibility of the financial sector, through risk-based (charges) assessments. Namely, the Dodd–Frank Act does not provide for a pre-funded orderly liquidation fund, although the establishment of such a fund was included in the original Senate proposal released in March 2010 by ex-chairman of Senate Banking Committee Christopher Dodd (D-CT). The reason for this omission is that these proposals were met by strong opposition by Senators who claimed that a pre-funded resolution fund would give rise to moral hazard and encourage the use of the orderly liquidation process, undermining market discipline.

To fund the 'orderly liquidation' process Title II establishes an 'Orderly Liquidation Fund' within the Treasury. The Fund will be managed by the FDIC.[129] Title II gives the power to FDIC to fund the costs of liquidating

---

[129] Section 210(n) of the Dodd–Frank Act provides: 'There is established in the Treasury of the United States a separate fund to be known as the "Orderly Liquidation Fund", which shall be available to the Corporation to carry out the authorities contained in this

a covered financial company by borrowing from Treasury, through the issuing of 'obligations', up to a maximum amount of:[130] (1) 10 per cent of the book value of the covered financial company's total consolidated assets during the first thirty days after the appointment of the FDIC as receiver; and (2) 90 per cent of the fair value of the covered financial company's total consolidated assets after the first thirty days.

Prior to drawing up any borrowing from the Treasury to fund an orderly liquidation, the FDIC must present to the Treasury for approval an 'Orderly Liquidation Plan' and a 'Mandatory Repayment Plan'.[131] The 'Orderly Liquidation Plan' must detail the liquidation actions the FDIC will adopt with regard to a covered financial company, including the provision and use of funds, payments to third parties, as well as steps to be taken to co-ordinate with other primary financial regulatory agencies. The 'Orderly Liquidation Plan' must also have a wider public interest/social dimension and describe actions to avoid or mitigate potential adverse effects on low income, minority or underserved communities affected by the failure of the covered financial company. The FDIC may, at any time, amend any 'Orderly Liquidation Plan' approved by the Treasury Secretary with his/her consent.

The 'Mandatory Repayment Plan' the FDIC presents to the Treasury for approval has two aspects.[132] First, it provides a specific plan and schedule to repay the borrowing (Mandatory Repayment Plan). Second, it demonstrates that income to the FDIC from the liquidated assets of the covered financial company and assessments will be sufficient to amortize the outstanding balance within the period established in the repayment schedule and pay the interest accruing on such balance, owed to Treasury within the time frame established in the repayment schedule.[133] If necessary to repay the debt to Treasury and the costs of any liquidation, the FDIC must impose risk-based assessments (charges) to the financial sector.[134] Any claimant who received more money in the

title, for the cost of actions authorized by this title, including the orderly liquidation of covered financial companies, payment of administrative expenses, the payment of principal and interest by the Corporation on obligations issued under paragraph (5), and the exercise of the authorities of the Corporation under this title'.

[130] Section 210(n), Dodd–Frank Act.
[131] Section 210(n)(9)(A), (B), Dodd–Frank Act.
[132] Section 210(n)(9)(A), Dodd–Frank Act.
[133] Section 210(n)(9)(B), Dodd–Frank Act. Treasury and the FDIC must submit a copy of the repayment schedule to Congress within thirty days of the receipt of funding by the FDIC.
[134] Section 210(o), Dodd–Frank Act.

FDIC's resolution than such claimant would have received in liquidation proceedings under the US Bankruptcy Code or in a Securities Investor Protection Corporation (SIPC) proceeding, must refund the difference. The assessments (charges) shall next be imposed, if necessary, on BHCs with total consolidated assets of US$50 billion or more and non-bank financial companies regulated by the FRB. The Dodd–Frank Act contemplates that the assessments criteria will be risk-based, taking into account a financial company's business.

The graduated assessments imposed by the FDIC will be based on a risk matrix developed by the FDIC in consultation with the FSOC. The Act requires the FDIC and FSOC to take the following factors into account when developing the risk matrix:[135] (1) general economic conditions; (2) assessments imposed on a financial company or any affiliate that is an insured depository institution, SIPC member or insurance company; (3) risks presented by the financial company to the financial system; and (4) the extent to which the financial company has benefitted, or is likely to benefit, from the orderly liquidation of a financial company under Title II (compared to a liquidation under the US Bankruptcy Code or other liquidation scheme). Assessment of the latter should take into account, *inter alia*: (1) the amount, categories and concentration of a financial company and its affiliates' on- and off-balance sheet assets and liabilities; (2) the activities and relevant market share of the financial company; (3) the extent to which the financial company is leveraged; (4) the amount, maturity, volatility and stability of the financial company's liabilities and its reliance on short-term funding; (5) the stability and variety of the financial company's sources of funding; (6) the financial company's importance to households, businesses and governments as a source of credit and liquidity to the financial system; and (7) the extent to which the financial company manages, rather than owns, assets, and the extent to which any ownership is diffuse.

The Miller–Moore amendment included in the original bill passed by the House of Representatives granted the FDIC the authority to impose haircuts of up to 10 per cent on certain secured creditors providing short-term funding. The Dodd–Frank Act did not include this amendment or any similar provision. Instead Section 215 requires that no later than one year after enactment of the Dodd–Frank Act, the FSOC shall conduct a study and submit a report to Congress evaluating the importance of maximizing protection of US taxpayers and promoting market discipline

---

[135]   Section 210(o)(4)(A)-(C), Dodd–Frank Act.

with respect to the treatment of fully secured creditors under the orderly liquidation authority.

6.3   Evaluation

The Dodd–Frank resolution framework is a very important reform and will prevent to the extent possible future bail-outs. Nonetheless, as should be expected of legislation that became so politicized, it also presents a number of loopholes. First, it largely ignores the cross-border dimension which is the most difficult and challenging part of financial group bail-outs/resolutions in modern markets. The lack of any attempt for substantive law convergence and of dedicated structures dealing with cross-border resolution in Dodd–Frank is coupled with an *ex post* form of financing resolution which is bound to make fiscal burden sharing arrangements between the US and other jurisdictions even more unlikely. Second, although the restriction on the use of Federal Reserve's emergency lending authority is based on a valuable principle – curbing the FRB's discretion to single out individual firms for rescue – it might not prove enough to prevent future bail-outs. Skeel observes that regulators can always pressurize other systemically important firms to fund a bail-out – as they did when the Long Term Capital Management, a hedge fund, collapsed in 1998. Also other forms of assistance may be offered, provided that OLA proceedings have not been initiated. [136]

Another area of concern should be the model chosen by Dodd–Frank legislators to fund resolution. Opting for an *ex post* resolution funding model could prove perilous. The value of bank assets is cyclical and the failure of an institution is more likely to happen during a downturn when asset prices are substantially lower than their valuations during boom times, when most banks assets tend to be created, due to the relaxed conditions governing credit extension. Returns on the sale of the distressed institution's assets may prove insufficient to cover the costs of resolution even when the economy is in a good phase. During liquidation interested buyers will try to obtain the assets of the failed institution at the lowest possible prices. Furthermore, risk assessed charges imposed on the financial sector to fund resolutions might prove an unbearable burden on banks if they coincide, as is likely, with an economic downturn when the financial sector will already be under stress.

Another aspect of OLA that is bound to prove problematic relates to legislators' insistence that a bank that enters OLA should be liquidated. In

---

[136] Skeel, 'The New Financial Deal', p. 12

some cases preserving the institution as a going concern for a while might be a better option for all parties concerned, including creditors, and the best approach for preserving systemic functions. Finally, if, contrary to what was said above, the market is persuaded that a future public bail-out is indeed unlikely, then the cost of funding for US financial institutions could increase affecting their profitability and business expansion, since competitor banks from other jurisdictions might still enjoy the safety of an implicit government guarantee.[137]

7.   The proposed EU crisis management and resolution framework

7.1   General principles

The Commission has issued a number of Communications and other documents that set out its thinking regarding a new EU architecture for the management of financial sector crises, especially cross-border crises, and the resolution of individual financial institutions and EU-based financial groups.[138] The EU crisis management plan is very ambitious, since it extends from early intervention to bank and (systemically significant) investment firm resolution. If implemented it is bound to cast aside shareholder and creditor rights that constitute serious obstacles for the timely and efficient resolution of financial institutions in certain EU jurisdictions. For this reason, the Commission proposals are not expected to be implemented without opposition, since the differentiated bank insolvency regimes in the EU are also used by certain member states as a means of shoring up the competitiveness of their national banks.[139]

The main objective of the new framework is to ensure that distressed 'institutions of any type and size, and in particular systemically important

---

[137]   For the possibility of 'OLA' creating competitive disadvantages to US banks, see Scott, 'Testimony'.

[138]   EU Commission, 'An EU Framework for Cross-Border Crisis Management in the Banking Sector' COM(2009) 561; EU Commission, 'An EU Framework for Crisis Management in the Financial Sector' COM (2010) 579. Cf. European Parliament, 'Cross-Border Crisis Management in the Banking Sector' A7–0213/2010, Committee on Economic and Monetary Affairs, rapporteur: Elisa Ferreira.

[139]   For an overview of bank insolvency law discrepancies in EU member states, see Annemarie van der Zwet, 'Crisis Management Tools in the EU: What Do We Really Need?', De Nederlandsche Bank Occasional Studies 9/2, March 2011, pp. 12–18, available at www.dnb.nl/binaries/os0902_tcm46-249429.pdf.

institutions, can be allowed to fail without risk to financial stability whilst avoiding costs to taxpayers'.[140] Unlike the Dodd–Frank Act the proposed EU framework does not create a special resolution regime for SIFIs. The crisis management framework the Commission is developing comprises three classes of measures: preparatory and preventative measures; early supervisory intervention; and resolution tools and powers. It is based on seven principles/objectives:[141]

(1) give priority to prevention and preparation;
(2) minimize the risk of contagion and secure 'continuity of essential financial services, including continuous access to deposits for insured depositors';
(3) enable fast and decisive action, by putting in place clear resolution powers and processes, which should also eliminate uncertainty about when authorities can intervene and what actions they can take;
(4) reduce moral hazard 'by ensuring an appropriate allocation of losses to shareholders and creditors and protecting public funds';[142]
(5) lead to a smooth resolution of cross border groups;
(6) ensure legal certainty, through: (a) the establishment of appropriate safeguards for third parties; and (b) restriction of any interference with property rights to what is necessary and justified in the public interest;
(7) limit distortions of competition, which derive from public support/ rescue interventions. As a result, state aid granted under the resolution framework must be compatible with the Treaty rules and the internal market.

The EU's proposed design for the resolution of both national and cross-border groups consists of the following mechanisms/tools:

(1) recovery planning, including conditions for intra-group financial support;
(2) resolution planning
(3) early intervention
(4) resolution which comprises: (a) conditions for resolution; and (b) resolutions tools and powers.

The Commission is placing increased importance on financial group resolution. Nonetheless, in the absence of any plans to establish a single EU resolution authority for cross-border groups the Commission simply

---

[140] EU Commission, 'Framework for Cross-Border Crisis Management, 2010', p. 4.
[141] *Ibid.*, p. 5.   [142] *Ibid.*, p. 4.

attempts to provide a regime harmonized in its most important characteristics and opts for the IMF contractual (mutual recognition) model of regulatory and cross-border co-ordination of resolution by different supervisors.[143] Furthermore, the Commission intends to introduce legislation to restrict asset transfers between different credit institutions and certain investment firms within a group and place safeguards on intra-group financing, especially when those entities experience liquidity stresses.

7.2   Preparation, early intervention and prevention

The Commission intends to minimize the risk of failure for EU financial institutions through the adoption of a series of preparatory and preventive measures, including a stricter supervision regime, for certain institutions, which also facilitates early intervention (also called Prompt Corrective Action (PCA)) to prevent the triggering of the resolution process, which is bound to prove highly disruptive for the markets and seriously damaging to shareholder and creditor interests.

EU credit institutions and (systemically) significant investment firms will have an obligation to draw up recovery and resolution plans. Recovery and resolution plans will be required both at entity and group level. They are bound to prove an effective tool both for the in-depth understanding of a financial institution's business by its supervisors and for the minimization of disruption in the event of an institution's failure.

7.2.1   Strengthened supervision

Failures of supervision at the national and the cross-border level preceded the crisis in the EU and contributed to its magnitude.[144] In response the Commission has, in tandem with the structural changes discussed in the previous chapter, suggested a plan for strengthening the supervision of credit institutions and of certain (systemically) important investment firms. The strengthened regime includes:[145]

---

[143] IMF, 'Resolution of Cross-Border Banks'.
[144] EU Commission, 'An EU Framework for Crisis Management 2010', p.5.
[145] DG Internal Market and Services, 'Working Document Technical Details of a Possible EU Framework for Bank Recovery and Resolution', 6 January 2011, available at ec.europa. eu/internal_market/consultations/docs/2011/crisis_management/consultation_ paper_eu.pdf, (hereinafter Commission Working Document). Commission Working Document, pp. 16–18.

(1) *Annual preparation of supervisory programmes for each institution on the basis of a risk assessment.* These should include annual examination programmes, which may indicate how the supervisors would carry out their tasks and allocate their resources. It could identify which credit institutions would be subject to enhanced supervision and make provision for such supervision, and include provision for on-site inspections at any of the premises used by a credit institution (including its branches and subsidiaries);[146]

(2) *robust stress testing involving annual supervisory stress tests of credit institutions*, in addition to those conducted by EBA. The purpose of the stress tests is to evaluate the resilience of credit institutions, which will be tested against conceivable adverse economic developments, including shocks which are of low probability but high impact, with the purpose of ascertaining institutions' ability to absorb shocks;

(3) *powers to undertake enhanced supervision* of: (a) credit institutions for which the results of the stress tests, or the outcome of the supervisory review process, indicate significant risks to their continuing financial soundness or breaches in their compliance with the requirements of the Capital Requirement Directives (CRD) (Comprising Directive 2006/48/EC and Directive 2006/49/EC); (b) credit institutions that pose systemic risks to the financial system; and (c) any other credit institution that supervisors consider should be subject to enhanced supervision.

Enhanced supervision, in particular, could, according to Commission proposals, include the means necessary to enable supervisors to monitor the development of risks to the financial soundness of the credit institution and to ensure that compliance breaches are rectified, such as:

(1) more frequent on-site inspections at the premises of the supervised institution;

(2) the establishment or maintenance of a permanent presence of supervisors at the premises of the institution concerned;

(3) requiring additional or more frequent reporting by the supervised institution;

---

[146] Commission Working Document, para. A1, p. 16. This provision will remedy situations where supervisors often take years to carry out a significant examination of the supervised institution's functions and riskiness as was the case with FSA's supervision of Northern Rock. See FSA, Internal Audit Division Report, 'The Supervision of Northern Rock: A Lessons Learned Review', March 2008, available at www.fsa.gov.uk/pubs/other/nr_report.pdf. For analysis of these failures see The Run on the Rock, (House of Commons, Treasury Committee, Fifth Report of Session 2007–08, 24 January 2008).

(4) additional or more frequent review of the operational, strategic or business plans of the credit institution and thematic examinations for the purposes of monitoring specific risks that are likely to materialize.

On the other hand, as the Commission Communication does not make any distinction between systemically important and non-systemically important banks, there is a danger that smaller institutions will struggle to cope with the level of regulatory intrusion the Commission intends to impose on them and the costs enhanced supervision entails.

7.2.2   Restrictions on inter-group asset transfers and intra-group financing

The Icelandic banks' failure and the Lehman Borther's collapse, discussed in Chapter 5, have underscored the importance of placing limits and safeguards on intra-group financing and asset transfers. On the other hand, intra-group financing and transfers of assets from one group entity to another are at the heart of modern banking and create significant, even critical, efficiencies in the operation of banking groups. However, both methods may also be used to weaken the financial position of one group entity and strengthen another. In addition, host country regulators who wished during the GFC to request the parent entity to provide funding support to a subsidiary or branch operating in their territory had no formal powers to do so. The Commission considers whether the provision of financial support by parent credit institutions and EU parent financial holding companies and subsidiaries, which are credit institutions or investment firms, should be allowed subject to strict requirements.[147] The Commission has proposed a number of conditions to be included in intra-group financing agreements acting as safeguards of proper use of such support.[148] The most important of these requirements are the following:

(1) there must be a reasonable prospect that the support provided will redress the financial difficulties of the entity receiving the support;
(2) the provision of financial support should have the objective of preserving or restoring the financial stability of the group as a whole;

---

[147] Financial support might involve the parent institution or the holding company providing to its subsidiaries or the subsidiaries to the parent finance, in the form of a loan, the provision of guarantees, or the provision of assets for use as collateral in the form of a loan, the provision of guarantees or the provision of assets for use as collateral.
[148] Commission Working Document, para. C4, pp. 22–3.

(3) the financial support should be provided for consideration given to the entity providing the support by the entity that receives it;

(4) the financial support may only be provided if it is reasonably certain that the loan will be reimbursed or the consideration for the support will be paid by the entity receiving the support;

(5) the financial support may only be granted if it does not jeopardize the liquidity or solvency of the entity providing the support;

(6) the financial support provided in accordance with the agreement may only be granted if the entity providing the support is in compliance when the support is granted and continues to be in compliance at the least with the capital requirements of Directive 2006/48/EC.

The decision of the management body of the entity providing financial support should indicate how the financial support is justified by an economic, commercial or financial common interest of the group as a whole, including the interest of the legal entity providing the support, and preserves or restores the financial stability of the group as a whole. Management must also confirm that the financial support does not exceed the financial capacities of the legal entity providing the financial support and that the provider of support will continue to meet its solvency obligations under Directive 2006/48/EC. The supervisor of the entity providing the group financial support has the right to prohibit or restrict the provision of financial support if the conditions for group financial support, set out above, are not met, or if the provision of financial support jeopardizes the financial stability in the member state where the entity providing it is established. A decision of the supervisor to prohibit or restrict the financial support should take into account the views of the supervisor of the member state in which the legal entity receiving the support has been licensed, and the potential impact of its decision on the financial stability of that country.[149] Moreover, the Commission is considering giving supervisors of financial institutions in distress the power to require the management body of the parent company to provide financial support. It is, however, hard to see how this power may be reconciled with the power of the parent supervisor to deny the provision of such assistance. Arguably, this is another gaping hole in the proposed resolution framework which underscores the pressing importance of establishing an EU resolution authority.

[149] If the supervisor responsible for the entity receiving the support disagrees with the decision to prohibit or restrict the financial support, it should be able to request the assistance of the EBA.

7.2.3   Asset transfers

In the absence of the concept of group interest, especially in cross-border insolvencies, transfers of assets from one member of the group to another are often restricted by member state laws, since the recovery of these assets is a very difficult process in insolvency due to the doctrine of separate legal entity. Moreover, where the concept of group interest has been developed as a result of court decisions, it lacks the required clarity to create legal certainty. The proposed resolution framework just intends to introduce rules governing the conditions under which assets may be transferred between entities of a cross-border banking group in stressed situations, but not when the institution has entered bank insolvency proceedings.[150]

The first requirement is that there should be a shareholders' agreement setting out the conditions for asset transferability and enabling the management to carry out asset transfers when these conditions are met. The shareholders' agreement should be approved by the supervisor of the transferor and be included in the recovery plan of the potential transferee and in the group recovery plan.[151] The purpose of the agreement is to ensure that managers can act with confidence and limit the legal challenges that minority shareholders and creditors may bring against the management. The parent credit institution and subsidiaries should file an application with the consolidating supervisor. The supervisors concerned would then work together in order to reach a joint decision within a certain period of time (e.g., six months). The EBA or another ESA could act as mediator when the members of the college of supervisors disagree. In the event of continuous disagreement, the Authority could decide to ask the supervisors to take a specific action or refrain from it. The most important concern generated by asset transfers will of course refer to the stability of the transferor and the impact of the transferor's weakened position in the stability of the financial system of the home country. As a result, the Commission is contemplating giving to the supervisor of the transferor the power to prohibit or restrict a transfer of assets pursuant to the agreement when this transfer threatens the liquidity or solvency of the transferor.

While the safeguards suggested by the Commission sound reasonable, in practice they are bound to create insurmountable problems for cross-border financial groups, unless the required procedures are substantially simplified. Within a financial group it is not uncommon at all that the

---

[150] Commission Working Document, p. 23.   [151] *Ibid.*

entire asset book moves overnight, on the basis of a loan or agency agreement, or something similar, from one entity of the group to another, located in a different part of the globe. While such transfers could make it impossible to locate the entity that is the rightful owner of the assets within a group in the event of resolution or insolvency, such practices sit at the heart of financial group operation in the fast moving world of modern markets. Thus, a balance will have to be struck between resolution preparation and creditor protection on the one hand and group operating efficiencies on the other.

7.3   Recovery plans and group recovery plans

Reflecting similar provisions in the Dodd–Frank Act and the aforementioned recommendations of the FSB regarding supervision of SIFIs, the Commission recommends the imposition on credit institutions and significant investment firms[152] of a requirement to draw up and keep updated recovery and resolution plans, also known as 'living wills'. These should: (1) set out the measures that the institution or group concerned sould be ready to take in different scenarios to address liquidity problems, raise capital or reduce risk;[153] and (2) be detailed and realistic without assuming access to any support from public funds. Supervisory and resolution authorities must be involved in the drawing up of such plans and when they refer to group plans they should be agreed jointly in the context of resolution colleges. Thus, they constitute one of the main pillars of the Commission's preparation and prevention strategy and should prepare the institution *ex ante* for the orderly transfer of the bank or of a business division or for its winding down should it fail.[154]

---

[152] According to the Commission the requisite criteria are 'the size of the firm, the nature of its sources of funding and the degree to which group or other sectoral support would be credibly available'. EU Commission, 'An EU Framework for Crisis Management', p. 5.

[153] EU Commission, 'An EU Framework for Crisis Management', pp. 5–6. The possible content of 'living wills' was first discussed in Richard Herring, 'Wind-Down Plans as an Alternative to Bailouts: The Cross-Border Challenge', in Kenneth E. Scott, George P. Shultz and John B. Taylor (eds.), *Ending Government Bailouts as We Know Them* (Stanford, CA: Hoover Institution Press, 2010), pp. 125–62.

[154] For example, resolution plans would require a detailed description of group structure, intra-group guarantees and service level agreements, contracts and counterparties, debt liabilities, custody arrangements, as well as operational information about IT systems and human resources. EU Commission, 'An EU Framework for Crisis Management 2010', p. 6. Recommendations regarding the potential content of resolution plans that are reflected in the Communication had been made, *inter alia*, in Herring, 'Wind-Down

Group plans should be agreed jointly. Supervisory authorities must assess whether such recovery plans are comprehensive and likely to restore the viability of the institution. According to the Commission Communication, at a minimum recovery plans should contain information regarding:[155]

(1) arrangements and measures to restore the credit institution's own funds;
(2) arrangements and measures to ensure that the credit institution has adequate access to liquidity to ensure that it can carry out its operations and meet its obligations as they fall due;
(3) arrangements and measures to reduce risk and leverage;
(4) preparatory arrangements to facilitate the sale of assets or business lines in a time frame appropriate for the restoration of financial soundness;
(5) possible arrangements for intra-group financial support adopted in accordance with any voluntary agreement for group financial support; and
(6) other management actions or strategies to restore financial soundness and the anticipated financial effect of those actions or strategies.

The supervisors examining recovery plans should assess the extent to which the plan satisfies the following criteria:[156] (1) the arrangements proposed in the plans are credible, realistic and sufficient to restore the viability of the institution or prepare it for an orderly winding-down of the problematic activities; and (2) the plans could be implemented without causing systemic disruption, even if several firms implemented similar recovery plans within the same period. Naturally, the question of whether supervisors are in a position to accurately assess *ex ante* whether the plans will provide credible recovery solutions *ex post* remains the biggest obstacle to the effectiveness of such plans.

One critical innovation suggested by the Commission is the drawing up by EU parent credit institutions or EU parent financial holding companies of group recovery plans, which could include recovery plans for each group entity. Group recovery plans should be submitted to the consolidating supervisor. The objective of a group level recovery plan should be to

---

Plans as an Alternative to Bailouts', pp. 125–62 and Avgouleas, Goodhart and Schoenmaker, 'Bank Resolution Plans as a Catalyst for Global Financial Reform'.
[155] Commission Working Document, p. 19.
[156] *Ibid.*, p. 20.

restore the viability of the group where part of the group, or the group as a whole, experiences a material deterioration in its financial situation. A group recovery plan would set out the circumstances under which a group level approach should be pursued, and could also include arrangements to ensure the co-ordination and consistency of recovery plans of group entities with the group recovery plan. The consolidating supervisor could review the group plan with representatives from the college of supervisors and assess, in co-operation with the other relevant supervisors, the extent to which the plan satisfies the above criteria. In addition the plan should provide assurances that measures taken at group level or the measures included in the recovery plans for each group entity would be sufficient to ensure the viability of each credit institution of the group or to prepare for an orderly winding down of the activities causing the problems.[157]

If supervisors decide that the recovery plan would not be likely to restore the viability of the credit institution under conditions of financial stress, or to prepare for an orderly winding down of the activities causing the problems, or that there are impediments to the timely and effective implementation of those arrangements the supervisors should require appropriate measures to address the shortcomings. Where supervisors assess that the arrangements and measures set out in a group recovery plan would not be likely to restore the viability of the group on a con-solidated basis and of each credit institution member of the group or that there are impediments to the timely and effective implementation of those measures and arrangements, the consolidating supervisor should notify the EU parent credit institution or EU parent financial holding company of this assessment and require measures to address the shortcomings.[158]

7.4   Resolution plans

The most important role of resolution plans should be to ensure that there are no significant impediments resulting from the legal, operational or

---

[157] *Ibid.*, pp. 21–2.
[158] For example, relevant supervisors will be able to require the EU parent credit institution to submit a revised group recovery plan and demonstrate how shortcomings have been addressed and/or to take any necessary measures to ensure that there are no impedi-ments to the implementation of the plan in situations of financial stress. The consoli-dating supervisor should take into account the views expressed by other supervisors when requiring the credit institution to take action. In case of disagreement about the assessment of the group recovery plan or of any action that the credit institution should be required to take as a result of that assessment, there is a mediation procedure through a reference to the EBA. Commission Working Document, p. 21.

business structures of the credit institution to the effective and timely application of resolution tools and exercise of resolution powers. In particular, the authorities should satisfy themselves that critical functions could be legally and economically separated from other functions so as to ensure continuity and avoidance of disruption of economic activity in the event of a credit institution failure.[159] In the process, they should ensure that supervisors gain a thorough and detailed picture of the institution's (and the group's) structure and business lines. If, following an assessment of the resolution plan, a resolution authority identifies significant impediments to the application of the resolution tools or the exercise of the resolution powers, it should, in consultation with the competent supervisor, draw up a list of measures that are required to address or remove those impediments. The Commission suggests a number of key measures to address or remove impediments:[160]

(1) require the credit institution to draw up service level agreements (whether intra-group or with third parties) to cover the provision of critical economic functions or services;
(2) require changes to legal or operational structures of the entity for which the resolution authority is responsible. Implementation of those changes may reduce structural complexity, making supervision easier and ensuring that critical functions could be legally and economically separated from other functions in the context of exercising the resolution tools;
(3) require the credit institution to limit or cease certain existing or proposed activities;
(4) restrict or prevent the development or sale of new business lines or products;
(5) require the credit institution to limit its maximum individual and aggregate exposures; and
(6) require the credit institution to issue additional convertible capital instruments.

Modifications (1) and (2) can significantly simplify the resolution process and minimize disruption of critical functions in the event of institution failure. In addition, modifications (3)–(6) may significantly strengthen the financial position of the institution concerned. Specifically, modification (4) can prevent further weakening of an institution in distress. Moreover, the existence of additional capital cushions in the form

[159] *Ibid.*, pp. 33–4.   [160] *Ibid.*

of convertible debt can (in conjunction with the debt write down tool) preserve the relevant institution as a going concern and avoid a winding up that would inevitably create market turmoil. Finally, measure (5) will inevitably involve asset sales, which, as discussed in Chapters 3 and 5, undermine rather than strengthen financial stability if they lead to fire sales. Thus, apart from the stability of the institution concerned the stability of the financial system should be a consideration when such measures are requested.[161]

Modifications (3) and (4), are bound to face significant opposition from the European banking industry, since the supervisors will acquire through scrutiny of resolution plans almost unfettered power to interfere with such institutions' business plans and models as well as with their mergers and acquisitions strategy. As explained in Section 6.1 above, this is exactly the case under the enhanced SIFI supervision regime introduced by Dodd–Frank. On the other hand, had this power been available and exercised both in the case of Northern Rock and Royal Bank of Scotland (RBS), it is likely that the two banks would not have failed or at least their failure would have been less dramatic. Northern Rock mainly failed due to the glaring holes in its business model and especially the funding basis of its asset book.[162] RBS, on the other hand, was allowed to buy a part of ABN Amro for £50 billion even after the Northern Rock failure and the 'freezing' international credit markets. Yet, as these measures will require exercise of regulatory discretion, further safeguards are required to first avoid an intra-EU supervisory race to the bottom and second extensive recourse to judicial review, which will mean that the courts instead of managers and, where appropriate, regulators will be the decisive actor with respect to key areas of bank business management.

The consolidating supervisor, within the meaning of Directive 2006/48/EC, would be responsible for deciding any changes required at group level. When measures to address or remove impediments to effective resolution are applied to the whole group, the Group Level Resolution Authority is considered as the authority responsible for the group as a whole (including the group members' entities for the purposes of group – rather than specific entity – resolution). The resolution authorities responsible for subsidiaries of an EU parent credit

---

[161] *Ibid.*, p. 34.
[162] See Emilios Avgouleas, 'Bank Supervision and the Special Resolution Regime of the Banking Act 2009: The Unfinished Reform' (2009) 4 *Capital Markets Law Journal* 201–35.

institution or an EU parent financial holding company should consult each other and do everything within their power to reach a joint
decision on the application of measures to address or remove impediments to effective and timely resolution. The Group Level Resolution
Authority, in co-operation with the consolidating supervisor, should
prepare and submit a report analysing the impediments to effective
group resolution and exercise of the resolution powers in relation to
the group, and recommend any measures necessary or appropriate to
remove those impediments. If within six months the resolution authorities fail to reach a joint decision, the Group Level Resolution Authority
should make its own decision on appropriate measures in relation to
the group as a whole. But again, as such decision shall not, in principle, be binding on subsidiary resolution authorities, it will just leave
another loophole in the (proposed) group resolution regime.

The EU Commission proposes that the exercise of preventative powers by resolution authorities should be subject to a set of strong general
principles:

(1) the assessment of the capacity of an institution should focus only on
the legal form, operations and business structure of the institution in
question and not on the capacity of the resolution authority to carry
out the task;

(2) before proposing measures to address or remove impediments to the
application of resolution tools or the exercise of resolution powers,
resolution authorities should consider:

(a) the impact that such measures would have on financial stability
in other member states, and not propose measures that will have a
significant adverse impact on financial stability,

(b) whether the measure is non-discriminatory in terms of the location of the registered office;

(c) whether the measure is justified by an overriding reason relating to the public interest and for this purpose, the public interest
should be understood by reference to the ability of the resolution
authorities to achieve the *resolution objectives*;

(d) proportionality: the measures should be suitable for achieving the
exclusive objective of addressing or removing impediments to the
application of resolution tools or the exercise of resolution powers
and should not go beyond what is necessary to attain that objective. To the extent possible the least restrictive measures should be
used;

(e) judicial review: affected credit institutions will have a right of appeal to the courts or a right of judicial review of any requirement imposed by resolution authorities.

7.5   Early intervention powers

Again much in accord with similar provisions of Dodd–Frank, discussed above, and FSB recommendations (on regulation of SIFIs), the Commission has proposed an early intervention regime that would give the power to supervisors to ask financial institutions, including local branches of banks based in other member states, to take PCA, when a credit institution does not meet the requirements of the CRD or is likely to fail to meet the requirements of the CRD. When exercising early intervention, supervisors should only take actions or steps that are proportionate to the nature of the breach in question and appropriate to address that breach and restore compliance with the requirements of the CRD. More specifically, through an expanded Article 136(1) CRD supervisors would have the power to require the credit institution concerned to:

(1) take steps to increase its own funds, including asking the institution to use net profits to strengthen the capital base;
(2) restrict or prohibit distributions[163] by the credit institution (including payments to hybrid instrument holders);
(3) request intra-group financial support;
(4) replace one or more board members or executive directors or require their dismissal;
(5) impose additional or more frequent reporting requirements, including reporting on capital and liquidity positions;
(6) draw up and implement a specific recovery plan;
(7) draw up a plan for negotiation on restructuring of debt with some or all of its creditors; and
(8) carry out a thorough review of its activities, according to stringent stress test requirements, to be able to have a full and accurate picture of the situation, to be submitted to the competent authority for validation.

---

[163] This partly reflects the relevant definition of discretionary payments under the capital conservation buffer of Basel III and refers to discretionary distributions of assets to shareholders including cash dividends, fully or partly paid bonus shares, share buy backs and other equivalent forms of distributions.

Also, it is proposed that supervisors shall have powers similar to those given to the FRB by Section 121(a) of the Dodd–Frank Act, being able to intervene with the business running of a credit institution and restrict or limit the business and operations of credit institutions, including asking for the divestment of activities that are regarded to create excessive risks to the soundness of a credit institution.

In addition to the list of very extensive intervention powers enumerated above, supervisors could have the power to appoint a special manager to run the institution for a limited period of up to one year. The special manager may take over the management, or assist the existing management, of an institution that is failing or is likely to fail to meet the requirements of the CRD and either has not submitted a credible recovery plan or fails to implement that plan effectively. A special manager would have all the powers of the management of the credit institution under the statutes of the credit institution and under applicable national law.[164]

The primary duty of a special manager would be to restore the financial situation of the credit institution by implementing the recovery plan or prepare for winding-down when it is apparent that recovery cannot be achieved within a reasonable timeframe on the basis of the credit institutions' own resources or any other means being made available at market terms. This duty should override any other duty of management under the statutes of the institution or national law, insofar as they are inconsistent. As this is the most drastic of the proposed early intervention powers, it is poised to give rise to the biggest reactions by shareholders and creditors. Thus, the Commission proposes that supervisors that would use this power could not be held liable to the shareholders or creditors for any actions, decisions taken by, or any failure to take an action or decision by the special manager.

Where the conditions for the imposition of requirements under Article 136(1) of the CRD, the requirements for the appointment of a special management or the requirements for the implementation of a recovery plan are met in relation to the EU parent credit institution or two or more subsidiaries, the consolidating supervisor, in co-operation with the supervisors involved within the supervisory college, should assess whether coordination is desirable, taking into account the following considerations:[165]

---

[164] Commission Working Document, p. 42.
[165] *Ibid.*, p. 43.

(1) whether the implementation of a group recovery plan, the co-ordination of measures under Article 136(1) or the co-ordinated appointment of special managers is more likely to restore the viability of the individual entities and preserve the financial soundness of the group as a whole than separate decisions by the individual supervisors; and

(2) whether the measures taken by one or more supervisors, including the consolidating supervisor, are likely to have an adverse impact on other entities of the group.

Any relevant decision should be taken promptly (for example, within twenty-four hours of the assessment by the relevant supervisor that the conditions referred to above are met).

7.6   Resolution powers and tools

7.6.1   Overview

The resolution framework must provide legal tools that enhance market discipline and reduce moral hazard by ensuring that losses will mostly fall on the shareholders and the creditors of the failing entity. If there is not enough equity or debt to cover the losses of the financial institution concerned the rest of the financial sector may be called to contribute either in the form of specially designed resolution funds or through reconfigured deposit guarantee schemes.[166] Accordingly, under the proposed EU resolution regime forcing a bank or a covered investment firm into resolution is an action justified only in order to achieve the following objectives (together called the *resolution objectives*): (1) ensure the continuity of essential financial services; (2) prevent any adverse effects on financial stability, including avoiding contagion; (3) protect public funds; and (4) protect insured depositors.[167]

Echoing the Dodd–Frank approach, the Commission suggests that the general rule should be that financial institutions should be liquidated under the general bankruptcy rules. Alternatively, and more plausibly, orderly winding down through resolution should be available, in order to pursue the aforementioned *resolution objectives* and maximize the value of remaining assets, facilitating their return to productive use in the private sector. A very important aspect of the suggested EU framework is

---

[166] Commission Working Document, p. 9.
[167] *Ibid.*, pp. 47–8. It must be noted that the resolution objectives should be of equal significance, and resolution authorities should balance them as appropriate to the nature and circumstances of each case.

the group resolution approach, namely, a (non-binding) framework for the resolution of cross-border financial groups. This framework reflects to a considerable extent the model proposed by the IMF of cross-border resolution, discussed in Section 5.2.3 above. However, in the absence of mandatory cross-border resolution agreements and clear burden sharing arrangements, the success of the EU group resolution scheme is far from assured. Finally, another innovation of the proposed regime is the separation of the supervisory from the resolution authorities/colleges.

7.6.2   Resolution tools

Given the magnitude of private and public interests at stake placing a bank or a covered investment firm into resolution is no simple decision. On the one hand, it should be taken only if all other options have been exhausted, since it is bound to greatly interfere with shareholders' and creditors' rights.[168] On the other hand, any delays in taking the relevant decision might lead to higher costs for the institution's resolution.[169] Thus, the threshold conditions must be properly calibrated. The Commission is trying to avoid the risk of delayed action by national resolution authorities by harmonizing the indicators that should trigger a resolution decision. In this context, the Commission considers a number of overlapping options regarding the assessment of the solvency and liquidity problems of distressed institutions. These include a supervisory assessment which indicates that:[170]

(1) 'the institution has incurred or is likely to incur losses' that will diminish its regulatory capital;
(2) the relevant institution's assets are likely to be less than its liabilities (rendering it technically bankrupt);
(3) it is unlikely that the institution concerned shall be able to pay its obligations in the normal course of business; or
(4) it does not have adequate resources to carry on its business.[171]

A qualitative assessment may also be involved ascertaining that an institution is no longer in a position to meet, or is expected to fail to meet, 'the conditions of its licence to carry on banking or investment business'.[172]

---

[168] For an overview of possible conflicts, see Kern Alexander, 'Bank Resolution Regimes: Balancing Prudential Regulation and Shareholder Rights' (2009) 9 *Journal of Corporate Law Studies* 61–93.
[169] EU Commission, 'An EU Framework for Crisis Management, 2010', p. 7.
[170] *Ibid.*   [171] *Ibid.*   [172] *Ibid.*, p. 7.

In addition, resolution authorities should apply the resolution tools and exercise the resolution powers only if:

(1) there is no reasonable prospect that the institution in question will be able, by using its own or other private means, to remedy the situation that triggered the resolution decision within a period that is reasonable;
(2) liquidation under the general insolvency regime would not meet the *resolution objectives*; and
(3) the application of resolution tools or exercise of resolution powers is taken to serve the public interest, namely, to meet one or more of the *resolution objectives*.

The Commission has proposed a set of general principles that should guide actions by resolution authorities. The general principles are intended to be subordinate to the *resolution objectives* and echo to a significant degree the FSB's recommendations for the resolution of SIFIs and more importantly the approach adopted by the OLA under the Dodd–Frank Act. Accordingly the exercise of resolution tools under the proposed EU regime should ensure that:[173]

(1) the losses of the credit institution first fall on shareholders;
(2) unsecured creditors bear the residual losses;
(3) where appropriate, senior management of the credit institution is replaced and held liable for losses in accordance with its responsibility (as determined by requisite laws);
(4) creditors of the same class are treated fairly and equitably and no creditor incurs losses greater than they would have incurred under liquidation;
(5) interference with property rights should not contravene the European Convention on Human Rights and fundamental freedoms;
(6) in determining which resolution tool and power to exercise, resolution authorities should seek to minimize the overall costs of the resolution.

Provided that the threshold conditions are satisfied the following resolution tools will be available to resolution authorities:[174] (a) sale of business; (b) bridge bank; (c) asset separation; and (4) debt write off.[175]

---

[173] Commission Working Document, pp. 49–50.
[174] Commission Working Document, pp. 51–5.
[175] For an evaluation of the resolution tools see van der Zwet, 'Crisis Management Tools in the EU', pp. 18–25.

Sale of business is a resolution tool that enables resolution authorities to effect a sale of the credit institution or the whole or part of its assets and liabilities to one or more purchasers on commercial terms, without requiring the consent of the shareholders or complying with procedural requirements that would otherwise apply. It is effected through the exercise of a share transfer or property transfer power.

The bridge bank is a resolution tool that enables resolution authorities to transfer all or part of the business of the credit institution to a company or other legal person (the bridge bank) which is wholly owned by one or more public authorities (which may include the resolution authority). The acquisitions shall be financed, in principle, by national resolution funds, which may also guarantee the liabilities of the bridge bank to ensure its continuous access to credit. The bridge bank/or bridge investment firm must be licensed in accordance with Directive 2006/48/EC (part of the CRD) or with the Market in Financial Instruments Directive (Directive 2004/39/EC), and must have the necessary national authorizations to carry on the business resulting from the transfer of rights, assets or liabilities. Even more controversial from a legal perspective is the Commission's stated intention that the bridge bank should be regarded as a continuation of the institution that is being resolved and thus carry the same rights as the failing institution, including the same right to operate within the EU internal market as that institution. When they exercise the bridge bank tool, the resolution authorities should be able to use on a repeat basis property transfer powers with respect to: (1) rights, assets or liabilities moving from the distressed credit institution to the bridge bank; and (2) rights, assets or liabilities moving back from the bridge bank to the affected credit institution.

Apart from the legal implications, the exercise of the bridge bank tool may prove a daunting task in the case of big banks or, worse, in the case of banking groups. In these cases treasury and cash management services as well as IT and back office functions may be highly centralized and prove difficult to disentangle and transfer to the bridge bank, upsetting the functional architecture of the affected institution and long-standing business arrangements. In addition, the use of the property transfer power – both in the context of the bridge bank and the asset separation tool – could also prove a rather complicated process bound to trigger early termination clauses in most of the commercial contracts of the failing institution. This may especially prove to be the case with derivatives contracts. Thus, the Commission, endorsing the IMF and FSB recommendations discussed above, intends to place transfers between the affected credit institution and the bridge bank under a set of special legal rules (safeguards for partial property transfers), which should protect specific kinds of financial contracts such as derivatives contracts and creditor rights. However, the success of such safeguards will have to be proved in practice and, until then, strong doubts remain regarding their effectiveness.[176]

The resolution authority (or another public authority) should be able to appoint directors and managers of the bridge bank. The ultimate objective of the bridge bank tool should be to facilitate the sale of the bridge bank, or the whole or part of its business, to one or more purchasers on commercial terms. The management of the bridge bank should aim at maintaining rather than expanding the business. The operations of a bridge bank are temporary, and its operations should be terminated within one year or extended under specified circumstances to two. If the bridge bank is not sold at the end of this period it should be wound up.[177]

Asset separation is a resolution tool that should be used to enable resolution authorities to transfer certain assets of a credit institution to an asset management vehicle for the purpose of facilitating the use or ensuring the effectiveness of another resolution tool.[178] Thus, the use of the asset separation tool will effectively create a 'good bank'/'bad bank' solution. This tool borrows several characteristics of the Swedish 'bad bank' model[179] and (in the asset purchase part) of the Troubled Asset Relief Program (TARP).[180] Through the asset separation tool assets of

---

[176] *Ibid.*, p. 21.
[177] Commission Working Document, p. 53. Shareholders of the affected credit institution, and its creditors, should not have any rights over the bridge bank or its property, except the right to any residual value realized from the sale of a bridge bank once all other creditors and claimants and expenses have been repaid in full. *Ibid.*, p. 54.
[178] *Ibid.*, p. 54.
[179] In 1992, due to a combination of factors, including lax regulation, the Swedish banking system was insolvent. The decision of the Swedish government to clean up the balance sheet of its banks and transfer problem or distressed assets to another entity, the 'bad bank', in addition to extending a state guarantee for bank liabilities and a recapitalization programme that was punitive to shareholders, enabled Swedish banks to return fast to financial soundness and profitability. Taxpayer costs were halved when bank assets held by the 'bad bank' subsequently increased in value and were disposed of at competitive prices. See 'The Swedish Model', *The Economist*, 28 January 2009, available at www.economist.com/blogs/freeexchange/2009/01/the_swedish_model and Carter Dougherty, 'Stopping a Financial Crisis, the Swedish Way', *New York Times*, 22 September 2008, available at www.nytimes.com/2008/09/23/business/worldbusiness/23krona. html.
[180] See Emergency Economic Stabilization Act 2008 (US) (PL 110–343). TARP also included the purchase of equity stakes in distressed banks in order to inject fresh capital and strengthen their balance sheet.

the affected credit institution are transferred – 'as a result of the level of risk they entail or of difficulties in establishing their value' for fair consideration to a separate 'asset management vehicle', which is a legal entity wholly owned by one or more public authorities. The resolution authority should appoint asset managers to manage the assets transferred to the asset management vehicle with the objective of maximizing their value through eventual sale. Shareholders of the affected credit institution, and its creditors, should not have any rights over the asset management vehicle or its assets.[181] In order for the tool to be effective, the Commission considers that the resolution authorities should be able to: (1) transfer assets from the affected credit institution to the asset management vehicle on more than one occasion; and (2) transfer assets back from the asset management vehicle to the affected credit institution, if this is necessary, to achieve the *resolution objectives*.

Transfers between the affected credit institution and the asset management vehicle would be subject to safeguards for partial property transfers. The exercise of the asset separation tool will be set up with public money as a way of absorbing losses and relieving the financial burden to the part of the business that is being sold or transferred to a bridge bank with a view to being sold in the near future. As a result, very significant moral hazard and other issues are associated with this resolution tool. To minimize moral hazard, the Commission suggests that the asset separation is only used in conjunction with another resolution tool. Moreover, in order to minimize distortions of competition between banks and between member states, state aid rules will need to be complied with.[182] However, what is left unanswered is how the valuation of distressed assets will be conducted,[183] a key factor in determining whether the 'no use of public money' principle is observed, or resolution will have to be financed by the resolution fund or taxpayers in the end. Finally, no guidance is given as to who covers the asset management company's loss if no willing buyers

---

[181] Commission Working Document, pp. 54–5.   [182] *Ibid.*, p. 54.
[183] On the issue of asset valuation in such situations, see TARP Congressional Oversight Panel, February Oversight Report, 'Valuing Treasury's Acquisitions', 6 February 2009, pp. 4–11, available at cop.senate.gov/documents/cop-020609-report.pdf: 'The valuation report concludes that Treasury paid substantially more for the assets it purchased under the TARP than their then-current market value'. More specifically the Panel found that the Treasury made a substantial loss for assets purchased under the asset relief part of TARP in October 2008. 'The Panel's review of the ten largest TARP investments the Treasury made during 2008 raises substantial doubts about whether the government received assets comparable to its expenditures … Overall, in the ten transactions, for each \$100 spent, the Treasury received assets worth approximately \$66'. *Ibid.*, pp. 4–5.

are found for those assets or the price offered for them does not cover the initial acquisition price.

The debt conversion tool (bail-in) is a mechanism that would enable resolution authorities to write down the claims of some or all of the unsecured creditors of a failing institution and, possibly, to convert debt claims to equity. Namely, it is a mechanism to force private sector creditors to share the costs of a bank rescue/recapitalization.[184] As discussed in Section 4.1 above, the bail-in mechanism is also a good alternative to liquidation. It might protect better financial stability which might be threatened by the liquidation of a financial institution. Also, in contrast to liquidation, it does not endanger the continuous provision of systemically critical services of a large commercial bank, such as payments infrastructure and lending functions. This business may be too large to sell to other banks in the prevailing conditions without government support or without a significant anti-competitive impact, while if it is wound down its market functions may not be readily replaced by existing or new entrants.

7.6.3   Bail-in debt mechanism

The bail-in debt mechanism suggested by the EU Commission fosters market discipline, in the ways discussed in Section 4.1 above, as it leads to the writing down of all equity and the conversion of the debt of a troubled institution into equity,[185] to restore an institution's capital position so as to allow it to continue (either temporarily or permanently) as a going concern.[186] According to what the Commission suggests the debt write

---

[184] Nuriel Roubini, 'Bail-In, Burden-Sharing, Private Sector Involvement (PSI) in Crisis Resolution and Constructive Engagement of the Private Sector. A Primer: Evolving Definitions, Doctrine, Practice and Case Law', mimeo, September 2000, available at pages.stern.nyu.edu/~nroubini/papers/psipaper.pdf.

[185] This would entail changes in EC company law, because it is generally not possible to recapitalize banks without shareholder approval under the Second Council Directive 77/91/EEC of 13 December 1976 on co-ordination of safeguards which, for the protection of the interests of members and others are required by member states of companies within the meaning of the second paragraph of Article 58 of the Treaty, in respect of the formation of public limited liability companies and the maintenance and alteration of their capital, with a view to making such safeguards equivalent, OJL026/1, 31 January 1977.

[186] The Commission has referred the key trigger and conversion issues to further consultation, considering: (1) whether the mechanism should be based on a statutory power for authorities to write down or convert debt under specified conditions, or on mandatory contractual terms for write down or conversion; (2) the classes of debt that should be covered by a relevant statutory power (N.B. the position and the alteration of the ranking of trade creditors, derivatives, wholesale deposits, secured debt, intra-group liabilities raise very delicate issues); (3) the impact on the institution's cost of funding;

down tool shall be used only where:[187] (1) the application of the standard resolution tools is not possible because of the nature of the failing institution or its business; or (2) in the opinion of the resolution authorities, other tools would not be sufficient to achieve the resolution objectives. In practice, this tool could prove most useful in the case of 'too-big-to-fail' institutions (SIFIs) or in the context of a generalized crisis when it is unlikely to find a large pool of potential third party purchasers. Creating a bridge bank or transfer of assets through a 'good bank, bad bank' split may not be possible in the time available for 'too-big-to-fail' SIFIs given the size and complexity of a particular institution's asset or trading book or the interconnectedness within the same group or externally.

Accordingly, unlike other CoCo structures discussed in Section 4.1 above, the bail-in-able debt envisaged by the Commission will be converted at a much later stage when the bank will be very close to being a 'gone concern'.[188] As a result, debt write down will not be used in isolation but is proposed to accompany significant restructuring measures, including the closure or sale of parts of the business, removal of problem assets and management replacement to return the institution to viability. In the course of restructuring, the affected bank is likely to face a run by wholesale lenders and its depositors, which might lead it to liquidity problems. Thus, resolution fund money or central bank funding should be available to support the institution undergoing restructuring.

In some cases the writing off of all equity and subordinated debt will not be sufficient to ensure that an institution in difficulty returns to viability so as to maintain market and creditor confidence when the markets next open.[189] For this reason, the Commission is considering providing resolution authorities with additional write down powers that would extend to senior creditors on the basis of two (non-mutually exclusive) possible models: *the comprehensive* approach and the *targeted* approach. Implementation of proposals to write off senior (bail-in-able) debt would amount to a radical change of well established legal doctrine, especially in those member state jurisdictions which give secured creditors very strong

---

(4) mechanisms to ensure recognition of any write down or conversion by foreign courts where the debt is booked in or governed by the law of a non-EU jurisdiction.

[187] For a good and critical analysis of the EU proposals on bail-in, see Clifford Chance, 'Sea of Change – Regulatory Reforms to 2012 and Beyond', April 2011.

[188] *Ibid.*, pp. 7–9.

[189] E.g., Royal Bank of Scotland balance sheet at the end of 2007 contained £38 billion in subordinated liabilities, while losses before tax in 2008 and 2009 amounted to around £43 billion. Commission Working Document, p. 87.

protection. On the other hand, in certain jurisdictions, such as the UK, it is entirely possible to implement the new regime through contract.[190] However, the fact that the UK courts would probably accept the terms of the issue allowing for restructuring of senior debt,[191] does not mean that, where the governing law of the instrument is English law, courts in other EU member states would not accept creditor petitions to block restructuring of senior debt. Given the strong public policy objectives involved in this case special national legislation will probably be required for the implementation of the bail-in mechanism.[192]

(a)   **Comprehensive approach**   The *comprehensive* approach[193] could make a broad range of senior creditors face the real risk associated with bank failure. It means that when an institution meets the trigger conditions for entry into resolution, the authority responsible for resolution has the power to write down by a discretionary amount or convert to equity all senior debt deemed necessary to ensure the credit institution is returned to solvency. The proposed scope of the resolution authorities' discretion in exercising this tool is very wide. They would be able to choose which classes of debt would be written down or converted in a particular case, the extent of the haircut and, where relevant, the rate of conversion. On the other hand, if regulatory discretion remains so wide, then, on the basis of the discussion of the mechanics of CoCos in Section 4.1 above, bail-in-able debt instruments will face two very serious problems. First, uncertainty about the exact class(es) of creditors that are to be wiped out and reliance on regulatory discretion will seriously hinder the market's ability to price (and rate) such uncertain future events. This uncertainty will further affect the marketability of these instruments to investors.

Although equity holders should be wiped out and subordinated debt should be written down completely before senior debt holders bear any losses, it is doubtless that the *pari passu* principle shall be violated. It is inevitable that certain classes of debt linked to swap, repo and derivatives counterparties and other trade creditors, retail and wholesale depositors, and secured debt holders would be excluded from the write down. Netting arrangements under master agreements should also be excluded from the ambit of the write down power. Otherwise, derivatives markets

---

[190]   Clifford Chance, 'Regulatory Reforms', pp. 12–13.
[191]   E.g., *National Bank of Greece and Athens S.A. v. Metliss* [1958] AC 509.
[192]   Clifford Chance, 'Regulatory Reforms', p. 13.
[193]   See Commission Working Document, pp. 87–8.

would enter into an era of increased legal uncertainty bound to create major disruptions and loss of liquidity.

The size of the write down will be determined by a valuation of the assets and liabilities of the institution, the amount deemed necessary to restore viability and maintain market confidence, the improvement in viability realized by actions taken on equity and subordinated debt holders, and the total amount of senior debt that is capable of being written down. A further limit to resolution authority discretion seems to be a question of whether the writing down of certain senior creditors might give rise to systemic risk.

The power to write down senior debt will not apply retrospectively as such a modification of debt contracts would mean a run on banks by creditors and a spate of litigation. To ensure that the power is exercised effectively in relation to debt that is booked in or governed by the law of a third country, new debt issued by EU credit institutions would be required to include a clause recognizing this statutory power. This contractual recognition should minimize the risk that any write down pursuant to the power would not be recognized or enforced by foreign courts.

(b)   Targeted approach   The *targeted*[194] approach could create a more focused tool for resolving SIFIs. In particular, resolution authorities will have the right to require SIFIs (only) to issue a fixed volume of 'bail-in-able' debt. Such debt would need to include a contractual term which would specify that the relevant resolution authority could use a statutory power to write down the debt when the institution meets the trigger conditions for entry into resolution. The amount of the write down or conversion rate could be either specified in the instrument, or it could be left to the discretion of the resolution authorities (subject to the principle that the affected debt holder should be 'no worse off than in liquidation'). The requirement could include a fixed minimum for all institutions (for example as a percentage of total liabilities), and the power for authorities to increase it further in the event that resolution plans identify impediments to resolution by other means.

7.6.4   Group level resolution

The Commission has signalled its clear preference for a pan-European resolution regime for cross-border financial institutions. But as the

---

[194]   See *ibid.*, p. 89.

Commission plausibly points out an integrated EU resolution regime for cross-border financial groups is not possible 'in the absence of a harmonised insolvency regime and of a Single European Supervisory authority for those entities'.[195] Since, implicitly, such a solution is regarded as politically untenable, the Commission proposes to endorse a group resolution framework that is based on national authorities' consent, reflecting the relevant IMF proposal (discussed in Section 5.2.3 above). In this context, group resolution would be considered in every case where more than one group member that is covered by the scope of the resolution regime meets the conditions for resolution. Because resolution powers are applied to individual legal entities and the competence for resolution will remain national, the group resolution scheme will not be binding.

The new EU framework will identify a 'Group Level Resolution Authority' for every EU consolidated cross-border group (or sub-group of an international banking group). This would be the resolution authority of the member state where the consolidating supervisor of that group or sub-group is located. Moreover, the Commission has proposed the establishment of resolution colleges for cross-border groups based on the core of the existing supervisory colleges through the inclusion of resolution authorities for group entities. Resolution colleges would be chaired by Group Level Resolution Authorities and would be responsible for crisis planning and the preparation of resolution plans including, if appropriate, principles for burden sharing.[196] The Group Level Resolution Authority should co-ordinate all activities of resolution colleges and chair all meetings.[197]

The group level colleges should facilitate and, in appropriate cases, 'prioritise group resolution (as opposed to the uncoordinated resolution of group entities at national level)'.[198] Specifically, the Commission suggests that in co-operation with colleges of supervisors, resolution colleges should:[199]

(1) develop group resolution plans and assess the impediments to effective application of the resolution tools and resolution powers;

[195] EU Commission, 'An EU Framework for Crisis Management 2010', p. 12.
[196] Ibid., p. 12.
[197] Commission Working Document, pp. 76–8.
[198] EU Commission, 'An EU Framework for Crisis Management 2010', pp. 12–13; Commission Working Document, p. 78.
[199] Ibid.

(2) develop common approaches to the application of resolution tools on an individual or group-wide basis;
(3) provide a framework for the agreement on group resolution schemes;
(4) co-ordinate decisions and actions by national resolution authorities, whether these are separate bodies or the central bank.

Group resolution means, in any relevant case:[200]

(1) the application of resolution powers and resolution tools at the level of the parent entity with a view to resolving two or more credit institutions of the group that meet the conditions for resolution and stabilizing the group as a whole; and
(2) the co-ordination of the application of resolution tools and the exercise of resolution powers by resolution authorities in relation to the legal entities of the group that meet the conditions for resolution.

Group resolution would be relevant where:

(1) the EU parent credit institution or EU parent holding company and at least one covered subsidiary meet the conditions for resolution; or
(2) two or more 'covered subsidiaries'[201] meet the conditions for resolution.

The Group Level Resolution Authority should have the power to decide in cases of group failure whether a group resolution scheme is appropriate. Pending that decision, which would need to be taken quickly, national authorities would be required to refrain from adopting national measures that could prejudice the effectiveness of the group resolution scheme. The Group Level Resolution Authority, in co-operation with the resolution authorities concerned, is the authority that should determine the desirability of group resolution taking into account the following factors: (1) whether the resolution objectives would be better achieved by group resolution than discrete or unco-ordinated national measures; (2) whether the measures that one or more resolution authorities are likely to take would have an adverse impact on different entities of the group; and (3) whether group resolution would avoid such adverse impact.

National authorities that disagreed with the scheme would not be prevented from taking independent action where they considered that

---

[200] *Ibid.*, p. 79.
[201] The term 'covered subsidiary' would mean any subsidiary that is a credit institution or an investment firm that falls within the scope of the EU resolution framework, *ibid.*, p. 79.

necessary for reasons of national financial stability, but in doing so would be required to consider the impact of that action on financial stability in other member states. A mechanism that adds 'teeth' to the group resolution scheme relates to giving to the Group Level Resolution Authority the power to sell fully-owned assets of the EU parent credit institutions, which may include the sale of fully-owned subsidiaries, subject to approval of change of control by the supervisor of the subsidiary. In case of non-fully owned subsidiaries, the sale of business tool would be applied by the authorities responsible for resolving the subsidiary, provided that the subsidiary meets the trigger conditions for resolution. The group level resolution authorities shall also have the power to exercise the bridge bank tool at group level (which may involve, where appropriate, burden sharing arrangements) to stabilize a group as a whole. Similarly the Group Level Resolution Authority has the power to apply the debt conversion tool to the parent institution and invite the supervisors of other entities within the group to do the same with those entities that also meet the trigger conditions for resolution.

The problem with the group level resolution approach is of course that, since it is not binding, in many cases it will prove to be not group level at all. The group authority may only exercise resolution tools to the parent entities without being impeded by the objections of other authorities within the resolution college. In fact, a resolution authority responsible for an entity covered by the Group resolution scheme may decide not to comply with the scheme and to take independent measures. The Commission suggests in this respect three rather vague and weak tests. First, the decision not to comply with the group resolution scheme and take independent measures should be based on reasonable considerations that such measures are necessary for reasons of national financial stability. Second, the decision to adopt national measures should be proportionate. Third, the national authority should consider the impact of that action on financial stability in other member states. Arguably, none of those tests provides any considerable constraint on national authorities to follow an unco-ordinated resolution approach, which might be the preferable route if taxpayer or national resolution funds' money is at stake. Yet, in the absence of legislation imposing a mandatory single resolution regime for cross-border groups and fiscal burden-sharing arrangements, the three tests would seem to be the only feasible ones and in full accord with general principles of EU law.

The Commission's approach to effective resolution of internationally active groups is based on mutual recognition and enforcement of measures

taken by resolution authorities in the relevant jurisdictions. It is suggested
that firm-specific co-operation agreements be developed between the
national authorities responsible for managing the failure of cross-border
groups to ensure effective planning, decision-making and co-ordination
in respect of international groups. Framework agreements may be concluded between the Commission and EBA or ESMA and third countries,
regarding the co-ordination of resolution of EU-based subsidiaries and
branches of third country credit institutions. Nonetheless, as neither the
Commission nor the EBA and ESMA have any powers of direct supervision or any fiscal responsibility to support an ailing financial institution,
the resolution authorities of the home member state of a credit institution
that has a subsidiary or a branch in a third country and the resolution
authorities of a member state responsible for resolving a credit institution
the parent undertaking of which has its head office in a third country, or
for resolving a branch of a credit institution having its head office in a
third country, must enter into firm-specific arrangements regarding the
resolution of any such institution.[202] It is, thus, very hard to foresee who
is going to resolve any ensuing co-operation disputes when issues of cost-
sharing arise in the context of a cross-border group rescue/resolution,
giving additional force to arguments in favour of implementing a single
resolution and insolvency regime in G-20 countries and importing binding fiscal burden-sharing arrangements.[203]

7.7   Financing resolution

In most cases a way to finance resolution should be found as shareholders'
and creditors' money will not prove enough. Availability of sufficient resolution financing can ultimately determine whether resolution is a credible
option or the expensive but tested route of public bank rescues should be
tried instead. Moreover, the ways resolution is financed at the national
level is bound to influence the effectiveness of cross-border resolution and
of authorities' willingness to co-operate. Thus, the Commission has proposed the establishment of privately financed national funds to support

---

[202] The resolution authorities responsible for resolving a third country branch in accordance with Directive 2001/24/EC and a credit institution, the parent undertaking of
which is a credit institution or a financial holding company, the head office of which is
in a third country shall assess whether the resolution arrangements in the third country
are adequate and compatible with EU arrangements and whether the resolution authorities may rely on or defer to the third country for taking the lead in resolution.
[203] Avgouleas, Goodhart and Schoenmaker, 'Bank Recovery and Resolution Plans'.

bank resolution.[204] This in many respects is a transitional measure as the Commission is ultimately in favour of a single EU resolution fund.[205]

The Commission regards the establishment of resolution funds as an essential component of any regime that counters the 'too-big-to-fail' phenomenon, since it will absorb the cost of resolution and avoid having recourse to public money. However, industry funded resolution funds are clearly unpopular in key member states, which favour other solutions,[206] and will face two further problems. First, there is no certainty that resolution funds will have enough money to finance resolution even if contributions are properly calibrated, since the level of their reserves is bound to be procyclical.[207] Second, they might give rise to heightened moral hazard or induce a tragedy of the commons situation, since contributions will not reflect each individual institution's riskiness. As regards the first issue, the Commission proposes a scheme that will be equal in size to the liabilities of domestic banks. With respect to the second issue, the Commission has suggested that resolution funds should only be used in conjunction with the exercise of resolution tools, especially the bridge bank tool. In addition, where the entity concerned is resolved as a going concern, through, for example, a debt write off, the Commission has indicated that temporary provision of any ancillary financing 'must be accompanied by appropriate measures to restructure the entity, remove culpable management, write down unsecured creditors and dilute or write off the claims of existing shareholders'.[208]

The Commission proposes that resolution funds will be funded *ex ante* by banks subject to the crisis management framework to ensure that

---

[204] European Commission, 'Bank Resolution Funds' COM (2010) 254 final, 26 June 2010.

[205] *Ibid.*, p. 6. See also speech by M. Barnier (the Internal Market Commissioner), 'Laying the Foundations for Crisis Prevention and Management in Europe', Conference on Building a Crisis Management Framework for the Internal Market, Brussels, 19 March 2010, available at europa.eu/rapid/pressReleasesAction.do?reference=SPEECH/10/112&format=HTML&aged=0&language=EN&guiLanguage=en. The European Parliament supports the idea of a single EU Financial Stability Fund under the responsibility of the EBA: A7–0213/2010.

[206] E.g., the UK and France want funds raised from bank levies to be used for general budgetary purposes and have implemented plans to raise levies for that purpose. See ECOFIN, 'State of Play on Financial Levies and Taxes: Report to the European Council', 19 October 2010.

[207] Dirk Schoenmaker, 'Do We Need a Separate Resolution Fund?', 14 January 2010, available at www.voxeu.org/index.php?q=node/4487. See also 'Written Statement by Prof. Dirk Schoenmaker', EP ECON Hearing on Cross-border Crisis Management, 16 March 2010, pp. 5–6.

[208] EU Commission, 'An EU Framework for Crisis Management 2010', p. 14.

financing is available irrespective of the size of the failed bank. Every credit institution and certain investment firms authorized in each member state shall regularly contribute to the fund. The contributions should also cover branches established in other member states. Branches established by a credit institution which has its head office outside the EU would have to contribute to the fund within the territory in which they are established. Unless otherwise decided by the member state, the contributions to the fund should be determined for each contributing institution prorata on the basis of its eligible liabilities. Where costs exceed the capacity of the resolution fund, they should subsequently be recovered from contributing institutions through extra-ordinary contributions. With respect to the amounts paid out to cover the costs incurred in connection with the use of resolution tools, the fund will have a priority ranking over all the other unsecured creditors of the credit institution that is under resolution.

National resolution funds may not necessarily be new structures but a redesigned Deposit Guarantee Scheme (DGS) will be available to resolution authorities for the sole purpose of covering the costs incurred in connection with the use of resolution tools and in accordance with the resolution objectives and the general principles governing resolution. The fund should have a target size, which the Commission suggests should be defined as a percentage of the total eligible liabilities of all contributing institutions, achieved by 31 December 2020.[209] The Commission recognizes the need to properly calibrate the size of resolution funds in order to also take into account the burden imposed by other recent financial sector reforms, which may also lead to safer banks. Yet the size of resolution funds will remain a thorny issue for the foreseeable future since measures to reduce resolution expenditure, such as the sale of a bridge bank, will much depend on the economic cycle and its impact on the 'fair' or market value of the assets held by the bridge bank.

7.8   Evaluation of the EU resolution regime

The crisis management and resolution framework suggested by the Commission introduces critical innovations. The proposed preventive measures and especially the obligation of banks and of important investment firms to draw up recovery and resolution plans and the early

---

[209] 'Eligible liabilities' should mean liabilities of contributing institutions net of Tier 1 capital and covered deposits, as defined under the DGS Directive. *Ibid.*

intervention powers should significantly improve the quality of supervision, especially of cross-border groups. On the other hand, the absence of substantive harmonization of bank insolvency and resolutions laws and of a single EU resolution authority are bound to prove very big obstacles to the effective operation of the new regime.[210] In the first instance, this absence has forced the Commission to propose a largely voluntary resolution framework for cross-border groups. Arguably this is bound to be abandoned when the next crisis hits or to fail in the face of the massive co-ordination challenges the new regime will inevitably give rise to, in the absence of a mandatory resolution regime and burden sharing.

Moreover, the exercise of resolution tools proposed by the EU Commission is far from unproblematic. Not only will partial asset transfers endanger the performance of derivatives, repo and other contracts concluded by the failing institution and backed by transferred assets but also the validity of the contracts themselves and their netting agreements[211] may become subject to dispute and even litigation.

The proposal to establish (a network of) national resolution funds has several shortcomings. These shall be underfunded under the Commission plan for almost a decade. In addition, member states will invariably choose to merge the national resolutions funds with their DGSs endangering also the solvency of the latter and weakening instead of strengthening the effectiveness of resolution. On the basis of the above observations, it is very hard to see how the Commission proposals resolve the 'too-big-to-fail' institution problem, which invariably is part of a cross-border group, or the problems of co-ordination between national regulators in the context of cross-border resolutions, which proved to be the biggest loophole in the previous EU framework.

8.   Summary and conclusions

This chapter surveyed the most critical part of recent reforms in the field of global market governance. It first discussed the emerging

---

[210] 'In principle, an integrated framework for resolution of cross border entities by a single European body would deliver a rapid, decisive and equitable resolution process for European financial groups, and better reflect the pan EU nature of banking markets', EU Commission, 'An EU Framework for Crisis Management 2010', p. 12.

[211] Philippe Paech, 'The Need for an International Instrument on the Enforceability of Close-out Netting in General and in the Context of Bank Resolution', UNIDROIT 2011 Study 78C – Doc. 2, available at www.unidroit.org/english/documents/2011/study78c/s-78c-02-e.pdf.

international approach to the regulation of G-SIFIs and minimization of moral hazard and systemic risk linked to their operation. Much attention was given to the issue of capital surcharges allocated, on the basis of G-SIFI riskiness and the disputed utility of CoCos. It has also discussed the recommendations of CBRG and FSB on cross-border resolution and the IMF's model that sets out general principles for the minimum harmonization of national resolution regimes and the foundations of a legal infrastructure to underpin international co-ordination between resolution authorities. Furthermore, the chapter has provided analytical overviews of the Dodd–Frank special resolution regime for SIFIs and EU proposals for a co-ordinated pan-European crisis management and resolution regime.

Arguably, the various regulatory approaches to the 'too-big-to-fail' problem have now crystallized and may be summarized as follows:

(1) additional capital requirements imposed on SIFIs either in the form of CoCos that turn into equity at some point before the institution is ordered to take PCA, or issuance of bail-in-able instruments, which might even be senior debt, where the write off or the conversion is triggered when the institution is close to entering liquidation and helps it to stay a going concern (proposed by the BCBS and the EU Commission);

(2) a capital surcharge imposed on G-SIFIs probably based on a grading scale of riskiness, reflecting principles similar to those applicable to environmental protection (promoted by the BCBS and the FRB);

(3) restrictions over engaging in certain investment banking activities, such as proprietary trading and hedge fund and private equity fund sponsoring and investment (adopted by the Volcker Rule);

(4) forms of separation of commercial from investment banking activities, which entail organizational restructuring and separate capitalization of the commercial banking business (adopted by the UK Independent Commission on Banking (Vickers Commission) and endorsed by the UK Chancellor). Implicitly, a similar approach that leads to de facto ring fencing and separate capitalization is taken by Dodd–Frank Act with regard to the 'swap' dealing divisions of US commercial banks that are no longer allowed to use 'federal assistance' to finance their 'swap' business;

(5) limitations of bank size by placing a cap on future expansion, the approach adopted by Dodd–Frank Act, which essentially halts further consolidation in the US banking sector;

(6) drawing up special resolution regimes, which operate outside of the restraints of ordinary insolvency (and company) law and intend to ensure continuity in the provision of systemic services and minimize recourse to public funds in order to bail-out SIFIs. Apart from the fact that resolution of cross-border financial groups on a unitary basis remains a largely unaddressed issue, national special resolution regimes may present marked differences in their philosophy. Thus, SIFIs must be properly liquidated in the US under the Dodd–Frank Act, whereas it is sufficient, under UK law[212] and EU proposals, to manage resolution properly through application of effective resolution tools;

(7) preparatory and preventive measures consisting of closer supervision of SIFIs and more regular stress testing as well as making compulsory the *ex ante* preparation of recovery and resolution plans (so called 'living wills').

A number of issues have emerged from the foregoing analysis that merit further discussion, to be provided in the next chapter. First, the EU, unlike the US, which through the Volcker Rule and Dodd–Frank approach to regulation of 'swaps' dealers, places size and activity restrictions on big banks, does not interfere with structural issues when it comes to SIFIs. EU restraint possibly reflects the continental European tradition of universal banking, or even more plausibly the fact that such intervention by the EU Commission would give rise to strong opposition by member states. It is reasonable that member states wish to be the authorities that determine the structural arrangements of their own banks and banking industry. Given, however, that the EU operates a common banking market this will give rise to disputes in the future that might undermine the 'single passport' facility, an undesirable and uncompetitive development. Moreover, US adoption of size and activity restrictions – arguably, a plausible response to risks commercial banks had undertaken in the pre-GFC period leading them to near collapse – signals a strong divergence in the way the worlds' two biggest jurisdictions tackle the regulation of 'too-big-to-fail' banks.

---

[212] On the UK special resolution regime, see Avgouleas, 'Banking Supervision and the Special Resolution Regime of the Banking Act 2009': and John Douglas, Randall Guyan, Dalvinder Singh and Hilary Stonefrost, 'Bank Restructuring and Insolvency Procedures', in Rodrigo Olivares Caminal *et al.*, *Debt Restructuring* (Oxford University Press, 2011), Chapter 8.

Second, the US resolution regime under the OLA and the EU proposals differ in a number of important areas, the most important of which are the approach to resolution outcomes and resolution funding. The OLA's absolute liquidation objective is bound to lead to regime clashes with the EU's more relaxed attitude to bank resolution. In addition, the EU's adoption of an *ex ante* approach to funding resolutions could mean that resorting to resolution might prove easier than under the OLA where resolution is funded *ex post*. Third, the IMF, FSB and BCBS proposals for the regulation of G-SIFIs lead to an ever more tightening global regulatory regime that still faces the challenge of national regulatory co-ordination, conflicting interests and divergence of objectives, which will hinder both its timely and effective operation.

The emerging resolution regimes for G-SIFIs and SIFIs constitute very considerable progress but still leave unanswered the issue of effective cross-border resolution of financial groups and burden sharing. While it is unclear if the new supervisory and resolution regimes for G-SIFIs and SIFIs will resolve the 'too-big-to-fail' problem, it should become a common admission that the new regimes require new global bodies, operating under a formal international law mandate, to carry out direct supervision of G-SIFIS and resolution of cross-border financial groups. In the next chapter, I outline a comprehensive model for the regulation and supervision of global markets and the resolution of cross-border financial groups, which in many respects constitutes the inevitable evolution and the missing part of the global governance jigsaw with respect to G-SIFI supervision and resolution.

8

An evolutionary model for global financial governance

'… Nothing excuses us, as responsible individuals, from the intellectual and moral duty of adopting a truly cosmopolitan perspective and from engaging in the thought experiment of devising the first best response…' The same sentiment should guide the effort to devise a new and stronger financial system. It should be global, it should be robust, it should be an effective servant of the real market economy. Being safe from disruption is a start, but it is not enough.[1]

1.   Introductory remarks

1.1   Overview

In the preceding chapters, I have provided an analytical discussion of the main functions and characteristics of the global financial markets, the causes of the Global Finance Crisis (GFC), and the governance structures for global finance in the pre-GFC period. I have also discussed at some length regulatory reform that is under way in the US, the EU and internationally mainly by means of the Basel Committee on Banking Supervision (BCBS) and the Financial Stability Board (FSB) initiatives. Relevant reforms constitute a marked improvement over previous arrangements in a number of areas, including OTC derivatives trading, financial institution resilience and national and regional systemic risk monitoring. However, as it has been repeatedly pointed out in the preceding chapters, the reforms provide very limited comfort when it comes to (1) the cross-border supervision of very big financial institutions, (2) the management of emerging risks due to unpredictable combination/ correlation of forces unleashed or shaped by financial innovation with other market and real economy forces, and (3) resolution of cross-border

---

[1] Andrew Crockett, 'What Financial System for the 21st Century?', Per Jacobson Lecture 2011, Bank for International Settlements, 26 June 2011, p. 19, available at www.bis.org/events/agm2011/spl10626.htm quoting the late Tomasso Padoa-Schioppa.

financial groups. Therefore, in the absence of a new governance system for global finance addressing the above shortcomings, the effectiveness of recent regulatory reforms will be greatly undermined.

This finding means that the entire project of financial globalization is also at peril, since it is impossible that the current environment of open markets will be able to sustain another crisis of similar magnitude as the current one. Yet, in terms of global economic development, this is the worst time possible to return to a closed markets system. World needs for credit and investment to finance development, sustainability and increased food production projects are on the rise.[2] These additional funds may only come from free and open global financial markets, notwithstanding the need, in certain cases, for very short-term capital controls in order to curb speculative capital flows. Yet financial globalization coupled with a host of financial innovations (together defined in this book as the financial revolution) led the world to the brink of collapse during the ongoing crisis and has pushed millions of the world's least protected citizens to experience the consequences of a deep global recession in the form of job losses and rising economic hardship. These were the exact people that had nothing to do with the causes of the crisis but their fates are these days very closely linked to global financial market development. For all their excesses and sometimes even outright criminal behaviour financial markets are one of the biggest stimulators of economic growth in the modern world and, as explained in Chapter 2, they also have a serious impact on poverty reduction. The multitude of the complex challenges financial globalization creates may not be resolved without solid and effective supra-national regulatory structures governing global finance. A workable system of governance for global financial markets may not be a panacea, but it is the essential foundation[3] that all global redistribution policies will have to rely on, since in the absence of financial stability, all other discussions/proposals look empty of content, no matter how good their intentions are.

In this Chapter, I provide an outline of a proposal for a new model of governance for global financial markets in order to address most of the

---

[2] Emma Rolwey, 'World needs $100 Trillion more Credit, says World Economic Forum', *The Telegraph*, 19 January 2011, available at www.telegraph.co.uk/finance/financetopics/davos/8267768/World-needs-100-trillion-more-credit-says-World-Economic-Forum.html.

[3] Stephen K. Aikins, 'Global Financial Crisis and Government Intervention: A Case for Effective Regulatory Governance' (2009) 10 *International Public Management Review* 23–43, available at www.ipmr.net.

above challenges in a way that would be more effective than the pre-existing regime or the architecture emerging as a result of the GFC. The most important value of the proposed governance system is that it would support effectively and further recent reforms protecting the ideal of open global markets and enhancing their legitimacy. The proposed global governance structure would have four pillars supported by a similar number of global administrative agencies: (1) macro-prudential; (2) micro-prudential; (3) financial policy, regulation, and knowledge supervisor; and, (4) a global resolution authority. The suggested governance system pre-supposes the negotiation and signing of an (umbrella) international treaty governing the most important aspects of international finance.

To many readers this might sound like an unrealistic 'academic' exercise requiring reform and expenditure on the grandest scale. Several valuable and insightful proposals for global financial governance reform[4] have been criticized or blocked on this basis or on grounds of lack of strong political will for reform. Clearly as regards the second obstacle, no amount of academic writing can really change the opposition of big stakeholders like the US or the EU to a supra-national governance system for global finance. It is possible that only an imminent financial catastrophe of a scale comparable with the GFC or bigger may be a threat big enough to set political minds to the task. On the other hand, academic writing and policy debates should have much to say regarding the first obstacle by attempting to provide structural reform proposals that present a realistic architecture/structure and attainable objectives.

The global financial governance model I outline below constitutes a global regulatory 'big bang', but it is not a new Bretton Woods, nor is it the answer to other global economic challenges, such as trade imbalances. For a number of years clear lines of responsibility and expertise have developed in the various corners of global financial governance. If one examines them carefully and puts the fragmented lines together, they automatically provide a rough guide to what is the right path to reform

---

[4] Among the most comprehensive ones are the UN Commission of Experts' proposal for the establishment of a Global Economic Coordination Council (United Nations, 'Report of the Commission of Experts of the President of the United Nations General Assembly on Reforms of the International Monetary and Financial System' New York, 21 September 2009, p. 87, hereinafter, UN Experts' Report) and John Eatwell's for the establishment of a global prudential (systemic risk) authority, suggested in many works, the most recent of which is Kern Alexander, Rahul Dhumale and John Eatwell, *Global Governance of Financial Systems: The International Regulation of Systemic Risk* (Oxford University Press, 2006).

and the most effective structural/institutional configuration. The next step of an academic work like this book should then be an attempt to shape the governance framework on the basis of knowledge we now have about: (1) the workings of global finance; (2) the causes of the GFC and the contours of the financial revolution; and (3) the other challenges modern markets/economies face such as (a) the widespread moral hazard 'too-big-to-fail' institutions give rise to and (b) the development objective. If this can be achieved, then the resulting governance framework for global finance would only require minimal expenditure and politically manageable tinkering with existing international arrangements.

1.2   Summary of the proposal

Accordingly, I submit here that a workable system of global financial governance to support and further recent reforms (discussed in Chapters 6 and 7) should be based on both the analysis of the challenges that a global financial governance structure would face and the default lines of authority already developed between the different bodies involved in the arena of international financial regulation, regardless of whether such bodies have a standing in international law. In proposing a global financial architecture with four pillars, I do not discard the debate on 'twin peaks'.[5] I just consider it not to be the most appropriate model in the international context where problems tend to be of a different nature. In the supra-national context the regulatory focus is on preventing cross-border contagion as much as protecting the stability of national financial systems and investor/consumer welfare. However, preventing cross-border spillovers is not a central objective of domestic regulatory systems to which the 'twin peaks' structure remains relevant.[6]

I also suggest that the first pillar, the global systemic risk (macro-prudential) supervisor that would monitor both macro-economic developments and the state of the global financial system, seen as encompassing national, regional and international financial systems and the shadow banking sector, should comprise a revamped IMF.[7] Assigning this duty,

---

[5] For an overview of this approach to regulation and discussion of its adaption by various jurisdictions (e.g., the Netherlands, Australia etc.) see Michael W. Taylor, 'The Road from "Twin Peaks" – and the Way Back' (2009) 16 *Connecticut Insurance Law Journal* 61. Many consider the term to have been coined by Michael Taylor.

[6] E.g., the new UK regulatory structures are clearly based on a 'twin peaks' plus approach.

[7] For a proposal to render the IMF into a global financial authority with a remit much wider than what is suggested here, see Luis Garricano and Rosa Lastra, 'Towards a New

by means of an international treaty, to a revamped IMF makes good sense, given also the IMF's monitoring role with respect to national balance of payments and sovereign indebtedness. In fact, the entanglement of financial sector stability and solvency with sovereign indebtedness and *vice versa* means that only a revamped IMF could effectively discharge the duties of a global macro-prudential supervisor.

The micro-prudential supervisor could exercise direct oversight over G-SIFIs, whether banks or other financial institutions, such as insurance companies, with a large cross-border asset or liabilities base. Its remit could gradually extend to cover certain wholesale segments of global derivatives and securities markets,[8] resolving the problem of regulation of mega-exchanges. It is suggested that this role should be assigned to a reconstituted and expanded FSB, where all G-20 banking and capital markets regulators are already represented. The Bank of International Settlements (BIS), minus its research 'division', would have to merge with the FSB. Accordingly, the new micro-prudential supervisor would essentially operate from existing BIS premises in Basel, ensuring its neutrality. The third pillar should comprise the OECD and the research 'division' of BIS and should be dedicated to the task of production of new regulation and examination/evaluation of emerging risks, especially by means of various financial innovations. The new body could be called the Global Financial Policy, Regulation and Knowledge Organization and should be the directing mind of international financial regulation. The fourth pillar should comprise a newly established Global Resolution Authority which should deal with the resolution of big cross-border financial groups on the basis of a single resolution and insolvency model.

The legitimacy of the proposed structure is premised on three arguments. First, abstract ideas of distributive justice in the international (cosmopolitan) context. These should be seen as having comparable importance with other core ideas/values of humanity, such as the protection of human rights, with which all democratic societies tend to abide.[9] Second, the suggested formal supra-national structure would be a much

---

Architecture for Financial Stability: Seven Principles' (2010) 13 *Journal of International Economic Law* 597–621.

[8] Cf. Donald C. Langevoort, 'Global Securities Regulation after the Financial Crisis' (2010) 13 *Journal of International Economic Law* 799–815.

[9] Thomas Cottier, 'Multilayered Governance, Pluralism, and Moral Conflict', (2009) 16(2) *Indiana Journal of Global Legal Studies* 647, 659–61. See also David Held, *Democracy and the Global Order: From the Modern State to Cosmopolitan Governance* (Stanford University Press, 1995), Chapter 11.

better guardian of the global public good[10] of systemic stability than national/ regional regulators and the existing Transnational Regulatory Networks (TRNs). Third, the new structure will contain an explicit set of shared values (in the form of general principles and sub-principles of governance), which would not only secure its coherence but also be much more cognizant of an additional (to financial stability) global public good: economic development and its impact on poverty eradication. Existing soft law structures do not have any mandate to consider this aspect of financial systems and systemic stability, vesting with considerable legitimacy advantages formal governance structures that would do so.[11]

Furthermore, it would have been very appealing to have been able to specifically suggest that the new governance structure should be based on a (concrete) social contract theory model that would incorporate a Rawlsian approach to distributions.[12] Right after the outbreak of the GFC,

[10] There is no universal definition of global public goods, but this does not mean that there are no credible scholarly attempts to define them. The departure point in the analysis is the distinction between public and private goods in the domestic context, where, in market economies, provision of public goods and services is the duty of governments, either because of a failure of the markets to provide them or failure to provide them in sufficient quantities to satisfy societal/re-distribution goals. An extension of this approach in the global sphere has described global public goods as 'goods [which] can be grouped into two sets. The first is that their benefits have strong qualities of publicness – i.e., they are marked by nonrivalry in consumption and nonexcludability. These features place them in the general category of public goods. The second criterion is that their benefits are quasi universal in terms of countries (covering more than one group of countries), people (accruing to several, preferably all population groups), and generations (extending to both current and future generations, or at least meeting the needs of current generations without foreclosing development options for future generations). This property makes humanity as a whole the *publicum,* or beneficiary of global public goods.' Inge Kaul, Isabelle Grunberg and Marc A. Stern, 'Defining Global Public Goods', in Inge Kaul, Isabelle Grunberg and Marc A. Stern (eds.), *Global Public Goods: International Cooperation in the 21st Century* (New York: Oxford University Press, 1999), Chapter 1, p. 2. See also Anthony B. Atkinson, 'Innovative Sources to Meet a Global Challenge', in Anthony B. Atkinson (ed.), *New Sources of Development Finance* (Oxford University Press, 2005), pp. 1–3.

[11] See Allen Buchanan and Robert O. Keohane 'The Legitimacy of Global Governance Institutions', in Rudiger Wolfrum and Volker Roben (eds.), *Legitimacy in International Law* (Berlin: Springer, 2008), Chapter 2, especially pp. 27–8.

[12] Rawls essentially argues that if people are rational agents and act only in their own self-interest they will choose two principles of justice: first, each person is to have an equal right to the most extensive basic liberty compatible with a similar liberty for others; second, social and economic inequalities are to be arranged so that they are both (1) reasonably expected to be to everyone's advantage, and (2) attached to positions and offices open to all. See John Rawls, *A Theory of Justice* (Cambridge, MA: Harvard University Press, revised edn, 1999), pp. 52–3.

the then UK Prime Minister Gordon Brown called for a new social contract between the public and the global financial services industry.[13] This is a very attractive political approach but much more scholarly analysis will have to be conducted before it is accepted as the normative foundation of a formal governance system for global finance. A possible basis for a social contract approach to governance of international finance would have been an examination of the (implicit) terms of banks and other financial institution's licensing by national regulators. But, in practice, such analysis would have nowhere to go in a global, as opposed to national, context. The biggest part, in terms of turnover, of global markets is the shadow banking sector and hedge funds and shadow banks are normally not licensed by any regulatory body representing the wishes of an elected (or not) government of the people. So, I have reluctantly come to accept that currently such an approach cannot successfully serve as the normative foundation of the proposed system of governance and further work is required in this area. Therefore, it is for future works to try to develop a sound theoretical framework that will incorporate a Rawlsian system of distributions into supra-national governance structures for global financial markets, if that is at all possible, given the limitations of Rawls' model in a cosmopolitan context.[14]

The remainder of this chapter is divided in two sections. Section 2 below sets out in more detail the global governance structure suggested in this chapter and explains the advantages of the proposal. Section 3 concludes.

2.   The proposed global regulatory framework

2.1   General principles: the importance of shared values

As mentioned in Chapter 5, the existence of a set of commonly accepted shared values is of cardinal importance for both the effectiveness and legitimacy of a multi-layered governance structure like the one suggested

---

[13] 'There has always been an implicit economic and social contract between financial institutions and the societies they serve … The new contract must recognise the two new characteristics of modern financial institutions – their global scope and their interconnectedness', Gordon Brown, 'How Can we Restore Trust in Financial Institutions', *Financial Times*, 9 November 2009, p. 15.

[14] Allen Buchanan, 'Rawls's Law of Peoples: Rules for a Vanished Westphalian World' (2000) 110 *Ethics* 697–721.

in this chapter.[15] The same applies to the nexus of relationships between the proposed supra-national governance system and member states and other constituents, such as the financial institutions overseen by the scheme. Therefore, the statutes of the bodies involved in the proposed system would have to be amended, making all four organizations accountable, for their regulatory mandate, to a Treaty-established *governing council* of twenty five representatives, which would comprise the G-20 members (Ministers or Heads of State), the EU as an organization separate from its members, the United Nations, as an organization separate from its members, the World Bank and the three most important national economies from those that are not represented in the G-20. The governing council could be convened every six months or whenever important matters have to be discussed. In addition, the head of the governing council, a post held by members of the governing council on a rotating basis, would have to file an annual report about the work of the new authorities before the UN General Assembly. In addition, key NGOs should be sitting on the board of the financial policy authority and even be given voting rights when debating issues within the NGOs' area of expertise.

Within the proposed structure, the four authorities would be of equal status and they would be mandated to co-operate in full, especially when it comes to exchange of information, initiation of joint regulatory action or processing and evaluation of data. The important decisions of the suggested system of global financial governance would be jointly decided by the heads of the four authorities. However, each authority would have the decisive vote in its respective governance field: systemic risk supervision, micro-prudential supervision, regulation production and resolution. Any critical disagreements would be referred to the chairman of the governing council or the council plenary but this right would cover only planning decisions and not instances where speedy action would be required, such as imposition of sanctions, prevention of an activity that threatens systemic stability or initiating resolution. Naturally, in the process more detailed rules would have to be instilled to allow the system to take effective and responsible action without fears of abuse. Thus, the system would eventually develop its own set of global administrative law rules. These arrangements would provide clarity in the relationship between the different authorities of the proposed scheme.

[15] See Cottier, 'Multilayered Governance'; Rolf H. Weber, 'Multilayered Governance in International Financial Regulation and Supervision' (2010) 13 *Journal of International Economic Law* 683–704.

The scheme could not come into existence unless G-20 countries, the rest of the EU members, and other key economies sign an international treaty establishing a supra-national governance structure for global finance. Thus, it would become mandatory for participating jurisdictions. Beyond participating members the scheme would be voluntary. Unsurprisingly, if all G-20 economies and the rest of the EU subscribe to the new governance scheme, following the signing of an international agreement, it would be impossible for the rest of the world not to join. Apart from the quality/credibility mark lent to institutions supervised under the scheme, the new governance system would also provide a further advantage. It is suggested that the scheme should provide to institutions falling under its remit full freedom of establishment in foreign jurisdictions and freedom to offer services on a cross-border basis, subject to local rules of conduct. Namely, it is proposed to give institutions governed by the scheme a 'single passport' facility similar to that granted by EU member states to any financial institution licensed in the EU.

The scheme could only be able to provide this facility if WTO signatories agreed a modification in the GATS rendering the 'prudential regulation carve out' inapplicable for financial institutions governed by the proposed governance scheme. This should not prove an insurmountable problem, since with the implementation of the suggested scheme, authorities would be taking important steps to safeguard systemic stability. This further liberalization of global trade in financial services should be able to return to the WTO negotiations agenda. The WTO structure is also instructive regarding settlement of disputes that would arise within the proposed scheme and perhaps existing WTO infrastructure could be used for the settlement of such disputes.[16]

The departure point for holding the regulatory bodies of the new structure to account would be their compliance not only with their charters but also with a set of general principles that should govern their actions. Several attempts have been made to first identify those principles and then define them,[17] also with reference to the general principles governing

---

[16] For a preliminary discussion of this issue see John H. Jackson, 'Introductory Note: The Quest for International Law in Financial Regulation and Monetary Affairs', (2010) 13 *Journal of International Economic Law* 525 and Michael Gadbaw, 'Systemic Regulation of Global Trade and Finance: A Tale of Two Systems' (2010) 13 *Journal of International Economic Law* 551. For a discussion of the WTO dispute settlement process, see Andreas Lowenfeld, *International Economic Law* (Oxford University Press, 2nd edn, 2008), Chapter 8, pp. 161–210.

[17] Garricano and Lastra, 'Towards a New Architecture', 606–20; Weber, 'Multilayered Governance', 693–4.

the operation of the leading international finance TRNs such as IOSCO.[18] In this context, I view three principles as beyond dispute. These are the need to:

(1) safeguard the global public good of financial stability;
(2) protect the robustness of financial infrastructure;
(3) safeguard the integrity of global markets and protect investors and consumers of financial services from abusive practices and products that may be unsuitable to their risk profile.

To these principles I would suggest that a fifth should be added, even though, it may only be seen as a supplement to the principle of financial stability. All actions of the new system should be cognizant of their impact on the ability of open and competitive financial markets to foster economic growth and reduce poverty, when the objective of financial stability is not compromised.

However general and abstract this principle might sound at this stage, it is a substantial leap forward. After all, it is not meant to provide the foundation for litigation or judicial review but to signal to the proposed regulatory bodies and the rest of the world that, first, financial crises and regulators' actions to prevent or contain them and, second, the preservation of open and competitive markets have significant impact on economic development and this reality may no longer be ignored.[19] Thus, the importance of this principle should not be underestimated in terms of the direction that it would provide to the new governance structures and the regulations they would produce.

I have explained elsewhere the possibility of creating very low risk weights under the Basel framework for certain classes of microcredit used to pursue an economic activity or buy a productive asset or for those that have an embedded borrower monitoring mechanism as group loans do.[20] Giving these loans a preferential treatment in terms of capital

---

[18] See IOSCO, 'Objectives and Principles of Securities Regulation' June 2010, available at www.iosco.org/library/pubdocs/pdf/IOSCOPD323.pdf.

[19] This observation only means that the principle will not be able to be litigated. It is not to say that domestic regulatory systems should not incorporate this principle in more binding terms given the importance of law in fostering development. See Ross Cranston, *How Law Works* (Oxford University Press, 2006), Chapter 9 and Douglas Arner, *Financial Stability, Economic Growth and the Role of Law* (Cambridge University Press, 2007).

[20] See Emilios Avgouleas, 'Access to Finance, Microfinance, and International Banking Regulation: A New Approach to Development' (2007) 4 *Manchester Journal of International Economic Law* 3–51.

regulations would provide a significant impetus to the industry without compromising financial stability.[21] The repayment rate of such loans sometimes touches 100 percent, but it is very hard for this fact to be clearly observed in the absence of written records or credit registries in the countries where such loans are mostly supplied. The suggested financial policy regulator could thus undertake its own independent examination of repayment rates for such loans, using a variety of formal and informal sources. Once satisfied with the outcome it could produce capital regulations that reflect the reality of low default ratios for those loans and not that formally appearing in the absence of technical infrastructure to document the true default rates. The same regulatory incentives (low capital requirements) route could be followed with debt to equity exchange schemes for loans to developing countries that go beyond exchanges between creditor and debtor nations[22] and extend to private institutions, once certainty is established, following relevant studies, that financial stability is safeguarded.

The existence of a set of commonly accepted values for the effectiveness and legitimacy of a multi-layered governance system like the one proposed here may not be overstressed. It is the foundation of any multi-layered system of governance and the material that holds it together reinforcing its legitimacy.[23] In addition, including the development objective in the new governance structure, notwithstanding the supremacy of the financial stability objective, would signal a marked re-orientation of global finance. This is of cardinal importance since it would emphasize to global finance operators and to people in developing nations the possibilities global finance holds in resolving several development issues. This, in turn, is a very good way to create a community of interests between the two and thus broaden the legitimacy of the proposed governance system. Binding global technocratic institutions, like the ones proposed here, to a set of 'shared values' that would promote global welfare objectives is, arguably, an excellent way to enhance their legitimacy.

---

[21] See Emilios Avgouleas, 'International Financial Regulation, Access to Finance, Systemic Stability, and Development' (2008) *LAWASIA Journal* 62–76.

[22] For a discussion of these schemes, see Ross Buckley, 'Debt-for-Development Exchanges: An Innovative Response to the Global Financial Crisis' (2009) 32 *University of New South Wales Law Journal* 620.

[23] As Cottier has perceptively noted: 'Multilayered governance thus relies upon a common and shared body of underlying constitutional values and legal principles ...' Cottier, 'Multilayered Governance', 657.

2.2   *The global macro-prudential supervisor*

Alexander, Eatwell and Dhumale had presciently observed in 2006:[24]

> Recent crises suggest that current international efforts to regulate financial systems lack coherence and legitimacy and fail to effectively manage systemic risk.

As explained in Chapters 4 and 5, this remains the case with TRNs and soft law structures, but cannot be said for the new US systemic risk supervisor, the Financial Stability Oversight Council (FSOC) or the European Systemic Risk Board (ESRB). Yet a closer examination will reveal two awkward truths for both newly established regimes for systemic risk supervision. First, their mandate is inevitably limited to the US and the EU borders. Accordingly, it is still open to question whose, if anybody's, job is the protection of global systemic stability. Second, although both the US and EU regimes will doubtlessly be geared towards global macro-prudential developments, from the movement of interest rates in other countries/regions to sovereign debt, they do not possess the tools to monitor properly the biggest channel of credit intermediation in the world: the shadow banking sector,[25] nor do they have any power of intervention. This shortcoming could undermine, through regulatory arbitrage, current regulatory efforts to create a safer financial system in very effective and invisible ways. For instance, it gives ample opportunity for regulated entities to evade the stricter leverage and liquidity requirements imposed by Basel III.[26]

The best way to remedy these shortcomings is the assignment, by means of an international treaty,[27] of the role of global macro-prudential

---

[24] Alexander *et. al.*, *Global Governance of Financial Systems*.

[25] The mechanics, operation and risks of shadow banking were analytically discussed in Chapter 2, Section 3.5 and Chapter 3, Section 2.2. For more extensive discussion of the ways in which shadow banking may be used to evade regulations and build 'hidden' systemic risks, see FSB, 'Shadow Banking: Scoping the Issues – A Background Note of the Financial Stability Board', April 2011, available at www.financialstabilityboard.org/publications/r_110412a.pdf.

[26] The FSB Report on Shadow Banking notes: 'If parts of the shadow banking system are able to operate without internalising the true cost of its risks and thus gain a funding advantage relative to banks where regulation aims to achieve such an internalisation, this is likely to create opportunities for arbitrage that might undermine bank regulation and lead to a build-up of additional leverage and risks in the system. Moreover, banks themselves may use shadow banking entities to increase leverage and find ways to circumvent their regulatory capital or liquidity requirements', *ibid.*, p. 8.

[27] For a discussion of the advantages of importing reforms in the sphere of international financial governance by means of a formal amendment of the IMF Articles of Agreement,

regulator to the IMF acting in co-operation with the ESRB and the FSOC. The IMF's monitoring of global markets on a consistent basis and its duty to conduct regular bilateral (FSAP) surveys and multilateral (global market) reviews (both discussed extensively in Chapter 4, Section 3.3) makes it the institution that presents the biggest advantages in terms of expertise, resources and economies of scale in global macroeconomic risk monitoring. This is also recognized by recent initiatives of the international community and the G-20 to strengthen the IMF's role in this area and make FSAP surveys compulsory.[28] Naturally, vesting the IMF with a formal role as global systemic risk supervisor would also solve the issue of quality of data provided to the IMF by domestic authorities during FSAP surveys and foster much stronger co-operation, within a formal framework.

In addition, the IMF should be given the tools to monitor closely the shadow banking sector in order to close the current supervisory discontinuities, especially as regards systemic risk data collection and processing. A possible way to do this would be to require all shadow banks and hedge funds[29] to register with the IMF and file regular reports with it. The scheme should be properly calibrated in terms of asset thresholds to capture only important shadow banking vehicles. Thus, it should provide for *de minimis* exemptions to avoid registration of small funds. In the unlikely event that it is proved that sovereign wealth funds are significant

---

which is, of course, an international law treaty, see Sean Hagan, 'Enhancing the IMF's Regulatory Authority' (2010) 13 *Journal of International Economic Law* 955–68. Sean Hagan is the general counsel of the IMF.

[28] See for an overview of these initiatives and the IMF's strengthened role in the post-2008 period, *ibid.*

[29] According to the FSA, hedge funds cause systemic risk through two channels: (1) the 'credit channel' which constitutes the direct link between hedge funds and the banking sector, namely the extent to which credit counterparties are exposed to hedge funds and the impact on them of a possible hedge fund failure and (2) the 'market channel' which refers to hedge fund trade strategies which can be correlated, with all hedge funds entering or exiting the market at the same time, since they often use similar trading strategies and risk management models. Aggressive and high-volume trading strategies can lead to 'large scale forced liquidations by hedge funds to disrupt market liquidity and pricing'. See FSA, 'Assessing Possible Sources of Systemic Risk from Hedge Funds – A Report on the Findings of the Hedge Fund Survey and Hedge Fund as Counterparty Survey', July 2010, pp. 1–2. Arguably, while the 'credit channel' could be controlled by placing position limits on regulated banks' exposure to hedge funds and other shadow banking vehicles, as the Dodd–Frank Act does, the market channel can only be contained if readily identified by a global systemic risk regulator that will have then to devise or implement existing strategies to cool off the market.

participants in the shadow banking sector, these funds would also have to register.

The IMF 'division' that would be assigned the tasks discussed above would be headed by the IMF leadership but its membership would be broadened to include the systemic risk regulators of the G-20 countries and outside experts. In addition, like the ESRB, the IMF should be entitled to recommend to national regulators or the global micro-prudential supervisor suggested here a course of defensive action against an emerging systemic threat. It should also be considered whether, in the context of the same treaty, it would be feasible to give the IMF the power that Dodd–Frank has already given to FSOC, and the ESRB can exercise indirectly, to require directly financial institutions to act upon emerging systemic risks that in its judgment give rise to significant concern that justifies adoption of remedial action. In both cases the global macro-prudential supervisor may only be involved where the risk concerned constitutes a threat to more than one jurisdiction or has the possibility of creating cross-border financial stability spillovers.

2.3   A global micro-prudential authority

As mentioned in the previous two chapters, many gaps remain in the supervision of large financial institutions/groups operating on a global basis. These fractures would almost certainly lead to three insurmountable problems that would make the operation of G-SIFIs a continuous source of moral hazard, notwithstanding the important new regulations that are underway to limit it. First, while the cross-border operation of financial institutions can give rise to cross-border contagion leading to a generalized financial crisis,[30] the incentives of the home supervisor to prevent this outcome could possibly be weak. As the collapse of the Icelandic banks discussed in Chapter 5 has shown, home country supervisors are certain to face weak incentives to intervene promptly, when the main asset/deposit base of the institution in trouble is in another jurisdiction. Supervisory colleges might make exchanges of information smoother, facilitating supervision, but they are unlikely to prove an

---

[30] For a good analysis of contagion channels opened by the cross-border operations of financial institutions, see Hans Degryse, Muhammad Ather Elahi and Maria Fabiana Penas, 'The Impact of Cross-Border Exposures on Financial Contagion', in Panagiotis Delimatsis and Nils Herger (eds.), *Financial Regulation at the Crossroads, Implications for Supervision, Institutional Design and Trade* (The Hague: Kluwer Law International, 2011), Chapter 1, especially. pp. 26–32.

effective crisis management and resolution mechanism. Since colleges do not have power of intervention, especially as regards Prompt Corrective Action (PCA) and resolution, it is unlikely that home supervisors will be forced to act when they stand to lose reputation and money (from the deposit insurance fund, the resolution fund, or due to a public bail-out), in order to protect/rescue depositors or other creditors of the financial institution concerned who are located in other jurisdictions. It should be noted that this was widespread behaviour during the GFC and it is not an assumption based on a theoretical model.[31] In addition, in the absence of a unitary supervision regime, regulatory co-ordination between home and host authorities is bound to be slow and incoherent, due to their conflicting objectives.[32] Second, inconsistent implementation and application of the new Basel III rules would more or less mean that different regulatory arbitrage channels are bound to open, undermining the effectiveness of reforms. Third, the multitude of national regulators that shall be involved in the calculation and application of the countercyclical buffer to G-SIFIs will prove to be an obstacle to its effective and consistent application to these institutions.[33]

Indicative of the severity and acuteness of the second obstacle is this statement by Daniel Tarullo, a member of the board of directors of the US Federal Reserve and bank regulation expert, in his June 2011 testimony to Congress:[34]

---

[31] 'During the current crisis one of the most commonly observed phenomena was discrimination against host country/foreign borrower', UN Experts Report, p. 56. In addition, in the tightly interconnected world of modern market economies regulatory forbearance in the home country can have a debilitating impact on economic growth in the host country, *ibid*.

[32] A group of leading EU experts had noted: 'During the financial crisis the situation of the banking system was assessed mainly at the national level and remedial action was also defined at country level in the European Union (EU). This may have prevented the efficient use of private resources and may have increased the overall cost to public finances. Coordination and cooperation between national supervisors have proved ineffective in the crisis management of multinational financial institutions where speediness was required (Fortis).' See Carmine Lamanda, *et al.*, 'Cross-border Banking in Europe: What Regulation and Supervision?', Unicredit Group Forum on Financial Cross-border Groups, Discussion Paper 1/09, March 2009, p. 8. See also *ibid*. pp. 18–19.

[33] For a discussion of this issue and for an insightful discussion of the several fractures presented by the emerging financial architecture, see Barry Eichengreen, 'Reforming the International Financial Architecture, 2011 Edition', Speech to the Bank of Korea, Seoul, 26 May 2011, especially pp. 2–4.

[34] Daniel K. Tarullo, 'Capital and Liquidity Standards', Testimony before the Committee on Financial Services, US House of Representatives, Washington, DC, 16 June 2011, p. 8, available at www.federalreserve.gov/newsevents/testimony/tarullo20110616a.htm.

> Despite extensive sharing of information on supervisory practices, the Basel Committee has, over the years, found it difficult to achieve what I have characterized as the second critical step in the implementation of international capital accords – that is, rigorous and consistent application of those rules by supervisors and firms across countries, as reflected in reported capital levels and amounts of risk-weighted assets of individual banks. An international process for monitoring implementation on a bank-by-bank basis has become increasingly necessary ... One area that has deservedly received attention of late is the potential for differences in the calculation of risk-weighted assets across banks, both currently and prospectively under the Basel III standards ... The Basel Committee leadership has acknowledged that failing to implement Basel III in a globally consistent manner could lead to a competitive race to the bottom and increase risks to the global financial system.

Although Tarullo continued by proposing mechanisms for effective cross-country monitoring, it is very obvious that political objections/realities notwithstanding, the only effective solution to the regulation of G-SIFIs is to subject international financial institutions with a strong cross-border asset or liabilities base (50 percent and over) to the direct supervision of a global micro-prudential authority,[35] to, inter alia, minimize the scope for regulatory arbitrage. In the same mode, a global micro-prudential authority supervising G-SIFIs on a consolidated and individualized basis is the only way to apply uniformly and effectively the countercyclical buffer, provided in Basel III, on financial institutions with large cross-border presence. As said earlier, the role of micro-prudential supervisor could gradually evolve into a fully fledged global markets regulator, which could eventually be asked to exercise oversight over mega-exchanges and wholesale derivatives markets. Thus, this duty should be assigned to a reconstituted FSB, where all national banking and capital markets supervisors are already represented.

The micro-prudential supervisor of G-SIFIs would monitor compliance with the globally accepted standards, such as the Basel III framework. As discussed in Chapters 6 and 7, transatlantic prudential regulation standards especially are on the path to convergence, but not entirely.[36] The Volcker Rule and Dodd–Frank approach to regulation of 'swaps' dealers are currently two clear areas of major divergence. It is likely that

---

[35] For similar views see Eric J. Pan, 'Challenge of International Cooperation and Institutional Design in Financial Supervision: Beyond Transgovernmental Networks' (2010) 11 *Chicago Journal of International Law* 243–84.

[36] See also on this point Morris Goldstein and Nicolas Veron, 'Too Big to Fail: The Transatlantic Debate', Peterson Institute for International Economics, Working Paper 11–2, January 2011.

divergence also exists among other G-20 member regimes that have not been examined in this study. Therefore, it is proposed that, in the absence of globally agreed standards, such as the Basel III framework, or BCBS proposals on CoCos and bail-able instruments, diverging home country prudential standards may apply to G-SIFIs. Therefore, it is more efficient that compliance of G-SIFIs with prudential standards is monitored by a global micro-prudential authority in order to avoid creating overlapping supervisory regimes. The global micro-prudential authority would be entitled to ask for the assistance of the home country supervisor, which is, in any case, responsible for monitoring compliance with national rules of conduct. Such an arrangement would eliminate scope for confusion or lax supervision and weaken home country opposition to the suggested supervisory scheme.

In fact, of all the parts of the proposed system of governance this is probably the most likely to be fiercely opposed. Strong national interest dictates that each country, which serves as the home jurisdiction of a big bank or other important financial institution, wishes to be the principal regulator of this institution, first for reasons of prestige and influence in global economic affairs and, second, for reasons of national economic interest, including job preservation and credit growth in the national markets. Yet the logic of the proposal is too strong to be dismissed out of hand. It eliminates the scope for regulatory forbearance and provides a framework for consistent application of the new Basel III rules, which, apart from regulating capital, extend to the key prudential areas of leverage and liquidity regulation.

Obviously, if there is a possibility for this part of the proposal to ever come to fruition, the issue of loss of sovereignty must be managed/contained as much as possible. Therefore, when the micro-prudential authority would have to take enforcement against a G-SIFI, it would need to act as a college – borrowing certain elements from the operation of the new EU supervisory authorities, discussed in Chapter 6 – allowing key national regulators to have a say and making it a truly multi-layered governance structure. Also strong accountability mechanisms would have to be established. If the finance minister of the home country is not a member of the new system's governing council, then it should be invited to attend proceedings, help with supervision and influence decisions, although it is the global body that would ultimately take the key supervisory decisions. For this reason, it would be an unassailable requirement that decisions concerning PCA, other supervisory decisions of equivalent force and resolution decisions would be taken only following the consent of the three authorities in the proposed system: the systemic risk supervisor, the micro-prudential supervisor, and the global resolution authority. It should be a requirement that the requisite PCA, resolution etc. decision is immediately implemented, unless the head of the governing council opposed such a decision in a reasoned manner. In that case disagreement between the consenting global regulators and the head of council would be resolved by a vote taken by the council's full membership in an extra-ordinary session convened as fast as possible.

The FSB has already assumed a global leadership role in a number of areas that are pertinent to G-SIFI oversight. First, it is instrumental in deciding which institutions should be regarded as G-SIFIs.[37] Second, it has taken a prominent review role with respect to the consistent implementation of the new regulations governing G-SIFIs.[38] Third, the FSB is trying to lead in another important area of supervision of G-SIFIs: the drawing up, scrutiny and viability testing of G-SIFI recovery and resolution plans.[39] In light of the above, the assumption by the FSB of a formal role as global micro-prudential authority should be seen as the natural progression of its existing functions in this area. Nonetheless, this finding

---

[37] '45. The PRC will periodically review, for consideration by the FSB, whether other significant institutions should be considered as (or no longer considered as) globally systemic.' FSB, 'Reducing the Moral Hazard Posed by Systemically Important Financial Institutions – FSB Recommendations and Time Lines', 20 October 2010, p. 9.

[38] '44. A Peer Review Council (PRC) will be established, comprising senior members of the relevant national authorities having G-SIFIs operating as home or host in their jurisdictions, with a mandate to assess and report to the FSB as to whether: the national G-SIFI policy measures adopted constitute reasonable choices from amongst the available set of policy options and potential trade-offs, on the basis of an evaluation framework agreed upon by the FSB in consultation with the standard setting bodies – the G-SIFI Recovery and Resolution plans and institution-specific cooperation agreements are robust and likely to be effective – the national G-SIFI policy measures are globally consistent and mutually supportive – additional loss absorbency measures have been implemented', *ibid.*, p. 8.

[39] 'A FSB working group will examine the legal and operational aspects of both contractual and statutory bail-in mechanisms providing for debt to equity conversions and/or write-downs in resolution. The working group will evaluate the market capacity and impact of such mechanisms and the legal requirements and contractual terms for their use in group structures and in a cross-border context. By end-2011, relevant home and host authorities should have drawn up for all G-SIFIs institution-specific cooperation agreements that specify the respective roles and responsibilities of the authorities at all stages of a crisis. The FSB will assess and report by end-2011 on the progress in the development of institution-specific recovery and resolution plans for G-SIFIs. It will report on practical measures taken to improve resolvability, addressing obstacles associated with booking practices, global payments, intra-group guarantees and information systems', *ibid.*, p. 8.

may not conceal the fact that considerable costs would be involved in transforming the FSB from its current status as a TRN into a global micro-prudential regulator and equipping it with the right amount of resources in order to discharge that role.

2.4   Global financial policy, regulation and risk knowledge authority

The third pillar of the proposed governance structure is a global financial policy body that would oversee the TRNs, including the BCBS, and IOSCO,[40] under arrangements that should be more binding than those underpinning the FSB, which currently performs this role. Suggested arrangements would not obliterate the importance of the BCBS and of other TRNs and their value as importers of private sector knowledge and interlocutors with the private sector. This approach would make the proposed scheme a truly multi-layered and hierarchical governance structure. TRN standards would have to pass a public interest test set by the financial policy body, which would primarily focus on financial stability and the ways any draft standard serves the other general principles of the proposed governance system. Once endorsed, the standards would become binding, automatically or through mandatory implementation legislation, to all jurisdictions that have opted into the proposed scheme and signed the treaty. The rule-making committees of the International Swaps and Derivatives Association (ISDA), the standard setting committee of the International Accounting Standards Board (IASB) and other important private sector rule-making bodies[41] would also come under the umbrella of the financial policy regulator and their standards would have to be endorsed by the regulator, provided that they met a public interest/financial stability test. This reform would secure coherence in standard-setting/rule-making in the field of international finance, eliminating the scope for rule conflict or uncertainty.

The same body should play the role of global risk knowledge bank and manager. I have already explained (in Chapters 2 and 3) the high costs of lack of knowledge and understanding of the mechanics and potential risks of innovative financial instruments and techniques and their interaction with global economic developments, such as market liberalization.

---

[40] A full discussion of the structure and work of these TRNs can be found in Chapter 4.
[41] A full discussion of these private sector bodies can be found in Chapter 4.

In the same chapters, I discussed the role of the financial revolution in both building up some of the conditions that led to the GFC and the wide amplification of its consequences. In the same mode, the financial revolution, like all knowledge revolutions, can bring very significant welfare benefits to the global economy if managed properly. Neither the risks nor the potential benefits of the financial revolution can be properly managed in the absence of painstaking research and even testing innovative financial instruments/techniques in real (or simulated) market conditions that would allow the global investment community to understand them properly and in their true dimensions.

For example, not only is the true impact of the financial revolution on tail risk correlations still not fully understood but also other significant aspects of the financial revolution remain largely unexplored. A case in hand is the interaction of the anthropological and psychological attributes of individuals and groups – as, for instance, the psychological rewards derived from risk-taking,[42] whether it is gambling or stock trading[43] – with the forces of the financial revolution which is very little studied and very poorly understood. Naturally, this might sound like a tiny matter that is not worth any serious scientific attention. Yet the truth is that it is very far from such an easy dismissal. Financial crises

---

[42] E.g., a British psychologist has postulated, drawing on anthropological studies of investor behaviour and an analysis of novels by and about financial professionals, that the theory of psychoanalysis 'suggests evidence that there is an element of masochistic satisfaction in the experience of running up losses, and that a full-blown crash is a source of euphoria as much as despair'. The financial crash, Crosthwaite argues, 'is the modern equivalent of the traditional Native American practice of "potlatch", a ritual ceremony in which the chiefs of rival tribes competed to destroy ever greater quantities of their own possessions. As with chiefs participating in a potlatch, the capacity to generate huge losses, just as much as huge profits, is experienced by investment bankers and financial traders as an expression of their power, prestige, and importance'. Paul Crosthwaite, 'Blood on the Trading Floor: Waste, Sacrifice, and Death in Financial Crises' (2010) 15 *Angelaki Journal of the Theoretical Humanities* 3–18.

[43] A mere browsing of two important books: a classic work of literature (Fyodor Dostoevsky, *The Gambler* (1867)) and a semi-satirical account of Wall Street attitudes by an industry insider who turned into a distinguished author (Mike Lewis, *Liar's Poker: Playing the Money Markets* (New York: W.W. Norton & Co., 1990)) should prove sufficient to convince even the most disbelieving and sceptical observer of the strong psychological connections between gamblers' and traders' attitudes (and addiction) to high stakes games. Of course, while Alexei (*The Gambler*'s central character, probably modelled on Dostoevsky himself) and other gamblers in human history in the end bring ruin only to themselves and perhaps their relatives, largely internalizing the cost of their actions, modern 'gambling' traders operate in a world of strong interconnectedness and the externalities caused by their actions are capable of wreaking havoc on the entire financial system.

throughout history tend to share a variety of characteristics, an issue extensively discussed in Chapter 3. Only one of these is however ever present both as a cause and effect: panic.[44] There is literally no crisis if one big group of stakeholders in financial markets do not lose their rational calm and become irrationally risk averse and panic sellers, regardless of whether they are sophisticated investors and creditors or the general public. At the same time, widespread herding is an ever present characteristic in all bubbles. There is little doubt that this sort of herding is triggered or boosted by socio-psychological reasons, whether irrational exuberance or just competition for the highest payment package among peer groups. But it may not be modelled with any degree of accuracy. Herding behaviour is ever present both in periods of growth and decline. In the latter case, the momentum game goes into reverse and panicking investors start selling.[45]

In spite of the grave threats to financial stability emanating from the largely unexplored risk correlations that might be generated through the use of innovative financial instruments/techniques and the forms of human behaviour discussed above, there is no private organization that would ever deem it profitable to engage in such research. Academic research, on the other hand, can make a valuable contribution especially with respect to development of research methodologies and even identification of the areas that hold hidden risks. But realistically academic research, due to either a lack of sufficient resources or appropriate expertise and experience, cannot close the knowledge gap that is still pervasive in global financial policy-making. Therefore, a global public body has to undertake this task and the results of its research output would have to be incorporated in international standards to make the expenditure worthwhile.

The need for a global public regulatory policy and risk knowledge body is even bigger in light of the marked and continuous criticism directed at credit rating agencies (CRAs) who are private sector's main financial risk knowledge processors and assessors in the global marketplace. I have given examples of CRAs flawed methods and rating unreliability in the wake of the GFC in Chapters 3 and 5. In addition, CRA ratings seem

---

[44] Charles P. Kindleberger and Rober Z. Alliber, *Manias, Panics, and Crashes: A History of Financial Crisis* (Hoboken, NJ: Wiley & Sons, 5th edn, 2005).

[45] For a discussion of how this can translate into escalating volumes of short sales see Emilios Avgouleas, 'A New Framework for the Global Regulation of Short Sales: Why Prohibition is Inefficient and Disclosure Insufficient' (2010) 15 *Stanford Journal of Law, Business & Finance* 376–425.

unpardonably procyclical or tend to de facto dictate international public policy. In the context of the ongoing sovereign debt crisis, CRAs have plausibly been accused of creating a string of 'self-fulfilling' prophesies with their aggressive downgrading of EU sovereign borrowers.[46]

Arguably, it would be easy to do away with credit ratings if they were only used for capital adequacy reasons, but their use is much wider. In practice, they are relied upon by all big institutional investors when they invest in corporate and sovereign bonds and a host of other instruments. As a result, they have the power to raise the cost of borrowing of nations. Respected commentators even reckon that they have become the masters of elected politicians.[47] This is too strong a power to entrust to private institutions. However, this is not to say that government policies should not be subjected to market scrutiny. Therefore, there is an urgent need for the establishment of a global body that would oversee CRAs and will not be attached to strong national or regional economic interests, as the CRAs new regulator in Europe, the European Securities Markets Authority (ESMA), is going to be. The regulator must also have the quality of staff and expertise that would allow it to provide true scrutiny of CRA methodologies and ratings back-testing.[48] I suggest that the global financial policy authority should also be entrusted with the risk knowledge task, fulfilling the duties described above with respect to market research and CRA oversight.

The body discharging the aforementioned tasks would be of enormous importance to global economic welfare and would have to be rich in resources, reliable and truly independent, since it would inevitably become subject to strong political pressure of all kinds and sometimes encounter deep mistrust. There is, however, a big global organization that has the resources, the credibility and the track record to provide all that.

---

[46] Given the long-running dispute between the CRAs and European governments, I only cite here the views of a neutral source: OECD chief economist Pier Carlo Padoan, who has stated: 'Lately, rating agencies have proved that they are strongly 'pro-cyclical' and produce self-realising prophesies … the agencies [do] not merely pass on information but express judgements, speeding up trends already at work … It's like pushing someone who is on the edge of a cliff. It aggravates the crisis.' See 'OECD Joins Criticism of Credit Rating Agencies', *EUbusiness.com*, 7 July 2011 available at www.eubusiness.com/news-eu/oecd-eurozone-debt.b5x/.

[47] Dirk Kurbjuweit, 'Essay: Die Politik im Griff der Finanzmärkte', *Der Spiegel*, 30 May 2011.

[48] An alternative solution would be to use this international body as an impartial CRA and mandate that its ratings would be given 50 per cent weight in all contexts with private ratings retaining another 50 per cent weight so that the true risk profile of an issuer or an instrument would be found by reference to both sets of ratings.

That organization is the OECD[49] and its lack of expertise in banking matters can be remedied by merging it with the research 'division' of the BIS. Not only would such a reform in the OECD's mandate revitalize a great organization that has been mostly a part player in the course of the GFC, it would also provide a cost effective and credible solution to the problem of global regulatory policy and risk knowledge. Finally, the new body should invite major civil society organizations such as Oxfam, Greenpeace and others to sit on its board and even have a vote on issues pertinent to their mission, broadening the accountability lines of the proposed governance structure and enhancing its legitimacy.

2.5   A global resolution authority

I have given in Chapters 3 and 5 an overview of the catastrophic consequences of Lehman Brothers' disorderly failure and the co-ordination challenges EU member state regulators faced in the case of Fortis. I have also discussed in Chapter 7 the regulatory steps taken by the US and the EU to remedy some of those problems as well as IMF and BCBS proposals on cross-border resolution. Whatever their shortcomings the proposed changes constitute a significant step forward, especially with respect to the orderly resolution of SIFIs with minimum involvement of public funding to minimize moral hazard. Yet another big problem remains that of the cross-border resolution of financial groups. There is nothing in the present reforms that provides a convincing answer to this problem[50] that is further intensified by the lack of a single regime for the resolution of cross-border financial groups on a unitary basis instead of holding separate proceedings for each group entity with different legal personality.

Accordingly, the fourth pillar of the proposed system of governance should be a (newly established) global resolution authority operating a single resolution model for G-SIFIs on a group basis.[51] This solution would

---

[49] Currently the OECD's main duty is to 'help governments foster prosperity and fight poverty through economic growth and financial stability. We help ensure the environmental implications of economic and social development are taken into account … OECD's work is based on continued monitoring of events in member countries as well as outside OECD area, and includes regular projections of short- and medium-term economic developments'. See OECD, 'What We Do and How', available at www.oecd.org/pages/0,3417,en_36734052_36761681_1_1_1_1_1,00.html.

[50] 50. 'The second aspect of the current reform process that I see as problematic is the continuing absence of a global regime for resolving troubled banks.' Eichengreen, 'Reforming the International Financial Architecture', p. 4.

[51] Cf. Thorsten Beck, 'Bank Resolution: A Conceptual Framework', in Panagiotis Delimatsis and Nils Herger (eds.), *Financial Regulation at the Crossroads – Implications*

of course be highly intrusive. Yet, given the grave doubts surrounding the effectiveness of current EU and IMF proposals on cross-border resolution and the side-stepping of the issue in the Dodd–Frank Act, a global regime is the only viable alternative to the territorial approach that would require the ring-fencing of subsidiaries and important branches in all host countries.[52]

Both the proposed EU resolution regime for financial institutions and the US special resolution regime for SIFIs (Orderly Liquidation Authority) will be financed, whether *ex ante*, as in the case of the proposed EU resolution funds, or *ex post*, as in the case of the US, by private sector contributions signalling an intention to use as little public money as possible. This inadvertently gives a serious boost to arguments for a global resolution regime for cross-border financial institutions and groups, since the argument about foreign authorities using domestic taxpayers' money, possibly an unconstitutional development in many jurisdictions and a politically charged issue, becomes irrelevant.

This does not mean that the new authority would be left with many options. Its resolution operations either must be supported by burden sharing arrangements between member countries, probably using assets to GDP ratios as a basis for contributions,[53] or a global resolution fund must be financed by levying a global tax on G-SIFIs. The best way to calculate such a levy would be on the basis of assessment of institution riskiness using a risk matrix developed jointly with the proposed financial policy authority and TRNs, such as the BCBS, that would work under its umbrella. Calibrating a levy on G-SIFIs in this manner could satisfy both the objective of financing resolution and curbing excessive risk-taking.[54] Any shortfall could be covered by a loan made available by the IMF to the global resolution authority and be repaid by the proceeds of liquidation and further charges levied on the financial institutions covered by the

---

for Supervision, Institutional Design and Trade (The Hague: Kluwer Law International, 2011), Chapter 3, especially pp. 67–9.

[52] See for a good defence of this approach Douglas Arner and Joseph Norton, 'Building a Framework to Address Failure of Complex Global Financial Institutions' (2009) 39 *Hong Kong Law Journal* 95–128.

[53] For this model and other forms of calculating burden sharing for bank bail-outs, see Charles Goodhart and Dirk Schoenmaker, 'Fiscal Burden Sharing in Cross-Border Banking Crises' (2009) 5 *International Journal of Central Banking* 141–65.

[54] 'Financial taxes can have three main objectives: (i) to limit excessive risk-taking, (ii) to provide an insurance or resolution fund for systemically important institutions and (iii) to help pay for global public goods', Kern Alexander, 'International Regulatory Reform and Financial Taxes' (2010) 13 *Journal of International Economic Law* 893, 894.

global scheme, with big central banks only opening liquidity lines to the global resolution authority, which may be made available on a short-term basis and until an IMF loan covers any shortfall, provided that the global resolution fund would have insufficient money to cover the cost of such resolution.

The establishment of a global resolution authority exclusively tasked with carrying out the resolution of G-SIFIs covered by the scheme would be expected to address issues of impartiality and mistrust that all cross-border resolutions are bound to face due to the multitude of conflicting (creditor, shareholder, employee and national) interests involved in the process. It would also remedy the continuous absence of special resolution regimes dealing with SIFIs in most G-20 countries, which obliterates the intended effect of special resolution regimes, namely the reduction of moral hazard associated with 'too-big-to-fail' institutions, diminishing the effectiveness of recent reforms.[55]

Furthermore, the global resolution authority may only operate effectively if participating countries and institutions accept its power of intervention and attendant modifications of their domestic laws that would be required in order for the global resolution authority to operate a single resolution and insolvency law for G-SIFIs. Country members of the scheme could create a *lex specialis* with respect to resolution of SIFIs. It is not the first time that most G-20 members and the rest of the EU countries would have to amend their national insolvency and security laws to accommodate the ends of global markets.[56] This has already happened

---

[55] A recent BCBS survey has found that the level of national implementation of Special Resolution Regimes is very low and the cross-border dimension has largely been neglected, while the issue of cross-border group resolution has been ignored. This is what the BCBS Press Release states in the customary diplomatic language of international bodies: 'Some jurisdictions continue to lack these and other important legal powers set out in the Basel Committee's 2010 recommendations or continue to rely on general corporate insolvency procedures. Such procedures are too slow, too costly and come too late to resolve a failing bank ... Further work is required on cross-border resolution as complications continue to arise from discrepancies among national regimes ... National authorities appear to be at different stages of developing recovery and resolution plans for systemically important financial institutions. In view of the importance of these plans for systemic stability, national authorities will need to move forward quickly in this area', BCBS, Resolution Policies and Frameworks – Progress So Far', July 2011, available at www.bis.org/publ/bcbs200.htm.

[56] E.g., 2002/47/EC of the European Parliament and of the Council of 6 June 2002 on financial collateral arrangements, OJL168/43, 27 June 2002 renders inapplicable certain provisions of member states' insolvency law that would, *inter alia,* inhibit the effective realization of financial collateral in the context of bilateral close-out netting. Examples of special provisions introduced by the Collateral Directive in 'violation' of general

with local implementation of ISDA close-out netting provisions.[57] Moreover, all financial institutions supervised by the proposed scheme would have to amend their statutes to incorporate the changes necessitated by the single model operated by the global resolution authority[58] in order to minimize shareholder and creditor litigation.

2.6   Other advantages of the proposed governance system

I have already explained that the main value of implementing a supranational governance system for global finance like the one suggested here is that it would address most of the weaknesses of recent reforms and enhance their effectiveness. It also promotes the ideal of open financial markets and their importance to global economic development. Other distinct advantages of the proposed system over existing structures are discussed below.

First, information would freely flow and be shared between the four pillars of the proposed system, facilitating effective supervision. Free flow of information and expertise would certainly allow the third pillar (the financial policy regulator) to provide higher quality rules and standards reflecting the realities of the market and emerging risks. At the same time, vesting the IMF with the role of a formal global systemic risk supervisor

---

insolvency law include the abolition of written notice, execution of any document, public filing or registration and title registration as requirements of financial collateral enforceability under a financial collateral arrangement, which may be made subject to close-out netting. Directive 98/26/EC of the European Parliament and of the Council of 19 May 1998 on settlement finality in payment and securities settlement systems, OJL166/45 and the Directive 2001/24/EC of the European Parliament and of the Council of 4 April 2001 on the reorganisation and winding up of credit institutions, OJL125/15, 5 May 2002 also strengthened the legal status of close-out netting arrangements.

[57] To give full force to the close-out netting clauses under the ISDA Master Agreement, ISDA has, in fact, drafted a Model Act on close-out netting, lobbying national authorities to adopt it. See 2006 ISDA Model Netting Act and 'Memorandum on the Implementation of Netting Legislation: A Guide for Legislators and Other Policy-Makers', March 2006, available at www.isda.org. Among the countries which have introduced legislation to enable or strengthen close-out netting (because it was already available) are: France, Germany, Spain, Sweden, Switzerland, Turkey, Australia, Brazil, Canada, Israel, Japan, the United States and 70 other countries. A current status report on the enforceability of close-out netting worldwide can be obtained from www.isda.org/docproj/stat_of_net_leg.html.

[58] An outline of a single insolvency model for G-SIFIs and cross-border financial groups has been given in Emilios Avgouleas, Charles Goodhart and Dirk Schoenmaker, 'Bank Resolution Plans as a Catalyst for Global Financial Reform' (2012) 8 *Journal of Financial Stability*, in press.

presents the tremendous advantage of creating a channel through which very important and critical knowledge/information could flow from other divisions of the IMF to a prospective supervisory division, creating the richest and most reliable global systemic risk data-bank. Second, the existence of an international micro-prudential authority for G-SIFIs makes the possibility of early intervention more likely and such intervention more effective, reducing the number of bank failures and attendant public rescue or resolution costs.

Third, the obvious objection that may be raised here is that the system solidifies a new super-class of financial institutions that would inevitably be seen as 'too-big-to-fail', 'contaminating' global markets with colossal amounts of 'toxic' moral hazard. But it is rather misplaced. The establishment of special resolution regimes for SIFIs and introduction of special capital requirements and surcharges for G-SIFIs, as proposed by the BCBS and the US FRB (discussed analytically in Chapter 7), have de facto solidified the ranks of this super-class of institutions, probably an unintended consequence of regulatory efforts to contain 'too-big-to-fail' risk. Thus, the proposed governance system is only a consequence of these proposals and, arguably, the best way to manage properly G-SIFI risk. An independent global supervisory body and an independent global resolution authority would be in a much better position to ensure that either preventive action would be taken early or a cross-border resolution of a G-SIFI would take place in an orderly manner, without causing tremendous disruption to the global financial system. Whereas the absence of a supra-national supervisory and resolution regime for G-SIFIs will perpetuate moral hazard, due to hesitation of home (or host) authorities to force a G-SIFI into resolution, because of fears of reputation damage and unintended cross-border consequences.

Fourth, resolution conducted at a domestic level is a highly politicized process and having a global body conducting the process for very big institutions might considerably de-sensitize it. In addition, the global resolution authority would be an impartial administrator of the resolution process and need not engage in 'asset grabbing' in order to favour local creditors and prejudice foreign creditors. When resolution is driven by home or host country authorities, regulators will inevitably feel obliged to resort to 'asset grabbing' in order to favour a domestic constituent, in most cases domestic depositors or local deposit guarantee schemes. Fifth, the existence of an integrated global financial structure would enable the adoption of truly global solutions to a variety of issues that require such solutions like short sales regulation or the regulation of CRAs.

Finally, having the same authority overseeing both ISDA and the CRAs can lead to a much better management of risk by both private and public actors in global markets. Indicative of the problem of unco-ordinated responses to threatening credit and market risks by private actors is the ongoing Eurozone debt crisis. ISDA, CRAs, lender clubs, sovereign lenders, such as the IMF, and sovereign debtors have never properly attempted to discuss what their common response to sovereign debt restructuring, rescheduling (extending maturities), or reprofiling (change of coupon payments) and interpretation of relevant actions under CDS contracts should be.[59] While CDS buyers need to be protected under the terms of their contracts, a coordinated interpretation of certain events would have meant that protection of CDS holders' interest would not be used to block the taking of action to relieve the debt burden of a sovereign borrower and hamper its chances of economic recovery, a very important public interest concern. In addition, if CDS holders' interests were given priority past sovereign restructuring plans, such as the issue of Brady bonds,[60] would not have been able to complete successfully, regardless of whether failure to restructure would have devastated both the South American economies and their creditors. This observation further underscores the importance of establishing a global financial policy body that would oversee CRAs

[59] During negotiations to restructure Greek debt, a very important source of global systemic risk, this move was often blocked by fears regarding the size of CDS pay-offs that will be triggered in such a case. It was feared that these payments would destabilize a still fragile financial system and as a result efforts to restructure with a haircut or extend the maturities of Greek debt were blocked condemning a country to misery and its creditors to even bigger future losses (haircuts) as the borrower's economy was descending into deeper recession and the crisis of confidence widened. This is how Reuters has described the situation: 'Rating agencies are playing hard ball. They would consider a Greek debt restructuring, a reprofiling and even a voluntary rollover of existing debt holdings when they mature – currently the most widely-touted solution to the crisis – as a default. A rollover has been championed by euro zone officials and would be unlikely to trigger the payment of default insurance taken out on Greek bonds under the rules of the International Swaps and Derivatives Association (ISDA), which has a final say on whether a credit event has occurred', Ana Nicolaci da Costa, 'Scenarios: Possible Impact of a Greek Ratings Default', *Reuters.com*, 24 June 2011, available at www.reuters.com/article/2011/06/24/us-greece-ratings-idUSTRE75N4AH20110624.

  See also Tim Bowden, 'S&P Slaps "Default" Label on Greece's $28bn Debt Restructuring Package – French and German Banks will now Seek a Deal that Rating Agencies Accept', *The Guardian*, 4 July 2011, available at www.guardian.co.uk/business/2011/jul/04/greece-greek-debt-austerity-default. Ultimately Greece managed to restructure its debt, yet precious time for the country's economic stability was lost due to the said loopholes in co-ordination.

[60] For a good analysis of methods of restructuring of sovereign debt, see Rodrigo Olivares-Caminal, 'An Introduction to Sovereign Debt Restructuring', in Rodrigo Olivares-Caminal *et al., Debt Restructuring* (Oxford University Press, 2011), Chapter 9.

and, in some cases, shape public sector reactions to emerging risks in co-ordination with private sector actors.

3. Conclusion

This book has argued that current regulatory reforms in the EU, the US, and through the BCBS and the FSB, analytically discussed in Chapters 6 and 7, are broadly in the right direction and constitute significant progress over pre-existing regimes that not only failed to predict or prevent the GFC, but also contributed to its magnitude. Current reforms whether already passed into law or still at the stage of planning seem to successfully target issues of perverse incentives, transparency of derivatives trading, adequate capitalization of financial institutions and adoption of workable leverage and liquidity coverage limits, and to tackle, to a certain extent, the 'too-big-to-fail' issue. Yet global rule-making is still largely left to TRNs and current reforms do very little to curb risk-taking in the shadow banking sector, notwithstanding the Dodd–Frank reforms in the US. Also, supervisory and resolution structures remain stubbornly domestic. As a result, they remain vulnerable to arbitrage and prone to the same co-ordination obstacles that cross-border crisis management and resolution faced during the last crisis. Namely, there is a serious and largely underestimated danger that current reforms, which are underpinned by territorial governance, may easily be undermined, even fail, in an era of global markets and interconnectedness. Arguably, the obvious remedy is to build strong global governance structures.[61] These ought to secure the effective implementation of current reforms through effective supervision of big financial institutions and resolution of cross-border financial groups. They should also tackle the remaining legitimacy problems, which have not been fully resolved in spite of the emergence of the G-20.

This chapter has offered an outline of a comprehensive and cost effective supra-national system for the governance of global finance to remedy the shortcomings and loopholes of current reforms. The proposed system would rely on four different authorities/pillars in order to both provide effective regulation and supervision and address the 'darker' and less explored parts of global financial markets. In this context, the chapter suggests the following reforms that should be based on a new international treaty:

---

[61] Cf. Crockett, 'What Financial System for the 21st Century?', pp. 18–19.

(1) build infrastructure for the proper regulatory understanding of emerging risks due to financial innovation and the production of financial regulation through a transparent process that would also utilize in full the expertise of TRNs and valuable private sector input. The international body that would provide this valuable public service for global markets should be based on the capabilities of the OECD and the research division of the BIS;

(2) give the IMF the role of a global systemic risk/macro-prudential supervisor and provide it with tools to identify risks emanating from the shadow banking sector properly and in a timely manner;

(3) establish a global structure for the micro-prudential supervision of G-SIFIs with large cross-border asset or liability bases in order to limit their room for regulatory arbitrage and to provide proper and consistent supervision on a global basis. This is the most sensitive of the suggested reforms and is bound to be met with the highest degree of opposition, especially political opposition. For this reason, key national regulators should be represented in such global authority and important decisions regarding G-SIFIs, such as the adoption of PCA measures or resolution, would be taken following discussions with key national regulators, and may only be taken following the concurrent consent of the proposed macro-prudential supervisor and global resolution authority;

(4) create a global resolution authority to provide effective, credible, and impartial cross-border resolution of financial institutions and especially of financial groups;

(5) establish a set of principles and sub-principles to underpin the actions of the proposed governance system that will have financial stability at its apex but will also give plenty of scope for the adoption of regulatory standards that without undermining financial stability have the potential to foster economic growth and poverty eradication, both prominent parts of UN's Millennium Development Goals.

Open global markets are the best way to achieve economic growth and global prosperity. But open markets also need proper governance structures to be in place, in order to prevent, to the extent possible, cross-border financial crises and more critically to manage properly and smoothly their consequences in order not to allow them to devastate real economy operators and household incomes. The financial crises the twenty-first century is going to experience are bound to be changeable in their characteristics, mostly due to the impact of the financial revolution that combines advanced technological infrastructure, open global markets and financial innovation.

Like all knowledge revolutions the new powers that the financial revolution has unleashed ought to have been harnessed to further the central goals of humanity. In the twenty-first century, these include the shift to sustainable development models, eradication of poverty and closing the funding gap that the pensions' time bomb poses for the developed world and some developing countries, such as China. So far this revolution has been so badly mismanaged, due to ignorance and insider rent-seeking, as to lead to colossal misallocation of resources, since it was one of the fundamental causes of the global financial crisis.

It is time to 'put things right'! The proposals made here are doubtlessly incomplete and very receptive to further improvement. Yet they provide realistic and relatively cost-effective solutions to an almost intractable problem. They are also geared towards prevention and containment of the next crisis rather fighting the last one. Therefore, if implemented, they have the potential to constitute a very important and critical first step towards a global governance model that both safeguards systemic stability and promotes global economic welfare.

INDEX

Lightning Source UK Ltd.
Milton Keynes UK
UKHW011400150819
348003UK00012B/257/P